THE UNITED STATES AIR FORCE

THE UNITED STATES AIR FORCE

A CHRONOLOGY

JOHN C. FREDRIKSEN

ABC-CLIO

Santa Barbara, California • Denver, Colorado • Oxford, England

Library of Congress Cataloging-in-Publication Data

Fredriksen, John C.
  The United States Air Force : a chronology / John C. Fredriksen.
    p. cm.
  Includes bibliographical references and index.
    ISBN 978–1–59884–682–9 (alk. paper) — ISBN 978–1–59884–683–6 (ebook)
1. United States. Air Force—History—Chronology. 2. United States. Army Air Forces—History—Chronology. 3. United States. Army. Air Corps—History—Chronology. 4. United States. Army. Air Service—History—Chronology. 5. United States. Army. Signal Corps. Aviation Section—History—Chronology.
6. Aeronautics, Military—United States—History—Chronology. I. Title.
UG633.F69   2011
358.400973—dc22   2010039860

ISBN: 978–1–59884–682–9
EISBN: 978–1–59884–683–6

15 14 13 12 11   1 2 3 4 5

This book is also available on the World Wide Web as an eBook.
Visit www.abc-clio.com for details.

ABC-CLIO, LLC
130 Cremona Drive, P.O. Box 1911
Santa Barbara, California 93116-1911

This book is printed on acid-free paper ∞

Manufactured in the United States of America

Contents

Introduction

The popular expression "Wild Blue Yonder" conjures up imagery of fleets of American warplanes, invincible in combat and in seemingly endless abundance. However, such popular notions belie the relatively humble origins of the U.S. Air Force, and its forebears. American military aviation is rooted in the U.S. Army Signal Corps, which operated reconnaissance balloons during the Civil War. It was not until airplanes became technologically feasible that the Signal Corps Aeronautical Division manifested in 1907, which, in turn, gave way to the Signal Corps Aviation Section in 1917. However, the United States had fallen far behind Europe in terms of military aviation by the advent of World War I, and it was not until May 1918 that the U.S. Army Air Service arose to manage the 10-fold increase in machines and personnel. Despite this shaky start, the Air Service acquitted itself well in combat, downing 756 enemy aircraft and 76 balloons at a cost of 289 aircraft, 48 balloons, and 237 crewmen. Success here stimulated cries for an independent air force, free of army control, and of which General William G. "Billy" Mitchell was the most vocal proponent.

Over the next decade a series of aviation boards and studies concluded that American air power merited greater recognition as a quasi-independent arm, so in 1926 the Army Air Corps was born. Despite a lack of funding brought on by the Depression era, America airmen managed to make significant technological and doctrinal strides with a number of historic flights, and new institutions such as the Air Corps Tactical School. Among the most significant creations was the General Headquarters Air Force (GHQ), which enjoyed a measure of autonomy from the Army and formed the kernel of American strategic bombing. By 1941, the inadequacies of the Army Air Corps forced it to give way to the new Army Air Forces (AAF), whereby commander General Henry "Hap" Arnold enjoyed coequal status and recognition with leaders of traditional ground forces. The war was also a turning point in American aviation history, for the AAF emerged as a conquering force of 1.2 million men and 160,000 airplanes, unprecedented in the annals of warfare. Significantly, AAF B-29s named *Enola Gay* and *Bock's Car* ushered in a defining moment in human history by dropping atomic bombs on Hiroshima and Nagasaki, respectively, and heralding the dawn of nuclear warfare.

The dream of an independent air arm was finally realized in 1947 when the U.S. Air Force emerged through the National Security Act of that year. The new organization performed splendidly during the Korean War, 1950–1953, the West's first challenge of the Cold War, and by decade's end had pioneered the development and deployment of new Atlas, Titan, and Minuteman intercontinental ballistic missiles. However, despite more capable aircraft and heroic sacrifices, the Air Force proved unable to materially change the course of events in the Vietnam War, or its collateral theaters in Laos and Cambodia. Thereafter, the Air Force concentrated on the acquisition of even more modern weapons systems, lavish in price and capabilities in combat, and proved itself capable of neutralizing the threat posed by the mighty Red Air Force. Ironically, its greatest challenge was mounted not by the Soviet Union but rather Iraq, during its invasion of neighboring Kuwait. The Air Force proved itself up to the challenge of defeating this modern, up-to-date adversary in an aerial campaign lasting 39 days, which enabled Operation DESERT STORM to triumph in only 100 hours on the ground. Since the end of the Cold War in 1991, the Air Force has continued displaying its global flexibility and capacities in Bosnia, Kosovo, Afghanistan, and Iraq, all of which reinforce its reputation as a high-tech, unbeatable adversary, and America's first line of defense in the war against terrorism.

This chronology is an attempt to capture the impressive historical sweep of the U.S. Air Force, and its antecedents, in a single volume. To that end, all important conflicts and personages are covered to properly contextualize military events at the time they occurred. Great care is also taken to mention important laws, military texts, schools, weapons systems, and occasional political developments affecting military affairs. Overall, this book should sketch out for lay readers the growth and maturation of American military aviation, while the detailed bibliography of the latest scholarship points the way to subsequent inquiries. It will also afford prospective researchers a workable time frame, or stepping-off point, from which they can investigate events and personalities of interest. The author would like to thank editors Padraic Carlin and Andy McCormick for their support and advice in compiling what the author hopes is a useful and relevant addition to any library shelf, public or private.

—*John C. Fredriksen, Ph.D.*

1861

JUNE 18   In Virginia, Professor Thaddeus S. C. Lowe sends the first aerial telegraph message from a balloon tethered to the vessel *Enterprise*.

SEPTEMBER 24   Over Washington, D.C., Professor Thaddeus S. C. Lowe flies a balloon 1,000 feet across the Potomac River; his messages assist Union gunners bombarding Confederate positions in Virginia.

OCTOBER 1   The U.S. Army establishes a Balloon Corps, which musters fifty men and five balloons. This is the first formation of its kind in military history.

1862

APRIL 16   Over Virginia, Professor Thaddeus S. C. Lowe uses a hydrogen balloon to assist Union General Fitz-John Porter. However, his tether line breaks and he drifts over Confederate territory, but Lowe waits for a breeze to blow him back across Union lines and he descends and relays his findings to Union headquarters.

MAY 31–JUNE 1   Over Virginia, the hydrogen balloon *Intrepid* is flown to convey military intelligence during the Battle of Fair Oaks (Seven Pines).

1892

JANUARY   In Paris, France, Lieutenant William A. Glassford purchases a balloon for the Signal Corps. It is subsequently named the *General Myer* and transferred to Fort Riley, Kansas, for the Signal Corps.

MAY 6   At Quantico, Virginia, Samuel P. Langley launches Aerodrome No. 5, the first pilotless, engine-driven, heavier-than-air craft. The device manages to fly from a catapult mounted on a houseboat for a distance of 3,300 feet and 2,300 feet in two flights.

1894

At Fort Logan, Colorado, the Signal Corps balloon detachment arrives from Fort Riley, Kansas, in search of better weather conditions.

1898

MARCH 25   In Washington, D.C., Assistant Secretary of the Navy Theodore Roosevelt recommends to the Secretary of the Navy that "scientific officers" be appointed to investigate the military applications of Dr. Samuel P. Langley's experimental "flying machine" under development.

APRIL 29   The first joint Army-Navy aeronautics board issues a report enunciating its findings relative to Dr. Samuel Langley's flying machine. This device is a developmental model with no practical military application, but they nonetheless recommend funding for continuing experimentation.

1900

OCTOBER   At Kitty Hawk, North Carolina, brothers Wilbur and Orville Wright successfully test their manned glider design.

1901

JUNE 26–27   In Dayton, Ohio, the Wright brothers confer with aeronautical theorist Octave Chanute over the concept of "flying machines."

JULY 27   At Kitty Hawk, North Carolina, the Wright brothers' 1901 Glider is successfully launched from sand dunes for the first time.

1902

SEPTEMBER 19   At Kitty Hawk, North Carolina, the Wright brothers begin testing their new, larger glider with technical information received from Octave Chanute. The device flies consistent with calculations that had been figured in advance. That winter the Wrights begin construction of a special four-cylinder motor and propellers for their glider.

1903

FEBRUARY 12   In Dayton, Ohio, the Wright brothers begin running their new four-cylinder engine, although it breaks down during testing.

MARCH 23   The Wright brothers file a patent with the U.S. Patent Office, based on their successful Model 1902 glider.

AUGUST 8   On the Potomac River, Washington, D.C., Samuel P. Langley, curator of the Smithsonian Institution, successfully launches a quarter-scale model of his Aerodrome A from an anchored houseboat.

DECEMBER 17   At Kitty Hawk, North Carolina, the world's first powered flight transpires when a heavier-than-air craft piloted by Orville Wright flies 120 feet during a 12-second sojourn. His brother, Wilbur Wright, then takes the

Original Wright Brothers 1903 Aeroplane ("Kitty Hawk") in first flight, December 17, 1903, at Kitty Hawk, NC. Orville Wright at controls and Wilbur Wright at right (first flight was 12 seconds). (National Archives)

machine up for a second flight lasting 59 seconds and covers 852 feet. A total of four successful flights are made and the new aviation age is launched.

1904

AUGUST 3   At Oakland, California, Captain Thomas S. Baldwin conducts the first American dirigible flight. He flies an airship, equipped with a Curtiss motor, in a complete circuit.

SEPTEMBER 20   At Dayton, Ohio, Wilbur Wright again makes aviation history with the first circular flight of a heavier-than-air craft around Huffman Prairie.

1905

JANUARY 18   In light of their success, the Wright brothers contact the government over possible sales to the U.S. Army, but no action is taken.

FEBRUARY 11   At West Point, New York, the 25-foot balloon *L'Alouette* rises from the siege battery there under Charles Levee; among those observing is Cadet Henry H. Arnold, Class of 1907.

OCTOBER 5   Wilbur and Orville Wright solve a difficult equilibrium (balance) problem in their nascent airplane, the Wright Flyer III. This is the first airplane capable of taking off, turning, flying for 30 minutes in a circular flight ranging 24 miles, then landing safely.

OCTOBER 27   In Washington, D.C., the War Department is again contacted by Wilbur and Orville Wright, who feel their new flying device has potential military applications. The Board of Ordnance, however, mistaking their letter as a request for funding, again turns them down.

1906

MARCH 2   Scientist Robert H. Goddard, jotting down thoughts in his Green Notebook, speculates that atomic energy might one day power spaceships during interplanetary flight.

MAY 22   Aeronautical pioneers Wilbur and Orville Wright finally, after three tries, win their first government-issued patent for their so-called flying machine.

SEPTEMBER 30   Over Scarborough, England, an army balloon piloted by Major Henry B. Hersey and Lieutenant Frank P. Lahm wins the first Gordon Bennett Balloon Race by traveling 402 miles from Paris, France.

1907

JUNE 4   Corporal Edward Ward becomes the military's first noncommissioned officer in the new balloon division, and he is ordered to learn balloon-manufacturing techniques.

AUGUST 1   In Washington, D.C., Army aviation is born once the Office of the Chief of the Signal Corps authorizes an "Aeronautical Division" to study and acquire balloons, heavier-than-air machines, and matters pertaining to military applications of manned flight. Captain Charles DeForest Chandler is appointed head of the new organization, but two more years lapse before the first military aircraft is acquired.

OCTOBER 17   Signal Corps Balloon No. 10 under Captain Charles DeForest Chandler flies 475 miles in 20 hours, moving between St. Louis, Missouri, and Walton, West Virginia. He wins the Lahm Cup for ballooning.

NOVEMBER 7   In Washington, D.C., the War Department awards the Army Signal Corps $25,000 to obtain an airship through the Board of Ordnance and Fortification.

NOVEMBER 30   At Hammondsport, New York, aeronautical pioneer Glenn H. Curtiss opens the nation's first airplane company.

DECEMBER 5 Wilbur Wright, in a letter to the Board of Ordnance and Fortification, proposes to build a military aircraft for $25,000. The board subsequently asks the Signal Corps for the desired specifications such a craft should include.

DECEMBER 6 Over Bras d'Or Lake, Nova Scotia, Lieutenant Thomas E. Selfridge rides the Cygnet I kite aloft as it is towed by a motorboat piloted by its inventor, Alexander Graham Bell.

DECEMBER 16 In Washington, D.C., Brigadier General James Allen, the chief signal officer, issues a call for bids to procure a lighter-than-air vessel, or airship.

DECEMBER 23 Brigadier General James Allen, the Army's chief signal officer, issues Specification No. 486, which outlines requirements for acquiring a military airplane. The new machine must be capable of carrying two passengers aloft for one hour at 40 miles per hour in any direction, and land safely.

1908

JANUARY 21 Brigadier General James Allen, the chief of the Signals Corps, issues specifications for lighter-than-air dirigibles capable of carrying two passengers at 20 miles per hour for at least two hours.

JANUARY 28 Over Oil City, Pennsylvania, a balloon piloted by Lieutenants Frank P. Lahm, Henry W. Alden, and J. G. Obermeier covers the 100-mile trip from Canton, Ohio, in only two hours and 20 minutes.

FEBRUARY 8 Wilbur and Orville Wright win the nation's first contract to build a military aircraft for the Army, at a cost of $25,000. The finished craft will be delivered no later than August 1909, and carry two people at 40 miles per hour over a distance of 125 miles.

FEBRUARY 10 The first-ever Army contract to acquire a heavier-than-air machine from the Wright brothers is signed by Captain Charles S. Wallace of the Signal Corps.

FEBRUARY 24 Captain Thomas S. Baldwin contracts with the Army to construct an airship for the fixed price of $6,750.

MARCH 8 In Washington, D.C., the Secretary of War approves the Wright brothers' bid to construct a viable military aircraft within 200 days.

MARCH 12 On Lake Keuka, Hammondsport, New York, the Red Wing aircraft designed by Lieutenant Thomas E. Selfridge successfully flies for the first time and reaches an altitude of 320 feet.

APRIL 4 In Massachusetts, inventor Robert H. Goddard coins the expression "jet propulsion" as a means of achieving space flight. He goes on to describe a primitive combustion chamber with a propulsion nozzle.

APRIL 11 Lieutenant Frank P. Lahm assumes responsibility for the Aeronautical Division, U.S. Army Signal Corps.

APRIL 22 Over Delaware City, Delaware, a balloon piloted by Captain Charles DeForest Chandler, with Theodore Roosevelt, Jr., the president's son, and Captain Fitzhugh Lee, the president's military aide, remains aloft for four hours and thirty minutes.

APRIL 30 Several enthusiasts in the 1st Company, Signals Corps, New York National Guard form an "aeronautical corps" to study ballooning. This is also the first documented instance of aviation in the National Guard.

MAY 6–14 In Dayton, Ohio, the Wright brothers modify their 1905 Flyer in order to accommodate a pilot and a passenger, pursuant to U.S. Army requirements. A successful flight is then performed at Kill Devil Hill, Kitty Hawk, North Carolina.

MAY 19 At Hammondsport, New York, Lieutenant Thomas E. Selfridge becomes the first American army officer to fly solo while piloting a machine called the *White Wing* designed by F. W. Baldwin. This is also the first aircraft to dispense with so-called "wing-warping" for turning in favor of mechanical ailerons.

JULY 6 In Washington, D.C., the U.S. Army Signal Corps creates the Aeronautics Board to test and evaluate dirigibles, balloons, and airplanes as they are acquired.

AUGUST 28 At Fort Myer, Virginia, Captain Thomas S. Baldwin concludes flight-testing Dirigible No. 1 for army officials, and it is accepted into service. The device can carry a crew of two and a 450-pound payload.

SEPTEMBER 9 Over Fort Myer, Virginia, Lieutenant Frank P. Lahm becomes the first military airplane passenger when he accompanies Orville Wright on a record flight of 57 minutes and 25 seconds in the Military Flyer. Lahm becomes one of the first 24 army aviators appointed by the Army.

SEPTEMBER 12 Orville Wright pilots a biplane for 1 hour, 14 minutes and 20 seconds, a new world's record.

SEPTEMBER 17 At Fort Myer, Virginia, the perils of airplane technology are underscored when Orville Wright crashes his machine, killing Army Lieutenant Thomas E. Selfridge. Wright sustains a broken hip and spends the next six months recuperating. The War Department suspends further flight-testing until 1909.

1909

MARCH 28 Wilbur Wright sails with his Military Flyer for Rome, Italy, to put on an aerial display for the Italian military.

JUNE 29 At Fort Myer, Virginia, Wilbur Wright resumes his Military Flyer practice flights, which were cancelled following the serious mishap of the previous September.

JULY 27 The Wright brothers' aircraft, flying before a crowd of 10,000 onlookers including President William H. Taft, passes all U.S. Army Signal Corps requirements, and even exceeds the one-hour duration specified by the contract. Orville Wright is accompanied by Army Lieutenant Frank P. Lahm.

JULY 30 Orville Wright performs a cross-country speed test in his Military Flyer with Lieutenant Benjamin D. Foulois as a passenger. He averages 42 miles and hour—two miles an hour faster than specified in the contract—and wins an additional $5,000 bonus.

AUGUST 2   General James Allen, chief signal officer of the U.S. Army, having observed several flights, authorizes acquisition of the first military airplane— a Wright Model A biplane. The machine is dubbed *Miss Columbia*.

AUGUST 25   At College Park, Maryland, land leased from the University of Maryland is to serve as its first Signal Corps airfield.

OCTOBER 23   At College Park, Maryland, Wilbur Wright gives Lieutenant Benjamin D. Foulois his first formal flight lessons.

OCTOBER 26   At College Park, Maryland, Lieutenant Frederick E. Humphreys becomes the first army officer to complete a solo flight, which lasts three minutes and three seconds. He then conducts several flights in concert with another early aviator, Lieutenant Frank P. Lahm.

1910

JANUARY 10   Near Los Angeles, California, the Aero Club of California hosts the first American air meet. Present in the audience is James H. Doolittle, who is inspired to join the U.S. Army and become a pilot.

JANUARY 19   Over Los Angeles, California, Lieutenant Paul Beck conducts the first "bomb run" when he drops three sandbags from his Farman biplane during a flying meet.

FEBRUARY 15   In an attempt to avoid wintry conditions, the U.S. Army Signal Corps transfers flight training operations from College Park, Maryland, to Fort Sam Houston, San Antonio, Texas, further south. Gusty winds encountered there, however, severely limit flying time.

MARCH 2   Over Fort Sam Houston, Texas, Lieutenant Benjamin D. Foulois is the first military aviator to fly west of the Mississippi River when he performs his solo flight. Foulois remains the only

pilot assigned to the Aeronautical Division, Army Signal Corps.

MARCH 19   At Montgomery, Alabama, Orville Wright opens a flying school; years hence, this becomes the future Maxwell Field (and Air Force Base).

JUNE 30   On Keuka Lake, New York, Glenn Curtiss conducts history's first aerial bombing test by dropping several dummy weapons. His target is a series of buoyed flags laid out in the shape of a battleship and 15 of his 17 projectiles score "hits." Several admirals observing the proceedings blithely dismiss any potential threat to capital vessels.

JULY 1   Captain Arthur S. Cowan gains appointment as head of the Aeronautical Division, Army Signal Corps.

AUGUST 18   At Fort Sam Houston, Texas, civilian mechanics add wheels to Signal Corps Airplane No. 1, therefore eliminating the need for rails and catapults while launching.

AUGUST 20 Over Sheepshead Bay Race Track, New York, Lieutenant Jacob E. Fickel is the first man to fire a weapon from an airplane when he shoots a .30-caliber Springfield rifle at targets from a Curtiss biplane; four passes result in two hits.

OCTOBER 10 At College Park, Maryland, Lieutenant Thomas DeWitt Milling takes his Wright Flyer aloft to test a bomb-sighting and -dropping device created by Riley E. Scott.

OCTOBER 11 Over St. Louis, Missouri, ebullient Theodore Roosevelt becomes the first former commander in chief to pilot an airplane.

1911

JANUARY 15 Flying in a Wright biplane at 1,500 feet, Lieutenant Myron S. Crissy drops a live 36-pound bomb on a target. The aircraft in question is flown by Philip O. Parmalee.

JANUARY 16 Over the San Bruno Hills, California, a Wright Flyer piloted by Lieutenant G. E. M. Kelly conducts the first aerial reconnaissance mission when he tries unsuccessfully to photograph and detect camouflaged troops from 2,000 feet.

JANUARY 17 At San Diego, California, Glenn H. Curtiss opens an aviation school on North Island, which subsequently serves as the Signal Corps Aviation School.

JANUARY 21 Over Selfridge Field, Michigan, a Wright Flyer piloted by Lieutenant Paul W. Beck relays the first radio-transmitted message while airborne. The test is conducted at an altitude of 100 feet and picks up a message 1.5 miles away.

FEBRUARY 7 Over Tijuana, Mexico, a biplane flown by Harry S. Harkness delivers a message to U.S. Army forces; the trip from San Diego, California, 25 miles distant, took only 25 minutes.

FEBRUARY 27 Near Fort McIntosh, Laredo, Texas, a Wright B Flyer piloted by Lieutenant Benjamin D. Foulois and Philip O. Parmalee demonstrates the potential of aircraft to cooperate with ground forces.

MARCH 3 In Washington, D.C., the Secretary of War authorizes the Army's first aviation appropriation of $125,000 to fund 51 members of its Aviation Section.

Over Texas, a biplane flown by civilian pilot Philip Parmalee and Lieutenant Benjamin D. Foulois travels between Laredo and Eagle Rock to demonstrate the utility of such technology for relaying military communications.

MARCH 17 A Curtiss D pusher aircraft becomes the first machine adopted by the U.S. Army Signal Corps to utilize tricycle landing gear and it receives the designation Aeroplane No. 2.

MARCH 21 Over Fort William McKinley, Lieutenant Frank P. Lahm flies Signal Corps No. 7, a Wright Flyer, in the first overseas flight of an American warplane.

MARCH 31 In Missouri, the National Guard Signal Corps detachment organizes an air section to teach aviation and ballooning for the first time.

APRIL 5   At Fort Sam Houston, Texas, the first provisional aero company is organized by the U.S. Army.

APRIL 11   At Augusta, Georgia, the Army establishes its first, permanent flying school outside College Park, Maryland, and seeks permission to build four hangars. Fliers train there during winter months, although the school eventually relocates to San Diego, California.

APRIL 21   Lieutenant Henry H. Arnold is ordered to Dayton, Ohio, for flight instructions at the Wright Flying School; he is accompanied by another early aviator, Lieutenant Thomas DeWitt Milling.

APRIL 27   At Fort Sam Houston, Texas, a Curtiss IV Model D and a Wright Type B become the second and third Signal Corps small aircraft.

MAY 4   In Washington, D.C., the War Department approves the transfer of Signal Corps Aeroplane No. 1, the Wright Military Flyer, to the Smithsonian Institution, where it will be put on display.

MAY 7–13   In Dayton, Ohio, Lieutenants Henry H. Arnold and Thomas DeWitt Milling arrive for flight instruction at the Wright Flying School. They graduate six days later.

MAY 10   At Fort Sam Houston, Texas, a Curtiss D pusher aircraft piloted by Lieutenant George E. M. Kelly crashes, killing him. His becomes the first fatality in Army aviation history, and Kelly Field, San Antonio, is named in his honor in 1917.

MAY 13   At Dayton, Ohio, Lieutenants Henry H. Arnold and Thomas DeWitt Milling graduate from the Wright aviation school.

Thomas DeWitt Milling and Lt. Sherman in airplane at Texas City after breaking American duration and distance record. (Library of Congress)

JUNE 7   At College Park, Maryland, Lieutenant John P. Kelly becomes the first medical officer assigned to the Signal Corps Aviation Field.

JUNE 20   Captain Charles DeForest Chandler replaces Captain Arthur S. Cowan as head of the Aeronautical Division, Army Signal Corps.

JULY 3   At College Park, Maryland, the Signal Corps Aviation School is formally established under Captain Charles DeForest Chandler. He employs two lieutenants, Henry H. Arnold and Thomas DeWitt Milling, who recently earned their wings at the Wright aviation school at Dayton, Ohio.

SEPTEMBER 4   Over Boston, Massachusetts, Lieutenant Thomas DeWitt Milling is the first army pilot to finish the 160-mile tri-state air race. He arrives at night, guided by the light of gasoline flares outlining the landing zone.

SEPTEMBER 26   Flying a Burgess-Wright biplane, Lieutenant Thomas DeWitt Milling wins the Rodman Wanamaker Trophy by flying a three-man flight for a duration of 54 minutes and 42 seconds.

SEPTEMBER 30   Over Nassau Boulevard, New York, Lieutenant Henry H. Arnold serves as a "stunt pilot" during filming of the movie *The Military Air Scout*.

OCTOBER 10   Lieutenant Thomas DeWitt Milling is the first army pilot to test drop live bombs from an aircraft while using a primitive bombsight invented by Riley E. Scott.

OCTOBER 18   Captain George W. McKay of the Michigan National Guard is the first member of that branch of service to become qualified as a pilot.

NOVEMBER 5   Calbraith R. Rodgers completes the first-ever cross-country flight by touching down at Long Beach California in a Burgess biplane. It has taken him seven weeks to cover 3,220 miles and he remains airborne for a total of 82 hours and four minutes—Rodgers only glided in after his engine completely failed.

NOVEMBER 28   The Signal Corps Army Aviation School temporarily relocates from College Park, Maryland, to Barnes Farm in Augusta, Georgia, to enjoy better flying conditions. However, the region suffers from one of its worst blizzards on record and operations are suspended until the spring.

1912

JANUARY 20–22   In Augusta, Georgia, the Signal Corps air detachment is visited by Wilbur Wright, who is seeking feedback to be used in the construction of a follow-on aircraft for the U.S. Army. In this capacity he thoroughly grills Captain Charles DeForest Chandler and Lieutenant Henry H. Arnold.

JANUARY 25   Over Augusta, Georgia, Army Lieutenant Henry H. Arnold establishes an altitude record by reaching 4,674 feet; it took him 59 minutes to reach that altitude in his Wright Flyer.

JANUARY 27   Clarence H. Mackay commissions the annual aviation trophy in his name, stipulating that it can be awarded by the War Department for the most meritorious flight of the year.

FEBRUARY 17 The U.S. Army publishes its first physical examination requirements for pilots.

FEBRUARY 23 In Washington, D.C., as the Army becomes more firmly wedded to airplanes, it issues *War Department Bulletin* No. 32 to establish new ratings for "military aviator," which also stipulate that prospective candidates must reach and hold an altitude of 2,500 feet in a 15 mile per hour wind, and also make a dead-stick landing within 150 feet of designated areas.

MARCH 1 Over Jefferson Barracks, Missouri, Captain Albert Berry jumps from a Bleriot pusher airplane and deploys a parachute for the first time; he lands safely from an altitude of 1,500 feet.

MARCH 11 In the Philippines, Lieutenant Frank P. Lahm opens an air school at Fort McKinley and accepts in two volunteer pilots, Lieutenant Moss L. Love and Corporal Vernon L. Burge, as his initial students.

MARCH 21 Over Fort William McKinley, the Philippines, Lieutenant Frank P. Lahm is the first American military pilot to fly in his Wright Model B, Signal Corps No. 7. Lahm commences instruction at the first air school in that region by taking Lieutenant Moss L. Love and Corporal Vernon L. Burge as students; the latter is the first enlisted man to receive flight training.

APRIL 15 In Marblehead, Massachusetts, the Burgess Company receives its first airplane order from the U.S. Army Signal Corps.

MAY 6 Over Maryland, three Signal Corps aircraft fly from College Park to Chevy Chase in the first multi-plane cross-country mission.

MAY 7 At College Park, Maryland, a Wright Flyer flown by Lieutenant Thomas DeWitt Milling is armed with a Lewis machine gun for the first time and Lieutenant Charles DeForest Chandler serves as his gunner.

JUNE 1 Over College Park, Maryland, Captain Charles DeForest Chandler performs the first official night flight. Concurrently, Lieutenant Henry H. Arnold also takes his Burgess-Wright biplane to a record-breaking 6,540 feet.

JUNE 5 In Augusta, Georgia, Lieutenant Colonel Charles B. Winder of the Ohio National Guard becomes the first guard officer to receive flight training.

JUNE 7 Captain Charles DeForest Chandler becomes the first person to fire an automatic weapon in flight when he looses off several rounds from a Lewis machine gun while flying with Lieutenant Thomas DeWitt Milling. However, the U.S. Army never adopts the flexible Lewis as a standard weapon.

JUNE 11 A Wright C pusher aircraft crashes, killing Lieutenant Leighton W. Hazelhurst and civilian Arthur L. Welsh. This is the earliest-known accident attributed to stalling.

JUNE 14 In the Philippines, Army Corporal Vernon Burge is the first American enlisted man to qualify as a pilot after passing through the Army Air School.

JULY 5 Captain Charles D. Chandler and Lieutenants Thomas D. Milling and Henry H. Arnold become the Army's first "Military Aviators," the first recipients of a new golden badge. Arnold becomes closely associated with the growth and maturation of American military air power in subsequent decades.

JULY 29–AUGUST 1   Lieutenant Benjamin D. Foulois, flying a Wright B Flyer, successfully concludes a series of airborne radio transmission tests, whereby his signals were received at distances of up to 10 miles away.

AUGUST 10–17   Over Bridgeport, Connecticut, Lieutenants Benjamin D. Foulois and Thomas DeWitt Milling participate in army maneuvers. This is the first time that aircraft have flown in conjunction with ground forces. Specifically, the craft is tested as a radio and reconnaissance platform for close cooperation with troops below.

SEPTEMBER 28   Over College Park, Maryland, the first fatal accident occurs when Signal Corps No. 4 (Wright B Flyer) crashes, killing Lieutenant Lewis C. Rockwell and Corporal Frank S. Scott, the first enlisted man to die in an airplane accident.

OCTOBER 1   A Wright Flyer flown by Lieutenants Henry H. Arnold and Alfred L. P. Sands experiences a series of stalls and nearly crashes, but pilot Arnold pulls out at the last minute and lands safely.

OCTOBER 9   At College Park, Maryland, Lieutenant Henry H. Arnold wins the first Mackay Trophy by successfully completing a triangular reconnaissance course. He comments that the trophy is so large it could easily hold four gallons of beer!

NOVEMBER 5–13   Over Fort Riley, Kansas, several aircraft employ direct communications (by radio, dropping cards, or smoke signals) in concert with artillery units; this is the origin of artillery "spotting."

NOVEMBER 27   The Army Signal Corps acquires three Curtiss F biplane flying boats; these also serve in the Navy under the designation C-1.

DECEMBER 8   At San Diego, California, the flying school established by Glenn H. Curtiss officially becomes the U.S. Army Signal Corps Aviation School. The first personnel to arrive there have all trained on Curtiss aircraft and are jocularly known as the "Curtiss Contingent."

1913

FEBRUARY 11   In Washington, D.C., West Virginia congressman James Hay introduces the first bill mandating an independent aviation corps, but it is defeated.

FEBRUARY 17   An autopilot device (gyrostabilizer) invented by Elmer Sperry is tested for the first time on a U.S. Army aircraft.

MARCH 2   The Army establishes flight pay at 35 percent over base pay for prescribed aviation duties, given the inherent risks of flying. Presently, only 30 officers qualify for such emoluments. The Army also mandate that not more than 30 officers could be involved in flying at any given time, and rank no higher than major.

MARCH 5   At Augusta, Georgia, the 1st Provisional Aero Squadron is formed with 5 pilots, 7 Wright pushers, and 21 enlisted men. The unit subsequently ships to Texas City, Texas, in response to a possible border crisis with Mexico, where it submits to additional training. This unit is also the lineal predecessor of the 1st Reconnaissance Squadron, the oldest formation in the U.S. Air Force.

MARCH 31   Over Texas, Lieutenant W. C. Sherman draws the first aerial map on a plane flown by Lieutenant Tommy Milling as he flies between San Antonio and Texas City.

MAY 27   In Washington, D.C., the War Department issues General Order No. 39, requiring all qualified pilots to receive a Military Aviator's Certificate, along with a badge. Presently, there are only 24 qualified army pilots.

MAY 28   Over Texas, Army Lieutenants Thomas D. Milling and W. C. Sherman set a flight endurance record of four hours and 22 minutes while flying between Texas City and San Antonio.

MAY 30   In Cambridge, Massachusetts, the Massachusetts Institute of Technology (MIT) initiates one of the first aerodynamics courses under the aegis of navy officer Jerome C. Hunsaker.

JUNE 12   The first Curtiss tractor-type (propeller in front) aircraft is accepted by the Army Signal Corps. Aerodynamically, this is a vast improvement over earlier pushers.

AUGUST 8   In Hawaii, Lieutenant Harold Geiger pilots a Curtiss E airplane over the island for the first time; he is the first graduate of the new aviation school at Fort Kamehameha.

SEPTEMBER 10   Command of the Aeronautical Division, U.S. Army Signal Corps, reverts to Major Samuel Reber.

OCTOBER 1   In Massachusetts, Dr. Robert H. Goddard finishes the paperwork to patent his "rocket apparatus."

DECEMBER 4   In Washington, D.C., General Order No. 75 is issued by the War Department to establish the Aero Squadron as a standard formation within the Aeronautical Division.

DECEMBER 18   Lieutenant Henry B. Post, flying Signal Corps airplane No. 23, establishes a new Army solo altitude record of 10,600 feet.

DECEMBER 29   A reconnaissance competition near San Diego, California, is won by Lieutenants C. J. Carberry and Fred Seydel, which results in their receipt of a Mackay Trophy.

1914

JANUARY 7   At San Diego, California, the 1st Aero Squadron is formally structured by the chief of signals at 8 airplanes, 20 officers, and 90 men.

JANUARY 15   In Washington, D.C., the War Department issues new safety regulations for pilots governing dress. Henceforth, all pilots are to be clad in helmets and leather coats while flying overland, and waterproof coats for overwater flying.

FEBRUARY 5 Lieutenant Joseph C. Morrow, Jr., is the last "Military Aviator" to be qualified under the original rules first established for the rating.

FEBRUARY 9 Tragedy strikes after Lieutenant Henry B. Post exceeds his old altitude record by reaching 12,140 feet, then his aircraft falls apart during its descent, killing him.

FEBRUARY 14 A Burgess H tractor aircraft flown by Lieutenant Townsend F. Todd and Sergeant Herbert Marcus sets an American duration and distance record of 244.18 kilometers in 4 hours and 43 minutes.

FEBRUARY 16 Over San Diego, California, Lieutenants Joseph E. Carberry and Walter R. Taliaferro set a new Army altitude record of 8,700 feet in a Curtiss aircraft.

FEBRUARY 24 At San Diego, California, a staff meeting at the Signal Corps Aviation School concludes that pusher-type aircraft are too dangerous to fly and are to be replaced with tractor-type machines such as the Curtiss Model J.

JUNE 24 At San Diego, California, the Signal Corps Aviation School accepts delivery of the first Curtiss J, a precursor of the famous JN-2 "Jenny." This is a tractor design with the engine mounted in front.

JULY 7–14 At Worcester, Massachusetts, Dr. Robert H. Goddard receives a government patent for his multistage rocket concept. He soon after receives another covering his liquid-fuel rocket design.

JULY 18 In Washington, D.C., Congress creates the new Aviation Section to replace the former Aeronautical Division

within the Army Signal Corps; it has an assigned strength of 6 aircraft, 67 officers, and 260 enlisted personnel under Lieutenant Colonel Samuel Reber. Moreover, all pilot candidates are to be unmarried lieutenants under 30 years of age.

JULY 28 At the Indian Head Proving Grounds, Stumpneck, Maryland, some early bombing tests are conducted by Lieutenant Victor D. Herbster and Ensign Bernard L. Smith. They drop both dummy and live bombs over the side of their craft from 1,000 feet and monitor the results.

On this fateful day, World War I commences after Austria-Hungary declares war against Serbia and a continent-wide mobilization commences.

AUGUST 17 At the Signal Corps Aviation School, North Island, California, Captain Lewis E. Goodier begins official testing of the Scott bomb-dropping device while flying a new Martin T aircraft.

SEPTEMBER 1 At San Diego, California, the 1st Aero Squadron is organized with 16 officers, 77 enlisted men, and 8 aircraft.

NOVEMBER 19 In a historic first, an airplane belonging to the U.S. Air Service completes a 429-mile cross-country flight from Fort Sill, Oklahoma, to Fort Sam Houston, Texas.

DECEMBER 11 Over Fort William McKinley, the Philippines, Army Lieutenants Herbert A. Dargue and Joseph O. Mauborgne successfully demonstrate two-way radio communication with ground stations 10 miles distant from their Burgess-Wright biplane.

DECEMBER 23 A reconnaissance contest won by Captain T. F. Dodd and

Lieutenant S. W. Fitzgerald results in receipt of a Mackay Trophy. They were the only competitors, as accidents and mishaps grounded all other aircraft during the event.

DECEMBER 30 The Signal Corps receives its first Burgess-Dunne armored aircraft; it does not go into production.

1915

JANUARY 15 Army Lieutenants Joseph E. Carberry and Arthur C. Christie set a two-man altitude record by reaching 11,690 feet in a Curtiss 100 tractor biplane; they remain aloft an hour and 13 minutes doing so.

Over San Diego, California, Army Lieutenant B. Q. Jones sets a one-man endurance record by flying 8 hours, 53 minutes in a Martin T biplane. He consequently receives a Mackay Trophy for the effort.

FEBRUARY 19 Dr. Robert H. Goddard begins experimenting with Coston signal rockets, which are propelled by solid fuel, in order to measure their thrust and efficiency.

MARCH 3 In Washington, D.C., Congress creates the National Advisory Committee on Aeronautics (NACA). This is the first government organization dedicated to advancing the state of aviation research and technology.

MARCH 4 In Washington, D.C., Congress allocates $300,000 for Army aviation during fiscal year 1916.

MARCH 12 Flying a Burgess-Renault biplane, Lieutenant Byron Q. Jones and Corporals Carl T. Hale and Robert H. Houser set a three-man endurance record of seven hours and five minutes.

APRIL 13 Lieutenants Thomas D. Milling and B. Q. Jones are detached from the 1st Aero Squadron and ordered to deploy along the Mexican border with a single airplane to find the location of bandit leader Francisco "Pancho" Villa.

APRIL 20 Along the Mexican border, a single plane piloted by Lieutenants Thomas D. Milling and B. Q. Jones of the 1st Aero Squadron fly the army's first combat reconnaissance mission.

APRIL 23 In Washington, D.C., Brigadier General George P. Scriven gains appointment as chairman of the National Advisory Council for Aeronautics (NACA).

MAY 20 The Curtiss JN-2 is selected by Army Aviation Service as the first mass-produced aircraft in the United States. It will also outfit the embryonic 1st Aero Squadron.

JULY 3 Above San Diego, California, Lieutenant Byron Q. Jones is the first army pilot to successfully loop and stall his aircraft without crashing.

JULY 6 At North Island, California, Captain V. E. Clark arrives for duty; he is the first air officer to receive a doctorate in engineering from the Massachusetts Institute of Technology.

JULY 12   Aviation mechanic examination requirements are adopted by the Signal Corps.

JULY 26   At San Diego, California, the 1st Aero Squadron under Captain Benjamin F. Foulois begins transferring its eight Curtiss JN-2 airplanes by rail to Fort Sill, Oklahoma, to participate in observations experiments with the Field Artillery School there.

JULY 29   At Fort Sill, Oklahoma, the 1st Aero Squadron transfers from August, Georgia, under Captain Benjamin D. Foulois. A crew and aircraft are subsequently flown to Brownsville, Texas, to support the Army's border patrol efforts.

OCTOBER 13   At Selfridge Field, Michigan, Lieutenant T. J. Koenig flies a LePere-Liberty 400 to victory in the Liberty Engine Builder's Trophy Race with a top speed of 128.8 miles per hour.

NOVEMBER 1   In Mineola, New York, the 1st Aero Company, New York National Guard, organizes under Captain Raynal C. Bolling. This is the first National Guard aviation unit and consists of four officers, forty enlisted men, and seven aircraft. The latter have been loaned by the New York City Aero Club.

NOVEMBER 18–19   At Fort Sill, Oklahoma, six Curtiss JN-3s of the Army Air Service begin the first squadron-level cross-country flight, which ends at Fort Sam Houston, Texas, 429 miles distant.

DECEMBER 11   At San Diego, California, the Signal Corps Aviation School hosts four Portuguese Army officers; these are the first foreign pilots trained in the United States.

DECEMBER 19   At Fort Sam Houston, Texas, the 1st Aero Squadron flies six Curtiss JN-3s in from Fort Sill, Oklahoma; this is also the first cross-country flight by an entire aviation unit.

1916

JANUARY 5   In the Philippine Islands, the 1st Company, 2nd Aero Squadron deploys as the first complete aviation unit assigned outside the United States.

JANUARY 17   The United States verges on the cusp of war with Germany, yet the Army Air Service only boasts 49 personnel and 25 aircraft. By the end of 1918 they will possess 19,068 aircraft, but the bulk of these are obtained from either France or England.

MARCH 15   At Columbus, New Mexico, the 1st Aero Squadron under Captain Benjamin D. Foulois begins readying pilots and equipment to support General John J. Pershing in Mexico. This is the first American tactical air unit committed to military operations in the field and it operates a handful of underpowered Curtiss JN-2 biplanes.

MARCH 16   Over Mexico, a Curtiss JN-2 makes aviation history's first recorded reconnaissance flight.

MARCH 21   In France, the French Air Service authorizes creation of the Escadrille Americaine, better known as the

Benjamin Foulois trains Philip O. Parmalee to be a part of the 1st Aero Squadron, 1916. (Library of Congress)

Lafayette Escadrille, to recruit volunteer pilots from the United States.

MARCH 27   The 1st Aero Squadron under Captain Benjamin D. Foulois begins making routine mail and dispatch flights for General John J. Pershing's Punitive Expedition.

APRIL 2   In San Diego, California, Colonel William Glassford arrives to take charge of the Signal Corps Aviation School at Rockwell Field.

APRIL 3   Command of the Aeronautics Division, Signal Corps, passes to Captain William "Billy" Mitchell.

APRIL 5   At San Geronimo, Mexico, the 1st Aero Squadron establishes a base camp for closer cooperation with ground units commanded by General John J. Pershing.

APRIL 7   Over Chihuahua City, Mexico, Lieutenant Herbert A. Dargue and

Captain Benjamin D. Foulois are fired upon as they deliver dispatches to the U.S. Consul; this is the first American airplane to receive hostile fire.

APRIL 16   At Luxeuil-les-Bains (Vosages), France, the Escadrille Americaine forms from American volunteer pilots and becomes part of the French Aeronautique Militaire. It sees extensive service in skies over the Western Front and, that December, it is renamed the Lafayette Escadrille after famed Revolutionary War hero Marquis de Lafayette.

APRIL 20   In France, Sergeant Major Elliot Cowdin is the first American aviator to receive the Medaille Militaire.

MAY 18   Over Thann, Alsace Region, France, Sergeant Kiffin Yates Rockwell of the Escadrille Americaine downs a German observer craft; this is the first aerial enemy kill by an American pilot.

MAY 20   Lieutenant Colonel George O. Squier assumes command of the Aviation Section, Signal Corps.

JUNE 3   In Washington, D.C., Congress passes the National Defense Act, which greatly enlarges the Signal Corps Aviation Section beyond its present 60 officers and 260 enlisted men.

JUNE 18   Over Verdun, France, aviator H. Clyde Balsley becomes the first American shot down while flying with the Escadrille Americaine. The French air commander subsequently flies to his airfield and presents the seriously wounded aviator with a Military Medal and a War Cross.

JUNE 23   Near Verdun, France, pilot Victor Emmanuel Chapman, flying with the Escadrille Americaine in France, is the first American pilot killed in World War I. Previously, Chapman had been shot down seven times in six weeks and also claimed four German kills.

JULY 13   At Mineola, New York, the 1st Aero Company, New York National Guard, mobilizes for service along the Mexican border. They are not deployed; however, they are the first National Guard air unit requisitioned into federal service.

AUGUST 28   Major Benjamin D. Foulois reports that his 1st Aero Squadron, despite severe operational conditions, managed to complete 540 reconnaissance flights, covering 19,533 miles and staying aloft for 346 hours without serious mishap.

AUGUST 29   In Washington, D.C., Congress appropriates $14 million for use by the Signal Corps to pursue military aeronautics. NACA also receives $82,500

to construct a large aeronautical laboratory at Langley Field, Virginia.

SEPTEMBER 2   Over North Island, California, two Signal Corps aircraft, flown by Lieutenants William A. Robertson and Herbert A. Drague, successfully exchange radiotelegraph messages in flight at a distance of two miles.

SEPTEMBER 6   Army aircraft test drop the first fragmentation bomb.

SEPTEMBER 13   In San Diego, California, the first aeronautics course for field officers is founded at the Signal Corps Aviation School.

OCTOBER 11   In Washington, D.C., the secretaries of War and the Navy agree to create a joint Aeronautics Board to evaluate the requirements for lighter-than-air machines.

NOVEMBER 18–20   At Mineola, New York, seven Curtiss JN-4s of New York's 1st Aero Company fly to Princeton, New Jersey, and back under Captain Raynal C. Bolling. They are there to attend a football game but also manage to showcase their cross-country flying ability to the public.

DECEMBER 20   The Army's new Balloon School is instituted at Fort Omaha, Nebraska.

DECEMBER 22   Elmer B. Sperry files a patent application for his "aerial torpedo," an unmanned airplane piloted by one of his gyrostabilizers.

DECEMBER 30   North of Hampton, Virginia, the Army establishes a new aviation school; it is now Langley Air Force Base, the Air Force's oldest active base.

1917

JANUARY 6 In Washington, D.C., the findings of a joint Army and Navy Board encourages the secretaries of War and the Navy to acquire several lighter-than-air ships based on the proven German Zeppelin design. Funding is also split between the two services, and a new board of three officers from each service arises to ensure close cooperation.

JANUARY 9 At San Diego, California, Captain Henry H. Arnold is dispatched to Panama as commander of the 7th Aero Squadron, which, presently, possesses neither bases nor airplanes.

At Fort Kameheha, Hawaii, Captain John F. Curry assumes command of the new 6th Aero Squadron.

William "Billy" Mitchell, ca. 1918. That year he directed the largest American air offensive of Wolrd War I. (Library of Congress)

FEBRUARY 3 In Washington, D.C., the United States formally severs diplomatic relations with Germany in response to the latter's resumption of unrestricted submarine warfare against neutral shipping.

FEBRUARY 10 The National Advisory Committee for Aeronautics (NACA) founds a patent subcommittee to help preclude legal actions threatening the entire industry.

FEBRUARY 19 Lieutenant Colonel John B. Bennett assumes command of the Aviation Service, Signal Corps, while his predecessor, Lieutenant Colonel George O. Squier, gains appointment as chief signal officer.

FEBRUARY 28 At North Island, San Diego, California, the first successful experiments with radiotelephones between aircraft and ground stations transpire. Previous attempts in aerial communication utilized telegraphs.

MARCH 13 Brigadier General George O. Squier, chief signal officer, authorizes the Intelligence subdivision of the Signal Corps; this marks the birth of Army Air Intelligence.

APRIL 6 When the United States enters World War I, the Aviation Section of the Signal Corps consisted of 35 pilots, 55 training aircraft, and 1,987 enlisted men. Such numbers are woefully inadequate by European standards.

APRIL 30 In Europe, Captain William "Billy" Mitchell becomes the first officer of the Army Air Service to fly over enemy territory in a French aircraft; he becomes an outspoken spokesman for American air power.

MAY 5   In Washington, D.C., the secretaries of War and the Navy consent to a "joint technical board" assembled for the standardizing the design and performance specifications of all forthcoming aircraft.

MAY 12   At San Diego, California, Captain W. A. Robertson sets a new altitude record of 17,230 feet over the North Island Flying School.

MAY 16   The Council of National Defense establishes the Aircraft Production Board and entrusts it to Howard Coffin, former CEO of the Hudson Motor Car Company. This body acts in an advisory capacity relative to aircraft development and procurement and signals a massive buildup of American aerial strength for use in World War I.

MAY 23   French premier Alexandre Ribot requests 5,000 American pilots, 4,500 aircraft, and 50,000 aircraft mechanics to assist the Allied war effort, and Major Benjamin D. Foulois is tasked with drawing up a plan for the government to achieve these goals.

MAY 26   Signal Corps Major Townsend F. Dodd gains appointment as AEF aviation officer to General John J. Pershing's staff. This is a boost to the Aviation Section's reputation.

MAY 29   In Washington, D.C., Colonel Edwin Deeds collaborates with several designers to conceptualize a standardized engine to American military aircraft. These endeavors culminate in the famous 12-cylinder, 400-horsepower Liberty engine, of which 15,000 are manufactured for the war effort.

JUNE 2   The Aviation Section, Army Signal Corps, is redesignated the Airplane Division.

JUNE 4   The Aircraft Production Board and the Joint Technical Board on Aircraft authorize five prototypes of 8- and 12-cylinder Liberty motors. These are exceptionally conservative in design, and expressly conceived for mass production.

JUNE 17   The Aircraft Production Board dispatches a joint Army-Navy aviation board under Major Raynal C. Bolling to Europe to study and possibly incorporate European production techniques in aircraft production at home.

JUNE 30   In France, Lieutenant Colonel William "Billy" Mitchell replaces Major Townsend F. Dodd as Aviation Officer, American Expeditionary Force (AEF).

JULY 4   Rantoul, Illinois, hosts the first military airfield in the United States for training purposes. Presently, the Army Air Service possesses only 55 obsolete aircraft. It ends the war with 16,801 combat aircraft in service, mostly obtained from France.

JULY 20   In the Shiloh Valley Township, Illinois, Scott Field is christened by the War Department in honor of Corporal Frank S. Scott, who was killed in a flying accident on September 28, 1912. This is the only base named after an enlisted man.

JULY 23   Command of the Airplane Division, Army Signal Corps, passes to Major Benjamin D. Foulois.

JULY 24   In Washington, D.C., Congress makes its first large appropriation for the Army Aviation Section, which receives $640 million. Significantly, the 4,500 new military aircraft manufactured in the United States are either naval patrol craft or army trainers powered by a reliable motor designed by the Packard Motor Car Company, the so-called "Liberty Engine," of which 15,131 are constructed by war's end.

Manufacturers Aircraft Association is created to implement a cross-licensing agreement, whereby member companies could access all patents at fixed low rates. This obviates the threat of lawsuits.

JULY 26   The Army-Navy Airship Board endorses a proposal by the Bureau of Mines to allot a grant of $100,000 and construct a small plant to produce helium in the United States.

JULY 27   A British-built De Havilland DH-4 two-seat bomber arrives in the United States to facilitate production of an American version. Roughly 4,500 are manufactured stateside with the popular 12-cylinder Liberty engine, but only a handful enter combat operations.

JULY 28   At Liverpool, England, the 29th Provisional Construction Squadron becomes the first American aero squadron deployed in Europe during the war.

AUGUST 5   In Columbus, New Mexico, the 1st Aero Squadron under Major Ralph Royce begins transferring its personnel to training facilities in Avord, France.

AUGUST 13   In New York, men and equipment of the 1st Aero Squadron set sail for Europe under Major Ralph Royce. This is the first such unit dispatched to the Western Front.

AUGUST 21   The Model F, constructed by the L.W.F. Engineering Company,

becomes the first airplane powered by the Liberty engine.

AUGUST 22   In the United States, mass production of air-to-ground radiotelephones commences.

AUGUST 25   The 12-cylinder, 300-horsepower Liberty engine passes its acceptance test with flying colors and is ordered into production as America's standard aircraft engine.

SEPTEMBER 3   Brigadier General William L. Kenly becomes chief of air service on the AEF staff, an act granting American aerial activities greater recognition and significance. Lieutenant Colonel William "Billy" Mitchell also becomes air commander of the Zone of the Advance.

SEPTEMBER 13   In France, the 1st Aero Squadron is the first aviation unit to reach operational status and begin training with the American Expeditionary Force (AEF). They are mostly involved in artillery spotting and tactical reconnaissance.

OCTOBER 16   At Langley Field, Virginia, radiotelephone devices installed on two aircraft transmit and receive signals at distances of 25 miles; those sent to ground stations can be heard 45 miles away.

OCTOBER 18   At Dayton, Ohio, the Signals Corps assigns McCook Field to serve as its new testing center to facilitate aeronautical research and development in the rapidly changing field of military aviation.

In Washington, D.C., the Aviation Medical Research Board is created by the U.S. Army Signal Corps.

OCTOBER 21   At Buffalo, New York, a new 12-cylinder Liberty engine enjoys a successful debut by powering a Curtiss HS-1 flying boat. The engine is adopted for use in both Army and Navy aircraft with great success.

OCTOBER 29   At McCook Field, Dayton, Ohio, test pilot Howard Rinehart pilots the first American-manufactured De Havilland DH-4 bomber. This is the first of several thousand constructed during the war years, although only a handful actually see combat.

NOVEMBER 7   Over France, Eugene J. Bullard is the first African American pilot to shoot down a German aircraft during World War I. Due to the intense racism encountered in America, Bullard joined the French army and subsequently flew with a French squadron.

NOVEMBER 27   Newly promoted Brigadier General Benjamin D. Foulois gains appointment as AEF chief of the air service under General John J. Pershing.

DECEMBER 22   At Cambridge, Massachusetts, an Aerography School begins instruction at the Massachusetts Institute of Technology; however, a major portion of the curriculum unfolds at the Blue Hill Observatory, Harvard University. Fifty-five men have passed through the program by war's end.

1918

JANUARY 19   In Mineola, New York, the School of Aviation Medicine opens under the aegis of Dr. William H. Wilmer. His job is to instruct medical personnel how to treat aviators and he helps construct the first pressure chamber to simulate high-altitude flying.

JANUARY 20   At Neufchâteau, France, Colonel William "Billy" Mitchell becomes chief of air service, I Corps.

JANUARY 23   Near Marne, France, the first American military balloon flight of the American Expeditionary Force (AEF) occurs.

FEBRUARY 1   In France, the U.S. Army Air Service forms its first operational squadrons, being largely equipped with French-built fighters, bombers, and observation craft. By war's end no less than 45 combat squadrons are present, with 800 pilots and 500 observer/tail gunners.

FEBRUARY 5   Over Saarbrücken, Germany, Lieutenant Stephen W. Thompson, 1st Aero Squadron, shoots down a German Albatros D.III fighter. This is the first American victory over an enemy aircraft; at the time he was serving as a volunteer tail gunner in a French Breguet aircraft.

FEBRUARY 7   The Joint Army-Navy Technical Board is created in light of the need to standardize instrumentation between Army and Navy aircraft.

FEBRUARY 8   Aircraft insignia of U.S. Army aircraft changes from a white star to concentric circles of red and blue around white.

FEBRUARY 16   In France, the 2nd Balloon Company deploys at Royamieux in the Toul sector of the Western Front; during the war, the Balloon Section makes 5,866 ascents (for a total of 6,832 hours in the air) for reconnaissance and artillery spotting purposes.

Rickenbacker, Eddie (1890–1973)

Army Air Service pilot. Edward Vernon Rickenbacker was born in Columbus, Ohio, on October 8, 1890, a son of Swiss immigrants. He developed a passion for automobiles, gained national attention as a racecar driver and, commencing in 1911, he was a regular contender at the Indianapolis 500. After the United States entered World War I, Rickenbacker was rejected by the U.S. Army for want of education, but he eventually served as General John J. Pershing's chauffeur. Rickenbacker, however, thirsted for combat and, assisted by his friend Colonel William "Billy" Mitchell, he obtained flight training at the Tours Aviation School. In March 1918, Rickenbacker joined the 94th Aero Pursuit Squadron, signified by its famous "Hat in the Ring" insignia, and shot down 26 German planes. As America's ace of aces, he returned home to accept a Congressional Medal of Honor, and also wrote his best-selling memoir, *Fighting the Flying Circus* (1919).

Back in civilian life, Rickenbacker returned to automobiles and founded the Rickenbacker Motor Company, and subsequently assumed the mantle as general manager of Eastern Airlines. Exercising great business acumen, Rickenbacker turned the company around in three years and became its president. In World War II Secretary of War Henry Stimson sent him on a tour of Pacific air facilities in 1942, but Rickenbacker's plane crashed, and he endured three weeks at sea in a lifeboat. Once rescued, he came home and wrote the popular book, *Seven Came Through* (1943). Rickenbacker retired from the industry in 1963, and toured the country on behalf of conservative causes before dying in Zurich, Switzerland, on July 27, 1973.

At Châtillon-sur-Seine, France, Major J. T. McNarney's 89th Aero Squadron arrives for the purpose of instructing aerial observers.

FEBRUARY 18   In France, the 95th Aero Squadron becomes the first American fighter formation deployed there, although combat patrolling does not commence for another month.

The French disband the famed Lafayette Escadrille and its 90 veteran pilots are inducted directly into the Army Air Service as the 103rd Aero Squadron. It is also one of the first American units equipped with French SPAD XIII fighters.

FEBRUARY 23–MARCH 5   At Toul, France, the 2nd Balloon Company joins the I Corps as the first unit of its kind deployed in support of field activities. It is ultimately joined by 35 other such companies.

MARCH 4   In France, the 94th Aero Squadron deploys, becoming only the second such unit to do so.

MARCH 8   At Mineola, New York, an early pressure chamber at the Signal Corps laboratory simulates conditions found at 34,000 feet for the first time. Majors Edward C. Schneider and James L. Whitney are the first two guinea pigs.

MARCH 11   Lieutenant Paul Baer of the 103rd Aero Squadron (formerly the Lafayette Escadrille) single-handedly tackles seven German fighters, downing one. He becomes the first American pilot to win the Distinguished Service Cross.

MARCH 12   Over France, Captain Phelps Collins becomes the first Air Service pilot killed when his SPAD XIII fighter crashes following a high-altitude dive.

MARCH 15   Over Villeneuve-les-Vertus, south of Epernay, France, American pilots fly Nieuport 28 fighters on their first independent patrols along the Western Front.

MARCH 19   In France, the 94th Aero Squadron ("Hat-in-the-Ring") becomes the first American aerial unit to operate over enemy lines.

MARCH 26   Over France, Colonel Raynal C. Bolling is killed on a ground reconnaissance mission, becoming the highest-ranking Air Service fatality of the war. Bolling Air Field, Washington, D.C., is dedicated in his honor.

APRIL 1   In Rome, Italy, the American Aviation Headquarters is opened, whereupon Italian fliers will begin training American pilots.

In England, the Royal Air Force becomes the world's first independent air service under Major General Hugh Trenchard; it is formed by combining the Royal Air Corps and the Royal Naval Air Service.

APRIL 6   Aerial reconnaissance takes a major step after Lieutenant J. C. McKinney uses magnesium flares for the first time to take night photographs of the ground.

APRIL 8   The 1st Aero Squadron becomes the first air squadron committed to combat operations along the Western Front. They operate two-seat SPAD aircraft and their first combat occurs four days later when they are attacked while conducting routine reconnaissance patrols.

APRIL 9   The 94th Pursuit Squadron becomes the first American fighter outfit assigned to the Western Front.

APRIL 14   Over the Toul Airdrome, France, Lieutenants Alan F. Winslow and Douglas Campbell of the 94th Squadron are the first army combat pilots to shoot down German aircraft; they are flying French-built Nieuport 28s.

Over France, Captain Edward V. Rickenbacker, soon to become America's highest-scoring "ace of aces" of this war, completes his first combat mission.

APRIL 23   In France, the first shipment of American-built Liberty engines arrives at Pauillac.

APRIL 29   Over Toul, France, Captain Edward V. Rickenbacker assists downing a German Albatros scout craft and receives half credit for the kill. A former racecar driver, he originally reached France as General John J. Pershing's chauffeur, but volunteered for combat.

At Langley, Virginia, NACA board members approve the designs for a wind tunnel to be constructed at the aeronautical laboratory.

MAY 5   Over Toul, France, the 94th and 95th Aero Squadrons are jointly administered as the 1st Pursuit Group; it survives today as part of the 1st Fighter Wing, the U.S. Air Force's senior unit.

MAY 7   Over France, Captain Eddie Rickenbacker downs a German Pfalz D.III fighter while flying a Nieuport 28. This is the first of 26 confirmed kills.

MAY 8   Captains John F. Gallagher, Robert J. Hunter, and Claude T. Uren are the first medical officers assigned as flight surgeons at U.S. Army airfields.

MAY 11   In France, the first Liberty engine-powered De Havilland DH-4 bombers built in America arrive for service with the American Expeditionary Force (AEF). A handful of these craft achieve operational status and most perform training functions.

MAY 15–16   Between New York City and Washington, D.C., airmail service begins as Lieutenants George L. Boyle and H. P. Culver fly rickety Curtiss JN-4H "Jenny" biplanes. After Boyle crashes in Maryland, Culver lands to retrieve the mail and continues on to New York.

MAY 17 In France, American-built DH-4 bombers are assembled from crates and make their first operational test flights.

MAY 18 At Amanty Airdrome, France, the 96th Squadron is the first bomber unit organized by the American Expeditionary Force (AEF). They begin familiarizing themselves with excellent Breguet 14 bombers purchased from the French.

MAY 19 Over France, Captain Raoul F. Lufbery, a naturalized American citizen and a famed fighter pilot of the Lafayette Escadrille, dies in combat flying; his final tally is 17 German aircraft.

MAY 21 In Washington, D.C., the Division of Military Aeronautics is detached from the Army Signal Corps and made a separate division under the Secretary of War's office. It is commanded by Major General William L. Kenly.

MAY 24 In Washington, D.C., the Army Air Service is established once the Division of Military Aeronautics and Bureau of Aircraft Productions merge.

MAY 29 Brigadier General Mason M. Patrick assumes command of the Air Service, American Expeditionary Force.

JUNE 6 Over Toul, France, the 91st Squadron, the Air Service's first dedicated Observation (reconnaissance) unit, begins making photo runs. Its subsequently performs useful service for the troops by spotting artillery behind enemy lines.

JUNE 12 Over France, French-built Breguet 14 bombers under Major Harry M.

Brown of the 96th Aero Squadron conduct their first offensive operation by bombing the Dommary-Baroncourt rail yards. By war's end, American bombers delivered 196 tons of bombs behind German lines, sometimes as far as 160 miles distant.

JULY 6 Over France, a German Albatros fighter shoots down a balloon belonging to the 2nd Balloon Company; this is the Air Service's first such loss.

JULY 14 Over France, Lieutenant Quentin Roosevelt is killed in action while flying with the 95th Aero Squadron. He is the youngest son of former president Theodore Roosevelt.

JULY 20 Near Dunkirk, France, the 148th Pursuit Squadron commences operational flying at the Royal Air Force base at Capelle Airdrome.

JULY 23 In Washington, D.C., the director of the Army Air Service instructs every Army airfield in the United States to have an air ambulance. This comes in response to experiments by medical officer Major Nelson E. Driver and Captain William C. Ocker, commander of flight training at Gerstner Field, Louisiana, to modify a JN-4 trainer to accept a patient in a semi-reclining position.

JULY 24 In France, AEF commanding general John J. Pershing finalizes aerial strategy for his upcoming ground offensive near St. Mihiel. His chief of air service, Colonel William "Billy" Mitchell, is to figure prominently in the scheme.

JULY 25 At Saints, France, Lieutenant Frank Luke, soon to gain renown as America's "Balloon Buster," arrives with a group of replacement pilots for the 27th Aero Squadron.

AUGUST 2   At Ourches, France, a formation of 18 DH-4 bombers from the 135th Observation Squadron completes a mission to and from their aerodrome. This action represents the combat debut of American-built warplanes.

AUGUST 7   In France, Chief of Air Service Colonel William "Billy" Mitchell requests the G-2 staff to provide him with targeting intelligence with respect to enemy airdromes, troop concentrations, and transportation choke points such as road intersections and railway stations.

AUGUST 17   The twin-engined Martin MB-1 bomber prototype performs its maiden flight. It was not available in time for combat in World War I, but served many years in the postwar decade as a mail carrier.

AUGUST 19–24   In France, Colonel William "Billy" Mitchell distributes Air Service Circular No. 1, which precisely lays out the targets to be attacked during the upcoming St. Mihiel offensive.

AUGUST 24   In France, a number of French bombardment units are subordinated to the U.S. Air Service, bringing aircraft strength up to 1,467. Moreover, British bomber forces, while independent, are coordinating their actions with Colonel William Mitchell's staff.

Over Chanute Field, Illinois, Major William R. Ream becomes the first flight surgeon to die in an aircraft accident.

AUGUST 28   In Washington, D.C., John D. Ryan gains appointment as the first director of the Air Service, which he holds simultaneously with the title Assistant Secretary of War.

SEPTEMBER 3   In France, General John J. Pershing orders American aerial reconnaissance units to photograph German positions prior to the commencement of ground and air offensive operations.

SEPTEMBER 7   In France, General John J. Pershing's staff headquarters issues Field Orders No. 9, which clearly delineates combat operations and daily objectives during the upcoming St. Mihiel offensive.

In Illinois, the first known instance of aerial troop transportation occurs when 18 soldiers are carried between two air bases.

SEPTEMBER 11   In France, Air Service Chief of Staff Lieutenant Colonel Thomas DeWitt Milling issues orders from Colonel William "Billy" Mitchell that the "Air Service will take the offensive at all points with the objective of destroying the enemy's air service, attacking his troops on the ground, and protecting our own air and ground troops." American air power is about to be born.

SEPTEMBER 12–15   Over France, Colonel William "Billy" Mitchell leads 600 aircraft in America's first, large-scale aviation offensive against St. Mihiel. Once supporting French, British, and Italian units are added to the mix, Mitchell commands a force of 1,476 aircraft and 30,000 servicemen. The first day's activities proceed well despite rain and overcast, and General John J. Pershing orders his airmen to continue attacks pursuant to Field Orders No. 9.

Lieutenant Frank Luke, soon renowned as the "Arizona Balloon Buster," claims his first German observation balloon.

SEPTEMBER 14   Over France, German aerial opposition begins to coalesce along the Hindenburg Line, with small groups of Fokker and Pfalz fighters rising to confront the Allied air offensive.

Luke, Frank (1897–1918)

Army Air Service pilot. Frank Luke was born in Phoenix, Arizona, on May 19, 1897, and he joined the U.S. Army Signal Corps during World War I. He received his flight training at Rockwell Field in San Diego, California, and in, January 1918, he shipped to France as a ferry pilot. Luke chafed under such restraints and began agitating for a combat assignment, so, in July 1918, he transferred to the 27th Aero Squadron, 1st Pursuit Group.

Luke was a loner by nature and not given to group tactics so essential to aerial warfare. Nonetheless, he shot down his first German plane by breaking formation, and received the first of several commendations and reprimands. Luke, however, silenced his critics by continually racking up his tally, and within six weeks he was credited with four aircraft and four observation balloons. The extremely dangerous practice of "balloon busting" became something of a career specialty for Luke. His tactics proved uncannily effective during a single week in September 1918, when he downed no less than 13 enemy craft.

Luke's solitary habits made him unpopular with other fliers, and he was teamed up with a newcomer, Lieutenant Joseph Wehner. The two men became close friends and fought well together, but their luck ended on September 19, 1918, when Wehner was killed. Thereafter Luke flew for revenge, and on September 29, 1918, he claimed two more Fokkers and three additional balloons before being damaged and crash-landing near Murvaux. Rather than surrender, Luke fought back desperately with his pistol until he was killed. He was the first American pilot to receive the Congressional Medal of Honor, posthumously.

SEPTEMBER 15 Over France, Major Carl A. Spatz (latter Spaatz) downs a German warplane, a Fokker D.VII, from a formation of five.

SEPTEMBER 18 At Dayton, Ohio, Major R. W. Schroeder establishes a world altitude record of 28,899 feet over McCook airfield.

SEPTEMBER 19 In France, daredevil pilot Lieutenant Frank Luke is grounded by superiors and ordered on a six-day leave in Paris. Over the past 17 days he has downed fourteen heavily armed balloons and four aircraft.

Over France, five bombers of the 20th Aero Squadron head for a target, but four of them return back to base for mechanical reasons. The aircraft piloted by Lieutenants Arthur F. Seaver and John Y. Stokes, Jr., continues on to the target and, despite the fact that enemy antiaircraft knocked out their engine, and they drop bombs while gliding. The two manage to thwart pursuing German fighters and crash-land behind Allied lines; both receive a Distinguished Service Cross.

SEPTEMBER 25 In France, Colonel William "Billy" Mitchell issues Battle Orders No. 7 to prepare for the upcoming Meuse-Argonne Offensive; this continues with little interruption until November 11.

Over Etain, France, Lieutenant Edward V. Rickenbacker, 94th Aero Squadron, single-handedly tackles seven German aircraft, shooting down a Fokker fighter and a Halberstadt observation craft. He consequently becomes the first American airman to win the Congressional Medal of Honor, although technical foul-ups prevent it being awarded until 1930.

SEPTEMBER 26 In France, the Air Service commits hundreds of aircraft and airmen to offensive operations during the Meuse-Argonne Offensive. By this date they claim to have downed 74 German aircraft and 15 balloons; the struggle here continues until the Armistice of November 11, 1918.

SEPTEMBER 29   At Murvaux, France, Lieutenant Frank Luke, 27th Aero Squadron, the celebrated "Balloon Buster" crashes behind German lines, refuses to surrender, and dies on the ground. With 17 airplanes and 18 balloons to his credit, he is the second-highest American ace of World War I and receives a posthumous Congressional Medal of Honor.

OCTOBER 2   At Dayton, Ohio, the pilotless Liberty Eagle (or Kettering "Bug") is successfully flown and tested, although actual military applications await.

OCTOBER 5   In the Argonne Forest, aircraft of the 50th Aero Squadron begin a limited airdrop of supplies to the "Lost Battalion" once it is cut off by German forces. This is the first sustained aerial resupply in aviation history.

OCTOBER 6   Over Binarville, France, Lieutenants Harold E. Goettler and Erwin R. Blecky, 50th Observation Squadron, are killed trying to deliver mail and supplies to the Army's "Lost Battalion"; both receive posthumous Congressional Medals of Honor.

OCTOBER 7   Over France, a plane from the 24th Aero Squadron flown by Lieutenants S. R. Keesler and H. R. Riley is attacked by German fighters while on a reconnaissance mission. Keesler tries driving the attackers off with his machine gun but is shot down behind enemy lines and dies; he receives a posthumous Distinguished Flying Cross.

OCTOBER 9   Over France, a force of 350 American bombers drops 32 tons of bombs on the region between La Wavrille and Damvillers, France. This is the largest single concentration of American airplanes to date.

OCTOBER 12   Over France, the 185th Aero Squadron performs the Army Air Service's first night missions.

OCTOBER 14   When Brigadier General William G. "Billy" Mitchell is appointed chief of the Air Service Army Group, the general staff disagrees and the position is abolished.

OCTOBER 30   Over France, Captain Eddie Rickenbacker claims his 25th and 26th German planes, becoming the leading American ace. He also receives of a Mackay Trophy for becoming America's "Ace of Aces."

NOVEMBER 6–7   At Aberdeen, Maryland, Dr. Robert H. Goddard test fires various solid-propelled rocket weapons for Army Air Service representatives. The direct military applications for such futuristic technology, however, remain more than two decades off.

NOVEMBER 9   In France, the 155th Night Bombardment Squadron is the final U.S. Air Service unit assigned to the American Expeditionary Force (AEF).

NOVEMBER 10   In France, airmen of the 94th Aero Squadron and the 104th Observation Squadron score the last American aerial victories of World War I during a final sortie over the Western Front. A wartime patrol occurs later that day, the last of the war, with aircraft of the 3rd Aero Squadron.

NOVEMBER 11   In France, the nascent Air Service has deployed 3,538 aircraft and balloons, 20,568 officers, and 175,000 enlisted men. An additional 4,865 aircraft are also in the United States.

NOVEMBER 14   William "Billy" Mitchell, newly promoted to brigadier general, becomes chief of the Air Service, Third Army, American Expeditionary Force (AEF).

NOVEMBER 21   At Mineola, New York, Major J. E. Booth and Lieutenant J. Spencer fly their De Havilland DH-4 bomber 700 miles nonstop from Mount Clemens, Michigan, in only four hours.

DECEMBER 4–22   At San Diego, California, a flight of four Curtiss JN-4s under Major Albert D. Smith lifts off from to begin the first coast-to-coast flight by Army pilots.

DECEMBER 12   Over Fort Tilden, New York, the C-1 dirigible lifts a Curtiss Army JN-4 trainer to 2,500 feet then releases it. The aircraft simply flies away and lands safely, demonstrating the practicality of carrying fighters on lighter-than-air vessels.

DECEMBER 22   At Jacksonville, Florida, Major Albert D. Smith coaxes his Curtiss JN-4 down after successfully completing the first coast-to-coast flight from San Diego, California, by Army pilots. His was the only machine to complete the trip.

1919

JANUARY 2   In Washington, D.C., Major General Charles T. Menoher assumes office as director of the Air Service.

JANUARY 6   Four Army Curtiss JN-4H Jennies fly 4,000 miles during a cross-country flight to select airfields for the forthcoming airmail service.

JANUARY 18   A Loening monoplane flown by Major Rudolph W. Schroeder and powered by a 300-horsepower Hispano engine reaches a record altitude of 19,500 feet.

JANUARY 24   Over Issoudun, France, Lieutenant Temple M. Joyce performs 30 consecutive loops without mishap, impressing onlookers.

FEBRUARY 21   The prototype Thomas-Morse fighter (MB-3) makes its maiden flight; it is eventually accepted into production as the first American designed fighter aircraft. Because 200 will be constructed, this constitutes the largest order for military aircraft for the next 17 years.

MARCH 10   In Washington, D.C., Brigadier General William "Billy" Mitchell gains appointment as commander of Military Aeronautics under the Director of Air Service.

APRIL 19   At New York City, a De Havilland DH-4B flown by Captain E. F. White and mechanic H. M. Schaefer arrives after traveling nonstop from Chicago, Illinois, in 6 hours and 50 minutes; an American distance record of 738.6 miles.

APRIL 28   At McCook Field, Ohio, civilian Leslie L. Irvin jumps from a DH-9 at 1,500 feet while wearing the experimental Model AA backpack parachute. Despite the fact he fractures an ankle upon landing, the Army orders 400 parachutes from his company.

MAY 17   In Washington, D.C., the War Department issues regulations making the national star a standard insignia on all American military aircraft.

MAY 19   Over McCook Airfield, Ohio, Sergeant Ralph W. Bottriell safely demonstrates the "Type A" parachute by jumping from an aircraft; he receives the Distinguished Flying Cross.

JUNE 1   In California, Major Henry H. Arnold, commanding Rockwell Field, California, begins the first fire patrol on the West Coast to assist the District Forester of San Francisco.

JULY 24–NOVEMBER 19   At Bolling Field, Washington, D.C., a twin-engine Martin MB-2 bomber piloted by Lieutenant Colonel R. S. Hartz, Lieutenant F. E. Harmon, and their crew, begins the first peripheral flight around the U.S. borders; the journey takes 155 hours and covers nearly 10,000 miles.

SEPTEMBER 1   At Aberdeen Proving Ground, Maryland, the first experiment in dive-bombing is conducted by a DH-4B flown by Lieutenant Lester B. Sweely (Air Service Reserve), which drops a fuselage-mounted 300-pound bomb.

SEPTEMBER 6   At Dayton, Ohio, Major Rudolph W. Schroeder and Lieutenant G. A. Elfrey set an unofficial two-man altitude record of 28,250 feet flying a Packard-LePere LUSAC II aircraft over McCook Field. To do so the aircraft was fitted with a special Moss Turbo Supercharger while Schroeder was fitted with an oxygen system.

SEPTEMBER 26   Near Arcadia, Florida, flight-testing begins on the Liberty Eagle pilotless flying bomb; of fourteen launches only five become airborne.

OCTOBER 7   At New York, a flight of 44 military aircraft departs for the West Coast on a reliability and endurance test; only 15 machines are available for the return flight, and only 10 of these actually complete the trip. Lieutenant B. W. Maynard wins the Mackay Trophy for coming in first, while Major Carl A. Spaatz registers the fastest west-east flight.

OCTOBER 12–15   At New York, a De Havilland DH-4 bomber flown by Lieutenant Belvin Maynard departs Roosevelt Field and flies roundtrip to San Francisco and back. He covers 5,400 miles in the first transcontinental flight.

OCTOBER 27   In Washington, D.C., Major General Charles T. Menoher, Director of the Air Service, rejects Congressional proposals to establish an independent air force that is free of Army control.

OCTOBER 30   At McCook Field, Dayton, Ohio, the first experiments with a reversible-pitch propeller are successfully conducted. This device slows an aircraft down while landing, allowing aircraft to brake on shorter runways.

1920

FEBRUARY 22   At San Diego, California, Lieutenant W. D. Coney makes the first solo transcontinental flight by flying his DH-4B to Jacksonville, Florida, in 22 hours, 27 minutes. This is also one of the earliest mail-service flights.

FEBRUARY 25   At Langley Field, Virginia, the first Air Service School is

established; it becomes the Air Corps Tactical School in July 1926.

FEBRUARY 27   Over Dayton, Ohio, a Packard-LePere LUSAC 11 biplane flown by Major R. W. Schroeder reaches a world-record altitude of 33,114 feet. The aircraft is powered by a modified Liberty 400 engine.

MAY 1   At Dayton, Ohio, the GA-1 triplane, the Army's first armored aircraft, debuts. This twin-engined bomber is heavily armed with eight machine guns and a 37mm cannon, but only flies at 105 miles per hour; it does not enter production.

MAY 14–16   At Bolling Air Field, Washington, D.C., the first Army Air Tournament, which features several captured German aircraft, draws a crowd of 10,000 people.

JUNE 4   In Washington, D.C., Congress passes the Army Reorganization Bill of 1920, which grants the Air Service permanent status on par with the infantry, cavalry, and artillery. The military rating of "airplane pilot" also arises, with authorized flight pay of 50 percent above existing base pay. Furthermore, the Air Service is authorized 1,514 officers and 16,000 enlisted men.

JUNE 5   To ease competition fears from the Navy, Congress passes legislation restricting the Air Service to land bases.

JUNE 8   Over San Antonio, Texas, Lieutenant John H. Wilson makes an unofficial world-record parachute jump from 19,861 feet.

JUNE 11   At Langley Field, Virginia, Wind Tunnel 1, which is only five feet in length, is successfully tested. Results obtained convince the National Advisory Committee for Aeronautics (NACA) that a larger device is necessary for meaningful results.

JUNE 28   Army and Navy representatives are encouraged by NACA to enroll air officers to the Massachusetts Institute of Technology (MIT) to study aeronautical science; among those assigned there is James H. Doolittle, who garners a doctorate.

JULY 1   In Ohio, the Wright Aeronautical Company constructs a Hispano-Suiza airplane engine capable of firing a 37mm cannon shell down the propeller shaft.

JULY 15–OCTOBER 20   At Mitchel Field, New York, four DH-4Bs under Captain St. Clair Streett fly to Nome, Alaska, and back; the trip covers 9,000 miles and is successfully concluded.

SEPTEMBER 11   At Langley Field, Virginia, three airships fly under radio communication and are directed while aloft and still in formation.

OCTOBER 3   On the Potomac River near Washington, D.C., a Huff-Daland HD-4 Bridget aircraft flown by Lieutenants Godfrey L. Cabot and Harold R. Harris retrieves a five-gallon can of gasoline from a float. This constitutes an early attempt at in-flight refueling.

OCTOBER 20   At Mineola Field, New York, a flight of four aircraft under Captain St. Clair Streett, who departed on the previous July 15, returns after a record 9,000-mile flight to Alaska and back. Streett wins a Mackay Trophy along with the Distinguished Flying Cross for his efforts.

NOVEMBER 1   At Langley Field, Virginia, Major Thomas DeWitt Milling assumes command of the Field Officers School, a precursor of the Air Corps Tactical School at Maxwell Field, Alabama. It arises to create new air doctrines and tactics for fast-changing times.

NOVEMBER 25   At Mitchel Field, New York, Lieutenant Corliss C. Moseley, flying a Verville-Packard 600, wins the first Pulitzer Air Race at an average speed of 156.5 miles per hour.

1921

JANUARY 10   At McCook Field, Dayton, Ohio, engineers test an experimental, 700-horsepower engine, which boasts three banks of six cylinders.

FEBRUARY 21–24   At Rockwell Field, California, Lieutenant William D. Conley stages a solo transcontinental flight to Jacksonville, Florida, covering 2,180 miles in 22 hours and 27 minutes of flying time.

MARCH 23   At Chanute Field, Illinois, Lieutenant A. G. Hamilton parachutes from 23,700 feet and survives.

JUNE 8   At McCook Field, Ohio, a DH–9 bomber flown by Lieutenant Harold R. Harris conducts the first experiments with a pressurized cabin.

JULY 13–21   Off Hampton Roads, Virginia, aerial avatar General William "Billy" Mitchell, Army Air Service, effectively displays air power by sinking the captured German battleship *Ostfriesland* with

Martin MB–2 bombers. He also proclaims, somewhat prematurely, that the eclipse of capital ships is at hand and the supremacy of air power beckons.

JULY 29   General William Mitchell leads a dozen Martin MB–2 bombers over New York City to demonstrate its vulnerability to air attack. He hopes to convince political authorities that the Navy can no longer defend America's coastline, and that that mission is best entrusted to the Air Service.

AUGUST   In Ohio, the Orenco D–1, the first U.S.-designed American fighter craft, is jointly manufactured by the Ordnance Engineering Corporation and Curtiss. The D–1 achieves production status but is only manufactured in small quantities.

AUGUST 1   The Bureau of Ordnance tests a gyroscopic-stabilized, World War I-type high-level bombsight designed by Carl L. Norden; this is a precursor to the famous Norden bombsight of World War II.

The *Ostfriesland, a captured German warship, sinks after being bombed by Martin MB-2 bombers of the First Provisional Air Brigade, Langley Field, 1921. (Library of Congress)*

AUGUST 3–4   At Troy, Ohio, a modified JN-6 Jenny flown by Lieutenant John A. Macready performs the first crop-dusting mission against caterpillar-infested trees.

SEPTEMBER 13   A private report written by Brigadier General William "Billy" Mitchell for Chief of the Air Service Major General Charles T. Menoher, which unequivocally calls for an aviation branch within the Department of National Defense, somehow leaks its way to the press.

SEPTEMBER 23   In Chesapeake Bay, Virginia, Air Service bombers send the obsolete battleship *Alabama* to the bottom with a 2,000-pound bomb.

SEPTEMBER 28   At McCook Field, Dayton, Ohio, a Packard-LePere fighter flown by Lieutenant J. A. Macready reaches a record altitude of 34,508 feet and he wins a Mackay Trophy. He assumes a circular flight path while climbing, the circumference of which reached 70 miles at the very top.

OCTOBER 5   In Washington, D.C., command of the Air Service passes to Major General Mason M. Patrick.

OCTOBER 18   At Mount Clemens, Michigan, Brigadier General William Mitchell pilots a Curtiss R-6 racer to a world speed record of 233 miles per hour.

NOVEMBER 12   At Long Beach, California, two JN-4 Jennies conduct the first in-flight refueling when Lieutenant Wesley May crawls along the wing of one aircraft to the other with a five-gallon can of gasoline strapped to his back, then empties it into the gas tank.

NOVEMBER 15   At Langley Field, Virginia, the *Roma*, the world's largest semirigid airship to that date, makes its initial flight with Captain Dale Mabry at the controls.

Wesley May climbs from one wing to another during the first in-flight refueling, November 12, 1921. (Bettmann/Corbis)

1922

FEBRUARY 21   Ner Hampton Roads Army Air Base, Virginia, the balloon *Roma*, purchased from the Italian government, strikes a high-tension wire; 34 of its 45-man crew are killed.

JUNE 12   At McCook Field, Dayton, Ohio, Captain A. W. Stevens pilots a supercharged Martin MB-2 bomber to 24,000 feet, a record altitude for that type of aircraft.

JUNE 16   At Bolling Field, D.C., Lieutenant Clayton L. Bissell commences a series of night flights to demonstrate that nocturnal flying is as safe as daylight flying. He concludes his experiment by touching down safely at Langley Field, Virginia.

JUNE 29   At Mitchel Field, New York, Lawrence Sperry's radio-controlled "aerial torpedo" covers 90 miles while being guided by a mothership. The concept is way ahead of its time, and neither the Army nor Navy expresses any interest in the technology.

AUGUST 2   At Dayton, Ohio, Lieutenant Leigh Wade, Captain Albert W. Stevens, and Sergeant Roy Langham reach an unofficial three-man altitude of 23,230 feet flying a supercharged bomber over McCook Field.

AUGUST 16   At McCook Airfield, Dayton, Ohio, the Sperry lighting system is demonstrated to assist aircraft landing at night.

SEPTEMBER 4   At San Diego, California, Lieutenant James H. "Jimmy" Doolittle arrives from Pablo Beach, Florida, in a modified DH-4B after covering 2,163 miles in 21 hours and 20 minutes.

This is also the first transcontinental flight completed in a single day.

SEPTEMBER 14–23   At Langley Field, Virginia, the non-rigid airship C-2, piloted by Major H. A. Strauss, flies cross-country to Foss Field, Arcadia, California, completing the first such flight for this type of airship.

SEPTEMBER 29   Dr. Robert H. Goddard compiles his report to the Smithsonian Institution relative to developments in multiple-charge rockets. However, Secretary Charles G. Abbot is less than impressed and cuts Goddard's funding.

OCTOBER 5   Over Rockwell Field, California, Lieutenants J. A. Macready and O. G. Kelly set an airborne endurance record of 35 hours, 18 minutes, and 35 seconds; they receive the Mackay Trophy.

OCTOBER 13   At Selfridge Field, Michigan, Lieutenant T. J. Koenig flies a LePere-Liberty airplane in the 257-mile-long National Air Race; he wins the Liberty Engine Builders Trophy with a speed of 129 miles per hour.

OCTOBER 14   At Detroit, Michigan, Lieutenant Harold R. Brown pilots a Curtiss R-6 racer, powered by a D-12 Conqueror engine, to an average speed of 193 miles per hour. Brown takes this year's Pulitzer Race Trophy and, significantly, Curtiss aircraft occupy the top four places.

OCTOBER 14–NOVEMBER 29   At San Diego, California, a pair of De Havilland DH-4Bs flown by Lieutenants Ben H. Wyatt and George T. Owen complete a round trip transcontinental flight, covering 7,000 miles in 90 hours of flight time.

OCTOBER 18   At Selfridge Field, Michigan, Brigadier General William G. Mitchell pilots a Curtiss R-6 racer to a new airspeed record of 222.96 miles per hour. This is also the first aerial record certified outside of France.

OCTOBER 20   Over McCook Field, Dayton, Ohio, Lieutenant Harold R. Harris is the first aviator saved by a parachute when his Loening PW-2A aircraft loses a wing in flight and he bails out.

OCTOBER 23   At Bolling Field, Washington, D.C., the American Propeller Company demonstrates its reversible propeller to the Army and Navy.

NOVEMBER 3–4   Lieutenants John A. Macready and Oakley G. Kelly pilot a Fokker T-2 aircraft to a record distance of 2,060 miles between San Diego, California, and Benjamin Harrison, Indiana; engine problems stopped them 800 miles of their destination at New York.

NOVEMBER 8   The new School of Aviation Medicine arises when the Air Service Medical Research Laboratory and School for Flight Surgeons are combined.

DECEMBER 18   At McCook Field, Dayton, Ohio, a de Bothezat helicopter rises vertically and flies 300 feet of ground; Major Thurmond H. Bane becomes the Army's first helicopter pilot.

1923

JANUARY 5   At McCook Field, Ohio, personnel from the Army Air Service and Cornell University make the first recorded attempt at "cloud seeding."

JANUARY 9   In Washington, D.C., a War Department board under Major General William Lassiter advocates expanding the Army Air Service. Moreover, the new force would possess its own general headquarters and perform strategic missions without interference from surface forces.

FEBRUARY 6   At Scott Field, Illinois, the Army airship D-2 reaches an altitude of 1,000 feet and maintains it for an hour.

FEBRUARY 7   At Selfridge Field, Michigan, Lieutenant Russell A. Meredith transports a physician to Beaver Island to treat a critically ill man; he receives the Distinguished Flying Cross for his actions.

MARCH 1   The TC-1 nonrigid airship, the largest such craft delivered to date by the Goodrich Tire and Rubber Company, is accepted into the Army Air Service.

MARCH 5   At Selfridge Field, Michigan, a Boeing MB3A fighter successfully jettisons an eternal auxiliary fuel tank for the first time. This device also increases the aircraft's range to 400 miles.

MARCH 27   Major General William Lassiter of the Lassiter Board declares that the Air Service requires operational freedom at the strategic level to strike targets beyond the reach of land and naval forces, to reach its fullest potential. He also notes it will probably require Congressional action to acquire such a function, given the entrenched resistance to airborne independence.

MARCH 29 Lieutenant R. L. Maitland pilots a Curtiss R-6 racer to a new air-speed record of 236.587 miles per hour.

APRIL 16 During a practice flight, Lieutenants John A. Macready and Oakley G. Kelly pilot a Fokker T-2 to new world distance, payload, and endurance records of 2,516 miles in 36 hours and 4 minutes while carrying 10,800 pounds of supplies.

APRIL 17 At Dayton, Ohio, Lieutenant Rutledge Irvine flies a Liberty engine-powered Douglas DT biplane to a Class C record of 11,609 feet. Concurrently, Lieutenant Harold R. Harris sets a new world speed record of 114.35 miles per hour over 1,500 kilometers while flying a Liberty 375-powered DH-4L.

APRIL 20 Over Rockwell Field, California, the first aerial refueling takes place, via a rubber hose extended through the air. Two DH-4s, directed by Major Henry H. Arnold, run a rubber hose between them in flight, and demonstrate the viability of gravity-flow air refueling.

MAY 2–3 At Rockwell Field, San Diego, California, Lieutenants John A. Macready and Oakley G. Kelly complete the first nonstop, transcontinental flight across the United States in a Fokker T-2. The mission originates at Roosevelt Field, New York, lasts 26 hours and 50 minutes, and traverses 2,500 miles. They are greeted by an estimated 100,000 spectators upon arrival.

MAY 14 The new Curtiss PW-8 pursuit (fighter) aircraft is accepted into Army service for flight trials. This is the first in the long series of "Hawk" fighters; the "W" signifies a water-cooled engine.

MAY 26 At Hamilton, Ontario, a DH-4B bomber flown by Lieutenant H. G. Crocker arrives from Houston, Texas, in an early south-to-north transcontinental flight of 11 hours and 55 minutes.

JUNE 20 At McCook Field, Dayton, Ohio, the prototype Gallaudet CO-1 monoplane, the Army's first all-metal aircraft, performs its maiden flight. The machine was designed and built by the Air Corps Engineering Division at the field, but proves unsuccessful.

JUNE 23 At Rockwell Field, San Diego, a DH-4 bomber piloted by Lieutenants Lowell H. Smith and John P. Richter perform the first air-to-air transfer of fuel over a hose extended from another DH-4 flown by Lieutenants Virgil Hine and Frank Seifert.

JULY 4 Lieutenants R. S. Olmstead and J. W. Shoptaw fly Army balloon S6 500 miles between Indianapolis, Indiana, and Marilla, New York, winning the National Elimination Balloon Race.

AUGUST 22 At McCook Field, Dayton, Ohio, the huge and experimental Barling XNBL-1 bomber makes its maiden flight. Gigantic for its age, the craft spanned 120 feet, was powered by six 400-horse-power Liberty engines, and flew at a top speed of 93 miles per hour; it is not accepted into service.

AUGUST 27–28 At Rockwell Field, California, a DH-4B bomber piloted by Lieutenants John P. Richter and Lowell H. Smith sets world distance and endurance records by covering 3,293 miles in 37 hours and 15 minutes.

SEPTEMBER 5 Near Cape Hatteras, North Carolina, General John J. Pershing watches as Army bombers sink the elderly battleships *Virginia* and *New Jersey* during bombardment tests.

Mitchell, William (1879–1936)

Army Air Service general. William "Billy" Mitchell was born in Nice, France, on December 29, 1879, and in 1898 he joined the army during the Spanish-American War. In 1915 he joined the aviation section, received his pilot's license at the advanced age of 36, and spent the next 20 years advocating the expansion of American air power. He was also a military observer in Europe when World War I commenced and, following America's entry in 1917, he served as a senior air commander. In September 1918, Mitchell orchestrated a mass aerial offensive against the St. Mihiel salient in concert with ground forces. He repeated his success in the Meuse-Argonne Offensive, rose to brigadier general, and was preparing a strategic bombardment campaign against Germany when the Armistice was signed. Mitchell returned to the United States, a decorated war veteran devoted to the primacy of air power.

Back home, Mitchell was outspoken in his assertions that aircraft had rendered navies obsolete and, to underscore that belief, on July 21, 1921 his Martin bombers sank the captured German battleship *Ostfriesland* off the Virginia Capes. However, in September 1925, when the navy dirigible *Shenandoah* crashed in a storm, he publicly accused War Department officials of criminal neglect and was court-martialed. Mitchell was found guilty of insubordination, but he resigned and continued touring the country to advocate air power. He also published several popular books on the subject before dying suddenly in New York City on February 19, 1936. The Japanese attack on Pearl Harbor, December 7, 1941, was one of Mitchell's many aerial prophecies to come true, and in 1946 Congress awarded him a posthumous Congressional Medal of Honor.

SEPTEMBER 13–DECEMBER 14 At Langley Field, Virginia, a Martin MB-2 bomber flown by Lieutenants J. F. Whitley and H. D. Smith departs on a transcontinental tour that ends at Rockwell Field, California, covers 8,000 miles, and last three months. They are testing possible routes for a national airway.

SEPTEMBER 18 A diminutive Sperry M-1 Messenger, one of the smallest airplanes ever designed for the Air Service, is flown by Lieutenant Rex L. Stoner and makes a successful "hook-up" with an Army D-3 airship in midair.

OCTOBER 6 In St. Louis, Missouri, Lieutenant Al Williams establishes a new speed record of 243.76 miles per hour at the Pulitzer Trophy flying competition.

OCTOBER 25 Over Ohio, the gigantic Barling bomber (NBX-1) piloted by Lieutenant Harold R. Harris sets a payload record by carrying 3,000 kilograms of cargo to 5,344 feet for 1 hour and 19 minutes.

At Camas, Washington State, a DH-4B flown by Lieutenants L. H. Smith and J. P. Richter fly nonstop 1,280 miles to Tijuana, Mexico, with three in-flight air refuelings.

The court martial of Brigadier General William G. "Billy" Mitchell begins; he is charged with insubordination and uses the occasion to make the case for air power as a separate branch of the military.

NOVEMBER 1 Dr. Robert H. Goddard successfully test launches a liquid fuel rocket powered by gasoline and liquid oxygen. The fluids are pumped into a combustion chamber and fired out a nozzle in the rear.

NOVEMBER 18 Over Kelly Field, Texas, tragedy strikes during an air show as an air refueling hose gets entangled in the wings of the two aircraft; the plane piloted by Lieutenant P. T. Wagner crashes, killing him.

DECEMBER 13   In the English Channel, a Sperry M-1 Messenger flown by Lawrence B. Sperry, son of the inventor, crashes during a cross-channel flight; the pilot drowns.

1924

FEBRUARY 22   An XC-05A piloted by Lieutenant John A. Macready reaches an altitude of 38,704 feet, a new record.

FEBRUARY 27   Over Kelly Field, Texas, Corporal C. E. Conrad vaults from a DH-4B bomber at 21,500 feet and parachutes safely down.

MARCH 4   Over North Bend, Nebraska, two DH-4 and two MB-2s unload bombs on the Platte River and break up surface ice to avert any chance for subsequent flooding. The bombing lasted for six hours.

MARCH 7   A DH-4B bomber piloted by Lieutenants E. H. Barksdale and B. Jones flies 575 miles between Mitchel Field, New York, and McCook Field, Ohio, by relying only on cockpit instruments.

MARCH 24   In Washington, D.C., the House of Representatives establishes the Lampert Commission to closely investigate the status and future of the U.S. Air Service.

APRIL 6   At Seattle, Washington, four Douglas World Cruisers christened *Boston*, *Chicago*, *New Orleans*, and *Seattle* depart on the first attempted round-the-world flight. This 26,350-mile mission is also the first transpacific flight and the first westbound crossing of the North Atlantic.

APRIL 30   In Alaska, the Douglas World Cruiser named *Seattle* crashes into a mountainside, although the crew survives and is rescued.

MAY 2   Over Dayton, Ohio, Lieutenants John A. Macready and Albert Stevens take an aerial photograph of the town, which covers 19 square miles; to do this, they make an unofficial altitude record in their LePere aircraft.

MAY 19   Over Dayton, Ohio, a LePere Liberty 400 piloted by Lieutenant John A. Macready reaches 35,329 feet, a new altitude record.

JUNE 23–24   At San Francisco, California, a Curtiss PW-8 fighter piloted by Lieutenant Russell I. Maughan arrives after covering 2,670 miles from Long Island, New York. The flight took 18 hours and 20 minutes by air, with an additional three hours and 20 minutes on the ground to refuel five times.

JUNE 28   A Curtiss bomber flown by Lieutenant John A. Macready sets an altitude record of 16,732 feet while carrying a payload of 3,306.9 pounds.

JULY 6   In California, Major Henry H. Arnold establishes a new speed record by flying 500 miles between Rockwell Field and San Francisco in only 4 hours and 25 minutes.

AUGUST 3   Over the North Sea, the Douglas World Cruiser *Boston* drops into the water after losing oil pressure. The craft is destroyed by pounding waves but the crew survives and is rescued.

SEPTEMBER 28   In Seattle, Washington, the remaining Douglas World Cruisers, *Chicago* and *New Orleans*, complete the first round-the-world flight by touching down. They covered 27,553 miles in only 175 days, which included 365 hours of flight time. Lieutenants Lowell Smith, Leslie Arnold, Erik Nelson, and John Harding are awarded a Mackay Trophy.

OCTOBER 28   At Bolling Field, Washington, D.C., an Army Air Service airplane seeds clouds with electrically charged sand for the first time; the experiment is a success.

1925

JANUARY 18   At Bolling Field, Washington, D.C., the new Loening amphibian is publicly displayed after a year in secret development; this all-metal biplane operates on either land or water and, carries three passengers for 700 miles.

AUGUST 22   The Army Air Service develops an in-flight system to record an aircraft's speed and bearing while aloft; this is a precursor to the modern-day "black box."

SEPTEMBER 3   At Cleveland, Ohio, a Granville GB racer piloted by Major James H. Doolittle reaches 294 miles per hour, a world speed record.

SEPTEMBER 12   In Washington, D.C., President Calvin Coolidge appoints an aeronautical advisory board under Dwight W. Morrow. He is to report on the state of American aviation and possible future trends.

SEPTEMBER 29   In Washington, D.C., Colonel William Mitchell testifies before Congress that the nation needs an independent air force. He further characterizes contemporary military attitudes respecting aviation as out of touch. Mitchell is court-martialed in consequence.

OCTOBER 15   At Mitchel Field, New York, Lieutenant Cyrus Betts takes the 1925 Pulitzer race in his Curtiss R3C-1 racer and also establishes a new world speed record of 248.9 miles per hour.

OCTOBER 26–27   In Baltimore, Maryland, a Curtiss R3C-2 floatplane flown by Lieutenant James H. "Jimmy" Doolittle wins the Schneider Cup Race with a top speed of 230 miles per hour. On the following day, Doolittle sets a new world record of 245.713 miles per hour in the same aircraft.

NOVEMBER 10   In New York City, an aircraft piloted by Major Thomas G. Lamphier touches down after covering 500 miles from Selfridge Field, Michigan, in 3 hours and 20 minutes.

NOVEMBER 30   In Washington, D.C., the Morrow Board presents its findings to President Calvin Coolidge. While falling short of recommending an independent air force, it recommends that the Air Service be renamed the Air Corps, that an assistant secretary of war for air be appointed, and that a five-year plan be adopted for expanding of the air arm.

DECEMBER 6   Dr. Robert H. Goddard successfully test fires a liquid-fuel rocket that produces 100 pounds of thrust and lifts its own weight for 10 seconds.

DECEMBER 14   In Washington, D.C., the Lampert Committee makes its report to the House of Representatives; they favor creation of a Department of Defense, greater aviation representation in higher military circles, and a pay raise for aviators.

DECEMBER 17 A military court finds Brigadier General William G. Mitchell guilty of insubordination. He is sentenced to rank and pay suspension for five years, but President Calvin Coolidge revises it to five years' suspension at half pay. Mitchell nonetheless resigns his commission to serve as a one-man spokesman on behalf of air power.

DECEMBER 24 In Connecticut, the Pratt and Whitney company constructs its famous Wasp radial engine.

1926

JANUARY 8 Over Scott Field, Illinois, Lieutenant Orvil Andersen pilots the RS-1, then the world's largest semi-rigid airship, being 282 feet long, 70 feet in diameter, and displacing 755,500 cubic feet when inflated. Andersen and his crew of eight circle the airfield at speeds of 40 miles per hour.

JANUARY 27 Brigadier General William G. Mitchell resigns from the Army, intending to champion American air power as a civilian. This move costs him retirement benefits commensurate with his rank, but he presses his beliefs with urgency.

JANUARY 29 At Dayton, Ohio, a XCO-5A flown by Lieutenant John A. Macready reaches 38,704 feet over McCook Field, a world record.

MARCH 8 At Clark University, Massachusetts, Dr. Robert H. Goddard tests an oxygen-pressure-fed rocket motor on a static stand for the first time.

MARCH 16 Near Auburn, Massachusetts, Dr. Robert H. Goddard successfully launches his first liquid-fueled rocket, a major technological development. The propellant burns but 2.5 seconds, yet propels the missile 184 feet. However, military implications for such new technology remain pending.

JULY 2 In Washington, D.C., Congress, cognizant of the growing importance of military aviation and recommendations of the Morrow Board, founds the Army Air Corps (AAC) as a separate branch of the service. This new arm is authorized at 16,650 men and 1,800 aircraft, and includes a new assistant secretary of war for air. Major General Mason M. Patrick is also appointed chief of the new Army Air Corps. Congress further mandates that no less than 20 percent of all military pilots must be drawn from enlisted ranks.

The Distinguished Flying Cross medal is established for all military individuals who distinguish themselves through some aerial activity; the award is retroactive to April 6, 1917.

JULY 16 In Washington, D.C., F. Trubee Davidson gains appointment as the first assistant secretary of war for air within the War Department.

DECEMBER 7 Flight surgeon Captain Charles T. Buckner, in the world's first study in aerospace medicine, flies a DH-4B to 28,000 feet without an oxygen tank to study the effects of high altitudes.

DECEMBER 21 At Kelly Field, San Antonio, Texas, five Loening AO-1A

Amphibians under Major Herbert A. Dargue commence a Pan-American Good-will Tour of South and Central America, covering 25 nations and 22,000 miles.

1927

MAY 2 At Bolling Airfield, Washington, D.C., President Calvin Coolidge awards eight Army pilots the Distinguished Flying Cross for flying from San Antonio, Texas, to South America, and back. The so-called "Goodwill Flight" lasted 122 days and covered 20,000 miles. The fliers also receive the Mackay Trophy for that year.

MAY 4 At Scott Field, Illinois, Captain H. C. Gray pilots an untethered balloon to an unofficial world record of 42,479 feet.

MAY 20–21 In Paris, France, Captain Charles A. Lindbergh, 110th Observation Squadron, Missouri National Guard, lands his Ryan monoplane named *The Spirit of St. Louis* after a historic solo flight across the Atlantic Ocean from New York. His flight covered 3,648 miles in 33 hours and 39 minutes and he receives the Distinguished Flying Cross and a special Congressional Medal of Honor.

MAY 25 Lieutenant James H. Doolittle performs the first outside loop in his Curtiss P-18 fighter.

JUNE 28–29 The Fokker C-2 *Bird of Paradise* piloted by Lieutenants Lester J. Maitland and Albert F. Hegenberger flies 2,407 miles between Oakland, California, to Oahu, Hawaii, in 25 hours and 50 minutes. They receive the Distinguished Flying Cross and the Mackay Trophy for their efforts.

OCTOBER 12 In Dayton, Ohio, McCook Field closes and is replaced by Wright Field, where aeronautical testing and development continues apace.

NOVEMBER 4 An Army hydrogen balloon flown by Captain Hawthorne C. Gray breaks all altitude records by reaching 42,470 feet, but he dies from lack of oxygen. His demise highlights the need for pressure suits and oxygen systems.

DECEMBER 10 In Washington, D.C., Colonel Charles A. Lindbergh is voted a Congressional Medal of Honor for his epic transatlantic crossing.

Charles A. Lindbergh, an Army reserve officer, poses next to his record-breaking Ryan aircraft, the Spirit of St. Louis. *(Library of Congress)*

DECEMBER 14   Major General James
Fechet, who rose from the enlisted ranks
to a command position, gains appointment as chief of the Army Air Corps.

1928

FEBRUARY 3   At Wright Field, Ohio,
Lieutenant H. A. Sutton receives a
Mackay Trophy for his work testing spin
characteristics of aircraft to improve aviation safety.

FEBRUARY 15   In Washington, D.C.,
President Calvin Coolidge authorizes
construction of a new Army Air Corps
training facility at San Antonio, Texas.
This is an innovative circular design
allowing squadrons to fly, train, and work
close to each other in different quadrants
of the housing circle and is subsequently
christened Randolph Field.

MARCH 1–9   A Loening OL amphibian
piloted by Lieutenants Burnie R. Dallas
and Beckwith Havens makes the first
transcontinental flight of an amphibious
aircraft; they complete their task in
32 hours and 45 minutes.

MAY 12   At Bolling Field, Washington,
D.C., a pair of Boeing PW-9 pursuit aircraft piloted by Lieutenants R. W. Douglas and J. E. Parker set a distance record
for fighter aircraft after arriving from
France Field, Panama Canal Zone.

   Over Florida, Army Air Corps lieutenant Julian S. Dexter finishes a two-month
mapping mission photographing 65,000
square miles of the Everglades.

JUNE 9   At Langley Field, Virginia, Lieutenant Earle Partridge wins his third consecutive Army Air Corps aerial gunnery
match.

JUNE 15   An Air Corps blimp flown
by Lieutenants Karl S. Axtater and
Edward H. White delivers a mail satchel
to the clerk of a moving train, thereby
completing the first aircraft-to-train mail
transfer.

JUNE 16   Over Wright Field, Ohio, a new
supercharger allows improved engine
performance at altitudes of up to 30,000
feet. Previously, aircraft engines were sus-
ceptible to power loss owing to the thin-
ness of the air.

JUNE 28   Langley Field, Virginia, is
ordered to serve as an experimental air
station for developing new aircraft and
technologies.

JUNE 30–JULY 1   In Detroit, Michigan,
Captain W. E. Kepner and Lieutenant
W. O. Eareckson win the Gordon Bennett International Balloon Race. The
distance covered is 460 miles; this is the
third consecutive victory by American
aircrews.

AUGUST 18   Randolph Field, San Antonio, Texas, is turned over to the Army
by city officials and quickly establishes
itself as a leading aviation center.

OCTOBER 10   At Wright Field, Ohio,
Captains St. Clair Streett and A. W.
Stevens set a world's record for aircraft
with more than one person in flight by
climbing to an altitude of 37,854 feet.

1929

JANUARY 1–7 Over Los Angeles, California, the Fokker C-2 Trimotor *Question Mark*, piloted by Army Major Carl Spaatz, Captain Ira C. Eaker, and Lieutenants Elwood Quesada and Harry Halveson, establishes a flight endurance record of 150 hours and 40 minutes. They are refueled 37 times by a pair of specially rigged Douglas C-1 transports.

JANUARY 9–16 A Fokker C-2 transport piloted by Major Paul Beck flies 3,130 miles from Wright Field, Ohio, to France Field, Panama Canal Zone, becoming the first military aircraft ferried abroad by the Army Air Corps.

FEBRUARY 23 At Wright Field, Ohio, the perfection of heated goggles, gloves, and oxygen bottles is announced by the laboratory there.

APRIL 14 In a major development, Edward A. Link patents his "flight trainer" (or flight control simulator), which becomes part of every pilot's basic flight instruction. By the advent of World War II, over half a million American and Allied pilots train on these devices en route to getting their wings.

MAY 16 In Hollywood, California, the World War I aerial drama *Wings* receives the first Oscar award for best picture. The film was shot with many real and reconstructed World War I fighter craft and highlights the nation's continuing interest in aviation.

The crew of the record-breaking Fokker C-2 aircraft Question Mark: *Major Carl Spaatz, Captain Ira C. Eaker, Lieutenants Harry Halverson and Elwood R. Quesada, and Sergeant Roy Hooe. (Library of Congress)*

MAY 21–22 In response to a directive from Assistant Secretary of War for Aviation Turbee Division, the Army Air Corps directs a Keystone bomber to fly roundtrip and nonstop from Dayton, Ohio, to New York. However, the mission is scrubbed when bad weather grounds the refueling aircraft. The bomber continues on to Washington, D.C., and, on the following day, rendezvous with the tanker.

MAY 30 In Washington, D.C., a Liberty-powered DH-4 completes cross-country air refueling tests while flying in from New York.

JULY 17 Near Auburn, Massachusetts, Dr. Robert H. Goddard successfully test launches a liquid-propelled rocket that carries a camera aloft which takes photos of a barometer and a thermometer on board.

AUGUST 15 In Spokane, Washington, Lieutenants Nicholas B. Mamer and Arthur Walker fly their Buhl Sesquiplane *Spokane Sun God* nonstop to the East Coast and back. They cover 7,200 miles while being refueled in the air 11 times.

SEPTEMBER 24 At Mitchel Field, New York, Lieutenant James H. Doolittle makes aviation history by successfully completing the first "blind" airplane flight. He flies his Consolidated NY-2 biplane for hours in a canvas-covered canopy using only instruments and no radio. Years later, Doolittle considered this feat his greatest contribution to aviation.

NOVEMBER 23 In New York, the Daniel Guggenheim Fund for the Promotion of Aeronautics awards Dr. Robert H. Goddard a $50,000 grant to assist his research with rockets.

NOVEMBER 29 Over Antarctica, a Ford Trimotor flown by Navy Commander Richard E. Byrd, Bernt Balchen, and Harold June makes an epic flight across the South Pole for the first time. They are accompanied by Army captain Ashley McKinley, who serves as the trip photographer.

1930

JANUARY 8–29 At Selfridge Field, Michigan, a flight of Curtiss P-1C Hawks under Major Ralph Royce departs for Spokane, Washington, to train under sub-zero flying conditions; he receives the Mackay Trophy.

APRIL 6 Army captain Frank Hawks flies 2,860 miles from San Diego, California, to New York City while piloting a glider that is towed by another aircraft.

APRIL 12 At Mather Field, California, Captain Hugh M. Elmendorf guides a flight of 19 Boeing P-19 fighters, 95th Pursuit Squadron, as they climb in formation to 30,000 feet, a new altitude record.

APRIL 21 Colonel Charles A. Lindbergh, accompanied by wife Anne Morrow, fly a Lockheed Sirius from Glendale, California, to Roosevelt Field, New York, covering 2,530 miles in a record in 14 hours and 45 minutes.

JUNE 20   At San Antonio, Texas, Randolph Field is inaugurated as the Army's newest flight training center for primary and basic pilot instruction. In this capacity it becomes a cradle of a generation of airmen who fight and win World War II, and subsequently serves as headquarters of the Air Education and Training Command. For this reason is regarded as the "West Point of the Air."

JULY 28   At Kelly Field, Texas, instrument flying is added to the regular curriculum at the U.S. Air Corps Advanced Flying School.

NOVEMBER 6   In Washington, D.C., President Herbert Hoover awards Captain Edward V. Rickenbacker the Congressional Medal of Honor he should have received in 1918, had the paperwork not become lost.

NOVEMBER 9–16   From New York, Captain Roy W. Ammel pilots a Lockheed Sirius Blue Flash 2,700 miles to the Panama Canal Zone in 24 hours and 35 minutes.

NOVEMBER 16   In Washington, D.C., Major General James E. Fechet, chief of the Army Air Corps, releases his annual report, which reveals the strength of the corps at 12,032, including 1,226 officers and 378 cadets.

DECEMBER 30   At Roswell, New Mexico, Dr. Robert H. Goddard's fifth liquid-fuel rocket rises to 2,000 feet at a speed of 500 miles per hour.

1931

JANUARY 9   In Washington, D.C., Army Chief of Staff Douglas MacArthur and Chief of Naval Operations William V. Pratt agree to allow the Army Air Corps to monopolize coastal defenses, while the Navy remains free to concentrate on carrier aviation and mobile air operations at sea.

FEBRUARY 15   At Selfridge Field, Michigan, the first nighttime deployment of aircraft unfolds when 19 planes take off, navigate nocturnally, then land safely at Bolling Field, Washington, D.C.

MAY 9   The War Department approves reproduction of the A-2 leather flying jacket as stand issue for aviators.

MAY 21–30   Brigadier General Benjamin D. Foulois directs a massive aerial training exercise, involving 667 aircraft and 1,400 crew members, as it commences across the nation. Every manner of aerial operation, including pursuit, bombardment, and observation, is successfully conducted; Foulois receives the Mackay Trophy for directing these ambitious maneuvers.

MAY 27   At Langley Field, Virginia, Army and NACA personnel construct the nation's first full-scale wind tunnel for testing full-size aircraft.

JULY 15–31   Maxwell Field, Montgomery, Alabama, becomes the new site of the Air Corps Tactical School. It becomes a hotbed of new air power theories throughout the ensuing decade. Foremost among them is the notion of long-range, daylight strategic missions employing precision bombing techniques. This becomes the backbone of American aerial strategy during World War II.

JULY 29   At Tokyo, Japan, Colonel Charles Lindbergh, accompanied by his wife, flies a Lockheed Sirius in from New York in one of the earliest transpacific flights.

AUGUST 11   At Maxwell Field, Alabama, Major John Curry gains appointment as commander of the Air Corps Tactical School.

SEPTEMBER 4   A Laird Racer flown by Lieutenant James H. Doolittle wins the first Bendix Transcontinental Race by flying from Los Angeles, California, to Cleveland, Ohio, in 9 hours and 10 minutes. He then refuels and continues on to Newark, New Jersey,

completing a coast–to–coast flight in only 11 hours and 16 minutes. Doolittle refuels again, returns to Cleveland to claim his trophy, then flies into St. Louis, Missouri, and home.

NOVEMBER 1   At Randolph Field, Texas, the aviation school enrolls its first class of 198 students, which includes members from West Point, the enlisted ranks, and civilian candidates.

DECEMBER 18   Over Hawaii, a glider flown by Lieutenant William A. Cooke sets an airborne record of 21 hours, 34 minutes, and 15 seconds.

DECEMBER 19   In Washington, D.C., Major General Benjamin D. Foulois gains appointment as commander of the Army Air Corps.

Arnold, Henry H. (1886–1950)

Army Air Forces general. Henry Harley Arnold was born in Gladwyne, Pennsylvania, on June 25, 1886 and he graduated from the U.S. Military Academy in 1907. He joined the Aviation Section, Signal Corps as one of the Army's earliest pilots, and in June 1912, he won the first Mackay Trophy for establishing a record altitude of 6,540 feet. Sidelined by a near-fatal crash, Arnold resumed flying in 1916 and over the next three decades he placed himself at the forefront of aviation with several record-breaking flights. In 1936 he conducted a flight of Martin B-10 bombers from Langley Field, Virginia, to Alaska and back and, two years later, Arnold became chief of the Army Air Corps following the death of Major General Oscar Westover. He was especially cognizant of aviation developments in Nazi Germany, and through the assistance of George Marshall, now Army chief of staff, he arranged a six-fold increase in military aircraft production.

On December 15, 1941, Arnold advanced to lieutenant general and, over the next four years, he surmounted daunting production, technological, and administrative challenges and allowed the Army Air Forces to expand from 22,000 men and 3,400 aircraft, to 2.5 million personnel and 63,715 warplanes. For orchestrating successful air strategies against the Axis, Arnold became a five-star general of the Army, the only airman so honored. After the war he remained in semi-retirement until 1947, then gained appointment as the first head of the newly independent U.S. Air Force through a special act of Congress. Arnold died in Sonoma, California, on January 15, 1950, a leading architect of American air power.

Doolittle, Jimmy (1896–1993)

Army Air Forces general. James Harold Doolittle was born in Alameda, California, on December 14, 1896, and in 1917 he joined the U.S. Army Signal Corps as a pilot. He became closely identified with General William "Billy" Mitchell's crusade for American air power and, in 1925, he graduated from the Massachusetts Institute of Technology with the first doctorate in aeronautical engineering. Doolittle next contributed to aviation by inventing such useful devices as the artificial horizon gauge, which he used to make the first blind takeoff and landing on September 24, 1929. In 1930 Doolittle left the military to represent the aviation branch of the Shell Oil Company, and applied his expertise to developing higher-octane aviation fuels. In 1940, shortly before American entry into World War II, he was returned to active duty by Army Air Corps chief General Henry H. Arnold, and spent several months touring aircraft factories and clearing up production bottlenecks.

In the spring of 1942 Doolittle conceived the plan to launch 16 B-25 land-based bombers from a carrier deck for the purposes of raiding Japan. These struck targets in and around Tokyo on April 18, 1942, and he consequently won a Congressional Medal of Honor and a double promotion to brigadier general. That year he arrived in the Mediterranean theater as a senior commander, and in January 1944 he transferred to London, England, to assume control of the Eighth Air Force. In 1945 Doolittle became the youngest lieutenant general in U.S. Army history, aged only 49 years. After the war, he resumed working for Shell Oil and the space division of TRW until his death at Pebble Beach, California, on September 27, 1993.

1932

JANUARY 1–31 Over Winslow, Arizona, bombers of the 11th Bombardment Squadron drop supplies and relief packages to snowbound Navajo and Hopi Indians. The squadron receives the Mackay Trophy for their humanitarian efforts.

JANUARY 11 Major Hugh J. Knerr proposes to establish a basic Air Corps transportation service with air depots based at Sacramento, California; San Antonio, Texas; Fairchild, Ohio; and Middletown, Pennsylvania.

MARCH 20 Boeing displays its XP-936 fighter plane, the first all-metal monoplane aircraft evaluated by the Army Air Corps. It enters service as the P-26 Peashooter, being the last Army pursuit craft with an open cockpit, fixed landing gear, and external wing-wire bracing.

MARCH 24 The Army Air Corps, delighted by the success rate of the Norden Mark XV bombsight in tests held the previous fall, requests 25 such devices for further evaluation.

MAY 9 Over Patterson, Ohio, Army captain Albert F. Hegenberger completes a 15-minute blind, solo flight in a "hooded" Consolidated NY-2; he wins the Collier Trophy for his effort.

AUGUST 31 Over Freyburg, Maine, an aircraft flown by Captain A. W. Stevens and Lieutenant C. D. McAllister reaches an altitude of five miles to help photograph a solar eclipse.

SEPTEMBER 3 At Cleveland, Ohio, Major James H. Doolittle pilots the dangerous Granville GeeBee Racer to 294 miles per hour, setting a new land aircraft speed record.

SEPTEMBER 21   At March Field, California, a Curtiss Condor bomber carries scientists from the California Institute of Technology skyward to measure the intensity of cosmic rays from high altitude. The aircraft are assigned from the 11th Bombardment Squadron of Lieutenant Colonel Henry H. Arnold.

1933

JANUARY 3   In Washington, D.C., General Douglas A. MacArthur instructs the Air Corps to conduct all land-based operations in defense of the United States and all overseas possessions.

FEBRUARY 10   Major Hugh J. Knerr, chief of the Field Service Section, Air Materiel Division, promulgates a scheme whereby each of four regional air depots will possess its own air transport squadron to haul men and equipment between the depots. They can also transport army troops on maneuvers.

OCTOBER 11   In Washington, D.C., a board headed by Major General Hugh A. Drum recommends creation of a General Headquarters Air Force (GHQ). This would consists of 1,000 aircraft and operate independently of all ground units; the report is subsequently approved by Secretary of War George H. Dern.

NOVEMBER 20   After departing from Akron, Ohio, Lieutenant Commander Thomas G. W. Settle and Major Chester L. Fordney are the first Americans to take a balloon to an altitude of 61,237 feet.

NOVEMBER 27   The first production Martin B-10 bomber is accepted into the Army Air Corps. This streamlined, all-metal monoplane features retractable landing gear, an internal bomb bay, and a power nose turret. It flies faster than contemporary fighters of the day.

DECEMBER 13   In Washington, D.C., Major Bryan Freeburg receives the first Air Mail Flyer's Medal of Honor from President Franklin D. Roosevelt.

1934

FEBRUARY 18   In Washington, D.C., President Franklin D. Roosevelt directs the Army Air Corps to commence regularly scheduled airmail service along 26 selected routes. This is because of perceived fraud connected with the commercial airlines contracted to perform the task; the effort, while earnest, is plagued with accidents and fatalities.

MARCH 10–19   The Army Air Corps temporarily suspends delivery of mail nationwide following a spate of accidents and nine deaths. Once proper night and bad-weather flying instrumentation is secured, the effort then resumes with fewer routes and numbers of flights.

APRIL 11   In Washington, D.C., Secretary of War George Dern convenes the Baker Board to evaluate the effectiveness of the U.S. Army Air Corps, and its equipment and training, in times of peace and war.

MAY 22   Captain W. T. Larson, who helped pioneer techniques pertaining to instrument flying and blind takeoffs and landings, wins a Mackay Trophy.

JUNE 1   Once commercial contracts have been renegotiated, the Army Air Corps is relieved of domestic airmail flight. Since February, Army pilots flew over 13,000 hours in the air, covered 1.5 million miles, and delivered 777,000 pounds of mail. The numerous accidents, however, revealed shortcomings in both pilot training and equipment, and the remedial efforts adopted place the American air arm on a much sounder footing.

Th Army Air Corps initiates a plan to employ civilian flying schools for the primary training of all flying cadets. These instructors allow the military to concentrate on advanced training and flying techniques.

JUNE 18   In Seattle, Washington, the Boeing Company stakes its future on the new Model 299, a large four-engine bomber that is accepted into service as the B–17 Flying Fortress.

JUNE 28   In Washington, D.C., the War Department is suitably impressed by Boeing's Model 299 and issues a contract to develop a prototype.

JULY 10   At Langley Field, Virginia, Lieutenant Colonel Henry "Hap" Arnold embarks on a stirring display of strategic air power by leading ten Martin B–10 bombers from to Fairbanks, Alaska, on a round-trip flight.

JULY 18   In Washington, D.C., a board headed by former Secretary of War Newton D. Baker concurs with the 1933 Drum Board report that a centrally controlled aerial strike force could enhance the Army Air Corps' effectiveness.

JULY 28   Over Nebraska, Army Major W. E. Kepner and Captains A. W. Stevens and O. A. Anderson rise in the pressurized balloon *Explorer* to 60,613 feet (14 miles). However, when the air bag tears, they bail out from extremely high altitude and safely land in a cornfield; all win the Distinguished Flying Cross.

AUGUST 20   At Bolling Field, Washington, D.C., Lieutenant Colonel Henry H. Arnold returns from Fairbanks, Alaska, with his Martin B–10 bombers after covering 7,360 miles without major mishap. This is also the first trip where radio communication was maintained with ground units for the duration of the venture; Arnold wins the Mackay Trophy and a Distinguished Flying Cross.

NOVEMBER 8   A passenger plane piloted by Captain Eddie Rickenbacker, Captain Charles W. France, and Silas Moorehouse sets a new speed record for this class of aircraft by flying nonstop from Los Angeles, California, to Newark, New Jersey, in 12 hours and 4 minutes.

NOVEMBER 17   At Selfridge Field, Michigan, an airplane flown by Captain Fred C. Nelson wins the Mitchell Trophy after hitting speeds of 217.832 miles per hour.

1935

JANUARY 15   A passenger plane flown by Major James H. Doolittle sets a new world record by flying between Los Angeles, California, and New York in 11 hours and 59 minutes.

MARCH 1   At Langley Field, Virginia, the Army Air Corps activates its General Headquarters Air Force (GHQ). This is an independent strike force under Brigadier General Frank M. Andrews, which reports directly to the Army chief of staff instead of a ground commander. It proves a seminal step towards the refinement of strategic air power, and creation of an independent air force.

MARCH 8   At Roswell, New Mexico, a liquid-fuel rocket launched by Dr. Robert H. Goddard reaches 1,000 feet at a speed of 700 miles per hour, then parachutes back to Earth. At 84 pounds, this is one of Goddard's largest rockets.

MARCH 28   At Roswell, New Mexico, a liquid-fueled, gyroscopically controlled rocket is launched by Dr. Robert H. Goddard; it reaches 4,800 feet at 550 miles per hour.

APRIL 1   In Los Angeles, California, the North American NA-16 prototype makes its maiden flight and is quickly adopted as an advanced training aircraft. It enters the Army as the AT-6.

MAY 31   Hickam Field, Hawaii, reaches operational status for Army aircraft.

JULY 22   Captain Albert F. Hegenberger wins this year's Collier Trophy for developing and demonstrating a new blind landing system.

JULY 28   Over Seattle, Washington, the Boeing Company flies its Model 299 heavy bomber prototype for the first time. It acquires the nickname Flying Fortress from inspired journalists.

AUGUST 20   Boeing's Model 299 (B-17) prototype flies from Seattle, Washington, to Wright Field, Ohio, for flight-testing.

It covers the 2,100-mile trip at 232 miles per hour, faster than most contemporary fighters.

AUGUST 24   Major Frank M. Andrews sets three speed-with-payload seaplane records while flying a Martin B-12W bomber equipped with pontoon floats between Langley Field, Virginia, and Floyd Bennett Field, New York, and back.

SEPTEMBER 17   At Scott Field, Illinois, TC-14, the world's largest non-rigid airship in the world, performs its maiden flight.

SEPTEMBER 26   The Army turns over Rockwell Field, San Diego, California; Luke Field, Ford Island, Hawaii; and Bolling Field, Anacostia, Washington, D.C. to the Navy, while the latter hands over its base at Sunnyvale, California.

OCTOBER 19   Over Selfridge Field, Michigan, Captain Ralph E. Gimmler wins the Mitchell Trophy Race by hitting a top speed of 212.96 miles per hour.

OCTOBER 30   At Wright Field, Ohio, the Boeing Model 299 bomber prototype crashes on takeoff because gust-locking mechanisms were not removed beforehand. The Army remains nonetheless interested in acquiring a fleet of such impressive heavy bombers.

NOVEMBER 11   Over Rapid City, South Dakota, the Army-crewed balloon *Explorer II* reaches 72,395 feet, taking photographs that show the Earth's distinctive curvature for the first time. Captains Orvil A. Anderson and Albert W. Stevens receive the Mackay Trophy and a Hubbard Gold Medal from the National Geographic Society.

DECEMBER 1   At Hamilton Field, California, 29 bombers of the 7th Bomb Group take off and land at Vero Beach, Florida, in 21 hours and 50 minutes.

DECEMBER 12   An amphibious aircraft flown by Lieutenant Hugh F. McCaferty and five crewmen travels from San Juan, Puerto Rico, to Miami, Florida, in record time, covering 1,033 miles faster than any previous craft of its kind.

DECEMBER 17   Over Santa Monica, California, the Douglas DC-3 prototype makes its maiden flight. It is adopted into military service as the C-47 and sees widespread service during World War II; 10,650 are constructed between 1935 and 1947, with many still flying today.

DECEMBER 22   In Washington, D.C., Brigadier General Oscar Westover gains appointment as commander of the Army Air Corps. He replaces Major General Benjamin D. Foulois, whose reputation suffered because of the airmail fiasco.

DECEMBER 27   At Hilo, Hawaii, bombers from the 5th Composite Group use bombs to divert a lava flow running down the slopes of the Mauna Loa volcano.

1936

FEBRUARY 19   In New York City, William G. "Billy" Mitchell, America's leading air power proponent, dies. Though not recognized at the time, many of his prophecies are strikingly realized during World War II.

JUNE 6   The Saucony-Vacuum Company uses the catalytic cracking method to produce the world's first 100-octane aviation fuel, use of which greatly boosts the performance of military aircraft.

JUNE 7   Major Ira C. Eaker performs the first-ever blind transcontinental flight as he pilots an airplane from New York to Los Angeles, California, relying solely upon instruments.

JUNE 16   On Long Island, New York, the Seversky Aircraft Company contracts with the Army Air Corps to manufacture its first all-metal fighter with enclosed cockpits and retractable landing gear. It enters service as the P-35.

JUNE 29   Major General Frank M. Andrews and Major John Whitney set a world airline record by flying a Douglas YOA5-2 1,430 miles between San Juan, Puerto Rico, and Langley Field, Virginia.

OCTOBER 13   At Roswell, New Mexico, the rocket facility operated by Dr. Robert D. Goddard, is visited by Army lieutenant John W. Sessums, who seeks to gauge possible military applications. He reports this technology might be useful in propelling gliders.

DECEMBER 2   In Washington State, Boeing's YB-15 prototype performs its maiden flight. This large aircraft, equipped with numerous gun blisters, is the epitome of the "aerial battleship" designed to fight its way into enemy airspace without fighter escort.

DECEMBER 9   The prestigious Columbian Trophy goes to the 3rd Attack Group, Army Air Corps for best flying safety record of the year.

1937

FEBRUARY 11 Major J. McDuffie leads a flight of eight Martin B-10 bombers from Langley Field, Virginia, to Airbrook Field, Panama, covering 4,000 miles without serious mishap. This is the first time that large land aircraft have operated over open water for an extended period.

MARCH 1 At Langley Field, Virginia, Boeing delivers its first YB-17A Flying Fortress to the 2nd Bombardment Group, Army Air Corps. This is the service's first four-engine, high-speed, high-altitude aircraft, possessing sufficient range and bomb load to serve as a strategic bomber.

MARCH 26 At Roswell, New Mexico, Dr. Robert H. Goddard launches a liquid-fuel rocket guided by moveable air vanes in the rocket exhaust and connected to a gyrostabilizer in the nose; it reaches an altitude of 9,000 feet.

APRIL 12 In England, a jet engine designed by Royal Air Force officer Frank Whittle is successfully tested at Cambridge University. Harnessing this technology takes almost a decade, but leads to breakthroughs in aviation speed.

MAY 7 A fully pressurized cabin is tested on the Lockheed XC-35 high-altitude research aircraft, winning the Collier Trophy. A novelty at present, pressurized cabins and passenger compartments eventually become standard equipment on most airplanes.

MAY 8 The Mackay Trophy is awarded to six officers and two enlisted men from the U.S. Army Air Corps for piloting three bombers from Langley Field, Virginia, to Allegan, Michigan.

JUNE 23 In Burbank, California, the Lockheed Corporation contracts with the U.S. Army Air Corps to develop its radical, twin-boomed XP-38 fighter. This eventually enters service as the Lightning.

JUNE 30 In Washington, D.C., Major General Oscar Westover, chief of the Air Corps, ends the Army's balloon program when Congressional funding ceases. Any remaining equipment is handed off to the Navy.

JULY 1 The Signal Corps Weather Service transfers over to the Army Air Corps.

JULY 20 At Langley, Virginia, the General Headquarters (GHQ) Air Force receives its own uniform insignia, signaling its status as an independent air unit.

JULY 26 Aviatrix Jacqueline Cochran, a newcomer to the male-dominated world of aviation, sets a women's American speed record of 203.895 miles per hour in a Beechcraft airplane.

AUGUST 5 Over Wright Field, Ohio, the XC-35 becomes the first aircraft to fly with a fully pressurized cabin.

AUGUST 23 Over Wright Field, Ohio, a Fokker C-14B piloted by Captain George V. Holloman performs the first completely automated landing by utilizing an autopilot designed by Captain Carl J. Crane; both men receive the Mackay Trophy and Distinguished Flying Crosses.

SEPTEMBER 1 At Buffalo, New York, Lieutenant Benjamin Kelsey takes the radical Bell XFM-1, multiplace, twin-engine pusher fighter on its maiden flight.

Eventually christened the Airacuda, it does not enter into production.

SEPTEMBER 21   Over Detroit, Michigan, gender barriers in aviation continue falling as aviatrix Jacqueline Cochran, flying a civilian version of the Seversky P-35 fighter, establishes a woman's speed record of 293 miles per hour.

OCTOBER 15   At Seattle, Washington, Boeing's gigantic XB-15 makes its maiden flight; though impressive in terms

of size, the XB-15 is grossly underpowered and only one is built.

DECEMBER 3   Major Alexander P. de Seversky flies an aircraft of his own design from New York City to Havana, Cuba, setting a new record of five hours and three minutes. This same day, aviatrix Jacqueline Cochran sets another new record by flying from New York to Miami, Florida, in four hours and twelve minutes.

1938

FEBRUARY 17   At Miami, Florida, Lieutenant Colonel Robert D. Olds leads six Boeing B-17A bombers to Buenos Aires, Argentina, to attend the inaugural of President Roberto Ortiz.

FEBRUARY 27   At Langley Field, Virginia, six Boeing B-17 bombers under Lieutenant Colonel Robert D. Olds return from a 10,000-mile round trip flight to Buenos Aires, Argentina, and back. The trip required 33 hours and 30 minutes of flying time and the crews receive the Mackay Trophy. Moreover, their success heralds that the age of strategic bombing is at hand.

APRIL 6   At Wright Field, Ohio, testing begins on the radically different Bell XP-39, whose engine is midway down the fuselage, behind the pilot's compartment, with a 37mm cannon mounted to fire down the fuselage centerline. During World War II nearly 5,000 P-39s are sent to the Soviet Union, where Russian pilots praised its heavy firepower and rugged construction.

MAY 1   Along the eastern seaboard, the Army stages three days of maneuvering to establish if airplanes can repel a seaborne attack. The exercise involves 220 aircraft and 3,000 men, and is judged successful.

MAY 12   Over the Atlantic, the Army Air Corps dispatches three B-17 bombers that intercept the Italian liner *Rex* 700 miles at sea. The Navy, suitably alarmed, demands that Army aircraft be limited to only 100 miles from the coast. The lead navigator in this stunt is Captain Curtis LeMay.

JULY 28   Lieutenant Harold L. Neely, flying a Seversky P-35 fighter, completes a transcontinental flight in 9 hours and 54 minutes flying time.

AUGUST 3–12   At Langley Field, Virginia, a flight of three Boeing B-17 bombers under Major Vincent J. Meloy, 2nd Bombardment Group, departs on a goodwill flight to Bogotá, Colombia, and back.

General Henry Harley "Hap" Arnold sits in his office at the Munitions Building in Washington, D.C. Arnold was a pilot, commander of the U.S. Army Air Corps from 1938 to 1941, commander of the U.S. Army Air Force from 1941 until 1945, and the first general of the Air Force in 1949. He is the only airman to achieve five-star rank. (Library of Congress)

AUGUST 19 At Mitchel Field, New York, the new Douglas B-18 Bolo bomber (adapted from the DC-3 transport) performs a transcontinental flight and arrives from Hamilton Field, California, in 15 hours and 18 minutes of flying time.

AUGUST 29 Major Alexander P. de Seversky sets a new east-to-west transcontinental speed record by covering 2,457 miles in 10 hours, 2 minutes, and 55.7 seconds.

SEPTEMBER 15 This year's Mackay Trophy is awarded to the Army Air Corps for its development of the XC-35 and its pressurized cabin.

SEPTEMBER 21 Over Burbank, California, Major General Oscar Westover, chief of the U.S. Army Air Corps, is killed when his Douglas A-17AS staff aircraft suddenly crashes. An accident inquiry concludes that unpredictable, gusty winds coupled with intense heat currents rising off the ground caused the mishap.

SEPTEMBER 29 Brigadier General Henry H. Arnold gains appointment as chief of the Air Corps to replace the recently deceased Major General Oscar Westover; he also becomes a major general.

OCTOBER 14 Over Buffalo, New York, the Curtiss XP-40 prototype fighter begins flight-testing. It enters Army service as the P-40 Tomahawk and during World War II 14,000 are built for the United States and its allies before construction ceases in 1944.

OCTOBER 26   At El Segundo, California, the Douglas Model 7B begins flight-testing. It enters service as the A-20 Havoc and, during World War II, it becomes the most-produced Army surface attack aircraft. A-20s are also widely exported to Great Britain, France, and the Soviet Union.

NOVEMBER 14   In Washington, D.C., President Franklin D. Roosevelt orders the mission of the Army Air Corps expanded and pushes for a 20,000-plane force. Major General Henry H. Arnold subsequently equates this secret conference to the "Magna Carta" as far as American air power is concerned.

1939

JANUARY 12   In Washington, D.C., President Franklin D. Roosevelt requests higher priority for the development and acquisition of modern military aircraft.

JANUARY 27   At March Field, California, the Lockheed XP-38 twin-boomed, twin-engined fighter performs its maiden flight. It enters service as the P-38 Lightning and serves throughout World War II with distinction.

FEBRUARY 10   Over Los Angeles, California, the North American NA-40 twin-engine bomber makes its initial flight. It enters service as the B-25 Mitchell and, during World War II, it becomes the most numerous medium bomber on the Allied side.

FEBRUARY 14   At Langley Field, Virginia, Major Caleb V. Haynes pilots the giant Boeing XB-15 prototype bomber during a mercy flight to assist earthquake victims in Chile. He arrives with 3,000 pounds of badly needed medical supplies in 29 hours and 53 minutes, winning a Mackay Trophy.

MARCH 1   At Langley Field, Virginia, Major General Delos C. Emmons is appointed commander of the General Headquarters force.

MARCH 21   A board of officers consisting of Colonel Hugo E. Pitz, Lieutenant Colonel Joseph T. McNarney, and Major George Kenney is assigned the task of evaluating permanent and auxiliary airfields in Puerto Rico.

MARCH 24   At Palm Springs, California, aviatrix Jacqueline Cochran sets another woman's altitude record of 30,052 feet in her Beechcraft.

APRIL 3   In Washington, D.C., President Franklin D. Roosevelt signs the National Defense Act into law, which gives the Army Air Corps $300 million and authorizes its expansion to 48,000 personnel and 6,000 aircraft. Significantly, it also allows African Americans to receive flight training for the first time.

APRIL 18   Major General Henry H. Arnold recalls Colonel Charles A. Lindbergh of the Missouri National Guard back to active duty; he is tasked with evaluating and uncovering weaknesses in American air power.

APRIL 27   In Washington, D.C., the Army Air Corps places an order for the first production batch of Lockheed P-38 Lightnings.

JUNE 1   Major General Henry H. Arnold, chief of the Army Air Corps, seeks to acquire as large a pool of trained pilots as possible, so he authorizes civilian flying schools to accept flying cadets as pupils.

JULY 1   In Washington, D.C., President Franklin D. Roosevelt issues an executive order mandating that the Aeronautical Board, the Joint Board (eventually Joint Chiefs of Staff), the Joint Economy Board, and the Munitions Board all function under the direction of the commander in chief.

JULY 15   The Army Air Corps acquires performance rights to the song "Wild Blue Yonder" by composer Robert Crawford; it subsequently becomes the theme song of the U.S. Air Force.

JULY 26   A Boeing B-17 Flying Fortress sets a new speed record of 204 miles per hour while carrying a 1,123-pound bomb load over a closed triangular course of 1,000 kilometers.

JULY 30   Over Wright Field, Ohio, the sole Boeing XB-15, piloted by Major Caleb V. Haynes and Captain W. D. Olds, reaches 8,200 feet while carrying a 15.5 payload and establishes a new payload-to-altitude record.

AUGUST 1   A Boeing YB-17A flown by Majors Charles M. Cunnings and Stanley Umstead carries a 11,023-pound payload to a new record of 34,016 feet.

AUGUST 26   Majors Charles M. Cunnings and Stanley Umstead pilot a B-17A from Miami, Florida, to the Panama Canal Zone. It reaches its objective in only six hours and underscores American ability to reinforce that strategic point by air.

SEPTEMBER 14   In Connecticut, the VS-300 helicopter, designed and flown by

Receipt of the YB-17 Flying Fortress by the GHQ Air Force at Langley, Virginia, gave the Army Air Corps its first taste of modern strategic airpower. (Library of Congress)

Igor Sikorsky, reaches a height of three feet for 10 seconds during a tethered test.

SEPTEMBER 15 Over Burbank, California, a Seversky AP-9 piloted by aviatrix Jacqueline Cochran sets a new speed record of 309.5 miles per hour over a 1,000-kilometer course.

NOVEMBER 7 The 2nd Bomb Group receives the Mackay Trophy for its B-17 flight from Miami, Florida, to Buenos Aires, Argentina, and then home to Langley Field, Virginia.

DECEMBER 16 At Langley Field, Virginia, Major General Delos C. Emmons gains appointment as chief of the General Headquarters Air Force (GHQ).

DECEMBER 29 Over San Diego, California, the Consolidated XB-24 prototype performs its maiden flight. It enters service as the B-24 Liberator and becomes the most numerous American warplane, with over 18,000 constructed.

1940

JANUARY 18 At Selfridge Field, Michigan, the 94th Pursuit Squadron wins the Luke Trophy Award for the highest gunnery average of the year. This is the lineal successor to Captain Eddie Rickenbacker's 94th Aero Squadron of World War I.

JANUARY 19 Major James H. "Jimmy" Doolittle is elected president of the Institute of Aeronautical Sciences.

JANUARY 23 At Hamilton Field, California, a force of 38 bombers from the 7th Bomber Group loads a battalion of the 65th Coast Artillery and flies them to a point 500 miles distant. This is a pioneering attempt at mass troop transport.

FEBRUARY 26 At Mitchel Field, New York, the Air Defense Command is established to coordinate defensive tactics and strategy by the U.S. Army Air Corps to thwart any possible air attack on the continental United States.

MARCH 15 At Mitchel Field, New York, Brigadier General James E. Chaney assumes command of the new Air Defense Command.

MARCH 25 In Washington, D.C., a liberalized release and export policy allows the Army Air Corps to sell modern aircraft to anti-Axis nations. This has the effect of boosting aircraft production domestically, broadening the production base for the Air Corps.

MARCH 26 At St. Louis, Missouri, the Curtiss CW-20T prototype flies for the first time. It enters service as the C-46 Commando and performs yeoman work as transport during World War II.

APRIL 1 In Oslo, Norway, 31-year old Captain Robert M. Losey, Army Air Corps Attache, is killed in a German air raid. He becomes the first American officer casualty of World War II.

APRIL 8 An Army Air Forces Douglas B-18 Bolo bomber flies nonstop for the first time between Denver, Colorado, and Miami, Florida.

APRIL 14   At Fairbanks, Alaska, the first detachment of Army Air Corps personnel and aircraft deploy.

APRIL 15   In Washington, D.C., the War Department issues Field Manual 1–5 relative to the tactical employment of air power, and imposes centralized control over all aerial assets.

MAY 16   President Franklin D. Roosevelt, having conferred closely with Major General Henry H. Arnold, appeals to Congress for a $1.18 billion defense appropriation. He seeks an increase in military aircraft production to 50,000 per year.

MAY 23–25   Near Barksdale, Louisiana, 300 Air Corps aircraft participate in large-scale wargames staged by the Third Army.

MAY 28   Major General Henry H. Arnold and Dr. Robert H. Goddard confer as to the possible military application of his rockets. Nothing material results, but Dr. Theodore von Karman is directed to pursue the possibility of rocket-powered assists for heavily laden bombers.

JUNE 11   Dr. Robert H. Goddard test fires a rocket engine that burns for 43.5 seconds, the longest duration yet achieved.

JUNE 27   In Washington, D.C., the Council of National Defense establishes the National Defense Research Committee to work on scientific projects with potential military applications. Among them is the Azon (azimuth only) guided bomb.

JUNE 29   In Washington, D.C., Congress approves a plan to procure 12,000 modern warplanes for the Army Air Corps by April 1, 1942. The Army will handle the training, organization, and procurement.

JULY 3   At El Segundo, California, the Northrop N-1M Flying Wing, a twin-engined pusher type aircraft that lacks a fuselage, is flight-tested.

JULY 8   Additional training facilities at Randolph Field, Texas; Maxwell Field, Alabama; and Moffett Fields, California, are established by the Army Air Corps.

JULY 16   At Lowry Field, Colorado, the Air Corps opens its first formal bombardier training school, whose initial cadre will serve as the instructors for subsequent classes.

AUGUST 17   Over Sussex, England, Pilot Officer William L. M. Fiske III is killed in an air battle while fighting with the Royal Air Force in the Battle of Britain. He is the first American pilot to die in World War II.

AUGUST 19   Over Inglewood, California, the North American NA-62, a highly modified NA-40 prototype, is successfully flight-tested; this version enters production as the famous B-25 Mitchell.

SEPTEMBER 16   In Washington, D.C., the War Department announces that the Civil Aeronautics Authority (CAA) will assist the Army to recruit and train African American aviation units.

OCTOBER 8   In Great Britain, the first Eagle Squadron forms from American volunteers serving with the Royal Air Force; it subsequently forms the basis of the 4th Fighter Group.

OCTOBER 12   Off the coast of Virginia, Curtiss P-40 Warhawks under Major Reuben Moffat, 33rd Pursuit Group, take off from the carrier *Wasp* to see how well land aircraft operate at sea.

OCTOBER 26   Over Inglewood, Los Angeles, the North American A-36 Apache, precursor to the famous P-51 Mustang fighter, flies for the first time. Built to British specifications, it is powered by the low-altitude Allison V-1710 liquid-cooled engine. It performs so impressively that the Army Air Corps decides to adopt it.

OCTOBER 30   In England, the first Eagle Squadron, composed primarily of American military personnel, is declared operational.

NOVEMBER 1   At Fort Shafter, Hawaii, the Hawaiian Air Force (later Seventh Air Force) is activated.

NOVEMBER 19   The General Head-quarters Air Force (GHQ) is taken from the chief of the Air Corps and assigned to the general commanding the field forces. This proves something of a setback for independent air power.

NOVEMBER 25   In Baltimore, Maryland, the Martin XB-26 makes its flying debut at the Martin Middle River plant. It enters service as the B-26 Marauder, and garners the reputation as a "hot" aircraft from its high performance.

In Washington, D.C., the National Advisory Committee for Aeronautics (NACA) declares it is building a $6.4 million engine research laboratory at the Cleveland Municipal Airport, Ohio.

DECEMBER 18   The Army Air Corps establishes new commands within its existing structure: Northeast Air District, Northwest Air District, Southeast Air District, and Southwest Air District.

1941

JANUARY   Officials from the radio manufacturer RCA propose designing and constructing a radio-controlled missile guided by a camera placed in the nose. The National Defense Research Committee, suitably impressed with the concept, agrees.

JANUARY 11   The Army Air Corps extensively tests radio-controlled airplanes, electronically tethered to ground facilities or other aircraft. Success prompts further development of guided glide bombs and torpedoes.

FEBRUARY   Reconnaissance expert Major George W. Goddard develops special, high-luminosity flares for nighttime aerial photography. Each flare can create several million candlepower for several minutes, lighting up to 20 square miles of terrain below as it dangles from a parachute. Cameras on the aircraft are then tripped by a photoelectric cell sensing the light.

MARCH 22   The 99th Pursuit Squadron, comprised solely of African Americans, organizes at Chanute Field, Illinois, under Captain Harold R. Maddux. It is the first of three units assigned to the all-black 332nd Fighter Group.

MARCH 26   The Air Corps Technical Training Command is founded.

APRIL 9   To circumvent possible German occupation, Denmark allows the United States to construct and employ military airfields in Greenland.

APRIL 11   The Army Air Corps, fearing that Europe would be under Nazi domination before the United States can intervene, approaches Boeing and Consolidated for a new, long-range strategic bomber that can perform missions from the United States. This is the origin of the Boeing B-29 Superfortress and Convair B-36 Peacemaker.

APRIL 15   In Washington, D.C., President Franklin D. Roosevelt signs an executive order allowing reservists serving in the Army Air Corps to temporarily resign and join the American Volunteer Group (AVG) under Claire L. Chennault. This unit, better known as the "Flying Tigers," is technically part of the Chinese Air Force.

At Stratford, Connecticut, engineer Igor Sikorsky completes the first flight of a helicopter in the Western hemisphere by flying tethered for 1 hour and 5 minutes.

APRIL 18   Near Fort Worth, Texas, Consolidated Aircraft Company invests $50 million in a giant aircraft factory to construct B-24 Liberators and B-32 Dominators.

MAY 6   Over Long Island, New York, the Republic XP-47 prototype makes its maiden flight. It enters service as the P-47 Thunderbolt and serves in every theater of World War II as a fighter and attack aircraft. This is also the lineal descendent of the earlier Seversky P-35.

MAY 13–14   At Oahu, Hawaii, 21 Boeing B-17D bombers of the 21st Bombardment Group arrive at Hickam Field after flying nonstop from Hamilton Field, California. This is the first mass bomber flight across the Pacific and consumed 13 hours and 10 minutes.

MAY 22   The Air Corps Ferrying Command is established to better facilitate the transfer of military aircraft to Great Britain. The United States also signs an agreement to assist training British pilots to operate these lend–lease aircraft.

MAY 31   In Washington, D.C., Major General George H. Brett gains appointment as chief of the Army Air Corps.

JUNE 3   The grade Aviation Cadet replaces the earlier designation of Flying Cadet; qualified fliers become commissioned officers once they acquire their wings.

JUNE 16   The Army Air Corps accepts delivery of its first Consolidated B-24 Liberator four-engine bomber. Equipped with a high-lift, low-drag Davis wing, it flies higher and faster than the Boeing B-17 and becomes the most widely produced American warplane, with 18,000 units manufactured.

JUNE 20   The new Army Air Forces (AAF) arises to supercede the old Army Air Corps and consolidate and better coordinate disparate air elements. Major General Henry H. Arnold gains appointment as commanding general, Army Air Forces (CGAAF), and reports directly to the Army chief of staff. The General Headquarters Air Force (GHQ) is also broken up and redistributed as the First, Second, Third, and Fourth Air Forces.

JUNE 27   Over Los Angeles, the gigantic Douglas XB-19 bomber takes performs its maiden flight with Lieutenant Colonel Stanley Umstead and Major Howard G. Bunker at the controls. While impressive to behold, it is underpowered and never enters into production.

JUNE 28 In Washington, D.C., President Franklin D. Roosevelt signs Executive Order 8807 to create the Office of Scientific Research and Development.

JUNE 30 In El Segundo, California, the Northrop Corporation receives a joint Army-Navy contract to develop an aircraft gas turbine (turboprop) engine weighing less than 3,215 pounds and generating 2,500 horsepower. It eventually enters production as the Turbodyne.

JULY 1 At Bolling Field, Washington, D.C., a B-24 Liberator piloted by Lieutenant Colonel C. V. Hayne flies to Scotland via Montreal and Newfoundland. This is the Army Air Forces' initial overseas flight by the new Air Corps Ferrying Command.

Aviatrix Jacqueline Cochran becomes the first woman to ferry a twin-engined Lockheed Hudson bomber across the Atlantic to England.

Two of the African American pilots known as the Tuskegee Airmen stand beside a plane during World War II. The Tuskegee Airmen were African American Air Corps officers who trained at the Tuskegee Army Airfield in Alabama, the only training facility for basic and advanced flight training open to black pilots during World War II. (Library of Congress)

JULY 8 The fabled Boeing Flying Fortress makes its combat debut over Wilhelmshaven, Germany, as part of the Royal Air Force. A force of 20 B-17Cs (or Fortress Is) proves largely ineffective owing to flaws in British bombing doctrine.

JULY 16 At Langley Field, Virginia, the A-1, a remote-controlled flying bomb, begins wind tunnel testing.

JULY 19 In Alabama, 12 African American pilots arrive at the Tuskegee Institute for flight instruction. Captain Benjamin O. Davis, a West Point graduate, will command the Tuskegee Airmen during the war. The U.S. Army Air Forces also dedicates the Tuskegee Air Field, which will be used exclusively for training African American pilots and personnel.

In China, Claire L. Chennault, presently aviation adviser to Generalissimo Jiang Jieshi, is called back into active duty with the Army Air Forces. He is currently organizing the American Volunteer Group (AVG) of American pilots in Chinese employ.

JULY 25 The 33rd Pursuit Squadron, consisting of thirty P-40 Warhawks and three trainers, is conveyed on the carrier *Wasp* to Reykjavik, Iceland.

AUGUST 1 In Washington, D.C., President Franklin D. Roosevelt attempts to restrain Japanese military aviation by forbidding the export of aviation fuel outside the Western Hemisphere, save for Great Britain and other countries resisting Nazi Germany.

AUGUST 4–12 In Washington, D.C., the Air War Plans Division (AWPD) of the Army Air Forces begins work on a war-winning air strategy intended to be used against Germany and Japan. Within eight days they conceive AWPD-1, which calls for an extensive strategic bombing campaign against enemy urban centers and industry.

AUGUST 6   Off Reykjavik, Iceland, Curtiss P-40s of the 33rd Pursuit Squadron fly off the deck of the carrier *Wasp* and deploy at their new base without serious mishap.

AUGUST 12   At Wright Field, Ohio, a Ercoupe civilian airplane piloted by Captain Homer Boushey, Jr., becomes the first plane to launch off the ground using rocket-assisted takeoff units (RATO). This system is intended to save valuable fuel during takeoff by heavily armed aircraft, thereby increasing their range and endurance.

AUGUST 23   At Wright Field, Ohio, the Ercoupe flown by Captain Homer Boushey, Jr., now takes off under the power of six rocket-assisted takeoff units under the wings alone, and flies a short distance.

AUGUST 27   Over Belgium, Pilot Officer William R. Dunn downs his fifth and sixth German aircraft, becoming the first American ace of World War II as a volunteer in the 71st Squadron, Royal Air Force. There are three RAF "Eagle Squadrons" fighting in Europe.

AUGUST 28   At Hickam Field, Hawaii, 35 Boeing B-17 bombers under Lieutenant Colonel Eugene L. Eubank, 19th Bombardment Group, begins a lengthy transfer to Clark Field, the Philippines. They have scheduled refueling stops at Midway, Wake Island, and Australia before arriving.

SEPTEMBER   Dr. Robert H. Goddard begins work on development of a functioning rocket system (RATO) to assist heavily laden aircraft during takeoff.

SEPTEMBER 5   In Hawaii, nine B-17Ds take off on a mass transpacific flight to Clark Field in the Philippines.

SEPTEMBER 6   In Seattle, Washington, the new Boeing B-17E makes its maiden flight. This variant features a totally redesigned tail section that sports a tail gunner, in addition to better armor and a higher stabilizer for better stability.

SEPTEMBER 12   At Clark Field in the Philippines, nine B-17Ds, having flown from Hawaii with scheduled stops at Midway, Wake Island, Port Moresby, New Guinea, and Darwin, Australia, deploy safely.

SEPTEMBER 17   In Louisiana, C-47 transports drop a company of paratroopers in a large military exercise for the first time.

SEPTEMBER 20   At Nichols Field, Luzon, the Philippine Department Air Force is created as a precursor of the Far East Air Force (FEAF) and the Fifth Air Force.

OCTOBER 9–16   In its first nationwide test, the U.S. air defense network employs 40,000 civilian aircraft spotters of the Aircraft Warning Service to begin scanning the skies. More than 1,800 individual stations are also tested as a viable communications network.

OCTOBER 30   A B-24 Liberator flown by Major Alva L. Harvey begins a record around-the-world flight by conducting Ambassador Averill Harriman between London and Moscow. The flight takes 17 days and covers 24,000 miles.

NOVEMBER 3   At Nielsen Field, Philippines, Major General Lewis H. Brereton assumes command of the new Far East Air Force (FEAF). This represents the largest single concentration of American air power outside North America and includes 107 Curtiss P-40 fighters and 35 Boeing B-17 strategic bombers.

NOVEMBER 7 The Army Air Forces tests the GB-1, the first guided glide bomb developed.

NOVEMBER 12 Project APHRODITE continues unfolding as the GB-8, the Army Air Forces' first radio-controlled glide bomb, is tested as part of a continuing quest for precision guided weapons.

NOVEMBER 14 Washington, D.C., is linked by air ferry to Cairo, Egypt, after a B-24 flown by Lieutenant Colonel Caleb V. Haynes and Major Curtis E. LeMay arrives with Major General George H. Brett. This is the first leg of a 26,000-mile round trip flight to Basra, Iraq.

NOVEMBER 30 This day Brigadier General Frank P. Lahm, the Army's first pilot, goes into retirement.

DECEMBER 1 In Washington, D.C., President Franklin D. Roosevelt signs an executive order creating the Civil Air Patrol (CAP), whose primary function is detecting enemy submarines offshore with small liaison aircraft. It is authorized recruit 17-year-old men ineligible for the draft.

DECEMBER 7 Japanese naval air forces achieve a complete tactical surprise at Pearl Harbor, Hawaii. Nonetheless, a pair of P-40s flown by Lieutenants Kenneth M. Taylor and George S. Welch, 47th Pursuit Squadron, depart Haleiwa Field and shoot down two and four Japanese aircraft, respectively. Four other Army pilots bagged one airplane apiece. Army losses are nonetheless heavy at 96 aircraft destroyed, mostly on the ground, along with 193 killed. Total American losses this day exceed 3,000.

Once alerted of the Pearl Harbor attack, six B-18s and twelve P-36s of the Alaska Defense Command are ordered

A captured Japanese photograph shows the smoke rising from Hickam Field during the attack on Pearl Harbor on December 7, 1941. In the foreground is the Navy's "Battleship row." (National Archives)

off from their fields to avoid being surprised on the ground.

By this date, the Air Corps Ferrying Command has delivered 1,350 aircraft from factories nationwide to airfields along the East Coast.

DECEMBER 8 In the Philippines, Japanese aircraft surprise the 19th Bombardment Group at Clark and Iba Fields, Luzon, the Philippines, inflicting devastating losses. They also strike the P-40s returning to various fields to refuel. Lieutenant Randall B. Keator manages to down the first enemy aircraft over the Philippines. However, no less than 17 B-17 heavy bombers and 55 P-40 fighters are destroyed for a total loss of 7 Japanese aircraft.

In Alaska, armed B-18 bombers of the Alaska Defense Command begin flying armed reconnaissance patrols between Anchorage and Kodiak.

Fearing a Japanese amphibious assault on the West Coast, the 1st Pursuit Group is sent to San Diego, California, from Selfridge Field, Michigan.

At Buffalo, New York, the Bell XP-63 Kingcobra, a larger version of the P-39 Airacobra, flies for the first time.

In Washington, D.C., Congress declares war on the Japanese empire.

DECEMBER 9 In the Philippines, Japanese aircraft launch another heavy raid at Nichols Air Field. By now, American air power has been reduced to 17 B-17s, 55 P-40s, and 3 P-35s. Most of the surviving four-engine bombers are dispersed to airfields at Luzon to prevent being destroyed on the ground.

In New York, fighters based at Mitchel Field are scrambled to intercept hostile aircraft allegedly approaching the East Coast; the alarm turns out to be false.

DECEMBER 10 In the Philippines, five Boeing B-17Ds of the 93rd Bombardment Squadron make the first American air raid of World War II by attacking Japanese warships and transport off Aparri, Luzon. One freighter is sunk but a bomber flown by Captain Colin Kelly is shot down; Kelly wins a posthumous Distinguished Service Cross for remaining in the burning craft long enough for his crew to bail out. He is also credited with sinking the battleship *Haruna*, an erroneous assertion as that vessel was not deployed with the invasion; he most likely scored several near misses against the heavy cruiser *Ashigara*.

DECEMBER 11 Over England, 19-year-old Pilot Officer John G. Magee, an American serving with the Canadian Air Force, dies in a midair collision. Previously, he had gained a degree of immortality in aviation circles by penning the poem "High Flight."

In Hawaii, six B-18 Bolo medium bombers commence sea-search missions from the islands, and soon they are joined by B-17s and A-20s in this same task.

In the Zone of the Interior (ZI), the Western Defense Command assumes control of the Second and Fourth Air Forces.

In Berlin, Germany, the Reichstag declares war on the United States and the United States responds in kind. Italy also declares war on America.

DECEMBER 12 Over the Philippines Captain Jesus Villamor, flying an outdated Boeing P-26 Peashooter, manages to shoot down a Japanese bomber; this is the P-26's only known aerial victory.

More than 100 Japanese fighters and bombers again strike at Clark Field, Batangas, and Olongapo, Philippines; the Americans can only muster a single B-17, which attacks enemy transports unloading at Vigan without scoring hits.

Major General H. A. Dargue is killed when his aircraft impacts a mountainside near Bishop, California.

DECEMBER 13   Over northern Luzon, Lieutenant Boyd D. Wagner, 17th Pursuit Squadron, flames four Japanese Ki-27 Nate fighters while on a reconnaissance mission.

DECEMBER 14   Over the Philippines, B-17s are dispatched to bomb the Japanese beachhead at Legaspi. Afterwards, Lieutenant Hewitt T. Wheless wins a Distinguished Service Cross for successfully making an emergency crash-landing at Cagayan.

DECEMBER 16   In the Philippines, Lieutenant Boyd D. "Buzz" Wagner, 17th Pursuit Squadron, shoots down his fifth Japanese aircraft over Vigan, Luzon, becoming America's first ace of World War II.

As B-17 bombers begin evacuating Luzon, Philippines, Captain Floyd J. Pell lands in Australia to arrange the use of local facilities by the Far East Air Force (FEAF).

DECEMBER 18   In China, a confrontation between Chinese peasants and Eriksen Shilling, a pilot with the American Volunteer Group ("Flying Tigers") who had been shot down, leads to the so-called "Blood chits," or hand-painted identification scarfs.

In California, Reaction Motors, Inc., is incorporated as the first American rocket company. It concentrates on liquid fuel-propelled designs· which eventually power the Bell XS-1 past the sound barrier in 1947.

DECEMBER 19   In the United States, the First Air Force is assigned to the Eastern Theater of Operations, subsequently known as the Eastern Defense Command.

DECEMBER 20   Over China, the American Volunteer Group (AVG), performs its first combat mission, and shoots down four Ki-48 light bombers near Kunming at the cost of one P-40, which ran out of fuel and crashed.

DECEMBER 22   In the Philippines, nine B-17s fly from Batchelor Field, Philippines, and bomb Japanese shipping at Davao Bay; the aircraft recover at Del Monte field.

DECEMBER 23   In the Philippines, four B-17s stagger aloft from Del Monte Field to bomb Japanese shipping in the Lingayen Gulf. A force of P-40s and P-35s also strafes Japanese troops coming ashore in San Miguel Bay.

Major General Lewis H. Brereton is ordered to establish his headquarters, Far East Air Force, at Darwin, Australia.

DECEMBER 24   In the Philippines, General Douglas MacArthur orders Major General Lewis H. Brereton to be evacuated to Australia by a Navy PBY, while his surviving aircraft find a temporary haven in the Dutch East Indies. Heavy bomber operations are no longer untenable.

As three B-17s bomb enemy airfields and shipping at Davao, Philippines, headquarters, Far East Air Force (FEAF), begins transferring from Manila to Darwin, Australia, to set up shop. Army Air Forces personnel on Luzon, mostly serving as ground forces, also relocate into the Bataan Peninsula with the rest of the army.

DECEMBER 25   The advanced echelon of Headquarters, Far East Air Force (FEAF) is formally established at Darwin, Australia, under Lieutenant Colonel Charles H. Caldwell.

DECEMBER 29   At Darwin, Australia, Major General Lewis H. Brereton arrives from the Philippines to coordinate activities of the Far East Air Forces (FEAF). All remaining air elements still in the Philippines are now commanded by Colonel Harold H. George.

The War Department responds to the Alaska Defense Command's incessant requests for reinforcements by dispatching the 77th Bomb Squadron, which arrives today, and a pursuit squadron, which lands a day later.

DECEMBER 30   The Army Air Forces tasks the National Defense Research Committee to develop functional, radio-controlled trajectory bombs; this is the origin of the Azon and Razon weapons, precursors of so-called "smart bombs" of the later 20th century.

1942

JANUARY 2   In Washington, D.C., Army Air Forces Chief Major General Henry H. Arnold orders the creation of a new numbered air force, soon to be christened the Eighth Air Force. By 1945 it becomes renowned as the "Mighty Eighth."

In the Alaskan Defense Command, aerial defenses now consist of two pursuit squadrons and three bombardment squadrons.

JANUARY 3   In Washington, D.C., the War Department orders that all Army and Navy planes will now receive a designated name in addition to a numerical and type designation. The practice is adopted from the British and includes such famous names as Mustang, Corsair, and Flying Fortress.

JANUARY 4   In the Philippines, a handful of P-40s launched from makeshift airstrips at Bataan try unsuccessfully to stem a large Japanese bomber raid against Corregidor. Many fighters are relocated from Mindanao after the mission.

JANUARY 5   A handful of B-17s staging from Malang and Samarinda, Netherlands East Indies, strike Japanese shipping at Davao Bay.

JANUARY 6   In Washington, D.C., President Franklin D. Roosevelt challenges the American aviation industry to manufacture 100,000 aircraft this year.

JANUARY 9   A small group of B-17s stage out of Kendari, the Philippines, and again attack Japanese shipping in Davao Bay.

JANUARY 10   At Wright Field, Ohio, the Army Air Forces Materiel Command begins researching ways to employ aerial refueling to fight the war in the Pacific.

On the Philippines, the handful of P-40 fighters still operational are completely relocated to the Bataan Peninsula from bases scattered about Luzon.

JANUARY 11   From Malang, Netherlands East Indies, a handful of B-17s drop bombs on Japanese landing forces coming ashore on the island of Tarakan.

JANUARY 13   On Long Island, New York, Igor Sikorsy's XR-4 helicopter flies for the first time; suitably impressed, the Army Air Forces issues a contract to obtain their first functional helicopters.

JANUARY 14   At Darwin, Australia, orders go out to relocate Far East Air

Eaker, Ira C. (1896–1987)

Army Air Forces general. Ira Clarence Eaker was born in Field Creek, Texas, on April 13, 1896, and in 1917 he became a pilot in the Aviation Section, Signal Corps. During January 1–7, 1929, he joined Carl A. Spaatz and Elwood Quesada on a seven-day nonstop endurance flight over Los Angeles that required 41 in-flight refuelings. In 1940 Eaker was selected to visit England and study the Royal Air Force in combat and, the following year, he received command of the 20th Pursuit Group at Hamilton Field, California. Once the United States entered World War II, Eaker gained temporary promotion to brigadier general and accompanied Spaatz to England to organize the VIII Bomber Command. A strong advocate of strategic bombing, he personally led the first American B-17 raid in Europe by striking rail yards at Rouen, France on August 17, 1942.

In the fall of 1942, Eaker replaced Spaatz as commander of the Eighth Air Force. In January 1943, during the Casablanca Conference, he personally convinced Prime Minister Winston Churchill to continue precision daylight bombing in concert with nighttime raids performed by the Royal Air Force. In June 1943 Eaker transferred to the Mediterranean, and in April 1945 Eaker returned to Washington, D.C., as deputy commanding general of the Army Air Forces, and its new chief of staff. He retired in 1947, and in 1979 Congress awarded him a special gold medal in recognition of his 40 years of distinguished service to the nation. Eaker died at Andrews Air Force Base on August 6, 1987, an accomplished pioneer of modern aerial warfare.

Force (FEAF) headquarters to the island of Java, to better coordinate Allied defenses there.

JANUARY 15   At Elmendorf Field, Alaska, the Alaskan Air Forces are activated under Lieutenant Colonel Everett S. Davis; a month later they are redesignated the Eleventh Air Force.

JANUARY 16   A force of six B–17s under Lieutenant Colonel Walter C. Sweeney fly to Palmyra Island en route to Canton Island. This is also the first significant wartime deployment of aircraft from Hawaii.

JANUARY 17   Small groups of B–17s staging from Malang, Netherlands East Indies, raid Japanese positions around Langoan Airfield and Menado Bay.

JANUARY 18   On Canton Island, the Pacific, newly arrived B–17s commence flying antisubmarine aerial patrols. Back in Hawaii, several aircraft launch an unsuccessful attack on what they believe was an enemy submarine.

JANUARY 20   In India, Major General George H. Brett halts the transshipment of aircraft to the Netherlands East Indies owing to heavy losses from Japanese aircraft while flying en route to Java.

JANUARY 22   From Malang, Netherlands East Indies, B–17s bomb Japanese ships moving through the Makassar Strait; over the next week they sink four transport vessels while losing several aircraft to wide-ranging Japanese fighters.

JANUARY 25   On Java, local defense are bolstered by the arrival of 13 P–40s under Major Charles A. Sprague, 17th Pursuit Squadron; they are arriving from bases in Australia.

JANUARY 26   In Washington, D.C., General Henry H. Arnold suggests to the Army chief of staff that the Army Air Forces in Britain (AAFIB) consist of a headquarters, and a bomber, interceptor, and base command.

In the Philippines, P–40s scrambled from airfields on Bataan bomb and strafe

Japanese targets on Nichols and Nielson Fields, damaging several aircraft and blowing up fuel depots.

JANUARY 28   In Savannah, Georgia, Brigadier General Asa N. Duncan assumes control of the newly formed Eighth Air Force headquarters. By war's end this will be the largest aerial strike force in history and senior partner in the Combined Bomber Offensive (CBO) with the Royal Air Force.

In the Pacific, a small force of B-17s lifts off from Malang, Netherlands East Indies, and attacks Japanese airfields at Kendari and Kuala Lumpur.

JANUARY 29   At Suva, Fiji, men and aircraft of the 70th Pursuit Squadron secure an aerial link between New Caledonia and Samoa; this unit subsequently operates from Guadalcanal.

On Palembang, B-17s sortie against Japanese airfields at Kuantan, destroying several aircraft hangars.

JANUARY 30   A force of B-17s departs Canton Islands and returns to Hawaii, having served there since January 16, 1942. This expedition provided valuable experience of the problems associated with long-distance flying over the Pacific region, along with navigation and aircraft maintenance.

JANUARY 31   Major General Ira C. Eaker is appointed the commanding general of Bomber Command, Army Air Forces in Britain (AAFIB), and ordered to depart for there immediately.

FEBRUARY   In   Washington,   D.C., Congress passes legislation which posthumously promotes the late William "Billy" Mitchell to major general.

FEBRUARY 1   In the Philippines, a handful of surviving P-40s from Bataan strafe and bomb Japanese landing barges coming ashore at Quinauan Point; heavy casualties are inflicted, but enemy forces are not deterred.

FEBRUARY 3–18   On Java, bad weather halts most B-17 offensive activity in the Netherlands East Indies. Two air strikes that manage to launch on February 8 and 9 against Singosari and Balikpapan are rebuffed by intense enemy fighter activity.

FEBRUARY 5   At Hickam Field, Hawaii, the Hawaiian Air Force is superseded by the new Seventh Air Force under Major General Clarence L. Tinker. The Far East and Caribbean Air Forces are likewise designated Fifth and Sixth Air Forces, respectively.

FEBRUARY 9–18   B-17s of the Fifth Air Force fly several air raids in the Southwestern Pacific, but they only claim three hits on Japanese vessels.

FEBRUARY 12   At Patterson Field, Dayton, Ohio, the new Tenth Air Force is established for service in the China-Burma-India (CBI) Theater.

In Washington, D.C., General Henry H. Arnold declares that no less than sixteen heavy bomber groups, three pursuit groups, and eight photoreconnaissance squadrons will arrive in Great Britain by the end of the year. The "Mighty Eighth" Air Force is beginning to assume a more permanent shape.

FEBRUARY 14   Over Wake Island, a B-17 of the Fifth Air Force runs one of the first photoreconnaissance missions to ascertain Japanese installations.

FEBRUARY 15   Over England, Lieutenant Colonel Townsend Griffiss is the first Army Air Forces airman killed in Europe when his transport is mistakenly attacked by Polish Spitfire pilots of the Royal Air Force.

FEBRUARY 19–20   In Java, a patched up group of Fifth Air Force A-24 dive bombers, B-17 heavy bombers, and P-40 fighters stage from Malang, Madioen, and Jogjakarta, Netherlands East Indies, to attack Japanese landing forces on the island of Bali; heavy damage is claimed. Other P-40s repel an attack by Japanese aircraft against the western portions of Java itself.

Over Port Darwin, Australia, a large Japanese air raid inflicts heavy damage on air and naval facilities. The Army Air Forces can only mount 10 P-40 fighters in its defense, and most of these are shot down.

FEBRUARY 20   In Washington, D.C., the War Production Board prioritizes aircraft construction to that of tanks and ships, and the allocation of resources are shifted accordingly.

In England, Major General Ira C. Eaker and six officers arrive to assess the condition of future air bases to be acquired there.

FEBRUARY 21   In Java, Major General George H. Brett informs the War Department that deteriorating defenses of Java compel him to evacuate Fifth Air Force aircraft and personnel back to Australia. This does not prevent his bombers from launching 20 air raids, usually in three-ship formations, against Japanese shipping in the Java Sea and on Bali. Some damage is inflicted, but the invasion force is undeterred.

FEBRUARY 23   In England, Major General Ira C. Eaker assumes command of VIII Bomber Command, Eighth Air Force, and his staff begins establishing a headquarters.

At Townsville, Australia, six B-17s that survived fighting in the Philippines launch the first Fifth Air Force strike against Japanese targets at Rabaul, New Britain. However, mechanical difficulties force five of the aircraft to abort, and only one drops its bombs on target.

The Army Air Forces Materiel Division suggests employment of the British lopped-hose refueling system for refueling American warplanes. This method entails using a 300-foot hose line dangled from the receiver aircraft, with an attached three-pronged grapple, which would then attach itself to a 100-foot weighted line towed behind the tanker aircraft.

FEBRUARY 24   At Bandoeng, Java, Major General Lewis H. Brereton and his staff is ordered to India to command the still-forming Tenth Air Force there. His primary task is organizing an aerial ferry over the towering Himalaya Mountains to support Major General Claire L. Chennault's new China Air Task Force (CATF) at Kunming.

Over Los Angeles, rumors of approaching Japanese aircraft result in a spate of wild firing against enemy "targets," although the Army subsequently deduces the mishap was caused by the misidentification of five local airplanes.

FEBRUARY 27–28   As an 80-ship Japanese convoy approaches Java, the Fifth Air Force launches every available A-24, B-17, P-40, and LB-30 against it, but only minor damage is inflicted. Immediately afterwards, most air and ground personnel are hastily evacuated by ship to Australia.

South of Tjilatjap, Java, Japanese land-based bombers strike an American convoy, damaging the seaplane tender *Langley* so heavily that it has to be scuttled. Its cargo of 32 Curtiss P-40 fighters intended for the 17th Pursuit Squadron is consequently lost.

MARCH 2 In Washington, D.C., the U.S. Army promulgates a new wartime structure: Army Air Forces (AAF) under Major General Henry H. Arnold, Army Service Forces (ASF) under Lieutenant General Brehon B. Somervell, and Army Ground Forces under Lieutenant General Lesley J. McNair. All report directly to Army Chief of Staff Major General George C. Marshall.

In the Philippines, a handful of Bataan-based P-40 fighters sortie to strike Japanese shipping in Subic Bay; some hits are claimed but four P-40s are shot down.

On Java, the few remaining Fifth Air Force aircraft at Jogjakarta airfield depart as Japanese land forces approach to within 20 miles.

MARCH 3 Disaster strikes at Broome, northern Australia, as Japanese aircraft strike American airfields and harbor installations without warning. No less than 2 B-17s, 2 B-24s, 12 seaplanes, and 2 Hudson bombers are destroyed on the ground while 20 U.S. servicemen are killed, along with 45 Dutch civilians.

MARCH 5 In India, General Lewis H. Brereton arrives from the Netherlands East Indies to take charge of the Tenth Air Force forming there. Presently, this consists of only eight B-17 bombers.

MARCH 7 In Alabama, Captain Benjamin O. Davis, son of the Army's first African American general, is among the first aviation school class to graduate from the Tuskegee Institute. Most fly Curtiss

P-40s, although several months pass before they are committed to combat.

MARCH 8 In India, 8 B-17s of the Tenth Air Force fly in 474 troops to Magwe, along with 29 tons of supplies, while also evacuating 423 civilians. The headquarters unit for the Tenth Air Force also departs the Zone of the Interior (ZI) and makes its way towards India.

MARCH 15 On New Caledonia, Southwestern Pacific, the 67th Fighter Squadron becomes the first Army Air Forces tactical unit to deploy for active duty.

MARCH 16 At Del Monte, the Philippines, three B-17s of the 435th Reconnaissance Squadron safely evacuate General Douglas MacArthur and his family and staff to Australia, where he is installed as supreme commander of the Southwest Pacific Area.

MARCH 19 In California, a group of scientists and engineers from the California Institute of Technology form the new Aerojet Engineering Company with Dr. Theodore von Karman as president. This soon becomes one of the largest rocket companies in the world and it manufactures liquid- and solid-fuel devices for both the Army and Navy.

MARCH 20 The Army Air Forces promulgates the "Plan for Initiation of US Army Bombardment Operations in the British Isles," which delineates broad outlines for attacking and reducing German national, economic, and industrial structure.

In Great Britain, Major General Ira C. Eaker finalizes a report detailing his analysis of Royal Air Force Bomber Command operations. In it he finds that British nighttime tactics dovetail nicely with American plans for precision daylight bombing, and that the two approaches complement each other.

MARCH 25   Over Europe, Major Cecil P. Lessig becomes the first American pilot from the Eighth Air Force to complete a combat mission when he flies one of 36 RAF Spitfires on a fighter sweep across the English Channel. However, the force withdraws after being approached by a larger German force.

MARCH 26   At Santa Monica, California, the Douglas C-54 Skymaster (DC-4) flies for the first time; it serves as a transportation workhorse for the Army Air Forces.

In the Philippines, a B-17 from the 435th Reconnaissance Squadron, 19th Bomb Group, safely evacuates President Quezon and his family to Australia.

MARCH 27   In Washington, D.C., the War Department and the Navy Department reach an agreement whereby the latter assumes responsibility for all antisubmarine operations along both coasts of the United States. Moreover, all Army units assigned to assist these missions will remain under Navy control.

MARCH 31   Major General Carl A. Spaatz suggests that the unassigned Eighth Air Force forming in Georgia become the nucleus of Army Air Forces in Britain (AAFIB).

APRIL 1   At Eglin Field, Florida, the Air Corps Proving Ground is redesignated the Proving Ground Command.

APRIL 2   From India, Major General Lewis H. Brereton leads three B-24 Liberators on the Tenth Air Force's first air strike; the targets are Japanese positions on Port Blair, Andaman Islands, in the Indian Ocean. Earlier, a two-aircraft raid against Rangoon is scrubbed after one B-24 crashes and the other experiences mechanical difficulties.

APRIL 3   At Anasol, India, six B-17s from the Tenth Air Force attack warehouse and docking facilities in Rangoon, starting several fires; one bomber is lost to enemy action.

APRIL 8   At Calcutta, India, the first supply mission over the "Hump" (Himalayas) transpires as 10 DC-3s acquired from Pan American Airlines hoist 30,000 gallons of fuel to Yunnan-yi, southern China. The transfer occurs in anticipation of the arrival of 16 B-25 Mitchell bombers launched from the carrier *Hornet* against Tokyo.

APRIL 6–7   On Bataan, Philippines, Japanese troops break through American defenses, necessitating all remaining P-40 fighters on the peninsula to be evacuated to dispersed airfields on Mindanao. All are flown to Australia as of May 1.

APRIL 7–24   In California, an A-20 Havoc aircraft begins testing the safety and utility of liquid-propelled rockets (incorrectly designated as JATO, or jet-assisted takeoffs). The organization conducting such flights jocularly becomes known as the "Suicide Club."

APRIL 1   In Buffalo, New York, the Curtiss-Wright Company unveils the first production C-46 Commando air transport, which becomes the largest and heaviest twin-engine aircraft employed by the Army Air Forces. Enjoying distinct advantages in load capacity and high-altitude performance over the older Douglas C-47, it serves with distinction in Asia by flying over the Himalaya Mountains, or "Hump."

APRIL 12 In Washington, D.C., General Henry H. Arnold forwards plans for Operation BOLERO to General George C. Marshall in London, England. This directive calls for establishing the Eighth Air Force on British soil.

Captain Edward "Eddie" Rickenbacker requests of Lieutenant General Henry H. Arnold that his World War I "Hat in the Ring" squadron insignia be bestowed upon the new 94th Pursuit Squadron. In 1924 that unit had adopted the "Indian Head" emblem of the 103rd Aero Squadron.

At Mindanao, Philippines, three B-17s and ten B-25s under Brigadier General Ralph Royce, Fifth Air Force, stage through Mindanao and attack Japanese shipping and installations, before returning 4,000 miles to their main base at Darwin, Australia.

APRIL 13 Fifth Air Force B-25s stage through Valencia, the Philippines, to strike Japanese installations and shipping near Cebu and Davao.

APRIL 15 In England, General Ira C. Eaker establishes the VIII Bomber Command at Wycombe Abbey, High Wycombe.

APRIL 16 In India, six Tenth Air Force B-17s take off from Dum Dum near Calcutta and strike Japanese targets at Rangoon at night; bomb damage assessment is not possible in light of enemy searchlights.

APRIL 18 Sixteen North American B-25 Mitchell medium bombers under Lieutenant Colonel James "Jimmy" Doolittle fly from the deck of the carrier *Hornet* and strike targets 800 miles distant in Tokyo, Yokosuka, Yokohama, Kobe, and Nagoya, Japan, before crash-landing in China (one is forced down in Siberia). Damage proves slight but the attack is a

The first of eighteen B-25 Mitchell medium bombers lifts off from the carrier USS Hornet *during the first U.S. air raid on the Japanese mainland, April 1942. (National Archives)*

stunning psychological coup to the United States by finally staging a successful assault on an erstwhile invincible enemy.

APRIL 22   Transport and bomber aircraft from the Tenth Air Force begin an immediate evacuation of Allied personnel and supplies from Burma to India in the face of a surging Japanese offensive there. By mid-June, 4,499 passengers and 1.7 million pounds of freight have been removed.

APRIL 29   Rangoon is struck by another wave of Tenth Air Force B-17s, which bomb dock areas and facilities.

APRIL 30   On New Guinea, Fifth Air Force P-39s fly from Port Moresby and strafe Japanese airfields and fuel dumps at Lae and Salamaua. At the time, Australian forces are attempting to contain an enemy offensive across the Owen Stanley Mountains.

MAY 2   At Bolling Field, Washington, D.C., Major General Carl A. "Tooey" Spaatz gains appointment as commander of the Eighth Air Force currently assembling in England.

MAY 5   A night raid by four Tenth Air Force B-17 bombers hits the Japanese airfield at Mingaladon, Burma, wrecking a hangar and a row of parked aircraft. The Americans claimed 40 enemy aircraft destroyed, but the damage assessment is impossible to verify at night.

MAY 6   Japanese fuel dumps at Mingaladon, Burma, are struck for a second consecutive time by three Tenth Air Force B-17s; several fires are reputed burning.

MAY 8   In the Coral Sea, American and Japanese navies clash in the first naval encounter where the main battle fleets never sight each other. Both sides lose a carrier in a costly exchange. Army Air Forces aircraft perform useful reconnaissance work, but the experience highlights deficiencies in Army-Navy communications and coordination.

MAY 9   Fifth Air Force B-26 Marauders, led by a single B-17, bomb Japanese seaplanes and shipping at Deboyne Island.

MAY 10   Off the Gold Coast of Africa, the carrier *Ranger* launches 68 Army Curtiss P-40s, which then safely land at Accra.

MAY 11   At High Wycombe, England, the advanced echelon of the Eighth Air Force, numbering 39 officers and 348 enlisted men, deploys and prepares to receive forthcoming arrivals.

MAY 12   In India, four Tenth Air Force B-17s bomb Japanese airfields at Myitkyina, Burma, which fell to enemy forces on May 8. Enemy aircraft here pose a direct threat to the Allied base at Dinjan as well as to transport aircraft flying the "Hump" into southern China.

MAY 13   At High Wycombe, England, the 15th Bombardment Squadron (Light), flying Douglas A-20 Havocs, becomes one of the first American combat units to deploy. However, they arrive without aircraft of their own and utilize British versions of the bomber for the time being.

In New Britain, Fifth Air Force B-17s and B-26s strike major Japanese airfields and nearby shipping on Rabaul.

MAY 14   Over Burma, Tenth Air Force heavy bombers hit Japanese airfields at Myitkyina a second time, claiming several hits on the runway and adjoining buildings.

Long lines of A-20 attack bombers roll ceaselessly, night and day, through the Douglas Aircraft plant at Long Beach, California, ca. October 1942.

MAY 15 In Washington, D.C., the War Department directs that interceptor and pursuit organizations within the U.S. Army Air Forces receive the new designation of "fighter."

MAY 16 In India, Tenth Air Force headquarters completes its transfer to New Delhi as B-17s attack Japanese airfields at Myitkyina a third time, completely neutralizing the airfield and, with it, the threat to Allied communications.

Fifth Air Force B-25s, B-26s, and B-17s launch another round of air raids against storehouses on Lae, New Guinea, and seaplane bases on Deboyne Island.

MAY 17–30 At Wright Field, Ohio, Igor Sikorsky delivers the prototype XR-4 helicopter to Army authorities for testing. It is accepted into service as the R-4

Hoverfly, the only American helicopter deployed during World War II.

MAY 18 In the mid-Pacific, the Seventh Air Force begins receiving shipments of new B-17Es in anticipation of a Japanese attack against Midway Island. These begin replacing the older and less capable Douglas B-18 Bolos still in inventory, although these are also pressed into reconnaissance duties.

In Panama, the government signs an agreement with the United States allowing Army Air Forces aircraft to defend the Canal region from a number of bases.

MAY 19 In England, General Ira C. Eaker, head of Headquarters, Eighth Air Force, assumes control of all Army Air Forces units in the British Isles.

MAY 22   Continuing their air offensive, Fifth Air Force B-17s strike Japanese installations on Rabaul, New Britain, while B-26s attack enemy airfields and shipping at Lae, New Guinea.

MAY 24   In the Zone of the Interior (ZI), the 12th Bomb Group is shifted from Louisiana to California in the face of a perceived threat to the West Coast.

Over Rabaul, New Britain, Japanese A6M Zero fighters intercept and maul Fifth Air Force B-26s, shooting down and heavily damaging several.

MAY 26   Over Hawthorne, California, the prototype Northrop XP-61 performs its maiden flight; this is the first American aircraft designed from the ground up as a night fighter and enters service as the P-61 Black Widow.

In England, General Henry H. Arnold arrives at 10 Downing Street, London, to attend the first of several Anglo-American air conferences with Prime Minister Winston Churchill.

MAY 28   In the Aleutian Islands, an Eleventh Air Force B-17 performs the first armed reconnaissance mission from the secretly constructed airfield at Umnak, but no signs of enemy activity are uncovered.

MAY 30   In Seattle, Washington, the first B-17F Flying Fortress is rolled out. This features an enlarged bombardier's nose canopy, a revised tail section, and a tail turret. It is the first major production variant.

In London, England, General Henry H. Arnold presents his British counterparts with the "Program of Arrival of US Army Air Forces in the United Kingdom," which stipulates deploying 66 combat groups, exclusive of reconnaissance squadrons, no later than March 1943.

At Oahu, Hawaii, the Seventh Air Force begins shuttling B-17 heavy bombers to Midway Island in anticipation of a Japanese attack there.

Over Burma, Tenth Air Force B-17s raid Japanese airfields at Myitkyina a fifth time; no enemy activity can be discerned below, so further attacks here are suspended.

JUNE 1   In the Zone of the Interior (ZI) fear of an impending Japanese attack results in the cancellation of all transfers of men and equipment to Great Britain for the time being.

Over Rangoon, Burma, Tenth Air Force B-17s strike the dock areas again, and claim sinking one Japanese tanker.

JUNE 2   At Boston, Massachusetts, the 97th Bomb Group, slated for immediate transfer to the United Kingdom, is instead ordered to the West Coast to thwart a possible Japanese attack there.

JUNE 3   At Dinjan, India, six B-25s of the 11th Bomb Squadron fly a mission over the Himalayan Mountains en route to joining the China Air Task Force (CATF) at Kunming. They unload their bombs on Japanese positions at Lashio, Burma, but three aircraft are lost when they crash into mountainsides and another is lost when it runs out of fuel. Only two B-25s complete the journey intact.

At Midway Island, nine Seventh Air Force B-17s launch a bombing raid against five large Japanese vessels 570 miles distant; they claim five hits and several near misses.

Over Dutch Harbor, Alaska, Japanese carrier aircraft make a sudden attack on American facilities, killing 52 service members. Several P-40s at Umnak sortie to intercept the attackers but arrive 10 minutes too late and only end up shooting down two enemy craft.

JUNE 4   Over Alaska, Japanese carrier aircraft raid American facilities and airfield
at Dutch Harbor a second day. P-40
fighters intercept the raiders, downing
three bombers and one fighter at a cost
of one of their own. That afternoon
two Eleventh Air Force B-17s and five
B-26s attack the Japanese fleet, although
no hits are scored; two aircraft are shot
down.

Nine Boeing B-17Es from the Seventh
Air Force participate in aerial bombardment of the Japanese fleet at Midway,
although with indifferent results. A force
of four Martin B-26 Marauders, rigged
as torpedo planes, also fares poorly, with
only two survivors. Two B-17s are also
shot down but two Zero fighters are
claimed.

Over Rangoon, Burma, Tenth Air
Force B-17s make a final raid on docks
and facilities, losing one aircraft. Two
months of harassing raids is concluded
following the onset of monsoon weather.

JUNE 5   Off the Alaska coast, a force of 18
B-26s, 10 B-17s, and 2 LB-30s are dispatched by the Eleventh Air Force against
Japanese carrier forces, but no contact is
made. They bomb a target that radar
paints as ships, which turn out to be the
Pribilof Islands.

Near Midway Island, a force of six Seventh Air Force B-17s make several high
altitude raids against the retreating Japanese fleet, claiming several hits on a heavy
cruiser; one B-17 is shot down and
another crashes due to lack of fuel. Total
Army Air Forces losses in this, one of history's most decisive encounters, are two
B-17s and two B-26s.

JUNE 6   The Army begins procuring light
civilian aircraft to serve as reconnaissance
and artillery spotters (Grasshoppers); most
are based on the popular Piper Cub
design.

In the Aleutians, bad weather grounds
most Eleventh Air Force operations, but
a flight of P-38s en route to Umnak manages to mistakenly strafe a Soviet
freighter. Meanwhile, Japanese forces
come ashore on Kiska.

Near Midway Island, trigger-happy
B-17s of the Seventh Air Force mistakenly attack a U.S. submarine, but fortu-
nately miss their intended victim.

JUNE 7   Major General Clarence L.
Tinker, commanding officer of the
eventh Air Force, becomes the first
Army Air Forces general killed in com-
bat when his LB-30 fails to return from
a bombing mission over Wake Island.
He is succeeded by General Howard C.
Davidson.

JUNE 8   In Washington, D.C., President
Franklin D. Roosevelt appoints Major
General James E. Chaney to serve as
commander of the European Theater of
Operations (ETO).

JUNE 9   In Washington, D.C., President
Franklin D. Roosevelt awards the
Congressional Medal of Honor to newly
promoted Brigadier General James H.
Doolittle for his role in the recent raid
on Tokyo, Japan.

Over Lae, New Guinea, a B-26
Marauder carrying Lieutenant Colonel
Lyndon B. Johnson—the future 36th
president of the United States—
experiences engine trouble and is forced
to turn back. Johnson nonetheless wins a
Silver Star for his participation.

JUNE 11   Over Alaska, a mixed force of
five B-24 Liberators and five B-17 Flying Fortresses belonging to the Eleventh
Air Force strike the Japanese-held island
of Kiska, Aleutian Islands, for the first
time; one B-24 is shot down by antiaircraft fire.

JUNE 12   At Fayid, Egypt, Lieutenant Colonel Harry A. Halveson leads 12 Army Air Forces B-24 Liberators on a secret air raid (HALPRO) against Axis oil installations at Ploesti, Romania. The raid inflicts little damage, but anticipates greater efforts to come.

Over the Aleutian Islands, six B-17s and one B-24 of the Eleventh Air Force make bomb runs over Japanese shipping off Kiska, claiming hits on a cruiser and a destroyer.

JUNE 13   Japanese shipping at Kiska, Aleutian Islands, is struck for the third consecutive day by five B-17s and three B-24s of the Eleventh Air Force. Due to cloudy conditions, damage assessment cannot be accurately gauged.

JUNE 14   Over the Aleutians, B-17s and B-24s from the Eleventh Air Force bomb Japanese shipping in Kiska harbor a fourth time. The raid is made from only 700 feet and damages two cruisers. A Japanese seaplane is also claimed but two B-17s suffer heavily from antiaircraft fire.

JUNE 15   In the Mediterranean, seven B-24s accompany RAF Bristol Beauforts in an attack on the Italian battle fleet; the Liberators claim to damage a battleship and a cruiser while the RAF crews sink a cruiser.

JUNE 17   In the Zone of the Interior (ZI), Army Air Forces C-47s begin practicing with Waco troop gliders for the first time.

Off the coast of Midway Island, P-40s of the 73rd Fighter Squadron are launched off the carrier *Saratoga* to replace the Navy fighters lost in the battle a week earlier. They conduct aerial patrols of the region until being relieved on June 23.

JUNE 18   In London, England, Major General Carl A. Spaatz assumes command of the embryonic Eighth Air Force; presently no less than 85 airfields are being enlarged to handle B-17 and B-24 bombers.

Over the Aleutian Islands, Eleventh Air Force B-17s and B-24s make a precision daylight raid at high altitude against Kiska Harbor; a transport is sunk and

---

Chennault, Claire L. (1890–1958)

Army Air Forces general. Claire Lee Chennault was born in Commerce, Texas, on September 6, 1890, and he gained his lieutenant's wings in April 1920. He was a natural-born flier and held several important assignments including as commanding officer, 19th Pursuit Squadron, 1923–1926, and instructor at the Air Corps Tactical School, Maxwell Field, Alabama. Here, Chennault honed his interest in fighter tactics, and in 1935 he published an important book, *The Role of Defensive Pursuit.* He resigned from the Army on account of deafness in April 1937, but his career changed dramatically when he was hired by Madame Jiang Jieshi to serve as an adviser to the Nationalist Chinese government. In 1941 Chennault convinced the American government to organize a group of mercenaries called the American Volunteer Group (AVG) to fight the Japanese in China.

Chennault equipped three squadrons of Curtiss P-40s, and they began winning battles against the heretofore invincible Japanese Army air force over China and Burma. They soon became hailed as the "Flying Tigers" and claimed over 100 Japanese aircraft for the loss of 12 pilots. Chennault's group disbanded in July 1942, and in March 1943 he rose to major general in charge of the newly created 14th Air Force. By war's end Chennault's men claimed 2,600 enemy planes shot down and 1.2 million tons of shipping sunk. He resigned from the Army in August 1945 and remained in China as head of the Civil Air Transport (CAT). Chennault died in New Orleans, Louisiana, on July 27, 1958, one of history's finest aerial strategists.

another set afire. One B-24 crashes due to battle damage and its crew is partially rescued.

JUNE 19 In Cairo, Egypt, Brigadier General Russell L. Maxwell is appointed commander of United States Army Air Forces in the Middle East (USAFIME).

JUNE 20 On Midway Island, Major General Willis H. Hales arrives to take command of the Seventh Air Force after the late Major General Clarence L. Tinker.

JUNE 21 In London, England, American and British representatives conclude the Arnold-Portal-Towers agreement; this act commits the United States to a gradual building up of air power in Europe under the codename of Operation BOLERO.

Over Libya, nine B-24s of USAFIME stage a nighttime raid on Bengasi harbor after a RAF Wellington bomber marks the target area with flares.

JUNE 23 At Presque Isle, Maine, two B-17s and seven P-38s begin staging out for England even before Operation BOLERO is officially enacted.

JUNE 25 Major General Lewis H. Brereton, facing a new crisis in the Middle East, departs India with all available heavy bombers of the 9th Bomber Squadron. Meanwhile, command of the Tenth Air Force reverts to Brigadier General Earl L. Naiden, who commands few aviation assets for the time being.

JUNE 26 A force of three Seventh Air Force LB-30s stage at Midway, then proceed to drop bombs on Japanese-held Wake Island.

JUNE 28 In Cairo, Egypt, Major General Lewis H. Brereton arrives to serve as commander of United States Army Middle East Air Forces (USAMEAF).

He has at present B-24s of the 9th Bombardment Squadron.

JUNE 29 In Europe, Captain Charles G. Kegelman, commander of the 15th Bomb Squadron, becomes the first member of the Eighth Air Force to drop bombs on German targets when he accompanies 12 RAF Bostons (A-20s) on a raid against the Hazebrouck marshalling yards. Meanwhile, Lieutenant Alfred W. Giacomini ditches his Spitfire in the English Channel and drowns, becoming the first casualty of the Eighth Air Force.

JUNE 30 Over North Africa, USAMEAF B-24s drop bombs on German and Italian positions at Bengasi, losing the first aircraft lost in the Middle East. General Lewis H. Brereton is also forced to relocate his detachment from Cairo, Egypt, to Palestine, as the Afrika Korps under General Erwin Rommel advances.

JULY 1 In Washington, D.C., the War Department revised Operation BOLERO downward from 66 combat groups down to 54 owing to commitments in other theaters.

At Polebrook, England, B-17s from the 97th Bombardment Group land after an uneventful Atlantic crossing; it takes a month before the entire group assembles there.

Over China, four B-25s and an escort of P-40s of the embryonic China Air Task Force (CATF) launch from Hengyang and attack the docks at Hankow; in light of poor weather conditions, the damage inflicted is not substantial.

JULY 2 Over China, CATF B-25s and P-40s strike the docks at Hankow a second time, inflicting considerable damage. The Japanese retaliate by launching a night raid against their base in Hengyang, but fail to destroy any aircraft.

JULY 3   Over North Africa, B-17s and B-24s of USAMEAF bomb Tobruk city and harbor.

B-25s and P-40s of the China Air Task Force (CATF) attack the Japanese airfield at Nanchang, damaging and destroying several parked aircraft. That evening, the Japanese launch another retaliatory raid against Hengyang, but fail to hit the airfield.

JULY 4   Over Holland, Army Air Forces pilots of the 15th Bombardment Squadron accompany Royal Air Force Boston bombers on their first raid over occupied Europe. Their six A-20 Havocs attack German airfields; one American airman is lost and another becomes the first American taken prisoner in Europe. Captain Charles C. Kegelman, squadron commander, nurses his crippled Havoc back to England and receives the Distinguished Service Cross.

In China, the American Volunteer Group (AVG), famously known as the "Flying Tigers," is disbanded once the China Air Task Force (CATF) activates under Major General Claire L. Chennault; it is eventually designated the 23rd Pursuit Group under Colonel Robert L. Scott.

Over Kweilin, China, P-40s of CATF intercept a formation of Japanese light bombers, and claim to shoot down 13.

JULY 6   In the Zone of the Interior (ZI), M-8 4.5-inch air-to-ground rockets are test fired by a Curtiss P-40 Warhawk for the first time.

Off the coast of Panama, aircraft of the 59th Bomb Squadron, Sixth Air Force, attack and damage the German submarine *U-153*; this vessel is subsequently sunk by U.S. Navy destroyers a week later.

In England, the Royal Air Force allows Eighth Air Force personnel to join various operational committees handling targeting, operational research, fighter interception, and bombing operations.

In China, B-25s of the China Air Task Force (CATF) strike the docks of Canton for the first time. This marks the first raid against coastal facilities along the China coast.

JULY 7   Off Cherry Point, North Carolina, a Lockheed A-29 Vega of the 369th Bombardment Squadron attacks and sinks the German submarine *U-701*; this is the first such victory by an AAF aircraft.

Over the Aleutian Islands, Eleventh Air Force B-24s fly to bomb Japanese targets in Kiska, Attu, and Agattu, but are turned back by bad weather.

Major General Millard F. Harmon gains appointment as commanding general of the South Pacific (COMGENSOPAC).

JULY 8   In Alaska, the Eleventh Air Force gains additional offensive muscle in the form of B-24s of the 404th Bomb Squadron; this unit was originally destined for North Africa before the Japanese invaded the Aleutians.

Over China, a single China Air Task Force (CATF) B-25 piloted by Colonel Caleb V. Haynes attacks Japanese headquarters at Tengchung, China, near the Burma border.

JULY 9   In England, seven P-38 Lightnings of the Eighth Air Force arrive, becoming the first single-seat Army Air Forces aircraft to successfully cross the Atlantic in stages.

JULY 10   In Washington, D.C., Operation BOLERO is revised upwards to include 137 Army Air Forces groups deploying in the British Isles by December 1943.

Over El Segundo, California, the prototype Douglas XA-26 light bomber debuts; it enters service as the A-26 Invader, the most capable aircraft in its class.

JULY 12   Over France, six RAF Boston (A–20) light bombers with Eighth Air Force aircrews attack German airfields at Abbeville and Drucat.

JULY 13   Over Bengasi, Libya, USA-MEAF B–17s and B–24s attack the harbor and enemy shipping; one B–24 is lost to antiaircraft fire.

JULY 16   At Kweilin, China, four B–25s of the China Air Task Force (CATF), with a P–40 escort, attack a storage area at Han-kow, starting several fires. The aircraft recover at Hengyang but are attacked by Japanese bombers and have to take off quickly. In the confusion, a P–40 mistakenly attacks a B–25 and shoots it down; this is the CATF's first bomber loss.

JULY 17   In the Aleutians, three B–17s and seven B–24s of the Eleventh Air Force attack Japanese shipping in Kiska Harbor; one B–17 is shot down by enemy fighters.

JULY 19   Over China, the China Air Task Force (CATF) dispatches two B–25s in support of Chinese forces besieging the Japanese-held town of Linchuan; immediately after the attack, Chinese forces are enabled to enter the city.

JULY 20   Over China, three B–25s and four P–40s of the China Air Task Force (CATF) bomb and strafe targets at Chinkiang on the Yangtze River. Several junks are reported sunk.

JULY 21   In England, General Dwight D. Eisenhower tasks the Eighth Air Force, assisted by the Royal Air Force, with achieving air superiority over Western Europe by April 1, 1943. This is an essential move to facilitate a cross-channel invasion.

Over New Guinea, Fifth Air Force B–26s attack a Japanese invasion convoy off Salamaua to forestall enemy reinforcements from reaching Buna.

JULY 22   At New Caledonia, four B–17 squadrons belonging to the 11th Bombardment Group deploy from Hawaii; this is also the first heavy bomber group in the region.

Over New Guinea, Fifth Air Force P–40s and P–39s attack Japanese landing craft as they come ashore at Gona; the aim of the attack is to halt a Japanese drive across the Stanley Owen Mountains to capture Port Moresby.

JULY 23   On New Guinea, the Fifth Air Force unleashes B–17s, A–24s, B–26s, and fighter aircraft against Japanese shipping, landing barges, and storage dumps at Buna and Gona as Japanese forces begin pushing down the Kokoda Trail.

In the South Pacific, seven B–17s of the Seventh Air Force make a photo-reconnaissance mission over Makin Island, soon to be the object of an overpowering attack by marine raiders.

JULY 24   In Washington, D.C., the Joint Chiefs of Staff announces that forces allocated to Operation BOLERO in England will be further depleted once several heavy and medium bomber groups are to be shifted to North Africa in support of Operation TORCH. They also determine to dispatch 15 combat groups to the Pacific theater.

Over New Guinea, Fifth Air Force B–26s and A–24s continue striking Japanese positions in and around Gona as enemy forces continue pouring down the Kokoda Trail.

JULY 25   The Fifth Air Force unleashes B–25s and P–39s against landing barges and troop concentrations at Gona as Japanese troops advance to within six miles of the Kokoda Trail at Oivi.

JULY 26   Over France, Lieutenant Colonel Albert P. Clark, executive officer of the 31st Fighter Group, is shot down on a fighter sweep, becoming the first officer of the Eighth Air Force taken prisoner.

Over New Guinea, Japanese air defenses repel a raid by Fifth Air Force B-25s at Gasmata; B-26s also attack shipping off Gona, but fail to score any hits. Meanwhile, Australian troops at Kokoda are evacuated in the face of a Japanese jungle onslaught.

JULY 27   As the Eighth Air Force begins gathering its offensive strength, Major General Ira C. Eaker agrees with RAF officers to employ Spitfire IXs as high-altitude escorts for B-17 bombers until VIII Fighter Command is fully operational. This will also pit Spitfire IXs against superlative Fw-190s for the first time.

At Auckland, New Zealand, Major General Millard F. Harmon arrives to take charge of the newly created U.S. Army Forces in the South Pacific (USA-FIPA); he moves quickly to transfer his headquarters to Nouméa, New Guinea, as preparations for a Solomon Islands offensive develops.

JULY 28   Over North Africa, B-17s and B-24s of USAMEAF strike docks and shipping at Bengasi, scoring probable hits on two merchant vessels.

In Australia, General George F. Kenney arrives to take charge of Allied Air Forces as B-26s of the Fifth Air Force bomb Japanese troops at Gona.

JULY 29   In the Aleutians, Eleventh Air Force B-24s and B-17s strike Japanese installations at Kiska, although bomb damage assessment is unobtainable due to cloud coverage.

On New Guinea, Japanese forces capture Kokoda as Fifth Air Force A-24s and P-39s continue working over shipping and supply depots in their rear areas. These constant attacks slow, but do not halt, the enemy's advance upon Port Moresby.

JULY 30   Over China, a major air battle unfolds as the Japanese dispatch 120 aircraft to strike the main China Air Task Force (CATF) base at Hengyang. P-40s of the 23rd Fighter Group maul the attackers over the next 36 hours, downing 17 aircraft and preventing them from reaching the base; three P-40s are also lost.

In the South Pacific, B-17s of the 11th Bomb Group deploy on Espiritu Santo as a reconnaissance and strike force in anticipation for the Marine Corps offensive at Guadalcanal, slated for August 7.

JULY 31   In Palestine, the USAMEAF is strengthened by the arrival of P-40s belonging to the 57th Fighter Group, and B-25s of the 12th Bomb Group. These add greater tactical flexibility to the B-17s and B-24s already in theater.

Over Guadalcanal, Fifth Air Force B-17s bomb Japanese positions on Kukum Beach and Lunga as marine amphibious forces depart New Zealand for the invasion. Other B-17s from the 11th Bomb Group on Efate under Colonel LaVerne G. Saunders attack the landing strip on Lunga Point. Saunders will execute another 56 sorties against the island up through the invasion of August 7.

Over Wake Island, a B-17 reconnaissance aircraft is pounced by six Japanese Zeroes, and its gunners claim four kills.

AUGUST 1   In the Mediterranean, B-24s of USAMEAF attack an Axis convoy headed for North Africa, sinking a large transport vessel. One B-24 crash-lands back at base and is written off.

AUGUST 2 Over New Guinea, a Fifth Air Force B-17 bombs Japanese shipping and targets south of Salamaua while another unloads ordnance on Gona; neither attack is particularly successful.

AUGUST 3 In Brisbane, Australia, Lieutenant General George H. Brett, commanding the Fifth Air Force, is recalled to the United States for reassignment.

AUGUST 4 Over China, China Air Task Force (CATF) P-40s attack Japanese headquarters at Linchuan, and also strafe barracks and transports in the river.

AUGUST 5 Over France, 11 aircraft of the 31st Fighter Group, VIII Fighter Command, make the unit's first practice sweep from across the English Channel.

In Egypt, General Lewis H. Brereton issues his first strategic estimate of Middle Eastern objectives, committing the USA-MEAF to the destruction of the Afrika Korps by supporting the British Eighth Army on the ground, securing control of air over the Mediterranean, and the gradual reduction of oil facilities at Ploesti, Romania, and the Caucasus, should they fall to the Germans.

Over China, Japanese aircraft make another attempted surprise attack at Kweilin airfields, but the Americans are tipped off by the Chinese warning net established by General Claire L. Chennault. P-40s engage bombers over the target, shooting down two and driving the rest off.

AUGUST 6 In a sharp counterstrike, B-25s of the China Air Task Force bomb the Tien Ho airfield, damaging the runway and several parked aircraft.

AUGUST 6–7 Captain Harl Pease, Jr., leads B-17s of the 93rd Squadron, 19th Bomb Group, on a strike against Rabaul,

New Britain, from which he does not return. Pease, who had earlier evacuated General Douglas MacArthur from Mindanao, Philippines, to Australia, posthumously receives a Congressional Medal of Honor.

AUGUST 7 Over Vunakanau. New Guinea, 13 B-17s of the Fifth Air Force attack Japanese airfields to neutralize them in anticipation of the forthcoming Guadalcanal invasion. B-26s also strike enemy positions at Lae.

AUGUST 8 Over Canton, China, B-25s of the China Air Task Force (CATF) bomb Tien Ho airfield, claiming two Japanese fighters shot down.

In the Lower Solomons, B-17s stationed in the South Pacific begin flying lengthy reconnaissance missions in order to detect any Japanese reinforcements steaming towards Guadalcanal.

AUGUST 9 Over China, P-40s of the 23rd Fighter Group attack Japanese ground forces at Linchuan in support of the Chinese army. Meanwhile, four B-25s and a fighter escort stage through Nanning, to bomb and strafe docks at Haiphong, French Indochina (Vietnam) for the first time.

AUGUST 10 In China, the 23rd Fighter Group under Colonel Robert L. Scott strafes and bombs Japanese warehouses and ammo dumps at Sienning, destroying a mountain of supplies intended for use against American air bases at Hengyang.

AUGUST 11 In England, General Carl A. Spaatz, speaking in reference to operations in North Africa, makes it his opinion that only the United Kingdom is well positioned as the only base from which air superiority over Germany can be achieved.

In China, China Air Task Force P-40s strike Japanese airfields at Yoyang and Nanchang, from which bombers have been attacking American bases at Hengyang.

AUGUST 12   At Westhampnett, England, the 31st Fighter Group is declared operational. It is the first fighter unit of the Eighth Air Force to reach that status, but it remains under operational control of the Royal Air Force until it acquires meaningful combat experience.

AUGUST 13   Off the coast of northern New Guinea, a Japanese convoy carrying 3,000 construction troops is attacked by Fifth Air Force B-17s, then a wave of B-26s closer to the shore.

AUGUST 14   Off the coast of Iceland, a pair of P-40s flown by Lieutenants Joseph D. Shaffer and Elza E. Shahan share credit for downing a four-engined Fw-200 Kondor patrol bomber; this is the first victory scored by the Army Air Forces in the European Theater of Operations (ETO). At the time, Shaffer and Shahan were ferrying their aircraft to England.

AUGUST 17   Over France, 12 B-17s under Colonel Frank A. Armstrong, 97th Bomb Group, stage the first large air raid in Europe by hitting the marshalling yards at Rouen-Sotteville. The attack proves a deceptively easy, for German resistance proves negligible and all aircraft return without damage. Sergeant Kent R. West also downs an Fw-190 German fighter, becoming the first Eighth Air Force gunner to score a kill.

AUGUST 18   In India, General Clayton R. Bissell is appointed the new commander of the Tenth Air Force; General Earl L. Naiden is bumped over to take charge of the India-China Ferry Command.

AUGUST 19   As Allied forces storm ashore at Dieppe, France, 22 B-17s from the Eighth Air Force drop 30 tons of bombs on German airfields at Abbeville and Drucat as a diversion. Lieutenant Sam F. Dunkin, 31st Fighter Group, also becomes the first active-duty American pilot to down a German fighter while flying from England.

AUGUST 20   At Bolling Field, Washington, D.C., the new Twelfth Air Force is activated for service in North Africa and the Mediterranean. There they will specialize in ground support missions with light and medium attack bombers.

In England, the Eighth Air Force formalizes its principles of coordinating day and night bombing with the Royal Air Force by issuing its "Joint British/American Directive on Day Bomber Operations involving Fighter Cooperation."

AUGUST 21   In England, General Carl A. Spaatz becomes Air Officer ETOUSA (European Theater of Operations) to insure that theater air forces are adequately represented at all levels of operational planning.

The Eighth Air Force dispatches 12 B-17s to strike shipyards at Rotterdam, the Netherlands, but they abort after being attacked by 25 German fighters. Promised Spitfire escorts failed to materialize, highlighting the problems of proper coordination between the two forces.

AUGUST 22   Off the Panama Canal Zone, aircraft of the 45th Bomb Squadron, Sixth Air Force bomb and sink German submarine *U-654*, the AAF's second confirmed kill of the year.

Bell P-400s (export version of the P-39 Airacobra) belonging to the 67th Fighter Squadron are the first Army Air Forces aircraft deployed at Henderson Field,

Guadalcanal. They join Navy and Marine Corps fighters and dive bombers of the so-called "Cactus Air Force," already present.

AUGUST 24   The Eighth Air Force dispatches 12 heavy bombers to hit the shipyard at Ateliers et Chantiers de la Seine Maritime at Le Trait, France. Meanwhile, General Carl A. Spaatz is pleased to report that the attitude of RAF officials toward daytime precision bombings is now one of grudging approval.

Over Rabaul, New Britain, Fifth Air Force B-17s strike at Japanese positions and airfields at Gasmata.

In the Solomon Islands, seven B-17s join Navy aircraft from the carriers Enterprise and Saratoga in attacking a Japanese reinforcement convoy steaming for Guadalcanal; the carrier *Ryujo* is sunk.

AUGUST 25   On Goodenough Island, New Guinea, P-40s from Milne Bay strafe and sink a number of Japanese troop barges. An enemy convoy bound for Milne Bay from New Ireland is also struck, but the attack is spoiled by poor weather. Meanwhile, P-400s attack airfield and antiaircraft positions at Buna.

In the Solomon Islands, B-17s flying from Espiritu Santo attack a Japanese troop convoy, sinking the destroyer *Mutsuki*; after a mauling from Navy aircraft, the convoy retreats.

AUGUST 26   At Yunnani, southern China, CATF P-40s attack the rail center at Lashio, Burma, shooting down at least two intercepting fighters.

At Milne Bay, New Guinea, Fifth Air Force B-17s, B-25s, B-26s, and P-40s work over Japanese troop concentrations, sinking a large transport and destroying several supply dumps. They are joined by several Lockheed Hudsons flown by the Royal Australian Air Force.

AUGUST 27   Over New Guinea, Fifth Air Force P-40s continue pounding Japanese forces at Milne Bay while B-26s and P-400s attack enemy positions at Buna.

AUGUST 28   In Washington, D.C., the War Department orders the Air Training Command to allocate aircraft and personnel to evacuate sick and wounded American servicemen throughout the world.

Over France, a force of 15 Eighth Air Force B-17s bomb the Avions-Potez aircraft factory, which is serving as a Luftwaffe repair base.

Over China, eight B-25s of the China Air Task Force (CATF) bomb ammunition dumps at Hoang Su Phi and Phu Lo, Indochina (Vietnam). This is both the largest bomb raid staged by CATF and the first staged without a fighter escort.

AUGUST 29   Over Burma, China Air Task Force B-25s attack Lashio, starting several warehouse fires.

Over New Guinea, Fifth Air Force B-26s and P-400s continue raiding Japanese airfields at Buna, while P-40s work over enemy positions at Milne Bay. However, enemy ground forces continue driving on Port Moresby despite this hard pounding.

AUGUST 30   Over Burma, P-40s from the China Air Task Force (CATF) strike Japanese airfields at Myitkyina for the first time. Fighters from this base could threaten Dinjan, an important stop on the Assam-Burma air ferry.

AUGUST 31   In North Africa, USAMEAF B-25s begin around-the-clock attacks on targets in Tobruk while P-40s of the 57th Fighter Group escort RAF bombers on a raid against Maryut. Other aircraft hit German and Italian positions along the El Alamein line as the Battle of Alam el Halfa unfolds.

At Milne Bay, New Guinea, Australian troops take to the offensive, assisted by close support missions by Fifth Air Force P-40s, while B-17s attack supply dumps at Buna, and B-26s and A-20s strike airfields at Lae.

SEPTEMBER 1   In North Africa, P-40s of the 57th Fighter Group assist the British Eighth Army during the Battle of Alam el Halfa with fighter sweeps while B-25s of the USAMEAF strike enemy tanks and trucks.

On Milne Bay, New Guinea, Fifth Air Force P-40s attack Japanese headquarters at Wagga Wagga while P-400s strafe enemy columns in the Kokoda Pass in the Owen Stanley Range.

SEPTEMBER 2   In North Africa, P-40s and B-25s of USAMEAF continue working closely with the RAF and Eighth Army, delivering hammer blows against the Afrika Korps along Alam el Halfa ridge. Trucks and tanks remain priority targets.

Over China, wide-ranging CATF P-40s strike rice-laden barges in the Poyang region, airfields at Nanchang, railroad stations at Hua Yang, and manage to destroy a train in the Wuchang Peninsula.

Over New Guinea, P-400s resume strafing and bombing attacks against Japanese forces pressing through the Kokoda Pass but fail to stop their offensive toward Port Moresby.

On Guadalcanal, low-altitude P-400s shift from air defense missions, where they are at a disadvantage, to ground support missions for marines on the ground. They prove much better suited for these sorties and attacks against enemy shipping.

SEPTEMBER 3   Over the Aleutian Islands, six bombers and five P-38s of the Eleventh Air Force strike Japanese targets in Kiska Harbor, destroying several

seaplanes. This is also the longest over-water flight—1,260 miles—of the war to date.

In North Africa, USAMEAF B-25s and P-40s continue providing close support missions for the British Eighth Army as the Battle of Alam el Halfa rages; one enemy fighter is claimed in combat.

At Brisbane, Australia, Major General George C. Kenney arrives to take command of the Fifth Air Force, also receiving promotion to lieutenant general. He replaces Lieutenant General George H. Brett, who has been ordered back to the United States.

Over New Guinea, Fifth Air Force P-400s continue bombing and strafing Japanese columns advancing upon Port Moresby from Kokoda, while B-25s and A-20s strike the Mubo-Busama-Salamaua region.

A North American B-25 bomber swoops in low over Hanoi, dropping bombs on a Japanese aerodrome and inflicting considerable damage. This is the first American air raid over that city.

SEPTEMBER 4   Over North Africa, USAMEAF B-24s attack an Axis convoy approaching at sea, sinking at least two transports. Meanwhile, B-25s and P-40s continue assisting their RAF counterparts in hammering German positions and vehicles near Alam el Halfa.

At Milne Bay, Australian forces begin mop up operations near Goroni, assisted by Fifth Air Force P-40s. The Japanese, thoroughly bested, begin evacuating the region.

SEPTEMBER 5   In London, Major General Carl A. Spaatz convinces Lieutenant General Dwight D. Eisenhower that Eighth Air Force operations in Europe should be temporarily scaled back to support Operation TORCH in North Africa.

Kenney, George C. (1889–1977)

Army Air Forces general. George Churchill Kenney was born on August 6, 1889 and he joined the Aviation Section of the Army Signal Corps in June 1917. He arrived in France during World War I as a fighter pilot and downed two German aircraft. Kenney spent the next 20 years at the forefront of aeronautical developments by passing through the Army Air Corps Tactical School (1926), the Army Command and General Staff School (1927), and the Army War College (1933). He was also an accomplished aviator, and in May 1938 he flew the lead B-17 bomber that intercepted the Italian liner *Rex* at sea. Following the onset of World War II, he ventured to Europe as a military observer, was shocked by the tactical efficiency of the German Luftwaffe, and wrote a scathing appraisal of America's obsolete aviation technology. He rose to brigadier general in 1941, but the turning point in his career occurred when he was appointed to the staff of General Douglas MacArthur in August 1942.

From his headquarters in Australia, Kenney adopted innovative approaches to render aircraft as deadly as possible, and pioneered low-level "skip bombing" to penetrate the sides of enemy vessels. Proof of his efficiency came in the March 2–3, 1943 Battle of the Bismarck Sea, where his aircraft obliterated a 12-vessel Japanese convoy. In March 1945, Kenney advanced to full general and commander of all Allied air power in the Pacific. After the war, he became chief of the new Strategic Air Command in 1946, then headed the Air University at Maxwell Air Force Base until his retirement in 1951. He died in Miami, Florida, on August 9, 1977, one of the finest aerial tacticians of World War II.

Over France, the Eighth Air Force commits 31 B-17s—its largest raid to date—against the marshalling yards at Rouen-Sotteville.

Over North Africa, USAMEAF P-40s and B-25s continue their relentless ground support attacks as the Afrika Korps falters and begins retreating from the Alma el Halfa ridge.

On New Guinea, with Japanese forces in retreat from Milne Bay, Fifth Air Force P-400s redouble their attacks on enemy troops along the Kokoda Trail. P-40s and A-20s also attack enemy airfields in the vicinity of Buna.

SEPTEMBER 6 Over Meaulte, France, VIII Bomber Command suffers its first combat losses when two Boeing B-17s are shot down as they bombed the Avions-Potez aircraft factory. Meanwhile, 12 DB-7s (A-20s) attack German airfields at Abbeville-Drucat.

Over North Africa, USAMEAF P-40s shoot down three Ju-87 Stukas near the Dayr Ar Depression; other fighters continue escorting RAF bomber missions.

On New Guinea, Australian forces continue falling back closer to Port Moresby while, overhead, Fifth Air Force P-400s, A-20s, and B-17s attack enemy positions at Myola, Mubo, Kokoda, Eora Creek, and Milne Bay.

SEPTEMBER 7 The Eighth Air Force dispatches 29 B-17s to bomb the Wilton shipyards in Rotterdam, the Netherlands, but bad weather forces back all but 7. These make an ineffectual bomb run over the target area, but also claim to have shot down 12 German fighters trying to intercept them.

Over New Guinea, Fifth Air Force P-400s and A-20s continue pounding away at Japanese forces in the Owen Stanley Mountains, especially at Myola Lake and Efogi. Meanwhile, P-40s escort Australian Hudsons, Beauforts, and Beaufighters against enemy warships 17 miles off the coast. By this time all organized resistance at Cape Milne has ceased, an impressive, if improvised, Allied victory in which air power played a significant role.

View of the pyramids of Egypt from an Air Transport Command C-47 in 1943. Loaded with urgent war supplies and materials, this plane was one of a fleet flying shipments from the United States across the Atlantic and the continent of Africa to strategic battle zones during World War II. (National Archives)

SEPTEMBER 8 In England, Major General Carl A. Spaatz suspends all tactical operations in Europe and redirects units involved to support upcoming Operation TORCH in North Africa. For this reason the new Twelfth Air Force has priority over units slated to arrive in the United Kingdom.

Over New Guinea, Fifth Air Force P–400s continue bombing and strafing runs against Japanese forces still forcing the Australians back towards Port Moresby. Meanwhile, B–17s and RAAF Hudsons attack enemy warships off the coastline.

SEPTEMBER 9 In Washington, D.C., General Henry H. Arnold reveals AWPD-42, the blueprint for aerial warfare against the Axis, to General George C. Marshall. It is subsequently approved by President Franklin D. Roosevelt within two months and is scheduled to be launched in 1943. This document is basically a continuation of the Combined Bomber Offensive previously agreed upon.

Over New Guinea, Fifth Air Force P–40s attack parts of Goodenough Island as final mop up operations continue near Milne Bay. A–20s also bomb enemy forces surrounding Australian troops in the Efogi Spur region.

SEPTEMBER 10 In Washington, D.C., the secretary of war orders the Women's Auxiliary Ferrying Squadron formed to transport aircraft from factories directly to U.S. Army airfields across the nation.

SEPTEMBER 11   Over New Guinea, Fifth Air Force A-20s and B-26s continue hammering Japanese forces at Efogi and Menari in the Owen Stanley Range and airfields near Buna. Meanwhile, B-17s assist RAAF Hudsons in attacking enemy destroyers 20 miles off the coast; a B-17 scores a direct hit on the *Yayori*, sinking it.

SEPTEMBER 12   At Bushey Hall, England, the 4th Fighter Group, VIII Fighter Command, becomes operational to provide long-range escorts for bombers of the Eighth Air Force. They are composed mainly of fighter pilots who previously saw service in the Royal Air Force's Eagle Squadrons.

Over New Guinea, the Fifth Air Force dispatches P-400s, B-26s, A-20s, and B-17s against Japanese airfields and transport barges at Buna while mop up operations and air attacks continue on Goodenough Island. Over Buna, New Guinea, aircraft from the 89th Attack Squadron, 3rd Bomb Group, also drop the first parachute-retarded bombs of the war on parked Japanese aircraft.

SEPTEMBER 13   In the Aleutians, an Eleventh Air Force LB-30, escorted by 2 P-38s, conducts an reconnaissance run over Kiska harbor; enemy fighter damage the bomber, losing 1 floatplane aircraft to the escorts.

SEPTEMBER 14   Over the Aleutian Islands, a force of Eleventh Air Force B-24 Liberators, escorted by 14 P-38s and 14 P-39s, launches from Adak to bomb Japanese positions on Kiska, 250 miles distant. The attackers claim five floatplane fighters downed and one flying boat destroyed in the water, while two P-38s are lost in a collision.

SEPTEMBER 15   In Cairo, Egypt, the 57th Fighter Group becomes the first USAMEAF unit to transfer there from Palestine.

SEPTEMBER 15–29   At Brisbane, Australia, the 126th Infantry Regiment, 32nd Infantry Division, is airlifted to Port Moresby, New Guinea. Both military and civilian transport are utilized to assist hard-pressed Australian land forces being pushed back towards Port Moresby by a Japanese offensive. It is a stunning display of modern air power's tactical flexibility by Lieutenant General George C. Kenney.

SEPTEMBER 17   In Birmingham, Alabama, the headquarters, Twelfth Air Force is activated and proceeds directly to North Africa as part of upcoming Operation TORCH.

Throughout the Mediterranean, USAMEAF B-24s are actively bombing targets at Bengasi, Libya, and Khalones and Pylos, Greece.

Over New Guinea, Fifth Air Force B-17s attack Japanese positions on Rabaul, New Britain, while P-400s, P-40s, and P-39s continue strafing runs against enemy troops at Buna. The Japanese offensive to Port Moresby also halts, having run into impenetrable Australian defenses along the Imita Range.

SEPTEMBER 19   Over Lungling, Burma, a raid by China Air Task Force B-25s proves ineffective owing to bad weather, but post-strike reconnaissance missions reveal a high degree of Japanese troop activity along the Burma Road toward Salween.

SEPTEMBER 20   Over New Guinea, Fifth Air Force A-20s bomb and strafe Japanese troops and installations at Sangara, Arehe, and Popondetta-Andemba in the Owen Stanley Range.

SEPTEMBER 21 Over Renton, Washington, Boeing's giant XB-29 prototype flies for the first time, and immediately goes into production as the famous B-29 Superfortress. This is the most technologically advanced bomber in the world and displays such novel features as powered gun turrets and a pressurized fuselage for operations at high altitude. By war's end 2,132 B-29s will be delivered and equip 21 bomb groups.

SEPTEMBER 22 Over New Guinea, Fifth Air Force A-20s and P-40s continue working over withdrawing Japanese columns at Kokoda and Buna, bombing and strafing all targets of opportunity including huts and barges. Meanwhile, B-17s are dispatched to hit enemy airfields on Rabaul, New Britain.

SEPTEMBER 23 In England, Brigadier General James H. Doolittle arrives to take command of the Twelfth Air Force, which is also known as the "Eighth Air Force, Junior."

Over the Aleutians, a Navy PBY patrol plane makes a reconnaissance run over

View through the nose of B-29 bomber showing target of bombing run during World War II. (Library of Congress)

Kiska, escorted by two Eleventh Air Force P-38s; the fighters surprise and sink a Japanese submarine at Amchitka.

SEPTEMBER 25 In the Aleutians, the Eleventh Air Force commits nine B-24s, one B-17, eleven P-39s, and seventeen P-40s on a large air raid against Kiska. They are accompanied by a detachment of P-40s flown by the Royal Canadian Air Force (RCAF). Heavy damage, fires, and explosions are noted and at least five floatplane fighters are claimed destroyed.

Over Indochina (Vietnam), four B-25s and ten P-40s of the China Air Task Force attack the Gia Lam airfield, shooting down nine enemy fighters attempting to intercept them.

SEPTEMBER 26 Over New Guinea, Fifth Air Force A-20s support an Australian counteroffensive along the Kokoda trail by bombing and strafing Japanese forces. B-17s are also dispatched to Rabaul, New Britain, to hit enemy airfields.

SEPTEMBER 27 In the Aleutians, Eleventh Air Force B-24s, P-39s, and P-40s attack the shore and harbor areas of Kiska, although bad weather forces 13 fighters to turn back.

Over southwestern China, B-25s of the China Air Task Force (CATF) bomb Mengshih, and claim to have destroyed 30 trucks and 400 troops. Concurrently, three flights of P-40s bomb and strafe troop columns along the Burma Road, claiming 15 trucks destroyed.

In New Guinea, Japanese forces are in full retreat as Fifth Air Force A-20s attack them at Ioribaiwa, Myola, and Menari.

SEPTEMBER 28 In the Aleutians, seven B-24s, one B-17, and seventeen P-39s are dispatched by the Eleventh Air Force to hit Japanese positions on Attu and Kiska. Five enemy floatplane fighters are shot down in exchange for one P-39.

Over New Guinea, Fifth Air Force P-40s and P-400s continue to bomb and strafe Japanese forces retreating along the Kokoda Trail.

SEPTEMBER 29   In England, volunteers from the three American Eagle Squadrons transfer to the new 4th Fighter Group, VIII Fighter Command, and stiffen its cadre with experienced leadership.

Over North Africa, P-40s of USAMEAF fly interception missions against Ju-87 Stukas near the El Alamein battlefront.

SEPTEMBER 30   In the Aleutians, nine B-24s of the Eleventh Air Force drop bombs on Kiska and Attu, scoring a direct hit on at least one vessel in the harbor.

OCTOBER 1–2   At Muroc Army Base, California, the Bell XP-59, America's first jet fighter, performs its maiden flight. The craft is powered by two General Electric I-16 engines, which are patterned after the British Whittle design. The following day Colonel Lawrence C. Craigie takes it aloft, becoming the first military officer to pilot a jet aircraft.

OCTOBER 2   At the Aeromedical Laboratory, Wright Field, Ohio, Major J. G. Kearby enters an altitude chamber simulating 60,200 feet to test a full-body pressure suit.

In the Aleutians, Kiska Harbor is again raided by Eleventh Air Force B-24s, which bomb several vessels in the harbor and claim four floatplane fighters shot down.

Off the coast of French Guiana, an aircraft of the 99th Bomb Squadron attacks and sinks the German submarine *U-512*.

Over New Guinea, Fifth Air Force A-20s and P-400s continue bombing and strafing runs against retreating Japanese forces at Myola and Siorata.

Over France, 30 B-17s are dispatched by the Eighth Air Force to hit the Avions-Potez aircraft factory at Meaulte and some nearby airfields. They are escorted by 400 fighter escorts, and no bombers are lost.

OCTOBER 3   At Peenemunde, Germany, an ominous development occurs as the German A-4 (or V-2 Vengeance weapon) becomes the world's first military ballistic missile. This five-and-a-half ton rocket has a range of 120 miles while carrying a large conventional warhead; the Allied powers can develop no effective counter other than bombing its launching sites.

Over the Aleutians, the Eleventh Air Force launches six B-24s, four P-38s, and eight P-39s against Kiska Harbor, striking a beached freighter and downing six float fighters.

In India, the India Air Task Force (IATF) is organized under Colonel Caleb V. Haynes to support Chinese forces along the Salween River by hitting Japanese supply lines in south and central Burma. At present Haynes can call upon the 51st Fighter and 7th and 341st Bomb Groups.

OCTOBER 6   Over Bengasi, Libya, B-24s of USAMEAF drop bombs in and around the harbor; two aircraft are lost to fighters and heavy flak.

In the Aleutians, the Eleventh Air Force unleashes eight B-24s, ten P-39s, and eight P-38s against Japanese shipping in Kiska Harbor; several vessels are struck and at least six float fighters are strafed on the water.

OCTOBER 8   In England, Major General Ira C. Eaker reveals plans to develop highly skilled pathfinder units capable of navigating in bad weather. Eaker intends to use bad weather to cloak small blind-bombing missions against selected targets.

Such attacks will keep German defenses on their toes during bouts of weather when regular air strikes cannot be mounted.

OCTOBER 9 In England, the Eighth Air Force launches its first 100-bomber raid, in which B-17s are accompanied by B-24s for the first time. They attack various steel, engineering, and locomotive works in Lille, France.

OCTOBER 10 Over New Guinea, Fifth Air Force B-17s raid Japanese installations at Rabaul, New Guinea, while A-20s and P-400s bomb and strafe Japanese forces retreating along the Kokoda Trail.

OCTOBER 11 Over the Solomon Islands, a SOPAC B-17 observes a Japanese task force of cruisers and destroyers sailing toward Guadalcanal, which are driven away on the morrow during the Battle of Cape Esperance.

OCTOBER 13 Over North Africa, USA-MEAF P-40s sweep the region around El Alamein, claiming two Me-109s shot down.

Off the coast of Guadalcanal, Japanese battleships *Haruna* and *Kongo* shell Henderson Field at night, inflicting heavy damage. This attack prompts all SOPAC B-17s operating there to withdraw the following day.

OCTOBER 14 On New Guinea, as Australian forces encounter stiff Japanese resistance near Templeton's Crossing, Fifth Air Force B-25s are called in to strike bridges in the vicinity of Lae.

OCTOBER 16 Over the Aleutians, the Eleventh Air Force launches six B-26s and four P-38s against Japanese shipping in Kiska Harbor, sinking two destroyers; one fighter is shot down.

OCTOBER 19 In North Africa, just as the British Eighth Army is preparing to attack German positions along El Alamein, B-25s of the USAMEAF are called in to bomb ground targets, while B-24s continue to attack shipping and supplies at Tobruk.

OCTOBER 20 Over North Africa, air activity over the El Alamein battlefield intensifies as USAMEAF B-25s assist the RAF in reducing German positions and equipment.

OCTOBER 21 Over France, the VIII Bomber Command dispatches 15 B-17s to strike U-boat pens at Lorient-Keroman for the first time. The Germans sortie several Fw-190 fighters in their defense and shoot down three bombers.

B-24 Liberators of the Indian Air Task Force (IATF) strike north of the Yangtze and Yellow Rivers for the first time by dropping ordnance on the Lin-hsi coal mine facilities near Kuyeh, China.

OCTOBER 22 The Westinghouse Electric Company begins construction of the first American-designed jet engine, the X-19A, which incorporates axial-flow technology. A working example emerges in five months.

The Twelfth Air Force relocates its headquarters from London, England, to North Africa to participate in Operation TORCH. Meanwhile, USAMEAF P-40s escort B-25s attacking dispersed aircraft, then bomb and strafe several German positions along the coastal road near El Hammam; two German fighters are claimed shot down.

OCTOBER 24–25 Over North Africa, B-25s of the USAMEAF provide close support to Field Marshal Bernard Montgomery's Eighth Army during his famous El Alamein offensive, which drives Germans under Field Marshal Erwin Rommel from Egypt. The bombers strike a variety of troop concentrations, tent areas, gun emplacements, and vehicles in concert with the RAF.

OCTOBER 25   In China, 12 B–25s and 7 P–40s of the China Air Task Force (CATF) bomb Hong Kong and the Kowloon Docks for the first time since the Japanese occupation. Several intercepting fighters are shot down for a loss of one B–25 and one P–40. That same evening, another six B–25s make CATF's first night raid by hitting other targets in Hong Kong. Meanwhile, Japanese aircraft bomb airfields at Dinjan and Chabua, India, to hobble the India–China air transport route; 10 aircraft are destroyed and 17 are damaged.

Over the Solomon Islands, a SOPAC B–17 observes another strong Japanese naval convoy off Santa Cruz Island and headed for Guadalcanal.

OCTOBER 26   In North Africa, the British Eighth Army halts its offensive to regroup while USAMEAF B–25s and P–40s continue attacking German positions, trucks, and tanks; four enemy planes are claimed shot down. Concurrently, 30 B–17s and B–24s are dispatched against enemy supply convoys off the Libyan coast.

In India, Japanese aircraft again raid airfields connected to the India–China transportation route, inflicting damage on ground facilities but striking no aircraft. Meanwhile, P–40s attack the Hong Kong–Canton area again, using dive-bomber tactics for the first time.

In the Solomon Islands, the Battle of Santa Cruz unfolds as B–17s attack the main Japanese convoy but score no hits. The U.S. Navy loses the carrier *Hornet*, but Japanese forces withdraw toward Truk.

OCTOBER 27   Over China, B–25s of the China Air Task Force attack Japanese airfields near Lashio, Burma, which have been hitting American facilities in India.

OCTOBER 28   Over North Africa, B–25s of USAMEAF continue pounding German supply and communications routes at El Alamein while P–40s provide escort, claiming three enemy fighters downed.

OCTOBER 29   In Washington, D.C., President Franklin D. Roosevelt assigns the production of 107,000 warplanes in 1943 the highest possible priority.

OCTOBER 30   In North Africa, the 9th Australian Division manages to trap a large portion of the Afrika Korps along the coast, supported by P–40s of USAMEAF, but German tanks manage to break through their lines and escape.

OCTOBER 31   In England, Major General Carl A. Spaatz informs General Ira C. Eaker that losses over heavily defended German submarine pens are too costly for the results they are achieving. He therefore intends to send the bomber in lower and accept the higher loss rate for better bombing results.

NOVEMBER 2   In North Africa, Field Marshal Bernard Montgomery launches Operation SUPERCHARGE against the Afrika Korps and USAMEAF B–25s continue bombing in support of the 9th Armoured Division as P–40s also strafe throughout the battle area.

Over New Guinea, Fifth Air Force B–26s strike Dili, B–17s attack Japanese shipping off the coast, and B–25s hit another convoy south of New Britain. All these efforts assist Australian forces as they capture Kokoda and surge across the Owen Stanley Mountains towards Buna.

NOVEMBER 3   Over North Africa, USA-MEAF B-25s and P-40s continue bombing and strafing retreating German columns as the Eighth Army continues its advance. They fly 400 sorties this day alone.

NOVEMBER 4   In North Africa, nine USAMEAF B-24s attack enemy shipping in Bengasi harbor while B-25s and P-40s continue attacking motor transports and retreating columns along the coastal zones. General Frank M. Andrews also replaces General Russell L. Maxwell as head of United States Army Air Forces in the Middle East (USAFIME).

In New Guinea, Fifth Air Force B-17s and B-25s strike Japanese positions and shipping at Salamaua while A-20s support Australian troops in their drive against Oivi. The remainders of the 126th Infantry Regiment, 32nd Division, are also flown by C-47s to Wangigela.

NOVEMBER 5   In North Africa, Field Marshal Bernard Montgomery declares victory at El Alamein as the Afrika Korps under Field Marshal Erwin Rommel retreats westward from Egypt. USA-MEAF B-25s and P-40s join their RAF counterparts in mercilessly harrying the defeated Axis forces.

NOVEMBER 7   In England the mass transfer to North Africa of units belonging to the Twelfth Air Force begins; several elements are on board convoys rapidly approaching the Algerian and Moroccan coasts.

NOVEMBER 8   Over Oran, Algeria, Supermarine Spitfires operated by the Army Air Forces' 31st Fighter Group are launched from Navy carriers in support

of landing operations there; they engage and down three Vichy French fighters which had attacked transport planes.

Colonel Demas T. Craw, XII Tactical Command, Army Air Forces, volunteers to land behind enemy lines at Port Lyautey, French Morocco, as an intelligence officer to secretly secure an armistice with the local French commander. However, he is killed shortly after landing, winning a posthumous Congressional Medal of Honor. His companion, Major Pierpont M. Hamilton, AAF, survives and reaches Casablanca about the truce in time to prevent an American attack by General George C. Patton; he also receives a Medal of Honor.

As Operation TORCH, the Allied invasion of North Africa, commences, C-47s from the 60th Troop-Carrier Group, Twelfth Air Force carry reinforcements to Senia. However, they are fired upon by Vichy French forces and several transports are shot down.

NOVEMBER 9   Over France, the Eighth Air Force dispatches 12 B-24s to bomb the U-boat pens at Saint-Nazaire from 18,000 feet, with average results. However, a flight of 31 B-17s that went in at 7,500 feet loses 3 aircraft to flak, along with 22 damaged. These losses spell the end of experimenting with low-altitude attacks.

Off the North African coast, several Army Air Forces Piper L-4 "Grasshoppers" (observation planes) are launched from LST decks to assist ground operations during Operation TORCH.

NOVEMBER 10   Off the North African coast, 100 Curtiss P-40 fighters belonging to the 33rd Fighter Group are launched from the escort carriers *Chenango* and *Archer*, and proceed to land at Port Lyautey, Morocco.

NOVEMBER 11   Over North Africa, USAMEAF B-24s again bomb shipping and dock facilities at Bengasi, Libya, as the Eighth Army drives German forces out of Egypt. P-40s sweeping through the Gambut area also shoot down three Ju-87 Stukas.

NOVEMBER 12   In Egypt, the Ninth Air Force under Major General Lewis H. Brereton arises to replace the U.S. Army Middle East Air Force (USAMEAF). Their initial task is providing close air support to British troops advancing west out of Egypt.

NOVEMBER 12–15   On Guadalcanal, Lockheed P-38s of the 339th Fighter Squadron arrive at Henderson Field to support local defenses; one Lightning is destroyed during a Japanese naval bombardment. Men and aircraft of the 11th Bomb Group, 69th, 70th, and 72nd Bomb Squadrons, and the 39th Fighter Squadron are on hand to assist the 339th over this three-day period.

NOVEMBER 13   In the Pacific, a raft containing World War I ace Edward V. Rickenbacker, Colonel Hans C. Adamson, and Private John F. Bartek is rescued by a Navy OS2U Kingfisher 600 miles north of Samoa. The trio survives a plane-ditching 21 days earlier.

NOVEMBER 14   In North Africa, the 79th Fighter Group and the headquarters, 19th Bomb Wing arrive from the United States as part of the Ninth Air Force.

NOVEMBER 15   Republic P-47s flown by Lieutenants Harold Comstock and Roger Dyer reach 725 miles per hour—exceeding the sound barrier—during experimental dives from 35,000 feet.

At Houston Municipal Airport, the first women's Flying Training detachment is redesignated as the 319th Army Air Forces Flying Training detachment.

NOVEMBER 16   Over North Africa, B-17 bombers of the 97th Bomb Group, having launched the first combat strike of the Army Air Forces in Europe, repeat that distinction by launching the first AAF bombing raid against German airfields at Bizerte, Tunisia. Meanwhile, Twelfth Air Force C-47 transports drop British paratroopers near Souk el Arba, Tunisia.

NOVEMBER 17   Over France, the Eighth Air Force unleashes 35 heavy bombers against the submarine pens at Saint-Nazaire, unloading 102 tons of bombs.

Over New Guinea, as Australian and U.S. troops gradually advance upon Japanese defenders at Buna-Gona, they are supported by Fifth Air Force B-26s. B-25s also hit airfields at Lae and Gasmata.

NOVEMBER 18   At Maison Blanche airfield, Algiers, several newly arrived P-38s of the 14th Fighter Squadron, Twelfth Air Force, are damaged in a German air raid.

NOVEMBER 20   In North Africa, German aircraft again bomb Maison Blanche airfield, Algiers, destroying several P-38 fighters on the ground.

Over Mandalay, Burma, eight B-24s from the India Air Task Force (IATF) strike marshalling yards as the Allied air effort intensifies.

NOVEMBER 21   Over New Guinea, Fifth Air Force A-20s and B-25s attack dug-in Japanese defenders at Buna and Sanananda in support of a joint Australian-American drive there. The Allies are stymied by a strong series of bunker positions.

NOVEMBER 22 Over New Guinea, Fifth Air Force A-20s provide close support to Allied troops advancing up trails near Sanananda as B-26s bomb Japanese positions at Buna.

NOVEMBER 23 Over Saint-Nazaire, France, Eighth Air Force heavy bombers continue attacking U-boat pens, although these heavily reinforced structures evince little damage for the effort. Air crews also report a change in enemy tactics as German fighters, aware of the relatively weak firepower at the front of their aircraft, are now resorting to frontal attacks.

Over Indochina (Vietnam), nine B-25s and seven P-40s of the China Air Task Force (CATF) sink a freighter and damage other vessels in the Gulf of Tonkin. Another force of six B-25s and seventeen P-40s strike Japanese air installations at Tien Ho, China, and claim to have destroyed 40 aircraft on the ground.

NOVEMBER 24 Over New Guinea, the Fifth Air Force launches A-20s, B-25s, B-26s, B-17s, P-40s, P-39s, and P-400s in a large series of raids against Japanese positions at Buna and Sanananda Point as Allied ground troops attack the region known as the Triangle.

NOVEMBER 26 Over the Aleutians, Eleventh Air Force B-26s and P-38s attack Japanese shipping in Holtz Harbor, and one large vessel is set afire.

NOVEMBER 27 Over Hong Kong, China, the China Air Task Force (CATF) mounts one of its largest bombing raids yet, with 10 B-25s and 20 P-40s. Several large warehouses are left in flames and some barges are claimed as sunk.

NOVEMBER 28 A force of nine B-24 Liberators of the 7th Bomb Group, Tenth Air Force, lift off from Gaya, India, fly 2,760 miles, and drop bombs on Japanese-occupied Bangkok, Thailand for the first time.

NOVEMBER 29 Over Tunis, North Africa, 55 C-47s from the 62nd and 64th Troop Carrier Groups, Twelfth Air Force, drop 530 British paratroopers in a failed attempt to seize Oudna Air Base; 300 casualties are incurred.

NOVEMBER 30 In London, the British Air Ministry reaches a joint decision to have British fighters provide aerial defense for American bases while Army Air Forces fighters will operate mainly as bomber escorts over the Continent.

DECEMBER 1 In London, England, Major General Ira C. Eaker gains appointment as head of the Eighth Air Force to replace outgoing Major General Carl A. Spaatz, recently transferred to North Africa as air aide to General Dwight D. Eisenhower.

In India, the India-China Division of the Air Transport Command is initiated to provide a constant airlift of supplies over the Himalayan Mountains to American air forces serving in China. This gradually becomes the greatest sustained aerial supply effort in wartime to this date.

The first issue of *Air Force Magazine* is issued to replace the Army Air Forces Newsletter.

DECEMBER 2 Over North Africa, Twelfth Air Force B-26s attack the airfield at Al Aouina while B-17s bomb Sidi Ahmed and Bizerte harbor. B-25s and P-38s also sweep in low over Gabes, destroying several vehicles.

DECEMBER 3 Over North Africa, Twelfth Air Force B-17s attack dockyards and enemy shipping in Bizerte harbor while German fighters mange to down two P-38 escorts. Other fighters, accompanying RAF Spitfires, make low-level sweeps and photo missions across Northwest Africa.

DECEMBER 4 From Egypt, a force of 24 Ninth Air Force B-24 Liberators strike at military and transportation targets at Naples, Italy, for the first time. Several hits on enemy vessels, including an Italian battleship, are claimed.

DECEMBER 5 In the Mediterranean, Major General Carl A. Spaatz becomes acting deputy commander in chief for Air, Allied Forces in Northwest Africa. Meanwhile, Twelfth Air Force B-17s hit docks and enemy shipping throughout Tunis; all raids are accompanied by P-38 escorts.

DECEMBER 6 Over Lille, France, the Eighth Air Force commits 36 heavy bombers against the Atelier d'Hellemmes locomotive works with diversionary raids on airfields at Abbeville-Drucat.

DECEMBER 7 Over North Africa, the Twelfth Air Force commits B-17s and P-38s to attack dockyards and enemy shipping at Bizerte while DB-7s (A-20s) strike enemy tanks at Tebourba. P-38s and P-40s also fly patrols and photo missions over the Gabes area.

DECEMBER 8 In England, a study released by VIII Bomber Command concludes that no current weapon in the American arsenal is capable of destroying heavily reinforced German U-boat pens along the French coast. However, several projects, such as APHRODITE, are underway to produce glide bombs capable of destroying such targets.

DECEMBER 9 In England, the Eighth Air Force releases a report on the first 1,100

bombers sent over France between August 17 to November 23, and it justifies the results of high-level, daylight precision bombing.

Over New Guinea, Fifth Air Force B-26s continue pounding the Buna region as Allied forces prepare for a final assault there. The village of Gona also falls to the Australians after hand-to-hand combat and intense aerial bombardment.

DECEMBER 11 Over Naples, Italy, Ninth Air Force B-24s raid the harbor area again with adequate results. In Tunis, P-40s also fly close support for the Eighth Army as it prepares to attack El Agheila.

DECEMBER 12 Over France, 17 heavy bombers from the Eighth Air Force strike marshalling yards at Rouen-Sotteville, although poor weather cancels an impending raid on air installations at Romilly-sur-Seine.

DECEMBER 13 Over North Africa, 15 B-17s of the 97th Bomb Group, Twelfth Air Force, attack the docks and enemy shipping at Tunis while 10 B-17s of the 301st Bomb Group also attack Bizerte. The latter is followed up by 19 B-24s of the 93rd Bomb Group, Eighth Air Force.

DECEMBER 14 Along the Mambare River, New Guinea, Fifth Air Force aircraft attack Japanese troops and troop-carrying destroyers as they attempt to land reinforcements.

DECEMBER 15 Over North Africa, nine B-24s from the 376th Bomb Group, Ninth Air Force, attack German and Italian positions at Sfax in a preliminary air campaign against enemy-held ports.

DECEMBER 16 Over New Guinea, Fifth Air Force A-20s and B-26s continue to savage enemy positions at Buna, and also strafe enemy troop barges coming up the Kumusi River.

DECEMBER 17 The Western Defense Command orders troops in Alaska to construct airfields on Amchitka Island, the Aleutians, once it has been secured by ground forces.

On Guadalcanal, the army's 132nd Infantry Regiment begins its final offensive in the Mount Austen region, receiving close aerial support from Marine Corp aircraft and SOPAC P-39s.

DECEMBER 18 Over North Africa, Twelfth Air Force B-17s and P-38s attack enemy shipping in Bizerte harbor, hitting at least one large vessel. German fighters manage to down one bomber and three escorts at a loss of three of their own.

DECEMBER 19 On New Guinea, Australian troops launch another determined attack against Japanese-held Buna, receiving close support from Fifth Air Force A-20s and B-25s. Meanwhile, B-17s and B-24s attack enemy transports off the coast of Mandang in Astrolabe Bay.

DECEMBER 20 Over the Aleutians, the Eleventh Air Force sorties four B-26s, five B-24s, four B-25s, and nine P-38s against Kiska Harbor, hitting an ammo dump and strafing several vessels offshore.

DECEMBER 22 Over New Guinea, Fifth Air Force B-25s continue bombing fanatical Japanese defenders at Buna, who have repelled yet another Australian attack.

DECEMBER 22–23 Launching from Midway, 26 B-24 Liberators of the 307th Bomb Group, Seventh Air Force, stage their first air raid by attacking Japanese installations on Wake Island.

DECEMBER 23 Over New Guinea, Fifth Air Force A-20s bomb and strafe Japanese positions near Gona while B-25s attack Cape Gloucester Airfield, New Georgia.

DECEMBER 24 SOPAC P-39s assist Navy and Marine Corps dive bombers to attack Japanese installations on Munda, New Georgia, destroying 24 aircraft without loss.

DECEMBER 26 Over Tunis, Twelfth Air Force bombers and escorts attack enemy installations at Bizerte again, losing two bombers and two P-38s to flak and enemy fighters; the P-38s claim to have shot down two Fw-190s.

DECEMBER 27 Over New Guinea, Lieutenant Richard I. Bong flames two Japanese aircraft in his twin-engine P-38 Lightning; 38 more follow for a total of 40, making him America's top-scoring ace of World War II.

DECEMBER 29 The Collier Trophy is jointly awarded to the Army Air Forces and private airlines companies of the United States for their sterling war efforts.

Over North Africa, Twelfth Air Force B-17s and P-38s strike against Sousse harbor while DB-7s and A-20s strike at La Hencha.

DECEMBER 30 Over the Aleutians, Eleventh Air Force B-25s, covered by 14 P-38s, make a low-level attack upon Kiska Harbor, and are intercepted by four Zero floatplane fighters. The Japanese down one B-25 and two P-38s for a probable loss of four of their own.

DECEMBER 31 Over North Africa, Twelfth Air Force B-17s bomb enemy positions at Sfax while B-26s attack an airfield near Gabes. P-38s and P-40s, flying escort, also bomb and strafe several enemy vehicles in the Bizerte-Tunis area.

1943

JANUARY 1   In North Africa, Brigadier General John K. Cannon is appointed commanding general of the XII Bomber Command, Twelfth Air Force.

JANUARY 2   Over Burma, P-40s of the China Air Task Force (CATF) bomb and strafe Japanese columns along the Burma Road near Loiwing while B-25s attack airfields at Monywa.

JANUARY 3   Over Saint-Nazaire, France, 68 VIII Bomber Command aircraft strike U-boat pens, losing 7 B-17s, with a further 47 damaged and 70 aircrew missing. This time, the Germans throw up a wall of predetermined flak instead of trying to track individual bombers. This is also the heaviest air raid to date against submarine facilities.

JANUARY 4   Over Burma, Tenth Air Force heavy bombers strike marshalling yards at Mandalay, while one B-25 and nine P-40s are assigned to strike rail targets at Naba.

JANUARY 5   In Northwestern Africa, the Allied Air Forces under Major General Carl A. Spaatz is officially activated by General Dwight D. Eisenhower. This consists of the Twelfth Air Force and some attached Royal Air Force units.

Brigadier General Kenneth N. Walker, head of V Bomber Command, Fifth Air Force, and an architect of AWPD-1, dies while leading an air raid over Rabaul, New Britain; he is awarded the Congressional Medal of Honor posthumously.

JANUARY 6   Over New Guinea, Fifth Air Force B-26s attack Japanese positions at Sanananda Point while B-17s, B-24s, and B-26s attack a Japanese convoy headed for Lae.

JANUARY 7   Over Italy, nine Ninth Air Force B-25s drop bombs on shipping in Palermo harbor; one B-24 with special bombs also attacks Maiouli Quay at Piraeus, Greece.

JANUARY 8   Over Lae, New Guinea, Fifth Air Force heavy bombers, medium bombers, and fighters assist RAAF aircraft in attacking a body of 4,000 Japanese reinforcements as they come ashore. Enemy aerial resistance is reported as fierce.

JANUARY 9   Over Burbank, California, the prototype Lockheed C-69, a militarized Constellation transport craft, makes its maiden flight; this is presently the largest transport aircraft in the world.

JANUARY 10   Over Burma, medium and heavy bombers dispatched by the Tenth Air Force attack the Myitnge Bridge, knocking out one span and temporarily severing Japanese supply lines.

JANUARY 11   Over North Africa, B-17s of the Twelfth Air Force attack enemy positions and bridges near the town of Gadames as escorting P-38s engage German interceptors in a swirling 25-minute dogfight; one German and two American fighters are downed.

JANUARY 12   Over Munda, New Georgia, SOPAC B-26s, P-38s, P-39s, and P-40s attack Japanese positions, while other P-39s strafe enemy troops on Guadalcanal.

JANUARY 13   On Espiritu Santo and New Caledonia, newly promoted Major General Nathan F. Twining takes command of the 13th Air Force ("The Jungle Air Force"). His instructions are to bomb all Japanese targets within the Southwest Pacific theater, commencing with Munda, New Georgia.

JANUARY 14 In England, one squadron of the 4th Fighter Group is the first Eighth Air Force formation to become fully equipped with P-47 Thunderbolt fighters.

JANUARY 14–23 At Casablanca, French Morocco, Major General Ira C. Eaker persuades Prime Minister Winston Churchill to accept the Army Air Forces' strategy of precision bombing during daylight hours. This will be performed to augment night-time saturation attacks by the Royal Air Force, and constitutes a major part of the Combined Bomber Offensive.

JANUARY 15 In the Central Solomon Islands, the Thirteenth Air Force dispatches B-17s, P-40s, P-39s, and P-38s to attack enemy shipping. On Guadalcanal, other P-39s assist mopping up efforts and also attack enemy vessels sighted off Kolombangara.

JANUARY 16 Over Yunnai, China, China Air Task Force (CATF) P-40s engage Japanese aircraft attempting to attack their airfield, claiming seven fighters shot down. Afterwards, Brigadier General Claire L. Chennault dispatches six B-25s and eleven P-40s to Lashio, Burma, in the expectation that the raiders will land there; none are found so they attack nearby enemy installations.

JANUARY 17 On Guadalcanal, Thirteenth Air Force P-39s continue assisting army units in their final mop up of Japanese holdouts near Mount Austen. At this time, B-17s based at Henderson Field are used to run in supplies and ammunition to the troops.

JANUARY 18 Over Lae, New Guinea, Fifth Air Force B-25s bomb Japanese

The B-24 Liberator bomber, designated C-87 when used as a heavy transport, could carry more than six tons of bombs and had a range of 3,000 miles, allowing it to penetrate deep into enemy territory. It was the most widely produced American warplane in history. (Library of Congress)

motor pool and supply dumps while two B-24s drop bombs on Malahang and Madang airfields.

JANUARY 19 Over North Africa, Ninth Air Force B-24s pound enemy ships and docks at Tripoli, Libya, while B-25s attack enemy motor transports and tanks as they withdraw up the coast.

JANUARY 20 Over North Africa, Twelfth Air Force B-17s strike Cape Mangin near Gabes, Tunis, while B-25s begin attacking enemy shipping in the Straits of Sicily.

JANUARY 21 In North Africa, American and British air leaders help formulate the "Casablanca directive," which declares that the purpose of bombing campaigns is to undermine the morale of the German people while also destroying military, economic, and industrial systems. For this reason, VIII Bomber Command is largely relieved of operations in North Africa and begins returning to England.

JANUARY 22 Over North Africa, Ninth Air Force B-25s attack the road junction near Tripoli, Libya, while the Eighth Army, closely supported by RAF and P-40s fighter-bombers, presses to within 17 miles of the city.

JANUARY 23 Over France, the Eighth Air Force unleashes 19 heavy bombers against U-boat pens at Brest while another 35 strike at Lorient-Keroman. Air crews report that the Germans are employing a new tactic of attacking in groups of six aircraft; five bombers are shot down.

JANUARY 24 Over Burma, the Tenth Air Force sends nine B-24s from the new 492nd Bomb Squadron on a raid against Rangoon, which sets several fires on the wharfs and sets a large freighter on fire. Meanwhile, P-40s are called in to strafe enemy positions at Shaduzup.

JANUARY 25 Over Wake Island, seven B-24s of the Seventh Air Force drop 60 bombs while also making a reconnaissance photo run; they previously staged through Midway.

JANUARY 26 In Hawaii, P-40s of the 73rd Fighter Squadron arrive after flying 1,400 miles from Midway Island. This is one of the longest overwater flights of the war by single-engine fighters.

JANUARY 27 Over Wilhelmshaven and Emden, Germany, the American daylight strategic bombing campaign against industrial targets accelerates when 55 B-17s and B-24s of the 1st and 2nd Bombardment Wings, Eighth Air Force, strike German port facilities. This attack constitutes the first American daylight raid against the enemy homeland; three bombers are lost and 22 fighters are claimed to have been shot down.

In the Pacific, Major General Nathan Twining, head of the Thirteenth Air Force, crashes in the ocean with 13 members of his staff and survives the next four days in a raft until being rescued on February 1. However, because their raft was not equipped with a radio for signaling purposes, dingy radio sets become standard equipment on all aircraft rescue rafts.

JANUARY 28 Over North Africa, the Twelfth Air Force unleashes 60 heavy and medium bombers to attack the harbor, airfields, and defenses around Sfax, Tunis. Meanwhile, P-40s support French and American land units as they seize control of the western exit of Kasserine Pass.

JANUARY 29   Over Germany, 86 heavy bombers from the Eighth Air Force bomb military targets in Frankfurt. However, a navigational error forces one formation to bomb Ludwigshaven by mistake; three bombers are shot down.

JANUARY 30   Over Rabaul, New Britain, Fifth Air Force B–17s attack enemy shipping and wharves. Meanwhile, at New Guinea, A–20s pound and strafe Japanese positions at Lae while a handful of B–24s attack vessels in Open Bay.

JANUARY 31   Over New Britain, Thirteenth Air Force P–39s assist Navy aircraft in attacks on enemy shipping in Vella Gulf. Other P–38s and P–40s attack Japanese positions at Munda.

FEBRUARY 1   Over North Africa, Twelfth Air Force B–17s bomb enemy facilities and shipping at Bizerte and La Goulette harbor while A–20s and P–40s strike tank and troop concentrations at Sidi Khalif.

FEBRUARY 2   In the Solomon Islands, Thirteenth Air Force B–17s, escorted by P–40s and P–38s, attack Japanese shipping off Shortland Island. Around 20 enemy interceptors rise to meet them, and the escorts claim shooting 9 down.

FEBRUARY 3   In Los Angeles, California, the first North America P–51A flies for the first time. An excellent, low–altitude design, it has yet to be fitted with a British Rolls Royce Merlin engine.

FEBRUARY 4   In England, Lieutenant General Frank M. Andrews is appointed commander, European Theater of Operations (ETO) while Lieutenant General Dwight D. Eisenhower becomes commander, North African Theater of Operations (NATOUSA).

Over the Aleutians, the Eleventh Air Force dispatches three B–17s, three B–24s, three B–25s, four P–38s, and eight P–40s on a raid against Kiska's North Head submarine base; three of five floatplanes rising to intercept are claimed shot down.

FEBRUARY 5   Over Burma, Tenth Air Force B–24s attack the railroad station at Rangoon while P–40s bomb the railway west of Meza and B–25s attempt to knock out the bridge at Myitnge, but fail.

FEBRUARY 6   Over New Guinea, Fifth Air Force A–20s attack Japanese positions from Mubo to Salamaua as P–39s, P–38s, P–400s, and P–40s tangle with a large intercepting force; they claim to shoot down 24 Japanese craft without loss.

FEBRUARY 8   Over Burma, 18 Tenth Air Force B–24s bomb the Rangoon marshalling yard, inflicting heavy damage, while 3 bombers are detached to hit the runway at Mingaladon.

FEBRUARY 10   Over the Mediterranean, Twelfth Air Force B–25s are dispatched to attack Axis shipping between Tunisia and Sicily, sinking one vessel and damaging others.

FEBRUARY 12   Over Burma, seven B–24s of the Tenth Air Force attack the bridge at Myitnge but fail to score any hits. This attack also marks the first time that 2,000–pound blockbusters have been used in the China–Burma–India (CBI) theater.

FEBRUARY 13   In the Solomon Islands, the Thirteenth Air Force sends six B–24s of the 424th Bomb Squadron on a raid against Buin and nearby Shortland Island. The Japanese mount fierce fighter resistance, and shoot down three bombers and three fighters.

FEBRUARY 14 Over North Africa, Twelfth Air Force A-20s bomb German tanks in the Faid Pass, Tunis, while P-40 fighters strafe vehicles and gun emplacements at El Guettar and Sened-Maknassy.

FEBRUARY 15 In England, Major General Ira C. Eaker is directed to head up the Eighth Air Force bombing campaign, while Major General Carl A. Spaatz relocates to the Mediterranean to direct Northwest African Air Forces during Operation TORCH.

Land-based aircraft operating in the southern Solomon Islands fall under a new command, Aircraft Solomons (Air-Sols). This force is both multiservice and multinational in nature.

FEBRUARY 16 Over France, Eighth Air Force B-17s and B-24s strike military targets at Saint-Nazaire; 8 bombers are lost and 30 receive damage.

FEBRUARY 17 In North Africa, Air Chief Marshal Sir Arthur Tedder assumes command of the new Mediterranean Air Command, which encompasses the Northwest African Air Forces of Major General Carl A. Spaatz, the Middle East Air Command, and the Royal Air Force Malta Command.

FEBRUARY 18 Boeing's giant XB-29 prototype bomber crashes during a flight-test, killing celebrated test pilot Edmund T. "Eddie" Allen.

At Bowman Field, Kentucky, the first class of 39 flight nurses graduates from the Army Air Forces School of Air Evacuation.

FEBRUARY 19 Over Burma, Tenth Air Force P-40s dive-bomb a Japanese headquarters at Hpunkizup and bomb a rail track passing through a defile, burying it under rubble.

FEBRUARY 20 In North Africa, bad weather prevents all but a handful of Twelfth Air Force P-39s from flying close support missions as Allied forces are staggered by a serious German counterattack through Kasserine Pass.

FEBRUARY 21 The 93rd Bombardment Group, having flown 43 missions from North Africa, including the famous Ploesti raid, is reassigned to the Eighth Air Force in England. All told, this unit completes 396 missions as a group, higher than any other unit.

FEBRUARY 26 In England, Major General James H. Doolittle assumes control of XII Bomber Command.

FEBRUARY 27 Over France, Eighth Air Force B-17s and B-24s bomb naval and dock facilities at Brest.

FEBRUARY 28 Over Tunis, fighters and fighter-bombers of the North African Air Force (NAAF) attack Axis troop, tank, and motor transport targets southwest of Mateur and adjoining areas.

MARCH 1 In Algeria, Major General Carl A. Spaatz is appointed head of the Twelfth Air Force. Meanwhile, B-17s of the North African Air Force (NAAF) bomb docks and shipping at Cagliari.

MARCH 2–4 In the Bismarck Sea, Fifth Air Force and Australian fighters and medium bombers attack and savage Rear Admiral Masatomi Kimura's 16-ship Japanese convoy, sinking 8 transports, 4 destroyers crammed with troops, and downing 25 aircraft. The loss of 3,500 men and 40,000 tons of shipping is a major blow to enemy plans for reinforcing Lae, New Guinea. This attack also employs low-level "skip bombing" techniques for the first time and constitutes one of Lieutenant General George C. Kenney's greatest achievements.

MARCH 10   At Kunming, China, the China Air Task Force (CATF) is reconstituted as the new Fourteenth Air Force under Major General Claire L. Chennault. His roster includes an entire wing of Chinese pilots who conduct reconnaissance missions from Kunming into Burma.

Over North Africa, the Twelfth Air Force dispatches B-17s to hit the harbor at Palermo, Sicily, while B-26s and B-25s strike at Axis positions in and around Faid Pass, Sidi bou Zid, and Kasserine, Tunis.

MARCH 15   Over the Aleutians, the Eleventh Air Force dispatches 6 B-25s, 11 B-24s, and 24 P-38s to strike Japanese positions at Kiska Harbor; 1 P-38 is lost while on a strafing run. Heavy damage and several fires are reported.

MARCH 18   Over Vegesack, Germany, Lieutenant Jack W. Mathis, lead bombardier of the 359th Bomb Squadron, is mortally wounded by flak during a bomb run, yet releases his bombs and dies at his post; he receives the Eighth Air Force's first Congressional Medal of Honor. He is replaced by his brother Mark, who sadly also dies on a mission in 1943.

MARCH 19   In Washington, D.C., Lieutenant General Henry H. Arnold, chief of the Army Air Forces, is the first airman promoted to the rank of full (four-star) general.

MARCH 26   Army Nurse Lieutenant Elsie S. Ott is the first woman to receive the Air Medal after faithfully escorting five patients across 10,000 miles from India to the Walter Reed Hospital in the United States.

MARCH 31   Over North Africa, B-25s of the Ninth Air Force attack enemy positions at Sfax, destroying six parked aircraft. Meanwhile, P-40s bomb and strafe enemy vehicles along the highway north of Gabes.

APRIL 1   Over China, 25 Tenth Air Force B-25s bomb rail yards at Maymyo and Ywataung. A dogfight also develops between twelve P-40s and Japanese fighters over Lingling, with seven of the latter being shot down in exchange for one P-40.

APRIL 2   The Army Air Forces School of Aviation Medicine opens a new research building that houses four altitude decompression chambers. The facility is staffed by 27 officers and 35 civilians.

APRIL 4   Over Paris, France, 85 Eighth Air Force bombers strike the Renault armaments factory, inflicting heavy damage. Aggressive German fighters manage to claw down four American aircraft.

APRIL 5–22   Allied air units in North Africa commence Operation FLAX, designed to interdict Axis supply and troop reinforcements in the Mediterranean; they also claim to shoot down 60 enemy airplanes.

APRIL 8   In England, the 4th Fighter Group, VIII Fighter Command, is bolstered by the arrival of the 56th and 78th Fighter Groups. P-47 Thunderbolts are now available in sufficient quantity to begin long-range escort missions to defend the heavy bombers. However, their limited range precludes them from accompanying the bombers into German airspace.

APRIL 12   In Washington, D.C., the War Department releases details about its highly secret Norden bombsight, which is highly accurate and designed to remain on target despite aircraft movements.

APRIL 14   Over France, a P-47 from the 4th Fighter Group shoots down a German aircraft for the first time.

In the Pacific, Fleet Radio Unit, Pacific Fleet, receives intelligence that Japanese Admiral Isoroku Yamamoto is planning an inspection tour of three bases near Bougainville. Admiral William F. Halsey then assigns a P-38 Lightning unit on Guadalcanal to intercept and kill him.

In the Zone of the Interior (United States) the new Weather Wing is activated to assume supervision of the Army Air Forces Weather Service from Headquarters AAF.

APRIL 15   Over the Aleutians, the Eleventh Air Force sends 20 B-25s, 23 B-24s, 25 P-38s, and 44 P-40s to raid Japanese positions at Kiska Harbor. These drop 85 tons of bombs on various targets; one B-24 is shot down.

Over New Guinea, the Fifth Air Force scrambles 40 P-38 and P-40 fighters to intercept a large Japanese air raid over Milne Bay; little damage is done to Allied facilities and the Americans claim 14 enemy aircraft downed.

APRIL 17   Over Bremen, Germany, the Eighth Air Force launches its first 100-plane air raid against the Focke-Wulf factory; German fighters and antiaircraft artillery shoot down 16 bombers for a total loss of 150 men. Consequently, a cry goes out for additional fighter groups as bomber escorts.

APRIL 18   Off the Tunisian coast, American P-40 fighters slaughter a force of German transport aircraft and they try desperately to airlift supplies to Panzer Armee Afrika; no less than 51 aircraft are bagged in the space of half an hour.

Over Kahili, Buin (Solomon Islands), a force of 16 P-38 Lightnings under Major John W. Mitchell expertly intercept and shoot down a Japanese bomber carrying Admiral Isoroku Yamamoto, commander in chief, Combined Fleet. The Americans were tipped off as to his impending arrival by cracking Japanese radio codes, and flew from Henderson Field, Guadalcanal, to kill him. Both Lieutenant Rex T. Barber and Captain Thomas G. Lanphier receive credit; one P-38 is shot down by the escorting Zero fighters.

APRIL 20   In the Pacific, Seventh Air Force B-24s stage out of Funafuti, Ellice Islands, and bomb Tarawa Atoll for the first time.

APRIL 22   Over Lashio, Burma, Lieutenant John S. Stewart, 76th Fighter Squadron, and Lieutenant Chin Hao, Chinese Air Force, commit the first joint reconnaissance mission in the China-Burma-India theater.

APRIL 24   The U.S. Army Air Forces graduates its first class of women pilots.

APRIL 29   The Civil Air Patrol (CAP) is transferred under the jurisdiction of the War Department. It is responsible for operating 4,700 light aircraft, 4,000 vehicles, and a 17,000-radio-station communications network.

APRIL 30   Over Sicily, B-24s of the Ninth Air Force strike dock facilities in the Straits of Messina while P-40s drop down to attack enemy shipping. They claim to sink four vessels, including one destroyer, along with five Me-109 fighters; three P-40s are lost.

MAY 1   Over Saint-Nazaire, France, the Eighth Air Force commits 56 heavy bombers in two waves against the U-boat pens, while also striking the shipyard. En route, Staff Sergeant Maynard H. Smith, 423rd Bomb Squadron, bravely administers to a wounded airman, mans waist guns, and fights flames as the rest of the crew bails out of his stricken craft. He becomes the first enlisted AAF man to win the Congressional Medal of Honor; only three others are so honored.

MAY 3 Over Iceland, Lieutenant General Frank M. Andrews, commanding the European Theater of Operations (ETO), is killed when his plane crashes into a mountainside. Previously, he had been instrumental in educating army senior staff officers in the proper application of air power.

MAY 4 Over Antwerp, Belgium, 65 Eighth Air Force bombers attack Ford and General Motors factories, while a smaller force launches a diversionary raid against the French coast. A force of 100 German fighters rises to oppose them but they fall for the feint, and the main strike force encounters little opposition.

MAY 6 Off Long Island Sound, New York, a Sikorsky XR-4 Hoverfly flown by Captain H. Franklin Gregory completes the first landing on a ship by a helicopter when he touches down on the deck of the merchant tanker *Bunker Hill*.

MAY 8 In the Mediterranean, the Italian island of Pantelleria is subject to heavy aerial attacks by Ninth Air Force B-26s, B-25s, and P-40s, assisted by Royal Air Force Wellington bombers. Concurrently, P-40 fighters strafe and bomb additional targets throughout the Gulf of Tunis.

MAY 14 In England, the VIII Bomber Command marks another aerial milestone when the first 200-bomber raid is launched against four targets on the European mainland. Submarine yards and naval facilities at Kiel, and factories

near Antwerp, Belgium, are the primary targets.

MAY 15 In England, the Eighth Air Force dispatches 135 heavy bombers to hit airfields and naval installations at Helgoland, Emden, and Wilhelmshaven.

Over China, a force of 35 Japanese bombers attacks Fourteenth Air Force airfields at Kunming, but their aim is poor and all bombs fall short of their target. They are attacked in turn by 28 P-40s, who claim to shoot down 13 fighters and 2 bombers.

MAY 17 In England, a B-17 Flying Fortress named *Memphis Belle* completes 25 combat missions over Europe under Captain Robert Morgan; they are allowed to return home to tour the United States and sell war bonds.

Over Holland, ten B-26 Marauders of the 322nd Bomb Group are shot down at low altitude by German defenses; only one aircraft returns to base. Such attacks are immediately suspended for all medium bombers.

MAY 18–25 In Washington, D.C., the Combined Chiefs of Staff approves plans for the Combined Bomber Offensive (CBO), which calls for alternating, around-the-clock attacks on German industrial centers by the Army Air Forces and the Royal Air Force. The destruction of German fighter factories is given the highest priority, followed by submarine bases, ball bearing plants, and oil production refineries. Secondary targets include synthetic rubber plants, tire factories, and military vehicle factories.

MAY 31 Over Italy, B-17s of the North African Strategic Air Force (NASAF) bomb airfields and marshalling yards at Foggia while medium bombers and fighters attack Axis positions on Pantelleria Island.

JUNE 1   In the Mediterranean, B-17s and P-38s of the North African Air Force (NAAF) attack the island of Pantelleria in the wake of an RAF raid. P-40s of the North African Tactical Air Force (NATAF) also strafe and bomb the seaplane base on Stagnone Island.

JUNE 2   Over Tunis, the first combat mission flown by the African American 99th Fighter Squadron is led by Lieutenants William B. Campbell and Charles B. Hall.

JUNE 10   The Combined Operational Planning Committee arises to coordinate daylight bombing of German targets by the Eighth Air Force and nighttime raids mounted by the Royal Air Force Bomber Command. Together their efforts constitute the Combined Bomber Offensive (CBO), whose around-the-clock attacks are intended to destroy German industry and morale.

JUNE 10–11   In the Gulf of Tunis, the Italian island of Pantelleria is continually attacked by British Wellington bombers of the North African Air Force and B-25s from the Ninth Air Force. A month later the island's garrison unconditionally surrenders in the first instance of a military objective being gained by air power alone.

JUNE 13   Over Kiel, Germany, an attack by 60 Eighth Air Force bombers underscores the need for fighter escorts when 26 aircraft are lost to enemy fighters.

JUNE 15   At Marietta, Georgia, the 58th Bombardment Wing is the first Army Air Forces unit outfitted with new Boeing B-29 Superfortresses.

Over the Solomon Islands, 120 Japanese aircraft approaching Guadalcanal are intercepted by 100 Army Air Forces, Navy, and New Zealand fighters. The

Allies claim to down 79 of the attackers at a cost of 6 of their own. However, the Japanese do manage to hit several ships and damage several land installations on the island.

JUNE 16   Over Buka, Solomon Islands, a B-17 flown by Captain Jay Zeamer, Jr., is attacked by an estimated 20 Japanese Zeroes. Zeamer, despite severe wounds, remains at his controls while his gunners shoot down at least five fighters. Lieutenant Joseph R. Sarnoski, who volunteered to serve as bombardier, also ignores severe wounds and mans his position, dying there. Both men receive Congressional Medals of Honor.

JUNE 17   Over Western Europe, Project WINDOW unfolds as American bombers drop chaff (tinfoil strips) to confuse German radar for the first time.

JUNE 22   Over Germany, 182 Eighth Air Force bombers strike industrial targets in the Ruhr Valley for the first time, including chemical works and synthetic rubber plants at Huls. Ford and General Motors plants at Antwerp are also struck by ancillary raids. Damage is extremely heavy and regular production cannot resume for six months.

JUNE 24   Over Ephrata, Washington, Lieutenant Colonel William R. Lovelace of the AAF Aeromedical Laboratory performs a record parachute jump from 42,000 feet.

JUNE 30   In England VIII Fighter Command is freed from RAF operational control, whereupon all fighter groups present revert to the 65th Fighter Wing.

General Douglas MacArthur initiates Operation CARTWHEEL, the aerial reduction of Rabaul, New Britain, into effect. American Army and Navy aircraft bomb and strafe the harbor and airfields over ensuing months to keep Japanese reinforcements from reaching Bougainville and New Georgia Island.

JULY 1 In Washington, D.C., General Henry H. Arnold receives a memo from Major General B. Giles stating that at least one fighter group is needed to escort every two bomber groups to avert present heavy loss rates.

JULY 2 Over the Aleutians, the Eleventh Air Force commits 17 B-24s and 16 B-25s on a major raid against Japanese positions at Kiska Harbor; two of the missions are radar-guided. Antiaircraft fire damages three bombers but several structures are left in flames as the aircraft depart.

JULY 4 In some noted events, a C-47 Skytrain completes the first transatlantic flight to Great Britain from North America; a Waco CG-4A glider is also safely towed 3,500 miles from England to Russia with medical supplies and other necessities.

JULY 7 In the Zone of the Interior (ZI), the Army Air Forces Training Command is established and assumes responsibilities formerly accorded the Technical Training and Flying Training Commands.

JULY 8 Colonel Malcolm G. Grow, a medical surgeon with the 8th Air Force, invents an armored vest and steel helmet for aircrews. For drastically reducing casualties, he receives the Legion of Merit for saving hundreds of American lives.

JULY 10 Over Sicily, hundreds of C-47 transports convey the 82nd Airborne Division in the first large American airborne assault of World War II. Several aircraft are shot down by U.S. Navy vessels which, not being informed of their mission, mistake them for German bombers.

JULY 15 Over Vella Lavella, the Thirteenth Air Force pits several fighters against an incoming Japanese force of 27 bombers and 40–50 escorts; in the ensuing scrape 3 American aircraft are lost against claims of 15 bombers and 30 Zeroes shot down.

JULY 19 Over Italy, 500 American heavy bombers of the North African Strategic Air Force, flying from Bengasi, Libya, strike German and Italian targets in and around the city of Rome. Special care is taken not to damage sites of cultural or religious significance, but 2,000 people are killed. The raid also underscores the preponderance of Allied air power in the theater.

JULY 21 Over Castelvetrano, Italy, Lieutenant Charles B. Hall, 99th Fighter Squadron, becomes the first African American pilot to score an aerial victory after he downs a German Fw-190 fighter.

JULY 22 In England, British intelligence reports that the Combined Bomber Offensive is slowly grinding down the vaunted German Luftwaffe, forcing it to deploy half its resources to defending the Fatherland and effectively weakening it along other fronts. It is also believed that German industry in the Ruhr Valley has been heavily damaged with respect to rubber, coal, iron, and fuel production.

JULY 24 Over Herøya, Norway, 167 Eighth Air Force bombers strike aluminum and magnesium plants; they employ "splasher beacons" for the first time to form up in poor weather conditions. At 1,900 miles round trip, this is also the longest mission to date.

JULY 24–AUGUST 3   Hamburg, Germany, is the first target of the Operation GOMORRAH, part of the Combined Bomber Offensive, as 750 British aircraft attack at night, followed up by 200 American Eighth Air Force bombers during the day. The U-boat installations at Kiel are also struck, and the ensuing firestorm kills an estimated 40,000 people. German defense is nevertheless tenacious and knocks down 19 American aircraft.

JULY 25–AUGUST 11   At Presque Isle, Maine, a flight of eight P-47s, accompanied by two B-24s and one C-87, departs on a transatlantic crossing to Prestwick, Scotland. One Thunderbolt is lost in a landing accident at Greenland while a second develops engine trouble en route and heads back to Iceland. This is the only such flight attempted by fighter aircraft during the war; the pilots are from the 2nd Ferrying Group and include Captain Barry Goldwater, a 1964 presidential candidate.

JULY 26   From Midway Island, 8 B-24 Liberators from the Seventh Air Force attack Japanese installations on Wake Island; they claim 11 intercepting Zeroes shot down.

JULY 28   Over Germany, the Eighth Air Force stages its deepest penetration raid by striking at aircraft factories and assembly plants in Kassel and Oschersleben. Twenty-two aircraft are lost from a total of three hundred; for the first time, German fighters also attack the bomber stream with unguided rockets. An escort of P-47 Thunderbolts could not accompany the bombers to the targets, but did shoot down nine aircraft for a loss of one.

Over France, Flight Officer John C. Morgan's B-17 is attacked by fighters that critically wound the pilot; he manages to control the wobbling aircraft for the rest of the mission and back, winning a Congressional Medal of Honor.

JULY 29   Over Messina, Sicily, the Ninth Air Force dispatches 200 P-40 Warhawks on a mission to bomb and strafe targets of opportunity; this is the largest sortie of the entire campaign to date.

JULY 30   Over Hengyang, China, a force of 39 Japanese fighters and 24 bombers attempt to raid Fourteenth Air Force airfields but are intercepted by 15 P-40s and driven off with a loss of 2 fighters and 3 bombers; 2 P-40s are shot down.

AUGUST 1   North of Bucharest, Romania, 177 B-24 Liberator heavy bombers from five bomb groups, Ninth Air Force, conduct Operation TIDALWAVE by striking the strategic oil fields of Ploesti. The attack, badly mishandled, inflicts 40 percent damage with 311 tons of bombs, while suffering a loss of 54 aircraft and 532 airmen. This is also the longest bombing mission thus far in the war, and five Congressional Medals of Honor are issued.

AUGUST 3   Over New Guinea, Fifth Air Force B-25s, B-17s, and B-24s work over Japanese positions at Lae, striking barges, airfields, villages, and military encampments.

AUGUST 5   The new Women Airforce Service Pilots(WASPs) arises after the Women's Flying Training Detachment merges with the Woman's Auxiliary Ferrying Squadron under noted aviatrix Jacqueline Cochran. Meanwhile, Nancy Harkness Love becomes an executive within the Ferrying Division of Air Transport Command. Both retain civilian status and are never considered members of the military establishment.

AUGUST 13 Bombers of the Northwest African Strategic Air Forces lift off from bases in Italy for the first time and attack German targets.

AUGUST 15 Over France and the Netherlands, the Eighth Air Force sends over 300 heavy bombers to strike at Luftwaffe airfields at Vlissingen, Lille, Merville, and Abbeville.

AUGUST 16 In the Southwest Pacific, P-38 Lightnings and P-47 Thunderbolts of the Fifth Air Force sweep down on Japanese targets at various locations, claiming 12 enemy aircraft downed. This is also the combat debut of P-47s in that theater.

AUGUST 17 Over Germany, on the one-year anniversary of the Eighth Air Force's first air raid, 315 B-17 Flying Fortresses stage their first attack on the ball bearing plants in Schweinfurt, Germany, and the Messerschmitt aircraft factory at Regensburg. This is the deepest American penetration of enemy airspace to date and 724 tons of bombs are dropped, but the bomber streams lose 20 percent of their number—60 B-17s—to ferocious resistance. Consequently, no further raids can be mounted until September 6.

A raid by 200 American aircraft flying off a secret airstrip 60 miles west of Lae, New Guinea, completely surprises Japanese air units in the Lae-Salamaua region, decimating them as a fighting force.

A C-87 Liberator flown by the Air Training Command conveys First Lady Eleanor Roosevelt on the tour of the Pacific theater to boost morale.

Four female World War II pilots, graduates of the four-engine school at Lockbourne Field, Ohio, walk past a B-17 in 1944. The Women's Air Force Service Pilots (WASP) division was a noncombat corps, charged primarily with transport of aircraft. (U.S. Air Force)

AUGUST 18   Over Wewak, New Guinea, 70 Allied bombers, escorted by 100 fighters, sweep over Japanese airfields, destroying aircraft on the ground and another 30 in the air. During the attack a B-25 flown by Major Ralph Cheli, Fifth Air Force, is severely damaged but he elects to continue flying the mission, then crashes into the sea. He is captured but does not survive the war, winning a posthumous Congressional Medal of Honor.

AUGUST 20   At New Delhi, India, Major General George E. Stratemeyer is appointed head of Army Air Forces, China-Burma-India (CBI).

AUGUST 21   In Alaska, Eleventh Air Force records reveal that 69 enemy aircraft have been shot down, 21 ships sunk, and 29 damaged, and 29 aircraft lost since June 3, 1942.

AUGUST 25   In England, Eighth Air Force planners commence Operation STARKEY, designed to prevent Germany from redeploying air assets to the Russian front and, instead, keeping them tied down in a war of attrition over the homeland.

Over Foggia, Italy, 140 P-38 Lightnings from the 1st and 82nd Fighter Groups, Twelfth Air Force, make the first mass, low-level strafing attack of the war. Zooming in at treetop level, they claim to destroy 143 enemy aircraft on the ground.

AUGUST 26   The U.S. Army Air Forces, in an attempt to improve high-altitude bombing results, introduces a new kind of perspective map, with targets rendered as they would be seen from the air.

AUGUST 27   Over Watten, Germany, 180 Eighth Air Force bombers unload their ordnance on V-1 and V-2 rocket-launching sites for the first time.

At Carney Field, Guadalcanal, 10 radar-equipped SB-24 "Snooper" bombers, capable of attacking targets in all kinds of weather, begin operations.

AUGUST 28   The 482nd Bomb Group, utilizing Oboe, H2X, and H2S blind-bombing radars, are the first operational Pathfinder unit of the Army Air Forces.

AUGUST 30   Over Rabaul, New Britain, fighter pilot Lieutenant Ken Walsh flames four Zeroes for a total of 20 air-to-air victories. He survives crashing in the water and subsequently wins the Congressional Medal of Honor.

AUGUST 31   Over Italy, a force of 150 North African Strategic Air Force (NASAF) B-17s bomb a marshalling yard in Pisa, inflicting heavy damage. Medium bombers and fighters of the North African Tactical Air Force (NATAF) also strike the railroad junction at Catanzaro and Sapri.

SEPTEMBER 1   In the United States, warplane production has manufactured 123,000 aircraft and 350,000 aircraft engines to date; in a war of protracted attrition, these are levels of production that Axis powers cannot sustain.

Over New Guinea, B-24 and B-25 bombers of the Fifth Air Force unload 201 tons of bombs over Alexishafen-Madang, its heaviest single mission tally to date.

Over China, seven B-25s and eight P-40s of the Fourteenth Air Force attack a Japanese destroyer anchored off of Shihhweiyao, although no hits are registered. Other P-40s bomb and strafe shipping and barges at Ichang at Swatow harbor.

SEPTEMBER 5   In the Mediterranean, the Ninth Air Force, having flown 1,060 missions, dropped 36 million pounds of bombs, shot down 666 Axis aircraft, and sunk 109 enemy ships, concludes its mission and begins transferring aerial assets back to England.

On northern New Guinea, the Fifth Air Force deploys 82 C-47 transports to drop paratroopers and seize Nadzab airfield west of Lae. Shortly afterwards, the Australian 7th Division is flown in by transports.

SEPTEMBER 6   Over Stuttgart, Germany, the Eighth Air Force conducts its first 400-bomber mission; poor weather fouls up bombing results and 45 bombers are lost despite P-47 fighter escorts.

SEPTEMBER 9   Near Paris, France, Operation STARKEY commences with a 300-bomber raid, but the Luftwaffe fails to mount serious opposition.

Over Italy, the Twelfth Air Force commences Operations AVALANCHE and SLAPSTICK in support of the Allied invasion, and which are continued for the rest of the year.

SEPTEMBER 13   At March Field, California, glider expert Richard Dupont is killed in a training accident; he was previously a special assistant to General Henry H. Arnold.

Over Salerno, Italy, 80 C-47s of the 52nd Troop Carrier Wing drop 1,200 men of the 82nd Airborne Division directly into the combat zone; the operation, though perilous, succeeds.

SEPTEMBER 15   Over Indochina (Vietnam), five Fourteenth Air Force B-24s are sent to bomb a cement factory in Haiphong; Japanese fighters manage to shoot down four of the aircraft and the sole surviving B-24 claims ten fighters had been shot down.

SEPTEMBER 18   Over the Gilbert Islands, a combined force of Army B-24 Liberators

and carrier-based aircraft from Task Force 15 under Rear Admiral Charles A. Pownall begin joint air strikes on Tarawa Atoll.

SEPTEMBER 20   Over Bougainville, a P-38 flown by Lieutenant Henry Meigs II, 6th Night Fighter Squadron, flames two Japanese bombers in just minutes.

SEPTEMBER 22   In an attempt to lessen heavy losses, Eighth Air Force B-17s fly a nighttime mission alongside Royal Air Force bombers; however, the Army Air Forces determines to stick to daylight, precision bombing.

After flying its final mission from North Africa, B-24s of the IX Bomber Command transfer to the Twelfth Air Force in Italy.

SEPTEMBER 27   In England, two significant firsts unfold: the first mission is flown with bombers guided by a pathfinder aircraft outfitted with British-developed H2S direction-finding radar, enabling them to bomb accurately through heavy overcast. P-47 Thunderbolts equipped with droppable belly tanks also provide fighter escorts for bombers from Emden and back, a distance of 600 miles. This act constitutes the beginning of long-range fighter escort missions over the German heartland.

SEPTEMBER 30   Over Italy, Twelfth Air Force P-38s, B-25s, and B-26s strike road, bridge, and rail lines at Ausonia, Piana, Castelvenere, Amorosi, and Capua, while fighter-bombers also strafe targets north of Naples.

OCTOBER 1   In England, Eighth Air Force intelligence reports that Germany fighter production, despite a terrific pounding, has actually increased thanks to moving production facilities underground; air resistance over the homeland remains as strong as ever.

Over Indochina (Vietnam), 21 Fourteenth Air Force B-24s, escorted by 21 P-40s, bomb power plant and warehouse areas of Haiphong. Many Japanese fighters rise to oppose them and down 2 aircraft, but lose 30 to the escorts.

OCTOBER 2   The Aerojet XCAL-200, the nation's first rocket-powered airplane, successfully flies for the first time.

OCTOBER 3   At the Lewis Flight Propulsion Laboratory, NACA technicians conduct the first successful test of a turbojet afterburner.

OCTOBER 5–6   In England, Major General James H. Doolittle temporarily replaces Lieutenant General Carl A. Spaatz as commander of the Twelfth Air Force.

OCTOBER 7   Over Paris, France, aircraft of the 422nd Bombardment Squadron, Eighth Air Force, complete their first nighttime drop of propaganda leaflets.

OCTOBER 8   Over Bremen and Vegesack, German, 350 Eighth Air Force bombers strike industrial targets and U-boat pens, losing 30 aircraft to enemy defenses. This is also the first mission to employ electronic jamming (Carpet equipment) against German radar.

OCTOBER 10   In a significant technological development, an Army Air Forces aircraft drone flies for the first time using a closed circuit television screen to monitor feedback.

Over Münster, Germany, 313 Eighth Air Force bombers make a determined raid against industrial targets, losing 33 aircraft shot down and 102 damaged.

OCTOBER 11   Over Wewak, New Guinea, Colonel Neel E. Kearby leads a flight of four P-47 Thunderbolts on a reconnaissance mission. He singlehandedly shoots down six Japanese aircraft, receiving a Congressional Medal of Honor.

OCTOBER 12   Over Rabaul, New Britain, 350 Allied fighters and bombers drawn from the Fifth Air Force and the Royal Australian Air Force launch a massive air strike against Japanese shipping and installations; 3 vessels and 50 aircraft are claimed to be sunk or destroyed.

OCTOBER 13   In Sunninghill Park, England, Major General Lewis H. Brereton assembles his staff and begins readying his Ninth Air Force for a new mission into Western Europe.

OCTOBER 14   Over Germany, 291 Eighth Air Force B-17s make a second bombing raid against ball bearing plants in Schweinfurt. Sixty-seven aircraft are lost to German fighters, which launch unguided rockets into the massed bomber streams; a further 138 aircraft are badly damaged. In the face of such losses, future deep penetrations of German airspace are cancelled unless fighter escorts are available.

OCTOBER 15   In England, Headquarters, U.S. Army Air Forces, United Kingdom, is established under Lieutenant General Ira C. Eaker to serve as a liaison between the Eighth Air Force and the Ninth Air Force, under Major General Lewis H. Brereton. The latter is arriving from the Mediterranean and will be employed as a tactical strike force.

Over New Guinea, the Fifth Air Force dispatches 50 P-38s and P-40s to intercept a Japanese force of 100 aircraft that is bombing Allied shipping in Oro Bay. They claim to shoot down no less than 40 of the attackers.

OCTOBER 16   General Henry H. Arnold recommends that the Fifteenth Air Force be established in Italy, where better weather conditions will allow it to bomb German targets during usually harsh winter weather. In said manner it will supplement the Combined Bomber Offensive already in play from England.

In Burbank, California, Lockheed Aircraft Company contracts with the U.S. Army Air Forces to design and build the XP-80, which becomes America's first operational jet fighter.

OCTOBER 22   For his role in developing air routes across Africa and the Middle East, Major R. C. Heffner receives a Distinguished Flying Cross.

OCTOBER 25   Over Rabaul, New Britain, 60 B-24s from the Fifth Air Force strike Japanese airfields, destroying 50 aircraft on the ground and in the air. These attacks, made in concert with a ground offensive on Bougainville, continue up through November 1.

OCTOBER 30   Over China, seven B-25s and twelve P-40s bomb and strafe a motor pool and barracks at Shayang while nine P-38s are dispatched to hit the dockyards at Chiuchiang.

NOVEMBER   Because of recent German advances, General Henry H. Arnold instructs greater effort on guided missile programs. Dr. Theodore von Karman, Arnold's principal scientific adviser, draws up extensive plans to acquire such long-range weapons.

NOVEMBER 1   In England, a Combined Bomber Offensive (CBO) progress report estimates that 19 German towns and cities have been almost completely destroyed, with another 9 also heavily damaged. The Ministry of Economic Warfare and

Air Ministry Intelligence Branch also issue a joint report that estimates at least 10 percent of Germany's war-making potential has likewise been eliminated.

At Tunis, Tunisia, General James H. Doolittle accepts command of the new Fifteenth Air Force, and prepares to relocate his men and heavy bombers to Italy for attacks against Germany proper.

NOVEMBER 2   Over Austria, the Fifteenth Air Force under Major General James H. Doolittle flies its first combat mission by launching 74 B-17s and 38 B-24s against industrial targets in Wiener Neustadt. They also enjoy the luxury of a P-38 fighter escort en route.

General Douglas MacArthur orders preemptive air strikes against Japanese forces gathering at Rabaul, New Britain, to forestall any possible offensive against operations at Empress Augusta Bay. The Fifth Air Force complies with B-25 Mitchells and P-38 Lightnings which send 94,000 tons of shipping to the bottom; American losses are 21 aircraft. During the attack Major Raymond H. Wilkins's B-25 is badly damaged by antiaircraft fire, but he manages to complete his bomb run before crashing; he wins a posthumous Congressional Medal of Honor.

NOVEMBER 3   Over Germany, a force of 530 Eighth Air Force B-17s and B-24s, guided by nine pathfinders employing H2X search radar, strike the port of Wilhelmshaven. The bomber stream enjoys a complete fighter escort of P-38 Lightnings for the first time.

NOVEMBER 5   In England, the 56th Fighter Group is the first Eighth Air Force fighter unit to destroy 100 enemy aircraft.

NOVEMBER 6–7   In India, B-24s belonging to the Tenth Air Force commence night mining operations along the Rangoon River, Burma.

NOVEMBER 11   Over Rabaul, New Britain, bombers and fighters of the Fifth and Thirteenth Air Forces strike Japanese airfields, in concert with Navy forces. This is the first time that the Thirteenth Air Force has mounted sorties here.

NOVEMBER 13   Bremen, Germany, witnesses the longest American fighter escort of the war thus far, as P-38 Lightnings accompany 115 Eighth Air Force bombers to their target and back; 7 of the fighters fall to stiff Luftwaffe resistance. Previously, poor weather forced over 100 other bombers back to their bases.

Over New Guinea, the Fifth Air Force launches 57 B-24s and 62 B-25s against airfields at Alexishafen and Madang, while other aircraft strike targets at Gasmata, Kaukenau, and Timoeka. This is one of the largest American raids in the region to date, and they are assisted by Bristol Beaufighters of the Royal Australian Air Force (RAAF).

NOVEMBER 14   Over Bulgaria, 90 B-25 Mitchells belonging to the Twelfth Air Force make their first-ever attack by hitting targets in Sofia with 135 tons of bombs.

NOVEMBER 15   Over New Guinea, 30 Fifth Air Force B-24s pound Japanese positions at Alexishafen. Meanwhile a force of 88 B-25s and 16 P-40s headed for Wewak are intercepted by Japanese fighters that are themselves escorting bombers on a raid to Gusap. The Americans claim 20 aircraft shot down at a cost of 2 P-40s.

NOVEMBER 20   In Salina, Kansas, XX Bomber Command is activated at Smoky Hill Air Field under Major General Kenneth B. Wolfe, being equipped solely with new Boeing B-29 Superfortresses.

In New York City, the play *Winged Victory*, written by Moss Hart and sponsored by the Army Air Forces, debuts on Broadway. It is concerned with the struggles of air cadets to earn their wings and features a cast of over 300 actors, virtually all of them active duty personnel.

NOVEMBER 22–26   In Cairo, Egypt, President Franklin D. Roosevelt and Generalissimo Jiang Jieshi discuss the possibility of using new B-29 bombers to attack Japan from Chinese bases. The plan, called Operation TWILIGHT, is the first aerial offensive launched from the China-Burma-India (CBI) theater.

NOVEMBER 25   Over France, P-47s of the VIII Fighter Command initiate the first fighter-bomber attacks by striking the Saint-Omer Airfield.

Formosa (Taiwan) is the subject of an attack by B-25s, P-38s, and P-51s of the Fourteenth Air Force for the first time.

NOVEMBER 26   Bremen, Germany, is the target of 440 Eighth Air Force bombers, which encounter poor weather and lose 29 aircraft to German defenses.

NOVEMBER 29   Over Sarajevo, Yugoslavia, 25 B-25 Mitchells from the Twelfth Air Force strike targets for the first time, including several rail yards.

NOVEMBER 30   Over Germany, the 78 Eighth Air Force heavy bombers strike targets in Solingen with the aid of blind-bombing equipment. This comes after nearly 200 aircraft had to abort owing to heavy cloud formations while assembling over England.

DECEMBER 1   Over Germany a force of 281 Eighth Air Force bombers strikes industrial targets in and around Solingen. The raid, originally intended for Leverkusen, was switched after Pathfinder equipment failed; the Germans manage to down 20 aircraft.

DECEMBER 2   In Washington, D.C., the Combined Chief of Staff directs the Allied Expeditionary Force to begin attacking so-called "ski sites" at Pas-de-Calais and Cherbourg, France, once they are positively identified as V-1 missile launchers.

DECEMBER 3   Operation POINTBLANK, designed to drain the Luftwaffe white prior to the cross-channel invasion of France, begins receiving top priority. Presently, its objectives are still well behind target.

DECEMBER 5   A force of North American P-51 Mustangs from the 354th Fighter Squadron, Ninth Air Force, escorts Eighth Air Force bombers to northern Germany and back, a total of 490 miles. This is the P-51's first escort mission of the war and proves essential for defeating the Luftwaffe in its own airspace.

Meanwhile, a force of 250 B-26 Marauders is forced to return to England on account of poor flying weather.

DECEMBER 8   In England, Lieutenant General Carl A. Spaatz becomes overall commander of American air operations for the forthcoming Operation OVERLORD.

DECEMBER 13   Over Germany, Bremen, Hamburg, and Kiel are targeted by 649 B-17s and B-24s of the Eighth Air Force, the first time an American bomber stream has exceeded 600 aircraft. The raid would have been even bigger but for poor weather that forced 100 bombers back to base.

DECEMBER 18   In Washington, D.C., General Henry H. Arnold finalizes his command list for 1944: General Ira C. Eaker, Mediterranean Theater of Operations (MTO); General Cannon, Twelfth Air Force; General Nathan Twining, Fifteenth Air Force; General Carl A. Spaatz, U.S. Strategic Air Forces; General James H. Doolittle, Eighth Air Force, and General Lewis H. Brereton, Ninth Air Force.

DECEMBER 20   Bremen, Germany, is the object of another massive raid by Eighth Air Force bombers, 27 of which are shot down by German fighters. This is also the first American mission to jettison strips of metal foil to confuse enemy radar. Tech Sergeant Forrest L. Vosler wins a Congressional Medal of Honor for ignoring serious injuries and assisting wounded crewmen on his aircraft after its ditches in the English Channel.

British Air Chief Marshal Arthur Tedder assumes command of the Mediterranean Allied Air Forces, while Lieutenant General Carl A. Spaatz heads up the North African Theater of Operations.

DECEMBER 24   The Eighth Air Force commits its largest bomber raid to date by dispatching 670 B-17s and B-24s against German V-1 launching sites at Pas-de-Calais, France. No aircraft are lost and, by this date, the Americans possess 26 bomber groups in the ETO. Such operations go under the Codename CROSSBOW, of which this is the first.

In the Pacific, Japanese positions on Cape Gloucester, New Britain, are hit by 190 B-25s, B-24s, and A-20s of the Fifth Air Force in relentless daylight attacks.

DECEMBER 2   Over Burma, a force of 25 Fourteenth Air Force P-40s strafe and bomb Japanese positions around Pailochi, and also claim 3 enemy aircraft destroyed.

Bombs destroy the vital Catapult Aircraft Merchantman ball-bearing plant and the nearby Hispano Suiza aircraft engine repair depot in Paris, France on December 31, 1943. This was part of the ongoing strategic bombing campaign against Hitler's "Festung Europa." (National Archives)

DECEMBER 26 Fifth Air Force bombers obliterate targets on Cape Gloucester, New Britain, while escorting P–40s, P–38s, and P–47s claim an additional 60 aerial victories. Hereafter, "Gloucesterizing" enters the military vernacular to imply the total destruction of a target.

DECEMBER 28 In another aviation first, the VIII Bomber Command assembles a "Radio Countermeasure Unit" consisting of 24 especially outfitted B–24 heavy bombers to defeat German radar and communications.

DECEMBER 31 Along the coast of northern France, the Eighth Air Force launches a 500-plane raid against targets, losing 25 bombers. A landmark is reached when the tonnage of bombs dropped by American bombers finally exceeds that delivered by the Royal Air Force.

Over New Georgia, Fifth Air Force A–20s continue pounding Cape Gloucester while 50 P–40s and P–47s intercept Japanese aircraft attempting to bomb the Arawe beachhead, claiming 12 kills. Meanwhile, 150 heavy and medium bombers strike Japanese positions at Madang, Alexishafen, and Bogadjim, New Guinea.

1944

JANUARY 1 In Pasadena, California, Project ORDCIT commences as the

California Institute of Technology (Caltech) begins researching a practical, long-range projectile. This is the origin of the Private A and Corporal tactical missiles.

The United States Strategic Air Force in Europe (USSAFE) is created to wield operational control over the Eighth Air Force (England) and the Fifteenth Air Force (Italy).

Over Saidor, New Guinea, the Fifth Air Force commits over 120 B-24s, B-25s, and A-20s against Japanese troop and supply concentrations in preparation for the coming Allied invasion there.

During a raid in Burma by B-25s and P-38s of the Tenth Air Force on a bridge spanning the Mu River, a bomber flown by Major Robert A. Erdin pulls up sharply to avoid hitting a ground obstacle, then releases his bombs. Two spans of the bridge are hit and collapse, giving rise to the "Burma Bridge Busters."

In Great Britain, the U.S. Strategic Air Forces is organized and initiated.

JANUARY 2 In Yenangyaung, Burma, oil and power plant facilities are struck by medium and heavy bombers belonging to the Tenth Air Force.

JANUARY 4–5 Over Germany, various ports are struck by 500 heavy bombers of the Eighth Air Force. Operation CARPET-BAGGER also begins that evening across Western Europe as Lieutenant Colonel Clifford Heflin flies the first supply mission aimed at bolstering the French underground; such missions originate from Tempsford, England.

JANUARY 6 In England, Lieutenant General Carl A. Spaatz gains appointment to command U.S. Strategic Air Forces in Europe (USSAFE); he also receives operational control of the Fifteenth Air Force. Furthermore, Lieutenant General James H. Doolittle becomes head of the Eighth Air Force in England, while

Lieutenant Ira C. Eaker transfers south to direct Mediterranean Allied Air Forces.

JANUARY 7 In the Pacific, Lieutenant General Hubert R. Harmon assumes command of the Thirteenth Air Force.

JANUARY 8 At Muroc Air Force Base, California, the Lockheed XP-80 christened *Lulu Belle* flies for the first time; it is destined to become the F-80 Shooting Star, America's first jet-powered fighter plane and the first to exceed 500 miles per hour in level flight. Noted aircraft constructor Clarence L. "Kelly" Johnson designed the prototype, which was constructed in only 143 days.

JANUARY 10 Over New Britain, P-39 Airacobras attack and strafe Japanese-occupied villages and barges, while Fifth Air Force heavy and medium bombers work over Madang, Alexishafen, and Bogadjim, New Guinea.

Waves of B-24s are dispatched by the Thirteenth Air Force against airfields and supply depots at Lakunai and Vunakanau. This is the beginning of a protracted night bombardment campaign, while Thirteenth Air Force fighters also assist the Navy covering carrier dive bombers as they strike targets at Cape St. George.

JANUARY 11 Over Germany, targets in Halberstadt, Brunswick, and Osc'hersleben are targeted by 600 Eighth Air Force bombers, which lose 60 of their number to an estimated 500 fighters. This is also the first mission to employ radar-equipped B-24 bombers as pathfinder aircraft to strike targets through overcast.

Over Halberstadt, Germany, a P-51 Mustang flown by Major James H. Howard shoots down three German fighters while singlehandedly engaging a formation of 30 aircraft to protect the bomber stream. He is the only Mustang pilot to receive the Congressional Medal of Honor.

A Fifteenth Air Force bombing mission over Piraeus, Italy, goes awry when six aircraft are lost to midair collisions in poor weather.

JANUARY 13 A force of 200 B-26 Marauders conducts another Noball raid by striking German rocket sites in northern France and reports being shot at by antiaircraft missiles.

At New Delhi, India, command of the XX Bomber Command passes to Lieutenant General Kenneth B. Wolfe. He is tasked with orchestrating the initial moves of Operation MATTERHORN, whereby B-29 Superfortresses will begin striking at Japan from bases on the Asian mainland.

JANUARY 13–14 Thirteenth Air Force B-24s launch another nocturnal air raid against Japanese airfields at Vunakanau and Malaguna. Army and Navy aircraft also strike targets near Buna, Wakuni, and Simpson Harbor, New Guinea.

JANUARY 14 Over Pas-de-Calais, France, 500 Eighth Air Force bombers strike at 20 V-1 weapon launch sites.

Over Italy, Twelfth Air Force bombers assist Fifth Army operations near Monte Trocchio, by launching scores of B-25s, A-20s, A-36s, and P-40s in close air support missions.

JANUARY 15 In Italy, command of Mediterranean Allied Air Forces (MAAF) formally passes to Lieutenant General Ira C. Eaker.

In the Pacific, nine B-25s from the Seventh Air Force stage from Tarawa and strike Japanese installations at Maloelap, inflicting heavy damage on installations and shipping; one B-25 is downed by antiaircraft fire.

JANUARY 18 Over New Guinea, the Fifth Air Force dispatches B-24s to bomb Japanese targets at Laha and Hansa Bay. Meanwhile, Madang and Bogadjim are hit by 70 B-25s while P-38 fighters conduct a sweep over Wewak; 3 Lightnings are lost.

JANUARY 21 Across northern France, German V-weapon sites are struck by more than 500 bombers of the Eighth and Ninth Air Forces; 19 targets are spared assault due to low overcast and 400 bombers are forced back to base.

JANUARY 22 Over Anzio, Italy, aircraft of the Twelfth and Fifteenth Air Forces conduct over 1,200 close air support and air superiority missions during the landing phase of Operation SHINGLE. German resistance remains tenacious and missions are required to be flown well into February.

Heavy and medium bombers belonging to the Thirteenth Air Force strike the airfields at Lakunai again, inflicting considerable damage. They are escorted by a force of more than 90 fighters.

JANUARY 27 Over Italy, fighters of the Twelfth and Fifteenth Air Forces conduct several sweeps over Rome and Florence, shooting down several dozen German aircraft in support of the Fifth Army there.

JANUARY 28 Over Bonnieres, France, Eighth Air Force B-24 Liberators strike German V-weapon launching sites with the new Gee-H blind-bombing radar system. This new system is more accurate than previous devices, but is limited to a range of 200 miles.

JANUARY 29 Over Frankfurt, Germany, a force of 763 Eighth Air Force bombers strikes numerous industrial targets with

1,900 tons of bombs. German fighters manage to claw down 30 of the giant craft; ominously for them, this is the first American attack mounting over 700 aircraft.

Japanese positions in the Gilbert Islands, Kwajalein, and Mille are struck by Seventh Air Force B-24s, which are then followed up by strafing attacks by P-39s. This "softening up" continues over the next few days until the Allied invasion is launched.

JANUARY 30 Over Germany, a second force of 700 Eighth Air Force bombers, guided by early bomb-guiding radar, strikes at targets around Brunswick and Hannover; fighter defenses claim 20 American bombers.

In Italy, the 451st Bomb Group (B-24s) joins the Fifteenth Air Force as its nine bomb group. Fighters of the Twelfth Air Force also continue conducting sweeps over the Anzio battleground, encountering no enemy resistance.

JANUARY 31 Over Saint-Pol/Siracourt, France, 74 Eighth Air Force B-24s attack V-1 launching sites while 70 P-47 fighter-bombers, escorted by 87 P-47 fighters and 47 P-38s, bomb and strafe the Gilze-Rijen airfield. The Germans throw up 84 fighters in a swirling combat; 6 P-38s are shot down while 13 German aircraft are claimed.

FEBRUARY The Army Ordnance Division and the Army Air Forces begin joint development of a guided, supersonic surface-to-air missile to intercept hostile aircraft. This is the origin of the Nike I antiaircraft missile.

The AAF deploys its first VB-1/2 Azon ("azimuth only") radio-controlled bombs in Europe. These primitive "smart weapons" are dropped from bombers and guided through a radio-equipped bombsight; a total of 15,000 Azons are manufactured through November 1944, although their record in combat is mixed.

FEBRUARY 1 In England, Command of IX Air Support Command reverts to Major General Elwood Quesada; this formation includes several fighter and reconnaissance units.

Fighter aircraft belonging to the Seventh Air Force deploy on newly captured airfields in the Gilbert Islands prior to beginning attacks on the Japanese-held Marianas (Operation CATCHPOLE).

Over Burma, 6 Tenth Air Force B-24s bomb Mingaladon Airfield while 32 P-51s and A-36s strike the main airfield at Myitkyina.

FEBRUARY 2 In Moscow, Soviet Union, Premier Josef Stalin approves plans to allow U.S. "shuttle missions" against targets in eastern Germany, after which American bombers will land at Soviet bases.

FEBRUARY 3 In England, the newly arrived 358th Fighter Group joins the 354th Fighter Group, Ninth Air Force, to fly escort missions. The Eighth Air Force also launches 1,200 B-17s, B-24s, and escort fighters against targets in Emden and Wilhelmshaven, Germany.

A force of five P-51 Mustangs under Colonel Philip G. Cochran flies the first air-commando mission in the China-Burma-India (CBI) theater.

Japanese airfields on Wewak are struck by fighters and bombers belonging to the Fifth Air Force; an estimated 80 enemy aircraft are destroyed. Enemy shipping in the Bismarck Sea is also struck by P-39s and B-25s.

FEBRUARY 7 This day, U.S. Army Air Forces fighters adopt a peculiar tactic known as the "Luftwaffe Stomp." If pursued by German fighters, the American pilot would suddenly stall and turn his aircraft, allowing his antagonist to zoom by and become the hunted.

FEBRUARY 8 In Italy, the 454th Bomb Group (B-24) joins the Fifteenth Air Force in Italy, bringing the total of bomb groups present to 10. Meanwhile, B-17s continue hammering targets at Orvieto, Piombino, and Prato, heavily escorted by P-47s and P-38 fighters.

FEBRUARY 9 As the Fifth Army operations resume around Cassino, Italy, it receives intense close air support missions by the Twelfth Air Force.

In the Pacific, a force of 250 fighters and bombers from bases ringing the Solomon Islands coordinate their efforts in a major attack against Japanese installations on Rabaul, New Britain.

FEBRUARY 11 Over Germany, Eighth Air Force bombers employ radar bombing techniques to strike chemical plants in poor weather.

FEBRUARY 13 In Washington, D.C., the Combined Bomber Offensive (CBO) is altered by the chief of staff to concentrate on German lines of communication, as well as the destruction of the Luftwaffe. This switch is undertaken in light of successful German attempts to disperse industrial targets and new tactical priorities for the upcoming Operation OVERLORD.

FEBRUARY 15 Over Indochina, four B-25s of the Fourteenth Air Force attack enemy shipping in the Gulf of Tonkin and also drop bombs on several targets in Haiphong harbor.

FEBRUARY 15–18 In Italy, German positions in and around the ancient Benedictine abbey at Monte Cassino are bombed by 254 B-17s, B-25s, and B-26 bombers belonging to the Twelfth Air Force. However, three days of constant bombing do little to dislodge the defenders and, by allowing them to occupy the wreckage, actually strengthens their position. The Allied drive spearheaded by the Fifth Army and the British Eighth Army remains stalled for several weeks.

FEBRUARY 18 At Cheddington, England, the 8th Reconnaissance Wing is activated to provide enhanced photographic capability in support of Operation OVERLORD. Command of the unit goes to Colonel Elliott Roosevelt, the president's son.

FEBRUARY 18–19 At Anzio, Italy, a serious German counterattack threatens the Allied beachhead, so Twelfth Air Force A-20 light bombers, A-36 dive bombers, and P-40 fighters bore in with 200 close-support sorties that drive them back.

FEBRUARY 19 Over Rabaul, New Britain, a 139-aircraft raid hits Japanese airfields and installations, claiming 23 enemy planes shot down. Consequently, all remaining Japanese aircraft are withdrawn from the island.

In Burma, the Tenth Air Force launches 60 A-36s, P-51s, and B-25s against Japanese fuel depots, rail cars, and river traffic to maintain pressure against enemy units.

In China, B-24s, B-25s, and P-40s belonging to the Fourteenth Air Force begin conducting sweeps between Formosa (Taiwan) and Indochina. These raids are seeking out targets of opportunity and three ships are sunk along with numerous bridges and trains wrecked.

As U.S. forces land and occupy Eniwetok, heavy bombers from the Seventh Air

Force bomb Japanese targets near Ponape and Wotje.

FEBRUARY 20–26   Over Germany, heavy bombers and escort fighters of the Eighth and Fifteenth Air Forces commence "Big Week," a maximum effort to cripple aviation production capacity and cripple the Luftwaffe's ability to resist. This is also the first time that the Americans get 1,000 bombers airborne. Their loss holds at six percent which, while, is acceptable. In contrast the Luftwaffe is hard pressed to reconstitute its strength.

Lieutenant William R. Lawley, severely wounded by the same blast that killed his copilot, gingerly nurses his damaged B-17 back to England after learning two of his crew are unable to bail out; he wins the Congressional Medal of Honor.

Lieutenant Walter E. Truemper, navigator, takes control of his damaged B-17 after his pilot and copilot are killed. Though desperately injured himself, he refuses to bail out and flies back to England only to die in a crash while landing; he wins a Congressional Medal of Honor. Sergeant Archibald Mathies, Truemper's gunner, dies with him and also becomes one of four enlisted airmen to receive a Medal of Honor.

FEBRUARY 21   Over Germany, the Eighth Air Forces unleashes 764 B-17s and B-24s against aircraft factories near Brunswick and Diepholz; results are unclear due to heavy overcast.

In the Pacific, Army bombers belonging to the Air Solomons Command (AirSols) sink two Japanese freighters attempting to evacuate ground crews from Eniwetok Atoll, Marshall Islands.

FEBRUARY 22   Over Germany, the Eighth and Fifteenth Air Forces put up 101 B-17s against Halberstadt, Germany, while a further 154 bombers hit aircraft production facilities near Regensburg; German fighters manage to claw down 50 American craft.

FEBRUARY 23   Over England, poor weather grounds most Eighth Air Force operations, but the Fifteenth Air Force manages to launch a B-24 attack against industrial targets in Steyr, Germany; escorting fighters claim 30 German fighters downed.

FEBRUARY 24   Over Germany, and following the onset of good weather, the Eighth Air Force hurls over 231 bombers at Schweinfurt, 238 against Gotha, and 236 against Rostow. Simultaneously, Fifteenth Air Force B-17s also strike Steyr and Fiume again, losing 19 aircraft. That evening the Royal Air Force strikes the same targets as part of the Combined Bomber Offensive (CBO).

FEBRUARY 25   Over Germany, aviation-related targets in Regensburg, Augsburg, Furth, Stuttgart, Zara harbor, and Fiume are struck by Eighth Air Force bombers in an attempt to lure Luftwaffe fighters up against their powerful escorts. Casualties are heavy on both sides, but the Germans cannot replace their losses as quickly.

FEBRUARY 26   In England, bad weather grounds operations on the final day of Big Week, but hereafter the Luftwaffe begins a precipitous decline towards irrelevance. American losses are steep but Lieutenant General James H. Doolittle's gamble pays huge dividends by D-Day, when German aerial resistance proves nonexistent.

FEBRUARY 28   Over New Guinea, the Fifth Air Force commits B-24 bombers to soften up Japanese airfields in Nubia, Awar, and Hansa Bay in preparation for Allied landings.

Bombs being loaded into the bays of one of the American B-24 Liberator bombers, the fleet known as the Travelling Circus, ready for another shuttle raid. (Hulton-Deutsch Collection/CORBIS)

Japanese positions on Rabaul, New Britain, are struck by waves of Thirteenth Air Force B-25s and P-38s at low altitude, then by B-24s at high altitude. Some of the attacks also involve glide bombs.

FEBRUARY 29 Over Italy, Twelfth Air Force B-26s strike German airfields at Viterbo and targets of opportunity along the west coast, while B-25s attack troops and gun positions west of Cisterna di Roma. Meanwhile, P-40s and A-36s conduct close support missions for the struggling Allied landing zone at Anzio.

Japanese air bases at Alexishafen, New Guinea, are struck by Fifth Air Force bombers. These attacks are carried out in concert with U.S. landings made on the Admiralty Islands, and part of an overall strategy to isolate the main Japanese garrison at Rabaul.

MARCH In Washington, D.C., the Office of War Information reports that the Soviet Union has received more than 7,800 aircraft under the Lend-Lease program to date.

The Bell XP-59 undergoes high-altitude testing at the hands of the NACA Lewis Laboratory to enhance the development of turbojet technology.

MARCH 1 At Shemya, Alaska, the XI Strategic Air Force becomes operational to patrol and defend the Aleutian Islands. It consists of the XI Bomber Command and XI Fighter Command.

Over the Admiralty Islands, the Fifth Air Force contributes more than 100 B-24 bombers in raids against Los Negros and Lorengau. Other aircraft go in and soften up Japanese positions at Wewak, New Guinea; these attacks persist up until the U.S. landing there on April 22.

Over China, 14 B-25s and 16 P-40s from the Fourteenth Air Force attack military targets in northeastern Nanchang.

MARCH 2   In Italy, the 459th Bomb Group joins the Fifteenth Air Force, while 300 heavy bombers, escorted by 150 fighters, support Army operations at Anzio.

MARCH 3   In the Caroline Islands, Operation FORAGER commences as Seventh Air Force bombers and fighters attack Japanese positions to neutralize enemy air activity around the Marianas. Their overarching purpose is to seize land bases capable of sustaining B-29 operations against the Japanese mainland.

MARCH 4   Berlin, Germany, experiences its first raid by aircraft of the VIII Bomber Command as 238 B-17s bore in towards Kleinmachnow. However, they are turned back by poor weather and a deceptive "recall" message broadcast by German intelligence. Only 31 B-17s from the 95th Bombardment Group actually reach the target and release bombs from 28,000 feet. Previously, Lieutenant General James H. Doolittle sought permission to lead the raid in person, but Lieutenant General Carl A. Spaatz refused.

MARCH 5   Over Burma, army gliders from Colonel Philip G. Cochran's Air Commandos insert 539 British and American troops under British brigadier general Orde C. Wingate 50 miles northeast of Indaw and deep behind enemy lines.

MARCH 6   Over Berlin, Germany, the Eighth Air Force returns with a vengeance as 658 heavy bombers unload 1,600 tons of bombs. German fighters and flak down 69 aircraft, the highest toll of any single mission day. This is despite the fact that the bombers are escorted by P-51 Mustangs, who claim 170 German craft.

MARCH 8   Over Germany, the Eighth Air Force unleashes 460 heavy bombers against industrial targets at Erkner; Wildau and Berlin are likewise struck by an additional 75 bombers. Thirty-six aircraft are lost this day.

MARCH 9   The German cities of Berlin, Brunswick, Hannover, and Nienburg are struck by 450 bombers belonging to the Eighth Air Force.

MARCH 11   On Kwajalein, Marshall Islands, B-24 bombers from the Seventh Air Force take off and strike at Japanese installations on Wake Island for the first time.

In India, Operation THURSDAY commences as Army Air Forces transports airlift 9,000 personnel and 1,400 mules to a point 200 miles behind Japanese lines in Burma.

MARCH 15   In a major tactical shift, P-51 Mustangs are released from escort duty and directed to go after German fighters on the ground and in the air.

Over Italy, the Fifteenth Air Force hurls 300 B-17s and B-24s against German positions at Monte Cassino in support of the Fifth Army; the bulk of aircraft are forced back by poor weather. Meanwhile, P-38s and P-47s sweep through the Viterbo-Canino region, encountering no organized opposition.

On Kwajalein, Marshall Islands, Seventh Air Force B-24s lift off from bases and strike at Truk Atoll for the first time. B-25 medium bombers on Tarawa also attack enemy positions at Maloelap.

Lieutenant General Hubert R. Harmon is appointed Commander, Air, Solomon Islands (COMAIRSOLS).

MARCH 16 The National Advisory Committee for Aeronautics (NACA) releases a study calling for a rocket-propelled research aircraft capable of transonic speeds; in 1947 it emerges as the Bell XS-1.

MARCH 18 Over Germany, 679 bombers of the Eighth Air Force strike industrial targets while under heavy escort. The Luftwaffe rises to the occasion, clawing down 43 bombers and 13 fighters while incurring heavy losses of its own. Constant attrition is slowly driving the Germans from the skies.

MARCH 19–MAY 11 Over Italy, Operation STRANGLE commences. This is a seven-week campaign conceived by General Ira C. Eaker to interdict and neutralize German supplies, railways, train yards, and ports across the peninsula. By the time the operation ceases, Allied aircraft fly over 50,000 sorties and unload 26,000 tons of bombs; however, it fails to sever German supplies as anticipated.

MARCH 20 Over Normandy, France, the 67th Reconnaissance Group completes 83 missions, and maps the entire region in advance of Operation OVERLORD. No aircraft are lost and 9,500 detailed photos are taken.

As U.S. Marines storm ashore on the Admiralty Islands, bombers from the Thirteenth Air Force attack nearby airfields to neutralize them. RADAR-equipped SB-24s also played a major role in covering the advance to the island.

MARCH 22 Near Naples, Italy, ancient Mount Vesuvius erupts, destroying or damaging aircraft belonging to the Twelfth Air Force.

MARCH 25 Over Italy, the Brenner Pass to Austria is completely interdicted by bombers and fighters of the Fifteenth Air Force, severely slowing the flow of supplies to German units from Austria. The Americans also employ their radio-guided VB-1 Azon bomb, a lineal predecessor to modern "smart bombs."

MARCH 26 Over France, Pas-de-Calais and Cherbourg are struck by 500 B-17s and B-24s belonging to the Eighth Air Force in an attempt to cripple V-weapon launching sites. Meanwhile, 338 B-26s strike motor torpedo boat pens at Ijmuiden, the Netherlands, while 140 P-47s and P-51s attack marshalling yards at Creil and other locations.

MARCH 27 Across France, 700 heavy bombers belonging to the Eighth Air Force strike multiple airfields and aircraft works.

MARCH 28 In England, the 801st Bombardment Group (Heavy) is activated by the Eighth Air Force; this unit is to conduct special missions throughout the ETO.

MARCH 28–APRIL 2 Over Italy, the Fifteen Air Force launches a series of heavy air raids in support of ongoing Operation STRANGLE when 400 B-17s and B-24s attack rail yards around Verona and Cesano. They are escorted by P-40s and P-38s and no aircraft are lost; this is also the Fifteenth's first 1,000-ton raid. This attack is followed by subsequent strikes against Turin, Milan, and Bolzano, where 6 bombers are shot down. Finally, 530 bombers pound ball bearing factories at Steyr, Germany, losing 19 aircraft.

MARCH 29 In Burma, the success of British Chindits in rear-area operations against Japanese units results in creation of the 1st Air Commando Group under Lieutenant Colonel Philip G. Cochran.

The unit had functioned on an ad hoc basis for several months previously, but now its operations are formalized.

Over Truk, B-24s from the Thirteen Air Force commit the first daylight raid against the atoll; two bombers are lost.

MARCH 30 Over Bulgaria, 350 B-17s and B-24s of the Fifteenth Air Force attack marshalling yards at Sofia, along with industrial zones and airfields at Imotski. Four bombers are lost, but escorting fighters claim thirteen enemy aircraft.

Over Hollandia, New Guinea, Japanese positions are struck by fighters and bombers from the Fifth Air Force. A variety of fuel dumps, troop concentrations, and airfields are targeted from Wewak to Madang.

APRIL 1 Over Germany, the Eighth Air Force sends 438 heavy bombers to destroy the chemical industry plants at Ludwigshafen, then the largest in Europe. However, poor weather forces the 192 B-27s launched to turn back while the remaining 246 B-24s become widely dispersed in heavy cloud cover. Several Swiss and French towns near the target are bombed by mistake.

APRIL 2 At Chakulia, India, the first operational Boeing B-29 Superfortress of the new XX Bomber Command lands under the command of Colonel Leonard F. Harman. As B-29s accumulate there in strength, they are shuttled off to bases in China to begin bombing the Japanese mainland for the first time.

APRIL 3 In England, IX Bomber Command adopts a new leave policy whereby crews receive one week's leave between their 25th and 30th missions. Between their 40th and 50th missions, they are entitled to take off an additional two-week respite.

APRIL 3–4 Over Budapest, Hungary, industrial targets are targeted for the first time by 450 Fifteenth Air Force bombers, while a 300-bomber raid is launched the following day; 10 B-24s are lost along with a score of German fighters.

APRIL 4 In Washington, D.C., the new XX Air Force is secretly activated. This unit is destined to employ giant B-29 Superfortress bombers against the Japanese mainland from China and India. The force is regarded as so significant that it is controlled by the Joint Chiefs of Staff (JCS) through General Henry H. Arnold.

APRIL 5 The refineries and marshalling yards at Ploesti, Romania, are struck by the Fifteenth Air Force; 13 bombers succumb to enemy fighters and flak.

APRIL 8 Over Germany, the Eighth Air Force launches 13 combat wings in three distinct waves. The city of Brunswick is the hardest hit, being the object of 192 B-17s; 34 bombers are lost.

At Hasselt, Belgium, the Ninth Air Force commits more than 163 B-26s and 101 P-47s in a major tactical raid against German-manned positions.

APRIL 9 Across Germany and Poland, 399 B-17s and B-24s belonging to the Eighth Air Force strike various targets, losing 32 aircraft to doughty German defenses; 3 aircraft also make forced landings in Sweden and are interned. The attack is escorted by 719 P-38s, P-47s, and P-51s culled from the VIII and IX Fighter Commands.

APRIL 11 Over Germany, the Eighth Air Force launches 800 B-17s and B-24s against fighter production factories and airfields; 64 bombers are shot down, the second-highest loss for a single day. Lieutenant Edward S. Mitchell, ignoring his own wounds, manages to fly his damaged B-17 to safety once his bombardier's parachute is damaged; he wins the Congressional Medal of Honor.

Across northern France, 300 B-26s, A-20s, and P-47s from the Ninth Air Force are committed against various military targets.

APRIL 13   In England, General Dwight D. Eisenhower receives authority to direct American aerial operations relative to Operation OVERLORD, especially those by the Eighth and Ninth Air Forces. Launching sites for V-weapons and German lines of communication remain priority targets.

530 bombers from the Fifteenth Air Force hit numerous targets in Hungary and southern Germany, and claim the destruction of 120 enemy aircraft.

APRIL 15   Over central and western Germany, 530 fighters of the Ninth and Tenth Air Forces sweep in low to shoot up airfields and targets of opportunity. Bad

U.S. Fifth Army Air Force planes bomb the Japanese-held base of Hollandia in New Guinea, 1944. (Hulton-Deutsch Collection / Corbis)

weather forces most of the aircraft to return to base, but they claim 58 enemy aircraft destroyed in air and ground attacks; 33 American fighters go missing with at least 19 attributable to unknown causes.

APRIL 16   Hollandia, New Guinea, is again hit by the Fifth Air Force, which dispatches 170 A-20s, P-38s, P-40s, and B-25s on the bombing mission. However, the onset of poor weather during the return flight leads to the loss of 37 aircraft—a higher loss rate than that experienced in combat.

APRIL 17   In South China, bases operated by the 308th Bombardment Group are threatened by a Japanese land offensive; this is the only American heavy bomber outfit then in China, and it is especially outfitted for stalking enemy shipping in the South China Sea.

APRIL 22   Over New Guinea, the Fifth Air Force provides close air support to Allied invading forces at Hollandia and Aitape. This comes after six weeks of continuous air raids on Wewak and Hansa Bay.

APRIL 24   In India, Lieutenant General Kenneth B. Wolfe, commanding the XX Air Force, pilots one of the first two B-29s to cross over the "Hump" (Himalayas) and land at Kwanghan, China. The American bomber offensive against the Japanese mainland originates here.

APRIL 25   Over France, the Eighth Air Force launches 114 B-117s to attack the Lyon/Bron airfield, while a further 177 B-17s hit the Clermont/Ferrand/Aulnat airfield. A further 22 P-38s and 21 P-47s also conduct a combination of high- and low-altitude bombing attacks on airfields at Orleans/Bricy. One heavy bomber and sixty-five fighters are shot down by German aircraft and flak.

Guam is the target of Seventh Air Force B-24 Liberators operating from Eniwetok for the first time; this is also the first raid by land-based bombers. A Navy PBY reconnaissance aircraft accompanies them to observe results.

In Burma, a Sikorsky YR-2 Hoverfly flown by Lieutenant Carter Harman, 1st Commando Group, executes the first helicopter rescue mission in history by extracting four downed airmen from the jungle.

MAY 1 In England, the Eighth Air Force sends over 500 heavy bombers to attack 23 V-1 rocket launching sites near Pas-de-Calais, France. Bad weather forces many aircraft to abort their mission.

In China, Operation MATTERHORN moves a step closer to reality with the opening of the first B-29 base at Chengtu. As bombers, supplies, and bombs accumulate, the aerial offensive against the Japanese mainland draws nearer.

MAY 5 Over Ploesti, Romania, the Fifteenth Air Force, enlarged to include 20 heavy bombardment groups, launches 640 bombers against the oil refineries. Over 240 fighter sorties are also launched to escort them; this is the largest raid to date by the Fifteenth Air Force.

MAY 7 Over Germany, the Eighth Air Force breaks its own record when it dispatches over 900 bombers against industrial targets in Münster and Osnabruck, Germany, while additional aircraft are dispatched against Liège, Belgium. This is the first time that the Eighth Air Force marshals over 900 aircraft one a single day.

MAY 9–11 Over France and Belgium, the Eighth Air Force begins a concerted bombing campaign against German airfields to render them inoperable during the build up to D-Day. Two days later

tactical aircraft of the Ninth Air Force are likewise thrown into the fray.

MAY 10 In China, Project CHENGTU concludes as 400,000 laborers finish work on five heavy bomber and six fighter bases near the city of Chengtu. The Chinese contribution to the project was unglamorous and largely unheralded, but also essential to the project. B-29 air raids against the Japanese mainland will commence shortly.

MAY 11 In Italy, Operation STRANGLE concludes apace, having delivered 26,000 bombs against German lines of communication and supply since March 19. However, it has failed to completely disrupt German supply lines.

MAY 12 Over Germany, the Eighth Air Force dispatches 800 bombers against oil production facilities in Merseburg, Chemnitz, and Brux; the Luftwaffe manages to down 46 American aircraft.

The Ninth Air Force begins Operation EAGLE as a dress rehearsal for airborne operations over Normandy. This maneuver tests the tactics and techniques for all specific missions to be executed on June 5.

The Fifteenth Air Force, having reached its authorized strength of 21 bombardment groups, launches 730 bombers against German headquarters at Massa d'Albe and Monte Soratte, Italy. This is the Fifteenth's largest raid to date and includes 250 escort fighter sorties.

MAY 13–14 In northern Italy, the Twelfth Air Force commits light bombers and fighter-bombers to assist the Fifth Army as it assaults the German Gustav Line. They are joined by 700 heavy bombers from the Fifteenth Air Force, which conduct interdiction missions against German supply lines.

MAY 15   Over Bougainville and Shortland Island, the Thirteenth Air Force puts up 25 B–25s and 40 P–40s, P–38s, and P–39s to attack antiaircraft positions, villages, trails and other targets of opportunity.

MAY 17–18   Over New Guinea, the Fifth Air Force dispatches more than 100 B–24s against Japanese targets as Allied forces come ashore unopposed at Arare and Sarmi. Another 100 medium bombers are dispatched against enemy positions around Wewak.

MAY 19   In Italy, German aerial opposition north of Rome disappears once the Fifteen Air Force begins pushing attacks into that region.

MAY 25   Over Anzio, Italy, the Twelfth Air Force harries retreating German forces as they withdraw, and also cover the Fifth Army as it breaks out from the beachhead.

MAY 27   Across Europe, the Eighth, Ninth, and Fifteenth Air Force put up 2,000 warplanes, which strike targets across France, Germany, and Italy; 24 heavy bombers are lost. From this point forwards, air raids by the Eighth Air Force routinely number 800 aircraft or more.

At Nanchang, China, P–40 fighters from the Fourteenth Air Force fire air-to-ground rockets at Japanese troop positions for the first time.

On Biak, Japanese positions are worked over by B–25s and B–24s operated by the Fifth Air Force. Other medium bombers continue providing close air support for Allied forces at Wewak, New Guinea.

MAY 29   An A–20 test aircraft named *Alcad Nag* is used for target practice by gunners who fire .50 caliber machine guns loaded with "frangible bullets."

These shatter after hitting an aerial target, leaving only a small mark for scoring purposes.

MAY 31   In the Zone of the Interior (ZI), the VB–7 (vertical bomb) is tested for the first time; this device employs radio-controlled fins and television for guidance to targets.

Over Italy, medium bombers of the 43rd and 57th Bomb Wings, Twelfth Air Force, are unleashed on a ground support mission to assist the Fifth Army and its drive on Rome. Concurrently, A–20s of the XII Tactical Air Command begin blasting German troop concentrations, tanks, and motor vehicles throughout the same region. Incredibly, despite this literal deluge of bombs, the Germans continue mounting fierce resistance.

JUNE 1   In the Pacific, XIII Bomber Command relocates from the New Hebrides to Los Negroes. Meanwhile, B–25s attack parts of Rabaul while 30 P–38s and P–40s strike at Talili Bay.

JUNE 2   Across northern France, the Eighth and Ninth Air Force contribute 1,000 bombers and fighters for around-the-clock air strikes against airfields and communication facilities, especially at Pas-de-Calais, to deceive German intelligence; 8 bombers are lost.

In Italy, the Twelfth Air Force continues launching heavy air raids north of Rome to support the Allied drive.

Lieutenant General Ira C. Eaker leads Operation FRANTIC, the first shuttle-bombing run from Italy to targets at Debreczen, Hungary, and then lands at Poltava in the Soviet Union. The strike force consists of 130 B–17s and 70 P–51 fighter escorts.

JUNE 4   In England, Lieutenant General Dwight D. Eisenhower delays Operation

OVERLORD for 24 hours in the face of severe weather, although 500 tactical air strikes continue. The storm also provides a convenient cover for the amphibious operation.

In Italy, the Twelfth and Fifteenth Air Forces continue supporting Allied ground troops as they advance towards the German Gustav Line; aircraft are being siphoned off to support Operation ANVIL/DRAGOON, the invasion of southern France.

JUNE 5   Over northern France, as part of the wind-up to Operation OVERLORD, 629 heavy bombers from the Eighth Air Force attack coastal forces; 6 are lost to German flak. Lieutenant Colonel Leon R. Vance, Jr., badly wounded by a direct hit on his B-24, flies his craft long enough to allow it to ditch in the English Channel and save the crew; he wins the Congressional Medal of Honor.

Over Southeast Asia, a force of 75 B-29s of XX Bomber Command strike Japanese rail targets in Bangkok, Thailand. A total of 98 aircraft were launched, but 5 of the new bombers are lost to mechanical problems while others abort for the same reason.

Over Wadke, New Guinea, Japanese fighters attack the Allied airfield, destroying and damaging several aircraft.

JUNE 5–6   Over Normandy, France, Operation OVERLORD kicks off at midnight as 1,400 C-47s of the IX Troop Carrier Command, Ninth Air Force, begin dropping three full divisions of American and British airborne troops behind German lines. Army Air Forces and Royal Air Force tactical aircraft also fly 15,000 sorties in support of the amphibious operation over the next 24 hours. Heavy bombers of the Eighth Air Force, now up to its assigned strength of 40 bomb groups, drop an additional 3,600 tons of ordnance on German

supply and communications centers further back from the beaches. Moreover, 1,800 fighter sorties are flown in support of the landings; 36 aircraft fall to enemy flak.

Throughout northern Italy, aircraft of the Twelfth Air Force continue striking German positions and communications for the rest of the war.

From Italy, Fifteenth Air Force heavy bombers continue making shuttle runs against Ploesti, Brasov, and Turin. Oil refineries and storage facilities remain priority targets.

JUNE 6   Over Normandy, France, the Eighth, Ninth, and Royal Air Forces conduct over 15,000 interdiction, close air support, and airlift sorties in support of ongoing landing operations. The Luftwaffe can mount only token opposition.

JUNE 7   At Freeman Field, Indiana, Colonel E. T. Rundquist initiates the Army Air Forces' helicopter training program.

Over Normandy, France, the Eighth and Ninth Air Forces fly 2,000 sorties in support of five beachheads established during Operation OVERLORD. Transport aircraft also drop 356 tons of supplies to the troops. Despite the deluge of bombs, however, German resistance remains resolute.

In Italy, the Fifteenth Air Force reaches its peak strength as its 21 heavy bomber groups are activated; here, as well as in the rest of Europe, American aircraft are flying thousands of sorties daily in the cause of victory.

JUNE 8   In England, Lieutenant General Carl A. Spaatz declares that Axis oil production and storage facilities are the highest priority targets of American air power in Europe.

JUNE 9   Only three days into Operation OVERLORD, the first Allied air units begin operating from airfields in northern France.

JUNE 11   At Poltava, Soviet Union, B-17s and P-51s complete Operation FRANTIC by launching against oil and refinery targets in Eastern Europe and returning to home bases in Italy.

JUNE 12   At Normandy, France, General Henry H. Arnold accompanies the Joint Chiefs of Staff as they cross the English Channel to inspect the recently acquired beachheads.

In the Russell Islands, Special Task Force Air Group I deploys as the first guided missile unit deployed to the Pacific.

JUNE 13   In a portent of things to come, the Germans launch V-1, or "vengeance weapons," from sites in France and Belgium against Great Britain; one of the pilotless flying bombs strikes Swanscombe, Kent, and General Henry H. Arnold personally inspects the damage inflicted.

JUNE 15   In England, the Eighth Air Force dispatches 1,225 heavy bombers to strike the oil refinery at Misburg, along with airfields, bridges, marshalling yards, and other targets in northern France.

At Brisbane, Australia, General George E. Kenney becomes commander of the new Far East Air Force (FEAF), which incorporates the Fifth and Thirteenth Air Forces. Meanwhile, aircraft from the former strikes a Japanese airfield south of Bougainville while bombers of the latter continue pounding enemy positions at Rabaul.

At Chengtu, China, a force of 68 Boeing B-29 Superfortresses under Brigadier General LaVerne G. Saunders of XX Bomber Command fly 1,500 miles to bomb steel factories at Yawata, Kyushu. This is the first major air raid against the Japanese mainland since the famous "Doolittle Raid" of April 1942.

However, bombing results are poor owing to encounters with the jet stream at high altitude.

JUNE 21   Over Germany, the Eighth Air Force mounts its first 900-bomber raid against Berlin, escorted by 900 fighters provided by the Ninth Air Force. Additional aircraft attack rocket launching sites at Siracourt, France.

JUNE 22   On Saipan, the 19th Fighter Squadron, 318 Fighter Group, Seventh Air Force, deploys on Aslito Airfield. Over the next week they will help pioneer close support using napalm bombs.

JUNE 22–23   Operation FRANTIC continues as 144 bombers belonging to the Eighth Air Force bomb targets in Eastern Europe and land at bases in the Soviet Union. That evening, German bombers raid Poltava, destroying 43 B-17s and damaging 19 more parked there.

JUNE 23   From England, aircraft of the Eight and Ninth Air Force continue pounding suspected V-1 launching sites throughout northern France.

Over Ploesti, Romania, the Fifteenth Air Force launches 400 bombers and 300 fighter escorts against oil refineries; resistance is fierce and costs the Americans 100 aircraft. Lieutenant David R. Kingsley, who refuses to bail out when ordered and instead assists the crewmen to escape—even giving his parachute to the tail gunner—dies when his B-17 crashes, but wins a Congressional Medal of Honor.

The 52nd Fighter Group also scores 12 kills over Romania for a total of 102 aerial victories in only 30 days. This record is never equaled by any other American fighter group in Europe.

JUNE 24   On Saipan, P-47 fighter-bombers of the Seventh Air Force provide close air support to army and marine units fighting on nearby Tinian.

JUNE 25   At Cape Kurubai, Aleutians, two B-24s of the Eleventh Air Force bomb a suspected Japanese airfield. This is despite the fact that the Kiska campaign had ended in August 1943.

JUNE 26   Over Saipan, the night skies are patrolled by Northrop P-61 Black Widows, while P-47 Thunderbolts attack Japanese positions during the day.

JUNE 27   Over Germany, Brigadier General Arthur W. Vanaman becomes the first Army general captured in Europe when his bomber is shot down on a raid; he spends the rest of the war at Stalag Luft III, southeast of Berlin.

JUNE 30   Over Burma, 47 Tenth Air Force B-25s continue airdropping ammunition to hard-pressed British forces defending Imphal, while an additional 17 B-25s carry gasoline to Kamaing. Other B-25s and P-38s continue striking at Tamu and Wauinggyo.

JULY 1   In the Mariana Islands, Seventh Air Force P-47s are dispatched to make strafing runs over Saipan, Tinian, and Rota while B-24s, staging through Eniwetok, bomb Japanese naval facilities at Truk.

JULY 2   In the Southwestern Pacific, fighters and bombers belonging to the Far East Air Forces (FEAF) strike at Japanese positions near Kamiri on Noemfoor Island in preparation for an amphibious attack.

JULY 3   Over France, the Northrop P-61 Black Widow, the sole American aircraft designed as a night fighter, begins flying nocturnal missions.

At New Guinea, the 54th Troop Carrier Wing drops the 1st Battalion, 503rd Parachute Infantry Regiment over the Japanese airfield at Kamiri.

JULY 5   Over Harper Dry Lake, California, the rocket-powered Northrop MX-324 performs its maiden flight. Originally designed as a glider, its sports an Aerojet XCAL-200 rocket motor and is unofficially known as the "Rocket Ram."

JULY 6   Over Saipan, a Japanese G4M bomber is flamed at night by a P-61 Black Widow flown by Lieutenant Francis Eaton, Lieutenant James Ketchum, and Sergeant Gary Anderson. This is the first confirmed kill for the P-61.

In China, the Fourteenth Air Force launches myriads of P-40s, P-51s, and B-25s against Japanese targets along the Yangtze River; ground support missions for Chinese forces are also flown at various locations.

JULY 7   Over Germany, the aerial campaign against petroleum, oil, and lubricant (POL) targets intensifies as aircraft of the Eighth, Twelfth, and Fifteenth Air Forces stage 3,000 sorties against them; German defenses claw down 60 aircraft.

JULY 8   In occupied France, a C-47 flown by Lieutenant Colonel Clifford Heflin touches down for the first time to rescue down Allied airmen.

JULY 9   Over Ploesti, Romania, Fifteenth Air Force bombers employ Pathfinder navigation devices for the first time; escorting P-38 and P-51 fighters claim 14 German aircraft. Lieutenant Donald D. Puckett flies his damaged B-24 long enough to allow most of his crew to bail out; he dies when it crashes, winning a posthumous Congressional Medal of Honor.

At Wright Field, Ohio, a wrecked Fieseler Fi. 103 (V-1) is delivered for technical inspection. Slightly over two weeks later, a working copy of its pulse-jet engine is replicated by Ford Motor Company engineers; copies of the V-1 enter the American arsenal as JB-1 Loons.

JULY 11   On Saipan, Seventh Air Force P-47s take off to strike Japanese positions in the Marianas Islands, especially Tinian and Pagan, in anticipation of forthcoming amphibious landings there. B-24s also stage out of Eniwetok and bomb Tinian over the next several days until the landings are affected.

JULY 11–16   Over Germany, the Eighth Air Force commits over 1,000 bombers and 800 escort fighters in a series of repeated strikes against rail yards and aircraft engine factories in Munich.

In southern France, the Fifteenth Air Force begins attacking ground targets in support of Operation ANVIL/DRAGOON. However, heavy bombers are also detailed to strike oil-related targets in Romania.

JULY 12   Over Italy, Operation MALLORY MAJOR is begun by U.S. Army Air Forces tactical bombers to systematically destroy all bridges over the Po River.

JULY 15   Over China, the Fourteenth Air Force sorties over 100 B-25s, P-40s, and P-51s, which attack Japanese positions at Sinshih, Chuzhou, Siantan, Siangsiang, Sungpai, and Chaling. Meanwhile, a force of 26 additional P-40s provide ground support to Chinese forces in the Salween area.

JULY 17   Over Coutances, France, P-38 Lightnings drop napalm (jellied gasoline) on German fuel depots for the first time; it proves to be a frightening and highly destructive weapon.

JULY 18   Over southern Germany, a P-51 Mustang flown by Lieutenant C. D.

"Lucky" Lester, an African American flying with the 100th Fighter Squadron, 332nd Fighter Group, downs three German fighters while escorting heavy bombers. Ultimately, black fighter pilots complete 15,000 missions and claim 261 enemy aircraft.

JULY 19   Over Germany, 1,100 bombers from the Eighth and Fifteenth Air Forces strike against Munich and other industrial targets, while escorted by nearly 1,000 fighters. Munich is struck by similar raids for the remainder of the month.

In the Pacific, scores of B-24s from the Far East Air Forces (FEAF) strike Japanese targets on Yap, Ngulu, and Sorol Islands while fighter-bombers provide close support to Allied troops in the Sarmi-Sawar sector of New Guinea.

JULY 21–AUGUST 10   As the struggle for Guam unfolds, bombers and fighters of the Seventh Air Force continue striking Truk and Tinian to pin down Japanese forces and prevent them from interfering.

JULY 22   From Italy, Operation FRANTIC continues as 76 P-38s and 38 P-51s of the Fifteenth Air Force attack airfields near Ploesti, Romania, then fly on to bases in southern Russia. This is the first all-fighter shuttle mission.

JULY 24–AUGUST 1   Over Tinian, P-47s belonging to the Seventh Air Force drop napalm bombs on heavy jungle vegetation to deny Japanese defenders tactical cover as U.S. Marines advance inland.

JULY 25   At Normandy, France, 1,495 heavy bombers of the Eighth Air Force commence Operation COBRA by carpet bombing German positions around St. Lo and creating paths for American ground forces to pour through. The elite Panzer Lehr tank training division is nearly annihilated by American air power, whose bombs leave the surrounding landscape as cratered as the moon's surface. However, several bombs fall short and kill Lieutenant General Leslie McNair, commander of U.S. Ground Forces, along with 102 soldiers. A further 1,500 fighter-bombers of the Ninth Air Force continue hammering enemy positions as they begin to give way.

JULY 29 Over Anshan, China, the Showa Steel Works is struck by B-29s of XX Bomber Command. One bomber is lost to enemy fighters while another, badly damaged, is forced down at Vladivostok, Soviet Union, and the crew is interned. This particular aircraft serves as the model for the Tupolev Tu-4 BULL, the first Soviet strategic bomber which flies in 1947.

JULY 30 In the Pacific, B-25s and P-47s launched from Tarawa continue pounding Japanese positions at Saipan as B-24s stationed in the Marshall Islands bomb naval installations on Truk.

Over Burma, constant attacks by Tenth Air Force fighter-bombers result in a Japanese withdrawal from Myitkyina; after issuing the order, the Japanese commander commits suicide.

At the western tip of New Guinea, Far East Air Forces (FEAF) aircraft mount an aerial diversion by striking Japanese positions at Wewak and Aitape are likewise attacked.

AUGUST 1 Over France, 191 Eighth Air Force B-17s drop supplies to underground forces as 320 more hit targets in Paris, and a force of 75 heavy bombers strike at Tours. B-24s meanwhile conduct numerous raids against V-1 launching sites across northern France.

At Fort Shafter, Hawaii, Lieutenant General Millard F. Harmon becomes commander of the new Army Air Forces, Pacific Oceans Areas (AAFPOA). He also serves as deputy commander of the XX Air Force, reporting directly to General Henry H. Arnold.

On Saipan, P-47s and P-61s of the Seventh Air Force continue their day and nighttime patrolling actions over Guam, Rota, and Pagan, in support of Allied ground forces fighting there.

AUGUST 4 Over Pas-de-Calais, France, several worn-down and pilotless B-17s and B-24s participate in the first project APHRODITE mission; the aircraft are packed with several tons of explosives and flown by a crew of two that bails out over the English Channel, whereupon a pacing aircraft guides them along via radio control to their target. Considering the dangers such missions pose to the crew, they are abandoned shortly after and television-guided bombs receive increased emphasis.

AUGUST 4–6 Over Western Europe, 1,250 heavy bombers are launched by the Eighth Air Force against multiple targets in Germany and northern France, and the raids are repeated over the next two days. Targets include four oil refineries, four aircraft factories, coastal batteries at Calais, and the rocket research facility at Peenemunde. Concurrently, Operation APHRODITE continues as radio-controlled B-17 drones, packed with 20,000 pounds of explosives, are launched against V-1 rocket sites at Pas-de-Calais, France.

Over the Balkans, the Fifteenth Air Force launches another Operation FRANTIC mission by dispatching 70 P-38s and P-51s to targets in Eastern Europe. This attack is in response to a request by the Soviet high command, the first of its kind.

AUGUST 5 The 63rd Bombardment Squadron, Fifth Air Force, commences the first night attack with a single radar-equipped B-24 Snooper II aircraft, which strikes the Sasa Airdrome on the island of Mindanao.

AUGUST 6 Over Brandenburg, Germany, a P-51 Mustang flown by Major George E. Preddy tangles with a horde of intercepting German fighters, and he downs six in only five minutes. Before his death by flak on December 15, 1944, Preddy becomes the highest-scoring Mustang ace, with 25 victories.

AUGUST 8 In England, command of the Ninth Air Force is assumed by Lieutenant General Hoyt S. Vandenberg.

Over China, a major air raid by the Fourteenth Air Force strikes Japanese communication and storage facilities at Hengshan, Hamoy, and Swatow, China. Several radio stations and storage facilities are likewise destroyed.

AUGUST 9 Over the Seine River, France, a B-26 Marauder flown by Captain Darrell R. Lindsey is set aflame by flak. Lindsey continues flying his crippled bomber until the crew bails out, then dies in the ensuing crash; he posthumously receives a Congressional Medal of Honor.

AUGUST 10 On Guam, Tinian, and Saipan, construction crews begin repairing and enlarging airfields for mounting B-29 operations against the Japanese homeland. These islands have not yet been declared secure and fighting continues.

Over Iwo Jima, Bonin Islands, the Seventh Air Force commits the first B-24 operations against Japanese positions, preparing them for an amphibious invasion six months hence. They also attack Chichi Jima and the Carolines throughout the period leading up to the U.S. assault.

AUGUST 10–11 In China, B-29s of XX Bomber Command flying from Chengtu

strike industrial targets in Nagasaki, Japan. Another force staging from China Bay, Ceylon (Sri Lanka), hits oil refineries at Palembang, Sumatra, 3,900 miles away; this is the longest mission flown by B-29s in the war.

AUGUST 10–14 In the Mediterranean, the Twelfth Air Force launches hundreds of B-25s, B-26s, and P-47s in strikes along the French and Italian coasts west of Genoa. Shortly after, the Fifteenth Air Force unleashes heavy bombers to soften targets for the intended invasion of southern France.

AUGUST 11 To further assist American ground forces in eastern France, the Eighth Air Force launches 956 heavy bombers and 578 escort fighters to strike transportation facilities and other German military targets.

AUGUST 13 At LeHavre, France, American aircraft unleash two television-guided GB-4 glide bombs against U-boat pens as part of Project APHRODITE.

AUGUST 14 Throughout the Pacific, the Seventh Air Force is reorganized into a hard-hitting tactical force whose aircraft, on this day, strike Japanese targets across a vast arc, including Iwo Jima, Pagan, Rota, Ponape, and the Wotje Islands.

AUGUST 14–15 In the Mediterranean, hundreds of heavy and medium bombers from the Twelfth and Fifteenth Air Forces pound German positions in the Toulon-Nice-Genoa area in support of Operation ANVIL/DRAGOON. They are escorted by 200 fighters, although resistance is almost nonexistent. This is the largest effort mounted by the Mediterranean Allied Air Forces during the war, which flies 4,249 sorties and lands 9,000 airborne troops.

AUGUST 15 Over Belgium and the Netherlands, the Eighth Air force launches 850 heavy bombers against German airfields, assisted by RAF Mosquito raiders and 607 VIII Fighter Command sorties. The Americans lose 17 bombers and 6 fighters while claiming 27 aircraft downed along with 29 locomotives destroyed. Another force of 33 P-47s also dive bombs a locomotive repair ship at Braine-le-Compte.

AUGUST 16 Over Merseburg, Germany, a flight of B-17 bombers is attacked by Me-163 Komet rocket-propelled fighters for the first time. Though spectacular at 590 miles per hour, the Komet proves ineffective against heavily armed bombers; only 279 are constructed.

In India, following the defeat of a determined and bloody Japanese offensive, the Tenth Air Force commits fighter-bombers and bombers to targets in northern Burma, where they harass retreating enemy columns.

AUGUST 18 In northern France, waves of B-26 and A-20 bombers strike at enemy fuel and ammunition dumps, covered by more than 1,000 escort fighters. The German army is beginning to crack and retreat under the weight of these incessant aerial onslaughts.

AUGUST 20 On Saipan, the Seventh Air Force launches B-24s against Yap for the first time, while Marshall Islands-based aircraft continue bombing enemy positions on Truk.

AUGUST 23 Over Burma, the Tenth Air Force commits 32 P-47 fighter-bombers to provide close air support during a British advance. Troop concentrations, batteries, and headquarter buildings are all ravaged.

AUGUST 24 In the Mariana Islands, a B-29 piloted by Brigadier General Edmund "Rosie" O'Donnell, 73rd Bomb Wing Headquarters, deploys. This is the first aircraft of the XX Air Force to deploy there.

AUGUST 26 In another series of major raids, the Eighth Air Force commits 997 heavy bombers and 897 fighter escorts against targets in France, Belgium, the Netherlands, and Germany. Enemy resistance remains sharp and downs 13 bombers and 13 fighters while a further 148 bombers and 15 fighters receive damage.

AUGUST 28 Over Germany, P-47 pilots Major Joseph Myers and Lieutenant Manford O. Croy, Jr., team up to down the first Messerschmitt Me-262 jet fighter claimed by American fighters. This is the first operational jet fighter, packing a top speed of 540 miles per hour, and a formidable bomber destroyer. It also stimulates Army Air Forces interest in acquiring jet bombers to counter the threat, and planning for the North American XB-45 begins this year.

Brigadier General Haywood Hansell takes charge of the new XXI Bomber Command, equipped with B-29s, while Brigadier General Lauris Norstad is appointed chief of staff with the Twentieth Air Force.

AUGUST 29 Major General Curtis E. LeMay becomes commander of the XX Bomber Command. LeMay, a hard-hitting strategist, is determined to wring out the best possible performance from his new and expensive B-29s.

AUGUST 31 Over Romania, the Fifteenth Air Force unleashes 45 P-51s against airfields at Reghin, while an additional 97 fighters strafe and bomb airfields at Oradea and Kecskemet. They claim to have destroyed over 150 aircraft on the ground. Meanwhile, at Bucharest, 36 B-17s begin evacuating U.S. airmen interned in Romania as that city falls to the Red Army.

SEPTEMBER 1   In England, the Eighth Air Force sorties 950 heavy bombers for raids in France and Germany, but most are recalled due to poor flying conditions. Meanwhile one P-47 fighter group makes strafing attacks along the Brussels-Antwerp region of Belgium, as an additional seven groups attack rail lines through northeastern France.

Over the Philippines, a force of 555 Fifth Air Force B-24s attack dispersal areas at three airfields near Davao, Mindanao, losing two of their number to Japanese antiaircraft fire. Enemy fighters also damaged several of the lumbering craft, but post-strike photography reveals 22 wrecked airplanes on the ground.

SEPTEMBER 3–11   Over Germany, the 55th Fighter Group shoots down 106 enemy fighters and earns a Distinguished Unit Citation.

SEPTEMBER 4   At Kunming, China, Brigadier General William H. Tunner is appointed commander of Air Transport Command and he orchestrates the conveyance of thousands of gallons of gasoline and bombs over the "Hump" (Himalayas).

SEPTEMBER 5   Over Germany, Captain William H. Allen, 55th Fighter Group, bags five enemy fighters in a few minutes, becoming an ace. The rest of his flight downed a further 11 aircraft in the same dust up.

SEPTEMBER 8   In a major technological breakthrough, one portending ominous implications for future warfare, the

Germans launch their first V-2 rockets. Suburbs in Paris and London are struck, and heavy damage ensues. The Allies possess no comparable technology.

Over France and Belgium, Ninth Air Force bombers drop leaflets—not bombs—while scores of transports drop supplies and pick up wounded troops as a large aerial supply line to the front deploys in force.

Over Anshun, China, 100 B-29s arrive from Chengtu to bomb the Showa Steel Works again. In retaliation, Japanese bombers stage at night attack against Chengtu's airfields, damaging a B-29 and a C-46.

In England, the Allied high command issues its "Joint British-American Directive on Day Bombing Operations Involving Fighter Cooperation," which solidifies the outline of around-the-clock attacks on Germany's industrial base.

SEPTEMBER 10   At Hagerstown, Maryland, the Fairchild XC-82 cargo plane prototype, which employs twin tail booms, performs its maiden flight. After the war it enters service as the "Flying Boxcar."

Over south central Germany, the Eighth Air Force commits over 1,000 bombers against industrial targets, while aircraft of the Ninth Air Force continue chewing up railroad targets to sever enemy supply lines.

In central France, as forces of Operations OVERLORD and ANVIL/DRAGOON link up, they are supported by 800 transports belonging to the Ninth Air Force.

In the China-Burma-India (CBI) theater, Air Transport Command missions begin averaging 300 flights per day to China bases and back.

SEPTEMBER 11   Chemnitz, Germany, is the object of a 1,000-bomber raid by the Eighth Air Force as factories, motor transport parks, and a jet engine facilities are struck. This is also the last shuttle raid whereby the aircraft are recovered in the Soviet Union.

SEPTEMBER 12 Over Germany, the Luftwaffe hurls 400 fighters against a stream of 800 Eighth Air Force bombers, shooting down 45 aircraft along with 12 P-51s. Though crippled, they remain a dangerous adversary.

SEPTEMBER 13 Over Hungary, Eighth Air Force bombers attack and destroy the Diosgyor Steel Works.

SEPTEMBER 14 Colonel Floyd B. Wood, Major Harry Wexler, and Lieutenant Frank Reckord intentionally fly their Douglas A-20 Havoc into a hurricane to gather meteorological data. They acquire the nickname "Hurricane Hunters."

SEPTEMBER 15 Over Greece, 276 B-17s and B-24s of the Fifteenth Air Force attack military targets in Salamis, Tatoi, Eleusis, and Kalamaki. Meanwhile, escorting P-38s and P-51s swoop down

Paratroopers, planes, and gliders litter the skies during Operation Market-Garden *in September 1944, during which the Allies dropped more than 20,000 paratroopers and landed more than 13,500 glidermen behind German lines in the Netherlands. (Corbis)*

low to bomb and strafe enemy units attempting to withdraw from the region.

SEPTEMBER 16 Over Germany, a stream of Eighth Air Force bombers, escorted by no less than seven fighter groups, savage targets in Hannover, Bremen, and Osnabruck. Other aircraft are detailed to attack targets in Ahlhorn, Mannheim, and Kaiserslautern.

SEPTEMBER 17–30 Over the Netherlands, Operation MARKET GARDEN commences as 1,546 Allied transports and 476 gliders convey 35,000 men of the First Allied Airborne Army near Arnhem to seize the Rhine River bridges. German defenders manage to down 16 B-24s and 21 fighters over the next two weeks.

SEPTEMBER 20 At Farmingdale, New York, the Republic Aircraft Company rolls out its 10,000th P-47 Thunderbolt fighter-bomber. Another 5,000 machines are manufactured over the next 10 months.

SEPTEMBER 21 In France, in order to relieve pressing fuel shortages experienced by ground units, the Eighth Air Force begins delivering gasoline to bases. Within a week, 200 spacious B-24 Liberators are acting as flying fuel pumps.

SEPTEMBER 23 In New Guinea, the Thirteenth Air Force relocates it base of operations to Noemfoor Island from Hollandia. Meanwhile, B-24s of the Seventh Air Force continue pounding Japanese positions on Chichi Jima, Haha Jima, and Ani Jima in the Bonin Islands.

In La Spezia Harbor, Italy, a force of 24 B-25s from the 340th Bomb Group attack and sink the light cruiser *Taranto*.

SEPTEMBER 24 Over Kurabu Cape, Aleutians, B-24s of the Eleventh Air Force are attacked by Japanese fighters, whereupon one damaged Liberator force lands in Soviet territory, and the crew is interned.

SEPTEMBER 28   In China, the Fourteenth Air Force dispatches 100 camera-equipped fighters over targets in southeastern China and Indochina (Southeast Asia).

SEPTEMBER 30   Over Germany, the Eighth Air Force unleashes 850 heavy bombers that strike airfields at Bielefeld, Hamm, and Münster. They are escorted by 13 fighter groups, while 2 additional fighter groups sweep in low over the region.

OCTOBER 1   In Italy, the Fifteenth Air Force reaches its fully authorized strength through the addition of the 5th Photo Group, Reconnaissance. It also possesses 21 heavy bomber groups and 7 fighter groups.

Over China, 18 B-25s from the Fourteenth Air Force bomb Japanese airfields at Tien Ho and White Cloud while over 100 P-40s and P-51s strafe and bomb military targets south of the Yangtze River.

OCTOBER 2   Over Germany, beginning today and continuing over the next 30 days, the Eighth Air Force launches 1,000-bomber raids against varied locales over two 3-day intervals. Airfields, oil production facilities, and aircraft factories remain priority targets, while Cologne is also hard hit. Another six lesser raids include 450 heavy bombers each, while the number of escorting groups numbers between 5 and 17 per mission.

Over Austria, Lieutenant Valmore Beaudrault is credited with shooting down the first Me-262 jet fighter claimed by the Ninth Air Force.

OCTOBER 2–16   Throughout the China-Burma-India (CBI) theater, transport

aircraft of the Tenth Air Force haul supplies and troops to distant points in the region, sometimes accomplishing as many as 250 sorties per day.

OCTOBER 12   Over Bologna, Italy, Operation PANCAKE unfolds as the Twelfth Air Force unleashes 700 heavy bombers, escorted by 160 fighters. The targets sought are ammunition and fuel dumps, repair facilities, and munition factories. This action is undertaken in support of Fifth Army offensive operations in northern Italy.

Over Germany, Lieutenant Chuck Yeager is credited with shooting down five German aircraft in one encounter; though better known as a test pilot, his final wartime tally is 12 victories.

On Saipan, Brigadier General Haywood Hansell personally lands *Joltin' Josie, the Pacific Pioneer*, the first XX Bomber Command B-29 bomber to reach that island. Elements of the 73rd Bomb Wing also arrive throughout the day.

OCTOBER 14   At Chengtu, China, the XX Air Force launches 100 B-29s on a strike against an aircraft factory at Okayama, Formosa (Taiwan). The raid coincides with American actions on Leyte, Philippines.

OCTOBER 15   Over Germany, over 1,000 Eighth Air Force heavy bombers attack marshalling yards and a gas unit plant at Cologne; they are escorted by less than twelve fighter groups. Another two P-47 groups swoop in low to bomb and strafe targets in Hannover and Münster-Kassel.

Aslito Airfield, Saipan, is repaired and enlarged for operations by B-29 Superfortresses. From here the Japanese homeland will be within striking distance.

OCTOBER 17   Over Cologne, Germany, a roused Luftwaffe downs 52 bombers and 15 fighters. Several of these fall to futuristic Me-262s; four of the jets are downed in turn.

OCTOBER 20–24   At Tacloban, Philippines, ground elements of the 308th Bombardment Wing, the Fifth Air Force, and the 475th Fighter Group come ashore with General Douglas A. MacArthur's invasion force to set up shop as quickly as possible for aerial echelons to follow.

OCTOBER 22   Over Ceram, Netherlands East Indies, P-38s of the 12th Fighter Squadron, 18th Fighter Group, drop napalm on oil storage tanks at Boela. At this time the squadron has been staging out from Sansapor, New Guinea.

OCTOBER 24   Over the Hannover-Kassel region of Germany, the Eighth Air Force dispatches 415 P-47s and P-51s to perform tactical fighter-bomber strikes against military targets.

OCTOBER 26   Over China, Fourteenth Air Force B-24s and B-25s strike Japanese shipping and rail yards off the Luichow Peninsula and Hsuchang. During the raid, the Liberator flown by Major Horace S. Carswell is crippled by antiaircraft fire, yet he refuses to abandon his burning craft until his crew bails out. He dies once the bomber crashes into a mountainside, winning a posthumous Congressional Medal of Honor.

OCTOBER 27   At Tacloban, Philippines, 34 P-38 Lightnings of the 9th Fighter Squadron become the first American fighters to operate from the islands since 1942. Major Richard I. Bong, the highest-scoring American ace of World War II, is among them and chalks up several aerial kills.

OCTOBER 27–DECEMBER 31   The Japanese aerial units make 1,050 sorties over Leyte while pilots of the V Fighter

---

Bong, Richard I. (1920–1945)

Army Air Forces pilot. Richard Ira Bong was born in Poplar, Wisconsin, on September 24, 1920, and he was attending Wisconsin State Teacher's College when the United States entered World War II. Bong enlisted in the Army Air Forces, and was initially assigned as an instructor at Luke Field, Arizona. He also underwent flight training in twin-boomed Lockheed P-38 Lightnings and evinced a desire to see combat. In September 1942, Bong arrived in Australia as part of the 9th Fighter Squadron, 49th Fighter Group. He proved himself a dervish in combat, downing his first five Japanese planes by January 1943. Promoted to captain, Bong rotated home the following August to serve as an instructor. He next reported to Fifth Air Force headquarters, New Guinea, in February 1944, although now as the officer in charge of replacement airplanes. The aggressive Bong chafed in this secondary role and, pressing his superiors for combat assignments, he gradually worked his score up to 28 kills. In May 1944, Bong, now the leading American Pacific ace, rotated back home again as a gunnery instructor at Forster Field, Texas.

In October 1944, Bong returned to New Guinea, serving as a gunnery training officer. In between his usual duties, he constantly volunteered for combat missions over Borneo and Leyte Gulf in the Philippines, increasing his score to 40 Japanese aircraft. Bong, now America's ace of aces, was grounded by General George C. Kenney, who ordered him back home for his own safety. Beforehand, General Douglas MacArthur personally awarded him a Congressional Medal of Honor. Bong died on August 6, 1945, when his P-80 Shooting Star flamed out on takeoff over Burbank, California.

Command are credited with 314 confirmed aerial victories and 45 additional probables.

OCTOBER 28   On the Marianas, a small force of B-29s belonging to XXI Bomber Command fly their first mission from when they strike submarine pens on Dublin Island; the aircraft flown by Brigadier General Haywood Hansell aborts due to mechanical difficulties.

OCTOBER 29   Over Leyte, Philippines, the 49th Fighter Group downs its 500th Japanese airplane.

OCTOBER 30   Over Burma, 10 Tenth Air Force B-25s attack bridges at Namhkai, Wuntho, Theygyaung, and Nankan while 50 P-47s are dispatched to perform similar works at Hpao Nam and other locations.

NOVEMBER 1   In Pasadena, California, the new Jet Propulsion Laboratory (JPL) is created at the California Institute of Technology; it serves as the locus of American rocket research.

In England, the Eighth Air Force sorties over 300 heavy bombers against synthetic oil plants at Gelsenkirchen, Germany, the bridge at Rüdesheim, and airfields at Koblenz and Hamm.

Over Tokyo, Japan, an F-13 (reconnaissance version of the B-29) becomes the first American warplane to fly over the city since the Doolittle raid of April 18, 1942.

NOVEMBER 2   Over Germany, a huge air battle erupts over the synthetic fuel plant at Merseburg/Leuna, as 1,100 heavy bombers of the Eighth Air Force run into determined resistance; 40 bombers and 28 fighters are lost, although 150 German aircraft are also claimed. Navigator Lieutenant Robert E. Femoyer, severely wounded by flak, refuses a morphine

injection so that he can complete his bomb run and finally dies from loss of blood; he receives a posthumous Congressional Medal of Honor.

NOVEMBER 3   Fifth Air Force P-38 fighters begin attacking targets throughout the Philippines, particularly on the Celebes and Halmahera. These sorties continue unabated until all Japanese resistance is eliminated.

NOVEMBER 4   Over Germany, the Eighth Air Force unleashes 1,100 B-17s and B-24s, which strike military and industrial targets at Hamburg, Hannover, and Saarbrucken.

In Italy, the Twelfth Air Force launches 300 medium bombers against German lines of communication in the Brenner Pass and along the Po Valley. Four P-47s also strafe a hotel in Milan where Hitler is supposedly staying.

NOVEMBER 5   Over Vienna, Austria, the Fifteenth Air Force launches 500 B-17s and B-24s, escorted by 350 fighters, against the Floridsdorf oil refinery. This turns out to be the Fifteenth's largest single operation directed against a single target.

In the Pacific, 24 B-29s from the XX Air Force lift off from the Marianas to strike Japanese targets on Iwo Jima, Bonin Islands. Another 53 Superfortresses depart Calcutta, India, to bomb the King George VI Graving Dock in Singapore for the first time since 1942.

NOVEMBER 6–DECEMBER 24   Off the Bonin Islands, the Seventh Air Force dispatches B-24s on mining operations to prepare that region for an amphibious invasion in the spring.

NOVEMBER 7   General Henry H. Arnold asks Professor Theodore von Karman to investigate possible future trends in aviation technology and their implications for national defense. His report is ultimately issued as *Towards New Horizons*, which establishes the scientific foundation for the new U.S. Air Force.

NOVEMBER 8   From Saipan, the XXI Bomber Command dispatches 17 B-29s on a strike against Iwo Jima; one Superfortress is lost after it is damaged by phosphorous bombs dropped by Japanese aircraft into its formation.

NOVEMBER 9   The Eighth Air Force commits 1,100 heavy bombers in support of Third Army maneuvers near Metz, Thionville, and Saarbrucken, France; German resistance proves fierce and 40 aircraft are lost. A B-17 flown by Lieutenant Donald J. Gott sustains heavy damage over Saarbrucken, yet he refuses to bail out, in order to save several wounded crewmen by crash-landing in friendly territory; the plane explodes on contact, killing all on board; Gott receives a posthumous Congressional Medal of Honor. Another B-17 flown by copilot Lieutenant William E. Metzger is also crippled over Saarbrucken, he attempts to crash-land to save his gravely injured pilot and radio operator, but all die upon impact; Metzger is also awarded a posthumous Congressional Medal of Honor.

NOVEMBER 10   Over Ormoc Bay, Philippines, the Fifth Air Force unleashes 36 B-25 medium bombers upon Japanese shipping; 3 vessels are sunk.

NOVEMBER 12   To avoid burnout, the combat tour length for fighter pilots is set at 270 flight hours.

NOVEMBER 15   The large Boeing XC-97 cargo plane, based on the B-29 Superfortress, flies for the first time. It enters production in the postwar period as the Stratofreighter.

In light of recent German advances, the Army Ordnance Department commences Project HERMES to research and develop ballistic missiles of it own.

Over Indonesia, Far East Air Forces (FEAF) B-25s and fighter-bombers offer close support to amphibious landings at Mapia Island while B-24s and P-38s strike Japanese positions at Lahug. Other targets in the Celebes and Mindanao, Philippines, are also bombed.

NOVEMBER 16   In eastern France, as the American First and Ninth Armies commence a new offensive, they are supported by 4,000 bombers and 750 fighters, which drop 10,000 tons of bombs. This is the largest single ground-support mission flown to date.

NOVEMBER 18   Over Italy, the Fifteenth Air Force dispatches 680 heavy bombers and 186 P-51 escorts to strike airfields at Aviano, Villafranca di Verona, Udine, and Vicenza.

NOVEMBER 21–25   Over Germany, the Eighth Air Force launches another 1,000-plane raid at oil refineries in Merseburg/Leuna, losing 35 aircraft. Four days later 900 bombers return in poor weather, guided by Pathfinders, and hit the same targets; 65 aircraft become lost in the overcast and make emergency landings on airfields in France.

NOVEMBER 22   A Japanese air raid against Morotai (Indonesia) strikes Far East Air Forces installations on the ground, killing two and wounding fifteen. A further fifteen aircraft are destroyed and eight damaged.

NOVEMBER 24   Over Tokyo, Japan, 88 B-29 heavy bombers under General Haywood S. Hansell of XXI Bomber Command, operating from Guam, Saipan, and Tinian, strike the Musashino Aircraft Factory for the first time since April 18, 1942. The mission is dogged by technical problems and 17 B-29s are forced to abort en route. One B-29 is lost after it is rammed by a fighter, and another ditches once it runs out of fuel.

NOVEMBER 30 Over Germany, synthetic oil plants in Bohlen, Zeitz, Merseburg/Leuna, and Lutzkendorf are struck by 1,200 heavy bombers from the Eighth Air Force. These are escorted by no less than 19 fighter groups, but German flak and fighters are relentless and 41 bombers are lost.

From Saipan, 23 B-24s of the Seventh Air Force make a bombing run over Iwo Jima, Bonin Islands. Another 37 Liberators launched from Angaur also strike Japanese installations on Legaspi.

DECEMBER 1 Over Burma, the Tenth Air Force commits 30 P-47s to support Allied ground forces in the vicinity of Bhamo. Meanwhile, a like number of Thunderbolts strike troop concentrations, supply dumps, and bridges at Myitson, Mingon, and Old Lashio. Transport aircraft also fly 240 supplies sorties to the forward areas.

DECEMBER 1–16 At Camp Irwin, California, technicians from the Jet Propulsion Laboratory (JPL) fire off two-dozen Private A rockets developed over the past 11 months as part of Project ORDCIT.

DECEMBER 5 Over Germany, 500 heavy bombers of the Eighth Air Force and P-47s and P-51s from the Ninth Air Force struggle with 300 German fighters over Berlin and Münster; dozens of aircraft are lost on either side.

DECEMBER 8 In the Pacific, Lieutenant General George Kenney, Far East Air Forces (FEAF), recommends Major

Richard I. Bong for the Congressional Medal of Honor after he downs eight Japanese aircraft on a series of sweeps over Balikpapan, Borneo. His score now stands at 38 kills, making him America's leading ace.

Japanese aerial raids against the Mariana Islands destroy 11 B-29s and damage 43, so the XX Air Force launches 60 of the giant bombers against airfields on Iwo Jima to stop them. By the time the raids stop in February 1945, 11 B-29s are destroyed and 43 more are damaged.

DECEMBER 13 Over Nagoya, Japan, the XX Air Force launches another large B-29 raid against the Mitsubishi aircraft engine factory, inflicting considerable damage.

DECEMBER 15 Over the Bay of Biscay, a Noorduyn C-64 Norseman carrying Major Glenn Miller, director of the Army Air Forces Band, disappears without a trace.

Over western Germany, 300 A-20s, A-26s, and B-26s of the Ninth Air Force attack German troop concentrations, ammunition dumps, and oil storage areas at Heimbach, Wollseifen, Ruthen, and Dorsel. Close support missions are also flown for the 2nd and 99th Infantry Divisions along the Westwall fortifications, and the 78th Infantry Division at Kesternich.

DECEMBER 17 At Wendover Field, Utah, the 509th Composite Group forms under Colonel Paul W. Tibbets, Jr.; this is a highly classified unit tasked with delivering the atomic bomb once it is developed.

Over the Ardennes, Belgium, poor weather grounds most American bombers, but over 1,000 fighters belonging to the Ninth Air Force sortie to provide close air support to hard-pressed Army units in the Battle of the Bulge. All aircraft are then grounded the following day and remain inoperative until the 23rd.

Major Richard I. Bong shoots down his 40th Japanese airplane over Mindoro, Philippines, making him America's top-scoring ace of World War II. Lieutenant General George Kenney immediately grounds him and arranges his transfer back to the United States.

DECEMBER 18 Over Hankow, China, the docks are the object of the first firebombing raid conducted by XX Bomber Command B-29s, assisted by 200 aircraft belonging to the Fourteenth Air Force.

DECEMBER 19 Over Santa Monica, California, fighters of the Fourth Air Force are scrambled after receiving reports that Japanese balloons have been spotted over the city; none are intercepted.

DECEMBER 21 In Washington, D.C., General Henry H. Arnold gains promotion to five-star general of the Army; he is the first and only aviator so decorated.

DECEMBER 23 In Belgium, bad weather lifts sufficiently over the Ardennes region, allowing clouds of A-20 and B-26 bombers from the Ninth Air Force to strike German tank and infantry formations during closing phases of the "Battle of the Bulge"; the Americans lose 31 bombers, but claim to down scores of German aircraft.

DECEMBER 24 Over western Europe, the Eighth Air Force launches 2,000 heavy bombers, escorted by no less than 13 fighter groups, at select targets across Europe, including 11 airfields, 14 communications centers, and 5 cities. The Germans muster 200 fighters and lose approximately 50 in swirling aerial actions. One B-17 piloted by Brigadier General Frederick W. Castle is crippled by German fighters, but he flies on, allowing his crew to bail out; he receives a posthumous Congressional Medal of Honor and Castle Air Force Base, California, is named in his honor.

Over Belgium, fighter-bombers and medium bombers of the Ninth Air Force brave poor weather to fly thousands of sorties in support of the Army's III, VIII, and XII Corps along the southern fringes of the Ardennes. They persist until the U.S. 4th Armored Division breaks the siege of Bastogne.

DECEMBER 26 Over Luzon, Philippines, P-38 fighters sweep over Mabalacat Aerodrome, encountering numerous Japanese fighters. Major Thomas B. McGuire, the Army's second-highest scoring ace, downs four fighters while defending a crippled bomber, raising his tally to 38—second only to Major Richard I. Bong.

DECEMBER 31 Above Germany, 1,200 Eighth Air Force bombers attack a series of refineries, aircraft plants, U-boat yards, and airfields across northern Germany. Over Hamburg, 14 escorting fighter groups tangle with 150 German interceptors, claiming to down 60; 14 bombers are lost to fighters and flak.

Brigadier General Haywood Hansell relocates his XXI Bomber Command headquarters from Saipan to Guam, a sign that the air war is moving ever closer to the Japanese mainland.

This year the Far East Air Forces (FEAF) conducted 163,397 sorties throughout the Pacific region, dropping 92,134 tons of bombs and destroying 2,518 Japanese aircraft. FEAF lost 2,584 aircraft of all kinds, mostly to antiaircraft fire.

1945

JANUARY 1   In England, the Eighth Air Force redesignates its three Bomb Divisions as Air Divisions. Hundreds of sorties are also flown against German troop concentrations and communication lines, despite the bad weather.

Meanwhile, 700 heavy bombers are dispatched to strike Rhine River bridges, rail junctions, and airfields in 10 German cities. The 14 fighter groups flying escort engage 120 German interceptors over Frankfurt/Main and Hannover, claiming 17 kills.

Over Belgium, Holland, and France, the Luftwaffe launches Operation BODENPLATTE, a surprise attack on Allied forward air bases. They manage to destroy around 120 aircraft on the ground only to lose 460 to German antiaircraft crews, who assumed they were enemy formations.

JANUARY 2   Over China, troop carriers attached to the Tenth Air Force fly 546 sorties to resupply troops on the front line; amazingly, this becomes the daily operational average for the rest of the year.

In the Philippines, Far East Air Forces (FEAF) P-38s and A-20s strike Japanese targets around San Fernando Harbor while B-24s pound Clark Field and B-25s blast enemy airfields near Batangas.

JANUARY 3   Over Nagoya, Japan, 57 of 87 B-29s have been equipped with fire-bombs as part of a test-bombing mission. Results are inconclusive, giving the erroneous impression that Japanese fire-prevention systems are working well.

JANUARY 5   In China, Operation GRUB-WORM, the aerial transfer of two Chinese infantry divisions, their headquarters, and all attached units, concludes. It took 1,300 transport sorties to relocate the

force from Burma to the front lines, but was accomplished with the loss of only 3 aircraft.

JANUARY 7   Over northern Luzon, Philippines, the Far East Air Forces (FEAF), in concert with carrier aircraft from the Third Fleet, contributes 130 light and medium bombers to attack Japanese airfields. This is also one of the largest joint missions in the Southwest Pacific campaign.

JANUARY 9   Over the Philippines, the Far East Air Forces (FEAF) continues providing close air support at various points, especially in the Lingayen Gulf region.

Over Iwo Jima, B-24s equipped with H2X bombing equipment attack Japanese airfields near Suribachi Bay.

JANUARY 10   The Thirteen Air Force begins shifting bases of operation from New Guinea to Leyte, Philippines, to support the American offensive there.

JANUARY 11   Over Luzon, Philippines, a reconnaissance version P-51 Mustang (F-6D) piloted by Captain William A. Shomo shoots down seven Japanese aircraft while his wingman bags three; considering that reconnaissance pilots rarely engage in combat, he wins the Congressional Medal of Honor.

JANUARY 17   From Chengtu, China, the XX Bomber Command unleashes 91 B-29 heavy bombers over military targets at Shinchiku, Formosa (Taiwan). This is the last such raid mounted from Chengtu, and by March the force transfers to the Marianas to be closer to Japan. The 58th Bomb Wing, meanwhile, remains active in India and provides tactical help to British

General Curtis E. LeMay orchestrated the highly successful strategic bombing campaign against Japan. (Library of Congress)

forces in Burma, with an occasional raid against Singapore and the East Indies.

JANUARY 20   On Guam, Major General Curtis E. LeMay takes command of the XXI Bomber Command, replacing Brigadier General Haywood S. Hansell. LeMay is expected to take revamp the largely unsatisfactory strategic bombing campaign against Japan. In India, Brigadier General Roger M. Ramey also assumes control of the XX Bomber Command.

JANUARY 22   Over Formosa (Taiwan), Fifth Air Force B-24s and P-38s mount their first air raid against Japanese targets, while other aircraft continue supporting ground operations on Luzon, Philippines.

JANUARY 24   Over Attu, Alaska, fighters of the Eleventh Air Force down an armed Japanese Fu-Go balloon.

Iwo Jima, Bonin Islands, is the object of a bombing campaign by B-24s from the Seventh Air Force and B-29s from the XX Air Force.

B-24s attached to the Far East Air Forces (FEAF) commence a three-week bombing campaign against Japanese positions on Corregidor, Philippines.

JANUARY 25–26   Over Southeast Asia, the XX Bomber Command launches 70 B-29s heavy bombers, which sow mines in Singapore Harbor, Cam Ranh Bay, Pakchan River, and Phan Rang Bay; this is also the largest single mining operation of the entire war.

JANUARY 27   The Twentieth Air Force completes a difficult transfer from Chengtu, China, to bases in India prior to a final move to the Marianas Islands in March.

In the Marianas, the XXI Bomber Command launches 130 B-29 heavy bombers, which strike targets in Tokyo, Japan. Five of the giant craft are lost to fighters while a further four ditch or crash-land due to mechanical failures. American gunners also claim to have shot down several enemy fighters.

JANUARY 28   Over Germany, this being the third anniversary of the Eighth Air Force's founding, a 1,000-plane air raid is launched over selected targets. By this date it has flown 250,000 bomber and 210,000 fighter sorties, dropped 518,000 tons of bombs, and shot down 13,000 enemy aircraft.

Transport aircraft in the China-Burma-India theater (CBI) continue averaging 500 sorties every day over the Hump (Himalayas), despite the fact that the Burma Road is reopened. The recent departure of B-29s based at Chengtu, China, allows more supplies to be available to the Tenth and Fourteenth Air Forces operating there.

The famous B-17 formed the backbone of the American strategic bomber fleet in European skies. (Library of Congress)

JANUARY 31   Over Austria, good weather allows the Fifteenth Air Force to put over 760 B-17s and B-24s over oil refineries at Moosbierbaum and marshalling yards at Graz and Manibor. The former is struck once more by 300 bombers on the following day.

FEBRUARY 1   Over Germany, the Eighth Air Force hurls 600 heavy bombers against three airfields at Mannheim, Ludwigshafen, and Krefeld while 6 fighter groups provide escort.

FEBRUARY 3   From England, the Eighth Air Force launches the largest air raid of the war to date with 1,200 B-17s and B-24s against targets in Berlin and Magdeburg, dropping 2,266 tons of bombs. They are escorted by over 900 escort fighters, most of which accompany them to Berlin and back.

In the Marshall Islands, B-29s of XXI Bomber Command attack industrial targets in Kobe, Japan, dropping 159 tons of bombs and 13.6 tons of incendiaries; 1,039 buildings and structures are destroyed.

FEBRUARY 4   From the Marianas, the XX Air Force launches 100 B-29 heavy bombers against targets in Kobe and Natsusaka; nearly 100 fighters rise to oppose them, but only 1 B-29 is lost, while 35 are damaged.

FEBRUARY 5   Over Italy, the Twelfth Air Force launches 270 medium bombers against German targets in the Po Valley region; an additional 730 heavy bombers from the Fifteenth Air Force fly across the Alps to strike oil refineries at Regensburg. Both operations are escorted by far-ranging P-38 and P-51 fighters.

On Corregidor, Philippines, Japanese defenses are struck by a force of 60 B–24s from the Far East Air Forces while B–25s provide close air support for ground troops.

FEBRUARY 7 In San Diego, California, the Consolidated Vultee XP-81 prototype performs its maiden flight. This innovative design employs a turboprop engine in the nose and a turbo jet in the tail, but does not progress beyond the experimental stage.

FEBRUARY 10 Over Ota, Japan, the Nakajima aircraft factory is the target of 84 B-29s heavy bombers from the XXI Bomber Command; in the absence of fighter escorts the defenders shoot down 12 of the giant bombers.

View of the wreckage of Dresden, Germany after it was firebombed by the Allies in 1945 during World War II. The bombing, which targeted the civilian population, was one of the most devastating aerial raids in history and was mounted in retaliation for German V-2 rocket attacks on London. Four years after the blaze, the city still appeared as a wasteland; most of its buildings were gutted, including many 1,000-year-old structures that had been completely destroyed. It took Germany decades to rebuild the city. (Library of Congress)

FEBRUARY 12–14 Over Iwo Jima, Bonin Islands, two dozen B-29s attack Japanese antiaircraft batteries while other aircraft fly reconnaissance missions for the U.S. Navy. The island's defenses are also struck by tactical aircraft from the Seventh Air Force, softening it up for the impending invasion.

FEBRUARY 14 Over Germany, the historic city of Dresden, having suffered from a destructive nighttime raid by the Royal Air Force, is struck again by waves of American bombers. The ensuing firestorm flattens 1,600 square acres and kills an estimated 250,000 people—more than the destruction of Hiroshima and Nagasaki combined. The attack comes as revenge for continuing V-2 attacks against London.

FEBRUARY 16 Over Corregidor, Philippines, C–47 transports drop 2,000 parachutists while tactical aircraft of the Far East Air Forces (FEAF) strike targets in and around that island in support of the invasion there.

In China, Tenth Air Force transports exceed their own record by flying 600 sorties on this day, a pace they will maintain until war's end. Ultimately, the Air Transport Command delivers 700,000 tons of supplies at a cost of 910 aircrew.

FEBRUARY 19 On the Marianas, and in an attempt to draw Japanese reinforcements away from Iwo Jima, the XX Air Force launches 150 B-29 heavy bombers to strike at targets in and around Tokyo, Japan; enemy fighters shoot down 6 bombers.

FEBRUARY 20 In Washington, D.C., Secretary of War Henry Stimson authorizes construction of a rocket testing area at White Sands, New Mexico. He had been warned that the Soviets would probably win a postwar race to build long-range ballistic missiles.

FEBRUARY 22–23   Over Western Europe, Operation CLARION unfolds as fighters and bombers of the Eighth, Ninth, Twelfth, and Fifteenth Air Forces systematically destroying German transportation networks in occupied territories, including Holland, Belgium, and Italy. Collectively, they unleash over 9,000 aircraft to hit targets in occupied Europe over the next 24 hours. On the following day additional fighter sorties are launched to cover the Rhine River crossings.

FEBRUARY 24   Over Singapore, 105 B-29 heavy bombers are launched by XX Bomber Command against the Empire Dock area. The aircraft carry incendiary weapons, and the resulting firestorm burns 40 percent of all warehousing. This is also the last time the India-based B-29s sortie in such large numbers.

FEBRUARY 25   The Bell XP-83 turbojet fighter, essentially a scaled-up version of the earlier P-59 Airacomet, makes its initial flight; it is not pressed into production.

In Washington, D.C., the Pentagon hatches Project PAPERCLIP, which is designed to recruit German rocket scientists after the war.

From the Marianas Islands, the XXI Bomber Command throws three bomb groups of B-29s against targets in the Tokyo area. This is the largest raid mounted by the XXI to date and the first employing incendiaries at high altitude. Over 15 square miles of the downtown section are burned out.

In Burma, B-25s of the Tenth Air Force provide close air support to British and Chinese forces advancing.

FEBRUARY 26   In the Pacific, a B-24 Liberator carrying Lieutenant General Millard F. "Miff" Harmon, commander of Army Air Forces, Pacific Ocean Area

(AAFPAC), disappears while flying between Kwajalein and Hawaii.

FEBRUARY 27   In India, the last remaining B-29 wing begins deploying to the Marianas Islands; the movement continues until June 6.

FEBRUARY 28   In Washington, D.C., General Henry H. Arnold reveals the existence of the new Lockheed P-80 Shooting Star. This is the first American jet fighter to reach operational status, but it arrives too late to see service in the war.

Over Germany, the Eighth Air Force dispatches 1,104 bombers and 737 escort fighters to hit enemy transportation targets; P-51 and P-47 groups also perform low-level attacks against airfields and factories.

MARCH 1   Over Austria, 630 B-24s and B-17s from the Fifteenth Air Force bomb the oil refinery at Moosbierbaum with a 200-strong fighter escort, while 47 other P-38s make strafing runs against rail traffic around Graz and Vienna.

MARCH 4   On Iwo Jima, Bonin Islands, the first damaged B-29 Superfortress makes an emergency landing on the airfield while Marines continue battling for control of the island; before the war ends, thousands of American lives are saved by the airfield.

MARCH 6   On Iwo Jima, Bonin Islands, 28 P-51 Mustangs and 12 P-61 Black Widows of the Seventh Air Force arrive to begin fighter escort service for B-29 formations.

MARCH 9   In the Marianas, Lieutenant General Curtis E. LeMay of XXI Bomber Command strips his B-29s of armament and loads them with 2,000 tons of incendiaries, then launches a devastating "fire raid" against Tokyo, Japan. Nearly 16 square miles, one-fourth of the city, is destroyed, and 100,000 casualties inflicted—more than Hiroshima and Nagasaki; Japanese defenses down 14 of the giant bombers. To enhance effectiveness and reduce casualties, the raid was conducted from altitude between 4,000 feet and 9,200 feet. It is considered one of the most devastating attacks in aerial history.

MARCH 11–12 Over Germany, a force of 1,000 heavy bombers strikes the town of Essen, Germany, dropping a record total of 4,378 tons of bombs.

The XX Air Force unleashes 285 B-29 heavy bombers against industrial targets in Nagoya, Japan, dropping incendiaries at low altitude at night with devastating effect.

MARCH 13 Over central Burma, P-47s and P-38s of the Tenth Air Force continue providing close air support to the Chinese 50th Division, then driving along the Namtu River.

Osaka, Japan is struck by 274 B-29s of the Twentieth Air Force; incendiaries destroy eight square miles in the city center.

MARCH 14 Over the Balkans, the Fifteenth and Twelfth Air Forces dispatch heavy bombers to Hungary and Yugoslavia to assist the advancing Red Army; P-38s and P-51s also attack targets in Austria.

MARCH 16 Over Kobe, Japan, 300 B-29 heavy bombers belonging to XXI Bomber Command firebomb industrial targets. This is the largest raid mounted by the XX Air Force and the 2,300 tons of ordnance delivered burns down one-fifth of the city.

MARCH 18 Over Germany, the Eighth Air Force launches 1,250 heavy bombers

and 670 fighters against Berlin's transportation network, dropping 3,000 tons in the process; this is also the largest daylight air raid of the entire war.

Over Nagoya, Japan, the XXI Bomber Command hurls 300 B-29 heavy bombers against industrial targets, again flown from low altitude with devastating effect.

MARCH 21 Over Reno, Nevada, a P-63 Kingcobra shoots down a Japanese Fu-Go balloon that had drifted; the fighter refueled in order to reach the target area.

Over Rutland, Germany, a P-51 Mustang flown by Lieutenant John Kirk espies a German Me-262 jetfighter as it dives through a B-17 formation. Kirk kicks his wing over and pursues, disabling his adversary and making him bail out.

MARCH 24 Across Wesel, Germany, Operation PLUNDER–VARSITY unfolds as 1,000 heavy bombers from the Eighth and Ninth Air Forces strike at rail yards, flak positions, and communications systems in support of the Rhine River crossings.

To facilitate the Allied crossing of the Rhine River, 2,000 transports drop two airborne divisions under Major General Matthew Ridgway near Wesel, Germany; 50 aircraft and 11 gliders are destroyed.

Over Germany, 150 heavy bombers from the Fifteenth Air Force attack Berlin, and drop 150 tons of bombs for the first time.

MARCH 27–28 One hundred B-29 heavy bombers depart the Marianas on their first mine-laying mission in the Shimonoseki Strait between Honshu and Kyushu, Japan. Simultaneously, another 150 B-29s strike targets on Okinawa, Ryukyu Islands, which is slated for a major invasion.

MARCH 29–30 In India, XX Bomber Command launches it final mission when

24 B-29s attack oil fields on Bukum Field, Singapore, at night.

MARCH 31 Over Omura and Tachiari, Japan, 137 B-29 heavy bombers of XX Bomb Group strike industrial targets at as a diversion for the upcoming invasion of Okinawa.

APRIL At the Aberdeen Proving Ground, Maryland, Dr. Theodore von Karman begins testing the concept of swept-back wings in a supersonic wind tunnel for the first time.

APRIL 1 Over Burma, Tenth Air Force B-25s attack Japanese rear areas and lines of communication while transports fly 478 sorties as the British 36th Division pushes down the railroad from Mandalay to Rangoon.

APRIL 1–13 At Fort Bliss, Texas, JPL technicians test launch 17 Private F Rockets within the Hueco Range.

APRIL 2 Over Japan, the XX Air Force unleashes a large force of B-29 heavy bombers that mine waters around Kure and Hiroshima harbors, and also bomb the Nakajima aircraft factory near Tokyo.

APRIL 4 In Burma, a YR-4 helicopter of the Air Jungle Rescue Detachment, Tenth Air Force, retrieves a PT-19 pilot down in the jungle.

APRIL 4–11 Over Germany, the Eighth Air Force unleashes 1,000 heavy bombers at industrial, transportation, and communication targets in several concerted attacks. The Nazi national infrastructure is eroding from the constant bombardment.

APRIL 7 At Iwo Jima, the XX Air Force is finally able to dispatch 91 P-51 Mustangs as fighter escorts on a raid by 280 B-29s

against the Japanese mainland. The fighters claim to shoot down 21 opposing aircraft.

APRIL 10 Over Germany, a force of 50 German Me-262 jet fighters shoot down 10 American bombers near Berlin; this is the largest single loss to enemy jets during the war. Conversely, turret gunners and fighter escorts claim to have downed 20 German jets.

APRIL 12 Over Koriyama, Japan, Staff Sergeant Henry E. Erwin picks up a phosphorous smoke flare that had backfired into his B-29 and tosses it out the navigator's window. He suffers severe third-degree burns, but survives and wins a Congressional Medal of Honor; he is one of only four enlisted airmen so honored.

APRIL 13 Over the Aleutian Islands, Alaska, P-38s and P-40s of the Eleventh Air Force intercept and shoot down nine explosive Fu-Go balloons.

Over Japan, a night raid by 330 B-29 heavy bombers belonging to the XX Air Force strikes industrial targets around Tokyo.

APRIL 15 Over Germany, 850 bombers from the Eighth Air Force drop napalm weapons on German fortifications and other targets as an experiment. However, these weapons prove ineffective delivered from high altitude and the attempt is discontinued.

In northern Italy, the Fifteenth Air Force dispatches 830 B-17s and B-24s against German supply and communication targets amply escorted by P-38s. Other fighters provide close air support for units of the Fifth Army and they continue advancing. The 1,412 sorties executed and tons of bombs dropped in this 24-hour period are a record for the Fifteenth.

Over Japan, the Japanese cities of Tokyo and Kawasaki are struck by 300 B-29 heavy bombers during the night.

In Los Angeles, California, the North American XF-82 Twin Mustang prototype flies for the first time.

APRIL 16 From Iwo Jima, P-51 Mustangs attack ground targets on the Japanese mainland for the first time. They are guided to and from Kanoya by a B-29 accompanying them for that purpose.

APRIL 17–MAY 11 Bombing priorities of the XX Air Force are shifted from strategic targets on the mainland to tactical airfields on Kyushu and Shikoku, from which waves of kamikaze attacks are launched against the American fleet off Okinawa.

APRIL 21–26 In Italy, A-20s and B-26s from the Twelfth Air Force maul German units retreating up through the Po Valley, dropping bridge spans and destroying 1,000 vehicles. These attacks severely infringe upon the enemy's ability to retreat.

APRIL 24–25 Over Germany, a P-47 flown by Lieutenant Raymond L. Knight accounts for 14 aircraft during strafing attacks at numerous aerodromes. When Knight's own aircraft is damaged by flak on the second day of attacks, he refuses to abandon his wingman and crashes into a mountainside; he wins a posthumous Congressional Medal of Honor.

APRIL 25 Eighth Air Force B-17s and B-24s hit armament works at Pilsen-Skoda, Czechoslovakia, and Traunstein, Germany; this is the last time they reduce industrial targets to rubble.

APRIL 26 Over Germany, Eighth Air Force fighters sweep the skies clean of enemy fighters as they raid Luftwaffe installations; a record 74 German aircraft are brought down in one day.

APRIL 27 The authorized strength of bomber groups is reduced from 68 to 48 planes, while fighter groups shrink from 96 to 75 machines. This is the first step towards postwar demobilization.

MAY 1 Over Austria, B-17s of the Fifteenth Air Force ignore poor flying conditions and strike marshalling yards at Salzburg, Austria. They are escorted, as usual, by swarms of P-51s and P-38s. This is also the final sortie by the Fifteenth Air Force during the war.

In Chungking, China, Lieutenant General George E. Stratemeyer assumes command of the Tenth and Fourteenth Air Forces as head of Army Air Forces China Theater, and he directs medium bombers and fighters to interdict and harass Japanese ground units as they withdraw from southern China.

MAY 1–7 Over the Netherlands, Operation CHOWHOUND unfolds as 400 Eighth Air Force bombers deliver 8,000 tons of food to starving citizens in the Netherlands. An agreement had been reached with the Germans to proceed without interference.

MAY 2 In Germany, several missile engineers, including Wernher von Braun, turn themselves over to the Americans near the Austrian border. Many are secretly relocated to Fort Bliss, Texas, to facilitate the transfer of V-2 technology to the United States. This clandestine move is essential seeing how the Red Army has occupied the German rocket test grounds at Peenemunde. During the war, the Germans fired off an estimated 20,000 V weapons, including 2,700 V-2 weapons against England and Western Europe.

MAY 3   Over Czechoslovakia, the 9th Bombardment Division makes its final raid when 132 A-26 Invaders strike the Stod ammunition plant.

Once Rangoon, Burma, is recaptured by Allied forces, the Tenth Air Force disengages and concentrates its assets at Piardoba, India. Only a single P-38 squadron remains behind to patrol and protect the Burma Road into southern China.

MAY 8   Over Western Europe, all combat missions halt, although the Twelfth Air Force continues flying evacuation and supply missions. Aircraft of the Ninth Air Force also make "demonstration missions" over previously hostile target areas and liberated concentration camps.

MAY 9   In Europe, the Air Tactical Command (ATC) commences Projects GREEN and WHITE to relocate personnel and equipment, respectively, back to the United States.

MAY 10   In England, Lieutenant General James H. Doolittle departs the Eighth Air Force and is reassigned to Army Air Forces Headquarters in Washington, D.C.; his replacement is Major General William E. Kepner.

Over Japan, a force of B-24s from the Eleventh Air Force successfully raids enemy shipping at Kataoka naval base, sinking several vessels. A force of 16 B-25s based on Attu, Aleutian Islands, also attacks Japanese vessels within their grasp.

MAY 14   Over Nagoya, Japan, the XX Air Force launches 472 B-29 heavy bombers from four complete bomb groups (58th, 73rd, 313th, and 314th) against industrial targets; 11 aircraft are lost.

MAY 16   Over Luzon, Philippines, 100 P-38s from the Far East Air Forces

(FEAF) make the largest napalm attack of the entire war by striking Japanese targets in the Ipo Dam area.

MAY 17   478 B-29 heavy bombers strike southern Nagoya, Japan, in the predawn darkness.

MAY 18   On Tinian, the advanced echelon of the 509th Composite Group deploys and begins setting up for operations. Their purpose is to drop atomic bombs on Japan if the government refuses to surrender.

MAY 19   Hamamatsu, Japan, succumbs to 272 B-29 heavy bombers belonging to the XX Air Force.

MAY 23–24   Over Japan, the XX Air Force dispatches 562 B-29 heavy bombers against industrial targets on the west side of Tokyo harbor. This is also the largest single B-29 raid of the war; 17 bombers are lost.

MAY 25   Wartime production of American military aircraft is slashed by 30 percent as total victory approaches.

Tokyo, Japan, is raided again by 464 B-29 heavy bombers of the XX Air Force, and 26 aircraft go down; this is the largest single loss suffered by B-29s during the war. Meanwhile, the VII Fighter Command on Iwo Jima is assigned to the XX Air Force.

MAY 29   Over Japan, the XX Air Force resumes firebombing attacks by dispatching 454 B-29 heavy bombers against targets in Yokohama, Japan; nine square miles of the downtown section are completely destroyed. The mission is escorted by 190 P-51s from VII Fighter Command on Iwo Jima; stiff resistance claims 7 bombers and 3 fighters.

Aerial view of Kobe docks during an air raid using 500 B-29 bombers. Smoke obscures most of the city, with more bombs falling, 1945. (Corbis)

MAY 31   The Army Air Forces receives the last models of the 18,188 B-24 Liberators constructed during World War II. This is the most numerous American warplane ever built, and several hundred also serve in the Navy as PB4Y Privateers.

JUNE 1   Osaka, Japan, is the target of 458 B-29 heavy bombers of the XX Air Force, of which 10 are shot down. The escort of 148 fighters from VII Fighter Command is disrupted by heavy turbulence and only a handful accompany the bombers; 27 are lost through collisions.

Over China, six B-25s from the Fourteenth Air Force strike the Sinsiang rail yards while four B-25s and four P-47s attack the bridge north of Linmingkuan.

JUNE 5   Over Japan, the XX Air Force launches 473 B-29 heavy bombers loaded with incendiaries against targets in Kobe, and four square miles of the city is reduced to ashes; 11 bombers are shot down.

JUNE 7   Osaka, Japan is the objective XX Air Force B-29s; this is also the first mission to utilize radar bombing technology and 55,000 buildings are destroyed. Meanwhile, the Shimonoseki Strait is mined by other aircraft.

JUNE 9   Over Japan, factories in Akashi, Nagoya, and Narao are struck by a force of 110 B-29s from the XXI Air Force.

Over the Kamchatka Peninsula, Soviet Union, a B-25 belonging to the Eleventh Air Force is downed by Soviet anti-aircraft fire while another is damaged and makes a forced landing at Petropavlovsk. This is the first recorded incident of Russian harassment of American aircraft.

JUNE 11   On Tinian, specially modified B-29 aircraft (Silverplate) belonging to the top secret 509th Composite Group begin arriving. These aircraft have modified propellers fitted, gun turrets removed, and special radio and monitoring equipment installed.

JUNE 15   Osaka, Japan, is again hit by the 44 B-29 bombers of the XX Air Force, who conduct the final firebombing of the war against a large city.

JUNE 17–18   The XX Air Force switches targeting priorities by sending 450 B-29 bombers loaded with incendiaries against smaller Japanese cities such as Omuta, Hamamatsu, Yokkaichi, and Kagoshima. Other aircraft sow the waters off Kobe and Shimonoseki with mines.

Seventh Air Force P-47 and P-61 fighters begin day and night intruder missions over Kyushu and the Ryukyu Islands.

JUNE 19   At Wright Field, Ohio, Dr. Frank L. Wattendorf of the Army Air Forces Scientific Advisory Group suggests that a new aeronautical research center be constructed near cheaper sources of electricity. Its principal activity will be the development of ballistic missiles and supersonic aircraft; in 1950 it emerges as the Arnold Engineering Development Center, Tullahoma, Tennessee.

JUNE 19–20   Over Japan, the XX Air Force dispatches B-29 heavy bombers against Toyohashi, Fukuoka, and Shizuoka, while mining operations continue around the mainland.

JUNE 22   Over Borneo, heavy bombers attached to the Far East Air Forces (FEAF) strike Japanese positions at Balikpapan in anticipation of an Allied landing there.

The naval arsenal at Kure, Japan, is the object of 300 B-29s from the XX Air Force.

JUNE 25   At White Sands, New Mexico, construction begins on a new missile proving ground. Over the ensuing months, dozens of captured German V-2 rockets will be launched as the Americans begin constructing their own liquid-fueled weapons.

JUNE 26   Over Japan, the XX Air Force dispatches 450 B-29 heavy bombers against industrial targets in the city of Tsu; this time the target is oil refineries instead of urban areas.

JUNE 28–29   487 B-29 heavy bombers of the XX Air Force strike targets in Okayama, Sasebo, Moji, and Nobeoka, Japan, with incendiary bombs.

JUNE 30   On Tinian, Mariana Islands, planes and crews of the 509th Composite Group begin training missions with flight profiles closely mimicking an atomic bomb strike. These entail dropping 10,000-pound practice bombs affectionately called pumpkins.

An official summary of wartime production reveals that 297,000 aircraft were manufactured in the United States between July 1940 and July 1945.

JULY 1   Over Japan, the XX Air Force unleashes 530 B-29 heavy bombers loaded with incendiaries against industrial targets in Ube, Kure, Shimonoseki, and Kumamoto, Japan. The aerial mining campaign also continues in Japanese waters.

Fighters and bombers of the Far East Air Forces (FEAF) supply close air support to Australian units as the landing at Balikpapan, Borneo, unfolds. B-24s, B-25s, and P-38s continually attack enemy airfields and troop concentrations.

On Okinawa, the Seventh Air Force unleashes 33 B-25s, which sweep north and bomb Chiran Airfield on Kyushu, Japan. Meanwhile, VII Fighter Command launches 84 P-51s, which bomb and strafe targets at Kasumigaura, Itami, Hamamatsu, and Nagano.

JULY 3   In the Pacific, the Fifth Air Force commits its first fighter sweeps over the Japanese mainland.

Over Japan, the XX Air Force dispatches 560 B-29 heavy bombers loaded with incendiaries against industrial targets in Kochi, Himeji, Takamatsu, and Tokushima.

JULY 6   Over Japan, the XX Air Force launches 517 B-29 heavy bombers to firebomb industrial targets in Chiba, Akashi, Shimizu, and Kofu.

In China, command of all Army Air Forces passes to General George E. Stratemeyer.

JULY 9   The cities of Sendai, Sakai, Gifu, and Wakayama, Japan, are firebombed by XX Air Force B-29s, while an additional 60 aircraft hit the oil refinery at Yokkaichi.

JULY 12   Over Japan, 453 B-29 heavy bombers is launched by the XX Air Force to firebomb Utsunomiya, Ichinomiya, Tsuruga, and Uwajima, while a further 53 aircraft strike petroleum centers at Kawasaki.

JULY 13   In New Mexico, the White Sands Proving Ground opens as a center of rocket research and development.

JULY 14   In the Pacific, the Seventh Air Force is formally assigned as part of Far East Air Forces (FEAF). The entire force relocates to Okinawa with the next two weeks.

JULY 16   At Harmon Field, Guam, Major General Curtis LeMay gains appointment as commander of the XX Air Force; previously it had been controlled by the Joints Chief of Staff (JCS) and General of the Army Henry H. Arnold. General Carl A. Spaatz also assumes control of the U.S. Army Strategic Air Force in the Pacific.

Over Japan, the XX Air Force directs 466 B-29 heavy bombers against Numazu, Oita, Kuwana, and Hiratsuka.

Near Alamogordo, New Mexico, a seminal moment of human history unfolds as American scientists explode the "Gadget," the first atomic bomb, under the direction of physicist J. Robert Oppenheimer. The total yield is an impressive 19 kilotons (19,000 tons of TNT) while the trademark "mushroom cloud" soars to 35,000 feet. This is also the prototype for the "Fat Man" bomb that will be employed against Nagasaki, Japan.

JULY 19–20   Over Japan, 420 B-29 heavy bombers from the XX Air Force strikes oil facilities at Amagasaki, Japan, along with cities of Fukui, Hitachi, Chosi, and Okazaki.

JULY 20   At North Field, Tinian, B-29s of the top secret 509th Composite Group conduct military operations to gain experience over target areas in Japan for the forthcoming atomic bomb. They are also trying to condition the Japanese to get used to observing small groups of B-29s overhead, as if they were reconnaissance aircraft.

JULY 24   Over Japan, 570 B-29 heavy bombers from the XX Air Force strike at industrial targets at Hando, Nagoya, and Takarazuka. Osaka, Tsu, and Kawana are likewise hit.

JULY 26   At Potsdam, Germany, President Harry S. Truman, Prime Minister

Winston Churchill, and Jiang Jieshi issue an ultimatum for Japan to surrender immediately or face "utter destruction."

At Tinian, Marianas, the cruiser *Indianapolis* drops off components for the first atomic bomb, or "Little Boy." The unit is then assembled and delivered to the 509th Composite Group there.

JULY 26–27 Three hundred fifty B-29 heavy bombers from the XX Air Force strike targets at Matsuyama, Tokuyama, and Omuta, Japan.

JULY 28 In New York City, a B-25 Mitchell bomber accidently crashes into the 79th floor of the Empire State Building during foggy weather; 19 people are killed and 29 injured.

Over Japan, the XX Air Force unleashes 471 B-29 heavy bombers against Tsu, Aomori, Ichinomiya, Ujiyamada, Ogaki, and Uwajima. The oil refineries at Shimotsu are also singled out by a force of 76 additional bombers. Despite this pounding, the Japanese government belligerently fails to respond to the Potsdam ultimatum, thereby ensuring that atomic bombs will have to be dropped.

JULY 29 Far East Air Forces (FEAF) aircraft from Okinawa and Ie Shima are unleashed against numerous targets on the Japanese mainland; Douglas A-26 Invaders debut in the Pacific by raiding a naval base and engine works in Nagasaki.

AUGUST 1 Over Edwards Air Force Base, California, the YP-80 Shooting Star jet prototypes easily move past slower fighter escorts and successfully "attack" bombers in mock air battles.

Over Japan, the XX Air Force dispatches a record 825 B-29 bombers from bases in the Marianas, which unload a record 6,520 tons of bombs on Hachioji, Toyama, Nagaoka, and Mito. A further

27 bombers drop mines throughout the Shimonoseki Strait. This is the largest single B-29 sortie of the war but, to lessen losses, the raids are conducted at night.

Over Indonesia, B-24 bombers from the Far East Air Forces (FEAF) strike Japanese targets along Makassar Strait, while 50 B-24s are dispatched to hit targets at Nagasaki, Japan. No less than 80 P-47s also bomb and strafe railroad bridges and other targets at Sendai.

AUGUST 2 In Washington, D.C., President Harry S. Truman signs the top secret operational orders to drop an atomic device on the city of Hiroshima, southern Honshu, Japan. This is also the headquarters of Japanese units defending the large island of Kyushu. In light of continued Japanese belligerence, he feels he has no choice.

On Guam, Major General Nathan F. Twining is appointed commander of the Twentieth Air Force while Major General Curtis E. LeMay serves of chief of staff with U.S. Strategic Air Forces, Pacific.

AUGUST 3 On Okinawa, VII Fighter Command launches 100 P-51 Mustangs on a major raid over Tokyo, Japan, strafing and bombing airfields and railways.

AUGUST 5 From Luzon, Philippines, the Far East Air Forces (FEAF) commences a widespread bombing campaign against Kyushu, Japan, involving 330 aircraft.

AUGUST 5–6 As 470 XX Air Force B-29 heavy bombers strike targets in Saga, Maebashi, Imabari, and Nishinomiya-Mikage, a further 100 aircraft are detailed to eliminate the coke processing plant in Ube.

On Okinawa, the VII Fighter Command is transferred to the XX Air Force for the duration of the war.

AUGUST 6   Over Burbank, California, Major Richard I. Bong, America's "Ace of Aces," dies when his Lockheed P-80 Shooting Star flames out on takeoff, and he ejects at low altitude.

Over Hiroshima, southern Honshu, the atomic bomb christened the "Little Boy" weapon, packing 20 kilotons (20,000 tons) of TNT, is delivered by Colonel Paul W. Tibbets, 508th Composite Group, whose B-29, christened *Enola Gay*, executes the difficult mission flawlessly. Two other B-29s accompany the flight to take photographs and drop measuring equipment. An estimated 70,000 people perish, and the devastation shocks the Japanese public, but militarists controlling the government refuse to capitulate. Humanity has nonetheless crossed an important threshold.

Atomic bomb cloud begins to mushroom over Hiroshima on August 6, 1945, just two minutes after the explosion. This attack, plus the subsequent bombing of Nagasaki a few days later, prompted the Japanese government to surrender unconditionally. (Corel)

On Iwo Jima, the XX Air Force commits 100 P-51 Mustangs to strike targets in and around Tokyo, Japan.

Over Japan, Far East Air Forces (FEAF) aircraft strike targets in Kyushu, and the southern Korean coast; they continue doing so until the end of hostilities.

AUGUST 7   Over Japan, as XX Air Force B-29s strike industrial targets in Kyushu, they are escorted by new, long-range P-47N fighters of the Far East Air Forces (FEAF).

AUGUST 8   In Virginia, scientists working at the NACA Langley Memorial Aeronautical Library publish an essay suggesting that an aircraft powered by atomic engines may one day be able to circumnavigate the globe several times without landing to refuel. Incredibly, they predict it would be powered by a fuel source no larger than a brick.

Over Japan, the combined wrath of Far East Air Forces (FEAF) and the XX Air Force is unleashed against the Nippon Oil Refinery in Kyushu, while a further 60 B-29s hit targets that evening in Tokyo and Fukuyama.

AUGUST 9   To force Japan's surrender and spare that nation, and the United States, the prospect of a horrifically costly conventional invasion, President Harry S. Truman orders a second atomic bomb dropped on Kokura. However, cloud cover forces the B-29 bomber *Bock's Car* under Major Charles W. Sweeney to drop the "Fat Man" weapon against Nagasaki, which kills 35,000 people and devastates the city. Unlike the previous mission, Sweeney is plagued by technical glitches like a faulty fuel pump that force him to make an emergency landing on Okinawa.

Over Japan, 95 B-29 heavy bombers are dispatched by the XX Air Force

Spaatz, Carl A. (1891–1974)

Army Air Forces general. Carl Andrew Spaatz was born in Boyertown, Pennsylvania, passed through the U.S. Military Academy in 1914, and in 1916 switched over to aviation. During World War I, he served as an instructor at Issoudun, France, with his two most successful students being Frank Luke and Eddie Rickenbacker. Spaatz also managed to join a British unit against orders, shot down two German planes, and crash-landed after running out of fuel; he received a Distinguished Service Cross and a severe reprimand. On January 1–7, 1929, he joined Ira C. Eaker and Elwood Quesada in setting a nonstop endurance record over Los Angeles that covered 11,000 miles and required 41 in-flight refuelings. In 1935 Spaatz attended the Command and General Staff School at Fort Leavenworth, Kansas, and in 1940 he arrived in England to observe the Battle of Britain first-hand, which convinced him of America's inferiority in terms of aviation.

During World War II, Spaatz functioned as commander of American air power in Europe, and he reached an agreement with the Royal Air Force for around-the-clock raids against German industry. After a stint in North Africa as a temporary lieutenant general, Spaatz returned to England in January 1944 as head of the Strategic Air Force in Europe. In concert with General James H. Doolittle, he advanced the strategy of allowing fighter escorts to concentrate on destroying the Luftwaffe. Spaatz became a general as of March 1945, and he was the Army Air Forces' last commander following the retirement of General Henry H. Arnold. He died in Washington, D.C., on July 14, 1974, a major aerial architect of victory in World War II.

to strike the Nippon Oil Refinery near Amagasaki. During this mission the Superfortesses are armed with 20,648 pounds of bombs and incendiaries apiece.

AUGUST 10 In China, command of the Fourteenth Air Force passes from Major General Claire L. Chennault to Major General Charles B. Stone.

In Baltimore, Maryland, American rocket pioneer Dr. Robert H. Goddard dies. He launched the first liquid-fueled rocket back in 1926 and, while his experiments were ignored at home, the Germans were keen to incorporate his research efforts into their own.

AUGUST 12 Over China, aircraft of the Fourteenth Air Force attack Japanese troop convoys moving through the Changsha corridor.

AUGUST 13 Over Japan, six B–24s belonging to the Eleventh Air Force make that

unit's final bomb run of the war by striking targets at Kashiwabara by radar.

AUGUST 14–15 Over Japan, the XX Air Force mounts its largest sortie ever—754 bombers and 169 fighters—on a final wave of bombing raids against the Japanese mainland. Targets at Hikari and Osaka are struck. The P–51s complete their mission by attacking airfields en route to returning to Iwo Jima. That night 160 B–29s make the final incendiary raid of the war by attacking Kumagaya and Isezaki. A smaller sortie from the Marianas to Tsuchizakiminato covers 3,650 miles round-trip—the longest such mission of the entire war. Before the bombers can return to base, President Harry S. Truman announces Japan's unconditional surrender.

AUGUST 15 In Tokyo, Japan, Emperor Hirohito takes to the airwaves and orders his countrymen to surrender. The Japanese people are stunned by this, but unhesitatingly obey. Meanwhile, General Douglas MacArthur is appointed supreme commander of all United Nations powers, and all offensive actions against Japan are ordered to halt.

AUGUST 18 Over Tokyo, Japan, a pair of B-32 Dominators commits the final American reconnaissance mission of the war. They are attacked by Japanese fighters, which kill one American and wound two others while losing two aircraft to bomber defenses. This is also the final aerial combat mission of World War II.

AUGUST 27 Over China, B-29s of the XX Air Force begin airdropping supplies to prisoners of war in the Weihsien camp near Beijing. Ultimately, 4,470 tons of food and supplies are delivered to 154 camps and the 63,500 inmates housed.

AUGUST 29 Over Korea, a B-29 bomber delivering supplies to prisoners is attacked by Soviet fighters and shot down; this is the first brush with the Red Air Force.

AUGUST 30–SEPTEMBER 11 In Tokyo, Japan, Mission 75 commences as C-54 transport aircraft arrive and deliver the 11th Airborne Division, the 27th Infantry Division, and advanced echelons from General Douglas MacArthur's headquarters. They fly a total of 1,336 missions without a single mishap.

SEPTEMBER In Washington, D.C., the Bell XP-59, America's first jet fighter, arrives at the Smithsonian Institution for exhibition purposes. Today it resides at the National Air and Space Museum's Milestones of Flight gallery.

SEPTEMBER 3 In Japan, film and photos taken of the surrender ceremony in

Tokyo are placed onboard a C-54 Skymaster, which promptly arrives in Washington, D.C., a record 31 hours and 25 minutes later. Ironically, due to crossing the international dateline en route, the flight starts and finishes on the same calendar day!

SEPTEMBER 4 Near Hokkaido, Japan, Soviet fighters intercept two Eleventh Air Force B-29s as they conduct a high-altitude reconnaissance mission of Paramushiru and Shimushu.

SEPTEMBER 5 Over Santa Monica, California, the Douglas XC-74 prototype flies for the first time. This huge, four-engined transport enters service as the Globemaster.

SEPTEMBER 26 At the White Sands Range, New Mexico, the U.S. Army fires its first liquid-propelled rocket, the WAC Corporal, which reaches an altitude of 43.5 miles. This device is a copy of the German V-2.

SEPTEMBER 15 The U.S. Army Air Forces obtains its 1,391st JB-2 Loon guided rocket, after which production ceases.

SEPTEMBER 29 Project PAPERCLIP continues as German scientist Dr. Wernher von Braun and his scientific consorts arrive in the United States to assist in the American missile and space program.

OCTOBER 4 In Washington, D.C., an Army Air Forces C-54 Skymaster completes the first global flight for an aircraft of its kind by covering 23,279 miles in 149 hours and 44 minutes. This includes 33 hours and 21 minutes on the ground to refuel at various places.

OCTOBER 11 At the White Sands Proving Ground, New Mexico, a Tiny Tim rocket, the first liquid-fueled rocket of American origin, is fitted to the nose of a WAC (without altitude control) Corporal and fired, reaching an altitude of 43 miles.

OCTOBER 13   At Wright Field, Dayton, Ohio, the Army Air Forces sponsors a large open house to display American and captured aircraft to the public. The display draws one million visitors over the following week.

OCTOBER 20   In Washington, D.C., a flight of three B-29 bombers led by Lieutenant General Nathan F. Twining lands, having covered 13,000 miles from Guam in only 60 hours. There were refueling stops in India and Germany.

NOVEMBER 7   The Bell Aircraft Corporation flies a remote-controlled version of its P-59 jet fighter. A cockpit television camera projects instrument panel readings to a ground station.

NOVEMBER 19–20   In Washington, D.C., the B-29 bomber *Pacusan Dreamboat* piloted by Lieutenant Colonel G. R. Stanley completes a record 7,196-mile nonstop flight from Guam in only 35 hours.

NOVEMBER 25   From Savannah, Georgia, a Douglas A-26 Invader flown by Colonel Joseph Holzapple flies around the world in only 96 hours, 50 minutes of flying time, then lands in Washington, D.C.

NOVEMBER 29   At Maxwell, Alabama, the Army Air Forces School permanently relocates from Orlando, Florida. This institution becomes a major command and is the present-day site of the Air University.

DECEMBER 3   At March Field, California, the 412th Fighter Group is the first

American unit equipped with new Lockheed P-80A Shooting Star jet fighters.

DECEMBER 8   The ubiquitous, glass-domed Bell Model 47 becomes the first CAA-certified helicopter to fly commercially in the United States. It sees widespread civilian and military applications over the next three decades.

At Washington, D.C., the Douglas XB-42 Mixmaster flown by Lieutenant Colonel H. F. Warden and Captain Glenn W. Edwards arrives from Los Angeles, California, after a record transcontinental flight of five hours, 17 minutes, and 55 seconds. Though this was a propeller-pusher design, the XB-42 averages 433.6 miles per hour in flight.

DECEMBER 11   In New York, the B-29 *Pacusan Dreamboat* piloted by Colonel Clarence S. Irvine arrives from Burbank, California, having covered the 2,464-mile distance in a record 5 hours, 27 minutes, and 8 seconds. Its average speed was 450.38 miles per hour, a record for multiengine aircraft.

DECEMBER 14   The Bell Aircraft Company contracts with the Army Air Forces to construct three swept-wing, supersonic research aircraft; the three aircraft eventually emerge as the X-2.

DECEMBER 17   In Washington, D.C., General Carl A. Spaatz receives the Collier Trophy from President Harry S. Truman for successfully directing the air war in Europe.

DECEMBER 30   The Republic XF-12 Rainbow reconnaissance aircraft makes its maiden flight. This well-stocked flying photo laboratory carries five crewmen at 425 miles per hour, but the Army Training Support Center subsequently cancels its order for six additional aircraft.

1946

JANUARY 10   Over Stratford, Connecticut, a Sikorsky R–5 helicopter piloted by C. A. Moeller and D. D. Viner sets an unofficial world helicopter altitude record of 21,000 feet.

JANUARY 16   The U.S. government institutes the Upper Atmospheric Research panel for the purpose of testing and evaluating 60 captured German V–2 rockets. Their work inspires similar rocket programs at Johns Hopkins University, Maryland, and the Naval Research Laboratory.

JANUARY 19   Over Pinecastle Army Air Base, Florida, the Bell XS–1 rocket-powered research plane completes its first successful glide test with Jack Woolams at the controls.

JANUARY 26   At Eglin Field, Florida, the First Experimental Guided Missile Group is assembled to test and develop rocket propulsion technology.

A Lockheed P–80 Shooting Star piloted by Colonel William H. Councill completes a transcontinental flight in only 4 hours and 13 minutes. His plane averages 584 miles per hour.

FEBRUARY 3   The Army Air Forces reveals plans to develop a totally automatic flight profile system, whereby the onboard pilot will only be required to monitor controls in flight.

FEBRUARY 4   Lieutenant General James H. "Jimmy" Doolittle is installed as the first president of the new Air Force Association. This civilian organization exists to help promote aerospace power to the public, along with the strategic role it plays in national defense.

FEBRUARY 9   Command of the Army Air Forces (AAF) passes from General of the Army Henry H. Arnold to General Carl A. Spaatz, who formally assumes office as of March 1.

FEBRUARY 26   At Honington Air Station, Suffolk, England, the Army Air Forces officially closes the last of its 112 World War II–era bases. However, a snowstorm prevents the departure of the last remaining B–17 heavy bomber.

FEBRUARY 28   The Republic XP–84 prototype flies for the first time with Major William Lien at the controls. As the Thunderjet, it becomes the first postwar jetfighter acquired by the Army Air Forces (AAF).

MARCH   In Los Angeles, California, the new Project RAND is established in conjunction with the Douglas Aircraft Company to investigate the possibilities and potential uses of rockets, satellites, and supersonic aviation.

In light of the real hazard posed to the United States by V–2-type weapons, the Army Air Forces announces a new program to develop a ballistic missile defense system.

MARCH 8   The glass-domed Bell Model 47 becomes the first helicopter certified for flight by the Civil Aeronautic Agency. This mainstay of military aviation enters service as the UH–13.

MARCH 11   An early afterburner is tested at simulated high altitudes by the NACA Lewis Altitude Wind Tunnel.

MARCH 12   At Maxwell Field, Alabama, the new Air University replaces the Army

Air Forces School. As such it enjoys jurisdiction over the Air Command and Staff School, the Air War College, and bases offering support and training functions.

MARCH 15 At the White Sands Proving Ground, New Mexico, the Army Air Forces test fires a captured German V-2 rocket in static mode for the first time.

MARCH 21 The Army Air Forces activates three new organizations: the Air Defense Command (ADC), the Strategic Air Command (SAC), and the Tactical Air Command (TAC).

MARCH 22 A WAC rocket is the first American projectile to penetrate the Earth's atmosphere as it reaches an altitude of 50 miles. The device was a collaboration between Army Ordnance and the Jet Propulsion Laboratory.

APRIL 1 In Buffalo, New York, the Bell Corporation signs a few postwar missile contracts to develop Project MX-776, a guided tactical missile capable of hitting targets at distances of 100 miles. This is eventually known as the Rascal missile.

APRIL 16 At the White Sands Proving Ground, New Mexico, the Army Air Forces launches a German V-2 rocket for the first time. The United States is slowly entering the Space Age with captured enemy equipment and technology.

APRIL 19 In San Diego, California, the Consolidated Vultee Company contracts with the Army Air Forces to develop the first intercontinental ballistic missile (ICBM). This project goes under the name MX-774.

APRIL 22 In Maryland, the Glenn L. Martin Company signs a contract to construct a surface-to-surface guided missile

with a 600-mile range. This is the genesis of the Matador missile, or MX-771.

It is announced that the U.S. Weather Bureau is teaming up with the Army Air Forces, Navy, NACA, and several universities to collect data for a better understanding of weather and related phenomena. Among the devices employed are pilotless P-61 aircraft and manned gliders.

MAY 16 At Wright Field, Ohio, the Army Air Forces Institute of Technology is founded and is intended to graduate 350 officers annually after advanced studies.

MAY 17 In Los Angeles, California, the Douglas XB-43 becomes the first jet-powered American bomber to fly. This twin jet design, while impressive, does not go into production.

MAY 28 The Army Air Forces initiates Project NEPA to investigate the potential for atomic energy as a means of aircraft propulsion; work continues over the next decade.

MAY 29 In Washington, D.C., the War Department Equipment Board reports that tactical missiles and rockets will play an important role in future armed combat. They also recommend the development of no less than seven new systems, including surface-to-surface projectiles with ranges up to several thousand miles.

JUNE 3 A Lockheed P-80 Shooting Star flown by Lieutenant Henry A. Johnson sets a world speed record over a 1,000-kilometer course by averaging 462 miles per hour; he finishes in only 1 hour and 20 minutes.

JUNE 5 The Army Air Forces announces that it has decided to commence construction of two new multiengine jet bombers, the North American XB-45 and the Boeing XB-47.

JUNE 17   In Washington, D.C., Professor Theodore von Karman is appointed the first chair of the new Scientific Advisory Board (SAB) created at the Pentagon. This forms from the original 33 scientists and engineers cobbled together for Operation LUSTY, then tasked with acquiring secret German technology at the end of World War II. It remains in active service to present times.

JUNE 22   Two P-80 Shooting Stars take off from Schenectady, New York, with one proceeding to Washington, D.C., and the other to Chicago, Illinois. This act initiates the world's first jet-powered airmail delivery.

JUNE 26   The Army Air Forces and the Navy both adopt the knot (one nautical mile per hour) and the nautical mile

Atomic bomb explodes during the "Baker Day" test at Bikini Atoll in the Marshall Islands on July 25, 1946. This ground level image was taken about six seconds after detonation. The advent of nuclear weapons wielded an indelible impact on subsequent military strategy and tactics. (Naval Historical Center)

(1.15 of a statute mile) as standard units of measurement for speed and distance.

JUNE 28   In Seattle, Washington, the Boeing Company contracts with the Army Air Forces to design and develop a new generation of heavy jet bombers; it ultimately emerges as the B-52 Stratofortress.

JULY 1   At Bikini Atoll in the Pacific, Operation CROSSROADS unfolds as a B-29 christened *Dave's Dream* drops a Fat Man-type atomic bomb over an armada of 73 anchored test vessels. The bomb is off target yet still manages to sink five vessels and heavily damage nine more. Much valuable information is gathered following the detonation.

JULY 25   At Bikini Atoll in the Pacific, Operation CROSSROADS continues as a second atomic bomb is detonated 90 feet below the ocean surface; the ensuing blast sinks eight more ships and causes considerable radioactive contamination.

AUGUST 6   At Muroc Dry Lake, California, two remote-controlled B-17s successfully complete a flight that originated at Hilo, Hawaii.

AUGUST 8   At Fort Worth, Texas, the massive six-engine XB-36 prototype, which has been under development since 1941, flies for the first time. Thus huge craft enters service as the B-36 Peacekeeper.

AUGUST 12   In Washington, D.C., President Harry S. Truman signs legislation establishing the National Air Museum at the Smithsonian Institution. This remains the most visited museum in the world, with 100 million guests annually.

AUGUST 17   Over Ohio, Sergeant Larry Lambert becomes the first American to utilize an ejection seat after he vaults from a P-61 Black Widow and survives. At the time he was traveling 302 miles per hour at an altitude of 7,800 feet.

AUGUST 31   A Lockheed P-80 Shooting Star flown by Colonel Leon Gray wins the Jet Division of the first postwar Bendix Cup Race by flying from Los Angeles, California, to Cleveland, Ohio, in 4 hours and 8 minutes while averaging 495 miles per hour.

SEPTEMBER 30   At Muroc Field, California, the NACA Muroc Flight Test Unit arrives from Langley Laboratory to assist development of the Bell XS-1 program. This detachment consists of 13 scientists under the direction of Walter Williams. Ironically, friction arises between the scientists and the Army Air Forces over which group will be responsible for achieving supersonic flight. Nonetheless, they constitute the origins for the future NASA Flight Research Center at present-day Edwards Air Force Base.

OCTOBER 4–6   A B-29 christened *Pacusan Dreamboat*, piloted by Colonel C. S. Irvine, completes the first nonstop flight over the North Pole. Irvine's flight takes him from Hawaii, over the pole, to his final destination in Egypt, having covered 10,000 miles in 40 hours of flight time.

OCTOBER 7   In Buffalo, New York, the first Bell XS-1 rocket plane is shipped off to Muroc Dry Lake, California, for flighttests. A total of three are constructed, although they subsequently receive the more famous designation X-1.

OCTOBER 10   At White Sands Proving Ground, New Mexico, space science begins once a V-2 rocket goes aloft carrying specialized equipment for taking spectroscopic readings of the upper atmosphere.

OCTOBER 25   At White Sands Proving Ground, New Mexico, a DeVry 35mm camera fitted to a V-2 rocket is carried to an altitude of 65 miles to make the first film records of planet Earth from that height. At its apogee, the camera captures an area of 40,000 square miles.

DECEMBER 8   Over Muroc Dry Lake, California, the first Bell XS-1, piloted by Chalmers Goodlin, is successfully dropped by a B-29 carrier aircraft, ignites its rocket motors, then flies up to 35,000 feet and Mach 0.75.

DECEMBER 17   At Holloman Air Force Base, New Mexico, the National Institute of Health creates a space biology research program, which includes a high-speed rocket sled to study the effects of high-G (gravity) situations on human beings.

At the White Sands Proving Ground, New Mexico, a V-2 rocket reaches 166 miles in height and a speed of 3,600 miles per hour, both world records for a single-stage rocket. The device also carries fungus spore samples into space to test their reaction to cosmic rays.

1947

JANUARY 13   At White Sands, New Mexico, a V-2 rocket equipped with onboard telemetry equipment is launched into low Earth altitude as part of Project HERMES. This is the first time that a rocket's performance and flight has been electronically monitored by a ground station.

FEBRUARY 5 In Washington, D.C., President Harry S. Truman agrees with the Atomic Energy Commission (AEC) and the secretaries of the Army and Navy that nuclear weapons testing and production should continue.

FEBRUARY 10 Over Dayton, Ohio, a Sikorsky R-5A helicopter piloted by Major E. M. Cassell reaches an unofficial world's altitude record of 19,167 feet.

FEBRUARY 17 At the White Sands Proving Ground, New Mexico, a WAC Corporal missile reaches an altitude of 250,000 feet.

FEBRUARY 20 At White Sands, New Mexico, the Blossom Project begins as V-2 No. 20 ejects a canister after it reaches its apogee.

FEBRUARY 27 At LaGuardia, New York, an F-82 flown by Lieutenant Colonel Robert Thacker and John M. Ard flies 5,000 miles nonstop from Hickam Field, Hawaii. This is the longest nonstop unrefueled flight by a propellor-driven aircraft, and it lasts 14 hours and 33 minutes.

MARCH 16 At San Diego, California, the twin-engine Convair 240 transport prototype flies for the first time. It eventually enters into Air Force service as the T-29 navigator training aircraft.

MARCH 17 Over Muroc Field, California, the North American XB-45 four-jet bomber flies for the first time with George Krebs at the controls. In two years it enters Air Force service as the B-45 Tornado, which is America's first jet bomber.

APRIL 30 In Washington, D.C., the Army and the Navy standardize their guided missile nomenclature as A for air, S for surface, and U for underwater. The first letter regards the weapon's origin and the latter its target.

MAY 21 At Langley, Virginia, NACA engineers fit a small aircraft with a special five-bladed propellor and muffled exhausts; the result is a near-silent flying machine.

MAY 27 The Corporal E, the Army's first guided surface-to-surface missile, is successfully test fired for the first time, meeting or exceeding all technical specifications.

JUNE 5 At Holloman Air Force Base, New Mexico, the first AAF research balloon, which was designed and built by New York University and the Air Materiel Command, is launched.

JUNE 19 Over Muroc Dry Lake, California, a Lockheed P-80 Shooting Star piloted by Colonel Albert Boyd, the Army's chief test pilot, reaches a new world speed record of 623.8 miles per hour.

JUNE 25 In Seattle, Washington, the first Boeing B-50 makes its initial flight. This is an updated version of the B-29 with more powerful engines and a taller tail.

JUNE 30 At Wright Patterson Air Force Base, Ohio, a meeting of Army Air Forces officials and NACA representatives convenes to iron out their differences regarding the X-1 testing program. They agree to divide responsibilities, with the Army being tasked with breaking the sound barrier, while NACA will acquire technical details from research associated with the program.

JULY 1 In light of budgetary restrictions, the Army Air Forces cancels its MX-774 program. However, it is revived the following decade and emerges as the Atlas ICBM.

JULY 3   At Holloman Air Force Base, New Mexico, New York University scientists release a cluster of balloons with a 50-pound instrument panel to measure atmospheric conditions at 18,550 feet.

JULY 18   In Washington, D.C., President Harry S. Truman assigns a five-man working group under chairman Thomas K. Finletter to originate a broad-based plan to endow the United States with the greatest possible benefits from aviation, civil and military alike.

JULY 26   President Harry S. Truman signs the National Defense Act of 1947 into law, which makes provisions for a new, independent United States Air Force, which will enjoy equal status with the Departments of the Army and Navy. The Air National Guard also comes into being as a reserve component of the new force.

AUGUST 28   Over Texas, the first of 22 Convair B-36A Peacekeepers performs its maiden flight. This giant craft is assigned to training future B-36 aircrews as formal production gets underway.

SEPTEMBER 18   As of this date, the U.S. Air Force is officially a separate entity in the American military establishment. Stuart A. Symington, a hard-nosed business executive, also gains appointment as the first secretary of the Air Force.

SEPTEMBER 22   At Brize Norton, England, a robot-controlled Douglas C-54 becomes the first autoguided aircraft to cross the Atlantic from Stephenville, Newfoundland. The flight lasted 2,400 miles.

SEPTEMBER 25   At the White Sands Proving Ground, New Mexico, the first liquid-propelled Aerobee sounding rocket is successfully launched. Variations of this device will be used constantly until 1985.

SEPTEMBER 26   In Washington, D.C., General Carl A. Spaatz gains appointment as the first Air Force chief of staff. The official transfer of officers, bases, and equipment is also authorized by the James V. Forrestal, the new Secretary of Defense.

Major General William E. Kepner, formerly head of the VIII Fighter Command in World War II, is installed as the head of the Atomic Energy Division within the Air Force.

OCTOBER 1   Over Muroc Dry Lake, California, the North American XP-86 prototype flies for the first time with Major George Welch at the controls. This swept-wing design enters service as the F-86 Sabrejet, a legendary fighter aircraft.

At Bethpage, Long Island, the Grumman XJR2F-1 flying boat flies for the first time. It enters Air Force service as the SA-16 and HU-16 Albatross, which serves as a standard rescue aircraft for two decades.

OCTOBER 6   The Ryan Firebird XAAM-A-1, the Air Force's first guided air-to-air missile, is successfully test launched for the first time.

OCTOBER 14   Over Muroc Dry Lake, California, a Bell X-1 piloted by Captain Charles Yeager makes aviation history by flying through the sound barrier for the first time. Although several propellor-driven aircraft have also broken the sound barrier while diving, Yeager is the first achieve Mach 1.06 in sustained level flight.

OCTOBER 21   Over California, the Northrop XB-49, a tailless, four-jet design, flies for the first time. This radical craft is an outgrowth of the propellor-driven XB-35 which flew in 1946. While impressive to

Yeager, Chuck (1923–)

Air Force pilot. Charles Elwood ("Chuck") Yeager was born in Myra, West Virginia, on February 13, 1923. He joined the Army Air Corps in 1940, and he earned his pilot's wings at Luke Field, Arizona, in July 1942. Yeager subsequently flew P-51 Mustangs with the 363rd Fighter Squadron in England, where he shot down thirteen German aircraft, including five in one day. His most notable kill happened on November 6, 1944, when he downed a futuristic Messerschmitt Me-262 jet fighter. After the war, Yeager was selected to fly the top secret Bell XS-1 rocket research aircraft. On October 14, 1947, he broke the sound barrier at Mach 1 for the first time, winning a prestigious Mackay Trophy for the year's most outstanding flight. Yeager continued flying at Edwards Air Force Base, California, where, in December 1953, he piloted a new Bell X-1A to 1,650 miles per hour, three times the speed of sound.

In 1954 Yeager left flight-testing to command an F-100 Suber Sabre squadron in Germany, and he returned home three years later, a lieutenant colonel. In 1969 he resumed combat operations by commanding the 405th Tactical Fighter Wing, and performed 127 missions over Vietnam in B-57s. Yeager retired from active duty in 1975 as a brigadier general and, on October 14, 1997, the 50th anniversary of his record-breaking flight, he again broke the sound barrier for a final time in his F-15 Eagle jet at an Edwards Air Force Base air show; he has since retired and resides in Cedar Ridge, California. In an active career spanning 50 years, Yeager flew and tested no less that 330 different types of aircraft.

behold, the aircraft is intrinsically unstable and does not enter production.

NOVEMBER 4 At the White Sands Proving Ground, New Mexico, an Aerobee rocket is successfully launched and reaches 190,000 feet above sea level.

NOVEMBER 15 The Air Force announces that it has been experimenting with ramjet helicopter technology in the form of the McDonnell XH-20 Little Henry, operated by one man.

NOVEMBER 23 Over San Diego, California, the giant XC-99 transport aircraft flies for the first time. This is a transport version of the B-36 bomber then in production, although it does not enter production.

NOVEMBER 26 At Langley, Virginia, scientists successfully demonstrate the world's first hypersonic–flow wind tunnel.

DECEMBER 10 A high-speed rocket sled carrying Lieutenant Colonel John P. Stapp is launched to examine the effect of high acceleration rates on the human body. Much useful information is derived and Stapp, while bruised, is not harmed by the 2,000-foot journey.

DECEMBER 17 At Seattle, Washington, the futuristic Boeing XB-47 six-engine jet bomber flies for the first time. This is the first postwar American bomber to incorporate German swept–wing information in its design, and it enters service as the B-47 Stratojet.

1948

JANUARY 2 At Patterson, Ohio, the Air Force Technical Museum is organized.

JANUARY 4 At the University of California, scientists complete a pilot model for the world's first supersonic wind tunnel, a tremendous boon for the design of modern jet aircraft.

FEBRUARY 6 At the White Sands Proving Ground, New Mexico, V-2 rocket No. 36 blasts off under the aegis of a Hermes A-1 flight control system. This is an important step in the development of guided missiles.

FEBRUARY 16 Over Germany, B-29 bombers of the Strategic Air Command arrive as part of a long-distance exercise. En route they are "intercepted" by RAF fighters as they traverse southern England.

FEBRUARY 20 The Boeing B-50, a more powerful version of the venerable B-29, is accepted into Air Force service. In addition to higher range and performance, it is also capable of being refueled in the air.

MARCH 10 Over Muroc Dry Lake, California, the Air Force declares that a B-29 bomber recently dropped an explosive device weighing 42,000 pounds.

MARCH 11–14 By terms of the so-called Key West Agreement, military and aeronautical rocket research is not to be monopolized by any one branch of the armed forces, but rather split equally amongst them.

MARCH 22 Over Van Nuys, California, the Lockheed TP-80C, the prototype of the T-33 jet trainer, flies for the first time. This machine enjoys widespread service in the Air Force.

MARCH 28 A series of new aerial tanker aircraft, the KB-29M, completes final testing at the behest of the Strategic Air Command (SAC). This B-29 variant can carry 2,300 gallons of fuel aloft and dispense it through a hose and reel system mounted in the bomb bay.

APRIL 21 In Washington, D.C., Secretary of Defense James V. Forrestal assigns the U.S. Air Force a primary responsibility for defending the country.

APRIL 26 In concert with President Harry S. Truman's order to desegregate the military, the U.S. Air Force announces a policy to fully integrate African Americans into whatever sphere or technicality they are qualified for.

APRIL 30 In Washington, D.C., General Hoyt S. Vandenberg becomes the second Air Force chief of staff, to replace retiring General Carl A. Spaatz.

MAY 20 Over Inglewood, California, the first production F-86A Sabrejet fighter flies for the first time. Over 6,000 of these peerless dogfighters will be constructed over the next few years.

MAY 24 A new world speed record for flying over a 1,000-kilometer course is established by noted aviatrix Jacqueline Cochran, who reaches 432 miles per hour.

MAY 26 In Washington, D.C., President Harry S. Truman signs legislation creating the new Civil Air Patrol (CAP); this organization functions as an auxiliary of the U.S. Air Force in peace and war.

JUNE 1 Air Force and Navy transport commands are brought together in a new, unified entity, the Military Air Transport Service (MATS), which remains under Air Force purview.

JUNE 10 The Air Force announces that the Bell X-1 rocket plane has exceeded

Vandenberg, Hoyt S. (1899–1954)

Air Force general. Hoyt Sanford Vandenberg was born in Milwaukee, Wisconsin, on January 24, 1899, and he was assigned to the Air Service in 1923. Vandenberg won his wings at Kelly Field, Texas, and subsequently attended the Air Corps Tactical School, and the Command and General Staff School. During World War II, he served on the staff of General James H. Doolittle in North Africa, rising to brigadier general in December 1942. A year of distinguished service in the Mediterranean ensued, so in March 1944, Vandenberg rose to major general, and helped plan Operation OVERLORD in England. Shortly before World War II ended Vandenberg, who rose from lieutenant colonel to lieutenant general in only three years, became assistant chief of staff for the Army Air Forces.

In April 1947 Vandenberg became deputy chief of staff of the newly independent U.S. Air Force, succeeded Spaatz the following year, and became, aged 48 years, the nation's youngest four-star general. Vandenberg realized that, in an age of fiscal restraint, the greatest firepower available would be in the form of nuclear weapons, so he spent most of his budget on expensive systems like Convair's giant B-36 bomber and a host of new jet aircraft. In 1950 the Korean War broke out and Vandenberg helped articulate the strategy that saw the U.S. Air Force gain air supremacy over the region. During his tenure the service expanded from 49 to 90 combat wings, becoming the largest aerial force in the world. Vandenberg died of cancer in Washington, D.C., on April 2, 1954, a far-sighted aviation leader who put the new Air Force on a sound footing.

the speed of sound several times since its first successful attempt the previous March.

JUNE 11 In Washington, the Department of the Air Force releases its new Air Force Regulations 65-60 which updates aircraft designations. Henceforth, "P" for "Pursuit" is replaced by "F" for "Fighter"; "F" for "Fotographic" is replaced by "R" for "Reconnaissance"; and "R" for "Rotary wing" is replaced by "H" for "Helicopter." "B" for "Bomber" is unchanged. The Office of Air Force Chaplains is also created.

JUNE 16 In Washington, D.C., Colonel Geraldine P. May gains appointment as the first director of Women in the Air Force. She is also the first woman in the Air Force to reach colonel.

JUNE 18 At Davis-Monthan Air Force Base, Arizona, and Roswell AFB, New Mexico, the first two aerial refueling squadrons are equipped and organized to use KB-29Ms.

JUNE 26 In response to the provocative Soviet blockade of Berlin, East Germany, the first Air Force C-47 transports bring in 80 tons of supplies. General Curtis E. LeMay, the head of U.S. Air Forces in Europe (USAFE), begins organizing men and equipment for what becomes renowned as the Berlin Airlift.

At Fort Worth, Texas, the 7th Bombardment Wing accepts delivery of the first production B-36 intercontinental bombers. This is currently the world's largest airplane.

JULY 13 In California, the Convair MX-774 rocket is successfully test flown for the first time. This is the first device to employ movable (gimballed) engine nozzles that come to characterize all intercontinental ballistic missiles, including the Atlas ICBM of the late 1950s.

JULY 17 In England, several B-29s of the Strategic Air Command (SAC) arrive and deploy for the first time since World War II. Ostensibly there for training purposes, they are known to be capable of dropping nuclear weapons on Eastern Europe in the event of war.

JULY 20   At Selfridge Field, Michigan, Colonel David Schilling leads the first flight of 16 F-80 Shooting Stars on the first transatlantic deployment to Fürstenfeldbruck, West Germany, via Scotland. The mission takes them 9 hours and 20 minutes.

JULY 30   The Air Force accepts delivery of its first North American B-45A Tornado jet bomber. Though plagued with teething problems, it becomes the first jet bomber fitted to drop nuclear weapons.

AUGUST 6   B-29s *Gas Gobbler* and *Lucky Lady*, from the 43rd Bomb Group, fly a 20,000-mile flight around the globe in 15 days.

AUGUST 8   In Hawaii, a Convair B-36B Peacemaker flies nonstop from Fort Worth, Texas, completing a 9,400-mile flight without refueling.

AUGUST 16   Over Muroc Dry Lake, California, the Northrop XF-89 prototype flies for the first time. It enters service as the F-89 Scorpion, and is the Air Force's first all-weather interceptor jet.

AUGUST 23   The ongoing program to develop a "parasite fighter" carried in the bellies of intercontinental bombers, a McDonnell XF-85 Goblin is dropped from a B-36, but collides with the hookup trapeze while returning and shatters its canopy. Test pilot Ed Schoch manages to land safely and the experiment is run again, successfully, on September 16.

SEPTEMBER 3   Over England, Operation DAGGER unfolds as Air Force B-29s and RAF fighters take part in a joint air defense exercise.

SEPTEMBER 15   Over Muroc Dry Lake, California, an F-86A Sabrejet flown by Major Richard L. Johnson establishes a world's speed record of 671 mile per hour.

LeMay, Curtis E. (1906–1990)

Air Force general. Curtis Emerson LeMay was born in Columbus, Ohio, on November 15, 1906. He attended Ohio State University ROTC, and won his wings at March Field, California, in October 1929. In 1937 he transferred to bombers at Langley Field, Virginia, and demonstrated his navigating prowess in 1938 by intercepting the Italian liner *Rex*. During World War II, LeMay was colonel commanding the 305th Bombardment Squadron and, in August 1943, he personally led the first shuttle-bombing run from England to North Africa. In March 1944, he became the youngest major general since Ulysses S. Grant, and transferred to China to command the XX Bomber Command flying new B-29 Superfortresses. LeMay subsequently transferred to the XXI Bomber Command on Guam, and his low-altitude raid against Tokyo on March 9, 1945, burned out 16 square miles of the city and inflicted over 100,000 casualties. In August 1945 LeMay transferred again to the staff of General Carl A. Spaatz, and helped plan atomic bomb missions against Hiroshima and Nagasaki.

After the war LeMay served as deputy chief of Research and Development, and initiated development of America's first jet bombers. In 1948 he orchestrated Operation VITTLES, the famous Berlin Airlift, forcing the Russians to lift their blockade. He subsequently headed the Strategic Air Command (SAC), transforming it into an elite atomic strike force of nearly 2,000 jets. In June 1961 President John F. Kennedy appointed him to chief of staff of the Air Force, and, in 1965, LeMay concluded 37 years of distinguished service by resigning. He died in San Bernardino, California, on October 1, 1990, the foremost aerial strategist of the Cold War.

SEPTEMBER 18 At Edwards Air Force Base, California, the Convair XF-92 makes its maiden flight. This is the world's first jet-powered delta-wing aircraft based on the designs of Germany engineer Alexander Lippisch.

OCTOBER 15 In West Germany, Major General William H. Tunner takes charge of the Berlin Airlift, which consists of both American and British aircraft. During World War II, Tunner was also responsible for organizing the successful India-China airlift over "The Hump."

OCTOBER 19 General Curtis E. LeMay replaces General George Kenney as commander of the Strategic Air Command (SAC). This turns out to be one of the most significant appointments in aviation history.

OCTOBER 31 The Air Force announces that an F-80 fighter had been flown at high altitude using only two wingtip ramjet engines for propulsion. This is the first known application of ramjet technology on manned aircraft.

NOVEMBER 4 In Santa Monica, California, the RAND Corporation, an outgrowth of the earlier Air Force-Douglas RAND Project, is organized to bring scientific, industrial, and military expertise into a think-tank for Air Force decision-making.

NOVEMBER 5 The government announces that all Air Force warplanes will bear the markings "USAF," save for those operated by the Military Air Transport Service, which are marked MATS.

NOVEMBER 10–12 The first symposium to ponder the theoretical problems associated with spaceflight is sponsored by the School of Aviation Medicine.

NOVEMBER 30 A Douglas C-54 Skymaster equipped with Curtiss-Wright reversible-pitch propellers descends from 15,000 feet to 1,000 feet in only 1 minute and 22 seconds.

DECEMBER 1 The Continental Air Command (CAC) is activated for operations.

DECEMBER 2 The Beech Model 45 prototype makes its maiden flight; it enters the service as the T-34A Mentor, which remains in service as a primary trainer until 1961.

DECEMBER 9 In another stunning display of strategic air power, a B-36 and a B-50 fly nonstop from Carswell Air Force Base, Texas, to Hawaii. The gigantic B-36 flies nonstop while the B-50 refuels three times from a KB-29M over a 35-hour period.

DECEMBER 16 Over Muroc Dry Lake, California, the Northrop X-4 Bantam flies for the first time. This is a semi-tailless, swept-wing jet design and flies as part of a joint NACA-Air Force research program.

DECEMBER 28 Over Greenland, a ski-equipped C-47 flown by Lieutenant Colonel Emil Beaudry lands and rescues 12 men of a C-47 and a B-17 that had crashed at the same site on December 9. The flight also wins the Mackay Trophy.

DECEMBER 29 In Washington, D.C., Defense Secretary James V. Forrestal declares that the United States will endeavor to initiate an "earth satellite program" to study the viability of placing objects into an Earth orbit.

DECEMBER 31 Over Berlin, the airlift completes its 100,000th flight as part of Operation VITTLES. All told, the Soviet blockade of Berlin has been a propaganda disaster for Premier Josef Stalin.

1949

JANUARY 3–MARCH 15   The Air Force commences Operation HAYRIDE after a severe blizzard strikes several Midwestern states. Over 4,700 tons of livestock and supplies are lifted in 200 sorties.

JANUARY 5   Over California, a Bell X-1 flown by Major Charles Yeager establishes an unofficial climbing speed record of 13,000 feet per second. This is the only instance of an X-1 taking off under its own power.

JANUARY 19   At Holloman Air Force Base, New Mexico, the Martin XB-61 Matador tactical missile is successfully test fired for the first time. This is intended as a short-range, highly mobile tactical weapon.

JANUARY 25   The Air Force orders that World War II-era olive green outfits of Army origin be replaced by slate blue uniforms, although phasing in the new threads will take several months.

FEBRUARY 8   At Andrews Air Force Base, Maryland, a B-47 Stratojet arrives from Moses Lake airfield, Washington, after traveling 2,300 miles in only 3 hours and 45 minutes. This cuts the time of existing transcontinental records in half.

FEBRUARY 9   At Randolph Air Force Base, Texas, the School of Aviation Medicine creates the first Department of Space Medicine.

Berliners watch a Fairchild Flying Boxcar land at Tempelhof Airport in 1948 during the Berlin Airlift. The airlift was a massive transfer of essential supplies flown into Germany during 1948 and 1949 by British and U.S. forces after the Soviet Union prohibited ground access to West Berlin. This was also the first strategic test for the new U.S. Air Force, and it performed with flying colors. (U.S. Air Force)

FEBRUARY 24   At Cape Canaveral, Florida, a two-stage vehicle consisting of a German V-2 and WAC Corporal second stage is launched and reaches 244 miles in height at a speed of 5,150 miles per hour. This launch is part of Project BOMBER and demonstrates the utility of two-stage projectiles.

FEBRUARY 26–MARCH 2   At Carswell Air Force Base, Texas, the B-50 *Lucky Lady II*, flown by Captain James Gallagher, arrives after completing a 23,400-mile non-stop flight around the world in 94 hours. The flight requires four in-flight refuelings over the Azores, Arabia, the Philippines, and Hawaii using the probe-and-drogue system developed by the British. The flight also wins the Mackay Trophy.

MARCH 4   In East Germany, the Berlin Airlift (Operation VITTLES) has delivered over 1 million tons of coal, food, and supplies since the mission began the previous June.

MARCH 15   The Military Air Transport Service (MATS) creates the Global Weather Central to assist the Strategic Air Command (SAC) in its mission.

MARCH 26   A B-36D Peacemaker, outfitted with four J-79 jet engines in wingtip pods, flies for the first time. This new configuration can hoist a payload of 85,000 pounds at 440 miles per hour. It also puts the Navy on notice that it does not possess a monopoly on the delivery of nuclear weapons, which increases friction between the two services.

MARCH 30   In Washington, D.C., President Harry S. Truman signs legislation to create the nation's first chain of permanent defense radar stations.

APRIL 4   In response to increasing Soviet aggression, the North Atlantic Treaty Organization (NATO) is formed as a defensive alliance. Its creation triggers the rise of the Warsaw Pact behind the Iron Curtain.

APRIL 6   At Tempelhof Airport, West Berlin, Operation VITTLES achieves its operational highpoint once transport aircraft begin landing every four minutes for six consecutive hours.

APRIL 16   Over Van Nuys, California, the Lockheed YF-94 prototype makes its maiden flight. This is a modified, two-seat version of the F-80 Shooting Star and it enters service as the F-94 Starfire, an all-weather interceptor.

Over Berlin, West Germany, the airlift hits another highpoint once 12,940 tons of supplies arrive through 1,398 aircraft.

MAY 7   In Washington, D.C., Congress votes to make General Henry H. Arnold a five-star general of the Air Force; he remains the only officer so honored.

MAY 9   The Republic XF-91 jet/rocket hybrid fighter performs its maiden flight. The craft also features an inverse-taper, variable incidence wing, but it does not enter into production.

MAY 11   In Washington, D.C., President Harry S. Truman signs legislation to establish a guided missile test range for the Air Force, which eventually emerges as Cape Canaveral, Florida.

MAY 11–12   In Berlin, East Germany, the Soviet blockade is lifted although Operation VITTLES continues to stockpile supplies in the city.

MAY 21   Over Bridgeport, Connecticut, a Sikorsky S-51-1 helicopter piloted by Captain H. D. Gaddis reaches a world altitude of 21,220 feet.

JUNE 4   The Lockheed XF-90 prototype flies for the first time. Envisioned as a strategic fighter that would escort jet bombers to their target, it does not enter production.

JULY 1   Major General Malcolm C. Grow gains appointment as the first surgeon general of the Air Force and the USAF Medical Service is also established.

The first production F-94A Starfire prototype makes its maiden flight. This is the first Air Force all-weather interceptor equipped with an afterburner.

AUGUST 8   Over California, a Bell X-1 piloted by Major Frank K. Everest reaches an unofficial altitude of 71,092 feet, the highest this generation of research aircraft will reach.

AUGUST 10   In Washington, D.C., President Harry S. Truman amends the National Security Act, which renames the National Military Establishment to the Department of Defense.

AUGUST 25   A Bell X-1 flying at 69,000 feet suffers from a potentially disastrous decompression, but pilot Major Frank K. Everest is saved by his T-1 partial pressure suit and he lands his crippled aircraft safely.

SEPTEMBER 24   Over Inglewood, California, the North American T-28 prototype flies for the first time; its enters Air Force and Navy service as the Trojan and serves as an advanced trainer.

SEPTEMBER 30   Over West Berlin, East Germany, Operation VITTLES, the Berlin Airlift, is formally concluded. A combination of Air Force, Navy, and RAF transports lifted 2.34 million tons of supplies into the beleaguered city, which was accomplished in 277,000 flights.

OCTOBER 1   At Cape Canaveral, Florida, Major General W. L. Richardson assumes command of the Long-Range Proving Ground.

OCTOBER 14   The Chase Aircraft Company XC-123 prototype performs its maiden flight; it enters Air Force service as the C-123 Provider, which sees extensive service throughout the Vietnam War.

NOVEMBER 19   The Sikorsky YH-19A helicopter performs its maiden flight. This is the first helicopter to have its engine mounted in the nose below the cabin to afford pilots an unrestricted view. It enters service as the Chickasaw.

NOVEMBER 28   At RAF Marham, England, the Douglas C-74 Globemaster I, christened *The Champ*, arrives from Mobile, Alabama, after a 23-hour nonstop flight. It is also the first aircraft to cross the Atlantic while carrying more than 100 passengers.

NOVEMBER 29   The Douglas YC-124 Globemaster II prototype flies for the first time; this enlarged version of the Globemaster I can carry 50,000 pounds of cargo for 850 miles, and it sees widespread service with the Military Air Transport Service (MATS) and the Strategic Air Command (SAC).

At Desert Center, California, aviatrix Jacqueline Cochran flies an F-51 to a new speed record of 436.995 miles per hour on the Mount Wilson Course.

DECEMBER 2   At Holloman Air Development Center, New Mexico, the Air Force test fires an Aerobee RTV-A-1a research rocket for the first time.

DECEMBER 5   In Alaska, the Air Force begins construction of a $50 million network of early warning radar sites to guard

A Distant Early Warning Line Station in Bullen Point, Alaska. Radar of the Distant Early Warning Line across the arctic, coupled with a similar line across the midpoint of Canada allowed for early detection of incoming Soviet bombers across the Arctic Circle. (Library of Congress)

against incoming Soviet bombers. Each designated station will have a range of 300 miles.

DECEMBER 22   The North American YF-84D all-weather interceptor performs its maiden flight. It enters service as the F-86D Sabre Dog, an all-weather interceptor with a large radome nose and a retractable rocket tray to shoot down bombers.

DECEMBER 25   The Air Force unveils the existence of Stupalith, a ceramic product that expands when heated and contracts when cooled and, because it can

withstand temperatures as hot as 2,000 degrees, it will be used as insulation in jet and rocket engines.

DECEMBER 28   At Wright-Patterson Air Force Base, Ohio, Project SAUCER disbands after two years, having concluded after two years that flying saucers do not exist.

DECEMBER 29   At Desert Center, California, aviatrix Jacqueline Cochran pilots a modified F-51 Mustang to an international speed record of 436.995 miles per hour over the 500-kilometer Mount Wilson Course.

1950

JANUARY 15   At Sonoma, California, General of the Air Force Henry H. Arnold dies. One of the architects of

victory in World War II, his career spanned aviation from its infancy to the cusp of jets and rocket technology.

JANUARY 18   The Lockheed YF-94 Starfire prototype performs its maiden flight. This is the Air Force's first rocket-armed jet interceptor and enters service in 1953.

JANUARY 23   The Air Force creates its Research and Development Command to separate basic research functions from logistics and procurement activities performed by the Air Materiel Command.

JANUARY 31   In Washington, D.C., President Harry S. Truman, alerted to Soviet endeavors, orders the development of a new and more powerful thermonuclear weapon, the so-called hydrogen bomb.

MARCH 1   In Seattle, Washington, the first production B-47A Stratojet is rolled out and acquired by the Air Force for an engineering inspection before it makes a test hop. This version of the swept-wing, six-jet bomber will be used for training purposes only.

MARCH 15   The government tasks the Air Force with sole responsibility for developing and deploying strategic guided missiles, or ICBMs, once they become operational at the end of the decade.

MARCH 22   At RAF Marham, England, the Air Force transfers the first of four Boeing B-29s to the Royal Air Force under terms of the Atlantic Pact. It enters British service as the Washington.

APRIL 18   The Air Force declares that it will spend $1.2 billion to acquire 1,250 new aircraft.

APRIL 24   In Washington, D.C., Thomas K. Finletter gains appointment as secretary of the Air Force.

MAY 5   Over Hawthorne, California, the Northrop YRB-49A is flown for the first time. This is a reconnaissance version of the four-jet "flying wing," with two additional jet engines mounted in pods below the wing. Despite its spectacular appearance, it does not go into production.

MAY 12   Over California, the Bell X-1 No. 1 research aircraft makes its final flight before being donated to the Smithsonian Institution, where it remains on display to present times.

JUNE 2   At Rapid City Air Force Base, South Dakota, the first operational RB-36D arrives with the 28th Strategic Reconnaissance Wing. This version mounts four jet engines in addition to six propeller engines.

JUNE 3   The Republic YF-96A jet prototype flies for the first time; this is a swept-wing version of the F-84 and it enters service as the Thunderstreak.

JUNE 23   At Seoul, South Korea, North Korean Yak-9 fighters swoop down upon Kimpo Airfield, damaging a C-54 Skymaster on the ground. This is the first American aircraft lost in the Korean conflict.

JUNE 25   In an act of overt aggression, tanks and infantry from North Korea attack South Korea while Communist airplanes, flown by Russian pilots, attack Kimpo Air Base. In Japan, Major General Earl E. Partridge, commanding the Fifth Air Force, places his organization on alert and increases surveillance activities over the Korean peninsula.

JUNE 26   Over Inchon, South Korea, Air Force F-82 Twin Mustangs fly top cover as vessels begin evacuating American citizens for Japan.

JUNE 27   In Washington, D.C., President Harry S. Truman orders the Air Force to commence combat operations over North and South Korea. Meanwhile, transport aircraft assist evacuations at Seoul, covered by fighters and bombers overhead.

The Air Force scores its first-ever kill as an F-82 piloted by Lieutenants William Hudson and Carl S. Fraser, 339th Fighter All-Weather Squadron, down a Communist Yak-1 fighter near Seoul, South Korea. A total of seven Communist craft are destroyed, making this the highest-scoring day of 1950.

In Japan, B-26 light bombers begin flying strike missions over South Korea, although poor weather largely negates their efforts. The Fifth Air Force also deploys an advanced echelon at Itazuke Air Base, whereby RF-80s are poised to begin flying reconnaissance missions.

JUNE 28   Over South Korea, B-29 Superfortresses of the Far East Air Forces (FEAF) begin pounding North Korean formations in the vicinity of Seoul. B-26 Invaders of the 3rd Bomb Group also make a successful strike against Communist rail and road traffic near Musan, North Korea, near the 38th Parallel.

The first RF-80A jet reconnaissance mission of the Korean War is executed by Lieutenant Bryce Poe.

JUNE 29   Over North Korea, Japan-based B-26 Invaders drop bombs on the North Korea capital of Pyongyang for the first time in the war. Meanwhile, General Douglas MacArthur instructs Major General George E. Stratemeyer to bomb strategic bridges over the Han River and massed North Korean formations in that vicinity. F-82s defending the airfield at

Suwon also down five North Korean aircraft attempting to attack there.

As eight B-29s finish attacking Communist-held Kimpo Airfield, South Korea, they are attacked by North Korean fighters; one of these is downed by a Superfortress gunner. This is the first such aerial victory of the war.

Because military intelligence is sorely needed by United Nations forces, RB-29s based at Yokota Air Base, Japan, begin photo operations over North Korea. They are joined by aircraft of the 8th Tactical Reconnaissance Squadron (TRS) for operations over South Korea.

JUNE 30   In Washington, D.C., President Harry S. Truman orders full-scale aerial attacks on North Korea, along with a naval blockade of the peninsula and the use of U.S. ground forces to halt the Communist offensive.

In South Korea, the Royal Australian Air Force (RAAF) No. 77 Squadron arrives for duty and is assigned to operational control by the Fifth Air Force.

As North Korean forces swarm southward over the Han River, they are beginning to threaten Suwon airfield, which now houses some of the first tactical Air Control Parties dispatched by the Fifth Air Force. However, Far East Air Forces (FEAF) orders the place to be evacuated to new facilities at Kumhae near the port of Pusan.

JULY 1   At Itazuke, Japan, transport aircraft of the 374th Troop Carrier Wing (TCW) begin airlifting elements of the 24th Infantry Division to Pusan, South Korea, for the first time.

JULY 3   In Washington, D.C., Air Force Chief of Staff General Hoyt S. Vandenberg orders B-29s of the 22nd Bomb Group deployed to Northwest Asia for use in the Korean conflict.

The futuristic Northrop YB-49 Flying Wing was a most impressive aircraft at first glance, but it proved too unstable as a bombing platform and was not accepted into service. (Library of Congress)

Because large C-54 Skymaster transports are too heavy for most Korean runways and damage them, the Far East Air Forces (FEAF) orders smaller C-46s and C-47s to transport men and supplies there from bases in Japan.

JULY 6   Over Wonsan and Hungnam, North Korea, nine B-29s conduct the first strategic air raid of the Korean War when they attack oil refineries and chemical plants in the two cities.

Back in the States, the Harmon International Aviation Awards Committee designates James H. "Jimmy" Doolittle as "Aviator of the Decade" while Jacqueline Cochran is named "Outstanding Aviatrix."

JULY 8   At Yokota Air Base, Japan, Major General Emmett "Rosie" O'Donnell gains appointment as the head of Bomber

Command (Provisional) within the Far East Air Forces (FEAF). Previously, O'Donnell served as a high-ranking adviser to General Henry H. Arnold during World War II.

JULY 9   In South Korea, forward air controllers flying L-5G and L-17 Liaison aircraft begin calling in F-80 air strikes to assist hard-pressed UN forces.

JULY 10   North American T-6 Texan trainers are now used by the Fifth Air Force to call in close support as forward air controllers. These "Mosquito" runs are usually in conjunction with F-80 jets against columns of North Korean forces.

Over Pyongtaek, South Korea, a convoy of Communist vehicles is caught in the open by American B-26s, F-82s, and F-80s after it stops at a bombed-out bridge. The enemy formation is annihilated by

One of the world's greatest aviators, U.S. pilot Jackie Cochran overcame a hardscrabble existence to set 200 flying records, as well as abolishing the gender barrier in her field. Cochran was appointed to lead the Women's Air Force Service Pilots in 1943. (Library of Congress)

bombs and napalm, losing 117 trucks, 38 tanks, and 7 armored cars.

JULY 12 In Japan, four aircraft of the Military Air Transport Service (MATS) arrive from the United States carrying a shipment of 3.5-inch bazookas with shaped charges. These are intended to replace smaller weapons in South Korea that are incapable of destroying Soviet-made T-34 tanks.

At Barksdale Air Force Base, Louisiana, the first RB-50B is delivered to the Strategic Air Command's (SAC) 91st Strategic Reconnaissance Squadron.

Communist aircraft manage to shoot down a B-29, a B-26, and an L-5, scoring their first aerial victories of the Korean War.

JULY 13 Over Wonsan, North Korea, 49 B-29s from 22nd and 49th Bomb Groups, Far East Air Forces (FEAF), strike an oil refinery and marshalling yards. This is also the first strategic raid launched from bases in Japan, and it is conducted by an RB-29 piloted by Lieutenant Fred Spies.

Off the coast of Korea, an SB-17 of the 3rd Aircraft Rescue Squadron drops rescue boats to members of a downed B-29 crew for the first time.

JULY 14 In South Korea, the Air Force deploys its first units to operate directly on the peninsula, including the 35th Fighter-Interceptor Group at Pohang and the 6132nd Tactical Air Control Squadron at Taegu. The latter is responsible for orchestrating a close support mission to assist UN ground forces.

JULY 15 At Taegu, South Korea, the Mustang-equipped 51st Fighter Squadron (Provisional) flies the first F-51 combat missions of the war.

A directive from Fifth Air Force headquarters orders the designation/call sign of "Mosquito" to pertain to all airborne controllers using T-6 Texan aircraft.

JULY 19 Over Taejon, South Korea, three Communist Yak fighters are downed by F-80s of the Fifth Air Force; this is the highest daily kill rate for the rest of the month.

Over Pyongyang, North Korea, 7 F-80s of the 8th Fighter-Bomber Group initiate a strategy to acquire complete air superiority by destroying 15 Communist aircraft on the ground.

JULY 20 In Tokyo, Japan, Major General Otto P. Weyland gains appointment as vice commander of Far East Air Forces (FEAF) for operations.

Over South Korea, two Yak fighters are bagged by Fifth Air Force F-80 Shooting Stars. These are the last American aerial victories until November, when Communist air opposition is dramatically revived.

JULY 22 In Japan, the carrier USS *Boxer* arrives carrying 145 Air Force F-51 Mustangs.

At Taegu, South Korea, the first H-5 helicopter to see active service is deployed by the 3rd Air Rescue Squadron.

JULY 24 At Cape Canaveral, Florida, a German V-2 rocket with a WAC Corporal second stage becomes the first missile launched from the Joint Long Range Proving Grounds.

At Taegu, South Korea, the Fifth Air Force establishes a headquarters near Eighth Army headquarters to facilitate communication and coordination between the two services.

In Tokyo, Japan, General Douglas MacArthur is formally appointed commander of all UN forces and he appoints Major General George E. Stratemeyer, commander of Far East Air Forces (FEAF), to assume responsibility for all air actions over the Korean peninsula.

JULY 28 In Japan, the first Grumman SA-16 Albatross arrives for search and rescue missions in the Korean War.

JULY 30 Over North Korea, 47 Far East Air Forces (FEAF) B-29s attack explosive factories at Hungnam.

AUGUST 1 In Washington, D.C., Generals Joseph Collins and Hoyt S. Vandenberg conclude an agreement establishing cooperation between the Aerospace Defense Command and the Army Anti-Aircraft Command for the defense of the United States.

In Florida, Patrick Air Force Base is christened after Major General Mason M. Patrick, the first chief of the U.S. Army Air Service.

Over North Korea, 46 B-29s of the 22nd and 92nd Bomb Groups destroy the Chosen Nitrogen Fertilizer Factory at Hungnam; this is one of the largest chemical plants in Asia.

AUGUST 2–3 At Ashiya, Japan, the 374th Troop Carrier Group establishes a new record by flying 150 tons of equipment and supplies to the Eighth Army in Korea within a 24-hour time period.

AUGUST 3 In Tokyo, Japan, Lieutenant General George E. Stratemeyer, commander of the Far East Air Forces (FEAF) lays down the strategy for Interdiction Campaign No. 1, aimed at cutting enemy supply routes between the 37th and 38th Parallels.

Off the Korean coast, SA-16 Albatrosses begin flying rescue missions to assist downed UN flight crews.

AUGUST 4 Over North Korea, the Far East Air Forces (FEAF) commences Interdiction Campaign No. 1 by dispatching B-29 heavy bombers to destroy key bridges north of the 38th Parallel.

AUGUST 5 At Hamchang, South Korea, Major Louis J. Sebille wins the Air Force's first posthumous Congressional Medal of Honor by deliberately crashing his F-51 into a North Korean ground position. Because an Air Force medal is not approved until 1960, Sebille receives the Army Medal of Honor.

AUGUST 7 At Yokota Air Base, Japan, the newly arrived 98th Bomb Group commits 20 B-29s to their first air raid over North Korea.

AUGUST 10 In the United States, the Air Force mobilizes two Reserve units, the 437th Troop-Carrier Wing and the 452nd Bomb Wing, for active duty; these are the first of 25 such units called into service for the Korean War.

AUGUST 11 The Fairchild XC-120 performs its maiden flight; this novel craft is assembled from wings and tail sections of the C-119B Flying Boxcar, but it does not enter production.

At Tachikawa Air Base, Japan, Air Force C-119 Flying Boxcars airlift trucks and other heavy equipment directly into Taegu, South Korea.

AUGUST 16 A force of nearly 100 B-29s drops bombs on massed North Korean troops at Waegwan, South Korea, in a spoiling attack to prevent them from overrunning the Pusan Perimeter. This is the largest carpet bombing raid of its kind since Operation COBRA at Normandy in August 1944.

AUGUST 19 In South Korea, Air Force and Navy aircraft help blunt a North Korean drive across the Naktong River, allowing the Battle of Naktong to end in a UN victory.

AUGUST 22 Over North Korea, Chinese antiaircraft batteries open fire on B-29 formations from across the Yalu River in Manchuria. This is the first recorded hostility of Chinese Communists in the Korean War.

AUGUST 23 West of Pyongyang, North Korea, the Air Force makes its first Razon guided-bomb strike of the war, although only one weapon strikes its intended target.

AUGUST 25 In Tokyo, the Fifth Air Force is ordered to maintain constant armed surveillance of enemy airfields in North Korea to prevent enemy aerial activity during the upcoming Inchon landings.

AUGUST 26 In Washington, D.C., Air Force Chief of Staff Hoyt S. Vandenburg presents the Bell X-1 No. 1, the vehicle that broke the sound barrier, to the Smithsonian Institution.

At Barksdale, Louisiana, the 91st Strategic Reconnaissance Wing receives its first operational RB-45C Tornado.

At Ashiya, Japan, General William H. Tunner, who had previously directed the Berlin Airlift, organizes the new Combat Cargo Command (Provisional), which is built around the 1st Troop Carrier Task Force (Provisional). Meanwhile, orders go out from the Far East Air Forces to collect all C-46 transport aircraft in Asia to support a major UN offensive the following month.

AUGUST 27 Over Antung, China, two F-51 Mustangs accidentally cross the border and strafe a Chinese airstrip, thinking that they were attacking a North Korean field near Sinuiju. The Chinese government uses the affair for propaganda and diplomatic purposes.

AUGUST 31 Outside Pusan, South Korea, North Korean forces make a last-ditch effort to drive UN forces back into the sea, but they are partly thwarted by close air support missions flown by the Navy and Fifth Air Force.

Over North Korea, a force of 74 B-29s attack mining facilities and marshalling yards at Chinnampo. This is also the largest strategic bombing raid of the entire month.

SEPTEMBER 1 At Biggs Air Force Base, Texas, the first operational KP-29P tanker deploys with the 97th Air Refueling Squadron. This variant is the first American tanker craft equipped with an aerial boom, which replaces the British-style trailing hose equipment used on the KB-29M.

Outside of Pusan, South Korea, Fifth Air Force fighter-bombers and light bombers continue working over Communist armor and infantry formations with machine guns, rockets, and napalm to support the UN perimeter.

SEPTEMBER 4   Over South Korea, a Sikorsky H–5 helicopter piloted by Lieutenant Paul W. Van Boven performs the first rescue mission of a pilot, Captain Robert E. Wayne, then downed behind enemy lines.

SEPTEMBER 9   In order to retard the possible arrival of Communist reinforcements to the Inchon landing site, Far East Air Forces (FEAF) Bomber Command begins a rail interdiction effort north of Seoul, South Korea. Heavy and medium bombers begin hammering key marshalling yards and resupply points over the next week.

SEPTEMBER 15   At Inchon, South Korea, UN forces under General Douglas MacArthur stage a brilliant surprise landing behind enemy lines while medium bombers and fighters of the Far East Air Forces (FEAF) strike at targets near Pusan to assist the forthcoming breakout.

SEPTEMBER 15–18   At Bergstrom Air Force Base, Texas, 180 F–84Es of the 27th Escort Fighter Wing begin flying in relays to airfields in West Germany. The next wave completes the move on October 15–28.

SEPTEMBER 16   The USAF Research and Development Command is redesignated the Air Research and Development Center (ARDC).

At Pusan, South Korea, the Eighth Army breaks through encircling North Korean unit and moves up the peninsula, closely supported by Fifth Air Force fighters and bombers. Communist forces retreat helter–skelter to avoid being cut off.

SEPTEMBER 17   Near the Naktong River, South Korea, Fifth Air Force F–51s and

F–80s drop napalm on retreating North Korean columns, killing hundreds of enemy troops.

Over North Korea, the Far East Air Forces begins a psychological campaign by dropping four million leaflets over the battered inhabitants.

SEPTEMBER 18   For a second time, 42 B–29s from the 92nd and 98th Bombardment Groups, Far East Air Forces (FEAF), carpet bomb North Korean troop concentrations in and around Waegwan, removing a major obstacle to the Eighth Army's surging offensive.

The third anniversary of the U.S. Air Force as an independent service finds it deeply immersed in the first armed conflict of the Cold War.

SEPTEMBER 19–20   Over South Korea, the Combat Cargo Command begins airlifting men and supplies to Kimpo Air Base, Seoul, with a force of 32 C–54 Skymasters. These operations are flown around the clock to supply the surging UN offensive underway.

SEPTEMBER 21   Outside Pusan, South Korea, Air Force T–6 Mosquitos observe a column of 30 North Korean tanks advancing upon the U.S. 24th Infantry Division, and direct the requisite air strikes to thwart them; 14 tanks are destroyed and the rest flee in confusion.

SEPTEMBER 22   Operation Fox Able Four unfolds as Colonel David Schilling flies the first nonstop transit over the Atlantic Ocean by touching down safely at RAF Manston in Kent, England. The flight from Limestone, Maine took 10 hours, covered 3,000 miles, and required three in-flight refuelings. However, wingman Lieutenant Colonel William D. Ritchie ran out of fuel over Labrador and ejected; Schilling wins the Mackay Trophy for his efforts.

This reconnaissance photograph taken in 1952 depicts a power plant made unserviceable by United Nations Command (UNC) warplane attacks. The campaign against North Korean hydroelectric plants in the summer of 1952 was launched by the Far East Air Force in the hope of forcing the Communists to accept UNC truce terms. (National Archives)

Over Kunsan, South Korea, a T-6 Mosquito flown by Lieutenant George W. Nelson drops leaflets to a body of North Korean troops, urging that they surrender or face annihilation. The Communists comply by moving to a designated position, where they surrender to UN forces.

SEPTEMBER 23   At Pusan, South Korea, the headquarters of the Fifth Air Force packs up and relocates to Taegu to be closer to the front.

An SB-17 from the 3rd Air Rescue Squadron makes the first recorded classified flight during the Korean War.

SEPTEMBER 26   Fifth Air Force fighters and bombers continue supporting the UN drive northward towards the 38th Parallel as they unite at Osan.

Over Haeju, North Korea, a force of 20 B-29s from the 22nd Bomb Group attack and destroy a munitions factory and a power plant. A hydroelectric plant at Pujon is also bombed by another group of B-29s. These raids conclude the Far East Air Forces' (FEAF) first strategic bombing campaign.

SEPTEMBER 27   In Washington, D.C., the Joint Chiefs of Staff (JCS) decides to halt further strategic raids against North Korea for want of suitable targets.

SEPTEMBER 28   Over Holloman Air Force Base, New Mexico, a research balloon carries eight white mice to an altitude of 97,000 feet, then returns them unharmed.

At Yokota Air Base, Japan, the first three RB-45C Tornado reconnaissance jets arrive for duty with Far East Air Forces (FEAF). Officially, they are known simply as Detachment A, 84th Bomb Squadron.

SEPTEMBER 29   Over Holloman Air Force Base, New Mexico, Captain Richard V. Wheeler performs a record parachute jump from 42,449 feet and lands unscathed.

OCTOBER 2   Over Nanam, North Korea, Far East Air Forces (FEAF) B-29s carpet bomb North Korean troop training facilities to retard enemy attempts at reinforcements.

At Taegu, South Korea, the 8th Tactical Reconnaissance Squadron (TRS) is the first such unit deployed at K-2 airfield.

OCTOBER 6   As of this date, headquarters Far East Air Forces (FEAF) assumes control of all UN land-based aircraft, including several U.S. Marine Corps squadrons flying out of Kimpo.

In South Korea, No. 2 Squadron, South African Air Force deploys under the aegis of the Far East Air Forces (FEAF).

Outside of Seoul, South Korea, the Marine Corps relinquishes control of Kimpo Airfield, which was captured earlier in September.

Over Kan-Ni, North Korea, 18 Far East Air Forces (FEAF) B-29s attack a Communist arsenal while FEAF headquarters also orders attacks against bridges south of Pyongyang and Wonsan halted.

OCTOBER 8   The Air Force receives a new shipment of modified and more reliable Razon radio-controlled guided bombs, and bombing missions with them resume.

Over North Korea, two F-80 Shooting Stars accidentally cross the border and strafe a Soviet airfield near Vladivostok. An enraged Air Force Chief of Staff Hoyt S. Vandenberg orders the two pilots court-martialed and the group commander relieved.

OCTOBER 10   In the United States, the first Air National Guard units are mobilized for service in Korea. Ultimately, 66 such units, representing 45,000 personnel, will be deployed there.

In Europe, Lieutenant General Lauris Norstad gains appointment as commander of United States Air Force in Europe (USAFE).

OCTOBER 15   At Davis-Monthan Air Force Base, Arizona, the Air Force commences the B-47 phase-out program by retiring the first of its RB-47Es.

OCTOBER 20   Over Pyongyang, North Korea, over 100 C-47 and C-119s transport aircraft convey 4,000 Army paratroopers and their supplies on a battlefield drop 30 miles north of the Communist capital.

OCTOBER 25   In Tokyo, Japan, headquarters Far East Air Forces (FEAF), halts all B-29 air raids due to a lack of strategic

targets in North Korea. However, all restrictions are lifted on medium bombers and fighters so that they can provide close support missions up to the Manchurian border.

Over Korea, the Combat Cargo Command establishes a new daily record of 1,767 tons lifted and delivered.

In an ominous development, Communist China decides to enter the Korean War and begins infiltrating thousands of troops across the Yalu River.

OCTOBER 26   Over North Korea, C-119s of the Combat Cargo Command deliver 28 tons of ammunition and supplies to troops isolated on the battlefield.

OCTOBER 28   In Europe, F-84s of the 27th Fighter Escort Wing finish deploying from the United States. This first-ever mass transfer of jet aircraft across the Atlantic wins the Mackay Trophy.

NOVEMBER 2   At Yokota Air Base, Japan, the first RB-45C reconnaissance mission is flown over North Korea.

NOVEMBER 4   Over Chongju, North Korea, Fifth Air Force B-26s provide close air support to Eighth Army troops, killing hundreds of Communist soldiers.

NOVEMBER 5   Over Kanggye, North Korea, 21 B-29s from the 19th Bomb Group drop 170 tons of incendiaries and destroy 65 percent of the central sector. This target is only 20 miles south of the Manchurian border and marks the beginning of a new strategy by Bomber Command.

NOVEMBER 8   Over Sinuiju, North Korea, the largest incendiary raid of the Korean War unfolds as 70 B-29s drop 580 tons of fire ordnance directly next to the Chinese border. Various bridges along the Yalu River are also bombed for the first time.

Near the Manchurian border, Soviet-piloted MiG-15 jets, sporting North Korean markings, engage a flight of Air Force F-80 Shooting Stars for the first time. Lieutenant Russell J. Brown is credited with downing the first Communist jet in combat, although postwar records suggest that the MiG, while damaged, managed to return to base.

NOVEMBER 9   Over North Korea, B-29 tail gunner Airman Harry J. LaVerne shoots down the first MiG lost to a heavy bomber. However, LaVerne's own aircraft is heavily damaged in the exchange and it crashes in Japan, killing five crewmen.

NOVEMBER 10   The effectiveness of the MiG-15's bomber-killing cannon armament is underscored this day when a B-29 of the 307th Bombardment Group is brought down near the Yalu River. The crew manages to parachute to safety and spends the rest of the war as prisoners.

NOVEMBER 18   Jets of the 35th Fighter Interceptor Group (FIG) transfer from their base in South Korea to Yonpo airfield outside Hungnam, North Korea. This enables them to fly and fight much closer to the front lines.

NOVEMBER 19   Over Musan, North Korea, 50 B-26 Invaders stage the first-ever mass light bomber attack when they dump incendiaries and destroy most of the town's barracks complex.

NOVEMBER 23   Over North Korea, Far East Air Forces (FEAF) B-29s hammer Communist communications, bridges, and supply centers while Fifth Air Force fighters and medium bombers provide close support missions for UN troops. Transports of the Combat Cargo

Command also redouble their efforts as General Douglas MacArthur begins his final drive to the Yalu River.

NOVEMBER 25   In North Korea, Chinese Communist forces launch a massive counteroffensive that begins pushing UN forces back down the peninsula.

In Japan, a C-47 detachment from the Royal Hellenic Air Force arrives for duty and is subordinated to the Far East Air Forces (FEAF).

NOVEMBER 26   Over North Korea, as mass Chinese forces bear down on the Eighth Army and the X Corps, B-26 Invaders begin flying their first close air support missions at night.

NOVEMBER 28   Over North Korea, radar-equipped B-26 Invaders begin safely dropping bombs within 1,000 yards of UN lines for the first time.

Transports of the Combat Cargo Command begin evacuating hundreds of wounded and frostbitten marines from the Chosin region of North Korea while also dropping 1,600 tons of equipment and supplies to the front lines.

DECEMBER 4   Over Sinuiju, North Korea, the world's first jet bomber interception unfolds as a flight of Soviet-piloted MiG-15s down an RB-45C Tornado on a reconnaissance mission.

DECEMBER 5   This day C-47s of the Royal Hellenic Air Force begin flying with the Combat Cargo Command to supply UN forces in northeastern North Korea; most missions start and begin at a frozen airstrip at Hagaru-ri.

DECEMBER 6   At Itazuke, Japan, F-84s of the 27th Fighter Escort Wing begin flying close ground support missions to North Korea and back.

DECEMBER 7   Over North Korea, B-29s of the Far East Air Forces (FEAF) pound Communist troop concentrations near the Changjin Reservoir as marines and army troops prepare to break out of an encirclement. Crude airstrips are continually being built as they retreat to accommodate transports of the Combat Cargo Command.

Near the Chosin Reservoir, North Korea, eight C-119 Flying Boxcars parachute several bridge spans to U.S. forces so that they can cross a 1,500-foot-deep gorge. This is also the first time that a complete bridge has been airdropped.

DECEMBER 14   Over Huichon, North Korea, Air Force planes drop the first six-ton Tarzon bomb near a railroad tunnel. Like its predecessor, the Razon, this device fails to live up to expectations.

DECEMBER 14–17   Near Hamhung, North Korea, transports of Combat Cargo Command begin a three-day aerial evacuation, lifting 228 patients, 3,891 passengers, and 20,088 tons of cargo to safety as Chinese forces begin closing in on the airfield.

DECEMBER 15   In response to the MiG-15's appearance over North Korea, the 4th Fighter Interceptor Group (FIG) deploys the F-86 Sabrejets to Japan as a counter. The stage is now set for a classical aerial encounter.

B-29s of Bomber Command begin a new series of zone interdiction raids to stop surging Chinese forces in North Korea.

DECEMBER 17   Over North Korea, the F-86 Sabrejet draws first blood when Lieutenant Colonel Bruce H. Hinton shoots down a MiG-15. This is the first aerial victory between swept-wing jets in aviation history.

DECEMBER 20   At Kimpo, South Korea, Operation KIDLIFT commences as 12 C-54s of the 61st Troop Carrier Group begin lifting Korean orphans to an island off the coast of Pusan.

DECEMBER 22   Over North Korea, six Russian-piloted MiG-15s fall to the guns of one Navy and five Air Force jet fighters; this is also the highest daily victory toll for a single day since June. However, one F-86 is also shot down for the first time.

At Seoul, South Korea, headquarters, Fifth Air Force, relocates back to Taegu as Chinese forces advance upon the city from the north.

DECEMBER 23   In a daring move, 3 H-5 helicopters evacuate 11 U.S. and 24 South Korean soldiers trapped eight miles behind enemy lines.

DECEMBER 24   At Hungnam, North Korea, the last of 105,000 troops belonging to X Corps, along with 91,000 civilians, are evacuated as B-26s bombers and Navy gunfire pin down advancing Chinese forces.

DECEMBER 29   From Taegu, South Korea, the first RF-51 reconnaissance missions are staged. Though slower than RF-80s, the Mustangs have greater range and endurance in the air.

1951

JANUARY 1   The Air Defense Command (ADC), having been previously abolished, is restored under General Ennis C. Whitehead.

In South Korea, as half a million massed Chinese and North Korean forces pour over the 38th Parallel, they are heavily racked by fighters and bombers of the Fifth Air Force.

JANUARY 2   Over South Korea, flares dropped by a C-27 transport illuminate target areas for B-26 and F-82 night attacks on Communist troop concentrations and supply lines.

JANUARY 3–5   Pyongyang, North Korea, is staggered by 60 Bomber Command B-29s which drop 650 tons of incendiaries on the city; a follow-up raid is launched two days later. This day Far East Air Forces (FEAF) also achieve a one-day record by mounting 958 combat sorties.

JANUARY 4   Near Seoul, South Korea, the last remaining Air Force planes evacuate Kimpo Airfield for the second time in six months as Chinese forces approach the city. The landing strip is then heavily bombed to preclude any possible use by the enemy.

JANUARY 6   Over South Korea, transports of the Combat Cargo Command finish resupplying the U.S. 2nd Infantry Division as it fights to prevent a Chinese breakthrough in UN lines.

JANUARY 10   In Tokyo, Japan, Brigadier General James E. Briggs gains appointment as the new head of Bomber Command. The Strategic Air Command (SAC) has mandated that new commanders will be rotated every four months to grant wartime experience to as many senior leaders as possible.

JANUARY 12   Over South Korea, Far East Air Forces B-29s attack massed Communist troops with 500-pound bombs fuzed for aboveground airbursts, and the ensuing shower of steel fragments staggers their formations.

JANUARY 13   Over Kanggye, North Korea, a Far East Air Forces B-29 drops a six-ton Tarzon bomb on an enemy bridge, scoring a direct hit and destroying 60 feet of the structure.

JANUARY 16   At RAF Lakenheath, England, six B-36 Peacekeepers complete a nonstop 7,000-mile deployment from Bergstrom Air Force Base, Texas.

Project MS-1593 is initiated by the Air Force and Convair to acquire a viable intercontinental ballistic weapon; in time it emerges as the Atlas missile.

JANUARY 17   At Taegu, South Korea, F-86 Sabres are redeployed on the peninsula, only this time as fighter-bombers for close support missions.

JANUARY 17–18   Over South Korea, Combat Cargo Command launches 109 C-119 missions, which drop 550 tons of supplies and ammunition to UN forces on the front lines.

JANUARY 19   Because the Communist forces have greatly overextended their supply lines in their drive south, Far East Air Forces (FEAF) commences an extensive aerial interdiction campaign to deny them badly needed supplies and reinforcements.

JANUARY 21   Over North Korea, a big dogfight results in the loss of one F-86 and one F-84 to MiG-15s. However, Lieutenant Colonel William E. Bertram scores the first MiG-15 kill by an F-84.

JANUARY 23   Over Sinuiju, North Korea, an attack by 33 F-84s stirs a large number of MiG-15s from across the Yalu River, resulting in a 30-minute dogfight. This time, the Thunderjets get the better of it, downing three MIGs.

A combined force of 21 B-29s and 46 F-80s attack antiaircraft emplacements and airfields, heavily damaging both.

JANUARY 25–FEBRUARY 9   In South Korea, Operation THUNDERBOLT unfolds as UN forces counterattack in an attempt to recapture Inchon and the Suwon airfield. They are assisted by 70 C-119s of Combat Cargo Command, which deliver 1,162 tons of supplies as they advance.

JANUARY 26   Over South Korea, a C-47 heavily rigged with radios can maintain contact with all T-6 Mosquito aircraft and coordinate their efforts. This is an early attempt to field an airborne command and control center.

JANUARY 31   At Yonan, South Korea, an aircraft of the 21st Tactical Control Squadron drops off an agent just south of the 38th Parallel; this is the first spy mission of its kind in this war.

FEBRUARY 8   Throughout North Korea, Far East Air Forces (FEAF) aircraft mount a concerted effort to sever all rail lines in northeastern reaches of the peninsula.

In Tokyo, Japan, Brigadier General John P. Henebry becomes commander of the 315th Air Division, and responsible for all airlift operations in this theater.

FEBRUARY 13   Over South Korea, transports of the 315th Air Division relocate over 800 wounded soldiers from the front lines to facilities at Taegu and Pusan. However, this movement tied up so many C-47s that routine supply functions were impossible.

FEBRUARY 13–16   At Chipyong-ni, South Korea, as 3 Chinese divisions surround the U.S. 23rd Infantry and a

French battalion, 100 Air Force transports support the latter by dropping 420 tons of supplies and ammunition. They are further assisted by fighters and bombers of the Fifth Air Force, which provide close air support to the troops, and by H-5 helicopters, which help evacuate wounded men despite subfreezing weather and strong wind.

FEBRUARY 16   In South Korea, the Army begins using the L-19 Bird Dog as an artillery spotter, thereby reliving Air Force aircraft to perform other missions.

FEBRUARY 17–18   Over North Korea, the B-29 bombing raid employs shoran for the first time. This is a navigation system utilizing an airborne radar receiver and two ground beacons to plot accurate bombing.

FEBRUARY 23   Over South Korea, Bomber Command B-29s begin using MPQ-2 radar for accurately bombing a highway bridge near Seoul.

FEBRUARY 24   Over South Korea, transports of the Combat Cargo Command deliver a record 33 tons of supplies to UN forces on the front lines. C-119 Flying Boxcars again distinguish themselves for flying the bulk of these sorties.

MARCH 1   Over North Korea, a force of 22 F-80s, sent to escort a force of 18 B-29s over a target, miss their rendezvous and have to return to base. The bombers continue on and are attacked by Communist MiGs, who damage 10 of them, 3 so badly that they make forced landings in South Korea.

In Greenland, the Air Force opens Thule Air Base, which is 690 miles north of the Arctic Circle and the northernmost American air facility.

MARCH 4   Over South Korea, 15 C-119s provide the 1st Marine Division with

260 tons of supplies; this is also the largest single drop of the month.

MARCH 6   Over North Korea, F–86 Sabrejets begin patrolling along the Yalu River for the first time in several months.

MARCH 14   As Communist forces evacuate Seoul, South Korea, Fifth Air Force B–26s drop tetrahedral metal spikes to puncture enemy truck tires.

MARCH 15   In a significant development, a B–47 Stratojet is refueled in midair by a KC–97A tanker for the first time. This endows the B–47 with the range of a strategic bomber.

MARCH 16   Over all of Korea, Far East Air Forces (FEAF) aircraft perform a record 1,123 sorties.

MARCH 20   At South Ruislip, England, the 7th Division, Strategic Air Command (SAC) establishes its headquarters.

MARCH 23   Northwest of Seoul, South Korea, Operation TOMAHAWK unfolds as 120 C–119s and C–46s, escorted by 12 F–51s, drop the 187th Airborne Regimental Combat Team and two Ranger Battalions behind enemy lines. This transfer of 3,400 men and 220 tons of supplies behind enemy lines is the largest single airborne operation of the conflict.

Over northwestern Korea, a force of 22 B–29s from the 19th and 307th Bomb Groups, escorted by 45 F–86 Sabrejets, bomb two bridges used for supply purposes.

MARCH 24   In South Korea, the Air Force deploys its H–19 Chickasaw helicopters for the first time; this vehicle is considerably larger than the H–5 it replaces, with greater range and carrying capacity.

MARCH 29   Over North Korea, Far East Air Forces (FEAF) B–29s attack bridges spanning the Yalu River as the ice begins to thaw.

APRIL 2   Major General David M. Schlatter gains appointment as head of the new Air Research and Development Command (ARDC).

APRIL 3   Southeast of Pyongyang, North Korea, a service-test YH–19 Chickasaw helicopter of the 3rd Air Rescue Squadron saves a downed F–51 pilot while under Communist fire.

APRIL 6   In Washington, D.C., the Labor Department reveals that the number of people working in aircraft construction fields has risen to 100,000 during the first six months of the Korean conflict.

APRIL 9   At India, California, an F–51 flown by aviatrix Jacqueline Cochran sets a woman's speed record of 469.5 miles per hour over a 16-mile course. This is her fifth such aviation record in piston-powered aircraft.

APRIL 12   Over Sinuiju, North Korea, a force of 46 B–29s, escorted by 100 fighters, attacks the Yalu River Bridge until they are set upon by 100 MiG–15s. The latter shoot down three bombers and damage seven more for a loss of seven MiGs. The F–86s also claim four more Communist craft for a total of 11, although the bridge is not destroyed.

APRIL 17   In North Korea, Warrant Officer Donald Nicholas leads a special operations team that recovers parts of a MiG–15 wreckage and other technical information; he receives the Distinguished Service Cross.

APRIL 18   At Holloman Air Force Base, New Mexico, a monkey accompanies an Aerorocket into space but fails to survive the return trip to Earth.

APRIL 19   In South Korea, the first refurbished C-119 Boxcars, modified and reconditioned after a hiatus of several weeks, are returned to combat operations.

APRIL 21   The Fairchild XC-123 Provider, a four-jet version of the propeller-driven design, flies for the first time. It does not enter production but does represent the first U.S. jet transport.

APRIL 23   Over South Korea, Far East Air Forces (FEAF) aircraft complete 340 close support missions, one of the highest totals ever. Meanwhile, F-86 Sabrejets are deployed to Suwon airfield to cut down flying time to "MiG Alley" along the Yalu River.

APRIL 23–26   Over this three-day period, Far East Air Forces (FEAF) aircraft perform 1,000 combat sorties in support of UN ground forces in the face of a massive Chinese offensive.

APRIL 30   Aircraft of the Fifth Air Force reach a new daily total of 960 combat sorties.

MAY 9   In northwestern North Korea, aircraft of the Fifth Air Force and the 1st Marine Air Wing commit one of the largest joint counterair efforts of the war by launching 300 sorties against Sinuiju airfield.

MAY 16–26   For 10 straight days, transport aircraft based in Japan fly in an average of 1,000 tons of supplies and ammunition per day to UN forces locked in combat with Chinese troops in South Korea.

MAY 17–22   Over North Korea, B-29s from Bomber Command fly 94 close support missions for UN ground forces, mostly at night.

Jabara, James (1923–1966)

Air Force pilot. James Jabara was born in Muskogee, Oklahoma, on October 10, 1923, the son of Lebanese immigrants. He joined the Army Air Forces as a pilot in May 1942, and earned his wings in October 1943. Jabara was initially posted with the 363rd Fighter Group, Ninth Air Force, in England, where he shot down a German aircraft after losing his own canopy. He transferred home for a year as an instructor, then returned to combat with the 355th Fighter Group in February 1945. His wartime tally was one-and-a-half kills in the air, and four aircraft on the ground. Afterwards he passed through the Air Tactical School and began flying the new F-86 Sabrejet in 1949. He was serving as a major with the 334th Fighter Interceptor Squadron, Fourth Fighter Group, when the Korean War broke out in June 1950. Because the Soviet MiG-15 fighter was superior to all other American aircraft in that theater, Jabara accompanied the Fourth Fighter Group there in December 1950 to confront them. He scored his first MiG on April 3, 1951, and his fifth and sixth MiGs on May 20, 1951, becoming history's first all-jet fighter ace.

Jabara served as an instructor back home until January 1953, when he returned to combat over North Korea. In several sizzling encounters, he wracked up 9 more kills over the next six months, raising his total to 15 and becoming the first triple jet ace. After the war Jabara commanded F-104 Starfighters over the Taiwan Straits in 1958, and he also transitioned to B-58 Hustlers in 1961. Jabara was awaiting deployment in Vietnam when he was killed in an auto accident on November 17, 1966. This distinguished aviator was interred at Arlington National Cemetery.

MAY 20   Over North Korea, F-86 pilot Captain James Jabara downs his fifth MiG-15, becoming the world's first all-jet ace.

In Tokyo, Japan, Major General George E. Stratemeyer, commanding the Far East Air Forces (FEAF), is sidelined by a heart attack. He is replaced by Major General Earle E. Partridge.

MAY 21   In Tokyo, Japan, Major General Edward J. Timberlake is appointed the new commander of the Fifth Air Force.

MAY 27–28   Over North Korea, C-47s drop thousands of leaflets calling upon enemy troops to surrender to the U.S. Army IX Corps. Over 4,000 Communist troops do come over and report that morale is very low due to incessant air strikes.

MAY 31   Over North Korea, Operation STRANGLE unfolds as the Fifth Air Force makes a concerted effort to interdict all Communist supply lines by air.

JUNE   At Edwards Air Force Base, California, the Air Force Flight Test Center formally opens for business.

JUNE 1   In the United States, aeromedical researcher Major John P. Strapp subjects himself to rapid acceleration on a series of rocket-powered sleds to examine how well human bodies can adapt to high G forces. He survives unhurt and preliminary results suggest that high rates are more survivable than medical science had believed.

In Tokyo, Japan, Major General Frank K. Everest gains appointment as commander of the Fifth Air Force.

JUNE 3   Over South Korea, two C-119 Flying Boxcars are accidentally shot down by friendly ground fire during an air supply effort. New procedures for aircraft identification are the result of this accident.

JUNE 10   In Tokyo, Japan, Lieutenant General Otto P. Weyland gains appointment as the new commander of Far East Air Forces (FEAF).

JUNE 20   Over Edwards Air Force Base, California, the Bell X-5 variable-sweep (moveable) wing research jet takes to the skies for the first time.

The Marin B-61 Matador, a mobile tactical missile, is launched successfully for the first time.

JUNE 25   At Tullahoma, Tennessee, the Arnold Engineering Development Center is dedicated by President Harry S. Truman.

JULY 1   Over South Korea, Colonel Karl L. Polifka, commander of the 67th Tactical Reconnaissance Wing, is killed after his F-51 is struck by enemy ground fire and his parachute snags the aircraft's tail.

JULY 6   Over North Korea, a KB-29M from the Air Materiel Command, crewed and flown by a SAC crew from the 43rd Air Refueling Squadron, conducts the first aerial refueling exercise over hostile territory when it tanks up four RF-80 Shooting Stars on a reconnaissance mission.

JULY 14   In light of Cold War tensions and paranoia, the Ground Observer Corp begins an around-the-clock skywatch of the United States.

JULY 30   Over North Korea, a major air raid unfolds as 91 F-80s attack enemy air defenses while 354 Marine Corps and Air Force fighter-bombers attack ground targets. The Joint Chiefs of Staff declines to release information about this air strike to avoid any negative publicity during peace negotiations with Communist leaders.

AUGUST 17   Over Detroit, Michigan, Colonel Fred J. Ascani sets a new world speed record of 635.6 miles per hour in his F-86E Sabrejet. He wins both the National Air Race and a Mackay Trophy.

AUGUST 18   At Detroit, Michigan, an F-86A flown by Colonel Keith Compton finishes first in the Bendix Trophy transcontinental race by arriving from Muroc, California, in 3 hours and 27 minutes. His average speed is 553.8 miles per hour.

Over North Korea, Far East Air Forces (FEAF) extends Operation STRANGLE air strikes to include Communist railroads and marshalling facilities.

AUGUST 24   In Washington, D.C., Air Force Chief of Staff General Hoyt S. Vandenberg declares that testing of tactical nuclear weapons capable of being carried by jet fighters had been accomplished the previous February.

AUGUST 24–25   Over this two-day period, Fifth Air Force B-26s claim to have destroyed over 800 Communist trucks during various intruder (nighttime) attacks.

AUGUST 25   Over Rashin, North Korea, 55 B-29 bombers drop 800 tons of bombs on marshalling yards less than 20 miles from the Soviet border. They are escorted by Navy fighters, but no resistance is encountered.

AUGUST 28   The Lockheed XC-130 is declared the winner of an Air Force competition to secure a turboprop-powered transport. This enters service as the C-130 Hercules, which is still widely employed around the world to present times.

SEPTEMBER 5   The firm Convair contracts with the Air Force to modify a B-36 to utilize a small nuclear reactor as a power source. General Electric is also signed to construct the actual reactor. The NB-36H flies in 1955, but it is cancelled due to a host of unresolvable technical and environmental issues.

SEPTEMBER 9   Over Sinuiju, North Korea, a force of 28 F-86s is attacked by 70 MiG-15s but, the odds notwithstanding, Captains Richard S. Becker and Ralph D. Gibson both flame a MiG, bringing the total of all-jet fighter aces to three.

SEPTEMBER 13   At Cocoa, Florida, the Air Force creates the first pilotless bomber squadron at the Missile Test Center.

SEPTEMBER 14   During a night intruder flight, Captain John S. Wamsley, Jr., expends all his weapons attacking an enemy train, then lights it up with an experimental searchlight on his wing. The target is illuminated and destroyed by another B-26, but Wamsley's B-26 is shot down and he and two crewmen are killed; he wins a posthumous Congressional Medal of Honor.

SEPTEMBER 20   During a second attempt, Air Force scientists launch a monkey and 11 mice on an Aerobee rocket, which reaches an altitude of 230,000 feet, and returns all the animals safely back to Earth.

SEPTEMBER 23   Over Suchon, North Korea, eight shoran-guided B-29s bomb and severely damage a rail bridge over the Yalu River.

SEPTEMBER 25   Over Sinuiju, North Korea, a force of 36 F-86 Sabrejets is jumped by an estimated 100 MiG-15s but, despite the odds, the Americans down 5 Communist aircraft.

SEPTEMBER 27 Over South Korea, Operation PELICAN unfolds as a service-test C-124 Globemaster II successfully delivers 30,000 pounds of aircraft parts to Kimpo Airfield. The C-124 enjoys a highly successful career in the postwar period.

SEPTEMBER 28 Over Korea, an RF-80 completes a 14-hour and 15-minute reconnaissance mission, during which time it was refueled several times by two RB-29M tankers.

SEPTEMBER 30 In Tokyo, Japan, General Joe W. Kelly gains appointment as head of Bomber Command.

OCTOBER 16 Over North Korea, F-86s of the Fifth Air Force down nine MiG-15s in their largest single-day combat record to date.

OCTOBER 22 This day, two SA-16 Albatrosses rescue the 12-man crew of a B-29 that crashed at sea; this is the largest total saved in a single day.

OCTOBER 23 At MacDill Air Force Base, Florida, the first production B-47 Stratojet is received by the 306th Bombardment Wing. The B-47 serves capably as a nuclear attack bomber for a decade.

Over North Korea, a huge air battle erupts as MiG-15s intercept a large B-29 force escorted by F-84s. Three of the bombers and one of the Thunderjets go down in exchange for five MiGs.

NOVEMBER 4 Over Sinuiju, North Korea, a force of 34 F-86 Sabrejets tangle with an estimated 60 MiG-15s; the Americans down 2 Communist craft and damage 3 more.

NOVEMBER 9 A C-47 makes a perilous landing on the beaches of Paengnyong-do Island, off southwestern North Korea, where it rescues 11 members of a downed B-29 bomber.

NOVEMBER 16 Over North Korea, Fifth Air Force fighter-bombers continue to attack Communist rail lines across the country, as well as bridges, gun emplacements, warehouses, supply dumps, and freight cars.

NOVEMBER 30 Over North Korea, a large Communist aerial force is intercepted by F-86s who shoot down twelve bombers and damage three more. Major George A. Dais, Jr., becomes the first man to become an ace in both World War II and Korea.

DECEMBER 13 Over Sinanju, North Korea, a force of 29 Sabres encounters 75 MiG-15s, and claims to have shot down 9. Victories in other aerial battles raise the Air Force tally to 13 for the day.

DECEMBER 27 Over North Korea, Far East Air Forces (FEAF) aircraft complete 900 sorties, attacking locomotives, rail cars, buildings, vehicles—in sum, anything of use to the enemy. This is also the greatest number of missions flown for the month.

1952

JANUARY 7 In Washington, D.C., the Air Force declares that it is planning to enlarge its combat strength by 50 percent, or 143 operational wings and 1.27 million men. In May 1953, following the onset of peace in Korea, this will be pared down to 120 wings.

JANUARY 8–13 In the United States, Exercise SNOWFALL unfolds as 100 transports of the 516th Troop Carrier Wing airlift 8,600 troops and their equipment from Fort Campbell, Kentucky, to Wheeler-Sack Airfield, New York. This marks one of the largest peacetime troop airlifts to date.

JANUARY 12 Over North Korea, three F-84 Thunderjets manage to trap several Communist supply trains by bombing the entrance to a tunnel shut. The jets then systematically attack and destroy two locomotives and a series of boxcars.

FEBRUARY 1 The Air Force acquires a Univac I, a high-speed digital computer based on vacuum-tube technology.

FEBRUARY 9 Over North Korea, 10 medium bombers use radar technology to accurately drop 10 tons of 500-pound bombs on the Chongju rail bridge bypass.

FEBRUARY 10 Along the Manchurian border, a patrol of 18 F-86E Sabrejets led by Major George A. Davis encounters a flight of 12 MiG-15s and gives battle. Davis downs two Communist craft but is himself shot down and killed; his final tally is 14 jets and he receives a Congressional Medal of Honor.

FEBRUARY 20 In Washington, D.C., President Harry S. Truman appoints former lieutenant general James H. "Jimmy" Doo-little as head of a presidential commission tasked with helping to relieve airport congestion at large American cities.

MARCH Throughout the month, the Rocket Engine Advancement Program (REAP) is initiated by the Air Force to acquire the best combination of liquid oxygen and hydrocarbon fuels for rocket propulsion. In consequence, better formulas are employed for intercontinental ballistic missiles (ICBMs) like the Atlas when they arrive a few years hence.

MARCH 3 Over North Korea, the Air Force commences Operation SATURATE, a round-the-clock aerial interdiction of Communist supply lines.

MARCH 11 Over North Korea, Air Force aircraft unload 150 tons of bombs and 15,000 gallons of napalm over a four-square-mile training and supply storage area.

MARCH 19 In California, the F-86F Sabrejet flies for the first time. This enhanced version is equipped with all-power tail surfaces and modified wing leading edges for improved performance at high altitudes. Previously, the MiG-15 exhibited better characteristics above 30,000 feet.

MARCH 25 Over North Korea, Fifth Air Force aircraft perform 959 interdiction strikes on rail and highway targets stretching from Sinanju to Chongju.

APRIL 1 The Air Force changes its rank structure by discarding inherited Army grades private first class, corporal, and buck sergeant, to a comparable airman third, second, and first class.

Over North Korea, Fifth Air Force F-86 Sabrejets down ten MiG-15s for the loss of one F-86; Colonel Francis "Gabby" Gabreski bags a MiG to become the eighth all-jet ace of the conflict.

APRIL 10 In Japan, Brigadier General Chester E. McCarthy assumes command of the 315th Air Division for the rest of the Korean War.

APRIL 18   At Carswell Air Force Base, Texas, the Convair YB-60 prototype flies for the first time. This giant craft is a jet-powered version of the B-36, but it fails to go into production.

APRIL 29–30   Tragedy strikes as the 315th Air Division loses a C-47, a C-119, and a C-46 in 48 hours. A total of 16 people are killed, the greatest loss sustain by the division in the first half of the year.

MAY 3   At the North Pole, a ski-equipped C-47 flown by Lieutenant Colonels William Benedict and Joseph Fletcher makes the first successful landing there.

MAY 7   A B-29 bomber launches the Lockheed X-7 air-powered ramjet for the first time. In time this program evolves into the Bomarc antiaircraft missile.

MAY 8   Over North Korea, the Fifth Air Force musters 465 fighter-bomber sorties against a large ammunition depot southeast of Pyongyang. This is the largest single attack of its kind since the war commenced, and over 200 buildings, vehicles, and structures are destroyed or damaged. An F-86 is shot down while dive bombing, being the first Sabrejet lost in this fashion.

MAY 16–17   In Japan, 2,361 members of the 187th Airborne Regimental Combat Team are rushed to Pusan, South Korea, by C-119s, C-54s, and C-46s of the Combat Cargo Command. They are needed to help quell a prisoner insurrection at Koje-do.

JUNE 23   Over North Korea, a strike force of fighter-bombers and F-86 escorts attacks the Sui-ho hydroelectric power complex, severely damaging that vital installation.

JUNE 24   In the Korean theater, aircraft of the Far East Air Forces (FEAF) complete 1,000 sorties, its highest-ever daily tally. Many of these missions are redirected at the Sui-ho hydroelectric facilities, which sustains additional damage.

JULY 3   In South Korea, the first operational C-124 Globemaster II arrives for active duty.
   Over North Korea, C-47 transports drop 22 million leaflets as part of a psychological warfare strategy.

JULY 4   Over North Korea, a large MiG force tangles with 50 F-86s and 70 F-84s escorting a fighter-bomber force. Fifth Air Force pilots down 13 Communist craft at a cost of 2 Sabrejets, but the MiG-15s break through the fighter screen and effectively disrupt the bombing raid.

JULY 4–17   A force of 58 F-84Gs under Colonel David C. Schilling stage the first successful transpacific crossing by jet fighters. The mission covers 10,895 miles and requires seven ground stops and two in-flight refuelings.

JULY 10   Commencing this date and continuing over the next three weeks, transports of the 315th Air Division transfer the entire 474th Fighter Bomber Wing from Misawa, Japan, to Kunsan, South Korea. This represents the largest aerial unit transported by air to date.

JULY 1   Over North Korea, Operation PRESSURE PUMP unfolds as the Far East Air Forces (FEAF) mounts a maximum effort against 30 targets in and around the Communist capital of Pyongyang. Not only is this the largest single strike of the war, but the Ministry of Industry building is destroyed in its entirety.

JULY 13–31   At Prestwick, Scotland, two Sikorsky H-19 helicopters complete the first transatlantic crossing by flying in from Westover Field, Massachusetts. The aircraft in question have been named *Hop-A-Long* and *Whirl-O-Way*.

JULY 29   At Yokota Air Base, Japan, an RB-45C Tornado flown by Majors Louis H. Carrington and Frederic W. Shook and Captain Wallace D. Yancey completes the first nonstop, transpacific flight from Elmendorf, Alaska. They covered 3,640 miles in 9 hours and 50 minutes, winning a Mackay Trophy.

JULY 30–31   Over North Korea, a force of 60 B-29s pounds the Oriental Light Metals Company into ruins during a highly effective nighttime raid. No aircraft are lost despite the fact they approach to within four miles of the Yalu River.

AUGUST 6   A major dogfight erupts over North Korea with 34 F-86 Sabrejets engaging 52 MiG-15s, with the Americans downing 6 of the latter.

AUGUST 8   This day, Fifth Air Force fighters complete 285 close support missions, the highest daily total for the entire month. That evening B-26 bombers equipped with megaphone systems fly propaganda missions for four hours over enemy positions.

AUGUST 22–23   Over North Korea, three specially equipped C-47s fly propaganda broadcast sorties over enemy positions as UN forces increase their emphasis on psychological warfare.

AUGUST 29   Pyongyang, North Korea, is struck by one of the largest air raids of the war, with 1,400 ground sorties covered by F-86 Sabrejets and Australian Meteors. The action was requested by the U.S. State Department, which wished for it to coincide with a visit by Chinese foreign minister Zhou Enlai to Moscow; three UN aircraft are shot down.

SEPTEMBER 3–4   Over North Korea, B-29s complete 52 sorties, mostly against the Chosin hydroelectric power plant.

SEPTEMBER 4   North of the Chongchon River, 75 Fifth Air Force F-84 fighter-bombers bomb various targets, which draws out a large number of MiG-15s from across the Yalu River. These are set upon by the escort of 39 F-86 Sabrejets who shoot down a record 13 in one day. Major Frederick "Boots" Blesse downs his fifth MiG to become an ace, while four UN aircraft are lost.

SEPTEMBER 9   Over Sakchu, North Korea, 45 Fifth Air Force F-84s attack the military academy complex, losing three of their number to MiG-15s. Escorting F-86s manage to destroy five Communist craft at no loss to themselves.

SEPTEMBER 16   Over North Korea, B-26s flying a nighttime intruder mission employ new roadblock tactics against Communist road traffic; hence they end up destroying an estimated 100 vehicles.

SEPTEMBER 19   Southwest of Hamhung, North Korea, a set of Communist supply areas are struck by 32 B-29s and their F-86 escorts. This is also the first daylight raid by heavy bombers in 11 months. Pre-strike reconnaissance intelligence was gathered beforehand by an RB-45C Tornado.

SEPTEMBER 21   Over Pukchong, North Korea, an F-86 flown by Captain Robinson Risner downs two MiG-15s, making him the latest Air Force ace. He is helping to cover an air raid by 41 F-84 Thunderjets.

SEPTEMBER 30 The Bell GAM-63 Rascal strategic missile is successfully test launched for the first time. However, it does not go into production.

OCTOBER 4 In Tokyo, Japan, Brigadier General William P. Fisher is directed to take charge of Bomber Command.

OCTOBER 8 Over eastern North Korea, 10 B-29s execute another daylight raid in concert with carrier-based Navy fighter-bombers.

Over Seoul, South Korea, Communist PO-2 biplanes begin making harassment raids at night, earning the nickname "Bedcheck Charlies."

OCTOBER 20 Over California, the sleek Douglas X-3 Stiletto research jet flies for the first time. It is part of a program for testing titanium machining and construction, as well as the effect of short-span, low-aspect-ratio wings at high speed.

OCTOBER 31 On Eniwetok, Marshall Islands, the United States explodes the "Mike Shot," a thermonuclear weapon equal to 10 million tons of TNT. This new device is roughly 1,000 times more powerful than the weapons that destroyed Hiroshima and Nagasaki.

NOVEMBER 10 In Japan, the 315th Air Division crosses an important milestone after its transports evacuate the 250,000th patient from Korea.

NOVEMBER 12–13 Over Pyongyang, North Korea, six B-29s from the 98th Bomb Wing destroy four spans of the recently repaired railway bridges.

NOVEMBER 15 Over Japan, a C-119 Flying Boxcar crashes en route to South Korea, killing all 40 crew and passengers on board.

NOVEMBER 19 Over the Salton Sea, California, an F-86D piloted by Captain J. Slade Nash streaks to a new world record of 698.5 miles per hour.

North American Aviation test fires its XLR-43-NA-3 rocket motor for the first time. This is the first American rocket capable of producing over 100,000 pounds of thrust and is a critical step in the development of intercontinental ballistic missiles.

NOVEMBER 22 Over North Korea, an F-84 piloted by Major Charles J. Loring is struck by ground fire near Sniper Ridge, yet he deliberately crashes his aircraft into a Communist gun emplacement. He wins a posthumous Congressional Medal of Honor.

NOVEMBER 26 The Northrop N-25 Snark, a turbojet-powered cruise missile, is successfully test launched for the first time. When it becomes operational at the end of the decade as the B-62, it serves briefly as the nation's first intercontinental ballistic missile (ICBM).

DECEMBER 11 At Kunsan airfield, South Korea, a fully armed B-26 catches fire and explodes, wrecking three nearby B-26s and damaging six F-84s.

DECEMBER 16 The Tactical Air Command (TAC) activates the first Air Force helicopter squadron, equipped with Sikorsky H-19 Chickasaws.

DECEMBER 17 While patrolling near the Sui-ho Reservoir, two F-86s espy an Ilyushin IL-28 Beagle jet bomber escorted by two MiG-15s; one of the Sabrejets chases them back across the Yalu River.

1953

JANUARY 17–18   Over Pyongyang, North Korea, 11 B-29s bomb an underground radio station with special, 2,000-pound bombs. Accuracy is essential as the site is only 1,000 feet from a POW camp; 10 direct hits are scored but the ordnance fails to destroy the station.

JANUARY 23   In South Korea and Japan, the last remaining F-51 Mustangs are retired from combat operations and replaced by F-86 Sabrejets. This marks the end of propellor-driven fighter aircraft in the U.S. Air Force.

JANUARY 24   Over North Korea, sharp-shooting Captain Dolphin D. Overton II sets a record for becoming a fighter ace by downing five MiGs in only four days.

JANUARY 28   Over Sariwon, North Korea, a B-29 explodes over its target, being the fourth heavy bomber downed

since the previous December; it is also the last one lost during hostilities.

JANUARY 30   Over the Yellow Sea, an F-86 observes a Soviet-built Tu-2 bomber and shoots it down; this is the first Communist bomber claimed since November 1951.

Boeing's B-47E Stratojet performs its maiden flight; this is the first major production model, of which 1,300 are constructed. A further 255 RB-47E reconnaissance aircraft are also acquired by the Air Force.

JANUARY 30–31   Over North Korea, a B-29 of the 307th Bomb Wing is badly mauled by Communist MiGs and is forced to make an emergency landing in South Korea.

FEBRUARY 4   In Washington, D.C., Harold E. Talbott gains appointment as secretary of the Air Force.

McConnell, Joseph C. (1922–1954)

Air Force pilot. Joseph Christopher McConnell was born in Dover, New Hampshire, on January 30, 1922, and he enlisted in the Army in 1940. Though he intended to be a pilot, he ended up as a navigator and flew 60 combat missions over Europe in B-24s assigned to the 448th Bomb Group. After World War II, McConnell remained determined to win his wings and, in 1948, he finally passed through flight school at Lackland and Randolph Fields, Texas. There he became one of the earliest jet pilots and qualified in Lockheed P-80 Shooting Stars. The onset of the Korean War in June 1950 resulted in the deployment of new F-86 Sabrejets there to counter Soviet MiG-15 fighters; McConnell immediately volunteered for service overseas, but was judged "too old" for combat. He nonetheless persisted and, in August 1952, he shipped to Korea with the 51st Fighter-Interceptor Wing. He flew constantly over the next 10 months, and on January 14, 1953, McConnell downed his first MiG.

Within a month, McConnell had scored his fifth kill, but three victories later he was himself shot down and rescued. Returning to combat, he became a double ace and, on May 18, 1953, he downed victims number 14 and 15, becoming a triple jet ace That same afternoon he ventured back to "MiG Alley" and bagged number 16, becoming the highest-scoring American jet ace. After the war, McConnell arrived at Edwards Air Force Base, California, to serve as a test pilot. On August 25, 1954, he died after his new F-86H stalled, and he ejected too close to the ground.

FEBRUARY 8   The American Medical Association finally recognizes aviation medicine as a medical specialty, the first to have evolved from strictly military practices.

FEBRUARY 14   The new Bell X-1A makes its first successful test glide; this variant is longer and has greater fuel capacity than the original X-1.

FEBRUARY 15   Over North Korea, 22 F-84s strike the Shi-ho hydroelectric power plant with 1,000-pound bombs while 82 F-86 escorts tangle with 30 MiG-15s. The facility is heavily damaged and off line for several months.

FEBRUARY 16   Over North Korea, Captain Joseph C. McConnell, Jr., bags his fifth MiG-15, becoming the latest all-jet ace.

FEBRUARY 18   Over the Sui-ho reservoir, North Korea, 4 F-86 Sabrejets attack a formation of 48 MiG-15s, downing 2. Two other Communist craft enter uncontrolled spins and crash while turning with the Americans. Captain Manuel J. Fernandez also becomes an ace by claiming his fifth and sixth MiGs.

FEBRUARY 18–19   Southwest of Pyongyang, North Korea, 500 Air Force aircraft attack a Communist tank and infantry school, destroying 243 buildings in the process.

MARCH 5   Over North Korea, Fifth Air Force aircraft run 70 sorties, destroying 56 bunkers, gun positions, and various storage shacks. One flight of F-84s drops bombs on an industrial facility only 60 miles from the Siberian border.

MARCH 10   Near the border between West Germany and Czechoslovakia, two Communist MiG-15s attack two F-84 Thunderjets, downing one. The pilot ejects safely.

MARCH 14   Over North Korea, Air Force aircraft drop propaganda leaflets demanding to know where the Communist air force is after they bomb a target. It is hoped such taunting will provoke an aerial engagement.

MARCH 21–22   Over North Korea, Operation SPRING THAW unfolds as Fifth Air Force medium bombers knock down the two main bridges at Yongmi-dong and heavily damage a third.

MARCH 27   In a surprise move, two MiG-15s attack two RF-80 Shooting Stars and two Australian Meteors only 38 miles north of UN lines.

MARCH 31   In Korea, the final F-80C Shooting Star is retired from front-line service after a distinguished two-and-a-half years in combat.

APRIL 12   Over the Red Sea, an H-19 helicopter rescues Captain Joseph C. McConnell after he and his eighth victory apparently downed each other.

APRIL 7   In Washington, D.C., the Atomic Energy Commission declares that it employs Lockheed QF-80 drones to study radioactive clouds during atomic testing. These remote-controlled craft are flown directly into mushroom clouds under the direction of nearby aircraft.

APRIL 13   Over South Korea, the F-86 Sabrejet performs its first close support ground sortie.

APRIL 26–27   Over North Korea, Project MOOLA unfolds as B-29 bombers drop leaflets offering $100,000 to any Communist pilot who defects with his MiG-15.

United States Air Force F-86 airplanes prepare for combat on the flight line in May 1953. (National Archives)

MAY 13   North of Pyongyang, North Korea, 50 F-84Gs, attacking in four waves, bomb several irrigation dams that had heretofore been off limits. The ensuing floodwaters destroy six square miles of rice crop, the Sunan airfield, and two miles of a nearby highway.

MAY 16   Over North Korea, 90 F-84Gs bomb the Chasan irrigation dam, and the floodwaters destroy three railroad bridges and several acres of rice crop.

MAY 18   Over Edwards Air Force Base, California, aviatrix Jacqueline Cochran flies a Canadair F-86E to a new world's speed record of 652.3 miles per hour over a 100-kilometer course. This day she also becomes the first woman to exceed the speed of sound.

Over North Korea, Captain Joseph C. McConnell, Jr., bags 3 more MiG-15s, becoming the war's first triple jet ace and, with 16 kills, also the highest-scoring UN pilot.

MAY 25   Over Edwards Air Force Base, California, the North American YF-100 Super Sabre flies for the first time and easily exceeds the sound barrier. This is the first of 2,300 F-100s that pass into Air Force service.

MAY 27   In Washington, D.C., the Air Force Historical Foundation (AFHF) is established to preserve and perpetuate the history and heritage of U.S. aviation.

MAY 31   In Tokyo, Japan, command of the Fifth Air Force passes to Lieutenant General Samuel E. Anderson.

JUNE 8   At Luke Air Force Base, Arizona, F-84 Thunderjets of the 3600th Air Demonstration Team make its first unofficial public appearance in red, white, and blue painted aircraft. They become better known as the USAF Thunderbirds.

JUNE 11   Along the Manchurian border, 13 F-84s commit the deepest penetration of Communist territory by bombing an enemy airfield. No opposition is encountered.

JUNE 13–18   Over Toksan and Kusong, North Korea, Fifth Air Force F-84s and B-29s, assisted by Marine Corps F4U Corsairs, blast several irrigation dams to flood nearby airfields. However, the Communists anticipated the move, because they had lowered the water level beforehand, thereby decreasing the impact of the strikes.

JUNE 15   In Tokyo, Japan, leadership of Bomber Command passes to Brigadier General Richard H. Carmichael.

JUNE 16   This day the Fifth Air Force completes 1,834 combat sorties, with half aimed at enemy troops contesting UN forces in the Pukhan Valley region.

JUNE 18   Over Japan, a C-124 Globemaster II crashes after takeoff, killing all 129 passengers on board. For many years this was the worst aviation disaster on record.

JUNE 21   Over Cheyenne, Wyoming, the Air Force Thunderbirds make their first official demonstration for the public.

JUNE 30   In Washington, D.C., General Nathan F. Twining gains appointment as the new Air Force chief of staff.

Over North Korea, Fifth Air Force F-86 Sabrejets have a field day by downing 16 MiG-15s without loss, a new single-day record.

JULY 15   Over North Korea, Major James Jabara downs his 15th MiG, becoming the second triple jet ace in aviation history.

JULY 16   An F-86D piloted by Lieutenant William Barnes sets a new world speed record of 715.7 miles per hour. To do so he broke an earlier record established by another F-86D.

JULY 20   At Middle River, Maryland, the first Martin B-57A, the American-built version of the English Electric Canberra, performs its maiden flight. This is also the first foreign-designed aircraft accepted into the U.S. Air Force.

JULY 21–22   Over North Korea, 18 Bomber Command B-29s fly the final sortie for that type of airplane by bombing the Uiju airfield.

JULY 22   Over North Korea, the final dogfight of the Korean War unfolds as three F-86 Sabrejets tangle with four MiG-15s, whereby Lieutenant Sam P. Young makes the final MiG kill of the war.

JULY 27   Just hours before the armistice ends the Korean War, Captain Ralph S. Parr, Jr., downs a Soviet-built IL-2 transport, becoming a double ace. This is also the final aerial victory of the Korean War.

Over North Korea, a B-26 drops its bombs during a radar-directed, close support mission only 24 minutes before the armistice becomes official. Ironically, the squadron to which this aircraft belongs also flew the first bombing mission of the war in 1950.

Over North Korea, an RB-26 from the 67th Tactical Reconnaissance Wing performs that last photo mission of the Korean War.

JULY 28   At Fairford, England, a Strategic Air Command (SAC) B-47 Stratojet completes a record-making flight from Limestone, Maine, by crossing the Atlantic in only 4 hours and 43 minutes at a speed of 618 miles per hour.

JULY 29   Off the coast of Vladivostok, Soviet Union, an RB-50 operating from Yokota, Japan, is attacked by MiG-15s and shot down; 16 men perish and only 1 survives.

This day the Far East Air Forces (FEAF) releases its official tally of wins and losses for the Korean War. They claim 839 MiG-15 jets shot down with 154 listed as probable, and a further 919 damaged. Over the past 37 months, the Air Force lost 110 aircraft to hostile air activity, 677 to ground fire, and 213 in various accidents. Since that time, the number of Communist aircraft claimed has been revised downwards to roughly half this total.

AUGUST 3   At Cape Canaveral, Florida, the Air Force Missile Test Center fires a Redstone missile for the first time.

AUGUST 12   In an ominous development, the Soviet Union detonates its first thermonuclear weapon.

AUGUST 20   In Western Europe, Operation LONGSTRIDE unfolds as F-84 Thunderjets of the 40th Air Division, Strategic Air Command (SAC) deploy from the United States in the first mass deployment of fighter aircraft during a transatlantic flight. It is a vivid demonstration of SAC's ability to shift men and resources to distant points, and wins the Mackay Trophy.

AUGUST 25   The Air Force reveals the existence of its Fighter Conveyor (FICON) project, whereby a giant B-36 bomber has been modified to carry, launch, and recover an RF-84 in flight. However, the concept of a "flying aircraft carrier" does not catch on.

SEPTEMBER   Aviation history is made this month when a B-47 Stratojet is refueled in midair by a KB-47B tanker aircraft. This represents the first time that one jet aircraft has passed fuel to another.

SEPTEMBER 11   Over China Lake, California, the new AIM-9 Sidewinder air-to-air missile destroys an airborne target for the first time. Updated versions of this weapon are still in production.

SEPTEMBER 21   Over Kimpo Airfield, South Korea, a MiG-15 flown by Lieutenant Noh Kum Suk arrives as he defects to the West. He receives the $100,000 bounty and his aircraft is thoroughly tested and examined by Air Force authorities before being put on display at the Air Force Museum in Dayton, Ohio.

OCTOBER   This month the Air Defense Command is bolstered by the addition of 10 Lockheed RC-121 Super Constellations, which serve as early warning radar platforms.

OCTOBER 1   At McClellan Air Force Base, California, the 4701st Airborne Early Warning and Control squadron is formally activated, being the first organization of its kind in the Air Force.

OCTOBER 14   The X-10 (B-64 Navaho prototype) is test launched for the first time. This impressively sleek missile is intended as a ground-to-ground weapon capable of carrying nuclear warheads.

OCTOBER 23   The twin-rotor Piasecki YH-16 transport helicopter makes its maiden flight.

OCTOBER 24   Over Edwards Air Force Base, the delta-winged Convair XF-102 is flown for the first time. Overall performance is poor and it is not until a major redesign incorporating the use of "area rule" (a pinched-in fuselage) that it enters service as the F-102 Delta Dagger.

OCTOBER 29   Over the Salton Sea, California, the YF-100 prototype flown by Colonel Frank K. Everest sets a world speed record of 755.125 miles per hour over a nine-mile course.

OCTOBER 31   Trevor Gardner, special assistant to the secretary of the Air Force, is tasked with forming the new Strategic Missile Evaluation Committee under mathematician John von Neumann.

NOVEMBER 6   At RAF Brize Norton, England, a B-47 Stratojet makes a new transatlantic speed record by flying in from Limestone Air Force Base, Maine, in 4 hours and 57 minutes.

NOVEMBER 20   Over Edwards Air Force Base, California, A. Scott Crossfield flies the Douglas D-558-2 Skyrocket to twice the speed of sound. This represents the first time such stellar velocity has been reached.

DECEMBER 12   Over Edwards Air Force Base, the Bell X-1A flown by Major Charles E. Yeager reaches a speed of 1,650 miles per hour at an altitude of 70,000 feet. Yeager loses control of his aircraft and spirals down to 25,000 feet before righting it and making a safe landing. He wins the Harmon Trophy for his effort.

1954

FEBRUARY 10   The Air Force Strategic Missile Evaluation Committee announces a major breakthrough in the size and weight of nuclear warheads. It therefore recommends that a special group be tasked to help accelerate the development of intercontinental ballistic missiles.

MARCH 1   In the Marshall Islands, a 15-megaton bomb is tested by the United States for the first time. This device is a thousand times more powerful than the atomic bombs utilized during World War II.

MARCH 5   Over Edwards Air Force Base, California, the Lockheed XF-104 prototype performs its maiden flight. It subsequently enters service as the F-104 Starfighter.

APRIL 1   In Washington, D.C., President Dwight D. Eisenhower signs legislation creating the U.S. Air Force Academy. In lieu of a permanent campus, the first classes will be conducted at Lowry Air Force Base in Denver, Colorado.

The first Convair C-131A transports, the military version of the Model 240 Airliner, is accepted into the Air Force inventory.

APRIL 8   In Washington, D.C., the Air Force Assistant Chief of Staff for Guided Missiles is created at the Pentagon.

JUNE 18   The Martin B-57B Canberra flies for the first time. This model is specifically designed for ground interdiction purposes.

JUNE 4   Over California, a Bell X-1A research aircraft piloted by Major Arthur Murray sets a world altitude record of 90,000 feet.

JUNE 21   At Yokota Air Base, Japan, three 22nd Bombardment Wing B-47 Strato-jets commanded by Major General Walter C. Sweeney, Jr., make a 6,700-mile nonstop flight from March Air Force Base, California, in only 15 hours. The flight requires two in-flight refuelings from KC-97 tankers.

JUNE 26–JULY 17   In Indochina (Vietnam) Operation WOUNDED WARRIOR unfolds as transports of the 315th Air Division, Military Air Transport Service (MATS), evacuate 500 injured French soldiers back to France, via Japan.

JUNE 28   The Douglas RB-66 prototype reconnaissance aircraft flies for the first time.

JULY 1   The Western Development Division is established under Brigadier General Bernard A. Schriever. It is tasked with developing the Air Force intercontinental ballistic missile system, particularly as it relates to the ongoing Atlas program.

JULY 15   In Seattle, Washington, the Boeing KC-135, which is based on the

Davis, Benjamin O., Jr. (1912–2002)

Air Force General. Benjamin O. Davis, Jr., was born in Washington, D.C., on December 18, 1912, the son of an Army lieutenant destined to become that service's first African American general. Davis entered West Point in 1932 and, despite four years of racism, graduated 35th in a class of 275. He had expressed interest in flying but, because the Army Air Corps was segregated, Davis taught military science at the all-black Tuskegee Institute. However, American entry into World War II forced the Army Air Forces to recruit black pilots, and in March 1942, Davis received his wings and command of the 99th Pursuit Squadron, the first such formation composed entirely of African Americans. He led it to distinction in North Africa in 1943, and the following spring he assumed command of the all-black 322nd Fighter Group. Davis received a Silver Star for his harrowing actions over southern Germany, and after the war he commanded the 477th Composite Group at Godman Field, Kentucky.

In 1947, President Harry S. Truman ordered the American military desegregated, and Davis accepted command of Lockbourne Air Force Base, Ohio, in a pioneer integration program. During the Korean War he served as deputy of operations in the Fighter Branch, and in 1954 he made history by becoming the Air Force's first African American brigadier general. Four years later Davis rose to major general commanding the 12th Air Force in Europe, and also became the first black lieutenant general in 1965. He retired in 1970 after 35 years of active duty, and on December 9, 1998, he was elevated to four-star general on the retired list. Davis died in Washington, D.C., on July 4, 2002.

Model 707 airliner, makes its maiden flight. This aircraft enters service as the KC-135 Stratotanker, and serves as an essential component of the Strategic Air Command (SAC).

JULY 26 The distinction of serving as the first superintendent of the Air Force Academy goes to Lieutenant General Hubert R. Harmon.

AUGUST 5 The first production B-52 Stratofortress rolls off the assembly line. This eight-jet behemoth becomes the backbone of the Strategic Air Command for a decade and is still employed in front-line service to the present.

AUGUST 6–7 This day a pair of 308th Bombardment Wing B-47s flies nonstop from Hunter Air Force Base, Georgia, to French Morocco, and back. Concurrently, the 38th Air Division contributes two B-47s which also depart Hunter AFB on a simulated bomb run over French Morocco. Both units consequently win the Mackay Trophy.

AUGUST 23 The Lockheed YC-130 turboprop-powered transport prototype flies for the first time. This enters service as the C-130 Hercules, which remains in front-line service over half-a-century later.

AUGUST 26 Over Edwards Air Force Base, California, a Bell X-1A piloted by Major Arthur Murray reaches a record altitude of 90,440 feet, where the curvature of the Earth can be clearly observed.

SEPTEMBER 1 At Colorado Springs, Colorado, the Continental Air Defense Command establishes its headquarters under General Benjamin W. Chidlaw.

The Fairchild C-123B Provider prototype performs its maiden flight. This aircraft will see extensive service throughout the Vietnam War, a decade hence.

SEPTEMBER 27   At George Air Force Base, California, the F-100A Super Sabre jet fighter is declared operational.

SEPTEMBER 29   The McDonnell F-101A Voodoo all-weather interceptor flies for the first time. This is an outgrowth of the earlier XF-88. It serves with distinction throughout the Vietnam War as a reconnaissance platform.

OCTOBER 8   Over Edwards Air Force Base, California, the Bell X-1B rocket research aircraft flies for the first time with Major Arthur Murray at the controls.

OCTOBER 9   In Washington, D.C., the Department of Defense adds an additional $500 million to this year's guided missile budget in an attempt to accelerate development of the Atlas ICBM.

OCTOBER 12   Over Wichita, Kansas, the Cessna XT-37 jet trainer flies for the first time. This unique, side-by-side aircraft also serves with distinction as a light attack bomber during the Vietnam War.

OCTOBER 18–19   Distinguished scientist Theodore von Karman convenes the ad hoc committee of the Air Force Scientific Advisory Board for the purpose of considering nuclear power as a source of missile propulsion. They ultimately recommend that the issue remain closely studied to maintain cogency in this field.

OCTOBER 27   Colonel Benjamin O. Davis, son of the Army's first African American general, becomes the first minority brigadier general in Air Force history.

NOVEMBER 1   The venerable Boeing B-29 Superfortress, the aircraft that helped to end World War II, is finally retired from active service.

NOVEMBER 2   At San Diego, California, the Convair XFY-1 Pogo, a vertical lift-off fighter, performs its maiden flight from Lindbergh Field. After rising from the ground like a helicopter, it transitions to horizontal flight and then lands vertically. This spectacular vehicle does not enter into production.

NOVEMBER 7   Off the coast of Hokkaido, Japan, an RB-29 reconnaissance aircraft is attacked by Soviet MiG-15s and shot down.

NOVEMBER 17–19   A B-47 Stratojet flown by Colonel David A. Burchinal is forced by bad weather to remain aloft over England and France for 47 hours and 35 minutes. He is forced to refuel in the air nine times while waiting for clear weather to land.

DECEMBER 7   At Edwards Air Force Base, California, a fully automated approach and landing system successfully brings an X-10 Navajo missile back to base.

DECEMBER 10   Aviation medicine research Colonel John P. Strapp endures a rocket-sled test that accelerates him to 630 miles per hour, which is the same as ejecting from an aircraft at Mach 1.7. That he emerges unhurt demonstrates the resiliency of the human body.

DECEMBER 20   The revamped F-102A, now endowed with a "wasp waist" as per the new "area rule," is successfully tested for the first time. It enters service as the Delta Dagger, becoming the first Air Force jet armed solely with guided missiles.

DECEMBER 23   The Air Force, the Navy, and NACA sign a joint memoranda to begin shared development of a hypersonic research aircraft, which emerges as the X-15.

1955

FEBRUARY 26   Off the coast of California, test pilot George Smith is forced to eject from his F-100 Super Sabre at a speed of Mach 1.7. He is knocked unconscious by the blast of 64 g's while exiting the aircraft, but is safely conveyed to the water by his shredded parachute. Smith is the first man to survive a supersonic ejection.

MARCH 1   At Otis Air Force Base, Maine, the first operational Lockheed RC-121D airborne early warning platforms begin patrolling the East Coast of the United States.

In Washington, D.C., Trevor Gardner gains appointment as the first secretary of the Air Force for Research and Development.

MARCH 2   The Boeing Model 367-80 (KC-135) successfully demonstrates its new in-flight refueling system, which departs from the probe-and-drogue system pioneered by the British.

MARCH 6   In Washington, D.C., Air Force Chief of Staff General Nathan F. Twining announces that the Atlas, Navaho, and Snark programs will be accelerated in light of recent Soviet advances in missile technology.

APRIL 6   Above Yucca Flat, Nevada, a B-36 bomber releases a nuclear-tipped missile at 42,000 feet, which then climbs six miles before detonating.

APRIL 21   The Air Force launches its first Aerobee-Hi sounding rocket, which reaches upwards for 123 miles while carrying a 200-pound payload.

MAY 2   In Washington, D.C., the Department of the Air Force gives its nod towards the Western Development Division's suggestion to construct a second, more capable type of intercontinental ballistic missile, which emerges as the Titan.

MAY 10   The Air Force accepts the last of 448 Douglas C-124 Globemaster II transports into active service. This capable craft was known as "Old Shaky" to those who flew it.

Over Schenectady, New York, an experimental GE XJ-79 turbojet engine is test flown in the belly of a RB-45C aircraft. The J-79 engine goes on to power an entire generation of Air Force fighters and bombers.

MAY 15   The governments of the United States and Canada agree on the details of a major construction project to build the Distant Early Warning (DEW) line. This consists of a series of radar sites across the northern hemisphere that will detect any incoming Soviet bomber aircraft.

JUNE 11   At Wright-Patterson Air Force Base, Ohio, an experimental F-80C fighter partially constructed of magnesium alloys is used to test the strength and weight of new aviation alloys.

The first Atlas intercontinental ballistic missile is test fired for the first time. This liquid-fueled weapon is capable of accurately hitting a target several thousand miles away with a nuclear warhead.

JUNE 29   At Castle Air Force Base, California, the 93rd Bombardment Wing accepts delivery of the first production B-52 Stratofortress.

JULY 1   Dr. S. J. Gerathewohl is tasked by the Air Force with directing a research program on weightlessness. He initiates airborne parabolic flight profiles that temporarily induce zero-gravity conditions while descending.

JULY 11   At Lowry Air Force Base, Colorado, the first class of the U.S. Air Force Academy, consisting of 306 students, gathers for initial instruction.

JULY 20   The NB-36H Peacemaker research aircraft goes aloft for the first time, but the nuclear reactor it carries remains inactivated.

AUGUST 1   Lockheed F-80s and T-33s conduct the first zero-gravity research flight involving parabolic flight profiles.

AUGUST 4   At Groom Lake, central Nevada, the top secret Lockheed U-2 high-altitude reconnaissance aircraft flies for the first time.

In China, the Communist government releases the crew of the B-29 *Stardust 40*; they had been held in captivity since being shot down over North Korea on January 13, 1953. They have been held prisoner longer than any other captives from this conflict.

AUGUST 8   Over California, a Bell X-1A explodes prior to being dropped by a B-29 mother ship; pilot Joseph A. Walker manages to escape the crippled craft, which is then released from the bomb bay.

AUGUST 20   Over the Mojave Desert, California, an F-100 Super Sabre piloted by Colonel Horace A. Hanes, who is also the director of the Air Force Flight Test Center, Edwards Air Force Base, set a world speed record of 822.1 miles per hour at high altitude. He consequently wins the Mackay Trophy.

OCTOBER 5   Boeing contracts with the Air Force to construct an initial batch of 29 KC-135 tanker aircraft, although over 700 will ultimately be acquired.

OCTOBER 20   At Biggs Air Force Base, Texas, the last Boeing B-50 Superfortress is finally retired from the 97th Bombardment Wing.

OCTOBER 22   The Republic XF-105 prototype flies for the first time and breaks the sound barrier during its maiden flight. It enters service as the F-105 Thunderchief and serves with distinction throughout the Vietnam War.

NOVEMBER 8–14   Because President Dwight D. Eisenhower has pronounced the acquisition of ICBMs and IRBMs as the nation's highest priority, the Air Force proffers streamlined procedures for their development and adoption.

NOVEMBER 18   Over California, the Bell X-2 research plane drops from an EB-50A mothership with Lieutenant Colonel Frank Everest at the controls. On this initial flight it reaches Mach 0.95, or 627 miles per hour.

DECEMBER 10   The Ryan X-13 Vertijet makes its maiden flight. While designed for vertical lift-off, it is fitted with conventional landing gear for its initial foray and makes a conventional flight profile.

1956

JANUARY 1 A milestone is passed as the 1000th Boeing B-47 Stratojet is accepted into service by the Strategic Air Command (SAC). It continues on as the mainstay of American nuclear deterrence until the larger and more capable B-52s are available in greater numbers.

JANUARY 17 In Washington, D.C., the Department of Defense declares that an automated, electronic air defense system called SAGE (semi-automatic ground environment) has been developed and deployed. This is a complex phone system tied to computer centers for a rapid transfer of real-time information.

FEBRUARY 17 The first production Lockheed F-104 Starfighter makes its initial flight.

MARCH 9 The new Boeing B-52C Stratofortress, equipped with large underwing tanks for greater range, performs its maiden flight.

MARCH 24 Airman D. F. Smith is sealed in the Air Force space cabin simulator for 24 hours without ill effects.

APRIL 23 The Douglas C-133A Cargomaster flies for the first time. The Air Force acquires 50 of these giant transports to haul ICBMs and other missile systems around the country.

MAY 7 Off the coast of Cape Cod, the first Air Force "Texas Tower" early warning radar is constructed 100 miles at sea on the Georges Bank.

A SAGE (Semi-Automatic Ground Environment) terminal used during cold war to analyze radar data in real time to target Soviet bombers. The light pen, which was shaped similar to a handheld power drill or gun, is resting on the console. Notice the built-in cigarette lighter and the ashtray just left of the light pen. (U.S. Air Force)

MAY 21   Over Bikini Atoll, a B-52 piloted by Major David Crichlow drops a thermonuclear bomb from 50,000 feet. This is the first airborne delivery for such a weapon and the test is considered a success.

MAY 31   At Turner Air Force Base, George, the 4080th Strategic Reconnaissance Wing deploys the first RB-57D Canberra jet.

JUNE 4   Over Wichita, Kansas, the first B-52D Stratofortress flies for the first time; this version is especially equipped for long-range bombing missions.

JUNE 22   In the Caribbean, Operation SIXTEEN TON unfolds as Air Force Reserve transports begin their first sustained cargo airlift into that region.

JULY 4   At Wiesbaden, West Germany, the top secret Lockheed U-2 spyplane makes its first clandestine overflight of the Soviet Union by photographing airfields in the Baltics, Minsk, and Leningrad before returning home.

JULY 15   At Torrejon, Spain, the Sixteenth Air Force is created as part of NATO.

JULY 18   At Renton, Washington, the last Boeing KC-97G propellor-driven tanker aircraft is rolled out of the factory.

JULY 23   Over Edwards Air Force Base, California, the Bell X-2 rocket-powered research aircraft is flown by Lieutenant Colonel Frank K. Everest to a record speed of 1,900 miles per hour at an altitude of 75,000 feet.

AUGUST 27   At Edwards Air Force Base, California, the Thor rocket engine undergoes its first static test firing by the Air Force Flight Test Center.

AUGUST 31   At Renton, Washington, the first Boeing KC-135 Stratotanker is rolled off the assembly line.

SEPTEMBER 7   Over California, the Bell X-2 rocket research airplane is flown by Captain Iven C. Kincheloe to an altitude of 126,200 feet—the first time a human being has exceeded 100,000 feet. Kincheloe receives a Mackay Trophy for his endeavor.

SEPTEMBER 15   At Hahn Air Base, West Germany, the 701st Tactical Missile Wing deploys as part of the Twelfth Air Force. This is the first unit of its kind and operates Matador missiles.

SEPTEMBER 20   At Cape Canaveral, Florida, the three-stage Jupiter C missile is launched for the first time. It ventures 3,300 miles downrange after reaching an altitude of 680 miles.

SEPTEMBER 27   Over California, disaster strikes as the Bell X-2 rocket plane flown by Captain Milburn G. Ap loses control after reaching 2,094 miles per hour at an altitude of 65,000 feet. He manages to eject but dies after his capsule hits the desert floor.

OCTOBER 26   At Fort Worth, Texas, the Bell XH-40 helicopter prototype takes to the air. It enters production as the UH-1 Iroquois, or Huey, and sees widespread service in the Vietnam War.

NOVEMBER 6   At Cape Canaveral, Florida, the first Navajo ramjet ICBM is launched and breaks up after 30 seconds of flight.

NOVEMBER 11   At Fort Worth, Texas, the Convair XB-58 prototype completes its maiden flight. This sleek, delta-winged bomber enters production as the B-58 Hustler and is the first aircraft of its class to incorporate "area rule" in its design.

NOVEMBER 16   In California, parts of Camp Cooke are transferred to the Air Force by the Defense Department. This is the future site of Vandenberg Air Force Base and also the first active ICBM base.

NOVEMBER 26   In Washington, D.C., Defense Secretary Charles E. Wilson delegates operational jurisdiction over long-range missiles to the Air Force.

NOVEMBER 30   After a final successful test, the Martin TM-61 Matador is certified as operational. This is the Air Force's first tactical missile and it can reach 35,000 feet at a speed of 650 miles per hour.

DECEMBER 9   The 463rd Troop Carrier Wing accepts delivery of the first Lockheed C-130 Hercules transport. This versatile craft can carry 92 fully armed troops or 92 tons of cargo for 2,500 miles and operate from unprepared runways as short as 4,000 feet.

DECEMBER 10   In West Germany, Operation SAFE HAVEN begins as the Military Air Transport Service begins lifting 100,000 Hungarian refugees fleeing a Soviet invasion of their country. The operation lasts seven months.

DECEMBER 21   At Dayton, Ohio, Major Arnold I. Beck reaches a simulated altitude of 198,770 feet in an Air Research and Development Command chamber.

DECEMBER 26   At Edwards Air Force Base, California, the Convair YF-106 prototype makes its initial flight. It enters service as the F-106 Delta Dart and serves with distinction as a bomber interceptor.

1957

JANUARY 16–18   Three B-52s from the 93rd Bombardment Wing, including *Lucky Lady III* under mission commander Major General Archie J. Old, Jr., make the world's first nonstop, around-the-world jet flight from Castle Air Force Base, California. The voyage covers 24,325 miles, requires five in-flight refuelings, and takes 45 hours and 19 minutes to execute. This dramatic display by the Strategic Air Command (SAC) to hit any region on the globe results in a Mackay Trophy for the unit and a Distinguished Flying Cross for each crew member.

JANUARY 25   The Air Force unsuccessfully test launches the new Thor intermediate range ballistic missile (IRBM) for the first time; the prototype had been under construction for 13 months prior to this setback.

MARCH 27   The McDonnell F-101B Voodoo makes its initial flight; this is a two-seat version of the original interceptor and now carries a radar operator.

APRIL 1   The Strategic Air Command (SAC) begins transferring all of its fighter wings over to the Tactical Air Command (TAC) in order to concentrate on manned bombers and guided missiles.

Archie J. Old Jr. sticks his head out of the window of the B-52 after around the world flight, January 18, 1957. (Time & Life Pictures/Getty Images)

APRIL 11 The Ryan X-13 Vertijet prototype becomes the first jet aircraft to take off vertically, transition to a conventional flight profile, then land vertically. However, functional vertical takeoff and landing aircraft (VTOL) are still two decades away.

APRIL 19 At Cape Canaveral, Florida, the Douglas XSM-75 Thor missile is successfully launched, but the safety officer destroys it during the flight

MAY 6 The title of Department of Defense Special Assistant for Guided Missiles is conferred upon William M. Holaday.

JUNE 2 Over Minnesota, the balloon Man High I piloted by Captain Joseph W. Kittinger, Jr., reaches 96,000 feet during a flight of 6 hours and 34 minutes. This constitutes a new record for balloon endurance/altitudes, and is also the first time a solo balloon has reached the stratosphere.

At Laughlin Air Force Base, Texas, the first production model U-2 spyplane deploys with the 4080th Strategic Reconnaissance Wing.

JUNE 11 At Laughlin Air Force Base, the 4080th Strategic Reconnaissance Wing accepts its first U-2 as operational. In contrast with CIA-operated U-2s, which are painted black, Air Force vehicles retain their silver aluminum finish.

JUNE 28 At Castle Air Force Base, California, the first operational Boeing KC-135 Stratotanker deploys with the 93rd Air Refueling Squadron.

JULY 1 In Washington, D.C., General Thomas D. White gains appointment as Air Force chief of staff.

At Cooke Air Force Base, California, the first Air Force intercontinental ballistic missile base (ICMB) becomes operational. The 704th Strategic Missile Wing

Twining, Nathan F. (1897–1982)

Air Force general. Nathan Farragut Twining was born in Monroe, Wisconsin, and, in 1923, he received his wings at Brooks Field, Texas. Twining held down a succession of staff and command positions in the Army Air Corps, and rose to colonel at the Pentagon. During World War II, he became a brigadier general assigned to Southwest Pacific, coordinating an air strategy that destroyed Japanese air power over Bougainville and Rabaul. In November 1943, he transferred to Italy as head of the Fifteenth Air Force and, in May 1945, Twining returned to the Pacific to replace General Curtis E. LeMay as head of the Twentieth Air Force. Here he supervised fire bombings of major Japanese cities, and the atomic bombings of Hiroshima and Nagasaki, ending the war as a temporary lieutenant general.

During the Cold War, Twining filled several major administration positions, and in 1948 he gained appointment as vice chief of staff in the newly independent U.S. Air Force. In 1953 he succeeded General Hoyt S. Vandenberg as Air Force chief of staff, and Twining facilitated Eisenhower's "New Look" strategy by acquiring numerous jet bombers, and laying the groundwork for the first intercontinental ballistic missiles. In 1956, he also became the first American general to tour Soviet aviation facilities since World War II. Eisenhower next appointed him chairman of the Joint Chiefs of Staff in 1957, and he pushed for new Atlas and Jupiter missiles, the XB-70 jet bomber, and the Navy's Polaris submarine. Twining died at Lackland Air Force Base, Texas, on March 29, 1982, a highly respected and influential military leader of the Cold War period.

(SMW) located there operates the Northrop Snark, an early form of cruise missile.

The Far East Air Forces (FEAF) is redesignated the Pacific Air Command (PAC) with new headquarters at Hickam Field, Hawaii.

JULY 10 This day the Air Force reveals the existence of the B-58 Hustler to the American public.

JULY 13 In Washington, D.C., President Dwight D. Eisenhower becomes the first chief executive to fly in a helicopter when he boards an Air Force Bell UH-13J for a meeting at an undisclosed location.

JULY 19 A Douglas MB-1 Genie antiaircraft missile is fired by an F-89J Scorpion for the first time. This is the first weapon of its kind to be armed with a nuclear warhead and is intended to break up enemy bomber formations in a single blast.

JULY 24 The Distant Early Warning (DEW) line, which stretches across the northernmost reaches of Canada, is declared operational.

AUGUST 15 In Washington, D.C., General Nathan F. Twining becomes the first Air Force officer to serve as chairman of the Joint Chiefs of Staff (JCS).

AUGUST 19–20 Over Crosby, Minnesota, the balloon Man High II piloted by Major David G. Simmons sets a new altitude record for this type of craft by reaching 101,516 feet. He remains aloft for 32 hours before finally touching down at Elm Lake, South Dakota.

SEPTEMBER 3 The NACA report "Study of the Feasibility of a Hypersonic Research Plane" is delivered to the Air Force for its consideration. The outcome of this project is the X-15 rocket plane.

SEPTEMBER 4 The Lockheed CL-328 Jetstar transport makes its maiden flight; it enters service as the C-140 as a test bed for navigation and communications equipment.

SEPTEMBER 20   At Cape Canaveral, Florida, a Thor IRBM missile is successfully launched for the first time.

OCTOBER 1   At Cape Canaveral, Florida, an Air Force crew test launches a Northrop Snark intercontinental ballistic missile for the first time.

OCTOBER 4   The Space Age commences following the successful Soviet launch of *Sputnik I*, the world's first artificial satellite. This event serves as a catalyst for U.S. missile programs to prevent falling further behind the Russians.

OCTOBER 20   The Air Force's Project FAR SIDE unfolds as a three-stage rocket is launched from a balloon flying 19 miles above the Earth's surface. This flight is an attempt by the Office of Scientific Research to gather information about cosmic rays from an altitude of 4,000 miles.

OCTOBER 24   A call is made for a hypersonic glide rocket weapon system by the Air Force Research and Development Command (ARDC). The WS464L project eventually becomes the Dyna-Soar system.

NOVEMBER 7   In Washington, D.C., President Dwight D. Eisenhower appoints James R. Killian, president of the Massachusetts Institute of Technology (MIT), to serve as the first special assistant to the president for science and technology.

NOVEMBER 13   At Buenos Aires, Argentina, a Boeing KC-135 Stratotanker flown by Air Force Vice Chief of Staff Curtis E. LeMay arrives after traveling 6,350 miles in a new nonstop distance record. His return trip proves equally laudable, reducing his flying time to a record 11 hours and 5 minutes; LeMay wins a Distinguished Flying Cross.

NOVEMBER 21   The Air Force selects Warren Air Force Base, Wyoming, as the site for its first dedicated ICBM base.

Retired general James H. "Jimmy" Doolittle heads up a new committee exploring the challenges of space travel for the NACA.

NOVEMBER 27   RF-101C Voodoos of the 363rd Tactical Reconnaissance Wing complete Operation SUN RUN, whereby three existing transcontinental speed records are broken by refueling with KC-135 Stratotankers at high altitude.

In Washington, D.C., the Defense Department authorizes production of the Thor and Jupiter intermediate range ballistic missiles (IRBMs), which will be deployed with the Air Force.

NOVEMBER 29   In Washington, D.C., Air Force Chief of Staff Thomas D. White assigns intercontinental and intermediate range ballistic missiles to the Strategic Air Command (SAC).

DECEMBER 12   Over Edwards Air Force Base, California, a McDonnell F-101A Voodoo flown by Major Adrian Drew sets a new speed record of 1,207.6 miles per hour.

DECEMBER 15   At Patrick Air Force Base, Florida, the 556th Strategic Missile Squadron becomes the first operational unit equipped with Northrop SM-62 Snark missiles.

DECEMBER 17   The first Atlas intercontinental ballistic missile (ICBM) is successfully launched and delivers its nose cone capsule 500 miles downrange as predicted. This is a major step in perfecting these strategic weapons.

DECEMBER 19   A Thor IRBM makes a successful fourth test flight, this time being fully guided by an all-inertial guidance system.

DECEMBER 23   The Air Force contracts with North American Aircraft to design

and construction a prototype Mach 3 strategic bomber, which becomes the XB-70 Valkyrie.

1958

JANUARY 1–15   At Cooke Air Force Base, California, the 672nd Strategic Missile Squadron becomes the first Air Force unit to train and deploy the Bomarc interceptor missile. The 864th Strategic Missile Squadron, equipped with Jupiter IRBMs, also becomes operational.

JANUARY 29   In Washington, D.C., the Department of Defense declares it intention to create the National Pacific Missile Range at the Naval Air Missile Test Range, Point Mugu, California. Future long-range weapons will be tested here.

The United States had been surprised by the Soviet Union's Sputnik satellite, and now embraced the new "space race" with a vengeance. (Courtesy NASA/Jet Propulsion Laboratory)

JANUARY 31   At Cape Canaveral, a Jupiter C rocket carries *Explorer I*, the first American satellite, into Earth orbit. An onboard experiment designed by James A. Van Allen reveals the existence of a radiation belt around the planet.

FEBRUARY 1   At Warren Air Force Base, Wyoming, the 706th Strategic Missile Wing, the first to deploy Atlas missiles, is activated by the Strategic Air Command (SAC).

FEBRUARY 7   In Washington, D.C., the Department of Defense creates the Advanced Research Projects Agency (APRA) to assume control of the nation's space exploration program.

FEBRUARY 18   At Tullahoma, Tennessee, the Arnold Research Development Center creates a wind tunnel capable of creating an airflow speed of 32,400 miles per hour for one-tenth of a second.

MARCH 17   At Cape Canaveral, *Vanguard I*, the nation's second artificial satellite, blasts off into orbit. This small device carries solar-powered batteries with an anticipated 1,000-year life expectancy, while other data reveals that the Earth possesses a slight pear shape to it.

MARCH 21   At Holloman Air Force Base, New Mexico, a two-stage rocket pushes an unmanned sled to speeds of 2,700 miles per hour.

MARCH 26   An Astrodyne rocket motor strapped to an F-100D Super Sabre launches the aircraft from a rail system for the first time. Such a system negates the need for a lengthy runway, although it is never adopted.

MARCH 27   The Advanced Research Projects Agency (ARPA) tasks the Air Force Ballistic Missile System with launching three lunar probes through its existing Thor-Vanguard missile system.

APRIL 2   In Washington, D.C., President Dwight D. Eisenhower proposes a new National Aeronautics and Space Agency (NASA) that would absorb the NACA as well as conduct civilian space programs and military technical initiatives.

APRIL 5   At Cape Canaveral, Florida, an Atlas ICBM is successfully launched by the Air Force, and it travels 600 miles downrange to a designated impact area.

APRIL 8   At Lajes Field, Azores, a KC-135 Stratotanker makes a nonstop, unrefueled jet flight record after covering 10,288 miles from Tokyo, Japan.

MAY 7   Over California, an F-104 Starfighter piloted by Major Howard J. Johnson sets a new altitude record of 91,243 feet, very impressive for an air-breathing jet.

MAY 12   At Colorado Springs, Colorado, the joint U.S.-Canadian North American Air Defense Command (NORAD) becomes operational. It is tasked with defending the continent against enemy aerial attacks.

MAY 16   An F-104A Starfighter piloted by Captain Walter W. Irwin sets an absolute speed record of 1,404.2 miles per hour.

MAY 24   The open-cockpit Bell X-14 research plane, cobbled together from parts of a Beech T-34 and a civilian Bonanza, makes its transition flight from vertical to horizontal. It remained an Air Force test bed until 1960, when it was transferred to NASA.

At Holloman Air Force Base, New Mexico, a rocket sled exposes passenger Captain E. L. Breeding to 83 g's for a fraction of a second.

MAY 27   At Eglin Air Force Base, Florida, the first operational F-105B Thunderchiefs are deployed with the 335th Tactical Fighter Squadron.

The McDonnell Douglas YF4H-1 prototype flies for the first time. It enters service as the legendary F-4 Phantom II.

JUNE 3   NACA and Air Force officials reveal details of an inertial guidance system for the new X-15 rocket research aircraft. This device will assure correct pitch attitude for reentering the atmosphere during high-altitude flights in near space.

JUNE 4   At Cape Canaveral, Florida, a Thor missile is launched from a tactical-type launcher by Air Force crews.

JUNE 16   The Air Force contracts with the Martin Company and the Boeing Company to design and build the Phase I Dyna-Soar boost-glide orbital spacecraft.

JUNE 27   At Cape Canaveral, Florida, the 556th Strategic Missile Squadron makes the first military launch of a Northrop Snark intercontinental missile.

JUNE 30   In Washington, D.C., NACA declares that nearly half of all research it conducts is skewed towards missiles and problems associated with space flight.

JULY 14–15   In Lebanon, Operation BLUE BAT unfolds as Composite Air Strike Force Bravo transfers 2,000 fully equipped combat troops from camps in West Germany to the Middle East during a period of unrest.

JULY 26   At Edwards Air Force Base, California, an F-104 Starfighter crash takes the life of Captain Iven C. Kincheloe.

AUGUST 1   Over Johnson Island in the Pacific, a nuclear-tipped ICBM interceptor missile is detonated to assess whether such weapons are practical in neutralizing incoming enemy missiles.

AUGUST 2   An Atlas missile is launched for the first time with a full-power flight profile utilizing both sustainer and boost engines.

AUGUST 6   The Rocketdyne Division, North American Aviation, contracts with the Air Force to design and build a rocket motor capable of producing 1 million pounds of thrust.

In Washington, D.C., Dr. T. Keith Glennan and Dr. Hugh L. Dryden are sworn in as administrator and deputy administrator, respectively, of the new National Aeronautics and Space Administration (NASA).

AUGUST 21   Former general James H. "Jimmy" Doolittle convenes the final meeting of the National Advisory Committee for Aeronautics (NACA) once NASA is enacted.

AUGUST 23   In Washington, D.C. the Federal Aviation Administration (FAA) is created by Congress to oversee military and civil aviation matters and help locate new airports and missile bases.

SEPTEMBER 2   Along the Soviet border with Turkey, Russian MiG aircraft attack and shoot down a C-130 Hercules performing ELINT (electronic intelligence) work.

SEPTEMBER 3–9   In the Pacific, Operation X-RAY TANGO unfolds as F-100 Super Sabres, B-47 Canberras, and C-130 Hercules aircraft are rushed to the Pacific in response to Communist China's threats to Taiwan. This effective deployment over so wide an area gains a Mackay Trophy.

SEPTEMBER 9   A Boeing EB-50 test aircraft launches a Lockheed X-7 ramjet test platform, which accelerates to Mach 4.

SEPTEMBER 16   The North American NA-246 prototype flies for the first time. This six-seat passenger jet enters service as the T-39 Sabreliner.

SEPTEMBER 19   The Kaman H-43A helicopter flies for the first time. It enters Air Force service as the Husky, although its twin-rotor design leads to the nickname of "eggbeater." The H-43A is widely employed by the Tactical Air Command (TAC) as a firefighting and crash recovery helicopter.

SEPTEMBER 24   At Cape Canaveral, a Bomarc interceptor missile is launched from commands issued at a control station in Kingston, New York, and destroys an incoming target drone flying a 1,000 miles per hour at an altitude of 48,000 feet.

OCTOBER 26   The Boeing B-52G performs its maiden flight; this version is designed to carry two AGM-28 Hound Dog missiles under its wings.

The mighty B-52 Stratofortress was a mainstay of American nuclear deterrance from the mid-1950s up through the end of the Cold War in 1991. (U.S. Department of Defense for Defense Visual Information Center)

NOVEMBER 1 The turbine-powered Kaman H–43B performs its maiden flight; it is eventually redesignated the HH–43B.

NOVEMBER 8 At Cape Canaveral, Florida, the third Air Force attempt to launch a lunar probe fails when the third stage of a rocket fails to ignite and the *Pioneer 2* falls back to Earth. This is the last lunar shot attempted by the Air Force.

NOVEMBER 28 An Atlas intercontinental ballistic missile undergoes its first operational test launch; the vehicle flies 6,300 miles and lands in a designated area.

DECEMBER 3 At Pasadena, California, the Jet Propulsion Laboratory is transferred from the California Institute of Technology (Caltech) to NASA at the order of President Dwight D. Eisenhower.

DECEMBER 16 At Point Mugu, California, a Thor IRBM is launched by the Pacific Missile Test Range for the first time. Another Thor goes up at Cape Canaveral on the same day.

A Military Air Transport Service (MATS) C-133 Cargomaster sets a world payload record by lifting 117,900 pounds to an altitude of 10,000 feet.

DECEMBER 18–19 Project SCORE unfolds as the Air Force launches its first communications satellite into orbit on an Atlas rocket. A day later it broadcasts a taped message by President Dwight D. Eisenhower, who has the first human voice beamed in from outer space.

DECEMBER 23 At Cape Canaveral, Florida, the Air Force successfully test launches the first Atlas-C missile.

1959

JANUARY 4   In California, the Pacific Missile Range and Vandenberg Air Force Base becomes operational for missile test firings.

FEBRUARY   At Travis Air Force Base, California, the 5th Bombardment Wing deploys its first B-52Gs.

FEBRUARY 1   Control of the Distant Early Warning (DEW) line passes from the United States Air Force to the Royal Canadian Air Force.

FEBRUARY 6   The Air Force successfully launches its first Titan I intercontinental ballistic missile; this is a two-stage, liquid-fueled projectile with an effective range of 5,500 miles.

FEBRUARY 12   The Strategic Air Command (SAC) becomes an all-jet bomber force once the last remaining B-36 Peacekeeper is retired from active service.

FEBRUARY 17   At Cambridge, Massachusetts, Dr. J. Allen Hynek, associate director of the Smithsonian Astrophysical Observatory, advises the Air Force that they should assume scientific approach to recording all UFO sightings and keep the public informed of all existing policies towards them.

FEBRUARY 19   At Holloman Air Force Base, California, a two-stage rocket sled reaches 3,090 miles per hour, or Mach 4.

FEBRUARY 28   At Vandenberg Air Force Base, California, a Thor-Hustler rocket launch system successfully puts the *Discoverer I* satellite into Earth orbit. This is also the first satellite launched from the West Coast and the first placed in a polar orbit.

MARCH 10   At Edwards Air Force Base, California, the X-15 rocket research aircraft makes its first captive flight while strapped under the wing of an EB-50 mothership. At this time it is piloted by A. Scott Crossfield.

APRIL 9   This day NASA announces that the 7 Project MERCURY astronauts have been selected from 110 candidates. Three of them—Captains L. Gordon Cooper, Virgil I. "Gus" Grissom, and Donald K. "Deke" Slayton—are Air Force pilots.

APRIL 10   In California, the Northrop YT-38 prototype flies for the first time. It enters service as the T-38 Talon, one of the most successful and most popular jet trainers in aviation history.

APRIL 23   Over the Atlantic Missile Range, a B-52 bomber test fires the first Hound Dog air-to-ground, nuclear-tipped guided missile.

APRIL 28   The Douglas Aircraft Company contracts with the Air Force to construct a three-stage Thor-Vanguard rocket-launching system named the Delta.

MAY 6   At Cape Canaveral, a successful, 1,500-mile test launch of the Jupiter IRBM results in that rocket system being declared operational.

MAY 12   At Andrews Air Force Base, Maryland, the 1298th Air Transport Squadron is the first unit to receive the first of three VC-137A (Boeing 707) executive transport aircraft.

A Thor missile launch carries a GE Mark 2 nose cone to an altitude of 300 miles and 1,500 miles downrange; an onboard camera in the nose photographs the Earth from that vista.

MAY 15 The first reentry vehicle recovered from an intercontinental-range missile test is put on public display by General Bernard Schriever, head of the Air Research and Development Center.

MAY 25 The first operational F-106 Delta Dart deploys with the Air Defense Command; this supersonic fighter is designed to replace the older, slower F-102 Delta Dagger.

JUNE 3 At Colorado Springs, Colorado, 207 members of the first U.S. Air Force Academy class graduate out of an original total of 306 cadets.

JUNE 8 Over the Mojave Desert, California, the X-15 rocket research aircraft piloted by A. Scott Crossfield makes a non-powered test glide after being dropped by a B-52 bomber at 38,000 feet.

JUNE 23 At Tullahoma, Tennessee, the Arnold Engineering Development Center is instructed to prepare operational and design requirements for a major space test facility for military space weapons.

JULY 1 At Jackass Flats, Nevada, the first experimental nuclear reactor, named Kiwi 1, is tested at full power as part of the nuclear space rocket program.

JULY 24 Near Antigua, Air Force authorities recover capsule film of a recent nose cone separation sequence.

JULY 30 In California, the Northrop N-156F exceeds Mach 1 on its maiden flight. This is the prototype of what becomes the F-5 Freedom Fighter.

AUGUST 7 A pair of F-100 Super Sabres become the first jet aircraft to fly directly over the North Pole.

AUGUST 24 The Air Force test launches an Atlas-C missile, which travels 5,000 miles downrange at an altitude of 700 miles. The nose cone, which contains movie footage of one-sixth the Earth's surface, is subsequently recovered and analyzed.

AUGUST 29 The Lockheed Corporation contracts with the Air Force to construct a new, high-speed, high-altitude reconnaissance aircraft under Project OXCART for the Central Intelligence Agency. This is the origin of the SR-71 Blackbird.

SEPTEMBER 1 At Vandenberg Air Force Base, California, all Atlas ICBM operations are assumed by the Strategic Air Command (SAC).

SEPTEMBER 9 At Vandenberg Air Force Base, California, the first Atlas missile is launched under SAC auspices. The missile reaches 4,300 miles downrange at speed of 16,000 miles per hour, at which point SAC declares the system operational.

SEPTEMBER 17 Over California, the X-15 rocket research aircraft is piloted by A. Scott Crossfield as it is dropped from a B-52 bomber and zooms to 53,000 feet at Mach 2.11.

OCTOBER 1 At Brooks Air Force Base, Texas, the Air Force Aerospace Aeromedical Center is created by consolidating a number of medical facilities.

OCTOBER 2 In Washington, D.C., the Defense Department appoints Major General Donald N. Yates, commander of the Air Force Missile Test Center, as its representative for Project MERCURY support operations.

OCTOBER 6 At Cape Canaveral, Florida, an Atlas ICBM and a Thor IRBM are both launched to their full flight ranges.

OCTOBER 13   A B-47 launches a Bold Orion, an air-launched ballistic missile, which then soars to an altitude of 160 miles. At one point it passes to within four miles of the orbiting *Explorer 6* satellite.

OCTOBER 28–DECEMBER 19   In Asia, the 4520th Aerial Demonstration Squadron—or Thunderbirds—completes a successful tour of several countries. They win a Mackay Trophy for their efforts.

OCTOBER 31   A Series D Atlas ICBM goes on full alert status, becoming the first U.S. intercontinental ballistic missile capable of striking the Soviet Union with a nuclear warhead.

NOVEMBER 3   For the first time, a C-133 Cargomaster transport delivers an Atlas ICBM to an operational base. It is the first aircraft designed for this specific mission.

NOVEMBER 16   Captain Joseph W. Kittinger jumps from the balloon *Excelsior I* from a record altitude of 76,400 feet, breaking all previous records.

NOVEMBER 17   In Washington, D.C., the Defense Department assigns the Air Force to accept primary responsibility for the Discoverer, MIDAS, and SAMOS satellite projects after they are transferred from the Advanced Research Projects Agency (ARPA).

DECEMBER 8   Major General Don R. Ostrander, formerly of ARPA, transfers as director of NASA's Office of Launch Vehicle Programs. As such he is responsible for all subsequent development and operations.

DECEMBER 9   A twin-rotored Kaman H-43B helicopter reaches a record altitude of 29,846 feet.

Over Akron, Ohio, an Air Force Goodyear unmanned balloon rises to 100,000 feet, whereupon it takes a radar "picture" of the Earth's surface from a payload gondola.

DECEMBER 11   Captain Joseph W. Kittinger jumps from the balloon *Excelsior II* at 74,500 feet, then drops 55,000 feet before opening his parachute. This is also a world's freefall record.

Brigadier General J. H. Moore, flying an F-105B Thunderchief, sets a new world speed record of 1,126.5 miles per hour over a 100-kilometer course.

DECEMBER 14   Over Edwards Air Force Base, California, an F-105C Starfighter flown by Captain Joseph B. Jordan reaches 103,389 feet, the highest altitude yet achieved by an air-breathing aircraft.

DECEMBER 15   Over Edwards Air Force Base, California, an F-106A Delta Dart makes a new official speed record of 1,525.95 miles per hour in level flight.

1960

JANUARY 30   The Central Intelligence Agency orders 12 Lockheed A-12 high-altitude, high-speed reconnaissance aircraft. This is an early version of the SR-71 Blackbird.

FEBRUARY 9   At Bedford, Massachusetts, the Air Force initiates the National Space Surveillance Control Center (SPACE-TRACK).

FEBRUARY 24   At Cape Canaveral, Florida, a Titan ICBM is launched and reaches 5,000 miles downrange, its longest flight profile to date.

APRIL 1   At Cape Canaveral, Florida, an Air Force Thor-Able rocket booster launches *TIROS 1*, the first U.S. weather satellite. In time it completes 1,300 Earth orbits and relays back 22,952 pictures.

APRIL 13   *Transit 1B* is launched into orbit, becoming the first U.S. navigation satellite.

MAY 1   Over Svedlorsk, Soviet Union, a U-2 spyplane flown by CIA pilot Francis G. Powers is struck by fragments of an SA-2 missile and brought down. He is put on trial and jailed for espionage, until being exchanged for a Soviet agent in 1961.

MAY 19   The X-15 hypersonic research plane piloted by Major Robert M. White reaches 107,000 feet, its highest altitude yet.

MAY 20   At Cape Canaveral, Florida, an Atlas missile is test fired and reaches an apogee of 1,000 miles in altitude as it reaches 9,000 miles downrange into the Indian Ocean. This is the longest flight of an Atlas to date.

MAY 23   In Chile, Operation AMIGOS unfolds as Air Force transports begin massive amounts of humanitarian aid to assist victims of a major earthquake there. Over the next month, 10,000 tons of supplies will be flown in from 4,500 miles away.

MAY 24   *MIDAS II*, the first antimissile early warning satellite, is placed into Earth orbit.

JUNE 25   The Aerospace Corporation, a nonprofit civilian group tasked with managing the engineering, research, and development of missiles and space programs, is created by the Air Force.

JUNE 28   In Washington, D.C., a Langley Medal is posthumously awarded to American rocket pioneer Dr. Robert H. Goddard. This is also the Smithsonian Institution's highest award.

JULY 1   Over the Barents Sea, an ERB-47H of the 55th Reconnaissance Wing is shot down over international waters by MiG-17s. Only the pilot and copilot survive, and they are held as spies until being released the following January.

JULY 8   At Jackass Flats, Nevada, a nuclear reactor named Kiwi-A Prime is tested at full power as part of the nuclear-powered rocket program Project ROVER.

In the Democratic Republic of the Congo, Air Force transports begin a four-year effort to evacuate U.S. citizens and fly in UN peacekeeping troops during a period of civil war.

JULY 14   In Africa, Project SAFARI begins as 100 C-130 and C-124 transports airlift 38,000 UN troops to various locales.

JULY 17   A series of three Air Force balloons carry three NASA experiments to 130,000 feet. The 12 mice on board are subject to cosmic rays for 12 hours then brought back for examination.

At Carswell Air Force Base, Texas, the 43rd Bombardment Group receives the first operational B-58 Hustler. This delta-winged giant flies at twice the speed of sound and can hit the Soviet Union with nuclear weapons after only one in-flight refueling.

AUGUST 10–11   High above Earth, the Air Force *Discoverer XIII* satellite ejects a 300-pound capsule, which becomes the first man-made object ever recovered from space.

AUGUST 12   Over California, the X-15 rocket research aircraft piloted by Major Robert M. White reaches a record altitude of 136,500 feet.

AUGUST 16   Captain Joseph W. Kittingerr rides the *Excelsior III* balloon to 102,800 feet then jumps, setting the highest-ever parachute record. He falls for 17 miles, approaching the speed of sound during his freefall period.

AUGUST 18   At Vandenberg Air Force Base, California, the satellite *Discoverer XIV* is thrown into a polar orbit by the Air Force.

AUGUST 19   Over Honolulu, Hawaii, a C-119 flown by Captain Harold F. Mitchell snares the Discoverer XIV re-entry capsule at an altitude of 8,000 feet. Consequently, the 6593rd Test Squadron (Special) receives a Mackay Trophy.

AUGUST 26   At Arecibo, Puerto Rico, the Air Force helps direct construction of the world's largest radar, capable of bouncing signals off the moon and nearby planets.

AUGUST 30   At Warren Air Force Base, Wyoming, the 564th Strategic Missile Squadron, consisting of six Atlas ICBMs, is the first operational unit of its kind.

SEPTEMBER 10   Across the United States, civil aeronautical operations cease for six hours while Operation SKYSHIELD unfolds. This is a defensive operation sponsored by NORAD and involves several hundred Air Force aircraft.

SEPTEMBER 15   At Brooks Air Force Base, Texas, Captain W. D. Habluetzel and Lieutenant J. S. Hargreaves remain in a mock space capsule for 30 days during a simulated journey to the moon and back.

SEPTEMBER 21   At Nellis Air Force Base, Nevada, the first Republic F-105 Thunderchief, all-weather, nuclear attack aircraft is delivered to the Tactical Air Command (TAC).

OCTOBER 1   At Thule, Greenland, the initial Ballistic Missile Early Warning System (BMEWS) is declared operational. This system is to alert the Strategic Air Command (SAC) of an impending missile attack in enough time to allow a retaliatory response.

OCTOBER 12   Over El Centro, California, a C-130 makes a record parachute drop by delivering 541,470 pounds of cargo by air.

NOVEMBER 12   At Vandenberg Air Force Base, California, the *Discoverer XVII* satellite is placed into orbit by a restartable rocket motor for the first time.

NOVEMBER 14   The second midair retrieval of an ejected satellite capsule occurs when a C-119 snares the payload for *Discoverer XVII* as it parachutes in from orbit. The cargo in this instance is the first letter carried into Earth orbit from Air Force Chief of Staff General Thomas D. White to the Secretary of Defense.

NOVEMBER 23   A Thor-Delta rocket carries the *TIROS 2* weather satellite into orbit, becoming the 14th successful launching of the year.

DECEMBER 1 In Pasadena, California, a scale map of the first lunar landing site selected by NASA is delivered to the Jet Propulsion Laboratory.

DECEMBER 3 Disaster strikes at Vandenberg Air Force Base, California, as a nighttime refueling of a Titan I ICBM results in an explosion and fire.

DECEMBER 10 A C-119 piloted by Captain Gene Jones retrieves the reentry capsule from the *Discoverer XVIII* satellite; this particular payload carried samples of human tissue to test the effects of solar radiation.

DECEMBER 14 A B-52G from the 5th Strategic Bombardment Wing, Travis Air Force Base, California, sets a new world jet distance record by flying 10,079 miles in 19 hours and 44 minutes.

DECEMBER 16 At Vandenberg Air Force Base, California, the Strategic Air Command launches an Atlas-D with a Mark II nose cone; the projectile flies 4,384 miles downrange to Eniwetok Atoll.

DECEMBER 19 At Cape Canaveral, Florida, NASA launches a Redstone rocket booster to lift an unmanned Mercury space capsule into low Earth orbit. The device is carried 135 miles up into the atmosphere at a speed of 4,200 miles per hour, and parachutes down into the ocean 235 miles downrange.

1961

JANUARY 13 Major H. J. Deutschendorf breaks six world speed records in his B-58 Hustler by flying 1,200.2 miles per hour over a closed course while carrying a 4,408 pound payload and a three-man crew.

JANUARY 22 The Air Force selects the new Titan II launch vehicle to loft the Dyna-Soar into orbit.

JANUARY 31 At Cape Canaveral, a chimpanzee named Ham (Holloman Aero Medical) is blasted into orbit by a Redstone rocket. His Mercury capsule is safely recovered and Ham exhibits no ill effects from his 18-minute ride.

    At Point Arguello, California, an Atlas-Agena rocket booster launches *SAMOS II*, a 4,100-pound photographic test satellite, into orbit.

    At Cape Canaveral, an LGM-130 Minuteman ICBM is launched for the first time and travels 4,600 miles downrange. This is a three-stage solid-propellant weapon and designed to replace more dangerous, labor-intense liquid-fueled designs.

FEBRUARY 3 The Strategic Air Command initiates the new Looking Glass program. This entails keeping modified KC-135 tankers, converted into flying communication centers, airborne 24 hours a day, all year long. These craft are in constant touch with the Joint Chiefs of Staff and all SAC bases and airplanes should a preemptive enemy strike wipe out American command structures.

MARCH 6 At Wichita, Kansas, Boeing unveils its first B-52H Stratofortress, which is equipped with economical turbofan engines and is capable of carrying the GAM-87A Skybolt air-to-surface missile.

MARCH 7   The North American X-15 hypersonic research aircraft is flown by Major Robert M. White to 2,905 miles per hour; White thus becomes the first man to exceed Mach 4.

The GAM-72A Quail missile is authorized to serve as an electronic diversionary missile on B-52 bombers, enhancing its survivability.

MARCH 17   At Randolph Air Force Base, Texas, the first Northrop T-38 Talon jet trainer is deployed with the Air Training Command. It is still widely in use to present times.

APRIL 1   This day the Air Force Air Materiel Command is renamed the Air Force Logistics Command (AFLC), and the Air Research and Development Command becomes known as the Air Force Systems Command (AFSC).

APRIL 12   In another memorable event, Soviet cosmonaut Yuri Gagarin becomes the first human in space and the first to orbit the Earth.

APRIL 17   At Vernalis, California, a constant-altitude balloon designed by the Air Force Cambridge Research Center deploys at 70,000 feet for nine days while carrying a 40-pound payload.

APRIL 19   During the ill-fated Bay of Pigs invasion, four Air National Guard B-26 crew members are shot down over Cuba and killed.

APRIL 21   The X-15 hypersonic rocket airplane flown by Captain Robert M. White zooms to 105,000 feet at a speed of 3,074 miles per hour. This is the first aircraft to reach that velocity.

MAY 2   Over Paris, France, the B-58 Hustler *Fire Fly* touches down after traveling from New York in 3 hours and 56 minutes; this is a new transatlantic record.

MAY 3   At Vandenberg Air Force Base, California, the Air Force Systems Command (AFSC) launches the first Titan I ICBM from a hard "silo lift" launcher.

MAY 5   At Cape Canaveral, U.S. Navy commander Alan B. Shepard, Jr., becomes the first American in space when his capsule *Friendship* 7 is lofted into a suborbital flight of 15 minutes and 28 seconds.

MAY 26   In Paris, a B-58 Hustler flown by Major William R. Payne, Captain William L. Pollemus, and Captain Raymond Wegener, 43rd Bombardment Wing, arrives from New York in only 3 hours and 20 minutes. They average 1,300 miles per hour and win the Mackay Trophy for their flight, which commemorates the 34th anniversary of Charles Lindbergh's crossing.

JUNE 1   At Kincheloe Air Force Base, Michigan, the first Bomarc-B site becomes operational.

JUNE 3   Over Paris, France, the B-58 Hustler *Fire Fly* stalls and crashes at the Paris Air Show, killing all three crew members.

JUNE 9   The Military Air Transport Service (MATS) obtains its first C-135A Stratotlifter as the process of switching over from piston-powered aircraft to jets begins.

JUNE 23   The X-15 hypersonic research aircraft flown by Major Robert M. White reaches 3,603 miles per hour; White is the first man to exceed Mach 5.

JUNE 30   In Washington, D.C., General Curtis E. LeMay gains appointment as the new Air Force chief of staff.

JULY   The Strategic Air Command (SAC) orders 50 percent of all airborne assets on a 15-minute ground launch alert to deter a surprise attack.

JULY 1   The North American Air Defense Command (NORAD) begins cataloging all man-made space objects with a special detection and tracking computer system.

The Air Force Communications System (AFCS) begins and is tasked with communications and air traffic control at all Air Force bases around the globe.

JULY 12   An Air Force Agena-B launch rocket places the *MIDAS II* satellite in orbit using new "kick in the apogee" technology, whereby a second-stage booster is ignited at the apogee of the first stage, pushing the satellite out to 1,850 miles above the Earth's surface.

JULY 21   At Cape Canaveral, Florida, Air Force captain Virgil I. "Gus" Grissom becomes the second American in space when a Redstone booster blasts his *Liberty Bell* 7 Mercury capsule to a height of 118 miles at 5,310 miles per hour.

AUGUST 8   At Cape Canaveral, Florida, the Air Force test fires its first Atlas F missile. This version is designed for long-term storage of liquid-fuel propellants and will be deployed in hardened silos.

AUGUST 24   Aviatrix Jacqueline Cochran sets a new women's speed record of 844.2 miles per hour in a Northrop T-38 Talon.

AUGUST 25   Lockheed's improved C-130E Hercules transport performs its maiden flight.

SEPTEMBER 8   A T-38 Talon flown by aviatrix Jacqueline Cochran sets a new women's 1,000-kilometer closed course

---

Cochran, Jacqueline (ca. 1910–1980)

Aviatrix, Air Force officer. Jacqueline Cochran was born in Pensacola, Florida, and orphaned at an early age. In 1936 she married millionaire Floyd Odlum, who convinced her to take flying lessons. Cochran, barely literate, passed her flying exam orally and, in 1935, she became the first woman to fly in the Bendix Continental Air Race. In 1938 flamboyant aircraft designer Alexander P. de Seversky allowed her to fly his specially modified racer, and that year Cochran became the first woman to win the Bendix Trophy. Following the outbreak of World War II, General Henry H. Arnold appointed Cochran head of the new Women Airforce Service Pilots (WASPs), with a rank of lieutenant colonel. She oversaw more than 1,000 women pilots who flew 60 million miles while ferrying aircraft abroad. In 1945 Cochran also became the first woman to land an aircraft in Japan, and was present during surrender ceremonies in Tokyo harbor.

After the war, Cochran remained a lieutenant colonel in the Air Force Reserve and eagerly embraced the new jet age. Mentored by test pilot Chuck Yeager, she became the first woman to break the sound barrier, while flying an F-86 Sabrejet in May 1953. Five years later she became the first woman president of the Federation Aeronautique International, and in 1964 she set the woman's world speed record by piloting an F-104 Starfighter at 1,424 miles per hour. Cochran retired from the military as a full colonel in 1969, and two years later she was the first woman inducted into the U.S. Aviation Hall of Fame. She died in Indio, California, on August 9, 1980, having set over 200 flying records, many of which still stand.

speed record by hitting 639.4 miles per hour.

SEPTEMBER 15 Aviatrix Jacqueline Cochran sets another women's world distance record by flying 1,346.4 miles in a Northrop T-38.

SEPTEMBER 19 At Gunter Air Force Base, Alabama, a Bomarc B automated interceptor rises to 7 miles in altitude before destroying a supersonic Regulus II drone 250 miles away. To do so the Bomarc had to complete a 180-degree turn to intercept.

OCTOBER 1 With the Berlin Wall Crisis in full play, Operation STAIRSTEP unfolds, whereby 18,500 Air National Guardsmen report for active duty while ANG units are activated for service in Europe.

OCTOBER 11 The X-15 hypersonic rocket research aircraft flown by Major Robert M. White zooms to an altitude of 217,000 feet—becoming the first manned aircraft to exceed 200,000 feet above the Earth.

OCTOBER 12 Aviatrix Jacqueline Cochran flies her T-38 Talon to a new women's altitude record of 56,071 feet.

OCTOBER 18 An Air Force Kaman H-43B helicopter rises to a record altitude of 32,840 feet.

OCTOBER 20 In Southeast Asia, the first RF-101C Voodoos are dispatched to fly over North Vietnam to monitor Communist troops activities.

NOVEMBER 9 The X-15 hypersonic rocket research aircraft flown by Major Robert M. White reaches 4,000 miles per hour at 101,600 feet. This is the X-15's 45th flight and the first time it has exceeded Mach 6.

The Farm Gate Air Commando detachment arrives in South Vietnam to instruct Vietnamese pilots how to fly T-28 Trojan ground-attack aircraft. The advisers also bring along numerous SC-47s and B-26 Invaders.

NOVEMBER 15 At Saigon, South Vietnam, the 2nd Advanced Echelon, Thirteenth Air Force deploys for active duty, officially initiating U.S. Air Force participation in the Vietnam War.

NOVEMBER 17 At Cape Canaveral, Florida, a Minuteman ICBM is launched from a silo for the first time and travels 3,000 miles downrange as planned.

NOVEMBER 21 At Cape Canaveral, Florida, the 6555th Aerospace Test Wing launches an Air Force Titan ICBM with a nose cone designed for Nike-Zeus antimissile testing.

NOVEMBER 22 The Air Force launches a highly secret SAMOS reconnaissance satellite atop an Atlas–Agena rocket booster.

NOVEMBER 29 At Cape Canaveral, two chimpanzees are launched in a Mercury space capsule, which orbits the Earth twice before being safely recovered.

DECEMBER 1 At Malmstrom Air Force Base, Montana, the 10th Strategic Missile Squadron becomes the first active Minuteman unit.

DECEMBER 15 At Sioux City, Iowa, the North American Air Defense Command's SAGE system becomes operational after its 21st control center is finished and activated.

1962

JANUARY This month the Air Force disbands the Trailblazers, a precision flying demonstration team first formed in 1948.

JANUARY 7 At Tan Son Nhut Air Base, South Vietnam, C-123 Providers are assigned to Operation RANCH HAND, a massive defoliation campaign, to deny Communist units cover in the jungle undergrowth. This project lasts nine years and is not finally halted until January 7, 1991.

JANUARY 10–11 A B-52H flown by Major Clyde P. Evely sets a new unrefueled flight distance of 12,532 miles by flying between Okinawa to Madrid, Spain, in 22 hours and 10 minutes.

JANUARY 13 Over South Vietnam, Air Force C-123 Providers fly the first RANCH HAND defoliation mission.

JANUARY 29 At Cape Canaveral, Florida, the final Titan I ICBM test firing occurs; of 47 tests, 34 are successful while only 3 are complete failures.

FEBRUARY 2 Over South Vietnam, a RANCH HAND C-123 crashes while on a defoliant training mission, and Captain Fergus C. Groves, Captain Robert D. Larson, and Sergeant Milo B. Coghill become the Air Force's first fatalities in Southeast Asia.

FEBRUARY 11 In Berlin, East Germany, U-2 pilot Francis G. Powers is exchanged for a Soviet agent after serving a year and a half in a Russian prison for spying.

MARCH 5 A B-58 Hustler flown by Captains Robert G. Sowers, Robert MacDonald, and John T. Walton, 43rd Bombardment Group, establishes three world air speed records by flying from New York to Los Angeles and back in 4 hours, 41 minutes, and 11 seconds at an average speed of 1,044.5 miles per hour.

MARCH 16 At Cape Canaveral, Florida, the 100-foot tall Titan II missile is test launched for the first time.

MARCH 21 A B-58 Hustler, traveling at 870 miles per hour, test ejects an escape capsule at 35,000 feet. The passenger—a bear—lands safely after a seven-minute parachute descent.

MARCH 22 At Tan Son Nhut Air Base, South Vietnam, four Convair F-102 Delta Daggers are deployed from Clark Air Force Base, the Philippines, in response to sightings of unidentified aircraft over the region.

APRIL 18–20 At Lowry Air Force Base, Colorado, the 724th Strategic Missile Squadron (SMS) becomes the first operational Titan I unit. It possesses nine of the huge missiles, all stored in hardened underground silos. The first Titan goes on operational alert two days later.

APRIL 22 Aviatrix Jacqueline Cochran breaks 68 world records when she becomes the first woman to cross the Atlantic in a Lockheed Jetstar named *Scarlet O'Hara*. She is also the first woman to make a transatlantic crossing in a jet.

APRIL 26 The high-speed, high-altitude Lockheed A-12 makes its maiden flight; it is a forebear of the more famous SR-71 Blackbird.

APRIL 27   At Eglin Air Force Base, Florida, the Special Air Warfare Center is created.

JUNE 19   The classified Dyna-Soar space vehicle receives the designation X-20.

JUNE 29   At Cape Canaveral, Florida, a military crew launches a Minuteman missile for the first time and it flies 2,300 miles downrange.

JULY 9   Over Johnson Island in the Pacific, Operation DOMINIC unfolds as a 1 megaton warhead is shot to an altitude of 248 miles before being detonated. This is the highest thermonuclear blast and the electromagnetic pulse it generates is felt 800 miles away in Hawaii.

JULY 17   The X-15-1 hypersonic rocket aircraft piloted by Major Robert M. White reaches an altitude of 58.7 miles above the Earth's surface at a speed of 3,784 miles per hour. Because White is technically in space, he becomes the first Edwards test pilot to acquire astronaut's wings.

JULY 19   At Vandenberg Air Force Base, California, an Atlas missile is launched towards Kwajalein Island, where its nose cone is successfully intercepted by a Nike-Zeus antimissile missile. This marks the first time that an ICBM has been intercepted by a missile, the equivalent of one bullet hitting another.

AUGUST 1   At Vandenberg Air Force Base, California, an Atlas F missile is test launched for the first time from an underground silo, and it travels 5,000 miles downrange to the Pacific Test Range.

AUGUST 9   At Cape Canaveral, Florida, the Air Force simultaneously launches two Atlas D missiles to demonstrate its multiple countdown capabilities.

SEPTEMBER 14   NASA announces the names of the next nine astronauts selected for the new Gemini space program. Of these, four are Air Force officers: Major Frank Borman, and Captains James A. McDivitt, Edward H. White, and Thomas P. Stafford.

SEPTEMBER 18   A B-58 Hustler flown by Major Fitzhugh L. Fulton zooms to an altitude of 85,360 feet while carrying an 11,000-pound payload. The record remains unbroken to the present day.

OCTOBER 14   Over Cuba, a U-2 piloted by Major Steve Heyser, 4080th Strategic Reconnaissance Wing, photographs irrefutable evidence of Soviet ballistic missiles deployed there. This sets in motion a chain of events culminating in the Cuban Missile Crisis.

OCTOBER 17   High above the Earth, a Vela Hotel satellite detects a ground-based nuclear explosion for the first time.

OCTOBER 17–22   Over Cuba, the U.S. Air Force U-2s and RF-101Cs, backed by Navy RF-8 aircraft, continue high-speed reconnaissance flights and discover several Soviet IL-28 Beagle bombers on Cuban airfields.

OCTOBER 22   Once President John F. Kennedy declares a blockade of Cuba until all Soviet offensive weapons are removed, the Strategic Air Command (SAC) places all its units on 24-hour alert. All B-47s are dispersed for their protection while B-52s maintain a continuous orbit outside of Soviet airspace where they can easily be seen on radar.

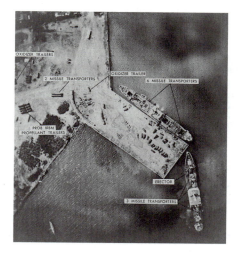

View from U.S. reconnaissance aircraft of Mariel Bay, Cuba. In October 1962, Soviet missile equipment and transport ships were photographed by U.S. U-2 spy planes, leading to the Cuban Missile Crisis. (Library of Congress)

OCTOBER 25   Over the Atlantic, the Strategic Air Command (SAC) sends RB-47s and KC-97 Stratotankers to assist the Navy to locate Soviet vessels heading for Cuba.

OCTOBER 27   Over Cuba, a U-2 piloted by Major Rudolph Anderson of the 4080th Strategic Reconnaissance Wing is shot down and killed by a Soviet missile. He is posthumously awarded the first Air Force Cross for his sacrifice.

At Malmstrom Air Force Base, Montana, all Minuteman I missiles of the 10th Strategic Missile Squadron are placed on high alert.

OCTOBER 28   After the Soviet Union agrees to remove all its offensive weapons from Cuba, the Air Force and other service elements begin to stand down. The United States, for its part, agrees to remove all obsolete Jupiter missiles from bases in Turkey.

OCTOBER 29   Over Cuba, photographic intelligence relayed by Air Force RF-101C Voodoos reveals that the Soviets are complying with the agreement to remove all missiles and jets from the island.

NOVEMBER 2   In the wake of the Chinese invasion of northern India, President John F. Kennedy authorizes Operation LONG SKIP to transfer over 1,000 tons of military equipment to Indian forces. The Miliary Air Transport Service (MATS) complies with its new C-135 jet transports and completes the task in only two weeks.

NOVEMBER 24   General Dynamics and Grumman contract with the Department of Defense to construct and build the new Tactical Fighter Experimental (TFX), a variable-swept wing, twin-engined jet fighter capable of carrying 20,000 pounds of ordnance at two-and-a-half times the speed of sound.

DECEMBER 5   At Cape Canaveral, Florida, the Atlas missile test program terminates with the 151st launch; 101 of these are successful.

DECEMBER 13–14   Over New Mexico, Project STARGAZER unfolds as Captain Joseph A. Kittinger and a civilian astronomer, William C. White, drift to 82,000 feet with a telescope in their gondola for the clearest possible view of the stars. They remain aloft for 18 hours.

DECEMBER 27   The Air Force orders six of the top secret Lockheed SR-71 high-speed, high-altitude reconnaissance aircraft; it enters service as the Blackbird.

1963

JANUARY 2   Over Ap Bac, South Vietnam, South Vietnamese aircraft attack suspected Viet Cong positions. Afterwards, Air Force Piasecki H-21 helicopters arrive to deliver supplies to troops there.

FEBRUARY 6   At Cape Canaveral, Florida, members of the 655th Aerospace Test Wing test launch a Titan II missile for the first time.

FEBRUARY 23   At Malmstrom Air Force Base, Montana, the 10th Strategic Missile Squadron becomes the first operational Minuteman ICBM unit.

APRIL 12   An F-104 Starfighter piloted by aviatrix Jacqueline Cochran sets a women's world speed record of 1,273 miles per hour over a straight course.

MAY 1   Over Edwards Air Force Base, California, aviatrix Jacqueline Cochran establishes another women's speed record by flying a TF-104 Starfighter at 1,203.7 miles per hour over a 10-kilometer course.

MAY 7   Over South Vietnam, an Air Force RB-57E flies a reconnaissance mission for the first time in conjunction with Operation PATRICIA LYNN.

MAY 15–16   At Cape Canaveral, Major L. Gordon Cooper is blasted into orbit in his *Faith* 7 Mercury capsule. He circles the Earth 22 times and lands safely after 34 hours and 19 minutes. Cooper is the first American astronaut to remain in space longer than one day and he is also the last American to fly alone.

MAY 24   At Wendover, Utah, a top secret Lockheed A-12 crashes while undergoing an extensive flight-test.

MAY 27   At St. Louis, Missouri, the McDonnell Douglas F-4C Phantom II makes its maiden flight; the Tactical Air Command acquires 580 of this model.

JUNE 8   At Davis-Monthan Air Force Base, Arizona, the 570th Strategic Missile Squadron becomes the Strategic Air Command's (SAC) first operational Titan II unit.

JUNE 17   The new Sikorsky CH-3C, which features a hydraulic rear ramp, performs its maiden flight.

JULY 20   The top secret Lockheed A-12 reaches Mach 3 in level flight for the first time.

JULY 20–21   Over South Vietnam, a C-47 piloted by Captain Warren P. Tomsett makes a dangerous landing at Loc Ninh, near the Cambodian border, to rescue six wounded Vietnamese soldiers. The mission requires careful planning and timing, yet goes off successfully; Tomsett and his crew consequently win the Mackay Trophy.

JULY 26   The Air Force launches *Syncon 2*, the first satellite placed in a geosynchronous orbit above the Earth. This leaves the satellite hovering over a fixed position in space.

AUGUST 1   The NASA satellite *Mariner II* is launched by the Air Force; this device is destined to travel 540 miles to orbit the sun.

AUGUST 7   At Groom Lake, Nevada, the YF-12A, a high-speed, advanced interceptor, performs its maiden flight.

AUGUST 22   The X-15 hypersonic research aircraft piloted by Joe Walker reaches 67 miles above the Earth's surface, placing it on the very edge of space. This is also the highest point achieved by the X-15 program.

OCTOBER 16 In concert with Project VELA HOTEL, the Air Force launches twin 475-pound satellites that assume circular orbits at opposite ends of the planet.

Operation GREASED LIGHTNING unfolds as a B-58 Hustler covers the 8,028-mile distance between Tokyo, Japan, and RAF Greenham Common, England, in 8 hours and 35 minutes.

OCTOBER 22 The Cessna YAT-37D prototype performs its maiden flight; this an armed, light attack version of the T-37 jet trainer.

NOVEMBER 29 Cape Canaveral, Florida, is renamed Cape Kennedy in honor of the recently assassinated President John F. Kennedy.

DECEMBER 10 In Washington, D.C., Defense Secretary Robert S. McNamara

tasks the Air Force with developing the new Manned Orbiting Laboratory.

Over Edwards Air Force Base, Colonel Chuck Yeager zooms up to 90,000 feet in a rocket-augmented NF-104A before entering a flat spin. He falls to 10,000 feet before being able to eject safely, although he suffers severe burns.

The Air Force cancels the X-20 Dyna-Soar program without ever launching a test vehicle.

DECEMBER 17 At Dobbins Air Force Base, Georgia, the Lockheed C-141A prototype performs its maiden flight. This giant jet transport enters service as the Starlifter.

DECEMBER 31 In Washington, D.C., President Lyndon B. Johnson authorizes the 4080th Strategic Reconnaissance Squadron to perform U-2 clandestine photographic missions over Southeast Asia.

1964

FEBRUARY 29 In Washington, D.C., President Lyndon B. Johnson acknowledges the existence of the Lockheed A-12 high-speed reconnaissance aircraft, although he mistakenly calls it the A-11.

MARCH 28 Near Anchorage, Alaska, Operation HELPING HAND unfolds as Air Force transports fly in 1,800 tons of relief supplies to assist earthquake victims. The endeavor lasts over the next three weeks.

APRIL 21 The Strategic Air Command (SAC) reaches a significant crossroads when the number of intercontinental ballistic missiles in its inventory equals its ground alert bombers.

MAY 11 An F-104G Starfighter flown by aviatrix Jacqueline Cochran sets a new women's speed record by reaching 1,429.3 miles per hour over a fixed course.

MAY 18 The first McDonnell Douglas RF-4C Phantom II reconnaissance aircraft performs its maiden flight; it acquires a significant career in the Vietnam War.

JUNE 9 Over Southeast Asia, KC-135 Stratotankers refuel eight F-100 Super Sabres for the first time during an air strike against Communist gun emplacements in Laos.

In Washington, D.C., President Lyndon B. Johnson acknowledges the existence of the Lockheed RS-71 high-speed high-altitude reconnaissance aircraft, although he misidentifies it as the SR-71; the name is retained.

AUGUST 5 In response to Communist aggression in the Gulf of Tonkin Incident, President Lyndon B. Johnson authorizes air strikes against military targets in North Vietnam. The Air Force is now directly involved in the Vietnam conflict and it begins deploying B-57s, F-100s, F-102s, RF-101s, and F-105s for combat operations.

AUGUST 14 At Vandenberg, California, the Air Force launches its first Atlas/Agena D rocket; this soon becomes a standard launch vehicle.

SEPTEMBER 21 Over Palmdale, California, the North American XB-70A Valkyrie performs its maiden flight. This is a large delta-wing configuration with moveable wing tips that angle down for greater stability at high speed.

NOVEMBER 1 At Bien Hoa Air Base, a Viet Cong mortar attack destroys 5 B-57s parked on the ramp and damages 15 more. The South Vietnamese Air Force also loses four A-1 Skyraiders.

NOVEMBER 10 Over Cuba, the first A-12 reconnaissance flight occurs, although the Central Intelligence Agency denies it happened.

NOVEMBER 12 In Zaire, Operation DRAGON ROUGE unfolds as a C-130 Hercules from the 464th Troop Carrier Wing delivers French paratroopers to help resolve a hostage situation and remove refugees. The unit receives the Mackay Trophy.

DECEMBER 9–10 Over Quang Tin and Binh Dinh Provinces, South Vietnam, Air Force A-1 Skyraiders attack exposed Viet Cong units, inflicting several casualties.

DECEMBER 10 The Air Force utilizes a Titan II rocket booster to put a 3,700-pound satellite into space using new "Transtage" technology, which places the third stage of the rocket in orbit before firing the satellite into a separate orbit.

DECEMBER 14 Over northern Laos, Operation BARREL ROLL commences as the Air Force begins flying armed reconnaissance and close support missions for allied forces.

DECEMBER 15 Over South Vietnam, a C-47 piloted by Captain Jack Harvey performs the first aerial gunship sortie by firing four side-mounted Gatling guns at Communist ground targets.

DECEMBER 21 At Fort Worth Texas, the General Dynamics YF-111A performs its maiden flight.

DECEMBER 22 Over California and Oregon, Operation BIGLIFT commences as Air Force transports deliver relief supplies to victims of recent flooding, delivering 1,500 tons through the following month.

The top secret Lockheed SR-71A Blackbird prototype flies its first one-hour mission, in this instance reaching 1,000 miles per hour.

1965

JANUARY 6   In Texas, General Dynamics begins extensive testing of the F–111A variable geometry (swing-wing) fighter-bomber by shifting the wings for the first time. No ill effects are experienced during the transition.

JANUARY 21   An Air Force Atlas ICBM is launched and carries the Aerospace Research Satellite into Earth orbit. This is also the first satellite slipped into a westward-facing orbit.

FEBRUARY 1   In Washington, D.C., General John P. McDonnell gains appointment as the Air Force chief of staff.

FEBRUARY 4   An Air Force Titan IIIC solid-fuel rocket booster is test fired for the first time, generating 1.25 million pounds of thrust. This output is 25 percent greater than calculated.

FEBRUARY 8   Over North Vietnam, Operation FLAMING DART unfolds in retaliation for Viet Cong attacks on allied air bases. This day Air Force F–100 Super Sabres make their first appearance in Communist airspace by flying top cover for South Vietnamese warplanes.

FEBRUARY 18   Over An Khe, South Vietnam, Air Force B–57 Canberras and F–100 Suber Sabres make their first aerial attacks on Communist positions.

MARCH 2–OCTOBER 31, 1968   Over North Vietnam, the United States commences Operation ROLLING THUNDER, a concerted aerial offensive against Communist military and economic targets. The onslaught involves both Air Force and carrier-based Navy aircraft. An F–100 Super Sabre flown by Lieutenant Hayden J. Lockhart is shot down on the

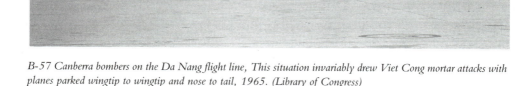

B-57 Canberra bombers on the Da Nang flight line, This situation invariably drew Viet Cong mortar attacks with planes parked wingtip to wingtip and nose to tail, 1965. (Library of Congress)

first day of the offensive; he remains in captivity over the next eight years.

MARCH 23 At Cape Canaveral, Florida, Major Virgil I. "Gus" Grissom becomes the first American astronaut when he blasts into orbit aboard Gemini II, accompanied by Navy Lieutenant Commander John W. Young.

MARCH 30–MAY 23 On Cyprus, Air Force C-124s transport 3,000 Danish UN peacekeepers and 76 tons of cargo during a period of unrest.

APRIL 3 Over Southeast Asia, Operation STEEL TIGER commences to interdict the Communist supply line known as the Ho Chi Minh Trail. This involves bombing targets in Laos and Cambodia for the remainder of the war.

APRIL 3–4 Over North Vietnam, two F-105 Thunderchiefs are shot down while trying to bomb the Thanh Hoa bridge. The attack fails to bring down any spans. These are also the first Air Force combat losses.

APRIL 20 A milestone is passed after the final production Atlas ICBM is placed in storage for use as a research vehicle, having been largely supplanted by solid-propellant missiles like the Minuteman.

APRIL 23 At Travis Air Force Base, California, the first operational Lockheed C-141 Starlifter is deployed.

APRIL 29–MAY 5 At Pope Air Force Base, North Carolina, Operation POWER PACK unfolds as Air Force C-130s and C-124s transport 12,000 troops and 17,000 tons of supplies during a stabilization and peacekeeping mission in the Dominican Republic. Personnel from the Air Force Reserve and Air National Guard are active throughout.

MAY 1 A Lockheed YF-12A flown by Colonel Robert L. Stephens establishes a new world's speed record by reaching 2,070 miles per hour in level flight. Consequently, the YF-12A/SR-71 Test Force receives a Mackay Trophy.

MAY 12–18 The United States suspends its bombing campaign to gauge North Vietnam's willingness to negotiate and to end the conflict—the gesture is not reciprocated.

MAY 22 Once the bombing of North Vietnam resumes, Air Force F-105s strike targets above the 20th parallel for the first time by bombing army barracks.

JUNE 3–7 In Earth orbit, Air Force astronauts and Majors Edward H. White and James A. McDivitt set an American endurance record in space by completing 63 orbits in 97 hours. On June 4, White also becomes the first American to depart his space capsule and drifts on a tethered line with a gas propulsion unit.

JUNE 18 On Guam, B-52s sortie to conduct the first ARC LIGHT (carpet bombing) missions against Viet Cong positions near Saigon, South Vietnam. This is also the giant bomber's baptism by fire.

A Titan III rocket launcher lifts a satellite weighing 10.5 tons into orbit by generating 2.5 million pounds of thrust. This system consists of a three-stage liquid-fuel rocket and two strap-on solid-fuel boosters.

JUNE 30 At Warren Air Force Base, Wyoming, the 800th Minuteman ICBM becomes operational, being the last of this variant deployed.

JULY 8   Control of NASA satellites *Syncom II* and *Syncom III* is assumed by the Air Force Satellite Control Facility for the Department of Defense. These geosynchronous devices relay communications and weather data.

JULY 10   Over North Vietnam, two Communist MiG-17s are shot down by F-4C Phantom IIs of the 45th Tactical Fighter Squadron. These are the first Air Force victories in Southeast Asia.

JULY 16   The North American/Rockwell YOV-10A Bronco performs its maiden flight as a COIN (counterinsurgency) light attack aircraft. It serves in Vietnam with distinction as a Forward Air Controller (FAC) vehicle.

JULY 23   Over North Vietnam, a Soviet-supplied SA-2 surface-to-air missile (SAM) downs an Air Force F-4 Phantom II jet for the first time.

AUGUST 5   The Saturn V first-stage booster is run at a full-power static test, whereby its five engines generate 7.5 million pounds of thrust for 2.5 minutes. The device is subsequently placed on display at the Smithsonian Institution.

AUGUST 21–29   At Cape Kennedy, Florida, the Gemini V space capsule is launched with Air Force astronaut L. Gordon Cooper and Navy counterpart Charles Conrad, Jr., on a week-long mission that completes 120 Earth orbits.

SEPTEMBER 15–21   In Southwest Asia, Operation NICE WAY commences as the Air Force evacuates 1,000 U.S. citizens as India and Pakistan fight another war.

OCTOBER 23   In South Vietnam, the 4503rd Tactical Fighter Squadron receives the first Northrop F-5E jet fighters sent to the region.

OCTOBER 31   At Grand Forks Air Force Base, North Dakota, the 447th Strategic Missile Squadron deploys the first 10 Minuteman II ICBMs. This weapon is larger and more capable than the first generation Minuteman I, but still squeezes into the same silo.

NOVEMBER 1   In Washington, D.C., Colonel Jeanne M. Holm gains appointment as director of the Women of the Air Force.

NOVEMBER 14–16   In South Vietnam, the costly battle of Ia Drang, the Vietnam War's first conventional encounter, is waged between U.S. and Communist forces. Air Force B-52s play a supporting role by pounding enemy positions; the battle ends with 71 Americans dead and 121 wounded while 2,000 Communists are estimated to have been killed.

DECEMBER 15   High above the Earth, the Gemini VI space capsule piloted by Navy captain Walter M. Schirra and Air Force major Thomas P. Stafford maneuvers close to Gemini VII under Air Force astronaut Frank Borman and Navy officer James A. Lovell.

DECEMBER 10   In order to facilitate aerial targeting, the U.S. Pacific Command divides North Vietnam into six "route packages"; those numbered 1, 5, and 6B were assigned to the Air Force and 2, 3, 4, and 6A went to the Navy.

DECEMBER 22   North of Hanoi, North Vietnam, F-105F Wild Weasels fly their first mission of the war and destroy a Communist Fan Song radar and an SA-2 missile site.

DECEMBER 23–JANUARY 23   At Hickam Air Force Base, Hawaii, Operation BLUE LIGHT unfolds as Air Force transports move the Army's 3rd Brigade, 25th Infantry Division to bases at Pleiku, South Vietnam. They deliver 3,000 troops and 4,600 tons of cargo in a month, which is one of the largest maneuvers of its kind to that point.

1966

JANUARY 1   The Military Airlift Command (MAC) is the new designation for the Military Air Transport Command (MATS). Concurrently, the Eastern Air Transport Force is renamed the Twenty-First Air Force and the Western Air Transport Force is now the Twenty-Second Air Force.

Over Southeast Asia, the Air National Guard commits men and resources to augment the Military Airlift Command to fly 75 airlift missions every month from bases in the United States.

JANUARY 7   At Beale Air Force Base, California, the 4200th Strategic Reconnaissance Wing receives the first operational SR-71 Blackbird.

JANUARY 17   Off the coast of Spain, a B-52 armed with thermonuclear weapons collides with a KC-135 tanker, killing 7 of 11 light crew members. All the weapons are recovered from the crash site, although the last had to be fished up from 2,500 feet down.

MARCH 4   Over North Vietnam, a flight of Air Force Phantom II jet fighters is attacked by three Communist MiG-17s, who make one pass then disappear back to their base.

MARCH 10   In the A Shau Valley, South Vietnam, an A-1E Skyraider flown by Bernard F. Fisher rescues the crew of another downed aircraft under enemy fire; he wins the first Congressional Medal of Honor granted an Air Force officer in the war, and the first designed especially for the Air Force.

MARCH 16–17   High in Earth orbit, the Gemini VII space capsule piloted by Navy astronaut Neil A. Armstrong and Air Force astronaut David Scott has to make an emergency splashdown after one of its maneuvering thrusters jams. This is also the first recovery mission in which Air Force aircraft participate.

MARCH 31   The Strategic Air Command (SAC) phases out the last of its B-47 Stratojets, ending the career of the first generation of swept-wing jet bombers.

APRIL 1   In Saigon, South Vietnam, the headquarters, Seventh Air Force under Lieutenant General Joseph H. Moore, becomes a subcommand of the Pacific Air Forces (PACAF).

APRIL 6   Tactical airlift aircraft of the U.S. Army are transferred to the Air Force, and are subsequently redesignated the C-7A Caribou and the C-8A Buffalo.

APRIL 11   East of Saigon, South Vietnam, Airman 1st Class William H. Pitsenbarger is mortally wounded while assisting in the evacuation of several wounded soldiers. He dies after refusing to be evacuated, winning a posthumous Congressional Medal of Honor.

APRIL 12 Over North Vietnam, B-52 bombers make their combat debut 85 miles north of the Demilitarized Zone by bombing supply lines at the Mu Gia Pass.

APRIL 25 The 447th Strategic Missile Squadron becomes the first Strategic Air Command unit to deploy Minuteman II ICBMs.

APRIL 26 Over Hanoi, North Vietnam, a Soviet-supplied MiG-21 fighter falls to an F-4C flown by Major Paul J. Gilmore and Lieutenant William T. Smith. This is the first kill of its kind and occurs while a flight of F-105s was being escorted to a target.

MAY 3 At Edwards Air Force Base, California, the Fulton Recovery System, designed to "snatch" a man from the ground to a moving airplane, is successfully tested by an HC-130H.

JUNE 3–6 High over the Earth, the Gemini IX space capsule piloted by Air Force astronaut Thomas Stafford and Navy astronaut Eugene Cernan experiences technical problems attempting to link up with an orbiting Agena Target Docking Adapter and the mission ends prematurely.

JUNE 8 Tragedy strikes as the second XB-70A Valkyrie I is struck by an F-104N Starfighter flying in close formation. Both aircraft are destroyed in the ensuing crash, which takes the lives of NASA chief test pilot Joe Walker and Air Force Major Carl Cross.

JULY 1 At Tan Son Nhut Air Base, South Vietnam, command of the Seventh Air Force passes to General William W. Momyer.

JULY 18–21 Above the Earth, the Gemini X space capsule flown by astronaut John Young and Air Force astronaut Michael Collins completes two rendezvous with an Agena target vehicle and then returns home.

AUGUST 20–29 In response to a destructive earthquake in Turkey, transports from the United States Air Forces in Europe (USAFE) bring in 50 tons of medical and relief supplies for the survivors.

SEPTEMBER 3 Over North Vietnam, large numbers of new MiG-21 jet fighters begin appearing for the first time. These are based at a series of airfields ringing Hanoi, which are off limits to U.S. bombing.

SEPTEMBER 20 At Edwards Air Force Base, California, a NASA M2-F1 "lifting body" is flown by Lieutenant Colonel Donald M. Sorlie, the first Air Force officer to test fly the vehicle.

NOVEMBER 11 Above the Earth, the Gemini XII space capsule flown by Navy astronaut James Lovell and Air Force astronaut Buzz Aldrin completes several docking maneuvers with an Agena target vehicle before returning safely.

NOVEMBER 14 On the Antarctic ice shelf, a C-141 Starlifter lands at McMurdo Sound after completing a 2,200-mile flight from Christchurch, New Zealand.

DECEMBER 14 Over Southeast Asia, Colonel Albert R. Howarth flies his aircraft coolly and effectively under fire; he wins a Mackay Trophy for the effort.

1967

JANUARY 2   Over the Red River Valley, North Vietnam, Operation BOLO commences as three flights of F-4 Phantoms under Colonel Robin Olds, the 8th Tactical Fighter Wing, mimic the usual routes flown by F-105 Thunderchiefs and lure a large party of unsuspecting MiG-21s into combat. The Communists are badly bested and lose seven MiGs—this is the largest single-day tally of the war.

JANUARY 18   An Air Force Titan IIIC launches eight defense communications satellites at a single throw.

JANUARY 27   Tragedy strikes Cape Kennedy, Florida, when the Apollo space capsule on the launching pad catches fire, killing Air Force lieutenant colonels Gus Grissom and Ed White, and Navy lieutenant commander Roger Chaffee.

FEBRUARY 22   Near the Cambodian border, Operation JUNCTION CITY unfolds as the 173rd Airborne Brigade drops into combat from 23 C-130 Air Force transports. This is the first such tactical deployment of the war and is part of a large search-and-destroy operation with the Army 1st U.S. Infantry Division.

FEBRUARY 24   Over Dalat, South Vietnam, a Cessna O-1 Bird Dog flown by Captain Hilliard A. Wilbanks, 21st Tactical Air Support Squadron, flies down low firing his rifle and smoke rockets in support of some South Vietnamese rangers; he is shot down and killed, winning a posthumous Congressional Medal of Honor.

MARCH 10   Over North Vietnam, an F-105 piloted by Captain Merlyn H. Dethlefsen, 354th Tactical Fighter Squadron,

makes repeated passes at Communist antiaircraft positions, allowing other aircraft to complete their bomb run; he wins a Congressional Medal of Honor. Another F-105 flown by Captain Max Brestel manages to down two MiG-17s in one day.

MARCH 10–11   Over North Vietnam, Air Force F-105s and F-4s operating out of Ubon, Thailand, strike the Thai Nguyen steel factory.

MARCH 11   Near Hanoi, North Vietnam, the Canal des Rapides bridges are attacked by Air Force warplanes.

MARCH 15   The Sikorsky HH-53B, the largest and fastest helicopter available in the Air Force inventory, performs its maiden flight.

MARCH 22   At U-Tapao, Thailand, a new B-52 base is constructed to alleviate the congestion at Andersen Air Base, Guam.

MARCH 25   At Eielson Air Force Base, Alaska, the primary role of strategic reconnaissance falls upon the 6th Strategic Wing, which flies a variety of RC-135 aircraft.

APRIL 3   In Washington, D.C., Paul W. Airey gains appointment as the first chief master sergeant of the Air Force. As such he is tasked with advising the service leadership on enlisted personnel issues.

APRIL 10   At U-Tapao, Thailand, B-52 bombers begin staging their first combat missions of the war. Due to their proximity to Vietnam, in-flight refueling is not necessary.

APRIL 19 Over North Vietnam, flying an F-105 Thunderchief, Major Leo K. Thorsness, 357th Tactical Fighter Squadron, completes his bombing sortie, then fights gamely against Communist jets and antiaircraft fire as a diversion for other aircraft; he manages to down two MiG-17s and wins a Congressional Medal of Honor.

APRIL 26 Over North Vietnam, Air Force bombers are finally allowed to attack Communist airfields at Kep and Hoa Lac. However, airfields within the boundaries of Hanoi remain off limits.

APRIL 28 At Ramstein Air Base, West Germany, Air National Guard KC-97Ls participate in Operation CREEK PARTY; this is the first time that the ANG has contributed to operations supporting military contingencies.

An Air Force Titan IIC missile hauls five Vela satellites aloft, which are designed to test the explosion of nuclear weapons back on Earth.

MAY 31 Over the Gulf of Tonkin, Vietnam, a KC-135 Stratotanker piloted by Major John H. Casteel, 902nd Air Refueling Squadron, manages to refuel six Navy fighters which were extremely low on fuel. Casteel and his men win the Mackay Trophy.

MAY 31 Over North Vietnam, the A-12 high-speed reconnaissance aircraft performs its first 3 hour, 40 minute mission. It is flown by CIA pilot Mele Vojvodich.

JUNE 1 In Paris, France, pair of Air Force helicopters recreates Charles Lindbergh's solo transatlantic flight in 31 hours and 9 aerial refuelings. This is also the first nonstop flight by helicopters from New York to Europe.

JUNE 5–11 At Wheelus Air Force Base, Libya, the Air Force relocates 8,000 U.S. and European citizens after the six day war erupts between Israel, Egypt, and Syria.

JULY 1 A Titan IIIC missile places six additional satellites into Earth orbit as part of the Initial Defense Communications Satellite Program (IDCSP).

JULY 30 At Fort Worth, Texas, the General Dynamics F-111 variable geometry (swing-wing) fighter performs its maiden flight.

AUGUST 10 In Washington, D.C., the Senate Appropriations Committee eliminates $172 million from the F-111B program intended for the U.S. Navy once critics felt the aircraft would be too big and heavy to land on carriers.

AUGUST 11 Over North Vietnam, two spans of the Paul Doumer Bridge is destroyed by F-105s of the 355th and 388th Tactical Fighter Wings, which flew in from bases in Thailand.

AUGUST 21 Over North Vietnam, a record 80 surface-to-air missiles are launched at attacking U.S. warplanes; this is the highest tally for the entire war.

AUGUST 24–SEPTEMBER 4 The American government enacts another round of bombing suspensions in a futile attempt to encourage peace talks with North Vietnam. The Communist regime fails to respond or reciprocate.

AUGUST 26 Over North Vietnam, an F-100 piloted by Major George E. Day is brought down; Day, captured and badly injured, makes several failed escape attempts; he receives a Congressional Medal of Honor.

AUGUST 28   The advanced Lockheed U-2R performs its maiden flight, although only six are acquired by the Air Force and six by the Central Intelligence Agency.

SEPTEMBER 9   Over South Vietnam, Sergeant Duane D. Hackney shows remarkable courage while rescuing a downed Air Force pilot and he becomes the first enlisted man to receive the Air Force Cross.

OCTOBER 3   The hypersonic X-15 research rocket plane piloted by William Knight reached a new world speed record of 4,543 miles per hour (Mach 6.7) at 102,100 feet.

In St. Louis, Missouri, the new McDonnell Douglas F-4E Phantom II is rolled out; this is the first version with an internally mounted 20mm cannon.

OCTOBER 16   At Nellis Air Force Base, Nevada, the first General Dynamics F-111 arrives for operational testing. In addition to featuring swing-wings, the craft can also fly nighttime, terrain-following flight paths.

OCTOBER 24   Over North Vietnam, the large aviation complex at Phuc Yen is struck by a joint force of Air Force, Navy, and Marine Corps warplanes.

OCTOBER 30   Over North Vietnam, Communist troops launch six SA-2 Guideline missiles at an A-12 passing overhead; none hit the aircraft, but missile fragments are subsequently found in a frontal fillet area.

NOVEMBER 9   Inside Laos, an HH-3E rescue helicopter piloted by Captain

Gerald O. Young is shot down while attempting to rescue an Army reconnaissance team. Though wounded, he refuses to be evacuated and evades capture for 17 hours until he can summon his own rescue mission. He wins a Congressional Medal of Honor.

Over North Vietnam, an F-4 Phantom II piloted by Captain Lance P. Sijan is shot down; he manages to eject but is badly injured and tortured. Sijan manages to escape but is recaptured, and he dies of illness on January 21, 1968. Sijan is the first U.S. Air Force Academy graduate to be awarded a posthumous Congressional Medal of Honor.

NOVEMBER 15   The X-14 hypersonic research plane piloted by Major Michael J. Adams breaks up in flight after entering into a spin at Mach 5, killing him. He wins a posthumous set of astronaut wings.

NOVEMBER 17–DECEMBER 29   Over Southeast Asia, Operation EAGLE THRUST unfolds as C-133 and C-141 transports convey 10,000 paratroops and 5,000 tons of equipment from Fort Campbell, Kentucky, to Bien Hoa Air Base, South Vietnam. This is also the longest-ranging aerial troop transfer of the war.

DECEMBER 8   Over Edwards Air Force Base, California, an F-104 crash takes the life of Major Robert H. Lawrence, the first African American selected by NASA to serve in the astronaut program.

DECEMBER 29   At Offutt Air Force Base, Nebraska, a chapter closes as the 55th Strategic Reconnaissance Wing retires its last remaining RB-47H.

1968

JANUARY 1   The Aerospace Defense Command is the new name for the Air Defense Command.

JANUARY 21   At Khe Sanh, South Vietnam, a Marine Corps garrison is surrounded by Communist forces for the next 77 days. The Air Force participates by flying in an average of 165 tons of equipment, weapons, and supplies every day while waves of B-52 bombers carpet bomb suspect enemy positions in the nearby hillside.

JANUARY 22   Over Greenland, a B-52 crashes while attempting an emergency landing at Thule Air Base. Radioactive debris from the four nuclear weapons it is carrying is spread across the sea ice at North Star Bay. Months of specialized cleaning are required before readings return to normal.

JANUARY 26   Over North Korea, an A-12 top secret reconnaissance flight unfolds in response to the seizure of the USS *Pueblo* three days earlier.

JANUARY 30–31   Communist forces launch their surprise Tet Offensive across South Vietnam which, while a military defeat, is a turning point in American opinion against the war.

FEBRUARY 27   In Southeast Asia, AC-130 Hercules gunships make their debut while attacking along the Ho Chi Minh Trail.

FEBRUARY 29   In Washington, D.C., a law is enacted which eliminates all obstacles against promoting women higher than the rank of full colonel. Consequently, Colonels Jeanne Holm, director of

Women in the Air Force, and Helen O'Day, assigned to the Air Force chief of staff's office, both become permanent colonels.

MARCH 25   Over North Vietnam, the General Dynamics F-111 performs its first combat missions as part of Operation COMBAT LANCER. This particular deployment is part of an operational testing scheme, and the jets are returned to the United States soon after.

MARCH 31   Once again, President Lyndon B. Johnson orders a partial bombing halt over North Vietnam in the hopes of stimulating peace talks. He also declares that he will not be seeking reelection in the fall.

APRIL 10   At Kadena Air Base, Japan, the 9th Strategic Reconnaissance Wing begins the first SR-71A missions over North Vietnam.

MAY 3   In South Vietnam, the 120th Tactical Fighter Squadron arrives from Buckley Air National Guard Base, Colorado, becoming the first ANG unit committed to combat operations.

MAY 12   At Kham Duc, South Vietnam, Air Force C-130s assist Army and Marine Corps helicopters to evacuate the outnumbered garrison while under enemy fire. Mortar fire strikes a C-130, killing all 150 people on board, and a total of eight aircraft are lost. Lieutenant Colonel Daryl D. Cole is awarded a Mackay Trophy, while four airmen receive the Air Force Cross. A C-123 under Lieutenant Colonel Joe M. Jackson also lands under intense fire to bring off a three-man combat control team; he is awarded a Congressional Medal of Honor.

A U.S. Air Force B-57 Canberra bombs a suspected Viet Cong jungle position in North Vietnam on March 17, 1967. The longest bombing campaign ever conducted by the U.S. Air Force, Operation Rolling Thunder lasted from March 1965 to October 1968. (AP/Wide World Photos)

JUNE 13   At Cape Kennedy, Florida, a Titan IIIC launch vehicle hoists eight communications satellites into orbit to augment the existing Defense Satellite Communications System.

JUNE 17   At Long Beach, California, the first McDonnell Douglas C-9 Nightingale is completed; this is intended as an aeromedical aircraft with United States boundaries.

JUNE 30   The Lockheed C-51 Galaxy, then the world's largest aircraft, performs its maiden flight. The Military Air Command (MAC) is slated to receive 81 of them.

AUGUST 1   In South Vietnam, General George S. Brown gains appointment as commander of the Seventh Air Force.

AUGUST 25   In South Vietnam, the North American OV-10 Bronco commences a 90-day combat evaluation period.

SEPTEMBER 1   Over Quang Binh Province, South Vietnam, an A-1H Skyraider piloted by Lieutenant Colonel William A. Jones III withstands a storm of enemy ground fire to land and rescue a downed pilot. Jones is badly injured in the action and his aircraft is shot up, so he receives a Congressional Medal of Honor.

SEPTEMBER 26   The Air Force LTD A-7D Corsair II light attack bomber flies for the first time.

OCTOBER 11   At Cape Kennedy, Florida, Air Force major Donn F. Eisele is one of three astronauts on the Apollo 7 mission, launched today on board a Saturn IB rocket.

OCTOBER 31   Over North Vietnam, the United States concludes Operation ROLLING THUNDER, its first sustained aerial offensive of the war.

NOVEMBER 1   Over Laos, Operation COMMANDO HUNT commences as all other aerial attacks on North Vietnam are suspended. However, reconnaissance missions are flown throughout the region.

NOVEMBER 26   Over Duc Co, South Vietnam, a UH-1F Huey helicopter piloted by Lieutenant James P. Fleming,

20th Special Operations Squadron, retrieves a six-man reconnaissance team under heavy enemy fire while being extremely low on fuel. Fleming receives a Congressional Medal of Honor.

DECEMBER 21–28   At Cape Kennedy, Florida, Apollo 8 is launched into space on a mission to orbit the moon. The three-man crew consists of Air Force colonels Frank Borman and William Anders, and Navy captain James Lovell. This is also the first space flight to actually leave Earth orbit.

1969

JANUARY 1   In South Vietnam, the 71st Special Operations Squadron, an Air Force Reserve unit, flies the first AC-119 Shadow gunship mission.

JANUARY 7   Northrop delivers it 1,000th T-38 Talon trainer to the Air Force.

FEBRUARY 4   At Edwards Air Force Base, the last surviving prototype XB-70 Valkyrie departs to be put on display at the National Museum of the U.S. Air Force in Dayton, Ohio.

FEBRUARY 9   A Titan IIIC rocket places *TACSAT 1*, the first tactical communications satellite, into orbit. This device relays messages between land, sea, and airborne tactical stations.

FEBRUARY 24   Over Bien Hoa Province, South Vietnam, an AC-47 gunship is struck by antiaircraft fire and Airman 1st Class John L. Levitow, though severely wounded, throws a magnesium flare that is burning in the cabin out the cargo door. He receives a Congressional Medal of Honor.

MARCH 3–19   The Apollo 9 space capsule conducts operational tests while in Earth orbit; the crew consists of Air Force colonels James A. McDivitt and David R. Scott and civilian Russell L. Schweickart.

MARCH 18   Over Cambodia, B-52 bombers begin covert bombing raids of Communist sanctuaries under the code-names of BREAKFAST, LUNCH, DINNER, and SNACK; by the time they end in May 1970, 43,000 missions will have been launched.

APRIL 4–10   As 72 F-4D Phantom IIs of the 49th Tactical Air Wing relocate from Spangdahlem Air Base, Germany, to Holloman Air Force Base, New Mexico, they complete 504 aerial refuelings without mishap. The unit receives the Mackay Trophy for its efforts.

APRIL 17   In California, the Martin X-24A lifting body piloted by Major Jerauld Gentry conducts its first glide test to validate the potential of reusable spacecraft.

MAY 14   In Ecuador, Operation COMBAT MOSQUITO unfolds as Air Force C-141s deliver 50 tons of pesticides to combat an outbreak of encephalitis. A pair of UC-123s also begins a spraying project to destroy mosquito breeding grounds; the outbreak is contained within a month.

MAY 18–26   Apollo 10 becomes the second spacecraft to orbit the moon, and includes the Command and service modules, plus the Lunar Extension Module (LEM). Air Force colonel Thomas Stafford and Navy astronaut Eugene Cernan fly the LEM to within 5.5 miles above the moon's surface as a dry run for Apollo 11.

MAY 21   The huge Lockheed C-5A Galaxy sets a new gross liftoff weight of 728,100 pounds.

JUNE   The U.S. Air Force Aerial Demonstration Squadron, or Thunderbirds, begins its new season flying F-4 Phantom II jets.

JUNE 5   Over North Vietnam, Air Force bombers resume bombing raids, the first since the previous November.

JULY 1   In Southeast Asia, the Air Force Air Rescue and Recovery Service (ARRS) flies its 2,500th mission.

JULY 8   In South Vietnam, Air Force C-141 Starlifters begin the withdrawal of 25,000 U.S. combat troops in accordance with President Richard M. Nixon's Vietnamization policies. The first wave is landed at McChord Air Force Base, Washington.

JULY 20   The Apollo 11 Lunar Extension Module (LEM) lands successfully on the surface of the moon and Navy astronaut Neil A. Armstrong becomes the first human to leave a footprint there. He is joined an hour later by Air Force astronaut Edwin P. "Buzz" Aldrin. Meanwhile, Air Force astronaut Michael Collins remains in orbit with the main capsule.

Astronaut Neil Armstrong, Apollo ll mission commander, at the modular equipment storage assembly of the lunar module "Eagle" on the historic first extravehicular activity on the lunar surface. Most photos from the Apollo 11 mission show Buzz Aldrin. This is one of only a few depicting Neil Armstrong. (NASA)

JULY 24   The Apollo 11 space mission successfully concludes after 8 days, 3 hours, and 18 minutes in space. They bring back 50 pounds of lunar rock samples.

AUGUST 1   In Washington, D.C., General John D. Ryan becomes the new Air Force chief of staff. Donald L. Harlow also becomes the new chief master sergeant of the Air Force.

AUGUST 19   In Mississippi, Air Force transports begin delivering tons of food, water, and relief supplies to assist victims of Hurricane Camille. They deliver 6,000 tons of goods within a month.

OCTOBER 8–14   At Wheelus Air Force Base, Libya, three HH-53 helicopters are sent to Tunis to assist victims of heavy flooding. Ultimately, they rescue 2,000 individuals.

NOVEMBER 6   At Holloman Air Force Base, scientists release the largest balloon ever constructed; it is over 1,000-feet long and carries a 13,000-pound payload into the air.

DECEMBER 18   At the Air Force Missile Development Center, crew test fire Maverick (AGM-65) air-to-surface television-guided missiles against moving targets for the first time.

1970

JANUARY 16   At Grissom Air Force Base, Indiana, the last few remaining B-58 Hustlers still in Air Force inventory are flown to their final resting place at the "bone yard," Davis-Monthan Air Force Base, Arizona.

FEBRUARY 17   In northern Laos, B-52 bombers drop bombs on Communist targets for the final time. These actions are not made public until March 6.

FEBRUARY 18   The HL-10 experimental lifting body piloted by Major Peter C. Hoag reaches Mach 1.86 at 65,000 feet. This is an unpowered glide test.

FEBRUARY 27   In Washington, D.C., the Defense Department selects Pratt and Whitney to build a new generation jet engine to power the McDonnell Douglas F-15 Eagle and the Grumman F-14 Tomcat then under development.

MARCH 15   A new telephone network called the "AUTOVON" is completed; this device is an automatic voice network linking all U.S. military bases.

MARCH 18   Over Cambodia, B-52s begin pounding suspected Communist positions as U.S. forces also make a limited incursion into the border region. The aerial blitz lasts two months, involves 4,300 sorties, and drops over 120,000 tons of bombs.

APRIL 11–17   The crippled Apollo 13 spacecraft makes a heroic return to Earth after being damaged while coasting to the moon; among the three-man crew is John L. Swigert, Jr., a former Air Force officer.

APRIL 14   At Hill Air Force Base, Utah, a C-141 Starlifter transports a Minuteman III missile to Minot AFB, North Dakota. This is also the first operational example of the new variant.

APRIL 17 At Minot Air Force Base, North Dakota, the first Minuteman III missile is handed off to the 741st Strategic Missile Squadron and declared operational.

MAY 4 At Kent, Ohio, rioting students are fired upon by the Ohio National Guard; four students are killed.

MAY 5 Across the nation, the Air Force Reserve Officer Training Corps (AFROTC) is opened to women for the first time.

MAY 8 Over Southeast Asia, an AC-119K Shadow gunship under Captain Alan D. Milacek loses 15 feet of the left wing to ground fire as it attacks heavily defended truck convoys along the Ho Chi Minh Trail. The aircrew successfully struggle to bring their plane back to base, winning a Mackay Trophy.

JUNE 2 In Peru, a disastrous earthquake compels the Air Force Southern Command to begin a major aerial relief effort. This entails delivering 750 tins of supplies and 3,000 medical personnel, and the evacuation of 500 patients.

JUNE 6 The first Lockheed C-51 Galaxy is delivered to the Military Airlift Command (MAC); this is the world's largest aircraft at the time.

JULY 31 At Keesler Air Force Base, Mississippi, the first class of South Vietnamese pilots graduates as part of the Vietnamization program.

AUGUST 24 At Da Nang Airport, South Vietnam, 2 HH-53 Sea Stallions arrive on the first nonstop transpacific helicopter crossing; they departed from Elgin Air Force Base, Florida.

SEPTEMBER 1 In South Vietnam, General Lucius D. Clay, Jr., gains appointment as commander of the Seventh Air Force.

SEPTEMBER 6 At Incirlik, Turkey, Operation FLAT PASS unfolds as USAFE deploys C-130s and F-4 Phantoms for the possible rescue of passengers from three airliners hijacked by Palestinian militants. The hostages are eventually released, but the three aircraft are blown up.

SEPTEMBER 28–OCTOBER 31 In Jordan, Operation FIG HILL commences as Air Force transports deliver 180 tons of supplies and equipment, along with Army and Air Force medical personnel to that beleaguered kingdom as it battles an uprising by the Popular Front for the Liberation of Palestine (PFLP).

OCTOBER 3 At Hurlburt Field, Florida, the Special Operations Center receives the first 2 Bell UH-1N Twin Hueys, the first of 79 such machines acquired. This is also the first Air Force unit to operate this twin-engined machine.

NOVEMBER 21 In North Vietnam, the American raid of Son Tay Prison commences with Air Force helicopters delivering Army Colonel Arthur D. "Bull" Simons to the camp. They are escorted by C-130E Combat Talon aircraft to recover the released prisoners. However, these had been relocated to another location previously and the raiders return empty-handed. The raid was also covered by F-4 Phantoms while F-105s flew diversionary raids elsewhere.

1971

JANUARY 28   Over South Vietnam, the final RANCH HAND defoliating mission is conducted by Fairchild UC-123B sprayer aircraft.

JANUARY 31–FEBRUARY 9   The Apollo 14 expedition arrives at the moon and safely returns. Air Force astronaut Stuart A. Roosa pilots the Command Module that remains in orbit.

MARCH 17   At Auburn University, Alabama, 2nd Lieutenant Jane Leslie Holley is the first woman to be commissioned through an Air Force ROTC program.

APRIL 26   An SR-71 Blackbird piloted by Lieutenant Colonel Thomas B. Estes and Lieutenant Colonel Dewain C. Vick sets a speed record for covering 15,000 miles in 10 hours and 30 minutes, nonstop; the flight wins a Mackay Trophy along with the Harmon International Aviator Award.

JULY 16   In Washington, D.C., Colonel Jeanne M. Holm is promoted to brigadier general, becoming the first female general in the Air Force. She remains as director of Women in the Air Force.

JUNE 16–JULY 18   Over India, Operation BONNY JACK unfolds as Air Force C-130s and C-141s transfer 23,000 refugees from East Pakistan (Bangladesh) during a civil war there. A further 2,000 tons of relief supplies are also delivered.

JUNE 26   At Phang Rang Air Base, South Vietnam, F-100 Super Sabres of the 35th Tactical Fighter Wing are relieved of front-line service as the unit redeploys back to the United States.

JULY 12   In Washington, D.C., retired general Benjamin O. Davis, the Air Force's first African American senior officer, is appointed Assistant Secretary of Transportation by President Richard Nixon.

JULY 26–AUGUST 7   At Cape Kennedy, Florida, an all-Air Force crew pilots Apollo 15 to the moon and back; this is the first mission to include a lunar rover.

JULY 29   The Air Force concludes research on the X-24A lifting body, information from which proved instrumental in the space shuttle program.

AUGUST 1   In South Vietnam, General John D. Lavelle gains appointment as the new commander of the Seventh Air Force.

SEPTEMBER 21   Over North Vietnam, 200 Air Force fighter-bombers conduct the first all-instrument bombardment of the war by employing loran (Long Range Air to Navigation) to destroy the fuel and storage area at Dong Hoi, burning 350,000 gallons of fuel.

OCTOBER 1   In Washington, D.C., Richard D. Kisling is appointed the new chief master sergeant of the Air Force.

NOVEMBER 7–8   Over North Vietnam, Air Force fighter-bombers strike Communist airfields at Dong Hoi, Vinh, and Quan Lang.

DECEMBER 26–30   Over North Vietnam, Air Force aircraft launch over 1,000 sorties against targets south of the 20th parallel. This is the largest raid of its kind since 1968.

1972

JANUARY 5 In Washington, D.C., President Richard M. Nixon declares that $5.5 billion has been budgeted for the new space shuttle program.

FEBRUARY 17 At Andrews Air Force Base, Maryland, a VC-137 Stratoliner from the 89th Military Airlift Wing conveys President Richard M. Nixon on his historic mission to Beijing, China.

FEBRUARY 20 In Illinois, an HC-130H Hercules sets a new world record by flying in from Taiwan during a nonstop, unrefueled flight.

MARCH 30 In Washington, D.C., the Joint Chiefs of Staff (JCS) authorizes 1,800 B-52 sorties throughout Southeast Asia. This total is up 600 sorties from a previous directive issued on February 8.

The massive Communist "Easter Offensive" erupts across South Vietnam as 40,000 North Vietnamese troops, backed by 400 tanks, attacks through the Central Highlands. They are largely halted by Air Force and Navy aircraft.

APRIL 6 In light of the Communist offensive in South Vietnam, Air Force and Navy aircraft resume their bombardment of North Vietnam for the first time since 1968.

APRIL 7 In South Vietnam, General John W. Vogt, Jr., gains appointment as head of the Seventh Air Force.

APRIL 7–MAY 13 In South Vietnam, Operation CONSTANT GUARD unfolds as 200 Air Force aircraft, stationed stateside, arrive to help contain the Communist Easter Offensive.

APRIL 16–27 Apollo 16 becomes the fifth successful lunar expedition as Air Force astronaut Charles Duke, Jr., and Navy astronaut John Young remain a record 71 hours on the moon's surface.

APRIL 27 Over North Vietnam, Air Force warplanes use 2,000-pound laser-guided Paveway I "smart bombs" against the Thanh Hoa Bridge, dropping several spans. Previously, 850 conventional attacks failed to seriously damage this structure.

MAY 5 The new Pave PAWS system becomes operational, being specifically design to detect incoming, sea-launched ballistic missiles.

MAY 10–OCTOBER 23 The Fairchild YA-10 prototype, conceived as a heavily armed and armored close support aircraft, flies for the first time; in January 1973 it enters production as the A-10 Thunderbolt II.

Over North Vietnam, Operation FREEDOM TRAIN commences as the Air Force resumes full-scale aerial attacks against military and economic targets. Early on, the name is changed to Operation LINEBACKER I. At one point in the campaign, F-4 Phantoms from the 8th Tactical Fighter Wing knock out Hanoi's Paul Doumer Bridge with precision-guided bombs.

MAY 13 Over North Vietnam, 14 F-4 Phantoms drop laser-guided and conventional ordnance against the Thanh Hoa Bridge, dropping several spans and rendering it useless for rail traffic for several months.

June 11 Over Hanoi, North Vietnam, laser-guided bombs dropped by B-52s destroy a major hydroelectric plant.

June 29 In Quang Tri Province, an A-10 Bronco piloted by Captain Steve L. Bennett, 20th Tactical Air Support Squadron, attacks enemy units preparing to ambush friendly forces, despite the fact that no other air support is available. After his plane is shot, Bennett orders his observer to bail out, but he dies in an attempt to ditch in some nearby water; he receives a posthumous Congressional Medal of Honor.

July 26 Rockwell International is declared to be the prime contractor to build a fleet of space shuttles for NASA.

July 27 The McDonnell Douglas YF-15A air superiority fighter performs its maiden flight; it enters production as the F-15 Eagle.

August 11 The Northrop F-5E Tiger II prototype is flown for the first time; this is a single-seat, armed version of the T-38 Talon trainer.

August 28 Over North Vietnam, Captains Richard S. Ritchie and Charles DeBellevue shoots down their fifth MiG-21, becoming the first Air Force aces of this war.

September 9 Over North Vietnam, weapons systems operator Captain Charles DeBellevue downs his sixth MiG-21, becoming the highest-scoring ace of the war.

September 11 Over North Vietnam, Air Force fighter-bombers drop precision-guided weapons on the Long Bien Bridge in Hanoi, destroying it.

October 2 At Vandenberg Air Force Base, California, an Atlas-Burner launch rocket carries two satellites aloft: *Space Test Program 72-1*, to measure radiation effects in space, and *Radcat*, a passive radar and optical calibration target.

Ritchie, Steve (1942–)

Air Force pilot. Richard Steven Ritchie was born in Reidsville, North Carolina, on June 25, 1942, and he passed through the U.S. Air Force Academy in 1964. He earned his wings at Laredo Air Force Base, Texas, in 1966, and arrived in Vietnam two years later flying F-4 Phantom II jet fighters. During his first tour, Ritchie pioneered the Fast FAC (forward air control) technique to better guide and support aerial bombing efforts. He flew 169 such missions before rotating back to the United States to attend the Fighter Weapons School at Nellis Air Force Base, Nevada. At the time, the Air Force was upgrading the flying skills of fighter pilots through the Red Flag program, which pitted them against instructors versed in Soviet-style tactics. Ritchie then returned to Vietnam in 1972 flying an improved model of the Phantom II, armed with better missiles and radar.

Ritchie deployed with the 555th ("Triple Nickle") Tactical Fighter Squadron based at Udon, Thailand, and he flew combat missions over North Vietnam to prevent the small but determined People's Air Force from attacking American bombers. On May 10, 1972, Ritchie and Weapons Officer Captain Charles DeBellevue shot down their first MiG-21. Three more consecutive kills followed and, on August 28, 1972, Ritchie and DeBellevue bagged their fifth MiG-21, becoming the first Air Force aces of the Vietnam War. Ritchie retired from active duty in 1974, although he remained active in the Air Force Reserve as a brigadier general in charge of recruiting activity at Randolph Air Force Base, Texas. He retired in January 1999, and presently resides in Colorado Springs, Colorado.

OCTOBER 13 Over North Vietnam, weapons officer Captain Jeffrey S. Feinstein shoots down his fifth MiG, becoming the final Air Force ace of the war. Feinstein, Richard S. Ritchie, and Charles B. DeBellevue all win the Mackay Trophy.

NOVEMBER 22 Over North Vietnam, a B-52 is damaged by a Communist SA-2 missile and the crew manages to eject over Thailand; this is the first heavy bomber lost.

DECEMBER 1 Colonel and astronaut Thomas P. Stafford is promoted to brigadier general in the Air Force, aged 42 years.

DECEMBER 18–29 Over North Vietnam, Operation LINEBACKER II kicks into effect in order to bring North Vietnam back to the Paris peace talks. All told, 741 B-52 sorties are flown, along with 796 flak suppression missions; 15 B-52s are downed, along with 2 F-111s, 3 F-4s, 2 A-7s, 2 A-6s (Navy), 1 EB-66, 1 HH-53, and 1 RA-5C (Navy). On the first day of the attack, B-52 gunner Sergeant Samuel O. Turner downs a MiG-21 as it tries to attack.

DECEMBER 24 Over North Vietnam, B-52 gunner Airman First Class Albert E. Moore shoots down the second MiG-21 scored in this fashion.

1973

JANUARY 8 Over North Vietnam, an F-4 flown by Captain Paul D. Howman and Lieutenant Lawrence W. Kullman shoots down the final MiG of the war with an AIM-7 Sparrow missile.

JANUARY 15 All Air force offensive operations against North Vietnam cease once the Communists agree to return to the Paris peace talks.

JANUARY 18 In Washington, D.C., the Defense Department contracts with Fairchild Republic to produce the A-10 close support aircraft, better known to its flight crews as the "Warthog."

JANUARY 28 Over South Vietnam, a B-52 bomber performs the final ARC LIGHT mission against suspected Communist positions. As of this date the war in Vietnam officially ends, although aerial campaigns are conducted in neighboring countries.

FEBRUARY 12 At Hanoi, North Vietnam, Operation HOMECOMING unfolds as Air Force C-141s arrive to transport the first of 591 prisoners of war to Clark Air Base, the Philippines, then home. Aircrews from the Military Airlift Command (MAC) involved in this humanitarian mission receive the Mackay Trophy.

FEBRUARY 21 Over Laos, a cease-fire between the government and Communist insurgents results in an end to B-52 air strikes. However, violations of the agreement result in a resumption of attacks through April.

MARCH 28 As the last remaining Air Force aircraft depart South Vietnam, the Seventh Air Force relocates its operations to Nakhon Phanom Air Base in Thailand.

APRIL 10 The Boeing T-43A prototype, a modified 737-200 airliner, performs its maiden flight.

APRIL 17   Over Laos, B-52 bombers from Guam launch air strikes on Communist positions in response to cease-fire violations.

MAY 15   Over Africa, Operation AUTHENTIC ASSISTANCE unfolds as C-130s perform 541 missions to deliver tons of relief supplies to drought-stricken regions of Chad, Mali, and Mauritania. The 19 aircraft involved deliver 9,200 tons by October.

JUNE 13   The Air Force deploys the first of its Boeing E-4A advanced airborne command posts.

AUGUST 15   Over Cambodia, B-52 bombers perform their final missions against Communist Khmer Rouge targets; this concludes an eight-year-long aerial campaign, most of it clandestine.

In Thailand, an Air Force A-7D Corsair II performs the final bombing raid of the Southeast Asian War while an EC-121 from Korat, Thailand, is credited with flying the last U.S. mission of this conflict. All told, the Air Force flew 5.25 million sorties since 1962 and lost 1,700 aircraft in combat.

AUGUST 20   In Pakistan, transports of the Military Airlift Command (MAC), the Tactical Air Command (TAC), and the Air Force Reserve (USAFR) convey 2,400 tons of supplies and relief equipment to assist victims of recent flooding.

OCTOBER 1   In Washington, D.C., Thomas N. Barnes gains appointment as the new chief master sergeant of the Air Force.

OCTOBER 12–APRIL 6   In the Middle East, Operation GIANT REACH unfolds as nine SR-71 Blackbirds perform reconnaissance missions launched from the United States as the violent Yom Kippur War between Israel, Egypt, and Syria rages.

OCTOBER 14–NOVEMBER 14   In Israel, Operation NICKEL GRASS begins transporting war materiel to make up for losses sustained in the Yom Kippur War. C-5A Galaxies and C-141 Starlifters bring in 22,400 tons of supplies to offset a similar effort by the Soviet Union to Egypt and Syria. This endeavor enables the beleaguered Jewish state to survive a well-coordinated Arab attack.

OCTOBER 6–24   In the Middle East, Operation NIGHT REACH commences as Air Force transports bring in UN peacekeeping forces to monitor the truce between Egypt and Israel.

DECEMBER 13   At Fort Worth, Texas, General Dynamics rolls out its prototype YF-16 lightweight air superiority fighter; it enters production as the F-16 Fighting Falcon.

1974

FEBRUARY 2   At Edwards Air Force Base, California, the YF-16 prototype performs its maiden flight.

APRIL 10   In the Middle East, Operation NIMBUS STAR unfolds as Air Force C-130

communication aircraft begin minesweeping efforts along the Suez Canal.

JULY 1   In Washington, D.C., General David C. Jones gains appointment as the new Air Force chief of staff.

JULY 25 On Cyprus, USAFE C-130s arrive with 10,000 blankets, 7,500 cots, 600 tents, and other items to assist refugees from the recent Turkish invasion of that island.

AUGUST 17 Operation COMPASS COPE continues as the first test of Teledyne remote pilotless vehicles is conducted by the Air Force.

SEPTEMBER 1 In London, England, an SR-71 Blackbird piloted by Majors James V. Sullivan and Noel Widdifield touches down after a record-breaking flight of 1 hour, 54 minutes, and 56 seconds from New York. Their average speed was 1,800 miles per hour.

SEPTEMBER 3 At Warren Air Force Base, Wyoming, the last remaining Minuteman I intercontinental ballistic missiles are removed and replaced by new Minuteman III missiles.

SEPTEMBER 13 At Los Angeles, California, an SR-71 piloted by Captains Buck Adams and William Machorek arrives from London after setting a new world record of 3 hours, 47 minutes, and 39 seconds. Their average speed was 1,436 miles per hour.

OCTOBER 24 Over the Pacific, a C-5A Galaxy transport releases a Minuteman I ICBM from 19,500 feet, which is then successfully launched.

DECEMBER 2 In Washington, D.C., the Department of Defense approves the Joint Air Force-Navy NAVSTAR global positioning satellite system. This new technology promises to revolutionize global navigation and weapons accuracy.

DECEMBER 23 In California, the Rockwell B-1A variable-geometry bomber performs its maiden flight.

1975

JANUARY 13 In Washington, D.C., Air Force Secretary John L. McLucas authorizes production of the General Dynamics F-16 Fighting Falcon.

JANUARY 16–FEBRUARY 1 The F-15 preproduction aircraft christened *Streak Eagle* sets eight time-to-climb world records while piloted by Air Force majors Roger J. Smith, David W. Peterson, and Willard R. MacFarlane, including 98,425 feet in 3 minutes, 27.8 seconds. The three men receive the Mackay Trophy.

FEBRUARY 7 The DIGITAC fly-by-wire computerized control system is first tested in a LTV A-7 Corsair II. This system is

designed to allow inherently unstable aircraft such as the F-117 to be safely flown.

MARCH 25 As Communist forces begin surging through Southeast Asia, the Military Airlift Command (MAC) begins organizing a major evacuation effort to assist refugees.

APRIL 4 In Saigon, South Vietnam, a C-5A Galaxy transport loaded with orphans crashes, killing most of the passengers. The aircraft is participating in Operation BABY LIFT.

In Phnom Penh, Cambodia, Air Force C-130 transports rush in to rescue 900 Cambodians who had been surrounded in the city by the Khmer Rouge.

APRIL 12   In Phnom Penh, Cambodia, Operation EAGLE PULL unfolds as Air Force and Marine Corps helicopters remove 280 refugees before the city falls to Communist forces.

APRIL 29–30   Over Saigon, South Vietnam, Operation FREQUENT WIND commences as Air Force helicopters operating off the deck of the carrier *Midway* help evacuate 6,000 people before Communist forces capture the city. Meanwhile, Operation NEW LIFT continues apace as C-141s and C-130s of the Military Airlift Command (MAC) remove a further 45,000 people, including 5,600 U.S. citizens, to a safe haven.

APRIL 29–SEPTEMBER 16   Throughout the Pacific, Air Force transports participating in Operation NEW ARRIVALS relocate 120,000 Indochinese refugees to processing centers prior to their resettlement in the United States.

MAY 14   At Koh Tang, Cambodia, eight Air Force HH-53 helicopters from the 3rd Aerospace Rescue and Recovery Group land 230 marines in an attempt to free the crew of the vessel SS *Mayaguez*, which had been seized two days earlier by Communist Khmer Rouge forces. They are backed by A-7s, F-4s, OV-10s, and AC-130s; three helicopters are shot down in heavy fighting. Major Robert W. Undorf is awarded the Mackay Trophy in this, the final U.S. military action in Southeast Asia.

JULY 15–JULY 24   Over the Earth, three American astronauts, including Air Force Brigadier General Thomas P. Stafford and Deke Slayton, link up with two Soviet cosmonauts in their Soyuz spacecraft.

JULY 31   The Air National Guard retires its last remaining Lockheed F-104 Starfighter after nearly two decades of service.

The E-3 Sentry Air Warning and Control System (AWACS) can detect, identify, and track enemy aircraft from great distances and direct fighter-interceptor aircraft to the enemy targets. AWACS has been a critical tool for allied forces during the U.S. wars in the Middle East. (U.S. Department of Defense)

AUGUST 8–15   In California, C-130s of the Air Force and National Guard drop 1,400 tons of fire retardant over a large forest fire.

SEPTEMBER 1   The Air Force's Daniel "Chappie" James, Jr., becomes the first African American four-star (full) general in American military history.

OCTOBER 31   Boeing's E-3A Sentry (AWACS) airborne command center performs its maiden flight.

NOVEMBER   The Air Force reveals the existence of the HAVE BLUE program to develop a "stealth" aircraft that is nearly invisible to radar.

NOVEMBER 29   Over Nellis Air Force Base, Nevada, the first "Red Flag" exercises are held to sharpen fighter pilot reflexes by flying realistic combat exercises. This is an outgrowth of the Vietnam War experience.

DECEMBER 6   The McDonnell Douglas F-4G Wild Weasel prototype performs its maiden flight; 116 F-4E aircraft will be so modified for the dangerous work of anti-air defense suppression.

1976

JANUARY 9   At Langley Air Force Base, Virginia, the 1st Tactical Fighter Wing accepts delivery of the first operational F-15 Eagle air superiority fighter.

JANUARY 31   In Thailand, the Air Force returns control of Udorn Air Base back to the Royal Thai Air Force; the Americans subsequently withdraw from Korat a month later.

FEBRUARY 5–MARCH 3   In Guatemala, Operation EARTHQUAKE unfolds as Air Force transports deliver 1,000 tons of relief supplies and 700 personnel to assist victims of a recent disaster there.

MARCH 1   At Taipei Air Station, Taiwan, the Air Force concludes operations following two decades of active service there.

MARCH 15   The Air Force communication satellites *Les-8* and *Les-9* are placed in orbit by an Atlas IIIC launch vehicle.

MARCH 21–JUNE 9   In the Philippines, a series of violent typhoons results in Air Force transports delivering help and medical supplies from bases on Guam. Air Rescue and Recovery helicopters are instrumental in saving 700 flood victims.

MARCH 22   At Davis-Monthan Air Base, Arizona, operational and evaluation testing of the Fairchild Republic A-10 Thunderbolt II commences.

In Thailand, the last Strategic Air Command (SAC) B-52 leaves U-Tapao Airfield after operating there for several years.

MARCH 26   At Edwards Air Force Base, California, the NASA Flight Research Center is renamed in honor of Hugh L. Dryden, a former deputy administrator.

APRIL 2   At Davis-Monthan Air Force Base, Arizona, the last Douglas C-118 Liftmaster flies to its final resting place in the "bone yard."

MAY 6–JUNE 5   At Aviano Air Base, Italy, local Air Force personnel assist victims of a recent earthquake in the northeastern portion of the country.

JUNE 28   At Colorado Springs, Colorado, the U.S. Air Force Academy admits the first women, eligible to graduate in the Class of 1980.

JULY 1   In Washington, D.C., the National Air and Space Museum, Smithsonian Institution, is opened to the public; it draws 20 million visitors in only two years and remains the most visited museum in the world.

JULY 15   At Mather Air Force Base, California, all military navigation begins training at one facility once Navy and Marine Corps navigators arrive for instruction.

JULY 27–28   Three flight records are established by three SR-71 Blackbirds: the first sets an absolute world speed record of 2,092 miles per hour with a 2,200 payload; the second does the same over a 15/25 kilometer course at 2,193 miles per hour; and the third

reaches a record 85,069 feet for sustained high-altitude flight.

AUGUST 1–2   Over Big Thompson Canyon, Colorado, two UH-1 Huey helicopters rescue 81 tourists stranded by a flood.

SEPTEMBER 9   At the White Sands Missile Range, New Mexico, the first fully guided test launch of an air-launched cruise missile (ALCM) is conducted; the missile in question carefully follows a flight path established by preset coordinates.

SEPTEMBER 29   At Williams Air Force Base, Arizona, 10 female students enter undergraduate flight training, being the first women admitted since World War II.

NOVEMBER 29–DECEMBER   At Incirlik Air Base, Turkey, C-130s and C-141s of the Military Airlift Command (MAC) arrive with relief supplies to assist victims of recent earthquakes.

DECEMBER 10   In the Atlantic, a U.S. balloonist crashes at sea and floats until he is discovered by Air Force search and rescue teams, which direct a nearby West German tanker to his locale.

1977

JANUARY 1   At Holloman Air Force Base, New Mexico, the 479th Tactical Training Wing forms with three squadrons of AT-38B Talons. These aircraft have been modified with gunsights and form the backbone of the Fighter Lead-in School.

JANUARY 8   At Marietta, Georgia, the first production C-141B "stretched"

transport rolls off the assembly line. This new version is 23 feet longer, and is capable of in-flight refueling for unlimited range.

JANUARY 31–FEBRUARY 11   At Buffalo, New York, and Pittsburgh, Pennsylvania, Military Airlift Command transports arrive with 1,160 tons of snow removal equipment following a massive blizzard.

MARCH 23 At Tinker Air Force Base, Oklahoma, the first Boeing E-3A is delivered to the Tactical Air Command (TAC). This airborne command and control station is characterized by a large rotating disk on its back.

MARCH 27–30 At Tenerife, Canary Islands, Air Force C-141s arrive to assist survivors of civil aviation's worst disaster when two Boeing 747s collide. C-130s also arrive with medical teams and equipment.

MAY At Colorado Springs, Colorado, the U.S. Air Force Academy selects the De Havilland DHC-6 Twin Otter for its parachute jump program. It receives the new designation UV-18B.

MAY 2 Lieutenant Christine E. Schott is the first woman to solo in a T-38 Talon trainer as part of the Air Force University undergraduate flying program.

MAY 19 A B-52 flown by Captain James A. Yule experiences a severe in-flight emergency, yet he manages to bring his aircraft in for a safe landing; he wins a Mackay Trophy.

JUNE 16 In Moscow, Soviet Union, a C-5A Galaxy arrives carrying a large superconducting magnet to support a joint U.S.-USSR energy research project. The flight, nonstop from Chicago, Illinois, required two in-flight refuelings and wins the crew a Mackay Trophy.

JUNE 30 In Washington, D.C., President Jimmy Carter cancels the B-1A bomber after four prototypes have been constructed; however, he also orders testing and research to continue.

AUGUST 3 At Colorado Springs, Colorado, Cadet Colonel Edward A. Rice, Jr., becomes the first African American Cadet Wing Commander at the Air Force Academy.

AUGUST 4 At Davis-Monthan Air Force Base, Arizona, the Air Force dispatches it last operational T-33 Shooting Star trainer to the "bone yard."

AUGUST 12 Over Edwards Air Force Base, California, the space shuttle *Enterprise* makes its first glide test with Air Force fighter pilot Fred Haise and Colonel C. Gordon Fullerton in control. It glides in safely from 22,800 feet while an estimated 70,000 onlookers cheer.

SEPTEMBER 2 Another gender barrier falls as the first 10 female Air Force pilots are given their wings.

SEPTEMBER 30 From Charleston, South Carolina, a C-141 Starlifter flies across the Atlantic without a navigator, being guided instead by a Delco inertial guidance system. This new technology leads to navigators being phased out.

OCTOBER 1 In the Panama Canal Zone, C-130s from the Air Force Reserve and Air National Guard arrive at Howard Air Force Base as part of a new series of quarterly deployments entitled Operation VOLANT OAK.

OCTOBER 12 At Colorado Springs, Colorado, the first five female navigators graduate from the Air Force Academy's undergraduate navigator training (UNT).

1978

FEBRUARY 8–17 In New England, Operation SNOW BLOW II unfolds as Air Force C-5As, C-141s, and C-130s deliver 2,300 tons of snow-removal equipment to help assist stranded motorists.

FEBRUARY 22 An Atlas F rocket places the first global positioning system (GPS) satellite into orbit. A total of 24 such satellites are planned by 1994, which promises to revolutionize navigation and weapons delivery.

MAY 16–27 In Zaire, Operation ZAIRE I unfolds as two C-5A Galaxy transports deliver French and Belgian troops to help local forces suppress rebels in Katanga Province. The aircrews are awarded a Mackay Trophy.

MAY 31–JUNE 16 Over Zaire, Air Force transports continue bringing in UN peacekeeping forces and evacuate French and Belgian troops. A total of 1,600 tons of cargo and 1,225 passengers are delivered in 72 sorties.

JULY 12 The last remaining Boeing KC-97L Stratotanker is retired from active duty following a quarter-century of service.

JULY 27 In England, new Fairchild A-10 Thunderbolt IIs of the 81st Tactical Fighter Wing deploy at Bentwaters/Woodbridge Royal Air Force Base for the first time.

AUGUST 14–16 In Khartoum, Sudan, 26 tons of relief supplies are delivered to flood victims by a single C-141 Starlifter.

AUGUST 17 At Fort Worth, Texas, the first production F-16 Fighting Falcon is accepted into Air Force service.

NOVEMBER 22–29 In Guyana, the 55th Aerospace Rescue and Recovery Squadron dispatches several HH-53 helicopters to assist in the removal of 900 bodies in the wake of a mass suicide at Jonestown. Once deposited at Georgetown, they are placed aboard C-141s and flown to the United States.

DECEMBER 9 In Tehran, Iran, Air Force C-5As and C-141s arrive to evacuate 900 U.S. citizens as the Shah's regime begins to crumble.

1979

JANUARY 6 At Hill Air Force Base, Utah, the first operational F-16 Falcon deploys with the 388th Tactical Fighter Wing. This multirole aircraft is capable of performing air superiority and close support missions.

JANUARY 29 E-3A Sentry AWACS aircraft are assigned responsibilities within the continental air defense mission.

FEBRUARY 27 At St. Louis, Missouri, the improved F-15C Eagle flies for the first time.

MARCH 9 Two E-3A AWACS aircraft participate in Operation FLYING STAR, as they are dispatched to Saudi Arabia in light of perceived threats from revolutionary Iran.

MARCH 31   Over the Yellow Sea, Major James E. McArdle, Jr., pilots an H-3 Helicopter which rescues 28 Taiwanese seamen whose ship had run aground; he wins the Mackay Trophy.

Following the nuclear accident at Three Mile Island, Pennsylvania, C-5 Galaxy, C-141 Starlifter, and C-130 Hercules transports begin flying in lead shielding and testing equipment to the afflicted area.

APRIL 3–5   At Nandi International Airport, Fiji, two C-141s of the Military Airlift Command (MAC) deliver 20 tons of food and supplies to assist survivors of Typhoon Meli.

APRIL 13   A C-141 Starlifter carrying 20 tons of vegetable seed is dispatched by the Military Airlift Command (MAC) to assist famished inhabitants of Kamina, Zaire.

APRIL 19–20   Transports of the Military Airlift Command (MAC) deliver 139 tons of humanitarian supplies to Titograd International Airport, Yugoslavia, after earthquakes ravage Adriatic coastal regions.

MAY   Sembach Air Base, West Germany, becomes the first forward operating base (FOB) for A-10 Thunderbolt IIs. This new tactical planning allows Air Force jets to operate closer to the front in the event of a Soviet invasion.

MAY 2–3   Two E-3A Sentry AWACS aircraft begin their first overseas training mission in central Europe.

JUNE 1   The Air Force Community College departs Lackland Air Force Base, Texas, for a new home as part of the Air University, Maxwell Air Force Base, Alabama.

RAF Fairford, England, becomes an active in supporting Strategic Air Command (SAC) tanker operations.

JUNE 5   In Washington, D.C., development of the new MX intercontinental ballistic missile (ICBM) is authorized by President Jimmy Carter.

JULY 8–16   Operation GLOBAL SHIELD 79 commences. This intricate nuclear war plan exercise also involves 100,000 members of the Strategic Air Command (SAC) and hundreds of bombers, tankers, and missiles being placed on alert or dispersed to various locations to test the Single Integrated Operational Plan (SIOP). GLOBAL SHIELD remains an annual SAC exercise for the rest of the Cold War.

JULY 26   At Vandenberg Air Force Base, California, the 400th Minuteman missile test is performed by Air Force crews.

AUGUST 31–NOVEMBER 21   Military Airlift Command (MAC) cargo planes begin delivering 2,900 tons of relief supplies to Caribbean islands devastated by Hurricanes David and Frederic.

SEPTEMBER 12   At RAF Fairford, England, Strategic Air Command (SAC) refueling operations are assisted by the first two KC-135 Stratotankers deployed there.

SEPTEMBER 15–22   Over Southern California, 732,000 gallons of water and flame retardant are dropped by Air Force Reserve and Air National Guard C-130s in a massive firefighting operation.

OCTOBER 1   The Air Defense Command (ADC) is gradually decommissioned as the Air Force begins phasing out its responsibilities to the Strategic Air Command (SAC) and the Tactical Air Command (TAC).

OCTOBER 19   At Yokota Air Base, Japan, specially-equipped C-141 Starlifters arrive to transport 38 severely burned marines to medical facilities at Kelly Air Force Base, Texas.

OCTOBER 26   At St. Louis, Missouri, McDonnell Douglas terminates F-4 Phantom II production after a run of 5,000 machines.

DECEMBER 2–21   The Military Airlift Command (MAC) transports begin delivering 650 tons of relief supplies and 250 medical personnel to Majuro Atoll, Marshall Islands, in the wake of Typhoon Abby.

DECEMBER 20   A Minuteman I missile carries an Advanced Maneuvering Reentry Vehicle (AMaRV) on board for the first time. This device employs an autonomous navigation system to avoid enemy antimissile weapons.

1980

JANUARY 2–4   Two C-141s from the 437th Military Airlift Wing, Military Airlift Command (MAC), deliver 700 tents and 1,000 blankets to earthquake victims on Terceira Island, Azores. Meanwhile, a C-141 from the 86th Military Airlift Squadron conveys 17 tons of relief supplies for victims of Cyclone Claudette on the Indian Ocean island of Mauritius.

JANUARY 8   In Washington, D.C., the government announces that 300 Air Force personnel had participated in military exercises in Egypt during the previous December, a sign of greater cooperation with that Muslim nation.

FEBRUARY 25–28   Off the Philippine coast, four Soviet Tu-95 Bear reconnaissance aircraft are intercepted by F-15 Eagles from Clark Air Base as they attempt to penetrate local air defenses.

MARCH 12–14   Two B-52 bombers from the 644th Bombardment Squadron fly around the world in order to locate Soviet warships in the Arabian Sea. They cover 22,000 miles in 43 hours, with an average speed of 488 miles per hour. This is the third time (since 1949 and 1957) that Strategic Air Command (SAC) bombers circumnavigate the globe nonstop; the crews win a Mackay Trophy.

MARCH 31   At Naha Air Base, Okinawa, the Air Force turns over control of facilities back to the Japanese government for the first time since 1945.

APRIL 6   At Beale Air Force Base, California, the C-141B Stratolifter flies to RAF Mildenhall, England, in 11 hours and 12 minutes. This is also the first operational mission of this aircraft and in-flight refueling is also necessary.

APRIL 7   In light of tensions between the United States and Iran, all Iranian military personnel currently attending the Air Training Command are forced to depart.

APRIL 18   At Vandenberg Air Force Base, California, a $3 million Data Transfer System is installed to help guide space shuttle, missile testing, and global positioning system (GPS) satellite network endeavors.

APRIL 22   Southeast of Manila, the Philippines, aircraft of the 33rd Aerospace Rescue and Recovery Squadron rescue 900 passengers from a ferry that sank.

MAY   Lieutenant Mary L. Wittick is the first female candidate to receive Air Force helicopter flight training.

MAY 18–JUNE 5   Aerospace Rescue and Recovery Service (ARRS), Military Airlift Command (MAC), and the 9th Strategic Reconnaissance Wing fly humanitarian and rescue missions to afflicted persons in the vicinity of Mount St. Helens. SR-71 Blackbirds also fly photographic sorties to assist ground rescue teams.

MAY 25   The Oregon National Guard dispatches radar-equipped OV-1 Mohawk reconnaissance aircraft to survey the condition of Mount St. Helens following its violent eruption.

JULY 8   The McDonnell Douglas FSD F-15B (F-15E Strike Eagle) flies for the first time; this is a two-seat version that includes a weapons systems officer (WSO) and is equipped for ground strike roles.

JULY 10–OCTOBER 3   At Moody Air Force Base, Georgia, Operation PROUD PHANTOM unfolds as 12 F-4E Phantom IIs deploy to Egypt. This training exercise is conducted with the Egyptian Air Force, which recently acquired Phantom IIs of its own.

JULY 28–30   At Tengah Air Base, Singapore, four F-4E Phantom IIs of the 3rd Tactical Fighter Wing arrive from Clark Air Base, the Philippines in the first goodwill mission mounted by the Air Force since Singapore gained its independence in 1965.

JULY 30–AUGUST 1   Over the San Bernardino National Forest, California, three C-130s dispatched from the 146th and 433rd Tactical Airlift Wings drop 10,500 gallons of fire retardant on raging forest fires.

AUGUST 7–16   The Air Force Southern Command deploys transports to deliver 61 tons of relief supplies and a 107-person cleanup crew after Hurricane Allen ravages Haiti and St. Lucia in the Caribbean.

AUGUST 14   At Dobbins Air Force Base, Georgia, the first C-5A with modified wings flies for the first time; all 77 aircraft will be similarly modified to extend their service life into the 21st century.

SEPTEMBER 2   At the Johnson Space Center, Houston, Texas, a detachment from the Air Force Air Weather Service assists NASA operations.

SEPTEMBER 10   At Osan Air Base, South Korea, an HH-3E Jolly Green Giant helicopter is dispatched to rescue 229 people struggling in the Sea of Japan following Typhoon Orchid.

SEPTEMBER 16   Over the Mediterranean, a Libyan MiG-23 fighter attacks an Air Force RC-135 electronic surveillance aircraft, which maneuvers drastically to avoid being hit. The United States has recently stepped up electronic intelligence missions along the Libyan coast.

SEPTEMBER 20   The Pacific Air Forces (PACAF) dispatch two F-15s and an E-3A on goodwill trips to New Zealand, Malaysia, Singapore, and Thailand.

OCTOBER 1   In the Persian Gulf, Operation ELF ONE places E-3A AWACS aircraft and KC-135 tankers in Saudi Arabia to closely monitor military communications. They remain in place over the next eight years as the bloody Iran-Iraq War continues.

OCTOBER 3   One hundred and twenty miles south of Yakutat, Alaska, an HH-3 Jolly Green Giant helicopter piloted by Captain John J. Walters rescues 61 passengers from the Dutch cruise ship *Prinsendam* after it catches fire; he receives a Mackay Trophy for his efforts.

OCTOBER 12–23   The Military Airlift Command (MAC) begins transporting 400 tons of relief supplies and medical personnel to El Asnam, Algeria, after a destructive earthquake that kills 6,000 people.

OCTOBER 20–23   Southern Air Division transport aircraft convey 40 tons of food and relief supplies to Nicaragua in the wake of severe flooding there.

NOVEMBER 12–14   At Hahn Air Base, West Germany, the United States Air Force in Europe (USAFE) instructs the 50th Tactical Fighter Wing to modify its wartime mission for a possible chemical warfare environment.

NOVEMBER 12–25   In Egypt, Operation BRIGHT STAR unfolds as Rapid Deployment Force elements of the United States Air Force in Europe (USAFE) participate in this first joint exercise held with Egyptian forces.

NOVEMBER 20   At RAF Lakenheath, the first operational Pave Tack F-111 deploys with the 48th Tactical Fighter Wing. The Pave Tack system allows bombing missions under 24-hour, high- and low-altitude bomb runs.

NOVEMBER 21   Over Las Vegas, Nevada, 310 guests are rescued from the burning 26-story MGM Grand Hotel by helicopters from Nellis Air Force Base.

NOVEMBER 23–DECEMBER 2   The United States Air Force in Europe (USAFE) dispatches transports with

An overall view of the camp set up for an unidentified exercise, 1980. A special operations C-130 Hercules aircraft is visible in the background. (U.S. Department of Defense for Defense Visual Information Center)

300 tons of blankets, tents, and medical supplies to assist survivors of severe earthquakes around Naples, Italy.

NOVEMBER 25 In England, the 26th Tactical Fighter Training Aggressor Squadron flies T-38 Talons for the last time and they are returned to the Air Training Command. They are replaced by F-5E Tiger II jets.

NOVEMBER 25–29 Transports of the Military Airlift Command (MAC) and the Air Force Airlift Readiness Center drop five tons of retardant on 11 fires raging in four different counties east of Los Angeles, California.

DECEMBER 10 From Ramstein Air Base, West Germany, four additional Boeing E-3A AWACS aircraft are deployed to help monitor military events throughout the Middle East. A further four E-3As are deployed to Europe to keep tabs on the ongoing crisis in Poland.

1981

JANUARY 10–11 At Griffiss Air Force Base, New York, the 416th Bombardment Wing receives the first two Boeing air-launched cruise missiles (ALCMs) for testing and maintenance training. These revolutionary weapons possess a 1,500-mile range, carry nuclear or conventional warheads, and navigate through a precise terrain-contour matching system allowing high-speed ingress to targets at low altitude.

JANUARY 12 In Puerto Rico, terrorists destroy nine parked A-7D Corsair II aircraft belonging to the 156th Tactical Fighter Group, Air National Guard.

JANUARY 23 Two hundred and forty miles west of Honolulu, Hawaii, two helicopters from the 6594th Test Group hoist an injured seaman from a merchant vessel.

JANUARY 25 At Wiesbaden, West Germany, an Air Force VC-137 transport flies 52 former American hostages to the United States and freedom.

FEBRUARY 10 In Las Vegas, Nevada, three U-1 helicopters dispatched by the 57th Fighter Weapons Wing rescue nine guests trapped on the roof of the 30-story Las Vegas Hilton.

FEBRUARY 26–MARCH 6 The 7206th Air Base Group, Hellenikon Air Base, assist relief efforts with supplies and equipment in the wake of severe earthquakes in central Greece.

MARCH 12 The Aerospace Defense Command selects Peterson Air Force Base, Colorado, as the backup facility for the North American Aerospace Defense Command (NORAD) in the event of technical failure.

MARCH 17 The first McDonnell Douglas KC-10 Extender is delivered to Strategic Air Command (SAC); this aircraft carries more fuel and cargo than the KC-135 Stratotanker it will replace.

MARCH 18 Eighty F-15 Eagles are delivered to the 18th Tactical Fighter Wing, which transfers its 79 F-4 Phantoms to other commands. This completes the conversion of the Pacific Air Forces to F-15 standards.

Freed American hostages greet a crowd on their arrival from Algiers after leaving Tehran, Iran, January 1981. They had been held hostage in the U.S. embassy by Iranian students since November 4, 1979. (Department of Defense)

APRIL 1　The Air Force deploys the 527th Tactical Fighter Training Aggressor Squadron to RAF Alconbury, England, to further hone the skill of its fighter pilots. It is equipped with Northrop F-5E Tiger IIs, which simulate Soviet fighters during air-to-air combat drills.

APRIL 12–14　At Cape Canaveral, Florida, the space shuttle *Columbia* is launched for the first time. This milestone flight involves taking off like a rocket then returning to Earth as a conventional airplane. Communications with the vehicle are also facilitated by the Aerospace Defense Command and the Air Force Communications Command.

MAY 2　At White Sands Missile Range, New Mexico, the Airborne Laser Laboratory (ALL) successfully downs an aerial target drone. This aircraft in question is a modified KC-135 carrying a carbon dioxide laser.

JUNE 14　The United States Air Force in Europe's (USAFE) 32nd and 36th Tactical Fighter Wings contribute seven F-15s to the Tactical Air Command's Red Flag exercise.

JUNE 18　At Tonopah Test Range, Nevada, the Lockheed F-117 Nighthawk stealth aircraft performs its maiden flight at night for security reasons. Extreme secrecy surrounds the test program until 1988.

JULY　South of Osan Air Base, South Korea, 118 people are assisted from rising floodwaters by helicopters of the 33rd Aerospace Rescue and Recovery Squadron (ARRS).

AUGUST 3　Air Force controllers are called in to fill in, after civilian air traffic controllers stage an illegal strike, to allow commercial air travel to continue safely.

AUGUST 15   At Griffiss Air Force Base, New York, the first air-launched cruise missiles (ALCMs) are fitted to B-52G bombers. This weapon adds new and potentially lethal capabilities to the aging aircraft.

SEPTEMBER 14   At Kunsan Air Base, South Korea, the Pacific Air Forces (PACAF) deploy the first operational F-16 Falcons in this theater.

SEPTEMBER 15   The first Lockheed TR-1A strategic reconnaissance aircraft are delivered to the Strategic Air Command (SAC); this latest version of the venerable U-2 spyplane is capable of all-weather operations from altitudes of 70,000 feet.

At RAF Lakenheath, the 494th Tactical Fighter Squadron, the first unit equipped with Pave Tack laser-guided weapons systems mounted on their F-111s, is deployed on operational status.

SEPTEMBER 21   Off the Philippine coast, members of the grounded Philippine destroyer *Datu Kalantiaw* are rescued by helicopters of the Aerospace Rescue and Recovery Squadron (ARRS); in the past 35 years, the ARRS has saved 20,000 lives.

OCTOBER   At Sheppard Air Force Base, the Euro-NATO Joint Jet Pilot Training program is initiated.

OCTOBER 1   At Mather Air Force Base, California, the Air Training Command

begins training German weapons systems officers for the European Tornado fighter-bomber.

OCTOBER 14   The Tactical Air Command (TAC) deploys two E-3A Sentry aircraft to monitor regional events in the Middle East following the assassination of Egyptian prime minister Anwar Sadat.

OCTOBER 21   At Sheppard Air Force Base, Texas, the new Joint Jet Pilot Training Program accepts candidates from NATO members.

NOVEMBER 5   At Mountain Home, Idaho, the first operational EF-111A Raven deploys with the 388th Electronic Combat Squadron (ECS). Popularly known as the "Spark Vark," it replaces EB-66 and EB-57 aircraft in electronic warfare and defense suppression missions.

NOVEMBER 23   Over Egypt, Operation BRIGHT STAR 82 unfolds as eight B-52 bombers fly 15,000 miles from North Dakota to drop training bombs on a practice airfield target. This is the longest B-52 bombing mission conducted to date and requires 31 hours and three air refuelings.

DECEMBER 31   At Hahn Air Base, West Germany, the 50th Tactical Fighter Wing receives the first operational F-16s assigned to the United States Air Force in Europe (USAFE).

1982

JANUARY 18   At Indian Springs, Nevada, tragedy strikes as four T-38 Talons belonging to the Thunderbirds demonstration team crash into the desert floor, killing four pilots.

JANUARY 26   At Edwards Air Force Base, California, Michael Collins, a major general and former astronaut, flies his final flight in an F-16, then retires from active duty.

JANUARY 28   In Georgia, the Lockheed plant receives the first C-5A Galaxy transport to receive new wings. The cost of modifying 76 transports costs $1.4 billion but extends the service life of these giant craft by several years.

FEBRUARY 5   The Northrop "Tacit Blue" stealth technology demonstrator makes its first secret flight to evaluate radar cross-reduction techniques. The so-called "Whale" makes a total of 135 clandestine flights during the flight program.

FEBRUARY 24   At Geilenkirchen Air Base, West Germany, the first Boeing E-3A Sentry AWACS aircraft assigned to NATO arrives; 17 more are planned.

MARCH 3   At Suwon Air Base, South Korea, Project COMMANDO unfolds and includes the first six A-10 Thunderbolt IIs to arrive in that theater.

MARCH 24   Comiso Air Base, Sicily, is appointed by the United States Air Force in Europe (USAFE) as a storage/launching site for new cruise missiles.

MAY 4–8   In Turkey, the Air Force deploys an E-3A Sentry AWACS plane to monitor Middle Eastern affairs for the first time.

JUNE 10   At Castle Air Force Base, California, an all-female crew flies a KC-135 aircraft belonging to the 924th Air Refueling Squadron, Strategic Air Command (SAC), for the first time. Their five-hour training mission includes a scheduled refueling with a B-52 bomber.

JUNE 14   At Hahn Air Force Base, West Germany, the first operational F-16 Falcon unit in the United States Air Force in Europe (USAFE) is the 313th Tactical Fighter Squadron.

JUNE 21   Over Antarctica, a Strategic Air Command (SAC) KC-10 Extender delivers 67,400 pounds of aviation fuel in support of Military Airlift Command (MAC) resupply operations. This is also the southern-most in-flight refueling by an American aircraft and occurs only 750 miles from the South Pole.

JULY 1   At RAF Greenham Common, England, the 501st Tactical Missile Wing becomes the first of six ground-launched cruise missile (GLCM) wings in Europe.

JULY 2   At Davis-Monthan Air Force Base, the 570th Strategic Missile Squadron decommissions its remaining Titan II intercontinental ballistic missiles (ICBM).

JULY 6–13   Over Africa, an Air Force C-130 Hercules transport conveys 113 tons of food supplies to assist refugees from the Chadian civil war.

JULY 15   At Vandenberg Air Force Base, California, the Strategic Air Command (SAC) conducts its 1,500th missile test.

AUGUST 4   A KC-135 tanker aircraft retrofitted with CFM-56 turbofan engines flies for the first time. These new powerplants will extend the life of the KC-135 well into the 21st century.

AUGUST 30   At Edwards Air Force Base, California, the Northrop F-20 Tigershark, a lightweight air superiority fighter, performs its maiden flight.

SEPTEMBER 1   At Peterson Air Force Base, Colorado, the Air Force Space Command becomes activated.

SEPTEMBER 2   At Edwards Air Force Base, California, B-1B prototype No. 4 departs on a nonstop flight to Farnborough, England. This is also the first overseas deployment of any B-1B.

SEPTEMBER 16   A B-52 piloted by Captain Ronald L. Cavendish suffers a crippling in-flight emergency, yet manages to land safely through superior airmanship; Cavendish receives the Mackay Trophy.

SEPTEMBER 21   At Griffiss Air Force Base, New York, a cruise missile is fired by a B-52G from the 416th Bombardment Wing during its first operational test. The bombers are undergoing modifications to carry six cruise missiles (ALCMs) under each wing.

NOVEMBER 14–19   At Eskisehir Air Base, Turkey, three F-5E Tigers of the 527th Tactical Fighter Training Aggressor Squadron are deployed to train the Turkish Air Force to cope with Soviet-style tactics.

NOVEMBER 16   At Edwards Air Force Base, California, the space Shuttle *Columbia* lands safely after orbiting Earth with four crewmen for the first time.

DECEMBER 16   At Griffiss Air Force Base, New York, the first air-launched cruise missiles (ALCM) are placed on alert by the 416th Bombardment Squadron.

DECEMBER 24–30   The Military Airlift Command (MAC) transport aircraft deliver 87 tons of supplies to Yemen, then staggered by a major earthquake.

1983

FEBRUARY   At Lagos, Nigeria, 15 tons of communications equipment are conveyed by a C-141 Starlifter to replace a telecommunication center that burned down.

FEBRUARY 1   In Honduras, a show of solidarity against regional Communist-inspired insurgencies unfolds as Air Force units participate in Operation AHUAS TARA I with forces from Central American countries. This maneuver is aimed at the Communist dictatorship in Nicaragua, then fomenting guerilla insurgencies throughout the region.

At Davis-Monthan Air Force Base, Arizona, the 868th Tactical Missile Training Squadron begins handling ground-launched cruise missiles (GLCMs) for future deployment in Europe.

FEBRUARY 2   At Luke Air Force Base, Arizona, pilots begin training to fly the new F-16 Fighting Falcon.

FEBRUARY 3   All Minuteman III intercontinental ballistic missiles are retrofitted with modified reentry systems designed to enhance retaliatory capabilities.

MARCH   At Langley Air Force Base, Virginia, the Air Force Thunderbirds demonstration team flies F-16 fighters for the first time.

MARCH 1   At Scott Air Force Base, Illinois, the Twenty-Third Air Force organizes to conduct missions involving combat rescue, weather reconnaissance, missile site security, and aircrew special operations training.

At Hurlburt Field, Florida, the 1st Special Operations Wing arrives and is reassigned from the Tactical Air Command (TAC) to the Miliary Airlift Command (MAC).

MARCH 7   In South Korea, three wings of B-52Gs simulate mine-laying operations off the coast as Team Spirit 83 unfolds.

MARCH 15–28   At the Pacific Missile Test Range, Kwajalein, a B-52 successfully fires three Navy AGM-Harpoon antiship missiles. The Strategic Air Command (SAC) is presently seeking ways of performing sea interdiction missions against the formidable Red Navy.

APRIL 1   The Strategic Air Command (SAC) yields 4 installations and 31 operational units to Space Command, as the majority of these are concerned with missile warning and space surveillance missions.

APRIL 1–8   In Colombia, floods and earthquakes prompt C-130 Hercules aircraft to transport 34 tons of shelters, medical supplies, and electric generators to assist survivors.

APRIL 5–10   After southeastern Louisiana is severely flooded by torrential rains, Air Force C-141 Starlifters convey 83 tons of food and medical supplies to victims.

APRIL 26   At Davis-Monthan Air Force Base, the first crews training to handle ground-launched cruise missiles (GLCMs) graduate and are assigned to tactical missile wings in Europe.

MAY 1   Over the Bahamas, Air Force aircraft surveillance missions commence to assist law enforcement agencies and help suppress drug smuggling operating offshore.

JUNE 4   At Hill Air Force Base, Utah, a final flyby is arranged for the few remaining F-105s in the Air Force Reserve before being retired from active service.

JUNE 17   At Vandenberg Air Force Base, California, an MX (Peacekeeper) missile is launched for the first time with multiple dummy warheads. These are programmed to splash down in the Kwajalein test range.

JUNE 26   In northwestern Peru, the Military Airlift Command (MAC) dispatches three C-130 Hercules aircraft to provide relief supplies for victims of recent flooding.

JULY 1   The Air Force deploys a provisional support squadron at Riyadh Air Base, Saudi Arabia, in light of the ongoing Iran-Iraq War. The oil-rich region of the Persian Gulf remains an area of vital strategic interest to the United States and the West.

JULY 7   At McEntire Air National Guard Base, South Carolina, the 169th Tactical Fighter Group is the first Guard unit to receive F-16As.

On this day, General Dynamics also completes its 1,000th Falcon of the 2,165 ordered by the Air Force.

JULY 24–AUGUST 6   In western Ecuador, the Air Force dispatches two UH-1 helicopters to deliver medical supplies and personnel to flood victims.

AUGUST   Over Minnesota, the 907th Tactical Airlift Group dispatches three

C-123 Providers to spray insecticide to fight an encephalitis epidemic in 11 counties.

AUGUST 1 At Andrews Air Force Base, Maryland, a microburst inflicts $465,000 in damages; the storm was packing 120-mile-per-hour winds.

AUGUST 10 In Washington, D.C., Secretary of Defense Caspar W. Weinberger announces that 100 MX (Peacekeeper) missiles will be deployed in existing Minuteman silos.

AUGUST 15–SEPTEMBER 15 The Air Force dispatches 12 Starlifters to convey 185 tons of cargo to the African nation of Chad in support of an ongoing security assistance program.

AUGUST 30 Lieutenant Colonel Guion S. Bluford becomes the first African American to ride in space on the space shuttle *Challenger*.

SEPTEMBER 1 Over Sakhalin Island, Soviet Union, a Korean Airlines 747 is shot down after it strays into Soviet airspace. Air Force HC130 transports of the 33rd Aerospace Rescue and Recovery Squadron deploy from Kadena Air Base, Okinawa, and comb the waters for survivors; all 269 passengers perish.

SEPTEMBER 3–25 In Lebanon, Operation RUBBER WALL commences as the Military Airlift Command (MAC) delivers 4,000 tons of supplies in 100 heavy-lift missions in support of marines operating there. The effort involves 85 C-141 Starlifters, 24 C-5 Galaxies, and 4 C-130 Hercules sorties.

SEPTEMBER 5 A Strategic Air Command (SAC) KC-135 piloted by Captain Robert J. Goodman refuels an F-4E Phantom II jet four times over water and even tows it along with the refueling

boom until it lands safely; Goodman receives the Mackay Trophy.

SEPTEMBER 28 The Air Force declares its EF-111A Raven electronic warfare aircraft operational after extensive testing; pilots dub it the "Spark Vark" because of its extensive electronic suite.

OCTOBER 1 At Davis-Monthan Air Force Base, Arizona, the last operational B-52D arrives for a final resting place in the "bone yard."

OCTOBER 4–5 Over Maricopa, Arizona, the 302nd Special Operations Squadron deploys four CH-3 helicopters to rescue 57 civilians trapped by floodwaters.

OCTOBER 6 Three B-52Gs are modified by the Strategic Air Command (SAC) to carry and fire the AGM-Harpoon anti-ship missile. These aircraft are intended to perform maritime interdiction missions against the Red Navy.

OCTOBER 23 In Beirut, Lebanon, transports of the Military Airlift Command (MAC) convey 239 dead and 95 wounded marines, the victims of a terrorist truck bombing, to European and American hospitals.

OCTOBER 25–30 Over Grenada, Air Force MC-130s drop paratroopers on Point Salines, Grenada. Lieutenant Colonel James L. Hobson, Jr., manages to keep his aircraft under control despite intense antiaircraft fire, guiding the mission to success; he wins a Mackay Trophy. Transports of the Military Airlift Command (MAC) and the Air Force Reserve also fly 11,389 passengers and 7,709 tons of cargo to facilitate Operation URGENT FURY. A total of 496 sorties are performed by C-141 Starlifters, C-5 Galaxies, and C-130 Hercules aircraft.

Members of the 82nd Airborne Division board a C-141 Starlifter aircraft at Point Salines Airport during Operation Urgent Fury, *November, 1983. (U.S. Department of Defense for Defense Visual Information Center)*

OCTOBER 26 At the Tonopah Test Range, Nevada, initial operational capability is achieved by the initial batch of five F-117 Nighthawks. Ongoing operations are conveniently covered by the activity of 18 A-7 Corsair IIs.

OCTOBER 27 B-52 Stratofortesses deploy at air bases for the first time in Spain.

NOVEMBER 1–5 After severe earthquakes rattle northern Turkey, four C-141 Starlifters and six C-130s Hercules transports are dispatched by the Military Airlift Command (MAC) to convey 234 tons of relief supplies to the survivors.

NOVEMBER 23 In Bonn, West Germany, the government ignores the KGB-orchestrated nuclear freeze movement and votes to deploy Air Force ground-launched cruise missiles (GLCMs) and Army Pershing II ballistic missiles as a counter to Soviet weapons of the same class.

DECEMBER 3 The Strategic Air Command (SAC) begins inactivating the 571st Strategic Missile Squadron and disbands its Titan II intercontinental ballistic missiles (ICBMs).

DECEMBER 6 At Langley Air Force Base, Virginia, the new National Transonic Wind Tunnel becomes operational. This device is expressly designed for researching the fastest jets being designed or under construction.

DECEMBER 23 The 390th Electronic Combat Squadron is the first operational unit equipped with General Dynamics EF-11A Ravens.

1984

JANUARY 1   The Air Force Space Command assumes control of the Global Positioning System (GPS).

JANUARY 21   An F-15 Eagle test launches the American antisatellite missile system for the first time against a dummy vehicle emulator.

JANUARY 28   At Hill Air Force Base, Utah, new F-16 Falcons replace aging F-105 Thunderchiefs in the 419th Tactical Fighter; this is also the first Air Force Reserve unit so equipped.

JANUARY 31   The new AGM-81A Firebolt target vehicle breaks world records for speed and altitude by reaching Mach 1.4 at 104,000 feet.

FEBRUARY 3   At RAF Upper Heyford, England, the 20th Tactical Fighter Wing deploys with the United States Air Force in Europe (USAFE), becoming the first EF-111A Raven unit in that theater.

FEBRUARY 23   The Tactical Air Command (TAC) officially replaces the aging F-4 Phantom II with the F-15C Eagle as its standard air superiority fighter.

FEBRUARY 24   The Air Force selects the McDonnell Douglas F-15E Strike Eagle over the delta-wing General Dynamics F-16XL to serve as its next dual-role fighter-bomber.

At Cherry Point, North Carolina, two C-141 Starlifter missions land after withdrawing U.S. Marines from Lebanon and Larnaca, Cyprus.

MARCH 6   Over the Northern Test Range, Canada, a B-52G from the 319th Bombardment Wing test launches an air-launched cruise missile (ALCM) for the first time.

MARCH 19–APRIL 9   An E-3A Sentry aircraft is dispatched to the Middle East following threats against Egypt and Sudan by Libya. Seventeen C-141 Starlifter and twenty-eight C-5 Galaxy missions also convey military supplies to the Egyptians as a precaution.

APRIL 6   The first of 80 Learjet C-21A aircraft are deployed with the 375th Aeromedical Airlift Wing, which phases out older Cessna CT-39 Sabreliner aircraft.

APRIL 11   The 375th Aeromedical Airlift Wing receives its first Beech C-12F operational support aircraft.

APRIL 19   Construction begins on the phased array, sea-launched ballistic missile warning system at Robins Air Force Base, Georgia.

MAY 16   At Peshawar, Pakistan, Afghan refugees receive 22 tons of medical supplies from C-141 Starlifters dispatched by the Military Airlift Command (MAC).

MAY 25   In Washington, D.C., the Vietnam War's Unknown Soldier returns home aboard a C-141 Starlifter for internment at Arlington National Cemetery. He is subsequently identified as Air Force Lieutenant Michael J. Blassie and is reburied at St. Louis, Missouri.

JUNE   At Golden, Colorado, a Schweizer TG-7A motor glider is delivered to the U.S. Air Force Academy for airmanship programs; it is relegated to the 94th Air Training Squadron.

JUNE 15   At Kansas City, Missouri, a C-130 Hercules from the Military Airlift Command (MAC) arrives with 4.5 tons of pumping equipment to assist flood-fighting efforts in that region of the state.

At Vandenberg Air Force Base, California, an MX (Peacekeeper) missile is test launched with a Mark-21 test reentry vehicle for the first time.

JUNE 16   At Fort Worth, Texas, the improved F-16C Falcon flies for the first time. This new version boasts improved heads-up display (HUD) instrumentation and more capable multimode radar.

JUNE 20   The first KC-135R Stratotanker aircraft deploys with the 384th Air Refueling Wing, Strategic Air Command (SAC). This variant is equipped with new CFM-56 fan-jet engines, possessing higher thrust and lower fuel consumption.

JUNE 21   Over Antarctica, a Military Airlift Command (MAC) C-141 Starlifter carrying supplies for U.S. bases at McMurdo Sound refuels en route with a 22nd Air Refueling Wing KC-10 Extender flying out of Christchurch International Airport, New Zealand.

JUNE 30   Hancock Field, New York, is closed by the Air Force after 32 years of constant operations.

JULY   At Loring Air Force Base, Maine, the 69th Bombardment Squadron accepts the first deliveries of AGM-84 Harpoon antiship missiles. These are intended for B-52 bombers during interdiction missions at sea.

JULY 31   At Davis-Monthan Air Force Base, Arizona, the 390th Strategic Missile Wing becomes the first Titan II unit to be decommissioned.

An RH-53D Sea Stallion helicopter is offloaded from a C-5A Galaxy aircraft, as Helicopter Mine Countermeasures Squadron 14 (HM-14) arrives to participate in Operation Intense Look, *August, 1984. (U.S. Department of Defense for Defense Visual Information Center)*

AUGUST 7–OCTOBER 2   In the Red Sea, Operation INTENSE LOOK unfolds as the United States begins minesweeping efforts in the Red Sea at the request of Egypt and Saudi Arabia. Air Force transports convey 1,300 tons of cargo and 1,000 military personnel to the region in support of this effort.

AUGUST 8   In Europe, the first C-23 Sherpa, a small cargo/liaison aircraft for flying between airfields and depot centers, begins operations.

AUGUST 19–20   On Johnson Island, 715 miles from Hawaii, two C-141 Starlifters from the 22nd Air Force evacuate 382 American military and civilian personnel as Typhoon Kell approaches.

AUGUST 28   At Florennes Air Base, Belgium, a C-5 Galaxy touches down with the first supply of ground-launched cruise missiles (GLCMs). Consequently, the noisy and KGB-orchestrated antimissile movement in Europe, sensing the futility of further opposition, begins disbanding.

AUGUST 29   At Sembach Air Base, Germany, the last OV-10 Broncos conclude a decade of service with the United States Air Force Europe (USAFE) and depart for the United States.

SEPTEMBER 2–3   In South Korea, 148 stranded civilians in a recent flood are saved by helicopters of the 38th Aerospace Rescue and Recovery Squadron (ARRS).

SEPTEMBER 4   At Palmdale, California, the first production B-1B Lancer intercontinental strategic bomber rolls out of the factory to begin flight-testing.

SEPTEMBER 14–18   Aeronaut Joe Kittinger, Jr., who is also a retired Air Force colonel, flies a balloon nonstop from Caribou, Maine, to Savona, Italy, in 84 hours. He also establishes a new balloon distance record.

OCTOBER 11–14   During a visit by Pope John II to San Juan, Puerto Rico, the Military Airlift Command (MAC) transports convey Secret Service vehicles for his use.

OCTOBER 18   At Palmdale, California, the first operational B-1B, christened *Star of Abilene*, flies for the first time ahead of schedule.

OCTOBER 18–20   The Air Force Rescue Coordination Center directs search and rescue operations and saves 47 lives after Colorado and New Mexico are struck by heavy snowstorms.

OCTOBER 23–24   In Baguio, Philippines, a fire breaks out at the Pines Hotel during a visit by General Douglas MacArthur's veterans. The 31st Aerospace Rescue and Recovery Squadron (ARRS) dispatches an H-3 helicopter, which lifts nine people trapped on the roof to safety. A C-130 Hercules transport subsequently conveys 48 injured people to Clark Air Base for treatment.

OCTOBER 25   Off the coast of Salto di Quirra, Sardinia, F-4Es of the 86th Tactical Fighter Wing participate in live missile exercises with U.S. Navy units.

NOVEMBER 2   At McConnell Air Force Base, Kansas, a Titan II missile bursts into flames as it is being drained of liquid fuel. This incident threatens to delay deactivation of this elderly system.

NOVEMBER 19   At Bogotá, Colombia, the Military Airlift Command dispatches two C-141 Starlifters to deliver vehicles, small arms, and ammunition to the U.S. Embassy, after drug lords threaten it.

NOVEMBER 20 In Washington, D.C., President Ronald W. Reagan authorizes creation of a unified United States Space Command.

DECEMBER 1 At Kelly Air Force Base, Texas, the Air Force Reserve accepts its first C-5A Galaxy.

DECEMBER 11–12 At Rhein-Main Air Base, West Germany, survivors and two wounded victims of a hijacked Kuwaiti airliner arrive onboard C-141 Starlifters before being flown to the United States.

DECEMBER 20 A collapsed tunnel in Huntington, Utah, results in two C-130 Hercules aircraft arriving with 23.8 tons of emergency equipment to rescue 27 coal miners trapped there; unfortunately, all had died from smoke inhalation beforehand.

DECEMBER 22–MARCH 1985 Eight Military Airlift Command (MAC) C-141 Starlifters are dispatched to Kassala, Sudan, with 200 tons of food and medical supplies to combat an ongoing famine there.

1985

JANUARY Headquarters, Strategic Air Command (SAC) determines that the recent fire at a Titan II silo at McConnell Air Force Base could have been avoided with better procedures. Once these changes are in place, deactivation of these elderly ICBMs continues as scheduled.

JANUARY 1 Lieutenant Colonel David E. Faught, 97th Bombardment Wing, having spent 13 hours of attempting to lower the nose gear of a KC-135, makes a successful nose gear–up landing without seriously damaging his aircraft; he receives a Mackay Trophy.

JANUARY 4 Major Patricia M. Young becomes the first female to lead an Air Force Space Command unit when she is appointed commander of Detachment 1, 20th Missile Warning Squadron.

JANUARY 5 An Eastern Airlines Boeing 727 crashes in the Andes Mountains, prompting the Military Airlift Command

(MAC) to dispatch a C-141 Starlifter with a Sikorsky S-70 helicopter to look for possible survivors.

JANUARY 18–23 Continuing C-141 Starlifter flights to the Sudan are ordered by the Military Airlift Command (MAC) to assist ongoing relief efforts; 62 tons of food are eventually delivered.

JANUARY 19–21 The 75th and 312th Military Airlift Squadrons send two C-5 Galaxies and one C-141 Starlifter with 186 tons relief supplies to Viti Levu, Fiji, after a hard pounding by Typhoon Eric.

JANUARY 24–27 At Cape Canaveral, Florida, Colonel Loren J. Shriver pilots the space shuttle *Discovery* on its first all-military mission; at 73 hours, 33 minutes, this is also one of the shortest shuttle missions.

JANUARY 28 At Kunsan Air Base, South Korea, two H-3 Jolly Green Giant helicopters are dispatched to help rescue 10 shipwrecked Korean fishermen.

FEBRUARY 3 At Howard Air Force Base, Panama, C-141 Starlifters of the Military Airlift Command (MAC) fly to Argentina in the wake of a devastating earthquake that results in 12,000 refugees.

FEBRUARY 4 The practice of gender-specific missile launch crews (either male or female) is instituted by the Strategic Air Command (SAC) for all Minuteman and Peacekeeper facilities. Women were previously restricted to Titan II launch sites.

MARCH 5–9 In Sudan, Niger, and Mali, Air Force transports complete four famine-relief missions by flying in 123 tons of food to victims.

MARCH 8 In the Bahamas, helicopters provided by the Military Airlift Command help police and U.S. Drug Enforcement Agency officials bust a $320 million cocaine-smuggling effort. This joint drug interception campaign continues through the following month.

MARCH 15 In Chile, a Military Airlift Command C-5 Galaxy delivers 1,000 rolls of plastic sheeting to assist victims of a devastating earthquake.

MARCH 25 The Air Force now allows women to function as forward air controllers (FAC) and as crew members on C-130 transports and gunships.

APRIL 4 In Washington, D.C., retired Air Force leader James H. Doolittle is elevated to full (four-star) general; he becomes the first Air Force Reserve officer so honored.

APRIL 5 Over drought-stricken western North Carolina, two C-141 Starlifters

and a C-130 Hercules arrive with 10 tons of firefighting equipment, 21,000 gallons of fire retardant, and 190 firefighters to contain a large fire which devastated 7,000 acres across six counties.

APRIL 20 The first B-52 crews completely trained in Harpoon antiship missile operations are graduated and deployed with front-line units.

APRIL 29–MAY 17 At Spangdahlem Air Base, West Germany, Salty Demo, an exercise to gauge the ability to defend bases against an attack and resume combat operations, is sponsored by the United States Air Force in Europe (USAFE).

JUNE 21–JULY 25 In southern Idaho, three C-123K Providers arrive for aerial spraying purposes. They cover 795,000 acres in 73 sorties to contain a severe locust infestation.

JUNE 29 The first Rockwell B-1B Lancer strategic bomber is accepted by the Air Force; only 100 are scheduled for acquisition owing to their considerable expense.

The 60th Bombardment Squadron becomes the second B-52G unit trained and equipped to fire Harpoon antiship missiles in an interdiction mission at sea.

At Naval Air Station, New Orleans, Louisiana, the 159th Tactical Fighter Group becomes the first Air National Guard (ANG) unit equipped with F-15 Eagles.

JUNE 30 At Vandenberg Air Force Base, California, the Air Force Space Command completes flight-testing of the new MX (Peacekeeper) intercontinental ballistic missile (ICBM).

JULY 1 At Carswell Air Force Base, Texas, the 7th Bombardment Wing becomes the first B-52H unit equipped to operate air-launched cruise missiles (ALCMs).

At Rhein-Main Air Base, West Germany, a C-141 Starlifter from the 438th Military Airlift Wing transports 39 passengers from TWA Flight 847, which had been hijacked and flown to Lebanon. Vice President George H. W. Bush is on hand to greet them upon arrival.

JULY 2–10   Over California and Idaho in C-141 Starlifters transport 285 firefighters to staging areas to combat a series of huge forest fires. Meanwhile, C-130s complete 200 sorties by spreading 450 tons of flame retardant across 1.5 million acres.

JULY 7   At Dyess Air Force Base, Texas, the first operational B-1B Lancers arrive at the 96th Bombardment Wing, Strategic Air Command (SAC).

JULY 15   Two B-52Gs from the 42nd Bombardment Wing simulate Harpoon missile launches for test and evaluation purposes during the United States Atlantic Command exercise Readex 85-2.

An air-to-air left side view of an F-15 Eagle aircraft releasing an anti-satellite (ASAT) missile during a test, 1985. (U.S. Department of Defense)

JULY 30   The Air Force officially terminates the Bomarc aerial target drone (CQM-10B) program.

AUGUST 12–15   In response to a request from the State Department, a C-5A Galaxy of the 436th Military Airlift Wing delivers 35 tons of food and equipment to assist famine victims in western Sudan.

AUGUST 23   At Vandenberg Air Force Base, California, a Minuteman III missile is "cold launched" out of its silo using compressed air for the first time. Through this procedure, the missile ignites once airborne, resulting in less damage to the silo and quicker reloading.

SEPTEMBER 10   The Lockheed C-5B Galaxy flies for the first time; the Air Force intends to acquire 50 of these giant transports by April 1989.

SEPTEMBER 13   A Vought ASM-135 anti-satellite missile is fired by an F-15 Eagle while 290 miles above the Earth, destroying the orbiting Defense Department satellite *P78-1*. This constitutes the first-ever satellite interception.

SEPTEMBER 21–30   A devastating earthquake in Mexico City, Mexico, results in Air Force transports delivering over 360 tons of food and medicine to survivors.

SEPTEMBER 23   First Lady Nancy Reagan is conveyed by a transport from the 89th Military Airlift Wing to Mexico City, Mexico, where she expresses condolences and presents the government with a check for $1 million.

OCTOBER 11   A C-141 Starlifter from the 438th Military Airlift Wing transports 11 American hostages from the *Achille Lauro* to Newark, New Jersey.

OCTOBER 15   At Edwards Air Force Base the T-46A next generation trainer flies for the first time.

OCTOBER 16   Two Air Force H-3 Jolly Green Giant helicopters rescue the crew of the shipwrecked Philippine vessel *Marcos Faberes*.

OCTOBER 18   A General Dynamics F-111A, modified with a mission adaptive wing (MAW) flies for the first time.

NOVEMBER 1   The Dutch government, ignoring protests from antinuclear groups and KGB-orchestrated peace movements, approves deployment of Air Force ground-launched cruise missiles at Woensdrecht, the Netherlands.

NOVEMBER 4   In the Shenandoah Valley, Virginia, the Air Force Rescue Co-ordination Center orchestrates helicopter missions that save 47 lives from rapid floodwaters.

NOVEMBER 15–18   In the wake of a severe volcanic eruption, Air Force transports lift 50 tons of food and supplies to Colombia.

DECEMBER 6   At Barksdale Air Force Base, Louisiana, the 19th KC-10 Extender aircraft arrives, completing the first fully operational tanker squadron to employ that aircraft.

DECEMBER 12   After a chartered Arrow Air airliner crashes near Gander, Newfoundland, Canada, killing 248 members of the 101st Airborne Division, Air Force C-141s and C-130s are required to airlift all the bodies back to the United States, along with 125 tons of cargo necessary for the cleanup; this remains the worst military aviation disaster.

DECEMBER 18   Off Lubang, Philippines, helicopters dispatched by the Western Pacific Rescue Coordination Center rescue 78 passengers from the sinking ship *Asuncion Cinco*.

DECEMBER 31   McDonnell Douglas contracts with the Air Force to build the new C-17A long-range, heavy-lift cargo transport. This aircraft will combine the lifting capability of the C-5A Galaxy, with the short field landing abilities of the C-130 Hercules.

1986

JANUARY 8   At Altus Air Force Base, Oklahoma, the Military Airlift Command (MAC) receives the first improved C-5B Galaxy transport aircraft.

At Eielson Air Force Base, Alaska, the first overseas meteorological data system circuit is installed by the Air Force to replace the obsolete weather teletype system already in place.

JANUARY 28   At Cape Canaveral, Florida, tragedy strikes when the space shuttle

Challenger explodes after liftoff. Among those killed are Air Force pilots Francis R. Scobee, Gregory B. Jarvis, Ellison S. Onizuka.

FEBRUARY 18–22   In Northern California, Air Force H-3s, HH-53s, and C-130s of the 49th and 129th Aerospace Rescue and Recovery Groups evacuate 500 civilians from along the Russian and Yuba Rivers after they were stranded by severe flooding. Three thousand sandbags are also delivered to Army troops on the ground.

FEBRUARY 25–26 In the Philippines, five H-3 Jolly Green Giant helicopters from the 31st Aerospace Rescue and Recovery Squadron (ARRS) convey President Ferdinand Marcos and 51 people from his palace to Clark Air Base for ultimate removal to Hawaii.

MARCH 3 At Shaw Air Force Base, South Carolina, the reconnaissance Cessna O-2 aircraft is replaced by the OT-38 Talon.

MARCH 4 In Egypt, operation BRIGHT STAR unfolds as aircraft from the United States and Egypt conduct their first joint exercise; this also marks the first time that foreign aircraft are refueled by Air Force tankers.

MARCH 5 Once over the Atlantic, a KC-10 aircraft, piloted by Captain Marc C. Felman, refuels another KC-10 and three Navy A-4 Skyhawks that were nearly our of fuel. For relieving this emergency situation by launched in zero visibility weather; Felman and his crew win a Mackay Trophy.

In Pakistan, the Air Force beings transporting Afghan refugees and patients to the United States in accordance with the 1986 McCollum Amendment. Afghanistan is then in the throes of a violent Soviet occupation.

MARCH 25 At Whiteman Air Force Base, Missouri, the first all-woman Minuteman missile crew, belonging to the 351st Strategic Missile Wing, is placed on active alert.

APRIL 5–6 At Osan Air Base, South Korea, a large jet fuel tank fire results in four C-141 Starlifters and one H-3 Jolly Green Giant helicopter from the 63rd Airlift Wing transporting fire-suppressant foam; burn victims are also conveyed to medical facilities in Seoul for treatment.

APRIL 14–15 Over Libya, Operation EL DORADO CANYON unfolds as 24 F-111F bombers from the Statue of Liberty Squadron, 48th Tactical Fighter Wing, launch from Great Britain and perform a retaliatory strike against Tripoli, Libya. Lacking overflight permission from Spain and France, they fly a 5,500-mile round trip around Continental Europe, and inflict heavy damage on the Jamahiriya Military Barracks and Benina Military Airfield. They are also carrier aircraft launched from the *America* and *Saratoga*; one F-111 is lost in action. Equally significant, 28 KC-10 Extenders and KC-135 Stratotankers are employed during the attack, and they refuel the strike force six times in complete radio silence.

APRIL 18 At Vandenberg Air Force Base, California, a Titan IIID rocket booster explodes after launching; Space Launch Complex Four sustains damage and cannot operate again until August 15.

APRIL 28–MAY 7 The Air Weather Service launches several WC-130s to track and analyze the radioactive fallout in the wake of a nuclear reactor accident at Chernobyl, Soviet Union.

JUNE 17 The last remaining UC-133K Provider is retired from spraying activities by the Air Force.

JULY The Air Force Reserve and Air National Guard receive their first C-141 Starlifter transports.

JULY 19 The United States Air Force in Europe (USAFE) declares Rapier surface-to-air missile units operational.

JULY 19–28   Operation SOUTHERN HAYLIFT unfolds once severe drought conditions across the southwestern United States result in 24 C-141s and 8 C-130s carrying 19,000 bales (536 tons) of hay to livestock farmers in afflicted areas.

JULY 27   At Rhein-Main Air Base, West Germany, an Air Force C-9 Nightingale transports Father Lawrence Jenco, recently released by Muslim extremists, to medical facilities.

AUGUST 27–29   In Cameroon, West Africa, a C-130 Hercules is dispatched from 50th Tactical Airlift Squadron with 250 tents for villagers fleeing volcanic fumes escaping from Lake Nyos.

SEPTEMBER 1   At Davis-Monthan Air Force Base, Arizona, the last operational Cessna O-2 Bird Dog arrives for disposal in the "bone yard."

SEPTEMBER 5   In Frankfurt, West Germany, a C-141 Starlifter transports Americans injured during a hijacking attempt to medical facilities. The flight originates in Karachi, Pakistan.

SEPTEMBER 18–20   At Luzon, Philippines, two C-5 Galaxies are dispatched by the 436th Military Airlift Wing with 93 tons of food and medical supplies as per the Foreign Assistance Act of 1985.

OCTOBER 10   The new LGM-118A (MX), or Peacekeeper, intercontinental ballistic missile achieves operational status for the first time. This weapon is capable of attacking up to 10 different targets with its multiple independent reentry vehicle (MIRV) warhead.

OCTOBER 11–16   After San Salvador, El Salvador, is destroyed by an earthquake, Air Force transports begin delivering food and relief supplies to survivors.

DECEMBER 7   A WC-130 Hercules of the 54th Weather Reconnaissance Squadron lands on Saipan, Mariana Islands, in the wake of Typhoon Kim, and delivers seven tons of relief supplies, food, and toys for children.

DECEMBER 10   Air Force helicopters rescue 19 members of the Norwegian research ship *Geco Alpha* several miles off the coast of Destin, Florida, after it caught fire; casualties are subsequently flown to Eglin Air Force base for medical treatment.

DECEMBER 14–23   From Edwards Air Force Base, California, the experimental *Voyager* aircraft, piloted by Richard G. Rutan and Jeana L. Yeager, flies 25,000 miles, nonstop and unrefueled, around the world; they win a Collier Trophy for this record, nine-day venture.

DECEMBER 18   In the South China Sea, the 31st Aerospace Rescue and Recovery Squadron (ARRS) dispatches two H-3 Jolly Green Giant helicopters that rescue 13 survivors from a sinking Filipino vessel. The injured are then delivered to medical facilities at Cubi Air Station, Philippines.

DECEMBER 22   At F. E. Warren Air Base, Wyoming, a tenth Peacekeeper intercontinental ballistic missile (ICBM) is deployed, leading to all weapons being placed on operational status.

DECEMBER 31   In San Juan, Puerto Rico, 75 people stranded on the roof of the Dupont Plaza Hotel during a fire are rescued by H-3 Sea King helicopters of Composite Squadron 8 (VC-8).

1987

JANUARY 16   Over the Tonopah Test Range, Nevada, a short-range attack missile (SRAM) is fired for the first time by a B-1B Lancer.

FEBRUARY 3   At Eglin Air Force Base, Florida, the first Sikorsky UH-60A Black Hawk helicopters are delivered to the 55th Aerospace Rescue and Recovery Squadron. The Pace Low III infrared system is retrofitted to them to facilitate long-range search and rescue missions.

FEBRUARY 13–15   On Vanuatu, New Hebrides, survivors of Typhoon Uma are assisted by two C-141 Starlifters and two C-130 Hercules, which transport 64 tons of tents and plastic sheeting for them.

FEBRUARY 16   In San Antonio, Texas, the Joint Military Medical Command, staffed by both Army and Air Force personnel, is activated.

APRIL 14   From Dyess Air Force Base, Texas, a B-1B Lancer flies 9,400 miles in 21 hours and 40 minutes, while utilizing five in-flight refuelings. This is the longest flight to date by a bomber of this type.

MAY 5   At Little Rock Air Force Base, Arkansas, the Air Force retires the last liquid-fueled Titan II intercontinental ballistic missile (ICBM) from active service. This is the largest ballistic missile fielded by the United States during the Cold War.

MAY 6   At Sembach Air Base, West Germany, the 43rd Electronics Combat Squadron receives the first EC-130H Compass Call aircraft.

JUNE 1   The Special Operations Command is established by the Air Force.

JUNE 10   At the Paris Air Show, France, the B1-B Lancer makes its first European debut.

JULY 4–SEPTEMBER 17   A Rockwell B-1B Lancer piloted by Lieutenant Robert Chamberlain establishes 12 new world records for speed and payload. Another Lancer flown by Major Brent A. Hedgpeth sets an additional 9 speed records. For their efforts, the B-1B System Program Office, Air Force Systems Command, wins the Mackay Trophy.

JULY 17   At Hurlburt Field, Florida, the Air Force Logistics Command delivers the first Sikorsky MH-53J Pave Low helicopter, and it begins operational service within a year. This machine is outfitted for poor weather/nighttime operations and is associated with Special Forces.

JULY 22–DECEMBER 21   In the Persian Gulf, Operation EARNEST WILL unfolds as Air Force E-3A Sentry aircraft begin routine patrols once the Iran-Iraq War begins spilling over into other countries. Moreover, C-5A Galaxy and C-141 Starlifter transports convey mine-sweeping equipment to the region, while Air Force tankers assist Navy aircraft patrolling the gulf waters.

AUGUST 31–SEPTEMBER 9   C-130 and C-141 aircraft deliver 2,511 tons of fire retardant across the coastal regions of Oregon and Northern California, to combat a fire consuming 970 square miles.

SEPTEMBER 17   A Rockwell B-1B Lancer piloted by Major Brent A. Hedgpeth sets

9 new world records during a five-hour sortie by carrying 66,140 pounds for 3,107 miles and at 655 miles per hour.

SEPTEMBER 24   Over Beijing, China, the Air Force Thunderbirds demonstration squadron entertains a crowd of 20,000 onlookers.

SEPTEMBER 28   A severe bird strike brings down the first B-1B during a training mission. The cost to the taxpayers is $100 million.

OCTOBER 1   At Onizuka Air Force Station, California, the Space Command takes command of the Air Force Satellite Control Network, a set of worldwide remote-tracking stations.

At Hickam Air Force Base, Hawaii, and Clark Air Base, Philippines, the Pacific Air Forces retire their T-33 jet trainers after 32 years of distinguished service.

NOVEMBER 19   In California, the Northrop Corporation contracts with the Air Force to design and construct the next generation of stealth aircraft, the B-2. While invisible to radar, projected costs per bomber are $1 billion, making them the most expensive aircraft ever built.

NOVEMBER 24   An air-launched cruise missile (ALCM) is successfully deployed by a B-1B Lancer for the first time.

DECEMBER 5   Six C-130 Hercules transports from the 374th Tactical Airlift Squadron arrive in Luzon, Philippines, bringing in 34 tons of supplies, clothing, and rice to assist the victims of Typhoon Nina.

1988

JANUARY 1   Mixed male/female teams to serve as Minuteman and Peacekeeper strategic missile crews are allowed by the Strategic Air Command (SAC) for the first time.

JANUARY 20   At Palmdale, California, the 100th Rockwell B-1B Lancer strategic bomber rolls off the assembly line. This is also the last example acquired.

JANUARY 25–28   In Manila, the Philippines, two C-5 Galaxy transports from the 60th Military Airlift Wing arrive with 102 tons of medical supplies to refresh the stocks of Americares, a private relief organization.

FEBRUARY 19–22   A C-141 of the 86th Military Airlift Wing conveys 50 tons of construction materials to repair housing in the Marshall Islands, recently battered by Typhoon Roy.

MARCH 16–28   In Honduras, Operation GOLDEN PHEASANT unfolds as Air Force transports convey 3,200 Army troops to counter Nicaraguan Sandinista threats to the region.

APRIL   In Panama, 8 C-5 Galaxies and 22 C-141 Starlifters from the Military Airlift Command (MAC) convey 1,300 security specialists once political instability threatens the safety of Americans living there.

APRIL 17–JULY 23   A C-5A Galaxy piloted by Captain Michael Eastman of the 436th Military Airlift Wing delivers nuclear test monitoring equipment to the Soviet Republic of Kazakhstan. This is in support of joint verification experiments, and Eastman wins the Mackay Trophy for the efforts.

APRIL 18   In the Persian Gulf, Air Force tankers actively refuel Navy aircraft during a confrontation with Iranian naval forces.

APRIL 30   At McConnell Air Force Base, Kansas, the final Rockwell B-1B Lancer arrives with the 384th Bombardment Squadron.

MAY   At Kadena Air Base, Okinawa, C-5 Galaxy transports convey 73 tons of relief supplies to Islamabad, Pakistan, to assist refugees fleeing the onset of civil war in neighboring Afghanistan.

JUNE 2–AUGUST 11   Sectarian warfare in southern Sudan prompts transports of the 60th and 436th Miliary Airlift Wings to convey 70 tons of plastic sheeting for shelters, along with food and medical supplies.

JULY 7   The last F-106 Delta Darts are ordered dropped from the Air Force inventory after three decades of distinguished service.

AUGUST 1   The last three F-106 Delta Darts are retired by the 177th Fighter Group; many surviving aircraft end up as remote-controlled target drones.

AUGUST 15–28   Air Force C-5 Galaxies from the Military Airlift Command (MAC) fly in 500 UN peacekeepers to help monitor a cease-fire between Turkey and Iraq.

AUGUST 22–OCTOBER 6   At Yellowstone National Park, the Military Airlift Command (MAC) transports 4,000

firefighters and 2,500 tons of equipment directly into a raging fire zone. Other transports, fitted with spraying equipment, apply flame retardant over thousands of acres.

AUGUST 25–31   In Somalia, a C-141 Starlifter belonging to the 41st Military Airlift Squadron delivers a 200-bed emergency hospital weighing 200 tons, after the onset of civil war creates an acute refugee problem.

AUGUST 28   On the island of São Tomé off the west coast of Africa, a C-141 Starlifter from the 20th Military Airlift Squadron delivers 29 tons of medical supplies and hospital equipment to various facilities.

SEPTEMBER   Over Seoul, South Korea, an Air Force E-3A Sentry aircraft, escorted by fighters, patrols the airspace above the peninsula to deter any North Korean aggression during the Olympic games there.

SEPTEMBER 10–15   In Bangladesh, no less than four Airlift Wings—the 60th, 62nd, 63rd, and 436th—bring 100 million tons of humanitarian supplies to the victims after catastrophic flooding leaves 28 million people homeless.

SEPTEMBER 29   At Cape Canaveral, Florida, *Discovery* is launched into orbit under Air Force Colonel Richard O. Covey. This comes two-and-a-half years after the *Challenger* space shuttle disaster.

OCTOBER 25   At Marikina, Philippines, severe flooding results in two HH-3 Jolly Green Giant helicopters from the 31st Aerospace Rescue and Recovery Squadron (ASSR) saving 27 stranded residents over an eight-hour period.

NOVEMBER 9 At Niamey, Niger, the 709th Military Airlift Squadron dispatches a C-5 Galaxy with a mobile dental clinic and two ambulances at the behest of the U.S. State Department.

NOVEMBER 10 The existence of the Lockheed F-117A Nighthawk is made known to the public. This light bomber employs the smallest radar cross-section of any aircraft at the time, and is virtually invisible to radar. The Air Force acquires 59 F-117s at $42.6 million apiece.

NOVEMBER 16–30 At Dakar, Senegal, aircraft of the 60th, 63rd, 437th, and 438th Military Airlift Wings deliver tons of insecticide to thwart major locust infestations.

NOVEMBER 22 At Palmdale, California, the new Northrop B-2 Spirit bomber is made public; it is reputedly invisible to radar, and also costs a whopping $1 billion per aircraft. The Air Force seeks to acquire 132 such aircraft as its front-line bomber.

NOVEMBER 29 The 60th and final KC-10 Extender is delivered to the Air Force. This newest version employs wing-mounted refueling pods to complement the traditional, centerline boom.

DECEMBER 12 In the Pacific Ocean, the 33rd Aerospace Rescue and Recovery Squadron (ARRS) dispatches a helicopter that saves 11 passengers on a life raft once their vessel sank. They are flown to Clark Air Base for treatment.

1989

JANUARY 7–20 At Monrovia, Liberia, MEDFLY 89, a joint-service humanitarian effort, unfolds as two C-130 Hercules from the 167th Tactical Airlift Group deliver needed medical supplies and personnel.

JANUARY 10 The AGM-136 Tacit Rainbow missile is tested by a B-52 bomber for the first time. This advanced weapon flies to specific coordinates then loiters until radar energy is detected and identified, whereupon it homes in and destroys the target.

FEBRUARY At Dakar, Senegal, the 63rd Military Airlift Wing dispatches two C-141 Starlifters carrying 20 tons of insecticide to control swarming locusts.

FEBRUARY 16 In California, the T-38 Talon production line is finally closed by Northrop after the 3,806th supersonic jet trainer is manufactured.

MARCH 27 In Alaska, Military Airlift Command (MAC) transports convey over 1,000 tons of cleanup equipment after 10 million gallons of oil are spilled by the tanker *Exxon Valdez*.

APRIL In Africa, the 436th Military Airlift Wing delivers 32 pallets of relief supplies to malnourished inhabitants of Gambia, Equatorial Guinea, and Chad.

APRIL 17 At Tinker Air Force Base, Oklahoma, a Boeing E-3A Sentry aircraft christened *Elf One* returns after serving eight years on station over Saudi Arabia.

The U.S. Air Force accepts the 50th and final Lockheed C-5B Galaxy transport.

MAY 13–18   In Panama, Operation NIM-ROD DANCER unfolds as the Air Force transports fly in 2,600 marines, along with 3,000 tons of equipment, in response to threats to U.S. military personnel.

MAY 16–JUNE 29   Continuing political unrest in Panama results in Operation BLADE JEWEL, whereby Air Force transports evacuate 6,000 nonessential personnel.

JUNE 9–11   In response to a terrible train wreck near Ufa on the Trans–Siberian Railroad, resulting in 850 casualties, the Military Airlift Command (MAC) sends several transports to the Soviet Union with humanitarian supplies for the victims.

JUNE 10   At Edwards Air Force Base, California, Captain Jacquelyn S. Parker becomes the first female graduate of the Air Force Test Pilot School.

JUNE 14   At Cape Canaveral, Florida, the new Titan IV heavy-lift rocket booster is launched for the first time and carries a Department of Defense satellite aloft.

JULY 6   In Washington, D.C., President H. W. Bush awards noted aviator James H. Doolittle the Presidential Medal of Freedom; he remains the only American to receive this and a Congressional Medal of Honor, the nation's two highest awards.

JULY 17   At Edwards Air Force Base, California, the new Northrop-Grumman B-2 Spirit stealth bomber flies for the first time.

AUGUST 16   The first Pacific Air Chiefs Conference is hosted by the Pacific Air Forces, and is attended by ranking airmen from Australia, Japan, the Philippines, Singapore, Malaysia, and Brunei. It seeks to promote regional cooperation and security through air power.

SEPTEMBER 19–21   The Military Airlift Command (MAC) conveys 4,300 tons of humanitarian supplies after Hurricane Hugo ravages the coast of South Carolina. Meanwhile, RF-4C Phantom II reconnaissance aircraft from nearby Shaw Air Force Base provide photo coverage to National Guard troops conducting rescue operations.

OCTOBER 1   General Hansford T. Johnson becomes the first U.S. Air Force Academy graduate promoted to full (four-star) rank.

OCTOBER 3   The last production U-2R spyplane is delivered to the Air Force by Lockheed; the clandestine fleet now consists of 9 U-2Rs, 26 TR-1As, and 2 TR-1Bs.

OCTOBER 4   A B-1B Lancer piloted by Captain Jeffrey K. Beene, 96th Bombardment Wing, makes a nose-wheel-up landing without seriously damaging the aircraft. Beene wins the Mackay Trophy.

Over Antarctica, a C-5 Galaxy from the 60th Military Airlift Wing lands for the first time at McMurdo Station without skids, and delivers two UH-1N Huey helicopters, 84 tons of supplies, and 72 passengers.

OCTOBER 17   After San Francisco, California, is heavily damaged by an enormous earthquake, transports from the Military Airlift Command (MAC) deliver 250 tons of supplies.

DECEMBER 14   Women serve as combat crew members on C-130 and C-141 airdrop missions for the first time.

DECEMBER 20–24   Over Panama, six F-117s of the 37th Tactical Fighter Wing and special operations AC-130H aircraft from Air Force Special Operations Command participate in Operation JUST CAUSE. Military Airlift Command (MAC) transports also airdrop 9,500 troops from Pope Air Force Base, North Carolina, in the biggest nighttime combat operation since the World War II. Furthermore, Air Force Reserve aircraft deliver in 6,000 passengers and 3,700 tons of supplies as hostilities unfold.

The 16th Special Operations Squadron, flying an AC-130H named *Air Papa 06*, distinguishes itself in combat during Operation JUST CAUSE by destroying numerous barracks and antiaircraft gun emplacements at La Comandancia (Panamanian Defense Force headquarters) without inflicting collateral damage to civilian buildings nearby. They win a Mackay Trophy for their mission.

DECEMBER 29–31   In Bucharest, Romania, two C-130 Hercules from the Military Airlift Command (MAC) deliver 30 tons of medical supplies to treat the victims in the wake of a bloody anti-Communist uprising.

1990

JANUARY 3   In Panama, captured dictator Manuel Noriega is packed onto an Air Force C-130 and extradited back to the United States to face drug trafficking charges in Miami, Florida.

JANUARY 31   Operation CORONET COVE, a decade-old maneuver that rotated Air National Guard units into the Panama Canal Zone, terminates after 13,000 sorties.

FEBRUARY   In Monrovia, Liberia, aircraft from the 436th Military Airlift Wing and the 463rd Tactical Airlift Wing arrive with 30 tons of relief supplies for refugees fleeing a civil war.

FEBRUARY–MARCH   In Western and American Samoa, transports of the 60th and 63rd Military Airlift Wing deliver 410 tons of relief supplies in the wake of Typhoon Ofa.

FEBRUARY 23   In Senegal, aircraft of the 435th Tactical Airlift Wing convey 11 tons of food, medical supplies, and 60 medics to combat an epidemic.

FEBRUARY 26   The Air Force retires the legendary Lockheed SR-71 Blackbird from active service owing to extreme operating costs, and improvements in satellite photography.

MARCH 6   In Washington, D.C., a Lockheed SR-71 Blackbird touches down after setting four transcontinental airspeed records, including 2,124 miles per hour on a transcontinental crossing. Once parked, it is handed over to the National Air and Space Museum, Smithsonian Institution for permanent display.

APRIL 11   In Europe, the first Pershing II missiles destined to be destroyed under provisions of the recent INF Treaty between the United States and Soviet Union are loaded onto a C-5 Galaxy.

APRIL 21   At Nellis Air Force Base, Nevada, the Lockheed F-117 Nighthawk is publicly displayed for the first time; it is beheld by an estimated 100,000 visitors.

MAY 4   The AIM-120A advanced medium-range air-to-air missile (AMRAAM) is approved by the Air Force for use on fighter craft.

MAY 22   The Twenty-Third Air Force gives rise to the Special Operations Command (SOC).

JULY 1   In Washington, D.C., General Michael J. Dugan becomes chief of staff, U.S. Air Force.

JULY 12   The final production F-117 Nighthawk is delivered by Lockheed to the Air Force; 59 are acquired in all.

JULY 17   Baguio, Philippines, is destroyed by a severe earthquake and the Air Force flies in 600 tons of relief equipment to

Two-ship formation of Lockheed F-117A Nighthawk Stealth fighter aircraft. This was the world's first military aircraft to boast a functional "invisibility" to enemy radar. (U.S. Department of Defense)

look for survivors; 2,475 passengers are also flown to medical facilities for treatment.

JULY 24   The EC-135 Looking Glass aircraft, intended to control and coordinate nuclear command posts in the event of a nuclear war, finally stands down. It flew continuously during three decades of service and hundreds of thousands of flying hours, yet never experienced a single accident.

AUGUST–SEPTEMBER   The Air Force Space Command (AFSPACECOM) initiates the first space system infrastructure capable of directly supporting a military conflict. It is capable of relaying communications, navigation and meteorological information, along with detecting short-range ballistic missile launches.

AUGUST 7   At Langley Air Force Base, Virginia, the 71st Tactical Fighter Squadron (TFS), 1st Tactical Fighter Wing, dispatches 24 F-15C Eagles on the 8,000-mile flight to Dhahran, Saudi Arabia. The flight concludes 15 hours later with the help of 12 in-flight refuelings.

AUGUST 8   At Dhahran, Saudi Arabia, an Air Force Reserve C-141 Starlifter lands, becoming the first American aircraft deployed in this theater. They are soon joined by F-15Cs from the 1st Tactical Fighter Wing. Additional AWACS aircraft also arrive to assist Saudi AWACS already orbiting the kingdom.

Air Force Vice Chief of Staff Lieutenant General Mike Loh orders the Air Staff planning group (Checkmate) under Colonel John Warden to initiate plans for conducting a strategic air war against Iraqi forces. This comes in response to a request from General H. Norman Schwarzkopf, the coalition commander.

AUGUST 9 The old Alaskan Air Command is designated the Eleventh Air Force, and it is assigned to the Pacific Air Forces (PACAF).

AUGUST 10 At Central Command (CENTCOM), MacDill Air Force Base, Florida, Colonel John Warren proffers a preliminary draft for air operations in the Persian Gulf to General H. Norman Schwarzkopf. General Charles Horner also draws up contingency plans in the event that Iraqi forces attack Saudi Arabia before the Americans deploy in force.

Detachments of F-16s and C-130s from Pope Air Force Base, North Carolina, begin filtering into Saudi Arabia.

AUGUST 12 At Dhahran, Saudi Arabia, the first 32 KC-135 tanker aircraft deploy, being the first of over 300 KC-135s and KC-10s scheduled there. These are joined by MH-53J Pave Low helicopters of the 1st Special Operations Wing.

AUGUST 14 In Washington, D.C., the presence of E-3 AWACS, KC-10s, KC-135s, and RC-135s in the Persian Gulf theater is announced by the Department of Defense.

AUGUST 15 At Tonopah, Nevada, top secret F-117 stealth aircraft of the 37th Tactical Fighter Wing (TFW) deploy to Saudi Arabia; they are soon joined by F-4G Wild Weasels flying in from George Air Force Base, California.

AUGUST 16 At Myrtle Beach Air Force Base, South Carolina, A-10 Thunderbolt IIs depart en masse for deployment to Saudi Arabia.

AUGUST 17 In Washington, D.C., the Civil Reserve Air Fleet is mobilized by President George H. W. Bush for the first time since 1952. Their aircraft are impressed as troop carriers to accelerate the Persian Gulf buildup.

General H. Norman Schwarzkopf approves the air campaign strategy, so Colonel John Warden is dispatched to Saudi Arabia to brief General Charles Horner as to its details.

The Air Force Space Command establishes the Defense Satellite Communications Systems (DSCS) to facilitate command links to Operation DESERT SHIELD.

AUGUST 19 At Mushait Air Base, Saudi Arabia, 18 F-117 Nighthawks from the 415th Tactical Fighter Squadron arrive for service during Operation DESERT SHIELD.

AUGUST 20 In Saudi Arabia, General Charles Horner declares that Saudi Arabia can now be defended against any Iraqi attack with the air power presently in the Gulf region. He is also briefed by Colonel John Warden as to the forthcoming campaign for waging a strategic air war.

AUGUST 21 In the Persian Gulf, the Air Force has deployed A-10s, C-130s, E-3 AWACS, F-4Gs, F-15s, F-15Es, F-16s, F-117s, KC-135, KC-10s, and RC-135s, being the largest concentration of military aircraft outside the United States since Vietnam.

The Air Force requests 6,000 reservists to join up and no less than 15,000 volunteer for service in Operation DESERT SHIELD.

AUGUST 22 Air Force Reserve personnel have flown 8,000 soldiers and 7 million tons of military cargo to Saudi Arabia for service in Operation DESERT STORM; 20,000 reservists and 12,000 Air National Guardsmen are also slated for service in the Persian Gulf.

Horner, Charles A. (1936–)

Air Force general. Charles A. Horner was born in Davenport, Iowa, on October 19, 1936, and he was commissioned a second lieutenant through AFROTC at the University of Iowa. Horner earned his wings as an F-100 pilot in 1960 and flew three years with the 492nd Tactical Fighter Squadron at RAF Lakenheath, England. In 1965 he performed 41 combat missions over North Vietnam then, between 1966 and 1967, he rotated back to Nellis Air Force Base, Nevada, to serve as an F-105 instructor. Horner next arrived in Thailand in May 1967, to fly an additional 70 combat missions as a Wild Weasel pilot. Horner handled his affairs capably and in July 1985 he rose to major general and deputy chief of staff for Plans, Headquarters Tactical Air Command at Langley Air Force Base, Virginia. In March 1987 he served as commander, 9th U.S. Air Force and U.S. Central Command Air Forces based at Shaw Air Force Base, South Carolina.

Horner's greatest challenge came in August 1991 after Saddam Hussein invaded Kuwait with a massive army, and he was appointed Commander in Chief Forward, U.S. Central Command. Once Operation DESERT STORM commenced the following January, Horner deployed 2,700 modern, sophisticated warplanes from 14 nations. Their accurate bombing gutted Iraqi air defenses, and allowed the ground attack to conclude after only 100 hours of fighting. Horner consequently advanced to general on July 1, 1992 and was appointed to head the North American Aerospace Defense Command and the U.S. Space Command. He retired from active service on September 30, 1994. During Horner's tenure in the Persian Gulf War, military air power was never more effective or decisive in terms of results.

AUGUST 23   At Andrews Air Force Base, Maryland, the 89th Military Airlift Wing deploys the first of two VC–25As (highly modified Boeing 747s). Whenever a president is on board, the aircraft receives the call sign *Air Force One.*

In Washington, D.C., Secretary of Defense Dick Cheney authorizes the Air Force reserve components to mobilize for service in the Persian Gulf; 20,000 are called to the colors.

AUGUST 24   At Birmingham, Alabama, six of its RF–4C Phantom IIs from the 117th Tactical Reconnaissance Wing are dispatched to the Persian Gulf region. They are soon joined by similar aircraft sent by the 67th Tactical Reconnaissance Wing, Bergstrom Air Force Base, Texas.

AUGUST 28   At Torrejon, Spain, F–16 fighters fly off on a new deployment to airfields in Qatar.

AUGUST 29   At Ramstein Air Base, West Germany, a C–5 Galaxy crashes on takeoff, killing 13 people. Staff Sergeant Lorenzo Galvin, Jr., wins the Airman's Medal for heroically assisting crash victims.

SEPTEMBER 5   In Saudi Arabia, five C–130 units from the Air National Guard (ANG) deploy for active duty.

SEPTEMBER 6   The U.S. Post Office issues a 40-cent stamp with a portrait of Lieutenant General Claire L. Chennault, who commanded the famous "Flying Tigers" of World War II.

SEPTEMBER 8   Colonel Marcelite Jordan Harris is the first African American woman promoted to brigadier general in the U.S. Air Force. She also gains appointment as director of Air Training Command's technical training.

In Saudi Arabia, the first wave of AC–130H gunships from the 16th Special Operations Squadron deploys for active duty.

SEPTEMBER 13   In Riyadh, Saudi Arabia, Air Force Brigadier General Buster

Glosson, deputy commander, Joint Task Force Middle East, briefs Generals H. Norman Schwarzkopf and Colin Powell on the final operational air war plan subsequent to Operation DESERT SHIELD.

SEPTEMBER 17   In Washington, D.C., Air Force Chief of Staff Michael J. Dugan is relieved by Secretary of Defense Dick Cheney for unauthorized comments made to the media about Operation DESERT SHIELD.

SEPTEMBER 18–28   In Jordan, transports of the 436th and 438th Miliary Airlift Wings deliver tons of blankets, tents, cots, and other impedimenta for the 100,000 foreign workers fleeing from Kuwait.

SEPTEMBER 29   The new Lockheed/General Dynamics YF-22A Raptor air superiority/stealth fighter prototype is ferried to Edwards Air Force Base, California, for testing.

OCTOBER 1   Control of Patrick Air Force Base, Florida, passes from the Air Force Systems Command to the Air Force Space Command.

OCTOBER 10   Throughout the Persian Gulf, Air Force fighter and fighter-bomber units begin exercises to familiarize them with desert warfare while F-15Cs begin performing combat air patrols (CAP).

OCTOBER 30   In Washington, D.C., General Merrill A. McPeak is appointed the new Air Force chief of staff.

Operation DESERT EXPRESS commences as Air Force transports expedite shipment of certain critical items to the Persian Gulf.

NOVEMBER 3   Over Edwards Air Force Base, California, the prototype YF-22A Advanced Technology Fighter (ATF) becomes the first jet aircraft to achieve supersonic speed through a process known as "supercruise." This does not require the use of afterburners.

NOVEMBER 17   Above the Indian Ocean a DSCS II satellite is placed by the Air Force Space Command to enhance DESERT SHIELD communications.

NOVEMBER 21   From Davis-Monthan Air Force Base, Arizona, additional A-10 Thunderbolt IIs deploy directly to Saudi Arabia.

DECEMBER 1–2   Off the Korean coast, 22 shipwrecked sailors from a grounded Panamanian vessel are rescued by two MH-60 Pave Hawk helicopters of the 38th Air Rescue Squadron.

DECEMBER 5   In Saudi Arabia, RF-4C Phantom IIs of the 152nd Tactical Reconnaissance Group begin arriving in theater.

DECEMBER 29   In the Persian Gulf, the 169th Tactical Fighter Group becomes the first Air National Guard (ANG) unit deployed for active duty in Operation DESERT SHIELD.

1991

JANUARY 2   In Saudi Arabia, the 4th Tactical Fighter Wing (Provisional) is cobbled together from Air National Guard F-16s of the 174th Tactical Fighter Wing and the 169th Tactical Fighter Group.

JANUARY 11   At Riyadh, Saudi Arabia, the two pre-production E-8A JSTARS aircraft deploy for use against Iraq; this highly advanced reconnaissance platform is capable of providing real-time surveillance over battlefields.

JANUARY 15   Command of Vandenberg Air Force Base, California, passes from the Strategic Air Command (SAC) to the Air Force Space Command.

JANUARY 16   Operation DESERT STORM commences as seven B-52Gs of the 2nd Bomb Wing launch from Barksdale Air Force Base, Louisiana, armed with new AGM-86C conventional air-launched cruise missiles (ALCMs). This is also history's longest bombing mission and requires 35 hours of flight time.

JANUARY 17   Over Kuwait, American and coalition aircraft begin attacking Iraqi military targets, missile sites, and communications facilities deemed useful to Saddam Hussein's occupying forces. They mount 750 attack sorties while carrier aircraft contribute a further 228. The aerial campaign continues without interruption for 38 days.

Among the first wave of aircraft to go in are AH-64A Apache helicopter gunships, guided by Air Force MH-53 Special Operations helicopters.

Seven B-52Gs from Barksdale Air Force Base, Louisiana, arrive over the Persian Gulf and unleash 35 super-accurate cruise missiles against communications and radar targets in Iraq.

Over Baghdad, Iraq, stealthy F-117 Nighthawks steal past Iraqi radar defenses and bomb strategic targets throughout the city as intense antiaircraft fire continuously lights up the darkness; they account for 31 percent of all targets struck on the first day.

Over Kuwait, Air Force C-130 transports deliver 14,000 troops and 9,000 tons of cargo belonging to the Army's XVIII Airborne Corps. This forward deployment suddenly places them on the Iraqi right flank.

An F-16C piloted by Captain Jon K. Kelk, 3rd Tactical Fighter Wing (TFW) downs the first Iraqi MiG-29 jet fighter.

JANUARY 17–FEBRUARY 28   C-130 transports of the 1650th Tactical Airlift Wing complete 3,200 combat sorties, while A-10 Thunderbolt IIs from the 706th Tactical Fighter Squadron fly 1,000 sorties against enemy targets. No Air Force Reserve aircraft are lost in combat despite this operational intensity.

JANUARY 18   Over Iraq, U.S. and coalition aircraft down eight Iraqi MiG-29 and Mirage F-1 fighters.

From Incirlik Air Base, Turkey, Air Force jets strike at military targets in northern Iraq to prevent them from concentrating against forces moving up from Saudi Arabia.

JANUARY 19   Over Iraq, two F-16Cs of the 614th Tactical Fighter Squadron are downed by missiles and the pilots are captured and paraded before television, along with six other coalition airmen.

JANUARY 21   Over Iraq, Captain Paul T. Johnson, piloting an A-10 Thunderbolt II, braves antiaircraft fire to destroy Iraqi vehicles threatening a downed Navy F-14 pilot; Johnson wins the Air Force Cross. Concurrently, an MH-53J Pave Low helicopter under Captain Thomas J. Trask, 20th Special Operations Squadron, successfully extracts the pilot; Trask wins the Mackay Trophy.

JANUARY 22   Over Iraq, an F-15E piloted by Colonel David W. Eberly and Lieutenant Colonel Tom Griffith is downed

The skies over Baghdad erupt with anti-aircraft fire as U.S. warplanes strike targets in the Iraqi capital early on January 18, 1991. (AP/Wide World Photos)

in combat; the two evade capture over the next three days, but are captured near the Syrian border.

JANUARY 22–27   At Al Asad Air Base, Iraq, MiG aircraft in hardened aircraft shelters are destroyed by F-111Fs using laser-guided "smart" bombs.

JANUARY 23   In Washington, D.C., General Colin Powell, chairman of the Joint Chiefs of Staff, declares that air superiority has been achieved over Iraq, as enemy positions are bombed with virtual impunity.

JANUARY 24   Over the Persian Gulf, a Saudi F-15C shoots downs two Iraqi Mirage F-1 fighters carrying Exocet anti-ship missiles. Also, this day coalition air forces mount 2,570 sorties; the total number over the past eight days is 14,750.

JANUARY 25   Over Iraq, Air Force fighter-bombers employ new I-2000

bombs against hardened aircraft shelters, destroying several MiG-29s sequestered inside.

JANUARY 26   Coalition forces begin concentrating their attacks on enemy ground forces in Kuwait as the Iraqi Air Force is effectively neutralized.

JANUARY 27   Over Kuwait, F-111s strike oil-pumping manifolds at the main terminal at Al Ahmadi with guided GBU-15 bombs to halt the flow of crude oil into the Persian Gulf. This is also the worst deliberate oil spill ever.

JANUARY 29   Over Al Khafji, Saudi Arabia, an AC-130H gunship is downed by a missile and all 14 crew members are killed.

FEBRUARY 2   Over the Indian Ocean, a B-52 bomber returning to its base on Diego Garcia experiences electrical problems while returning from a mission over

Iraq and crashes; three crew men are rescued, but three are killed.

FEBRUARY 6   Over Iraq, Captain Robert R. Swain, Jr., flying an A-10 Thunderbolt II, shoots down an Gazelle helicopter with his 30mm cannon; this is the only aerial victory attributed to a "Warthog."

FEBRUARY 9   Over Kuwait, A-10 Thunderbolt IIs begin the process of destroying individual targets with precision-guided munitions. To date, 600 enemy tanks and armored vehicles have been destroyed, roughly 15 percent of Saddam Hussein's military strength.

FEBRUARY 11   Today coalition air forces mount 2,900 strike sorties for a grand total of 61,862 over a 26-day period.

FEBRUARY 12   Over Baghdad, Iraq, Air Force fighter-bombers employ "smart bombs" against the Martyr's Bridge, the Republic Bridge, and the July 14 Bridge, destroying all three.

FEBRUARY 13   Acting upon a tip from military intelligence, F-117s bomb the Al Firdos bunker in downtown Baghdad, Iraq, suspected of housing Saddam Hussein. The building, a civilian communications center, is flattened with the loss of several hundred dead, but the elusive dictator was not there. Thereafter, coalition air authorities more closely supervise combat strikes in the capital city.

FEBRUARY 14   Over Saudi Arabia, an EF-111A "Spark Vark" crashes after a bombing mission over Iraq; the two-man crew ejects in their cockpit capsule, but apparently dies upon landing.

FEBRUARY 17   Coalition aircraft have since accounted for 1,300 of Saddam Hussein's 4,240 tanks and 1,100 of his 3,110 artillery pieces.

FEBRUARY 19   A combination of F-4Gs and F-16s launched from Turkish airspace attacks Baghdad, Iraq. Coalition forces also mount a record 3,000 sorties this day, for a grand total of 83,000.

FEBRUARY 21   At Freetown, Sierra Leone, a C-141 Starlifter of the 438th Military Airlift Wing arrives with 55 tons of food and medicine for victims of hardship.

FEBRUARY 23   Over Iraq, Air Force B-52Gs pound Iraqi Republican Guard positions as retreating Iraqi troops set Kuwaiti oil wells on fire.

FEBRUARY 24   Coalition aircraft perform 3,000 combat sorties, including reconnaissance, close air support, and interdiction, over the next three days.

FEBRUARY 25   Air Force F-16Cs bomb Iraqi forces preparing to attack a Army Special Force team, while a UH-60 Black Hawk helicopter swoops in to rescue them.

FEBRUARY 27   Over Iraq, the Air Force unloads two 4,700-pound GPU-28 bombs that demolish the so-called "impregnable" command bunker at Al Taji. Total air sorties mounted this day also top 3,500—a new record.

FEBRUARY 28   Operation DESERT STORM ceases at 8 A.M., and the Air Force has performed 59 percent of all coalition sorties. Moreover, its 2,000 aircraft represent 75 percent of all machines involved. The elusive F-117s, however, account for 40 percent of all Iraqi strategic targets knocked out in 1,270 combat sorties that delivered 2,041 tons of bombs.

DESERT STORM is also the first "space war" judging from the extensive use of satellite technology involved. The Air Force Space Command (AFSPACECOM) satellite systems were extremely active relaying meteorological information to combat headquarters, along with alerts of short-range ballistic missile launches.

MARCH 1   At Bucharest, Romania, C-5 Galaxies from the Military Airlift Command (MAC) arrive with 150 tons of relief supplies at a time of violent street confrontations and food shortages.

MARCH 8   At Vandenberg Air Force Base, California, the Martin Marietta two-stage Titan IV heavy-lift booster successfully launches for the first time.

MARCH 8–DECEMBER   In the Persian Gulf region, the Military Airlift Command (MAC) demonstrates its strategic flexibility by flying an influx of supplies, personnel, and environmental cleanup equipment. Forty-two C-5 Galaxies and three C-141 Starlifters of the 60th and 436th Military Airlift Wings also transport over 1,000 tons of firefighting equipment and crews necessary to extinguish 517 oil wells set alight by retreating Iraqi forces. This done, they next provide 7,000 tons of supplies to Kurdish refugees in southeastern Turkey.

MARCH 20   Over Iraq, an F-16C downs an Iraqi Su-22 caught violating the cease-fire agreement.

APRIL   In Lima, Peru, two C-5 Galaxies of the 436th Military Airlift Wing convey 200 tons of medical supplies to stave off a cholera epidemic threatening 150,000 people.

APRIL 7   In northern Iraq, Operation PRO-VIDE COMFORT commences as Air Force warplanes assist the Kurds by enforcing a no-fly zone above the 36th parallel.

APRIL 12   Off the Alaskan coast, a Soviet AN-74 Coaler transport aircraft is intercepted by forward-deployed F-15 Eagles stationed at Galena Airport for the first time.

APRIL 18   At Vandenberg Air Force Base, California, a Martin Marietta/Boeing MGM-134A intercontinental ballistic missile is launched for the first time. It travels 4,000 miles downrange to the Kwajalein Missile Range.

MAY 10–JUNE 13   Transports of the Military Airlift Command (MAC) begin Operation SEA ANGEL by carrying 3,000 tons of relief supplies to the city of Dacca, Bangladesh, after a tropical cyclone batters the coast with 150-mile-per-hour winds.

MAY 31   At RAF Greenham Common, England, the 501st Tactical Missile Wing is inactivated, being the final unit entirely armed with cruise missiles; this was also the first GLCM unit deployed in Europe.

JUNE–SEPTEMBER   The Military Airlift Command (MAC) transports fly 19 humanitarian missions to Addis Ababa, Ethiopia, to mitigate severe drought conditions.

JUNE 8–JULY 2   In the Philippines, once Clark Air Base is nearly destroyed by the eruption of nearby Mount Pinatubo, Operation FIERY VIGIL unfolds to evacuate 15,000 people from the disaster zone, while bringing in 2,000 tons of relief supplies. This is also the largest emergency evacuation since the fall of South Vietnam, 1975.

JUNE 25   In Nairobi, Kenya, transports of the 60th Military Airlift Wing fly in 60 tons of food and other supplies to help alleviate drought conditions.

JULY 7   In N'Djamena, Chad, drought conditions, exacerbated by civil war, result in 70 tons of food delivered by transports of the 436th Military Airlift Wing.

JULY 10   At Plattsburgh Air Force Base, New York, the final FB-111A nuclear strike aircraft is flown to its final desert storage at Davis-Monthan AFB, Arizona.

JULY 22   At Ulan Bator, Mongolia, transports of the 730th Military Airlift Squadron and 445th Military Airlift Wing carry 20 tons of medical supplies to help alleviate acute shortages.

JULY 31   In Washington, D.C., an amendment allowing women to fly combat missions in Air Force, Navy, and Marine warplanes is passed by Congress.

AUGUST 6–9   In Shanghai, China, transports of the Military Airlift Command carry 75 tons of blankets and medical supplies after severe flooding throughout the interior region.

AUGUST 22   The Air Force initiates the Gulf War Air Power Survey (GWAPS) to correctly evaluate the overall impact of air power during recent hostilities.

SEPTEMBER 15   At Long Beach, California, the new Boeing C-17A Globemaster III flies for the first time by relocating to Edwards Air Force Base. This aircraft will replace C-141s and C-5s in use. It can transport oversized cargo loads of C-5 Galaxies to remote and primitive landing zones used by C-130 Hercules.

At Edwards Air Force Base, California, the prototype Beech T-1A Jayhawk flies for the first time; it becomes a standardized trainer for tanker and transport pilots.

SEPTEMBER 27   In Washington, D.C., President George H. W. Bush orders the long-standing Strategic Air Command (SAC) alert discontinued. This has been a standard American military fixture since October 1957.

A KC-10A Extender takes off in the rain as it deploys to Saudi Arabia during Operation Desert Shield. In addition to fuel, this versatile aircraft could also carry large numbers of troops and their equipment. (U.S. Department of Defense for Defense Visual Information Center)

OCTOBER–NOVEMBER   Air Force transports deliver food and medical supplies
to the needy in Russia, Armenia, and
Byelorussia, as the former Soviet Union
begins unraveling.

Angola, having concluded a bloody,
16-year civil war, accepts aid from the
United States as transports from the
436th Military Airlift Wing accordingly
convey 275 tons of supplies to the capital
of Luanda.

OCTOBER 2   At Ulan Bator, Mongolia,
transports of the 834th Airlift Division
fly in 15 additional pallets of medical supplies, along with 8 ambulances, to thwart
endemic shortages caused by the Soviet
Union's collapse.

OCTOBER 23   In Kiev, Ukraine, Air
Force transports deliver 146 tons of medical and relief supplies after its economy
collapses with the Soviet Union's fall.

NOVEMBER   In Pakistan, transports of the
Military Airlift Command (MAC) perform their 100th humanitarian flight by
assisting Afghan refugees. Since
March 1986, they have also delivered
over 1,000 tons of aid to the region.

NOVEMBER 1   At Thule, Greenland, a C-
5 Galaxy from the Twenty-Second Air
Force flies with a 36-member search and
rescue team and two MH-60G Pave

Hawks to rescue 13 crew members of a
Canadian C-130 Hercules that crashed
near the North Pole.

NOVEMBER 14   In Freetown, Sierra
Leone, the 436th Military Airlift Wing
dispatches a C-5 Galaxy with 50 tons of
medical and relief supplies to mitigate
food shortages.

NOVEMBER 26   In the Philippines, the
Air Force closes Clark Air Base, ending a
90-year American military presence
there; this was also the largest overseas
Air Force base.

DECEMBER 6   The 834th Airlift Division
dispatches six C-130s to Kwajalein Atoll
with relief supplies after Typhoon Zelda
batters its facilities.

DECEMBER 17–22   In Russia, transports
of the 436th, 438th, and 439th Airlift
Wings deliver 238 tons of food and relief
supplies to Moscow and Saint Petersburg;
along with Minsk, Byelorussia; and Yere-
van, Armenia. Severe economic hard-
ships continue in the months following
the Soviet Union's collapse.

DECEMBER 21   The prototype Rockwell
AC-130U gunship flies for the first time.
This new variant possesses updated sensors, increased firepower, and enhanced
ability to locate ground targets.

1992

JANUARY 17   The Air Force accepts
delivery of the first production model T-
1A Jayhawk to upgrade its fleet of training
aircraft.

JANUARY 20–25   Continuing medical
shortages in Mongolia result in another

C-5 Galaxy from the 60th Airlift Wing
delivering 56 tons of supplies to Mongolia. They do so at the behest of
the U.S. State Department to curry
good relations with this former Soviet
state.

JANUARY 30   The Air Force Satellite Control Network is handed off to the Air Force Space Command (AFSPACE-COM) to consolidate control of all Department of Defense satellites.

FEBRUARY 6   In Lithuania, four C-130 Hercules transports of the 435th Tactical Airlift Wing carry food and medical supplies to this former Soviet state.

FEBRUARY 10–29   PROVIDE HOPE I, a mass humanitarian mission to the new Commonwealth of Independent States, which replaced the now-defunct Soviet Union, unfolds as Air Force C-5 Galaxies and C-141 Starlifters fly in thousands of tons of food and medical supplies.

FEBRUARY 29   In Eastern Europe, Operation PROVIDE HOPE II commences as Air Force transports continue providing food and medicine to former states of the defunct Soviet Union.

MARCH 4   In Russia, two B-52 bombers land on a friendship mission land on an airfield for the first time since World War II.

MARCH 15   In Turkey, C-5 Galaxy and C-130 Hercules aircraft transport 165 tons of medicine, blankets, clothing, and other supplies to the victims of a severe earthquake.

MARCH 19   Off the Alaskan coast, two Russian Tu-95 Bear aircraft are intercepted by F-15s for the first time since the demise of the Soviet Union.

MARCH 24   In Spain, the Air Force ends a 26-year tenure there once its final fighter aircraft return home.

APRIL   In Uzbekistan, five C-141 Starlifters deliver several tons of fire-fighting equipment after severe oil rig fires break out.

APRIL 1   In Antarctica, a C-141 Starlifter from the 437th Airlift Wing delivers 155 barrels of aviation fuel by parachute to a joint U.S.-Russian ice station; the fuel is to be used by their helicopters.

APRIL 17   C-141 Starlifters begin flying in humanitarian aid to the former Yugoslavian states of Bosnia-Herzegovina, Croatia, and Slovenia as their regional, centralized economies begin constricting.

APRIL 24   Off the coast of Peru, a C-130H Hercules of the 310th Airlift Squadron is attacked in international airspace by Peruvian Su-22s. The shooting injures six crewmen and kills one, who was sucked out of the cabin at 14,500 feet. The crew makes an emergency landing in the damaged plane, winning a Mackay Trophy.

MAY 1–10   In Los Angeles, California, transports of the Military Airlift Command (MAC) convey troops and police to help quell an outbreak of racial violence.

MAY 3–4   In Sierra Leone, a military coup prompts C-141 Starlifters and C-130 aircraft to evacuate 350 citizens and foreign nationals from that West African nation.

MAY 7–8   In Russia, the Air Force Reserve Command Band marches in a Moscow military parade.

MAY 12   The Air Force accepts delivery of Lockheed's 2,000th C-130 Hercules, making it one of the most successful transports aviation in history.

JUNE 1   With the Cold War successfully concluded, the Air Force embarks on a major organizational overhaul. The Strategic Air Command (SAC), the Tactical Air Command (TAC), and the Military

Airlift Command (MAC) are immediately discontinued and replaced by the new Air Combat Command (ACC), to operate SAC's bomber and missiles and TAC's fighters, and the Air Mobility Command (AMC), which inherits MAC's transports and SAC's tanker aircraft.

The new United States Strategic Command (USSTRATCOM) is created by the Department of Defense to oversee U.S. nuclear forces and their long-range delivery systems; General George L. Butler, the final SAC commander, assumes control.

JUNE 30 Transports of the Air Mobility Command (AMC), in accordance with President George H. W. Bush's Nuclear Forces Initiative, begin withdrawing remaning stocks of nuclear artillery shells, Lance missile warheads, and nuclear depth charges from depots throughout Western Europe.

JULY 1 The former Air Force Logistics Command (AFLC) and Air Force Systems Command (AFSC) are consolidated into a new entity, the Air Force Materiel Command (AFMC).

JULY 1–MARCH 15, 1996 In Sarajevo, Bosnia-Herzegovina, Operation PROVIDE PROMISE unfolds as Air Mobility Command (AMC) transports deliver thousands of tons of medicine and food to inhabitants of that region.

AUGUST 2–20 In Kuwait, Operation INTRINSIC ACTION commences as transports of the Air Mobility Command (AMC) bring Army reinforcements in response to recent threats made by Iraq.

AUGUST 12 In Angola, Air Mobility Command (AMC) transports conduct Operation PROVIDE TRANSITION, flying

thousands of demobilized soldiers home to participate in that nation's first democratic elections.

AUGUST 18 In Iraq, Operation SOUTHERN WATCH is established to keep Iraqi aircraft from flying above the 32-degree north latitude line.

AUGUST 21–DECEMBER 9 In Somalia, Operation PROVIDE RELIEF commences as transports of the Air Mobility Command (AMC) begin flying food, medicine, and other relief supplies to a region wracked by civil wars, drought, and famine. By February 28, 1993, over 3,000 missions are flown and deliver 23,000 tons of cargo.

AUGUST 25–OCTOBER 28 In southern Florida, Homestead Air Force Base is so severely damaged by Hurricane Andrew that it is abandoned. The Air Mobility Command (AMC) also dispatches 13,500 relief workers and 21,000 tons of equipment and supplies in 724 sorties.

AUGUST 26 Over Iraq, Operation SOUTHERN WATCH begins to enforce a no-fly zone and prevent Iraqi aircraft flying below the 32nd parallel. This is necessary to prevent Saddam Hussein from attacking the Shia community residing in the southern marsh regions.

AUGUST 28 At Bergstrom Air Force Base, Texas, Air Force RF-4C Phantom II operations conclude when the 67th Reconnaissance Squadron is deactivated.

AUGUST 31 In Minsk, Byelorussia, an Air Mobility Command (AMC) C-141 Starlifter transports 70 children stricken by cancer from the Chernobyl nuclear accident to Brussels, Belgium, for treatment.

SEPTEMBER 1–25 On Guam, transports of the Air Mobility Command (AMC) convey 750 relief workers and 2,000 tons of supplies after a hard pounding by Typhoon Omar.

SEPTEMBER 12–OCTOBER 18   In Kauai, Hawaii, Air Mobility Command (AMC) and Air National Guard (ANG) transports perform 600 sorties to deliver 9,200 tons of relief supplies and 8,600 passengers after Typhoon Iniki ravages the area.

SEPTEMBER 13–29   Transports of the Air Mobility Command (AMC) commence Operation IMPRESSIVE LIFT by conveying UN peacekeeping forces from Pakistan to Somalia, including 974 soldiers and 1,168 tons of equipment.

SEPTEMBER 23–25   In Liberia, two C-130 Hercules aircraft evacuate 96 Americans from impending civil strife.

OCTOBER 25   In Tajikistan, a spate of civil unrest in the former Soviet republic prompts the arrival of an Air Mobility Command (AMC) C-141 Starlifter to evacuate citizens and foreign nationals.

NOVEMBER 4–11   In Armenia, the Air Mobility Command (AMC) dispatches five C-5 Galaxies and one C-141 Starlifter with 236 tons of flour to relieve food shortages there.

NOVEMBER 30   Over Montana, disaster strikes once two C-141 Starlifters of the 62nd Airlift Wing collide during a nighttime air refueling mission.

DECEMBER 4   Over Somalia, Operation RESTORE HOPE unfolds as Air Mobility Command (AMC) transports commence the first of 1,000 airlift missions while Air Force Reserve crews perform an additional 190 sorties; all told, 50,000 passengers and 40,000 short tons of cargo are conveyed to the region.

DECEMBER 6–20   In Islamabad, Pakistan, the Air Mobility Command (AMC) dispatches six C-5 Galaxies with 415 tons of engineering vehicles and supplies to combat severe flooding.

DECEMBER 15   England Air Force Base, Eaker Air Force Base, and George Air Force Base are ordered closed as a cost-cutting measure.

DECEMBER 16   The new McDonnell Douglas C-17 Globemaster III jet transport sets several world altitude records with payload.

A B-52 piloted by Captain Jeffrey R. Swegel, 668th Bomb Squadron, suddenly loses four engines on its left wing. By adroit flying two engines are restarted and the bomber makes a safe emergency landing; Swegel wins the Mackay Trophy for his efforts.

DECEMBER 27   Over Iraq, an F-16C shoots down an Iraqi MiG-25 Foxbat violating the UN no-fly zone; this is also the first aircraft destroyed by the new AIM-120 AMRAAM air-to-air missile, or "Slammer."

1993

JANUARY 1   At Falcon Air Force Base, Colorado, the 7th Space Operations Squadron is the first Reserve space unit activated.

JANUARY 3   President George H. W. Bush and President Boris Yeltsin of Russia conclude the second Strategic Arms Reduction Treaty (START II), which eliminates all multiple, independently targeted reentry vehicles (MIRV), and reduces the number of nuclear weapons bombers can carry.

JANUARY 13   Over Iraq, Air Mobility Command (AMC) transports convey forces to support SOUTHERN WATCH II, the no-fly zone near Kuwait and Saudi Arabia.

Air Force Major Susan J. Helms becomes the first U.S. military female in space when she enters orbit in the space shuttle *Endeavor*.

JANUARY 17   Over Iraq, an F-16 detects a MiG-23 and destroys it with an AIM-120 "Slammer" missile as it covers an F-4G Wild Weasel mission against Iraqi antiaircraft sites.

JANUARY 18   Over Iraq, F-4G Wild Weasels shoot back at an Iraqi missile site that fired upon them; F-16s also bomb an airfield whose antiaircraft gun had opened upon them.

In Zagreb, Croatia, a joint air operations cell arises to coordinate airlifting supplies by aircraft of the United States, the United Kingdom, Germany, France, and Canada.

FEBRUARY 2   Air Force transports deliver medical and humanitarian aid to Zagreb, Croatia, as ethnic fighting in the former region of Yugoslavia intensifies. Operation PROVIDE PROMISE will expand this effort with direct airdrops to Muslims fleeing a Serbian advance.

FEBRUARY 13–MARCH 9   Operation PROVIDE REFUGE commences as Air Mobility Command (AMC) transports fly supplies from Hawaii to Kwajalein Atoll to assist 535 Chinese sailors who defected after their vessel broke down.

FEBRUARY 19   The 64th Flying Training Wing introduces the new T-1A Jayhawk trainer to prospective student pilots.

FEBRUARY 28   Over eastern Bosnia, Operation PROVIDE PROMISE continues as transports of the 435th Airlift Wing airdrop supplies to Muslim refugees fleeing Serb forces.

MARCH 13–14   In Florida, the 301st Rescue Squadron dispatches helicopters to save 93 victims of heavy flooding brought about by a blizzard blanketing the Gulf Coast region.

MARCH 31   Operation DENY FLIGHT, a no-fly zone over Bosnia, is established by the United Nations. It becomes effective on April 5 and is aimed at limiting Serbian use of airplanes in the Bosnian civil war.

APRIL 19–24   In Siberia, aircraft of the Russian and U.S. air forces conduct joint rescue operations for the first time.

MAY 17–29   Over Cambodia, Air Mobility Command (AMC) C-5s and C-151s fly 24 missions conveying UN troops to supervise the first free elections held since 1970.

JUNE 11   Over Somalia, AC-130 Spectre gunships participate in Operation CONTINUE HOPE by attacking Somali warlords who had shelled UN ground forces on June 5.

JUNE 14   At Charleston Air Force Base, South Carolina, the first C-17A Globemaster IIIs are accepted by the 437th Airlift Wing. This is the first Air Force transport capable of hauling oversized cargo loads to relatively short, unprepared runways.

JUNE 17   At Minot Air Force Base, North Dakota, Lieutenant Colonel Patricia Fornes assumes control of the 740th Missile Squadron, becoming the first woman to command a combat missile unit.

JUNE 29   At Wright-Patterson Air Force Base, Ohio, the prototype OC-135B aircraft flies for the first time, being designed to function over nations participating in the Open Skies Treaty.

JULY 1   The new Air Education and Training Command (AETC) absorbs the Air Training Command (ATC) and the Air University (AU).

The Twentieth Air Force, which controls and monitors daily operations of the intercontinental ballistic missile force, falls under the purview of the Air Force Space Command (AFSPACECOM).

At Vandenberg Air Force Base, California, the Fourteenth Air Force is assigned missile warning and space surveillance missions under the aegis of the Air Force Space Command (AFSPACE-COM).

JULY 5–12   In Macedonia, transports of the Air Mobility Command (AMC) deliver Army troops and their equipment from Germany to bolster UN peacekeeping efforts there.

JULY 11–AUGUST 1   In the Midwest a huge flood inundates eight states along the Mississippi and Missouri rivers. Air Force C-5 and C-141 transports deliver 800 tons of relief equipment, including 1 million empty sandbags, to assist the residents.

AUGUST 6   In Washington, D.C., Dr. Sheila E. Widnall gains appointment as the secretary of the Air Force; she is the first woman to hold the position.

AUGUST 11–15   In Nepal, the 436th Airlift Wing dispatches three C-5 Galaxies to Nepal after floodwaters wash out several bridges; they convey 190 tons of bridge components made in England.

AUGUST 18   At White Sands Missile Range, New Mexico, Air Force Space and Missile Center (SMC) personnel observe the first launch of the Delta Clipper Experimental (DC-X) vertical takeoff and landing rocket.

OCTOBER 1   At Barksdale, Louisiana, the 93rd Bomber Squadron becomes the first Air Force Reserve unit to employ B-52 bombers.

OCTOBER 2–4   In Bombay, India, the Air Mobility Command dispatches two C-5 Galaxies carrying 1,000 rolls of plastic sheeting, 950 tents, and nearly 19,000 five-gallon water containers for survivors of recent earthquakes.

OCTOBER 3–4   In Mogadishu, Somalia, Air Force pararescueman Technical Sergeant Tim Wilkerson rescues and treats five wounded U.S. Army Rangers; he receives the Air Force Cross.

OCTOBER 5–13   Over Mogadishu, Somalia, Operation RESTORE HOPE II commences once Air Mobility Command (AMC) C-5s and C-141s deliver 18 Abrams tanks, 44 Bradley fighting vehicles, and 1,300 troops to bolster the American peacekeeping force.

OCTOBER 8   Over Bosnia, Operation PROVIDE HOPE is the Air Force's longest, most continuous airlift operation; it is surpassed only by the Berlin Airlift, 1948–1949.

NOVEMBER   Lieutenant Colonel Betty Mullis takes control of the 336th Air Refueling

Squadron, becoming the first woman to command an Air Force Reserve unit.

DECEMBER 2–13 At Cape Canaveral, Florida, the space shuttle *Endeavor* goes aloft under the command of Air Force Colonel Richard O. Covey. Its mission is to repair the $2 billion Hubble space telescope which is in need of a "contact lens" to correct its malformed main lens.

DECEMBER 8 In accordance with the 1991 Strategic Arms Reduction Treaty, the Air Force begins destroying the first of 450 Minuteman II missile silos.

DECEMBER 17 At Whiteman Air Force Base, Missouri, the first B-2A Spirit bomber, *The Spirit of Missouri*, deploys with the 393rd Bomb Squadron.

1994

JANUARY 4 At Rhein-Main Air Base, Germany, the 435th Airlift Wing dispatches a C-130 Hercules with relief supplies to Bosnia. This unit consists of both Reserve and Air National Guard members.

JANUARY 10 Off the coast of Iceland, HH-60G Pave Hawk helicopters Air Rescue 206 and 208, 56th Rescue Squadron, save six sailors from a stranded tugboat amidst heavy seas; they receive a Mackay Trophy.

JANUARY 13 At Soesterberg Air Base, the Netherlands, the last remaining F-15s of the 32nd Fighter Group depart, ending a 40-year American presence there.

JANUARY 17–25 C-5s and C-141s deliver 150 tons of relief supplies and 270 medical personnel after parts of Southern California are struck by a powerful earthquake.

FEBRUARY KC-135 tanker aircraft supporting Operation DENY FLIGHT in Bosnia receive permission to overfly French airspace for the first time in 20 years.

FEBRUARY 3 At Hondo Field, Texas, the Air Education and Training Command receives the first T-3A enhanced flight screening aircraft.

FEBRUARY 5 A crew from the 317th Airlift Squadron, an Air Force Reserve unit, checks out in a new C-17 Globemaster III for the first time.

After a Serbian mortar attack in Sarajevo kills 68 and injures 200, four C-130s are dispatched to fly the wounded to medical facilities in Germany.

FEBRUARY 7 The Air Force Space Command launches a Titan IV/Centaur rocket which hurls the first Military Strategic and Tactical Relay Satellite into orbit. This device enhances ready, secure communications around the world during any conflict.

FEBRUARY 10 Lieutenant Jeannie Flynn becomes the Air Force's first female F-15E-qualified fighter pilot.

FEBRUARY 18 At Spangdahlem Air Base, Germany, the last remaining F-4G Wild Weasels depart for Nellis Air Force Base, Nevada.

FEBRUARY 25 Bitburg Air Base, Germany, is closed by the Air Force, which begins transferring F-15s of the 53rd

Fighter Squadron over to Spangdahlem Air Base.

FEBRUARY 28   Over Bosnia-Herzegovina, Operation DENY FLIGHT heats up when an F-16 piloted by Lieutenant Robert Wright, 526th Fighter Squadron, spots four Serbian J-1 Super Galeb attack aircraft violating the "no-fly zone." He brings down three with Sidewinder and AIM-120 Slammer missiles while another F-16 downs the final Jastreb. The F-16's aerial record is now 69 kills and no losses. This is also NATO's first-ever military action.

MARCH   The new T-3A flight screening aircraft is ordered to replace the older T-41 Mescalero trainer, which has been in service with the Air Force since 1964.

This C-141 flight from Bujumbura, Burundi took on passengers who were fleeing from fighting in Rwanda. Evacuees were transported to the safety of Nairobi by USAF after they had been processed by the Marines in Burundi. (U.S. Department of Defense for Defense Visual Information)

At Edwards Air Force Base, California, an AGM-84 Harpoon antiship missile is fired by an F-16 for the first time.

MARCH 13   At Vandenberg Air Force Base, two military satellites are placed into orbit for the first time by a Taurus booster rocket.

MARCH 15   In Washington, D.C., after the director of the Smithsonian Air and Space Museum unveils plans to exhibit the B-29 *Enola Gay* as a prop in a politically correct revisionist diatribe, an public outcry from Congress, veterans groups, and the news media halts the attempt in its tracks; the director is subsequently fired for distorting national history.

MARCH 18   In California, Norton Air Force Base, which has served as an important aircraft repair depot for 52 years, is ordered shut down.

MARCH 25   In Somalia, an Air Force C-5 Galaxy departs, removing the last American military personnel still there and ending Operation RESTORE HOPE.

MARCH 31   Aviano Air Base, Italy, is upgraded to become a NATO main operating base.

In light of ongoing aerial operations over Bosnia, two F-16 fighters arrive there to support them.

APRIL   At Ellsworth Air Force Base, the final 150 Minuteman II missiles are removed to comply with the 1992 Strategic Arms Reduction treaty.

APRIL 6–12   In Africa, Operation DISTANT RUNNER commences as Air Force transports evacuate citizens and foreign nationals from Bujumbura, Burundi, to Nairobi, Kenya. A genocidal civil war has broken out.

APRIL 7   A Rockwell B-1B Lancer piloted by Captain Michael S. Menser sets a world speed record of 599.59 miles per hour by flying between Grand Forks Air Force Base, North Dakota, and Mullan, Idaho. Concurrently, a Lancer flown by Captain R. F. Lewandowski sets another speed record of 594.61 miles per hour over the same course.

APRIL 10   Over Bosnia, two Air Force F-16Cs destroy a Bosnian Serb Army command post near Gorazde in retaliation for an attack on UN personnel. This is also NATO's first air-to-ground attack, and the first close support mission of Operation DENY FLIGHT.

APRIL 14   Over northern Iraq, F-15C fighters of the 53rd Fighter Squadron misidentify and accidentally down two Army UH-60 Black Hawk helicopters in the northern no-fly zone, killing 15 Americans and 11 international observers. The pilots believed they were Russian-built Mi-24 Hind gunships of the Iraqi Air Force.

MAY 3   At Davis-Monthan Air Force Base, Arizona, the last operational B-52G is retired to the bone yard. However, the fan-jet powered B-52H continues serving into the 21st century.

MAY 6   At Tucson, Arizona, Lieutenant Leslie DeAnn Crosby becomes the first female Air Force Reserve fighter pilot once she passes through the F-16 RTU.

MAY 7–9   In Yemen, the outbreak of civil strife prompts six Air Mobility Command (AMC) transports to evacuate 623 citizens and foreign nationals to safety.

MAY 8   The Air Mobility Command (AMC) dispatches five C-141 Starlifters in support of Operation PROVIDE PROMISE in Bosnia. By July 26, they will deliver 7,000 tons of supplies.

MAY 11–17   From Turkey, Operation PROVIDE ASSISTANCE unfolds as Air Mobility Command (AMC) C-141 Starlifters convey 329 tons of supplies to thousands of refugees in Rwanda; they ultimately deliver 10,000 rolls of plastic sheeting and 100,000 blankets.

JUNE–SEPTEMBER   As raging forest fires consume 2 million acres throughout six Western states, Air Force Reserve and Air National Guard C-130 aircraft douse afflicted regions with 5 million gallons of fire retardant.

JUNE 3   At Edwards Air Force Base, California, a C-17 Globemaster III piloted by Major Andre A. Gerner establishes a record 44,088 pounds to 6,600 feet.

JUNE 22–30   In to Uganda, Air Mobility Command (AMC) C-5 Galaxies and C-141 Starlifters transport armored vehicles to assist UN peacekeeping forces in neighboring Rwanda.

JUNE 24   The Lockheed F-117 stealth bomber receives the official designation "Nighthawk." Previously, air crews referred to it as the "Wobblin' Goblin" and "Black Jet."

JUNE 26   In the Ukraine, a C-5 Galaxy of the 60th Military Airlift Wing carries a 34-ton magnetic resonance imaging system for victims of the 1986 nuclear accident at Chernobyl.

JUNE 30   In Berlin, Germany, Detachment I, 435th Airlift Wing, is deactivated 46 years after the famous Berlin Airlift.

JULY   The last production McDonnell Douglas F-15 Eagle is delivered to the Air Force.

After Tropical Storm Alberto ravages the Georgia coastline, aircraft of the 507th Air Refueling Group flies in 1,000 pounds of supplies to assist flood victims.

JULY 1 In Kansas, the 184th Bomb Group becomes the first Air National Guard (Kansas ANG) unit to fly B-1B Lancers.

The Air Combat Command (ACC) yields responsibility for the nation's nuclear ballistic missiles to the Air Force Space Command (AFSPACECOM), and now manages all missile warning, space surveillance, space launch, and satellite control functions.

JULY 21 Over Bosnia, small arms fire damages a C-141 Starlifter, and humanitarian operations are temporarily suspended. The aircraft returns to Rhein-Main Air Base, Germany, with 25 holes in its fuselage and wings.

At Ramstein Air Base, Germany, the Air Force transfers F-16s of the 86th Fighter Wing to Aviano Air Base, Italy, thereby concluding all fighter operations there.

JULY 24–OCTOBER 6 Over Zaire, Operation SUPPORT HOPE begins as Air Mobility Command (AMC) transports fly in humanitarian relief to thousands of refugees in nearby Rwanda. A total of 3,660 tons of supplies is delivered by aircraft from 22 airlift wings.

AUGUST 2 At Barksdale Air Force Base, Louisiana, two B-52s from the 2nd Bomb Wing circumnavigate the globe in 47.2 continuous hours and five aerial refuelings, setting a new world record. They then land in Kuwait on the fourth anniversary of the Iraqi invasion.

AUGUST 3 A B-52 launches a Pegasus rocket at high altitude, which then successfully places a satellite in Earth orbit.

AUGUST 4 Brigadier General Susan L. Pamerleau becomes the first female commander of the Air Force Reserve Officer Training Corps.

In Kansas, two B-1B Lancers from the 384th Bomb Group and the 184th Bomb Group (Kansas ANG), fly a 19-hour nonstop mission to Hawaii in another display of strategic air power.

AUGUST 5 Over Bosnia, after heavy weapons are stolen from a UN compound, two A-10 Thunderbolt IIs destroy a Serbian armored vehicle near Sarajevo in retaliation.

AUGUST 24–25 On Johnston Island, Pacific Ocean, Air Force transports evacuate over 1,000 people as a huge typhoon approaches.

AUGUST 31–SEPTEMBER 10 In Cuba, Operation SAFE HAVEN unfolds as the Air Force transports thousands of Cuban and Haitian refugees from crowded facilities at Guantanamo Bay to Panama.

SEPTEMBER 9 At Cape Canaveral, Florida, the space shuttle *Discovery* lifts off with a crew of four Air Force officers and two civilian technicians.

SEPTEMBER 19 In Haiti, Air Force transports supply logistical support throughout the life of Operation UPHOLD DEMOCRACY.

SEPTEMBER 26 At Poltava Air Base, Ukraine, a B-52 Stratofortess, a B-1B Lancer, and a KC-10 Extender make the first appearance of American warplanes since the shuttle-bombing missions of World War II.

OCTOBER 4 F-16 Falcons replace the few remaining F-4G Wild Weasel air defense suppression aircraft.

OCTOBER 10   In Kuwait, Operation VIGI-
LANT WARRIOR unfolds as Air Force warplanes arrive to deter possible Iraqi
aggression in the Persian Gulf region.
Within days the number of aircraft
increases from 77 to 270, including F-
15s, F-16s, and A-10s.

OCTOBER 14–16   At Langley Air Force
Base, Virginia, two C-17 Globemaster
IIIs perform their first logistical mission
by conveying military supplies to Saudi
Arabia. This 17.2-hour jaunt is also the
longest flight logged by C-17s to date.

OCTOBER 26   In Washington, D.C.,
General Ronald R. Fogleman gains
appointment as the Air Force chief of
staff; he is also the first Air Force Academy graduate to hold this position. Chief
Master Sergeant David J. Campanale also
becomes chief master sergeant of the Air
Force.

OCTOBER 30   At Vladivostok, Russia, a
C-141 Starlifter arrives, loaded with
20 tons of medical supplies, blankets, and
tarpaulins to assist flood victims.

OCTOBER 31–NOVEMBER 1   In Kuwait,
a pair of B-1B Lancers fly nonstop for
25 hours from Ellsworth Air Force Base,
North Dakota, to reach a bombing range.

This mission also marks the B-1's operational debut in the Persian Gulf region.

NOVEMBER 6–8   In Egypt, a pair of C-
141 Starlifters arrives with 37 tons of
relief goods to assist the victims of recent
flash flooding.

NOVEMBER 21–23   Over occupied
Croatia, NATO and the Air Force strike
Serbian airfields and missile sites at
Ubdina, in retaliation for a Serb attack
on Bihac.
      In Kazakhstan, Project SAPPHIRE unfolds
as two C-5 Galaxies remove 1,300
pounds of enriched uranium to Dover
Air Force Base, Delaware, for safekeeping
from terrorists.

DECEMBER 17–21   In Albania, the 94th
Air Lift Wing dispatches a C-130 Hercules loaded with clothing, furniture,
and beds to assist orphan shelters there.

DECEMBER 22   At Edwards Air Force
Base, the first of three Lockheed SR-71
Blackbirds arrives; they have been reacti-
vated for research purposes.

DECEMBER 29   Off the coast of Ireland,
the 56th Rescue Squadron dispatches
helicopters that save eight Dutch sailors
from their sinking vessel.

1995

JANUARY 17   The 17th Airlift Squadron
becomes the first Air Mobility Command
(AMC) unit equipped with the C-17
Globemaster III and placed on active duty.

JANUARY 19   At Yokota Air Base, Japan,
the 374th Airlift Wing begins humanitarian missions to assist earthquake victims in
southwestern Honshu.

FEBRUARY 1–20   In Panama, Operation
SAFE PASSAGE unfolds after Cuban refugees
riot in their camps and C-5 Galaxy, C-
141 Starlifter, and C-130 Hercules aircraft transport 7,300 passengers back to
Guantanamo Bay, Cuba.

FEBRUARY 3   At Cape Canaveral, Florida,
Air Force colonel/astronaut Eileen M.

Collins becomes the first female space shuttle commander during a mission on the *Discovery*.

FEBRUARY 7   Over Nellis Air Force Base, Nevada, a Northrop B-2A Spirit makes the first live bomb drop as part of a Red Flag exercise.

FEBRUARY 3–10   In Haiti, eight C-141 Starlifters transport 300 Nepalese troops as part of UN peacekeeping force there.

MARCH 5   At Malmstrom Air Force Base, Montana, Russian arms inspectors arrive to monitor the destruction of Minuteman II intercontinental ballistic missiles (ICBMs). Their visit is in accordance with terms of the recent Strategic Arms Reduction Treaty (START II).

MARCH 10   The 11th Space Warning Squadron is the first unit able to detect launching ballistic missiles in a given theater, and warn battlefield commanders of their approach.

MARCH 16   At Keflavik, Iceland, the 56th Rescue Squadron dispatches an HH-60 Pave Hawk helicopter to save three skiers marooned by a sudden blizzard.

MARCH 24   At Vandenberg Air Force Base, California, Air Force technicians launch the last remaining Atlas E booster rocket; it hoists a satellite into polar orbit.

MARCH 31   At Barksdale Air Force Base, Louisiana, Lieutenant Kelly Flinn becomes the first female bomber pilot in the U.S. Air Force when she commences training with the 11th Bomb Squadron, 2nd Bomb Wing.

APRIL 8   In Sarajevo, Bosnia, as Operation PROVIDE PROMISE continues, a C-130 transport is hit 12 times by small arms fire from the ground.

APRIL 27   The Air Force Space Command (AFSPACECOM) declares the Global Positioning System (GPS) operational. This device provides accurate geographical coordinates for both navigation and guided bomb delivery purposes.

MAY 8–11   In Louisiana, a deluge of rain results in Air National Guard units rescuing thousands of flood victims over a two-day period.

MAY 10–17   In Kinshasa, Zaire, transports of the 60th and 349th Airlift Wings deliver several tons of medical supplies in the wake a deadly Ebola virus outbreak in Central Africa.

MAY 25–26   Over Bosnia, NATO high command commits aircraft strikes against Serbian artillery emplacements shelling Sarajevo, Bosnia. Air Force F-16s drop precision-guided munitions on gun emplacements while Marine Corps jets bomb Serbian ammunition dumps near the town of Pale.

JUNE 1   At Palmdale, California, the Dark Star Tier III Minus high-altitude unmanned aerial vehicle (UAV) is rolled out by Lockheed Martin and Boeing.

JUNE 2–3   At Dyess Air Force Base, Texas, pair of B-1B Lancers flown by Lieutenant Colonel Doug Raaberg and Captain Gerald Goodfellow fly around the world in 36 hours, 13 minutes, and 36 seconds. Raaberg's plane also sets an official speed record of 631.16 miles per hour. En route, the bombers refuel six times, and drop bombs on three ranges on three continents and in two hemispheres; air crews win the Mackay Trophy.

JUNE 2–7   Over Banja Luka, Bosnia, an F-16C flown by Captain Scott O'Grady is shot down by Serbian antiaircraft fire. He spends six days evading capture by subsisting on insects and rainwater.

JUNE 22   In Washington, D.C., Air Force Secretary Sheila E. Widnall declares that Beechcraft will develop the Joint Primary Aircraft Training System (JPATS), a modified Swiss Pilatus PC-9 turboprop aircraft that will replace aging Cessna T-37Bs and Beech T-34Cs.

JUNE 27–JULY 7   The Lockheed Martin F-22 Raptor prototype, an advanced air superiority fighter, begins construction.

JUNE 28   In Washington, D.C., the Smithsonian Institution puts the B-29 *Enola Gay* on public display, in a factual and straightforward exhibit, devoid of political correctness.

JUNE 30–AUGUST 10   In Croatia, Operation QUICK LIFT unfolds as Air Mobility Command (AMC) C-5 Galaxies and C-141 Starlifters transport British and Dutch peacekeepers.

JULY 7–AUGUST 5   In Washington, D.C. , the Department of Defense declares that the C-17 Globemaster, whose spotty performance record threatened it with cancellation, has since been repaired to the effect that the Air Force is now willing to purchase 120 of the giant craft.

JULY 8   This day the Minuteman III intercontinental ballistic missile (ICBM) achieves 100 million hours of operational duty.

JULY 23   In Byelorussia, a C-5 Galaxy from the 433rd Airlift Wing conveys 20 tons of medical supplies, blankets, clothes, and other supplies to alleviate economic deprivation there.

JULY 29   At Nellis Air Force Base, Nevada, the 11th Reconnaissance Squadron is activated as a UAV unit and equipped with the Tier II Predator for operational testing purposes.

JULY 31   At Whiteman Air Force Base, Missouri, the 351st Missile Wing deactivates its final Minuteman II missile.

AUGUST 13   A C-5 Galaxy of the 60th Air Mobility Wing delivers 75 tons of food from Germany to Croatia to feed victims of the recent civil war there.

AUGUST 17   The E-8C joint surveillance target attack radar system (JSTARS) begins final flight-testing. These will replace pre-production models that saw extensive and successful service during the 1991 Gulf War.

AUGUST 20–21   At Ramstein Air Base, Germany, a C-5 Galaxy flies to Zagreb, Croatia, to assist refugees of the ongoing civil war.

AUGUST 25   At Edwards Air Force Base, California, a B-52H piloted by Captain Russell F. Mathers arrives from Barksdale AFB, Louisiana, setting a world record of 549.45 miles per hour over a 6,200-mile course. They were airborne for 11 hours, 23 minutes.

AUGUST 25–29   In Kuwait, 11 new C-17 Globemaster IIIs of the 315th and 437th Airlift Wings haul 300 tons of troops and equipment; this is also their first major exercise as an operational unit.

AUGUST 31   Over Sarajevo, Bosnia, Air Force, Navy, Marine Corps, and NATO warplanes attack Serbian targets, including

US Air Force personnel from the 14th Airlift Squadron unload cargo from a C-17 Globemaster III aircraft at the Kuwait City International Airport, Kuwait during Operation Intrinsic Action, *1995. (U.S. Department of Defense for Defense Visual Information)*

air defense systems, ammunition dumps, and equipment storage facilities. A 24-hour suspension of aerial activities then ensues to encourage peace negotiations with recalcitrant Serbian leaders.

SEPTEMBER 1   The Air Combat Command (ACC) reactivates its remaining SR-71 Blackbird reconnaissance aircraft to resume missions previously handled by satellites.

SEPTEMBER 5   In Bosnia, peace negotiations between NATO and Serbian leaders break down, and air strikes of Operation DELIBERATE FORCE resume in full fury against remaining targets.

SEPTEMBER 6   Over Bosnia, an Air Force F-16C from the 23rd Fighter Squadron destroys a Serbian SA-6 radar site with a combination HARM (High-Speed Anti-Radiation) Targeting Pod System and an AGM-88 missile.

SEPTEMBER 7   Over Bosnia, Air Force and NATO warplanes deliver six strike packages against integrated targets, including six bridges and one chokepoint.

SEPTEMBER 8   In northwest Bosnia-Herzegovina, Operation DELIBERATE FORCE begins planning additional strike packages using standoff missiles against the Serbian integrated air defense system (IADS).

SEPTEMBER 9   Over Bosnia, three strike packages are flown against Serb targets using HARM missiles and 2,000-pound GBU-15 precision-guided glide bombs.

SEPTEMBER 10   In northwestern Bosnia, Air Force, Navy, Marine Corps, and NATO forces use Tomahawk Land Attack Missiles (TLAM), HARM, and other standoff ordnance to strike down Serbian antiaircraft defenses. Other sorties support UN positions near the Tulza airport that are being shelled.

At Eglin Air Force Base, Florida, the C-130 Hercules dubbed *First Lady*, which was the first production model accepted into the Air Force back in 1955, is finally retired as a museum exhibit.

SEPTEMBER 11   Over Bosnia, Operation DELIBERATE FORCE continues with four strike packages planned and delivered under favorable weather conditions. Reconnaissance efforts are also increased to provide accurate bomb damage assessments (BDA).

SEPTEMBER 14   Serbian factions finally come to terms with UN negotiators, and the NATO commander orders a halt to all aerial offensive operations in Bosnia.

SEPTEMBER 14–30   In Hanoi, Vietnam, transports of the Air Mobility Command (AMC) deliver 30 tons of medical supplies; this is the first American military visit to Vietnam since the war ended in 1975.

SEPTEMBER 15–21   Throughout the eastern Caribbean, Air Force, Reserve, and National Guard transports are mobilized in the wake of Hurricane Marilyn to bring relief aid. C-17 Globemaster IIIs also perform their first disaster relief effort.

SEPTEMBER 20   In Bosnia, Operation DELIBERATE FORCE formally concludes, having forced tough and professional Serb forces from their positions with air power alone.

SEPTEMBER 22   At Elmendorf Air Force Base, Alaska, an E-3B AWACS jet crashes on takeoff when two geese are ingested by the engines; all 24 crew members are killed, including 2 Canadians. This is also the first AWACS accident in 18 years of operation.

Two U.S. Air Force F-16C Fighting Falcon aircraft prepare to take off. This high-performance, light-weight fighter has been exported to several nations around the world and will continue serving well into the 21st century. (U.S. Department of Defense Visual Information Center)

SEPTEMBER 30 Castle Air Force Base, California, and Plattsburgh Air Force Base, New York, both former Strategic Air Command (SAC) bases, are closed down. The 93rd Bombardment Group, the first Air Force unit to operate B-52s, also deactivates after 47 years of service.

OCTOBER At Marietta, Georgia, the first C-130J Hercules, an advanced technology version, rolls off the assembly line; this is instantly recognizable by its six-bladed propellers.

OCTOBER 1 Chief Master Sergeant Carol Smits becomes the first woman selected as senior enlisted adviser in the Air Force Reserve.

At Shaw Air Force Base, South Carolina, the Air Combat Command activates the 609th Information Warfare Squadron.

These troops are in Bosnia in support of Operation Joint Endeavor. Operation Joint Endeavor is a peacekeeping effort by a multinational Implementation Force (IFOR), comprised of NATO and non-NATO military forces, deployed to Bosnia in support of the Dayton Peace Accords. (U.S. Department of Defense for Defense Visual Information)

OCTOBER 16–17 In the Gulf of Mexico, the 53rd Weather Reconnaissance Squadron dispatches aircraft to search for survivors of a Mexican pipe-laying barge that sank during Hurricane Roxanne. A single crewman is spotted and his location is relayed to the Coast Guard, who ultimately rescue 23 people.

OCTOBER 28–DECEMBER 18 In Bahrain, Operation VIGILANT SENTINEL unfolds as F-16Cs of the 20th and 357th Fighter Wings deploy quickly and en masse. This is also the first test of the air expeditionary force concept.

NOVEMBER 1 At Wright-Patterson Air Force Base, Croatian, Bosnian, and Serbian delegates meet to conclude a formal peace agreement. These are all former states of the by now defunct Yugoslavia.

NOVEMBER 2 Lieutenant Colonel Greg Feest is the first Air Force pilot to acquire 1,000 hours of flight time in the F-117A Nighthawk stealth fighter.

DECEMBER In Washington, D.C., New World Vistas, a forecast of air and space technology, is unveiled by Dr. Gene McCall of the Air Force Scientific Advisory Board (SAB). This study was commissioned by Secretary of the Air Force Dr. Sheila Widnall and Air Force Chief of Staff Ronald R. Fogleman.

DECEMBER 6 In Bosnia, Operation JOINT ENDEAVOR commences as Air Mobility Command (AMC) C-130 transports from the 37th Airlift Squadron deliver American peacekeeping troops and equipment. They arrive in anticipation of a comprehensive peace treaty previously arranged at Wright-Patterson Air Force Base.

DECEMBER 20   In Washington, D.C., the Air Force declares that its manpower levels have dipped below the 400,000 level for the first time since 1948.

1996

JANUARY 9   Over Bosnia-Herzegovina, Operation PROVIDE PROMISE begins coming to an end; Air Force transports have flown 4,597 sorties and delivered 62,000 metric tons of cargo to numerous refugees throughout the region. This is the longest sustained humanitarian airlift in aviation history.

FEBRUARY 14   Over the Balkans, the E-8A JSTARS aircraft flies its 50th mission in support of Operation JOINT ENDEAVOR; this is a highly advanced, joint surveillance and target attack radar aircraft.

FEBRUARY 24   The space shuttle *Endeavor*, commanded by Air Force colonel John H. Casper, completes a 10-day mission after spending 240 hours and 39 minutes in space and completing 160 Earth orbits.

MARCH 29   At Edwards Air Force Base, California, the Tier III Minus Dark Star unmanned aerial vehicle (UAV) flies for the first time. This is intended as a stealthy, jet-propelled reconnaissance system, but only five are built before the program is cancelled.

APRIL 3   Outside Dubrovnik, Croatia, an Air Force CT-43 transport jet from the 76th Airlift Squadron crashes into a mountain, killing Secretary of Commerce Ron Brown and 34 passengers.

APRIL 9–25   Over Monrovia, Liberia, Operation ASSURED RESPONSE commences as Air Force AC-130s, MC-130s, C-130s, and MH-53J Pave Low helicopters execute 94 missions to evacuate 2,000 citizens and foreign nationals.

APRIL 15   At Randolph Air Force Base, Texas, Navy and Air Force navigator trainees will jointly study in a single class for the first time.

APRIL 18   In Sierra Leone, Africa, a pair of C-17 Globemaster IIIs convey two MH-53J Pave Low helicopters to England, at a considerable savings in time and expense had they flown under their own power.

APRIL 30   The top secret Tacit Blue aircraft is publicly revealed for the first time; this formed the basis of the B-2A Spirit stealth bomber.

MAY 1   At Holloman Air Force Base, New Mexico, a German officer takes charge of the German tactical training center; this is the first time that a foreign officer commands a foreign unit within the United States.

MAY 31   The Air Force signs a $16.2 billion contract to purchase 80 additional C-17 Globemaster III transports. This is the most costly military order ever placed, bringing the total number of C-17s acquired to 120. These aircraft also allow the aging C-141 Starlifters to be phased out.

JUNE 6   Lieutenant Colonel Kai Lee Norwood assumes control of the 91st Logistic Group, becoming the first woman commander of a unit responsible for maintaining Air Force missiles.

JUNE 11   The Air Force accepts delivery of the first production Boeing E-8 JSTARS aircraft. Previously, several pre-production models had demonstrated their utility during Operations DESERT STORM and JOINT ENDEAVOR.

JUNE 21   At Randolph Air Force Base, Texas, Navy commander David J. Cheslak assumes control of the 562nd Flying Training Squadron. He becomes the first naval officer to lead an Air Force unit, which, in this instance, is responsible for training navigators for both services.

JUNE 25   At Dhahran, Saudi Arabia, a terrorist bomb explodes outside the Khobar Towers, killing 19 airmen and injuring hundreds of passersby.

JULY 27   At Fort Worth, Texas, the Air Force retires its last General Dynamics F-111s from active duty, ironically at the same plant where the first model was accepted 30 years earlier. The final unit operating F-111s, the 524th Fighter Squadron at Cannon Air Force Base, New Mexico, is reequipped with F-16 Falcons. The nickname Aardvark, which had been the unofficial moniker for the F-111 for years, also gains official status.

SEPTEMBER 3   The Air Combat Command (ACC) activates the 11th Reconnaissance Squadron as the first unit to operate RQ-1B Predators, an unmanned aerial vehicle (UAV). These are initially deployed to monitor the peace agreement in Bosnia.

SEPTEMBER 3–4   Over Iraq, Operation DESERT STRIKE commences following Iraqi seizure of the city of Ibril. Consequently, two B-52Hs depart Guam, fly to the Middle East, and launch 13 cruise missiles against antiaircraft and command and control centers. The mission requires the assistance of 29 tanker aircraft and wins the crew of Duke 01 the Mackay Trophy; this is also the first combat mission of the B-52H.

SEPTEMBER 3   Over Bosnia-Herzegovina, the 11th Reconnaissance Squadron becomes the first Air Force unit operating the new RQ-1 Predator unmanned aerial

A Crew Chief from the 9th Fighter Squadron salutes the pilot of a F-117 Nighthawk aircraft after final checks prior to takeoff for Operation Desert Strike against Iraqi air defense forces. (U.S. Department of Defense for Defense Visual Information)

vehicle (UAV). They help enforce peace treaty provisions.

SEPTEMBER 4 At Bujumbura, Burundi, a C-141 Starlifter from the 305th Air Mobility Wing arrives from McGuire Air Force Base to help evacuate 30 foreign nationals during a period of civil strife.

SEPTEMBER 14 In Bosnia-Herzegovina, Air Force security personnel are on hand to help provide security during the first free elections since their civil war.

SEPTEMBER 15–19 In northern Iraq, Operation PACIFIC HAVEN unfolds as Air Force transports convey two thousand Kurdish refugees to Andersen Air Force Base, Guam, for processing prior to settling in the United States.

SEPTEMBER 30 In Western Europe, the Seventeenth Air Force is inactivated after four decades of service.

OCTOBER 8 Over the Nellis Air Force Base Range, Nevada, three Northrop B-2A Spirit bombers score 16 hits on 16 targets using the live Global Position System-Aided Targeting System. The aircraft were dropping 2,000-pound bombs from 41,000 feet.

OCTOBER 21 Over Eglin Air Force Base, Florida, an F-16C Fighting Falcon successfully conducts the first guided launch of a GBU-31 Joint Direct Attack Munition (JDAM). The 2,000-pound bomb, released

from 20,000 feet, was partially guided by the Global Positioning System (GPS) and its own internal navigation system.

OCTOBER 22 Operational control of all C-130 Hercules transports and Learjet C-21 liaison craft in the United States is transferred from the Air Combat Command (ACC) to the Air Mobility Command (AMC), although aircraft deployed in Europe and the Pacific remain under their respective local commands.

NOVEMBER 5 In Washington, D.C., Chief Master Sergeant Eric W. Benken gains appointment as chief master sergeant of the Air Force.

NOVEMBER 21 In Washington, D.C., Secretary of the Air Force Dr. Sheila Widnall releases the policy projection paper Global Reach, Global Power, to the public. This far-sighted work conceptualizes Air Force power into the next century.

NOVEMBER 26 At Elgin Air Force Base, Florida, the first armed test of a GBU-31 Joint Direct Attack Munition (JDAM) transpires as an F-16C releases one from 20,000 feet; although the target was obscured by heavy cloud cover, the bomb fell within 9.2 meters of the target.

DECEMBER 4 At Hill Air Force Base, Utah, an F-16C piloted by Captain Kurt Gallegos, 388th Fighter Wing, flies the 5 millionth hour in the Air Force's Fighting Falcon fleet.

1997

JANUARY 1 In northern Iraq, Operation NORTHERN WATCH supersedes Operation PROVIDE COMFORT to enforce no-fly zone conditions north of the 36th north latitude line.

At Beale Air Force Base, California, two SR-71 Blackbirds are declared operational by the 9th Strategic Reconnaissance Wing.

The top secret machines had recently been brought out of retirement.

JANUARY 6 Abdullah Hamza Al-Mubarak is the first Muslim chaplain commissioned by the U.S. Air Force.

JANUARY 31 The Air Force activates the 31st Air Expeditionary Wing (AEW) as the first operational unit of its kind. This formation can be deployed or rotated anywhere around the world with little delay.

FEBRUARY 17 The Air Force Reserve is upgraded to the status of a major command within the Air Force and receives the new designation Air Force Reserve Command.

FEBRUARY 18–MARCH 3 In Liberia, Operation ASSURED LIFT commences as five C-130s of the 37th Airlift Squadron land 1,160 soldiers and 450 tons of cargo from several neighboring African nations to assist peacekeeping operations.

FEBRUARY 20 In San Diego, California, the Teledyne Ryan Aeronautical plant rolls out its first Global Hawk long-range reconnaissance unmanned aerial vehicle (UAV).

MARCH 17 In Zaire, Operation GUARDIAN RETRIEVAL commences as aircraft of the Special Operations Command (SOC) and Air Mobility Command (AMC) evacuate 532 individuals threatened by civil unrest. The mission requires 57 sorties and employs a variety of aircraft and helicopters.

APRIL 1 At Whiteman Air Force Base, Missouri, the 509th Bomb Wing is the first operational B-2 Spirit unit; they currently deploy six bombers.

All C-130 transports deployed in the continental United States with the Air Combat Command (ACC) are hereafter assigned to the Air Mobility Command (AMC).

APRIL 4 At Vandenberg Air Force Base, California, a Titan IIG rocket lifts a Defense Meteorological Satellite Program satellite into a polar orbit. This also constitutes the first time that a converted ICBM has been used as a launch vehicle.

APRIL 9 At Marietta, Georgia, the first production Lockheed Martin/Boeing F-22 Raptor, *Spirit of America*, rolls out of the factory in front of 3,000 attendees. This aircraft reflects doctrinal changes in Air Force thinking, from air superiority to air dominance.

APRIL 22–25 In Las Vegas, Nevada, Air Force Fifty, the 50th Anniversary of the U.S. Air Force's founding, unfolds with a meeting of all Global Air Chiefs; the event is capped off by an impressive air show at nearby Nellis Air Force Base.

MAY 12 At Zhukovsky, Russia, a group of U.S. Air Force test pilots from Edwards Air Force Base, California, visit the Russian Air Force Flight Test Facility at the Gromov Flight Research Institute for the first time. The Americans each get an orientation flight in a MiG-29 fighter.

MAY 17 Over Edwards Air Force Base, California, the Douglas X-36 remotely piloted research aircraft is successfully tested for the first time. This is a tailless, high angle of attack fighter drone.

JUNE 10 In England, the Air Force Special Operations Command directs an MC-130H Combat Talon II from the 352nd Special Operations Squadron to convey a European political survey crew into Brazzaville, Republic of Congo, then in the throes of political instability. They depart RAF Mildenhall, Great Britain, and ensuing flight lasts 13 hours, involves three aerial refuelings, and covers 3,179 nautical miles. Braving ground fire from rebels, the team lands, deposits their charge, and extracts 56 people from danger. Lieutenant Colonel Frank J. Kisner and his crew receive a Mackay Trophy.

JUNE 24 The Air Force issues a report entitled "The Roswell Report: Case Closed" to refute assertions that it is involved in a cover-up related to a 1947 UFO crash. However comprehensive, it fails to silence critics, who continue accusing the Air Force and government of a cover up.

JULY 28–AUGUST 1 Over the United States, a Russian Antonov An-30 transport conducts a practice overflight from the Open Skies Treaty to monitor information about military forces. Twenty-seven countries are signatories, but Russia, Belarus, and the Ukraine have yet to ratify the treaty.

SEPTEMBER 1 In Washington, D.C., General Ralph Eberhart gains appointment as temporary Air Force chief of staff to replace the retiring General Ronald R. Fogleman.

SEPTEMBER 7 At Dobbins Air Reserve Base, Georgia, the F-22 Raptor flies for the first time. This aircraft is intended to gradually replace F-15 Eagles after a four-year test program.

SEPTEMBER 12 At Maxwell Air Force Base, Alabama, Air University introduces the Air and Space Basic Course.

SEPTEMBER 14–15 Over Kazakhstan, C-17 Globemasters arrive nonstop from Pope Air Force Base, North Carolina, and airdrop 500 men from the Army's 82nd Airborne Division to participate in an exercise dubbed CENTRAZBAT '97. The 19-hour flight required three in-flight refuelings.

OCTOBER 6 In Washington, D.C., General Michael E. Ryan gains appointment as the 16th chief of staff, U.S. Air Force.

OCTOBER 12 In Indonesia, three C-130s of the 153rd Airlift Wing, Wyoming Air National Guard, arrive to help fight fires. They convey the Modular Airborne Fire Fighting System, capable of dropping 3,000 gallons of water or flame retardant per aerial sortie.

NOVEMBER 1 In Washington, D.C., F. Whitten Peters gains appointment as acting secretary of the Air Force.

DECEMBER 18 After a seven-year gestation, the Joint Stars airborne communication and monitoring system is declared operational.

DECEMBER 27–JANUARY 4 At Andersen Air Force Base, Guam, the Air Mobility Command (AMC) dispatches C-5s, C-141s, C-130s, and KC-135s with 2.5 million pounds of relief supplies in the wake of Typhoon Paka.

1998

FEBRUARY 11 At China Lake, California, a Joint Direct Attack Munition (JDAM) is

dropped by a B-1B Lancer for the first time. This is a 2,000-pound conventional bomb fitted with a highly accurate satellite guidance system.

FEBRUARY 28 At Edwards Air Force Base, California, the Teledyne Ryan Company RQ-4 Global Hawk unmanned aerial vehicle (UAV) flies for the first time. This jet-propelled device is a reconnaissance platform capable of reaching 65,000 feet and photographing an area as large as Kentucky in under 24 hours.

MARCH 23–APRIL 3 On Guam, the B-2A Spirit stealth bomber makes its first overseas deployment from the United States, proving its capacity for global operations.

MAY 27 Over Mount Torbert, Alaska, the 210th Rescue Squadron Alaska (ANG) dispatches a Guard HH-60 Pave Hawk helicopter to save six surveyors trapped in an airplane that had crashed on a glacier. The crew, braving extreme wind and temperature, safely extracts the passengers, winning a Mackay Trophy.

MAY 29 The Air Force transfers primary control of the Defense Meteorological Satellite Program to the National Oceanic and Atmospheric Institute. This constitutes the first transfer of an operational space system to a civilian agency.

SEPTEMBER 22 Destructive Hurricane George induces Air Force transports to deliver food and medical supplies to victims on Puerto Rico, the Dominican Republic, and along coastal Mississippi.

NOVEMBER 6 After powerful Hurricane Mitch cuts a swath of destruction through Central America, Air Force transports convey 3,500 tons of relief supplies in 200 sorties that last until March 1999.

DECEMBER 9 In Washington, D.C., Benjamin O. Davis attends ceremonies commemorating receipt of his honorary fourth star on the retired list. During World War II, he commanded the legendary Tuskegee Airmen.

DECEMBER 16–20 Over Iraq, Operation DESERT FOX commences in retaliation for Iraqi obstruction and deceit in connection with a UN arms inspection mission. Consequently, the Air Combat Command (ACC) contributes several B-1B Lancers, this being their combat debut in the Persian Gulf.

1999

FEBRUARY 17 At Keesler Air Force Base, Mississippi, the 403rd Wing accepts delivery of the first Lockheed C-130J, a high-tech version mounting six-bladed propellers.

MARCH 24–JUNE 10 Over Kosovo, Air Force and NATO warplanes commence Operation NOBLE ANVIL to halt Serbian forces committing "ethnic cleansing." This is the largest aerial offensive in Europe since World War II, and aims to stop Serbs under President Slobodan Milosevic from further atrocities. American aircraft constitute 723 out of 1,023 aircraft involved. This also witnesses the combat debut of the B-2 Spirit bomber. On the first day of the campaign, an F-16C piloted by Captain Jeffrey G. J. Hwang shoots down a pair of Serbian MiG-29s with new AIM-120 AMRAAM missiles in one quick action, winning a Mackay Trophy.

MARCH 27 Over Kosovo, a Lockheed F-117 stealth fighter is downed by Serbian missiles, but the pilot is rescued after being spotted by A-10 pilot Captain John A. Cherrey; Cherrey receives a Silver Star for his assistance.

APRIL 4 In Tirana, Albania, Operation SUSTAIN HOPE unfolds as Air Mobility Command (AMC) C-17 Globemaster IIIs fly 3,000 tons of relief supplies from Dover Air Force Base, Delaware, to refugees in Kosovo.

APRIL 8 Over Serbia, Air Force and NATO aircraft begin around-the-clock bombing sorties to convince President Slobodan Milosevic to withdraw from Kosovo.

APRIL 17 Over Serbia, the unmanned RQ-1 Predator drone performs its first known combat operation by firing a Copperhead missile.

MAY 1 The Air Force Reserve Command mobilizes its first tanker wing for active duty, this being the first of five wings facing activation over the next nine months.

In Kosovo, a Serbian bus plunges off a bridge recently bombed by NATO aircraft; there are 47 fatalities. By this point in Operation ALLIED FORCE, the American sortie rate has reached 150 per day.

MAY 2 Over Serbia, an F-16 is downed by ground fire, although the pilot is rescued by an MH-60 helicopter. This is the second and final aircraft lost during Operation ALLIED FORCE.

MAY 4 Over Kosovo, an F-16C pilot shoots down a MiG-29; this is the final Air Force victory of Operation ALLIED FORCE.

MAY 7 In Belgrade, Serbia, ordnance fired by a B-2A Spirit stealth bomber accidently strikes the Chinese embassy, killing three. The problem was incorrect coordinates provided by headquarters. Massive demonstrations break out in China as a result.

JUNE 10–JULY 6 Over Kosovo, Air Force and NATO air raids are suspended as Serbian forces begin withdrawing. This is also the first military campaign won by air power alone.

JULY 23–27 At Cape Canaveral, Florida, Colonel Eileen M. Collins becomes the first woman to command a space shuttle flight when she lifts off with the *Columbia*. The Chandra X-Ray Observatory is placed in orbit during this mission.

JULY 30 In Washington, D.C., F. Whitten Peters is named secretary of the Air Force in full capacity. Chief Master Sergeant Frederick J. Finch also gains appointment as chief master sergeant of the Air Force.

SEPTEMBER 20 In Dili, East Timor, aircraft of the Air Mobility Command (AMC) begin transporting Australian peacekeeping forces to restore stability to that island.

OCTOBER 1 Aerospace Expeditionary Force 1 is sent to Southwest Asia for the first time. This new system is designed to permit more effective deployments around the world while also rendering them more predictable to increase unit morale.

At Lackland Air Force Base, Texas, "Warrior Week" is initiated by the Air Education and Training Command to grant basic trainees a glimpse of the Aerospace Expeditionary Force concept. This also constitutes the biggest change in military training in half-a-century.

OCTOBER 6   At Langdon, North Dakota, 150 Minutemen III silos are destroyed in accordance with the Strategic Arms Reduction Treaty (START II) with Russia.

NOVEMBER 2   In the Panama Canal Zone, Howard Air Base is relinquished by American authorities; this had been an active airfield for the past 82 years.

DECEMBER 20–28   In Venezuela, Air Mobility Command (AMC) C-5, C-141, and C-130 transports convey humanitarian aid supplies to assist 200,000 victims of severe flooding.

2000

MARCH 2   In Mozambique, Operation ATLAS RESPONSE commences as Air Mobility Command (AMC) transports deliver humanitarian relief supplies from bases in Europe.

MAY 3   In Europe, General Joseph W. Ralston gains appointment as the supreme allied commander of the North Atlantic Treaty Organization (NATO); he is the first Air Force officer in 37 years to hold that position.

MAY 8   At Cape Canaveral, Florida, a Titan IVB rocket hurls a Defense Support Program (DSP) satellite into orbit. These function as early warning missile launching detection systems with global coverage.

MAY 23   At Randolph Air Force Base, Texas, the first production T-6A Texan II turboprop trainer deploys; it will replace the Cessna T-37 and Beech T-34 as a primary pilot training aircraft.

JULY 15   At Whiteman Air Force Base, Missouri, the final production B-2 Spirit bomber arrives for service. The Air Force will not add new heavy bombers to its inventory until 2035.

JULY 25   At Fort Worth, Texas, Bell Textron rolls out the Air Force CV-22 Osprey tilt rotor aircraft, which is modified for special operations.

SEPTEMBER 18   At Edwards Air Force Base, California, the first Air Force CV-22 Osprey arrives for testing. This hybrid design lifts off and lands like a helicopter, but flies like a regular airplane.

SEPTEMBER 27   At St. Louis, Missouri, the Boeing XB-45A unmanned air combat vehicle is unveiled to the public for the first time.

OCTOBER 15   At Norfolk, Virginia, aircraft from the 75th Airlift Squadron and the 86th Aeromedical Evacuation Squadron fly 28 victims of the *Cole* bombing from Yemen, a 6,000-mile trip; they receive a Mackay Trophy.

OCTOBER 24   At Palmdale, California, the new Lockheed Martin XF-35A Joint Strike Fighter, the world's most advanced warplane, performs its maiden flight by flying to Edwards Air Force Base for testing.

OCTOBER 27   In Tampa, Florida, General Charles R. Holland gains appointment as commander of the U.S. Special Operations Command; he is the first Air Force officer to hold this post.

NOVEMBER 22 At Edwards Air Force Base, California, Lieutenant Colonel Paul Smith flies the XF-35A Joint Strike Fighter (JSF) at supersonic speeds to 34,000 feet for the first time. This craft is then returned to the factory at Palmdale to begin conversion into the XF-35B short takeoff and landing (STOL) version.

2001

JANUARY 11 In Washington, D.C., a Congressional Space Commission report recommends that the Air Force receive increased responsibilities and increased organizational realignments.

JANUARY 20 In Washington, D.C., Lawrence J. Delaney becomes acting secretary of the Air Force.

JANUARY 22–26 "Schriever 2001," the first war game to include elements of space control, including countering hostile space capabilities, is conducted by the Air Force Space Command Warfare Center.

FEBRUARY 3 In India, Air Mobility Command (AMC) C-17 Globemaster IIIs convey relief supplies and food to victims of a recent earthquake. They are refueled while traversing the Pacific and Indian Oceans by KC-135s.

FEBRUARY 21 At Nellis Air Force Base, Nevada, an RQ-1 Predator pilotless drone has been modified to carry a Hellfire C missile, which it then fires to destroy a target. This becomes the first unmanned aerial vehicle (UAV) to do so.

FEBRUARY 24 At March Air Force Base, California, Lieutenant Colonel Stayce D. Harris takes control of the 729th Airlift Squadron, becoming the first African American woman to command an Air Force unit.

APRIL 22–23 At Edwards Air Force Base, California, the RQ-4 Global Hawk flies nonstop to Adelaide, Australia. This is the first transoceanic flight by an unmanned aerial vehicle and it covers 7,500 miles in 23 hours, a new world's record.

MAY 7 Off the China coast, an RC-135 aircraft from Kadena Air Base, Okinawa, resumes intelligence flights in international airspace.

MAY 8 In Washington, D.C., the Secretary of Defense declares that the Air Force has the sole executive control over the Pentagon's activities in space.

JUNE 1 In Washington, D.C., James G. Roche gains appointment as the new secretary of the Air Force.

JUNE 5 Major General James E. Sherrard, III, the Air Force Reserve commander, gains his third star to lieutenant general. He advocates a "total force" concept closely integrating Reserves into the regular Air Force.

JULY 13 Historic Kelly Air Force Base, Texas, the cradle of American military aviation, and McClellan Air Force Base, California, are closed due to budget cuts.

AUGUST 6 At Edwards Air Force Base, California, the XF-35B returns to Palmdale, signaling the end of another successful round of flight-testing. En route the aircraft reaches 34,000 feet at Mach 1.2, and sustains it for 3.7 hours, the longest flight of the test program so far.

AUGUST 24 At Minot Air Force Base, North Dakota, another Cold War milestone passes as the final Minuteman III missile silo, which formed the bulwark of American nuclear deterrence for three decades, is destroyed.

SEPTEMBER 6 In Washington, D.C., General John P. Jumper gains appointment as Air Force chief of staff.

SEPTEMBER 19 Lockheed Martin contracts with the Air Force to produce an initial production batch of 10 ultramodern F-22 Raptors.

SEPTEMBER 27 In Washington, D.C., Secretary of War Donald Rumsfeld declares that President George W. Bush has authorized military aircraft to shoot down commercial liners hijacked in American airspace if an emergency presents itself.

SEPTEMBER 29 At the Kodiak Launch Complex, Alaska, the Air Force launches its first space satellite. Heretofore, all space launches were from either Florida or California.

OCTOBER In Afghanistan, the Air Force and CIA begin operations against the Taliban with unmanned, remotely guided RQ-1 Predator aircraft. These high-flying drones are armed with television cameras and deadly Hellfire missiles.

OCTOBER 1 In Washington, D.C., General Richard B. Myers becomes the first Air Force officer to serve as chairman of the Joint Chiefs of Staff (JCS) in almost 20 years.

The Air Materiel Space and Missile System Center are now subordinated to the Air Force Space Command (AFSPACECOM). The latter organization now monopolizes all Air Force space concerns.

OCTOBER 7 Over Afghanistan, Operation ENDURING FREEDOM begins as United States and British warplanes begin a concerted aerial campaign to drive the Taliban and al-Qaeda from power. Lieutenant General Charles F. Wald is also the Joint Force Air Component Commander throughout this operation.

At Whiteman Air Force Base, Missouri, B-2 Spirit bombers of the 509th Bomb Wing fly to Afghanistan and back during the longest bombing mission in aviation history.

OCTOBER 8 Over Afghanistan, C-17 Globemaster IIIs perform their first combat mission by airdropping pallets of humanitarian daily rations to territory controlled by the Northern Alliance.

Coalition aircraft begin around-the-clock air strikes against Taliban positions throughout Afghanistan. This enables the Northern Alliance to counterattack.

OCTOBER 26 The Department of Defense awards the Lockheed Martin Corporation with a contract to develop the new and highly advanced F-35 Joint Strike Fighter (JSF) while Pratt and Whitney will develop the engine. This new aircraft will be deployed by Air Force, Navy, and Marine units.

OCTOBER 28–NOVEMBER 4 Over Afghanistan, coalition aircraft switch from bombing fixed assets of the Taliban and al-Qaeda, to front-line units opposing the Northern Alliance.

NOVEMBER 2   In Afghanistan, the crew of an MH-53J Pave Low helicopter of the 20th Special Operations Squadron lands behind enemy lines to rescue the crew of another MH-53 that crashed; they receive a Mackay Trophy.

NOVEMBER 28   Near Kandahar, Afghanistan, Operation SWIFT FREEDOM unfolds as Air Mobility Command (AMC) C-17 Globemaster III transports convey Army and Special Forces troops to an airstrip.

DECEMBER 4   Over Afghanistan, coalition aircraft bomb the mountain refuge of Tora Bora, a heavily fortified cave complex 55 miles south of Jalalabad, which holds an estimated 2,000 al-Qaeda Arab fighters.

DECEMBER 5   In Afghanistan, a 2,000-pound bomb dropped by a B-52 accidently strikes an American command post, killing three Special Forces soldiers and five Afghan allies. These are the first American fatalities of Operation ENDURING FREEDOM.

DECEMBER 12   Over the Indian Ocean, the destroyer *Russell* rescues the crew of a B-1B bomber that ditched en route to targets in Afghanistan. This is the first B-1B lost in combat, and also the first aircraft lost during Operation ENDURING FREEDOM.

DECEMBER 17   At Istres Air Base, France, Air Mobility Command (AMC) C-17 Globemaster IIIs convey French military forces to Afghanistan in concert with Operation ENDURING FREEDOM.

DECEMBER 26   In Washington, D.C., Undersecretary of War Pete Aldrich announces that the Pentagon approves acquisition of the one-ton, Joint Air-to-Surface Standoff Missile. This is an advanced, precision-guided weapon capable of destroying targets 200 miles distant.

2002

JANUARY 11   At Guantanamo Bay, Cuba, a C-17 Globemaster III deposits the first of 371 Taliban and al-Qaeda detainees.

JANUARY 21   In Iraq, after Iraqi antiaircraft weapons fire at coalition aircraft participating in Operation SOUTHERN WATCH, American and British jets retaliate with strikes against weapons emplacements at Tallil.

FEBRUARY 4   Over Afghanistan, an MQ-1B Predator unmanned aerial vehicle (UAV) fires a Hellfire missile at a group of senior al-Qaeda figures on the ground, killing them; this is also the first combat engagement by an UAV.

MARCH 1   At McGuire Air Force Base, New Jersey, Brigadier General Teresa M. Peterson assumes control of the 305th Air Mobility Wing, becoming the first active female duty officer to command an operational flying wing.

Over Eastern Afghanistan, Operation ANACONDA commences as Air Force B-52s, B-1Bs, AC-130s, A-10s, and F-15s support ground units attacking Muslim extremists near Gardez. Precision-guided weapons keep civilian casualties to a minimum while thermobaric bombs are dropped in caves, killing by depriving them of oxygen.

MARCH 2–10   In Afghanistan, an AC-130 Spectre gunship relieves a detachment of the 10th Mountain Division surrounded by enemy fighters. HH-60 Blackhawk helicopters then rescue them in rough terrain; the AC-130 crew wins a Mackay Trophy.

MARCH 4   Near Gardez, eastern Afghanistan, a helicopter assault on enemy troops results in the first Air Force combat losses during Operation ENDURING FREEDOM. Sergeant John Chapman receives a posthumous Air Force Cross for charging a Taliban gun emplacement, killing several enemy combatants.

APRIL 18   At Hanscom Air Force Base, Massachusetts, the experimental MC2A-X flies for the first time. This vehicle will provide electronic command and control functions over combat areas.

South of Kandahar, Afghanistan, an American warplane accidently kills four Canadian soldiers and wounds eight others in an errant bomb drop.

APRIL 19   The Air Force Space Command is formally elevated to a four-star Air Force Command; previously, it was led by the four-star general commanding the U.S. Space Command and NORAD.

APRIL 22   The Air Force promulgates a new organizational scheme for wings, basing them around four groups: operations, maintenance, mission support, and medical.

MAY 22   At Edwards Air Force Base, California, the X-45A unmanned combat aerial vehicle (UCAV) flies for the first time. This vehicle, while stealthy and capable, is terminated in 2006.

JULY 22   At McConnell Air Force Base, Kansas, the prototype YAL-1A, or "Airborne Laser," flies for the first time. This weapon system employs concentrated light beams to destroy enemy ICBMs while they are launching into the atmosphere (boost phase).

JULY 30   A Scramjet engine (air-breathing supersonic combustion engine) is successfully ignited at high altitude for the first time. Such futuristic technology has potential for revolutionizing air transportation.

AUGUST 21   At Cape Canaveral, Florida, the Lockheed Martin Atlas V launches for the first time. This is part of the Evolved Expendable Launch Vehicle program, consisting of a main rocket with as many strap-on boosters added as necessary for very heavy payloads.

OCTOBER 1   General Ralph Eberhart assumes command of the U.S. Northern Command. This organization monitors and guards the military security of North America, and consists of elements from all four U.S. armed services.

General John P. Jumper orders the Peacekeeper (MX) ICBM system deactivated. This is the largest and most capable nuclear missile deployed by the United States during the Cold War.

NOVEMBER 17–18   In Iraq, antiaircraft batteries fire on coalition aircraft patrolling the northern no-fly zone; the warplanes retaliate by dropping precision-guided munitions. This action coincides with a UN resolution authorizing strong actions against Iraqi transgressions.

DECEMBER 8   At Andersen Air Force Base, Guam, the Air Mobility Command (AMC) directs several C-5 Galaxies to bring 1,200 tons of relief supplies to survivors of Typhoon Pongsona.

2003

JANUARY 10 At Offutt Air Force Base, Nebraska, the U.S. Strategic Command (STRATCOM) is tasked with four new missions, including global strike, integrated missile defense, integrated information operations, and C4ISR (global command, control, communications, computers, intelligence, surveillance, and reconnaissance).

FEBRUARY 1 Two hundred thousand feet above East Texas, the space shuttle *Columbia* breaks up in the atmosphere, disintegrating only 15 minutes from touchdown. All seven astronauts die, including Navy Captain David M. Brown, Captain Laurel Clark, and Commander William C. McCool and Air Force Lieutenant Colonel Michael Anderson and Colonel Rick Husband. This is also the 113th shuttle mission, and the *Columbia's* 28th venture into space.

FEBRUARY 8 In Washington, D.C., the Department of Defense begins contracting with commercial airlines to deliver troops and supplies to the Persian Gulf region. This is in anticipation of another conflict with Iraq and involves activation of the Civil Reserve Air Fleet (CRAF).

MARCH 11 Over Eglin Air Force Base, Florida, a C-130 test drops a 21,500-pound Massive Ordnance Air Blast weapon for the first time; this is the largest non-nuclear explosive currently in existence.

MARCH 17 Over northern Iraq, the final mission connected to Operation NORTHERN WATCH is conducted.

MARCH 18–19 Just prior to war with Iraq, Air Force planes begin dropping informational leaflets on 20 civilian locations. An EC-130 Commando Solo aircraft also broadcasts messages for alert Iraqi citizens to take cover.

MARCH 19 Operation IRAQI FREEDOM commences as Air Force F-117 Nighthawks drop precision-guided munitions on Iraqi communication and command centers. Meanwhile, over southern Iraq, Operation SOUTHERN WATCH concludes over the southern no-fly zone.

MARCH 20 Over Iraq, swarms of 500 coalition aircraft, mostly from Great Britain and the United States, attack Iraqi antiaircraft and missile radar defenses, along with command and control centers. These include F-117 Stealth fighters and cruise missiles fired from at least six U.S. warships aimed at "leadership targets of opportunity." All told, coalition air and sea forces unleash 1,000 Tomahawks and over 3,000 precision-guided munitions against significant targets.

MARCH 21 In the Arabian Gulf, an Iraqi fast-attack patrol boat is tracked by a Navy P-3 Orion, then destroyed by an Air Force AC-130 Spectre gunship.

MARCH 22 Over Iraq, coalition force aircraft launch over 1,000 sorties and a like number of cruise missiles at military targets.

MARCH 23 Over Kuwait, an American F-16 knocks out a Patriot battery after its radar locks on to it; no casualties occur.

MARCH 24   Over Kirkuk, Iraq, coalition force aircraft bombard military targets near the oil-producing center over a 24-hour period.

MARCH 26   Over northern Iraq, Operation NORTHERN DELAY commences as 15 C-17 Globemaster IIIs insert 990 paratroopers onto Bashur Airfield. This is also the first time that parachutists have dropped from C-17s. The crew of the lead aircraft wins a Mackay Trophy for orchestrating an intricate maneuver.

APRIL 2   Over Iraq, B-52s drop CBU-105 cluster bombs on Iraqi armored units. These are armor-piercing, sensor-fused weapons, and devastate tank formations. Meanwhile, an F-15C fighter-bomber mistakes an MLRS missile launcher from 1st Battalion, 39th Field Artillery, for a Soviet-designed Iraqi vehicle and directs a laser-guided GBU-12 bomb to it; several soldiers are killed.

APRIL 7   Over Baghdad, Iraq, a B-1B Lancer from the 34th Bomb Squadron drops four GBU-31 satellite-guided joint direct attack munitions (JDAM) on a restaurant where Iraqi dictator Saddam Hussein and his two sons were lodged; Hussein is not there, but the attack kills several senior Iraqi leaders. A C-130 Hercules also deploys the first Army troops to Baghdad International Airport under the cover of darkness.

APRIL 8   Over Baghdad, Iraq, ground fire brings down an A-10 Thunderbolt II, although the pilot escapes capture and is secured by coalition forces near the airport. A surface-to-air missile also destroys an F-15E Strike Eagle, killing both crewmen.

APRIL 11   Over Iraq, a B-52 employs a Litening II advanced airborne targeting and navigation pod to hit Iraqi facilities on an airfield.

APRIL 12   At Holloman Air Force Base, New Mexico, a Missile Defense Agency rocket sled reaches 6,416 miles per hour at a high-speed test track; this is also a world's speed record.

MAY   In Washington, D.C., the Air Force declares it will lease 100 Boeing KC-767 tankers to replace its aging fleet of KC-135s.

MAY 1   Over northern Iraq, Operation NORTHERN WATCH, begun as a no-fly zone on January 1, 1997, finally ends.

AUGUST 29   The last of 14 Defense Satellite Communications System (DSCS III) satellites are placed in orbit, finishing a project that was begun in 1981.

2004

FEBRUARY   Over Edwards Air Force Base, California, an F/A-22 aircraft undergoes an icing test at altitude by being sprayed with water from a modified KC-135 tanker.

FEBRUARY 14   At Elmendorf Air Force Base, Alaska, F-15 fighters and 150 ground support crews transfer to Gwalior Air Force Station, India, to train with the Indian Air Force. This constitutes the first joint venture between the two services since the 1960s.

JUNE 23   At Cape Canaveral, a three-stage Delta II launch vehicle hurls a replacement satellite into orbit as part of the Air Force Global Positioning System (GPS).

JULY 23   In the Caribbean, a HC-130 from the 38th Rescue Squadron airdrops two pararescue men into the water. These deploy a rubber boat and paddle to a Chinese fishing vessel to assist a crewman who had a life-threatening chest injury.

SEPTEMBER 4–8   Patrick Air Force Base, Florida, is struck by a hurricane, and members of the 45th Space Wing response team are called in to survey the damage.

SEPTEMBER 14   Over Mountain Home Air Force Base, Idaho, an F-16 suddenly bursts into flame during a Thunderbird

exhibition, and the pilot is forced to eject. None of the 60,000 spectators are hurt.

SEPTEMBER 15   In Washington, D.C., ground-breaking ceremonies unfold for the site of the new Air Force Memorial, located near the Potomac River, and directly across from the Pentagon.

DECEMBER 3   Over Edwards Air Force Base, California, the Airborne Laser (ABL) aircraft goes airborne for the first time with an integrated battle management and Beam Control/Fire Control (BC/FC) systems onboard.

DECEMBER 12   At Edwards Air Force Base, California, the Airborne Laser (ABL) team concludes a successful round of tests with its high-energy beam weapon.

2005

JANUARY 3–8   In Sri Lanka, a C-17 Globemaster III aircraft delivers a pair of HH-60G Pave Hawk helicopters following a destructive tsunami. C-130s also arrive from Japan to convey 145 tons of relief supplies.

MAY 12   At Langley Air Force Base, Virginia, the first operational F-22A Raptor deploys with the 27th Fighter Squadron, 1st Fighter Wing. This is the most advanced fighter aircraft in the world, and incorporates such novel technologies as stealth and "supercruise."

MARCH 1   The Air Force declares the MQ-1 Predator unmanned aerial vehicle (UAV) operational.

MAY 13   Over Charleston Air Force Base, South Carolina, massed C-17 Globemaster IIIs deploy to Biggs Army Airfield, Texas;

this is also the largest C-17 formation to fly cross-country.

JUNE 16   Captain Nicole Malachowski joins the Thunderbirds aerobatic team as the first female demonstration pilot of any U.S. military high-performance jet team.

JUNE 22   Over Southwest Asia, a U-2 aircraft from the 9th Reconnaissance Squadron experiences a catastrophic failure in midair, and crashes; the pilot is killed.

JULY 29   In Rwanda, Air Force transports redeploy 1,200 soldiers to Sudan on yet the latest UN peacekeeping missions.

AUGUST 23–29   As Hurricane Katrina ravages the Gulf of Mexico, several Air Force bases in its path are evacuated in advance.

Two F-22A Raptors from the 27th Fighter Squadron, Langley Air Force Base, Virginia fly in formation. This is presently the world's most advanced fighter aircraft, and it combines high performance with advanced avionics and stealth capabilities. (U.S. Department of Defense Visual Information Center)

SEPTEMBER 2   In Washington, D.C., General T. Michael Moseley gains appointment as chief of staff, U.S. Air Force.

SEPTEMBER 10   Over Afghanistan, an all-female crew flies their first C-130 combat mission.

SEPTEMBER 24   Near Houston, Texas, the Civil Air Patrol (CAP) begins flying new GA-8 Airvan aircraft to assess damage in the wake of Hurricane Rita.

OCTOBER 15–18   From Langley Air Force Base, Virginia the 27th Fighter Squadron flies its F-22A Raptors to as part of Operation COMBAT HAMMER at Hill Air Force Base, Utah,. There they drop their first JDAMs on a target range.

SEPTEMBER 2   In Washington, D.C., Michael W. Wynne gains appointment as secretary of the Air Force.

NOVEMBER 5   At Randolph Air Force Base, Texas, the first TH-1H Huey training helicopters are deployed.

NOVEMBER–JANUARY 2006   At Camp Lemonier, Africa, Air Force C-130s support military exercises as part of the Combined Joint Task Force–Horn of Africa.

DECEMBER 7   In a sign of the times, the new Air Force mission statement includes cyberspace to the existing combat domains of air and space.

DECEMBER 15   The F-22 Raptor air superiority fighter is declared operational.

2006

JANUARY 14   At the San Antonio Monster Jam, Texas, the Air Force enters a monster truck christened *Afterburner* in a car-smashing contest; it loses to the equally huge competitor *Grave Digger*.

JANUARY 15   Over northwest Pakistan, a U.S. air strike in the Bajaur tribal region, intended for al-Qaeda second-in-command Ayman al-Zawahiri, kills several terrorists along with 18 civilians.

FEBRUARY 8   At Hickam Air Force Base, Hawaii, the first C-17 Globemaster III deploys to that state.

FEBRUARY 22–25   During a three-day aerial exercise off Okinawa, Japan, four F-15s of the 18th Fighter Wing simultaneously target and fire at aerial decoys for the first time.

MARCH 20   The Air Force deploys the first of its CV-22 Osprey tilt-rotor aircraft. Unlike the Marine Corps version, this variant is outfitted for special operations.

MARCH 22   At Davis-Monthan Force Base, Arizona, A-10 Thunderbolt IIs arrive for "Hawgsmoke 2006," an annual ground support exercise.

JUNE   Former astronaut Susan J. Helms takes command of the 45th Space Wing as a newly minted brigadier general.

JUNE 7   Near Baqubah, Iraq, an air strike by two Air Force F-16s kills terrorist ringleader Abu Musab al-Zarqawi at his hiding place. The raid was directed by nearby Special Forces.

JUNE 30   In Washington, D.C., Chief Master Sergeant Rodney J. McKinley gains appointment as chief master sergeant of the Air Force.

OCTOBER 14   In Arlington, Virginia, ceremonies mark the dedication of the new Air Force Memorial.

DECEMBER 15   The Lockheed Martin F-35 Lightning II Joint Strike Fighter performs its maiden flight.

2007

JANUARY 7   Over Somalia, an Air Force AC-130H Spectre gunship destroys a suspected al-Qaeda training camp.

JANUARY 24   AC-130H Spectre gunships conduct a second round of strikes against suspected al-Qaeda terrorist training camps in Somalia.

MARCH 29   In Washington, D.C., the Tuskegee Airmen are awarded a Congressional Gold Medal for their service

in World War II, and for helping to frame the civil rights issue in the postwar period.

AUGUST 1   Ceremonies are held marking the 100th anniversary of the founding of the U.S. Army Signal Corps, the lineal antecedent of the U.S. Air Force.

AUGUST 31   In Washington, D.C., Defense Secretary Robert Gates is notified as to the mistaken transport of six nuclear-tipped cruise missiles from Minot

Air Force Base, North Dakota, to Barks-dale Air Force Base, Louisiana, onboard a B-52 bomber.

OCTOBER 19   In Washington, D.C., the Air Force publicly acknowledges that six

nuclear-tipped cruises missiles were mis-takenly transported on a B-52 bomber; such incidents are referred to as a Bent Spear.

2008

JANUARY 29   In northwestern Pakistan, a missile strike launched by an unmanned Predator drone kills wanted terrorist leader Abu Laith al-Libi.

FEBRUARY 20   In Washington, D.C., the Defense Department declares that a U.S. missile has successfully destroyed a falling spy satellite to prevent its fuel tank from contaminating parts of the Earth as its orbit decays.

FEBRUARY 23   On Guam, a B-2A Spirit stealth bomber crashes shortly after take-off, although both crew members survive. This is the first accident involving a B-2, of which only 21 were built, and it sets the taxpayers back $1 billion.

MARCH 24   In Washington, D.C., Air Force and Defense Department officials admit that in 2006 a shipment of ICBM-related parts had been mistakenly shipped to the Republic of China (Taiwan) instead of helicopter batteries. The government at Taipei reported the inci-dent at the time, but it took nearly a year for military officials to rectify the mistake.

JUNE 5   In Washington, D.C., Secretary of Defense Robert Gates dismisses Secretary of the Air Force Michael W. Wynne and Air Force Chief of Staff T. Michael Moseley for an August 2007 incident whereby a B-52 bomber had

unintentionally flown with six nuclear-tipped cruise missiles from Minot Air Force Base, North Dakota, to Barksdale Air Force Base, Louisiana.

JUNE 21   In Washington, D.C., President George W. Bush nominates Michael B. Donley to serve as acting secretary of the Air Force.

JULY 6   In Nangarhar Province, Afghani-stan, an American air strike kills several Taliban militants, but Afghan govern-ment officials complain that 47 civilians at wedding party also died.

JULY 22   Off Guam, a B-52 bomber from the 36th Bomb Wing crashes, killing all six crew members.

AUGUST 12   In Washington, D.C., Gen-eral Norton A. Schwartz gains appoint-ment as the 19th Air Force chief of staff.

OCTOBER 2   In Washington, D.C., the U.S. Senate confirms Lieutenant General Craig R. McKinley, present director of the Air National Guard, to full (four-star) general and head of the National Guard Bureau. He is also the first Air Force officer to hold that post since 2002.

OCTOBER 17   In Washington, D.C., Michael B. Donley gains appointment as the 22nd secretary of the Air Force.

2009

JANUARY 1   At an undisclosed location, two senior al-Qaeda leaders, Usama al-Kini and Sheikh Salim Swedan, are killed by a missile launched from a U.S. Predator drone.

JANUARY 23   In North and South Waziristan, Pakistan, five missiles fired in two U.S. Predator drone attacks kill 14 Taliban militants. These are the first attacks since President Barack Obama took office and signal that these tactics will continue.

FEBRUARY 14   Near the town of Makeen, South Waziristan, Pakistan, two missiles by a U.S. Predator drone kill an estimated 30 Taliban militants.

FEBRUARY 16   In the Kurram Valley, Pakistan, missiles fired by U.S. Predator drones kill an estimated 30 Taliban militants.

MARCH 1   In Sararogha village, South Waziristan, Pakistan, missiles fired from U.S. Predator drones kill seven Taliban militants.

MARCH 12   Over Afghanistan, missiles fired from a U.S. Predator drone kill an estimated 24 Taliban militants.

MARCH 15   In Jani Khel, North-West Frontier Province, Pakistan, missiles fired from U.S. Predator drones kill four Taliban operatives.

MARCH 25   Over Edwards Air Force Base, California, the first ultramodern F-22A Raptor jet fighter crashes; the pilot is killed.
   Near Makeen, South Waziristan, Pakistan, missiles fired from a U.S. Predator drone kill seven Taliban militants riding in two vehicles.

MARCH 26   Over Essokhel, North Waziristan, Pakistan, a missile fired from a U.S. Predator drone kills four Taliban militants.

APRIL 1   In the Orakzai tribal area, Pakistan, a missile strike by a U.S. Predator drone kills 14 Taliban militants.

APRIL 4   In North Waziristan, Pakistan, a missile launched from a U.S. Predator drone kills 13 suspected Taliban.

APRIL 8   In Gangi Khel, South Waziristan, Pakistan, a missile launched from a U.S. Predator drone kills four Taliban militants in a vehicle.

APRIL 19   In South Waziristan, Pakistan, a missile launched from a U.S. Predator drone kills three suspected Taliban militants.

APRIL 29   In Kanni Garam village, South Waziristan, Pakistan, a missile launched from a U.S. Predator drone kills six Taliban militants.

MAY 2   In Canberra, Australia, Prime Minister Kevin Rudd announces the purchase of 100 Lockheed F-35 Lightning II Joint Strike Fighters as part of an overall military buildup and modernization program.

MAY 9   In Sararogha, South Waziristan, Pakistan, a missile launched by a U.S. Predator drone kills six Taliban militants.

MAY 12   In Sra Khawra village, South Waziristan, Pakistan, a missile launched from a U.S. Predator drone kills eight Taliban militants.

MAY 16 Over Sarkai Naki, North Waziristan, Pakistan, missiles fired from a U.S. Predator drone kill 25 Taliban militants.

MAY 22 At Edwards Air Force Base, California, a T–38 Talon jet trainer crashes, killing the pilot.

JUNE 4 In Washington, D.C., the Air Force reveals the existence of its Counter-Electronics High-Powered Microwave Advanced Missile Project. This new weapon is a cruise missile capable of emitting focused bursts of high-power microwaves (HPM) that fry enemy electronics without harming their operators. A $40 million prototype is expected to be operational within five years or less.

JUNE 6 At Cape Canaveral, Florida, the Air Force unveils the top secret X–37B unmanned space plane in anticipation of a January 2010 launch. This five-ton craft is only 27 feet long and 15 feet across, yet is capable of performing a variety of classified missions.

JUNE 14 In South Waziristan, Pakistan, missiles fired from a U.S. Predator drone kill five Taliban militants in a vehicle.

JUNE 18 In northwest Pakistan, a suspected U.S. missile strike kills eight people at the villages of Gharlamai and Nandaran; most were apparently Taliban guerillas, but two dozen villagers may also have been injured.

JUNE 22 The Air Force announces that it has developed a new bomb rack for the B–2 stealth bomber, enabling it to carry the advanced MOP (Massive Ordnance Penetrator), weighing 30,000 pounds.

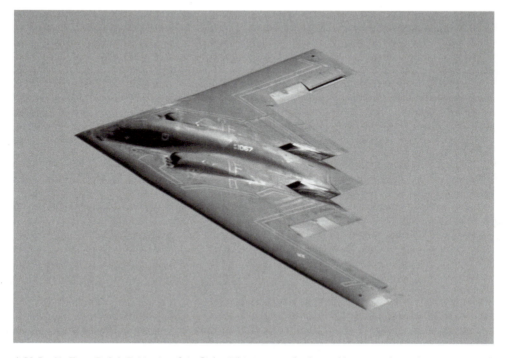

A U.S. Air Force B-2A Spirit aircraft in flight. This is presently the world's most advanced intercontinental strategic bomber and employs advanced stealth technology that render it virtually invisible to enemy radar. (U.S. Department of Defense Visual Information Center)

JUNE 23   In Makeen, South Waziristan, Pakistan, a U.S. Predator drone missile strike at a funeral for fallen Taliban leader Niaz Wali kills 45 guerillas in attendance. A concurrent missile strike in Neej Narai also kills eight suspected Taliban militants.

JUNE 24   In Washington, D.C., a commuter train crash kills nine people, including Major General David F. Wherley, Jr., formerly commander of the 113th Fighter Wing at Andrews Air Force Base. On September 11, 2001, he scrambled jets over the capital to thwart potential terrorist attacks.

JUNE 29   At Vandenberg Air Force Base, California, the 576th Flight Test Squadron launches a Minuteman III ICBM for test and reliability purposes, and it flies 4,300 miles downrange to targets near Kwajalein in the Marshall Islands.

JUNE 30   In Khost Province, along the Afghan–Pakistani border, U.S. airstrikes reportedly kill 12 Taliban militants hiding in a bunker complex.

JULY 3   Over Pakistan, a U.S. Predator drone launches missiles at Taliban training facilities, killing 17 people and wounding 27 others. The facility was operated by Baitullah Mehsud, wanted for the assassination of former prime minister Benazir Bhutto.

JULY 4   The Air Force announces that all F–22 Raptor fighters will be upgraded for ground attack missions. This is possible due to modifications to the onboard AN/APG-77 radar, which allow it to see realistic photo images on the ground.

JULY 7   In the Makeen area of South Waziristan, Pakistan, a U.S. Predator drone strike against Taliban targets kills 12 militants associated with the band of Baitullah Mehsud.

JULY 8   In South Waziristan, Pakistan, a U.S. Predator drone launches missiles at a

---

B-2 Spirit

Air Force stealth bomber. With the perfection of practical stealth technology in the late 1970s, the Air Force contracted with the Northrop Corporation to design and construct a bomber that would be invisible to Soviet-style radar defenses. The prototype XB-2 rolled out in 1988 as a flying wing incorporating stealth design features such as trailing wing edges in a double-W configuration. The aircraft was also fully automated and operated by a crew of two. The XB-2 first flew on July 17, 1989, but, by the time the first production models became available, the Soviet Union had collapsed and the Cold War was over. Given the great expense of the B-2, with a price tag of nearly $1 billion apiece, Congress capped acquisition at 21 aircraft. Nonetheless, it still reigns as the world's most advanced bomber, capable of penetrating all present radar systems without detection. It can deliver nuclear weapons, and can also be fitted with eighty 500-pound or sixteen 2,400-pound conventional bombs. Thus augmented, the B-2 can strike up to 60 targets in a single pass and, possessing a 6,000-mile range, can reach across the world with relative ease.

The Spirit made its combat debut over Kosovo in 1999, and accounted for 33 percent of all Serbian targets destroyed in an eight-week period. It has since been active in Operations ENDURING FREEDOM in Afghanistan and IRAQI FREEDOM in Iraq, performing bombing missions up to 60 hours in duration from the United States. These ultrasophisticated, ultraexpensive weapons are expected to remain operational well into the twenty-first century.

Taliban target, critically wounding Maulana Fazlullah and killing 45 associates.

JULY 10   In Ghazni Province, Afghanistan, a U.S air strike results in the deaths of 22 Taliban insurgents.

JULY 17   In Garhiwam Bahadur Khel, North Waziristan, Pakistan, a missile launched by a U.S. Predator drone strikes the home of militant Abdul Majid, killing five Taliban militants.

In Washington, D.C., Senators Carl Levin and John McCain argue for striking additional funding for the F-22 jet fighter; President Barack Obama has threatened to veto any defense appropriation bill containing more money than for the 187 aircraft requested.

JULY 18   In eastern Afghanistan, an F-15E Strike Eagle inexplicably crashes, killing two crew members. The cause of the loss remains speculative but enemy action is ruled out.

JULY 23   At an undisclosed location in Pakistan, a missile launched from a U.S. Predator drone reputedly kills the son of Saudi terrorist Osama bin Laden.

JULY 30   In a major policy shift, the U.S. government announces that Predator drone strikes in Pakistan will - refocus from neutralizing al-Qaeda targets to local Taliban efforts. The change will help shore up the Pakistani regime in the face of a protracted radical insurgency.

AUGUST 4   According to a national survey released by the Quinnipiac poll organization, 61 percent of Americans support the dropping of atomic bombs on Hiroshima and Nagasaki in August 1945; only 23 percent objected, while 16 percent were undecided.

AUGUST 5   In South Waziristan, Pakistan, a missile launched by a U.S. Predator drone strikes the home of wanted Taliban leader Baitullah Mehsud, killing one of his two wives.

AUGUST 7   In South Waziristan, Pakistan, a missile launched from a U.S. Predator drone kills Taliban leader Baitullah Mehsud as he lies on a rooftop. Mehsud, who suffered from diabetes, was observed having his legs massaged—a clear indication of who it was. This activity was clearly observed by television cameras onboard the Predator, and the attack followed.

AUGUST 8   In Ottawa, Canada, the government announces that it has possibly found the wreckage of a U.S. Army OA-10A Catalina amphibious aircraft that crashed in the St. Lawrence River on November 2, 1942. The United States and Canada will work to recover the wreckage and any human remains there.

AUGUST 10   The Strategic Air Command (SAC), which was disbanded in 1992 following the collapse of the Soviet Union, is revived in the form of the new Global Strike Command. The spit-and-polish attitude of SAC, along with instant dismissal of officers who do not measure up, becomes incorporated into the unit following a rash of nuclear-related mishaps.

In Afghanistan, U.S. and coalition officials point to declining numbers of Afghan civilians killed due to new restrictions and rules of engagement for dropping bombs. Taliban militants routinely use civilians as "human shields" to evade bombing attacks, but the tradeoff in terms of better public relations is viewed as worth such restraint.

AUGUST 11   In Kaniguram, South Waziristan, Pakistan, a missile launched from a

U.S. Predator drone strikes a house used by Taliban militants, killing 14 people.

AUGUST 21   In Dande Darpa Khel, North Waziristan, Pakistan, a missile launched from a U.S. Predator drone strikes a suspected Taliban hideout, killing 11 insurgents.

AUGUST 23   At Vandenberg Air Force Base, California, the Air Force launches another Minuteman III ICBM for testing purposes, which splashes down at a target range in the Kwajalein Atoll, 4,200 miles distant.

AUGUST 27   In Tapar Ghar, South Waziristan, Pakistan, a missile launched by a U.S. Predator drone strikes a Taliban hideout operated by Waliur Rehman, killing six militants.

SEPTEMBER 13   In the Bala Baluk district of Farah Province, Afghanistan, air strikes by U.S. and coalition warplanes kill several dozen Taliban militants.

SEPTEMBER 14   In the town of Mir Ali, North Waziristan, Pakistan, a missile launched from a U.S. Predator drone strikes a car, killing four Taliban militants.

SEPTEMBER 17   Over Pakistan, a missile fired by a U.S. Predator drone kills two dangerous al-Qaeda leaders, including Najmiddin Kamolitdinovich Jalolov from Uzbekistan.

SEPTEMBER 24   In the village of Dande Darpa Khel, North Waziristan, Pakistan, a missile fired from a U.S. Predator drone kills 12 Taliban militants.

SEPTEMBER 28   Off the Southern California coast, an amateur historian conducting a sonar search discovers the wreckage of a Lockheed T-33 jet trainer

that had been missing since October 15, 1955.

SEPTEMBER 29   In North and South Waziristan, Pakistan, missiles launched from a U.S. Predator drone strike two buildings operated by Taliban militants, killing 13 people including commander Irfan Mehsud.

SEPTEMBER 30   In Washington, D.C., the Senate votes 64–34 to continue production of the Boeing C-17 Globemaster III at a price of $2.5 billion; another 10 aircraft will be procured to keep the assembly lines open. Senator John McCain accuses President Barack Obama of caving in to special interests and not fighting the Chicago-based aerospace firm.

OCTOBER 13   In Washington, D.C., Pentagon officials announce that they are accelerating delivery of the 15-ton Massive Ordnance Penetrator (MOP), or "bunker buster." The move is viewed as a warning to Iran, which is digging underground nuclear facilities near the holy city of Qom. This weapon, which carries 5,300 pounds of explosives, is 10 times more destructive than the weapons it is designed to replace.

OCTOBER 16   Off the coast of South Carolina, two F-16Cs collide during training exercises; one aircraft makes it back to base safely, but the other and its pilot, Captain Nicholas Giglio, are missing.

DECEMBER 21   In Afghanistan, it is announced that the first MC-12W spyplanes, which are highly advanced and classified, will deploy under the aegis of the U.S. Air Force. This twin-engined aircraft is equipped with videocameras and other sensors, and is capable of beaming real-time intelligence to troops on the ground.

Bibliography

Alexander, Thomas E. *The Wings of Change: The Army Air Force Experience in Texas During World War II*. Abilene, Tex.: McWhiney Foundation Press, 2003.

Ambrose, Stephen E. *The Wild Blue: The Men and Boys Who Flew the B-24s Over Germany*. New York: Simon and Schuster Paperbacks, 2007.

Anderegg, C. R. *Sierra Hotel: Flying Air Force Fighters in the Decade After Vietnam*. Washington, D.C.: Air Force History and Museums Program, United States Air Force, 2001.

Aviation Nation Foundation. *60th Anniversary United States Air Force, 1947–2007: Heritage to Horizons—Commemorating 60 Years of Air & Space Power*. Las Vegas: Aviation Nation Foundation, 2007.

Ayres, Travis L. *The Bomber Boys: Heroes Who Flew the B-17s in World War II*. New York: NAL Caliber, 2009.

Bailey, Mike. *B-24 Liberator Groups of the 8th Air Force*. Walton on Thames, Surrey, Eng.: Red Kite, 2007.

Barbree, Jay. *"Live from Cape Canaveral": Covering the Space Race, from Sputnik to Today*. New York: Smithsonian Books/Collins, 2007.

Barnes, Pete. *Richard Bong: World War II Flying Ace*. Madison: Wisconsin Historical Society, 2009.

Bartsch, William H. *Every Day a Nightmare: American Pursuit Pilots in the Defense of Java*. College Station: Texas A&M University Press, 2010.

Beser, Jerome, and Jack Spangler. *The Rising Sun Sets: The Complete Story of the Bombing of Nagasaki*. Bloomington, Ind.: AuthorHouse, 2007.

Bowman, Martin W. *The USAF, 1947–99*. Stroud, Eng.: Sutton, 2000.

Bowman, Martin W. *Clash of Eagles: American Bomber Crews and the Luftwaffe, 1942–1945*. Barnsley, South Yorkshire, Eng.: Pen & Sword Aviation, 2006.

Bowman, Martin W. *B-17 Combat Missions: Fighters, Flak, and Forts: First-Hand Accounts of Mighty 8th Operations over Germany*. London: Greenhill Books, 2007.

Bowman, Martin W. *Bomber Bases of World War 2, 1st Air Division, 8th Air Force USAAF, 1942–45: Flying Fortress Squadrons in Cambridgeshire, Bedfordshire, Essex, Hertfordshire, and Northamptonshire*. Barnsley, Eng.: Pen & Sword Aviation, 2007.

Bowman, Martin W. *Bomber Bases of World War 2: 2nd Air Division, 8th Air Force USAAF, 1942–45: Liberator Squadrons in Norfolk and Suffolk*. Barnsley, Eng.: Pen & Sword Aviation, 2007.

Bowman, Martin W. *Bomber Bases of World War 2: 3rd Air Division, 8th Air Force USAAF, 1942–45: Flying Fortresses & Liberator Squadrons in Norfolk and Suffolk*. Barnsley, Eng.: Pen & Sword Aviation, 2009.

Bowman, Martin W. *On the Highways of the Skies: The 8th Air Force in World War II*. Atglen, Pa.: Schiffer Military History, 2008.

Bowman, Martin W. *Duxford and the Big Wings, 1940–45: RAF & USAAF Fighter Pilots at War*. Barnsley, Eng.: Pen & Sword Aviation, 2009.

Boyne, Walter J. *World War II Aircraft: Great American Fighter Planes of the Second World War*. San Diego: Thunder Bay Press, 2006.

Bowman, Martin W. *Beyond the Wild Blue: A History of the U.S. Air Force, 1947–2007.* New York: Thomas Dunne Books/St. Martin's Press, 2007.

Brown, Lee Frances. *Calvin J. Spann: Tuskegee "Red Tail" Fighter Pilot.* New York: iUniverse, 2009.

Bucholtz, Chris. *332nd Fighter Group—Tuskegee Airmen.* Westminster, Md.: Osprey Pub., 2007.

Burrows, William E. *By Any Means Necessary: America's Secret Air War in the Cold War.* New York: Farrar, Strauss, and Giroux, 2001.

Burton, John. *Fortnight of Infamy: The Collapse of Allied Airpower West of Pearl Harbor.* Annapolis, Md.: Naval Institute Press, 2006.

Caine, Philip D. *The RAF Eagle Squadrons: American Pilots Who Flew for the Royal Air Force.* Golden, Colo.: Fulcrum Pub., 2009.

Casey, Aloysius G., and Patrick Casey. *Velocity: Speed with Direction: The Professional Career of General Jerome F. O'Malley.* Maxwell Air Force Base, Ala.: Air University Press, 2007.

Chancey, Jennie E., and William R. Forstchen. *Hotshots: An Oral History of the Air Force Combat Pilots of the Korean War.* New York: William Morrow, 2000.

Cherny, Andrei. *The Candy Bombers: The Untold Story of the Berlin Airlift and America's Finest Hour.* New York: G.P. Putnam's Sons, 2008.

Clarke, Bob. *The Berlin Airlift: 10 Tons to Templehof.* Stroud, Eng.: Tempus, 2007.

Clodfelter, Mark. *The Limits of Air Power: The American Bombing of North Vietnam.* Lincoln: University of Nebraska Press, 2006.

Collins, Brian J. *Behind the Cyberspace Veil: The Hidden Evolution of the Air Force Officer Corps.* Westport, Conn.: Praeger Security International, 2008.

Collins, Martin J. *Cold War Laboratory: RAND, the Air Force, and the American State, 1945–1950.* Washington, D.C.: Smithsonian Institution Press, 2002.

Cooke, James J. *Billy Mitchell.* Boulder, Colo.: Lynne Rienner, 2002.

Cox, Douglas. *Airpower Leadership on the Front Line: Lt. Gen. George H. Brett and Combat Command.* Maxwell Air Force Base, Ala.: Air University Press, 2006.

Cox, Sebastian, and Peter Gray, eds. *Air Power History: Turning Points from Kitty Hawk to Kosovo.* Portland, Ore.: Frank Cass, 2002.

Craft, Stephen G. *Embry-Riddle at War: Aviation Training during World War II.* Gainesville: University Press of Florida, 2009.

Crane, C. Conrad. *American Airpower Strategy in Korea, 1950–1953.* Lawrence: University Press of Kansas, 2000.

Cunningham, Meghan, ed. *Logbook of Signal Corps No. 1: The U.S. Army's First Airplane.* Washington, D.C.: Air Force History and Museums Program, 2004.

Curtis, Duncan. *Rise and Defend: The USAF at Manston, 1950–1958.* East Yorkshire: Flight Recorder Publications, 2006.

Darlow, Stephen. *D-Day Bombers: The Stories of Allied Heavy Bombers during the Invasion of Normandy.* Mechanicsburg, Pa.: Stackpole Books, 2010.

Daso, Dik A. *Doolittle: Aerospace Visionary.* Washington, D.C.: Potomac Books, 2005.

Daso, Dik A. *U.S. Air Force: A Complete History.* Westport, Conn.: Hugh Lauter Associates, 2006.

Davies, Peter E. *F-4 Phantom II vs. MiG-21: USAF & VPAF in the Vietnam War.* New York: Osprey, 2008.

Davies, Steve. *Red Eagles: The Top Secret Acquisition and Testing of Soviet Combat Aircraft in the Cold War by the USAF.* Stroud, U.K.: Sutton, 2006.

Davies, Steve. *Red Eagles: America's Secret MiGs.* New York: Osprey, 2008.

Davis, Richard G. *On Target: Organizing and Executing the Strategic Air Campaign Against Iraq.* Washington, D.C.: Air Force History and Museums Program, 2002.

Davis, Richard G. *Bombing the European Axis Powers: A Historical Digest of the Combined Bomber Offensive, 1939–1945.* Maxwell AFB, Ala.: Air University Press, 2006.

DeBlanc, Jefferson J. *The Guadalcanal Air War: Col. Jefferson DeBlanc's Story.* Gretna, La.: Pelican Pub., 2008.

Dewez, Luc, and Michael P. Faley. *High Noon over Haseluenne: The 100th Bombardment Group over Berlin, March 6, 1944.* Atglen, Pa.: Schiffer, 2009.

Dorr, Robert F., and Thomas D. Jones. *Hell Hawks! The Untold Story of the American Fliers*

Who Savaged Hitler's Wehrmacht. Minneapolis, Minn.: Zenith Press, 2008.

Drury, Bob. *The Rescue Season: The Heroic Story of Parajumpers on the Edge of the World.* New York: Simon & Schuster, 2001.

Dutcher, Russell K. *Union Army Balloon Corps: Operations during the War of the Rebellion, 1861–1863.* Westminster, Md.: Heritage Books, 2009.

Dyson, George. *Project Orion: The True Story of the Atomic Spaceship.* New York: Henry Holt, 2002.

Ehlers, Robert S. *Targeting the Third Reich: Air Intelligence and the Allied Bombing Campaigns.* Lawrence: University Press of Kansas, 2009.

Eisel, Brick, and Jim Schreiner. *Magnum! The Wild Weasels in Desert Storm.* Barnsley, Eng.: Pen & Sword Aviation, 2009.

Endicott, Judith G., ed. *The USAF in Korea: Campaigns, Units, and Stations, 1950–1953.* Washington, D.C.: Air Force History and Museums Program, 2001.

Engel, Jeffrey A. *Cold War at 30,000 Feet: The Anglo-American Fight for Aviation Supremacy.* Cambridge, Mass.: Harvard University Press, 2007.

Ethell, Jeffrey L. *Warbirds: American Legends of World War II.* Ann Arbor, Mich.: Lowe & B. Hould Publishers, 2003.

Fagan, George V. *Air Force Academy Heritage: The Early Years.* Golden, Colo.: Fulcrum Pub., 2006.

Farmer, James H. *America's Pioneer Aces: A Historic Perspective on the First Pursuit Group's Remarkable Anomalies.* Upland, Calif.: BAC Publishers, 2003.

Farquhar, John T. *A Need to Know: The Role of Air Force Reconnaissance in War Planning, 1945–1953.* Maxwell Air Force Base, Ala.: Air University Press, 2004.

Frandsen, Bert. *Hat in the Ring: The Birth of American Air Power in the Great War.* Washington, D.C.: Smithsonian Books, 2003.

Frankum, Ronald B. *Like Rolling Thunder: The Air War in Vietnam, 1964–1975.* Lanham, Md.: Rowman & Littlefield, 2005.

Fredriksen, John C. *The B-45 Tornado: An Operational History of the First American Jet Bomber.* Jefferson, N.C.: McFarland Pub. Co., 2009.

Freeman, Roger A. *Wolfpack Warriors: The Story of World War II's Most Successful Fighter Outfit.* Mechanicsburg, Pa.: Stackpole Books, 2009.

Fremont-Barnes, Gregory. *American Bomber Crewman 1941–45.* Oxford: Osprey, 2008.

Galdorisi, George, and Thomas Phillips. *Leave No Man Behind: The Saga of Combat Search and Rescue.* Minneapolis, Minn.: MBI Pub. Co., 2008.

Gallagher, James P. *With the Fifth Army Air Force: Photos from the Pacific Theater.* Baltimore: Johns Hopkins University Press, 2001.

Gamble, Bruce. *Fortress Rabaul: The Battle for the Southwest Pacific, January 1942–April 1943.* Minneapolis, Minn.: MBI Pub Co. and Zenith Press, 2010.

Gault, Gary. *United States Air Force 60th Anniversary: Lessons Learned in Airpower Throughout the Ages.* Rosslyn, Va.: HQ USAF, 2007.

Geer, James. *The Republic F-105 Thunderchief: Wing and Squadron Histories.* Atglen, Pa.: Schiffer, 2002.

Gibson, Ramón. *The Way I Saw It: From Fighter Pilot to Test Pilot.* Dallas, Tex.: Brown Books Pub. Group, 2004.

Gladman, Brad W. *Intelligence and Anglo-American Air Support in World War Two: The Western Desert and Tunisia, 1940–43.* New York: Palgrave Macmillan, 2009.

Gordon, Doug. *U.S.A.F. Tactical Reconnaissance in the Cold War: 1945 to Korea, Cuba, Vietnam, and the Iron Curtain.* Barnsley, U.K.: Pen & Sword Aviation, 2006.

Graff, Cory. *Strike and Return: American Air Power and the Fight for Iwo Jima.* North Branch, Minn.: Specialty, 2006.

Graham, Roger D. *The Nimrods: A-26 Nimrods and the Secret War in Laos.* Bloomington, Ind.: AuthorHouse, 2007.

Granholm, Jackson. *The Day We Bombed Switzerland: Flying with the US Eighth Army Air Force in World War II.* Shrewsbury, Eng.: Airlife Pub., 2000.

Grant, Rebecca. *Airpower in Afghanistan: How a Faraway War is Remaking the Air Force.* Washington, D.C.: Mitchell Institute Press, 2009.

Gross, Charles J. *American Military Aviation: The Indispensable Arm.* College Station: Texas A&M University Press, 2002.

Guinn, Gilbert S. *The Arnold Scheme: British Flyboys, the American South, and a Daring Plan to*

Win the War. Charleston, S.C.: History Press, 2007.

Gushee, Edward T. *52-Charlie: Members of a Legendary Pilot Training Class Share Their Stories about Combat in Korea and Vietnam.* Tucson, Ariz.: Wheatmark, 2002.

Guttman, Jon. *USAS 1st Pursuit Group.* New York: Osprey, 2008.

Guttman, Jon. *SPAD XIII vs. Fokker D VII: Western Front 1916–18.* New York: Osprey, 2009.

Haave, Christopher E., and Phil M. Haun, eds. *A-10s over Kosovo: The Victory of Airpower over a Fielded Army as Told by the Airmen Who Fought in Operation Allied Force.* Maxwell Air Force Base, La.: Air University Press, 2003.

Hagedorn, Dan. *North American's T-6: A Definitive History of the World's Most Famous Trainer.* North Branch, Minn.: Specialty Press, 2009.

Hall, R. Cargill, and Clayton R. Laurie, eds. *Early Cold War Overflights, 1950–1956: Symposium Proceedings.* Washington, D.C.: Office of the Historian, National Reconnaissance Office, 2003.

Hallion, Richard P., et al. *Silver Wings, Golden Valor: The USAF Remembers Korea.* Washington, D.C.: Air Force History and Museums Program, 2006.

Hammond, James T. *Tom's War: Flying with the U.S. Eighth Army Air Force in Europe, 1944.* New York: iUniverse, 2007.

Handley, Phil. *Nickel on the Grass: Reflections of a U.S. Air Force Pilot.* New York: iUniverse, 2006.

Hannah, Craig C. *Striving for Air Superiority: The Tactical Air Command in Vietnam.* College Station: Texas A&M University Press, 2002.

Hanson, David S. *"When You Get a Job to Do, Do It": The Airpower Leadership of Lt. Gen. William H. Tunner.* Maxwell Air Force Base, Ala.: Air University Press, 2008.

Harder, Robert O. *Flying from the Black Hole: The B-52 Navigator-Bombardiers of Vietnam.* Annapolis, Md: Naval Institute Press, 2009.

Harrington, Daniel F. *"The Air Force Can Deliver Anything": A History of the Berlin Airlift.* Ramstein Air Base, Germany: USAFE Office of History, 2008.

Hawthorne-Tagg, Lori S. *On the Front Line of R & D: Wright-Patterson Air Force Base in the Korean War, 1950–1953.* Wright-Patterson Air Force Base, Ohio: Air Force Materiel Command, 2001.

Hawthorne-Tagg, Lori S. *Development of the B-52: The Wright Field Story.* Wright-Patterson Air Force Base, Ohio: History Office, Aeronautical Systems Center, 2004.

Hearn, Chester G. *Air Force: An Illustrated History: The U.S. Air Force from 1907 to the 21st Century.* Minneapolis, Minn.: Zenith Press, 2008.

Henriksen, Dag. *NATO's Gamble: Combining Diplomacy and Airpower in the Kosovo Crisis, 1998–1999.* Annapolis, Md.: Naval Institute Press, 2007.

Hill, Mike, and John Beitling. *B-24 Liberators of the 15th Air Force/49th Bomb Wing in World War II.* Atglen, Pa.: Schiffer Pub., Ltd., 2006.

Hill, Mike, and John M. Campbell. *Tactical Air Command: An Illustrated History, 1946–1992.* Atglen, Pa.: Schiffer Military History, 2001.

Hirsch, Michael. *None Braver: U.S. Air Force Pararescuemen in the War on Terrorism.* New York: New American Library, 2003.

Homan, Lynn M., and Thomas Reilly. *Black Knights: The Story of the Tuskegee Airmen.* Gretna, La.: Pelican Pub. Co., 2001.

Hoppes, Jonna D. *Calculated Risk: The Extraordinary Life of Jimmy Doolittle—Aviation Pioneer and World War II Hero; A Memoir.* Santa Monica, Calif.: Santa Monica Press, 2005.

Houchin, Roy F. *US Hypersonic Research and Development: The Rise and Fall of Dyna-Soar, 1944–1963.* New York: Routledge, 2006.

Hudnut, Herbert B. *That Fateful Day: The Story of Two Lieutenants in the American Balloon Service of World War I.* Glenn Falls, N.Y.: Glenn Falls Printing, 2006.

Hurley, Alfred F., and Robert C. Ehrhart, eds. *Air Power and Warfare: The Proceedings of the 8th Military History Symposium, United States Air Force Academy, 18–20 October 1978.* Honolulu: University Press of the Pacific, 2002.

Huston, John W., ed. *American Airpower Comes of Age: General Henry H. "Hap" Arnold's World War II Diaries.* 2 vols. Maxwell Air Force Base, Ala.: Air University Press, 2002.

Jamieson, Perry D. *Lucrative Targets: The U.S. Air Force in the Kuwaiti Theater of Operations.* Washington, D.C.: Air Force History and Museums Program, 2001.

Jamieson, Perry D. *Khobar Towers: Tragedy and Response*. Washington, D.C.: Air Force History and Museums Program, 2008.

Jenkins, Dennis R., and Tony Landis. *Experimental & Prototype U.S. Air Force Jet Fighters*. North Branch, Minn.: Specialty Press, 2008.

Johnson, E. R. *American Attack Aircraft Since 1926*. Jefferson, N.C.: McFarland, 2008.

Kan, Kenneth C. *First in the Air: The Eagle Squadrons of World War II*. Washington, D.C.: Air Force History and Museums Program, 2007.

Kaplan, Philip. *Two-Man Air Force: Don Gentile & John Godfrey, World War Two Flying Aces*. Barnsley, Eng.: Pen & Sword Aviation, 2006.

Kaplan, Robert D. *Hog Pilots, Blue Water Grunts: The American Military in the Air, at Sea, and on the Ground*. New York: Random House, 2007.

Kennedy, Gregory P. *Touching Space: The Story of Project Manhigh*. Atglen, Pa.: Schiffer Military History, 2007.

Kerns, Raymond C. *Above the Thunder: Reminiscences of a Field Artillery Pilot in World War II*. Kent, Ohio: Kent State University Press, 2009.

Kozak, Warren. *LeMay: The Life and Wars of General Curtis LeMay*. Washington, D.C.: Regnery Pub., 2009.

Lambert, John W. *The 8th Air Force: Victory and Sacrifice; A World War II Photo History*. Atglen, Pa.: Schiffer Pub., 2006.

Lambeth, Benjamin S. *NATO's Air War for Kosovo: A Strategic and Operational Assessment*. Santa Monica, Calif.: RAND, 2001.

Lambeth, Benjamin S. *Air Power Against Terror: America's Conduct of Operation Enduring Freedom*. Santa Monica, Calif.: RAND Corp., 2005.

Landis, Tony, and Dennis R. Jenkins. *U.S. Air Force Jet Fighter Prototypes: A Photo Scrapbook*. North Branch, Minn.: Specialty Press, 2009.

LaPointe, Robert L. *PJs in Vietnam: The Story of Airrescue in Vietnam as Seen Through the Eyes of Pararescuemen*. Anchorage, Alaska: Northern PJ Press, 2001.

Larison, Grey T. *Snafu Snatchers: Recovery of Downed Airmen: 13th Air Force, 2nd Air Sea Rescue Squadron, Clark Field, Philippines, 1946*. Bloomington, Ind.: AuthorHouse, 2009.

Leary, William M. *Anything, Anywhere, Any Time: Combat Cargo in the Korean War*. Washington, D.C.: Air Force History and Museums Program, 2000.

Lenderman, Laura L. *The Rise of Air Mobility and Its Generals*. Maxwell Air Force Base, Ala.: Air University Press, 2008.

Levis, Alexander H., ed. *The Limitless Sky: Air Force Science and Technology Contributions to the Nation*. Washington, D.C.: Air Force History and Museums Program, United States Air Force, 2004.

Lewis, W. David. *Eddie Rickenbacker: An American Hero in the Twentieth Century*. Baltimore: Johns Hopkins University Press, 2005.

Logan, Don. *USAF F-15 Eagles: Units, Colors & Markings*. Atglen, Pa.: Schiffer, 2000.

Logan, Don. *F-4 Phantom IIs of the USAF Reserve and Air National Guard*. Atglen, Pa.: Schiffer Pub., 2002.

Logan, Edward F. *"Jump, Damn It, Jump!" Memoir of a Downed B-17 Pilot in World War II*. Jefferson, N.C.: McFarland, 2008.

Mackay, Ron. *First in the Field: The 1st Air Division over Europe in World War II*. Atglen, Pa.: Schiffer, 2007.

Mann, Robert A. *Aircraft Record Cards of the United States Air Force: How to Read the Codes*. Jefferson, N.C.: McFarland Pub. Co., 2008.

March, Peter. *The Stealth Story*. Stroud, Eng.: Sutton, 2007.

Marion, Forrest L. *That Others May Live: USAF Air Rescue in Korea*. Washington, D.C.: Air Force History and Museums Program, 2004.

Marrett, George J. *Testing Death: Hughes Aircraft Test Pilots and Cold War Weaponry*. Annapolis, Md.: Naval Institute Press, 2006.

Marrett, George J. *Contrails Over the Mojave: The Golden Age of Jet Fighter Flight Testing at Edwards Air Force Base*. Annapolis, Md.: Naval Institute Press, 2008.

Martin, Michael N., ed. *Flight of Excellence: United States Air Force Academy 50th Anniversary*. Nashville, Tenn.: Turner Pub. Co., 2007.

McCarthy, Donald J. *USAF F-4 and F-105: MiG Killers of the Vietnam War, 1965–1973*. Atglen, Pa.: Schiffer Military History, 2005.

McCarthy, Donald J. *MiG Killers: A Chronology of U.S. Air Victories in Vietnam, 1965–1973*. North Branch, Minn.: Specialty Press, 2009.

McCarthy, Mike. *Phantom Reflections: The Education of an American Fighter Pilot in Vietnam.* Mechanicsburg, Pa.: Stackpole Books, 2007.

McDonough, James L. *The Wars of Myron King: A B-17 Pilot Faces WWII and U.S.-Soviet Intrigue.* Knoxville: University of Tennessee Press, 2009.

McGill, Earl J. *Black Tuesday Over Namsi: A True History of the Epic Air Battle of the Korean War.* Westminster, Md.: Eagle Editions, 2008.

Meilinger, Phillip S. *Airpower: Myths and Facts.* Maxwell Air Force Base, Ala.: Air University Press, 2003.

Meilinger, Phillip S. *Hubert R. Harmon: Airman, Officer, Father of the Air Force Academy.* Golden, Colo.: Fulcrum Group, 2009.

Meixsel, Richard B. *Clark Field and the U.S. Army Air Corps in the Philippines, 1919–1942.* Quezon City, Philippines: New Day Publishers, 2002.

Merlin, Peter W. *Mach 3+: NASA/USAF YF-12 Flight Research, 1969–1979.* Washington, D.C.: NASA History Division, 2002.

Mesko, Jim. *Air War Over Korea.* Carrollton, Tex.: Squadron/Signal Publications, 2000.

Michel, Marshall L. *The Eleven Days of Christmas: America's Last Vietnam Battle.* San Francisco, Calif.: Encounter Books, 2002.

Miller, Donald L. *Masters of the Air: America's Bomber Boys Who Fought the Air War Against Nazi Germany.* New York: Simon & Schuster Paperbacks, 2007.

Miller, Donald L. *Eighth Air Force: The American Bomber Crews in Britain.* London: Aurum, 2008.

Miller, Roger G. *To Save a City: The Berlin Airlift, 1948–1949.* College Station: Texas A&M University Press, 2000.

Miller, Roger G. *Like a Thunderbolt: The Lafayette Escadrille and the Advent of American Pursuit in World War I.* Washington, D.C.: Air Force History and Museums Program, 2007.

Mitchell, William. *Winged Defense: The Development and Possibilities of Modern Air Power.* Mineola, N.Y.: Dover Publications, 2006.

Molesworth, Carl. *23rd Fighter Group: "Chennault's Sharks."* New York: Osprey, 2009.

Moran, Jeff. *American Airborne Pathfinders in World War II.* Atglen, Pa.: Schiffer, 2003.

Moy, Timothy. *War Machines: Transforming Technologies in the U.S. Military, 1920–1940.* College Station: Texas A&M University Press, 2001.

Moye, J. Todd. *Freedom Flyers: The Tuskegee Airmen of World War II.* New York: Oxford University Press, 2010.

Mutza, Wayne. *Green Hornets: The History of the U.S. Air Force 20th Special Operations Squadron.* Atglen, Pa.: Schiffer Military History, 2007.

Mutza, Wayne. *Gunships: The Story of Spooky, Shadow, Stinger, and Spectre.* North Branch, Minn.: Specialty Press, 2008.

Nalty, Bernard C. *Air War over South Vietnam, 1968–1975.* Washington, D.C.: Air Force History and Museums Program, 2000.

Nalty, Bernard C. *Winged Shield, Winged Sword: A History of the United States Air Force. Vol. 1, 1907–1950.* Honolulu: University Press of the Pacific, 2003.

Nalty, Bernard C. *The War against Trucks: Aerial Interdiction in Southern Laos, 1968–1972.* Washington, D.C.: Air Force History and Museums Program, United States Air Force, 2005.

Natola, Mark, ed. *Boeing B-47 Stratojet: True Stories of the Cold War in the Air.* Atglen, Pa.: Schiffer Pub., 2002.

Nauman, Robert A. *On the Wings of Modernism: The United States Air Force Academy.* Urbana: University of Illinois Press, 2004.

Neufeld, Jacob, ed. *A Century of Air Power Leadership, Past, Present, and Future.* Washington, D.C.: Air Force History and Museums Program, 2007.

Neufeld, Jacob, and George M. Watson, eds. *Coalition Air Warfare in the Korean War, 1950–1953: Proceedings, Air Force Historical Foundation Symposium, Andrews AFB, Maryland, May 7–8, 2002.* Washington, D.C.: U.S. Air Force History and Museums Program, 2005.

Newman, Rick, and Don Shepperd. *Bury Us Upside Down: The Misty Pilots and the Secret Battle for the Ho Chi Minh Trail.* New York: Presidio Press/Ballantine Books, 2006.

Nichol, John, and Tony Rennell. *Tail-end Charlies: The Last Battles of the Bomber War, 1944–45.* New York: Thomas Dunne Books, 2008.

Noles, James L., and James L. Noles, Jr. *Mighty by Sacrifice: The Destruction of an American Bomber Squadron, August 29, 1944.* Tuscaloosa: University of Alabama Press, 2009.

Norton, Bill. *U.S. Experimental & Prototype Aircraft Projects: Fighters 1939–1945*. North Branch, Minn.: Specialty Press, 2008.

Olsen, John A. *Strategic Air Power in Desert Storm*. Portland, Ore.: Frank Cass, 2003.

Olsen, John A. *John Warden and the Renaissance of American Air Power*. Washington, D.C.: Potomac Books, 2007.

Pardoe, Blaine L. *Terror of the Autumn Skies: The True Story of Frank Luke, America's Rogue Ace of World War I*. New York: Skyhorse Pub., 2008.

Peebles, Curtis. *Twilight Warriors: Covert Air Operations against the USSR*. Annapolis, Md.: Naval Institute Press, 2005.

Polmar, Norman, and Robert S. Norris. *The U.S. Nuclear Arsenal: A History of Weapons and Delivery Systems Since 1945*. Annapolis, Md.: Naval Institute Press, 2009.

Pons, Gregory, and Philippe Charbonier. *9th Air Force: American Tactical Aviation in the ETO, 1942–1945*. Paris: Histoire & Collections, 2008.

Prados, John. *Vietnam: The History of an Unwinnable War, 1945–1975*. Lawrence: University Press of Kansas, 2009.

Pushies, Fred J. *U.S. Air Force Special Ops*. St. Paul, Minn.: Zenith Press, 2007.

Pushies, Fred J. *Deadly Blue: Battle Stories of the U.S. Air Force Special Operations Command*. New York: American Management Association, 2009.

Putney, Diane T. *Airpower Advantage: Planning the Gulf War Air Campaign, 1989–1991*. Washington, D.C.: Air Force History and Museums Program, United States Air Force, 2004.

Randolph, Stephen P. *Powerful and Brutal Weapons: Nixon, Kissinger, and the Easter Offensive*. Cambridge, Mass.: Harvard University Press, 2007.

Rehr, Louis S. *Marauder: Memoir of a B-26 Pilot in Europe in World War II*. Jefferson, N.C.: McFarland Pub. Co., 2009.

Rickman, Sarah B. *Nancy Love and the WASP Ferry Pilots of World War II*. Denton: University of North Texas Press, 2008.

Ringenbach, Paul T. *Battling Tradition: Robert F. McDermott and Shaping the U.S. Air Force Academy*. Chicago: Imprint Publications, 2006.

Ripley, Tim. *Air War Iraq*. Barnsley, Eng.: Pen & Sword Aviation, 2004.

Robertson, Linda R. *The Dream of Civilized Warfare: World War I Flying Aces and the American Imagination*. Minneapolis: University of Minnesota Press, 2005.

Rodman, Matthew K. *A War of Their Own: Bombers Over the Southwest Pacific*. Maxwell AFB, Ala.: Air University Press, 2005.

Rodrigues, Rick. *Aircraft Markings of the Strategic Air Command, 1946–1953*. Jefferson, N.C.: McFarland, 2006.

Roesler, Alan L. *An Arizona Aviator in France: The Life of Ernest A. Love, 147th Aero Squadron, USAS*. Mesa, Ariz,: Roesler Enterprises, 2007.

Rosenfeld, Susan C., and Charles J. Gross. *Air National Guard at 60: A History*. Arlington, Va.: Air National Guard, 2007.

Rosenthal, Jack. *Letters from an Airfield: The True Story of a GI Bride of the Mighty Eighth*. Stroud, Eng.: History Press, 2009.

Rubel, John H. *Doomsday Delayed: USAF Strategic Weapons Doctrine and SIOP-62, 1959–1962: Two Cautionary Tales*. Lanham, Md.: Hamilton Books, 2008.

Samuel, Wolfgang W. E. *I Always Wanted to Fly: America's Cold War Airmen*. Jackson: University of Mississippi Press, 2001.

Schemo, Diana. *Skies to Conquer: A Year Inside the Air Force Academy*. Hoboken, N.J.: John Wiley & Sons, 2010.

Scutts, Jerry, and Jim Laurier. *A-26 Invader Units of World War 2*. Oxford: Osprey, 2009.

Shaud, John A. *In Service to the Nation: Air Force Research Institute Strategic Concepts for 2018–2023*. Maxwell Air Force Base, Ala.: Air University Press, 2009.

Sheehan, Neil. *A Fiery Peace in a Cold War: Bernard Schriever and the Ultimate Weapon*. New York: Random House, 2009.

Sherwood, John D. *Fast Movers: Jet Pilots and the Vietnam Experience*. New York: Free Press, 2000.

Sinko, Benjamin A. *Echoes of the Dominator: The Tales and the Men Who Flew the B-32*. Minneapolis, Minn.: Up North Press, 2007.

Skinner, Stephen, and Mike Carr. *The Stand: The Final Flight of Lt. Frank Luke, Jr.* Atglen, Pa.: Schiffer, 2008.

Spires, David N. *Beyond Horizons: A History of the Air Force in Space, 1947–2007*. Peterson Air Force Base, Colo.: United States Air Force, 2007.

Stanaway, John. *479th Fighter Group: "Riddle's Raiders."* New York: Osprey, 2009.

Stanley, Roy M. *Asia From Above: 67th Reconnaissance Technical Squadron: Yokota Air Base, Japan—July 1957 to March 1971*. Bloomington, Ind.: AuthorHouse, 2006.

Steadfast and Courageous: FEAF Bomber Command and the Air War in Korea, 1950–1953. Washington, D.C.: Air Force History and Museums Program, 2000.

Strebe, Amy G. *Flying For Her Country: The American and Soviet Women Military Pilots of World War II*. Washington, D.C.: Potomac Books, 2009.

Sundloff, Frederick D. *Dien Bien Phu Remembered: A Chapter in United States Air Force History, Classified and Forgotten, February 5–July 19, 1954*.Indialantic, Fla.: Frederick D. Sundloff, 2003.

Tart, Larry, and Robert Keefe. *The Price of Vigilance: Attacks on American Surveillance Flights*. New York: Ballantine Books, 2001.

Tate, James P. *The Army and Its Air Corps: Army Policy Toward Aviation, 1919–1941*. Maxwell Air Force Base, Ala.: Air University, 2005.

Terry, Michael R., and Walter J. Boyne. *Winged Crusade: The Quest for American Air and Space Power*. Chicago: Imprint Publications, 2006.

Thomas, Andrew. *American Spitfire Aces of World War 2*. Oxford: Osprey, 2007.

Thompson, Thomas W. *The Fifty-Year Role of the United States Air Force in Advancing Information Technology: A History of the Rome, New York, Ground Electronics Laboratory*. Lewiston, N.Y.: Edwin Mellen Press, 2003.

Thompson, Warren. *F-86 Sabre Aces of the 4th Fighter Wing*. Oxford: Osprey, 2006.

Thompson, Warren. *F-86 Sabre Aces of the 51st Fighter Wing*. New York: Osprey, 2006.

Thompson, Wayne. *To Hanoi and Back: The United States Air Force and North Vietnam, 1966–1973*. Washington, D.C.: Smithsonian Institution Press, 2000.

Tillman, Barrett. *LeMay*. New York: Palgrave Macmillan, 2007.

Treadwell, Terry C. *America's First Air War: The United States Army, Naval, and Marine Air Services in the First World War*. Osceola, Wisc.: MBI Pub. Co., 2000.

Trest, Warren A. *Air Force Roles and Missions: A History*. Honolulu: University Press of the Pacific, 2005.

Tucker, Todd. *Atomic America: How a Deadly Explosion and a Feared Admiral Changed the Course of Nuclear History*. New York: Free Press, 2009.

Van Staaveren, Jacob. *Gradual Failure: The Air War Over North Vietnam, 1965–1966*. Washington, D.C.: Air Force History and Museums Program, 2002.

Veronico, Nicholas, and Ron Strong. *AMARG: America's Military Aircraft Boneyard*. North Branch, Minn.: Specialty Press, 2010.

Wallwork, Ellery D., and Kathryn A. Wilcoxson. *Operation Deep Freeze: 50 Years of U.S. Air Force Airlift in Antarctica*. Scott Air Force Base, Ill.: Office of History, Military Airlift Command, 2007.

Walsh, Kenneth T. *Air Force One: A History of the Presidents and Their Planes*. New York: Hyperion, 2003.

Ward, Ray. *Those Brave Crews: The Epic Raid to Destroy Hitler's Ploesti Oil Fields*. Waverly, N.Y.: Weldon Publications, 2003.

Warnock, A. Timothy. *Short of War: Major USAF Contingency Operations, 1947–1997*. Washington, D.C.: Air Force History and Museums Program, 2000.

Warnock, A. Timothy. *The USAF in Korea: A Chronology, 1950–1953*. Washington, D.C.: Air Force History and Museums Program, 2000.

Watkins, Robert A. *Battle Colors: Insignia and Aircraft Markings of the Eighth Air Force in World War II*. 2 vols. Atglen, Pa.: Schiffer Military History, 2006.

Watkins, Robert A. *Battle Colors, Volume III: Insignia and Tactical Markings of the Ninth Air Force in World War II*. Atglen, Pa.: Schiffer Publishing, 2008.

Watson, George M. *General James H. Doolittle: The Air Force's Warrior-Scholar*. Washington, D.C.: Air Force History and Museums Program, 2008.

Wayman, Charles R., and Candace R. Wayman. *Twenty-five Missions: A Bombardier's Story*. McKinleyville, Calif.: Fithian Press, 2009.

Weinstein, Michael L., and Davin Seay. *With God on Our Side: One Man's War Against an Evangelical Coup in America's Military*. New York: Thomas Dunne Books, 2006.

Whitcomb, Darrell D. *Combat Search and Rescue in Desert Storm*. Maxwell Air Force Base: Air University Press, 2006.

Whitcomb, Randall. *Cold War Tech War: The Politics of America's Air Defense*. Burlington, Ont.: Apogee Books, 2008.

Withington, Thomas. *Wild Weasel Fighter Attack: The Story of the Suppression of Enemy Air Defences*. Barnsley, U.K.: Pen & Sword Aviation, 2008.

Witters, Arthur G., and J. Bryce Hollingsworth. *Off We Go! The Real Story of How the United States Air Force Academy Was Created, Designed, and Built*. Chapel Hill, N.C.: Professional Press, 2009.

Wolf, William. *U.S. Aerial Armament in World War II: The Ultimate Look*. Atglen, Pa.: Schiffer, 2009.

Wolk, Herman S. *Fulcrum of Power: Essays on the United States Air Force and National Security*. Washington, D.C.: Air Force History and Museums Program, 2003.

Wolk, Herman S. *Reflections on Air Force Independence*. Washington, D.C.: Air Force History and Museums Program, 2007.

Wortman, Marc. *The Millionaires' Unit: The Aristocratic Flyboys Who Fought the Great War and Invented American Air Power*. New York: PublicAffairs, 2006.

Wrage, Stephen D., ed. *Immaculate Warfare: Participants Reflect on the Air Campaigns over Kosovo, Afghanistan, and Iraq*. Westport, Conn.: Praeger, 2003.

Y'Blood, William T. *MiG Alley: The Fight for Air Superiority*. Washington, D.C.: Air Force History and Museums Program, 2000.

Y'Blood, William T. *Down in the Weeds: Close Air Support in Korea*. Washington, D.C.: Air Force History and Museums Program, 2002.

Yenne, Bill. *The Story of the Boeing Company*. St. Paul, Minn.: Zenith, 2005.

Yenne, Bill. *The American Aircraft Factory in World War II*. St. Paul, Minn.: MBI Pub Co., 2006.

Yenne, Bill. *Aces High: The Heroic Saga of the Two Top-Scoring American Aces of World War II*. New York: Berkeley Caliber, 2009.

Yenne, Bill. *Convair Deltas: From SeaDart to Hustler*. North Branch, Minn.: Specialty Press, 2009.

Index

About the Author

JOHN C. FREDRIKSEN is an independent historian and the author of 20 reference books on various subjects. He received his doctorate in military history from Providence College.